科隆空间法评注

第二卷

Cologne Commentary on Space Law

（Volume Ⅱ）

斯蒂芬·霍贝
【德】伯恩哈德·施密特-泰德◎主编
凯-伍·施罗格

李寿平　吕卓艳　吴晓丹
杨　宽　王国语◎译

中国宇航出版社
·北京·

著作权合同登记号：图字：01－2023－1839 号

图书在版编目（CIP）数据

科隆空间法评注. 第二卷 /（德）斯蒂芬·霍贝(Stephan Hobe) 等主编 ；李寿平等译. --北京 ：中国宇航出版社，2023.8

书名原文：Cologne Commentary on Space Law (Volume Ⅱ)

ISBN 978-7-5159-2230-0

Ⅰ. ①科… Ⅱ. ①斯… ②李… Ⅲ. ①空间法一研究 Ⅳ. ①D999.1

中国国家版本馆 CIP 数据核字(2023)第 084182 号

责任编辑　赵宏颖　　　**装帧设计**　王晓武

出版发行	中国宇航出版社		
社　址	北京市阜成路 8 号　邮　编　100830 (010)68768548	版　次	2023 年 8 月第 1 版 2023 年 8 月第 1 次印刷
网　址	www.caphbook.com	规　格	700×1000
经　销	新华书店	开　本	1/16
发行部	(010)68767386　(010)68371900 (010)68767382　(010)88100613(传真)	印　张	33.5
		字　数	615 千字
零售店	读者服务部 (010)68371105	书　号	ISBN 978-7-5159-2230-0
		定　价	168.00 元
承　印	北京中科印刷有限公司		

本书如有印装质量问题，可与发行部联系调换

译者简介

（按章节顺序）

李寿平：教授，法学博士，国际宇航科学院社会科学学部院士，国家航天局空间法律中心主任，北京国际法学会会长，北京理工大学法学院院长、特聘教授、博士生导师，国家“万人计划”哲学社会科学领军人才（翻译总体介绍部分）。

吕卓艳：法学博士，国际空间大学讲师，研究方向为法律与科技、国际空间法、电信法和网络空间法。曾任空间一代咨询委员会商业航天项目主持人，国际宇航学会商业载人航天项目研究员，联合国法律事务总署法典编纂处研究员，联合国外层空间事务办公厅研究员（翻译《营救协定》）。

吴晓丹：法学博士，中央财经大学法学院副教授。深耕外空法研究近二十年，发表英文专著一本，在国内外多家权威期刊发表中英文论文。常年参与中国航天法律与政策以及重大项目和议题的起草和论证（翻译《责任公约》）。

杨　宽：法学博士，北京理工大学法学院长聘副教授、博士生导师，北京理工大学空天政策与法律研究院副院长，兼任国家航天局空间法律中心研究员、国际宇航联空间交通管理委员会专家、中国国际法学会理事、中国空间法学会理事（翻译《登记公约》）。

王国语：北京理工大学空天政策与法律研究院院长，法学院副教授，兼任国家航天局空间法律中心副主任、国际空间法学会常务理事，连续多年作为中国代表团成员参加联合国外空规则一线谈判，研究方向为国际空间法、航天法、国际空间政治（翻译《月球协定》）。

咨询专家委员会

Elisabeth Back Impallomeni 博士，教授

Karl-Heinz Böckstiegel 博士，教授

Jonathan Galloway 博士，教授

Gilbert Guillaume 法官

Peter P. C. Haanappel 博士，教授

Peter Jankowitsch 博士，大使

Nandasiri Jasentuliyana 博士

Vladimír Kopal 博士，教授

Abdul Koroma 法官

Gabriel Lafferranderie 博士

José Monserrat Filho 博士，教授

Vladlen S. Vereshchetin 法官

主编简介

主　编

Stephan Hobe 博士，教授

科隆大学航空与空间法研究所主任

科隆大学国际公法、欧洲法、欧洲与国际经济法首席教授

科隆大学科隆国际投资法中心联合主任

Bernhard Schmidt-Tedd 博士

德国宇航中心法律支持部主管

Kai-Uwe Schrogl 博士，教授

欧洲空间局局长首席顾问，成员国关系部主管

图宾根大学政治学研究所教授

助理主编

Peter Stubbe

文学硕士

德国宇航中心法律支持部项目经理和法律顾问

主编及作者名单

主编

Stephan Hobe 教授：德国科隆大学国际公法、欧洲法和国际经济法教授，是现任科隆大学航空与空间法研究所主任。他曾在德国慕尼黑大学、弗莱堡大学和哥廷根大学学习法律，在加拿大麦吉尔大学获得法学硕士学位，在德国基尔大学获得法学博士学位。霍贝教授是国际空间法学会的财务国际法协会空间法委员会的报告员。他是欧洲空间法中心、德国国际法学会等多个学会的理事。霍贝教授也是《德国航空与空间法》杂志的编辑，是《航空与空间法研究》系列丛书及《科隆国际公法和欧洲法研究》系列丛书的编辑。他也是《空间法——基本文件》活页集（十一国际出版/乌特勒支）的共同主编。他在国际公法、欧洲法、德国公法及航空与空间法领域发表文章150余篇。

Bernhard Schmidt-Tedd 博士：德国宇航中心联合国事务部的负责人，在吕讷堡大学和德国斯图加特大学空间系统研究所讲授空间法；并与德国科隆大学航空法、空间法和网络法研究所合作，指导面向实践的博士论文。他在科隆大学和日内瓦大学完成了法律学习，并在科隆大学（德国）获得法学博士学位。施密特-泰德博士是国际宇航科学院院士和俄罗斯齐奥尔科夫斯基宇航科学院通讯院士，也是国际空间法学会、欧洲空间法中心和德国航空航天协会的成员。他是《德国航空和空间法》杂志的编辑委员会成员，并发表了50多篇关于空间法法律发展的文章，特别是关于发射服务合同、国家空间立法、数据政策和商业空间应用。

Kai-Uwe Schrogl 教授：欧洲空间政策研究所主任。他作为代表团成员参与多次国际谈判，担任欧空局国际关系委员会和联合国外空委法律小组委员会关于发射国定义和登记实践工作组的主席。施罗格教授撰写和编辑了九部著作，在空间政策、法律及通信政策等方面发表了文章、报告100多篇。他是国际空间法学会主席，国际宇航研究院政策、经济和法律委员会主席和俄罗斯齐奥尔科夫斯基宇航科学院的会员。他是《空间政策年刊》和《空间政策研究》（均由施普林格在维也纳/纽约出版）系列丛书的主编。他也是《空间政策》《德国航空与空间法杂志》等国际期刊的编委会成员。他在德国图宾根大学作为荣誉教授讲授国际关系课程，经常在国际空间大学和欧洲空间法中心的暑期课程班授课。

作者

Urike M Bolmann 博士：欧空局法律主管（与Schmidt-Tedd、Malysheva、Stelmakh和Tennen共同承担《登记公约》的评注工作）。

Steven Freeland 教授：澳大利亚西悉尼大学国际法副教授，丹麦哥本哈根大学国际法访问教授（与Hobe，Jakhu，Tronchetti和Stubbe共同承担《月球协定》的评注工作）。

Stephan Hobe 教授，法学博士、名誉博士：德国科隆大学航空与空间法研究所主任兼国际公法、欧洲法、欧洲与国际经济法首席教授（与Jakhu、Freeland、Tronchetti和Stubbe共同承担《月球协定》的评注工作）。

Ram Jakhu 博士，教授：加拿大蒙特利尔麦吉尔大学法学院航空与空间法研究所副教授（与Hobe、Freeland、Tronchetti和Stubbe共同承担《月球协定》的评注工作）。

Armel Kerrest 博士，教授：法国布列斯特西布列塔尼大学国际空间和电信法研究所名誉教授和主席（与Smith和Tronchetti共同承担《责任公约》的评注工作）。

Irmgard Marboe 博士，教授：维也纳大学法学院欧洲、国际和比较法系国际法教授（在奥地利维也纳与Neumann和Schrogl共同承担《营救协定》的评注工作）。

Nataliya R. Malysheva 博士，教授：乌克兰国家科学院国际空间法中心副主任（在乌克兰基辅与Schmidt-Tedd、Bohlmann、Stelmakh和Tennen共同承担《登记公约》的评注工作）。

Julia Neumann 博士：律师（在德国柏林与Marboe和Schrogl共同承担《营救协定》的评注工作）。

Bernhard Schmidt-Tedd 博士：德国宇航中心联合国事务部主管（在德国波恩与

Bohlmann、Malysheva、Stelmakh 和 Tennen 共同承担《登记公约》的评注工作）。

Kai-Uwe Schrogl 教授：欧洲空间局政策所主任（在巴黎与 Marboe 和 Neumann 共同承担《营救协定》的评注工作）。

Lesley Jane Smith 博士，教授：德国吕讷堡大学国际和欧洲经济法教授；拉脱维亚大学里加研究生院前院长和教授；德国不来梅 Weber-Steinhaus & Smith 律师事务所律师和合伙人（与 Kerrest 和 Tronchetti 共同承担《责任公约》的评注工作）。

Olga S. Stelmakh 博士：国际空间商业研究所业务发展和国际事务主任（与 Schmidt-Tedd、Bohlmann、Malysheva 和 Tenne 共同承担《登记公约》的评注工作）。

Peter Stubbe 文学硕士：法律顾问，欧空局空间管理部，德国宇航中心/联邦经济事务和能源部空间政策部（在德国波恩与 Hobe、Freeland、Jakhu 和 Tronchetti 共同承担《月球协定》的评注工作）。

Leslie I. Tennen 博士：美国亚利桑那州凤凰城 Sterns 和 Tennen 律师事务所律师（与 Schmidt-Tedd、Bohlmann、Malysheva 和 Stelmakh 共同承担《登记公约》的评注工作）。

Fabio Tronchetti 教授：中国哈尔滨工业大学法学院空间法研究所副教授（与 Hobe、Jakhu、Freeland 和 Stubbe 共同承担《月球协定》的评注工作）

序

本书是《科隆空间法评注》(CoCoSL)的第二卷，该项目致力于为国际空间法提供逐条的注释。我特别欢迎这一努力，因为在支持和管理联合国和平利用外层空间委员会(COPUOS)工作的联合国外层空间事务办公室(OOSA)，我每天都看到现有的法律制度对于规范空间活动的根本意义，以及通过国家空间法和监管框架实施这些规则的各种持续努力。理解空间法对于其一贯的应用和有效性是极其重要的。

CoCoSL 的第一卷分析了《外层空间条约》(简称《外空条约》)，它作为解释《外空条约》所载空间法条款的一个重要参考资料，于 2009 年出版，受到了空间界的好评。它的成功基于两个重要的支柱：一是在这个项目中汇集了一批经验丰富的、代表不同法律传统的学术和实践专长的作者；二是该项目采用评注形式，是法律文献中系统分析书面规范的成功和成熟的媒介——在空间法的学术写作中构成了一个创新，使《科隆空间法评注》在各种同类出版物中具有独特的地位。同时，必须向 CoCoSL 的编辑，Stephan Hobe 教授，Bernhard Schmidt-Tedd 博士和 Kai-Uwe Schrogl 教授就 CoCoSL 第一卷的杰出成就表示祝贺。国际宇航科学院于 2010 年授予了《科隆空间法评注》社会科学图书奖，肯定了该出版物的卓越性。

本书延续了第一卷的成功经验，采用基于条款解释的既定方法，汇集了专家作者，阐述了 1968 年《营救协定》、1972 年《责任公约》、1975 年《登记公约》和 1979 年《月球协定》。前述公约加协定诞生于一个非常有成效的实体法制定时期，随后在外空委法律小组委员会的范围内得到了发展。此后，通过联合国大会的决议，空间法得到了进一步的发展。这四个国际条约具体规定，体现了《外层空间条约》的条款，所有五项文书构成了基于条约的外层空间活动的实质性法律制度。

2012 年是 COPUOS 法律小组委员会成立 50 周年，即 1961 年尤里·加加林飞向外层空间 50 周年纪念日的一年后。这两个历史性日期的重合标志着人类进入外层空间的进展与国际空间法的相应发展之间的密切关系。今天，技术进步和空间利用的新前景使得既定的法律规范体系必须适应不断变化的空间活动形式。一些国家对重返月球的兴趣增加，以及高度宣传的太空旅游飞行的前景，都强调了对国际空间法的正确理解，以维持现有法律秩序的有效性和适用性。

CoCoSL 的目的就在于促进对空间法的详细理解。第二卷完成了对基于条约的空间法的分析，从而对其条款进行了连贯而深入的分析。

在 COPUOS 法律小组委员会成立 50 周年之际，为了承认其在空间法发展中的重要作用，联合国外空事务办公室在其网站上继续开放空间条约准备工作的全面收集，供公众查阅。此外，联合国外空事务办公室在促进和协助空间法能力建设的进一步努力方面发挥了积极作用，特别是在发展中国家，其理由反映在法律小组委员会关于“空间法能力建设”的相应议程项目中。事实上，《科隆空间法评注》在这一努力中具有重要地位。

空间条约在利用外层空间方面继续发挥着至关重要的作用，对它们的理解，对促进其有效性具有极其重要的意义。我确信，本书将延续第一卷的成功，并在未来几年内被确立为解释联合国空间条约实质性规范的标准参考文件。

Mazlan Othman

联合国外层空间事务办公室主任

联合国维也纳办事处副总干事

维也纳，2012 年 9 月

编者按

在《科隆空间法评注》第一卷出版四年后，我们很高兴完成了第二卷。继《外层空间条约》（OST）的评注之后，本卷包含了所有其他联合国空间条约——《营救协定》（ARRA）、《责任公约》（LIAB）、《登记公约》（REG）和《月球协定》（MOON）。

上述条约的评注之间的协调需要在时间和内容方面做出巨大努力。为了方便不同部分的使用和定位，我们引入了一系列额外的结构要素。编辑们制定的非官方标题符合评注的标准，目的是使条例的内容可以直接查阅。目录的比较也突出了结构。

为了全面了解这些条约，有必要提出一个详细的历史概述，以了解标准术语和基本规则是如何发展的。事实上，本卷中的四个条约在很大程度上代表了《外层空间条约》的基本原则和之前联合国大会决议的进一步发展。作者希望强调，这五个条约确实是一个单一的空间法体系。研究条约文本的时间越长，对其相互关系的理解也就越深刻。

编辑们决定使用评注的概念，以便能够在有关空间法的个别出版物之外，对这些条约提供一个统一的概述。五个原始条约为任何与空间法有关的问题奠定了一个统一的基础，它们是自第一个联合国大会关于空间的决议以来相继发展形成的。即使在目前的条件下，这些文本也没有失去其说服力。存在的问题是，在那些在已知问题上没有任何发展的地方，往往缺乏实施的举措和政治意愿。

例如，就像任何其他类型的交通系统一样，只有在制定了交通规则之后，对外层空间物体造成损害的基于过失的责任规定才可以实现。鉴于目前在政治上不愿意制定相应的交通规则，而这些规则显然是相关的，但没有被法律政策认真处理，因此相当清楚，现有的五个空间条约的成就是多么的宝贵。

编辑们要感谢项目经理和助理编辑 Peter Stubbe，没有他们，这项工作就不可能实现。我们也感谢项目组的 Anne Hurtz、Lisa Küpers 和 Martin Reynders，他们在从文本创作到最后定稿的漫长过程中，负责编辑历史文件、文献和所有章节的正式一致性。项目组还组织了一系列的作者研讨会，这些研讨会伴随着文本的起草，提供了讨论与评注相关的具体法律问题的机会。其中，2012 年 6 月举行的“In Heaven as on Earth?”专题讨论会分析了一般国际法和空间法之间的相互关系。

最后，我们不应该忘记《科隆空间法评注》框架内的工作准则：严格遵守法治不仅是任何类型的国际公共法律条例的最宏伟目标，也是编辑们的信念，是维护地球和外层空间的国际和平的最佳目标。

Stephan Hobe，Bernhard Schmidt-Tedd，Kai-Uwe Schrogl

科隆/波恩/巴黎

2012 年 10 月/2017 年 1 月/2019 年 1 月

目　录

文件目录

条约简介

引用空间条约的参考日期

国际条约的缔结和生效的程序分为几个不同的阶段。文书的谈判阶段之后是文本的通过和认证，以及表示同意接受条约的约束，然后文书才最终生效。文本的通过标志着谈判的结束，对文本的形式和内容进行了表决。另一个程序性步骤是认证，通过具体的程序性行为确定最终的有效文本。确定最终文本后，愿意这样做的国家表示同意接受条约的约束。这可以通过通常在条约本身中规定的各种行为来实现。这些手段可以是签署、交换构成条约的文书、批准、接受、核准或加入或任何其他商定的手段。批准通常是在签署之后，而且往往是在条约中具体述及的，特别是在正式条约的情况下。它构成了在国际层面上同意接受约束的表达，不同于一国根据其宪法要求进行的内部批准行为。加入是允许未谈判或签署该文书的国家成为该条约缔约方的一种常见手段。各国可在条约中自由商定文书生效的要求。一旦条约拥有法律效力，条约的缔约方就必须真诚地履行条约（必须遵守条约）。

在制定联合国外层空间条约的实践中，条约的文本由联合国和平利用外层空间委员会（UNCOPUOS）法律小组委员会谈判，该委员会是联合国大会的主管附属机构，负责“研究探索外层空间可能产生的法律问题的性质”。这些条约草案随后被提交给联合国和平利用外层空间委员会，最终被提交给联合国大会通过。法律小组委员会的谈判结果不一定代表最终文本，即使在法律小组委员会提交后，谈判仍在继续。大会通过条约最后文本的决议——即表示结果适合各国接受——同时要求保存人，即条约指定的保存国（奥斯陆、阿拉伯联合酋长国、阿拉伯利比亚民众国）或联合国秘书长开放该条约供签署。

在缔结条约的一般程序中，联合国大会对条约文本的确认构成了通过阶段，通过这一阶段确定了条约文本的形式和内容。保存国政府或联合国秘书长开放供签署代表签署的文书最终文本的认证。这一日期决定了通常与各空间条约相关的年份。在大多数情况下，大会在条约开放供签署的前一年对其进行表决。通常确定的条约参考年份来自于后一个日期，因此这些文书被称为1967年《外空条约》、1968年《营救协定》、1972年《责任公约》和1975年《登记公约》。唯一的例外是1979年的《月球协定》，其文本由大会推荐未经投票通过，直接在1979年同年由秘书长开放供签署。表示同意受条约约束的方式在所有空间条约中是统一的。所有这些条约都规定，条约须经签署国批准，同时条约向所有国家开放供签署。所有条约还规定，条约在交存五份批准书后生效。在条约生效前没有签署相关条约的国家可以通过加入条约成为缔约国。

《联合国条约汇编》（UNTS）中空间条约的出版

根据《联合国宪章》第102条第1款，每项条约和国际协定都应在联合国秘书处登记，登记后，秘书处应公布所记录的条约。《联合国条约汇编》（UNTS）构成了这一出版物系列，其中包括条约或国际协定的原始语言文本。五个国际空间条约中的三个（《外空条约》《营救协定》《责任公约》）责成其保存国政府进行相应的登记。由于联合国秘书长是另外两个国际空间条约（《登记公约》和《月球协定》）的保存人，这些条约的登记工作由秘书处依职权进行。

所有国际空间条约都已在《联合国条约汇编》中公布。此外，还有另一份联合国出版物，题为“联合国外层空间条约和原则以及相关的大会决议”的册子，其中特别包括五项国际空间条约。这本册子中的文本与《联合国条约汇编》中公布的文本略有不同。这些差异不是实质性的，而是涉及正式的更正，可能是在册子出版过程中由编辑调整造成的。例如，对某些术语的拼写进行了调整：“co-operation”一词被改为“cooperation”（《月球协定》第4条）。另一个例子是修改了保存国政府和有效语言的顺序，例如《营救协定》的第7条和第10条。

因此，本评注在每一章的开头都转载了联合国贸易中心出版的有关空间条约的原文，以提供该文书的原始和真实文本。特定章节内的个别条款的复制是以联合国出版物为基础的。

文件目录

1910	International Convention for the Unification of certain Rules of Law relating to Assistance and Salvage at Sea of 23 September 1910 (done 23 September 1910, entered into force 1 March 1913)
1944	Convention on International Civil Aviation (done 7 December 1944, entered into force 4 April 1947) 15 UNTS 295
1945	Statute of the Statute of the International Court of Justice (26 June 1945) 1 UNTS 16 Charter of the United Nations (done 26 June 1945, entered into force 24 October 1945) 1 UNTS 16
1952	Convention on Damage Caused by Foreign Aircraft to Third Parties on the Surface, (signed on 7 October 1952, entry into force 4 February 1958) 310 UNTS 181
1959	The Antarctic Treaty (done 1 December 1959, entered into force 23 June 1961) 402 UNTS 71
1960	Convention on Third Party Liability in the Field of Nuclear Energy (opened for signature 29 July 1960, entered into force 1 April 1968) 956 UNTS 251
1961	Vienna Convention on Diplomatic Relations (opened for signature 18 April 1961, entry into force 24 April 1964), 500 UNTS 95
1963	Convention Supplementary to the Paris Convention of 29th July 1960 on Third Party Liability in the Field of Nuclear Energy (opened for signature 31 January 1963, entered into force on 04 December 1974) Vienna Convention on Civil Liability for Nuclear Damage (opened for signature 21 May 1963, entered into force 12 November 1977) 1063 UNTS 266 Treaty Banning Nuclear Weapon Tests in the Atmosphere, in Outer Space and under Water (done 5 August 1963, entered into force 10 October 1963) 480 UNTS 43
1967	Treaty on Principles Governing the Activities of States in the Exploration and Use of Outer Space, including the Moon and Other Celestial Bodies (done 27 January 1967, entered into force 10 October 1967) 610 UNTS 205
1968	Agreement on the Rescue of Astronauts, the Return of Astronauts and the Return of Objects Launched into Outer Space (done 22 April 1968, entered into force 3 December 1968) 672 UNTS 119
1969	Vienna Convention on the Law of Treaties (done 23 May 1969, entered into force 27 January 1980) 1155 UNTS 331
1972	Convention on International Liability for Damage Caused by Space Objects (done 29 March 1972, entered into force 1 September 1972) 961 UNTS 187
1975	Convention on Registration of Objects Launched into Outer Space (done 14 January 1975, entered into force 15 September 1976) 1023 UNTS 15
1979	Agreement Governing the Activities of States on the Moon and Other Celestial Bodies (done 18 December 1979, entered into force 11 July 1984) 1363 UNTS 3
1982	Memorandum of understanding on the Roentgensatellit program, (signed 8 August 1982, entered in to force 8 August 1982), TIAS 10669; 2000 UNTS 445 United Nations Convention on the Law of the Sea (done 10 December 1982, entered into force 16 November 1994) 1833 UNTS 396

续表

1986	Vienna Convention on the Law of Treaties between States and International Organizations or Between International Organizations (opened for signature 21 March 1986, not yet in force), International Legal Materials 1986 (25), p. 543
1988	Convention on the Regulation of Antarctic Mineral Resource Activities (done 2 June 1988, not in force) 27ILM 868
1994	Agreement between the Russian Federation and the Republic of Kazakhstan on the Basic Principles and Conditions of the Utilization of the Baikonur Cosmodrome (28 March 1994) Agreement relating to the Implementation of Part XI of the United Nations Convention on the Law of the Sea of 10 December 1982 (done 28 July 1994, entered into force provisionally 16 November 1994, entered into force definitively 28 July 1996) 1836 UNTS 3 Lease Agreement on the Baikonur Complex between the Government of the Russian Federation and the Government of the Republic of Kazakhstan (10 December 1994)
1995	Agreement between Russia and Kazakhstan On the Status of The City of Baikonur, Order of Formation and the Status of its Executive Bodies (23 December 1995)
1998	Agreement among the Government of Canada, Governments of Member States of the European Space Agency, the Government of Japan, the Government of the Russian Federation, and the Government of the United States of America Concerning Cooperation on the Civil International Space Station (done 29 January 1998, entered into force 28 March 2001), in: Böckstiegel, Karl-Heinz/Benkö, Marietta/Hobe, Stephan (eds.), *Space Law-Basic Legal Documents*, D. II. 4. 1
2001	IMO Convention on Civil Liability for Bunker Oil Pollution Damage (BUNKER), adopted 23 March 2001, entry into force 21 November 2008
2004	Agreement between the Russian Federation and the Republic of Kazakhstan on the Development of Cooperation Concerning the Effective Utilization of the Baikonur Cosmodrome (9 January 2004)
	联合国大会决议
1946	UNGA Res. 97 (I), Registration and Publication of Treaties and International Agreements: Regulations to give effect to Article 102 of the Charter of the United Nations, 14 December 1946
1949	UNGA Res. 364 B (IV), Registration and publication of treaties and international agreements, 1 December 1949
1950	UNGA Res. 482 (V), Registration and Publication of treaties and international agreements, 12 December 1950
1958	UNGA Res. 1348 (XIII), Question of the peaceful use of outer space, 13 December 1958
1959	UNGA Res. 1472 A (XIV), International co-operation in the peaceful uses of outer space, 12 December 1959
1961	UNGA Res. 1721 B (XVI), International co-operation in the peaceful uses of outer space, 20 December 1961
1962	UNGA Res. 1802 (XVII), International co-operation in the peaceful uses of outer space, 14 December 1962
1963	UNGA Res. 1884 (XVIII), Question of general and complete disarmament, 17 October 1963 UNGA Res. 1962 (XVIII), Declaration of Legal Principles Governing the Activities of States in the Exploration and Uses of Outer Space, 13 December 1963
1966	UNGA Res. 2222 (XXI), Treaty on Principles Governing the Activities of States in the Exploration and Use of Outer Space, including the Moon and Other Celestial Bodies, 19 December 1966

续表

1967	UNGA Res. 2260 (XXII), Report of the Committee on the Peaceful Uses of Outer Space, 3 November 1967 UNGA Res. 2345 (XXII), Agreement on the Rescue of Astronauts, the Return of Astronauts and the return of Objects Launched into Outer Space, 19 December 1967
1969	UNGA Res. 2601 (XXIV) B, International co-operation in outer space, 16 December 1969
1970	UNGA Res. 2625 (XXV), Declaration on Principles of International Law Concerning Friendly Relations and Co-operation among States in Accordance with the Charter of the United Nations, 24 October 1970 UNGA Res. 2733 (XXV) B, International cooperation on the peaceful use of outer space, 16 December 1970
1971	UNGA Res. 2777 (XXVI), Convention on International Liability for Damage Caused by Space Objects, 29 November 1971 UNGA Res. 2779 (XXVI), Preparation of an international treaty concerning the Moon, 29 November 1971
1973	UNGA Res. 3190 (XXVIII), Inclusion of Arabic among the official and working languages of the General Assembly and its Main Committees, 18 December 1973
1974	UNGA Res. 3235 (XXIX), Convention on Registration of Objects Launched into Outer Space, 12 November 1974
1977	UNGA Res. 32/151, Report of the International Law Commission, 19 December 1977, para. 7
1978	UNGA Res. 33/141, Registration and publication of treaties and international agreements pursuant to Article 102 of the Charter of the United Nations, 19 December 1978
1979	UNGA Res. 34/68, Agreement Governing the Activities of States on the Moon and Other Celestial Bodies, 5 December 1979
1980	UNGA Res. 35/219, Use of Arabic in the subsidiary organs of the General Assembly in the Security Council and in the Economic and Social Council: amendments to rules 51, 52, 54 and 56 of the rules of procedure of the Assembly, 17 December 1980
1982	UNGA Res. 37/91, Question of the review of the Convention on International Liability for Damage Caused by Space Objects, 10 December 1982
1986	UNGA Res. 41/66 Question of the review of the Convention on Registration of Objects Launched into Outer Space, 3 December 1986
1992	UNGA Res. 47/68, Principles Relevant to the Use of Nuclear Power Sources in Outer Space, 14 December 1992
1994	UNGA Res. 49/34, International cooperation in the peaceful uses of outer space, including the question of the review of the Agreement governing the Activities of States on the Moon and Other Celestial Bodies, 9 December 1994
2002	UNGA Res. 56/83, Responsibility of States for internationally wrongful acts, 28 January 2002
2004	UNGA Res. 59/115, Application of the concept of the "launching State", 10 December 2004
2006	UNGA Res. 61/63, Allocation of loss in the case of transboundary harm arising out of hazardous activities, Annex, 4 December 2006 (hereinafter Draft Principle on Allocation of Loss)

续表

2007	UNGA Res. 62/101, Recommendations on Enhancing the Practice of States and International Intergovernmental Organizations in Registering Space Objects, 17 December 2007 UNGA Res. 62/68, Consideration of prevention of transboundary harm from hazardous activities and allocation of loss in the case of such harm, Annex, 6 December 2007
2008	UNGA Res. 62/217, International cooperation in the peaceful uses of outer space, 22 December 2007, 1 February 2008

联合国和平利用外层空间委员会相关文件

简介

每份联合国文件都有一个独特的编号，可以明确地识别。联合国和平利用外层空间委员会（UNCOPUOS）的文件都带有“A/AC. 105”的编号。这个编号表明，该机构是联合国大会的一个附属机构（“A/”），它最初是作为一个特设委员会（“AC.”）成立的。

联合国和平利用外层空间委员会是根据 1958 年联合国大会第 1348（XIII）号决议设立的，后来根据 1959 年联合国大会第 1472（XIV）号决议转变为一个常设委员会。然而，尽管转变为常设机构，符号部分“AC.”一直沿用至今。UNCOPUOS 的两个小组委员会即科学和技术小组委员会和法律小组委员会成立于 1962 年（1962 年 3 月 30 日联合国文件 A/5109）。来自前者的文件用符号部分“C. 1/”表示，来自后者的文件可以用“C. 2/”表示。

关于联合国文件符号组成部分的概述

A/	联合国大会
A/AC. 105/	联合国和平利用外层空间委员会
A/AC. 105/C. 1/	联合国和平利用外层空间委员会科学和技术小组委员会
A/AC. 105/C. 2/	联合国和平利用外层空间委员会法律小组委员会
ST/SG/SER. E	按照《条例》规定提供的资料
/WG.	工作小组

续表

/CRP.	会议室文件
/INF.	信息系列
/L.	限量分发的文件(临时性文件,如草稿)
/PV.	逐字记录(procès-verbal)
/SR.	简要记录
/WP.	工作文件
/Add.	增编
/Corr.	更正
/Rev.	修订本

联合国和平利用外层空间委员会相关文件列表

Series A/	
1959	UN Doc. A/AC. 98/2, Report of the Legal Committee, 12 June 1959 UN Doc. A/4141, Report of the ad hoc Committee on the Peaceful Uses of Outer Space, 14 July 1959, UNGA Official Records, Fourteenth Session, Agenda Item 25
1962	UN Doc. A/5181, Report of the Committee on the Peaceful Uses of Outer Space, 27 September 1962
1967	UN Doc. A/8604/Add. 1, Report of the Committee on the Peaceful Uses of Outer Space, 27 September 1967 UN Doc. A/PV. 1640, United Nations General Assembly, Twenty-Second Session, Official Records 1640th Plenary Meeting, 19 December 1967
1971	UN Doc. A/8420, Report of the Committee on the Peaceful Uses of Outer Space, General Assembly Official Records, Twenty-Sixth Session, Supplement No. 20, 1971 UN Doc. A/8391, Treaty Concerning the Moon: Letter dated 27 May 1971 from the Minister for Foreign Affairs of the Union of Soviet Socialist Republics addressed to the Secretary-General, 4 June 1971
1978	UN Doc. A/33/20, Report of the Committee on the Peaceful Uses of Outer Space, General Assembly Official Records, Thirty-Third Session, Supplement No. 20, 7 August 1978
1979	UN Doc. A/34/20, Report of the Committee on the Peaceful Uses of Outer Space, General Assembly Official Records, Thirty-Fourth Session, Supplement No. 20, 14 August 1979
1994	UN Doc. A/49/20, Report of the Committee on the Peaceful Uses of Outer Space, General Assembly Official Records, Forty-Ninth Session, Supplement No. 20, 12 August 1994
2007	UN Doc. A/62/20, Report of the Committee on the Peaceful Uses of Outer Space, General Assembly Official Records, Sixty-second session, Supplement No. 20, 2007
2012	UN Doc. A/67/20, Report of the Committee on the Peaceful Uses of Outer Space, General Assembly Official Records, Sixty-Seventh Session, Supplement No. 20, 29 June 2012

续表

Series A/AC. 105/	
1962	UN Doc. A/AC. 105/INF. 1, Letter dated 6 March 1962 from the Acting Secretary-General addressed to the Chairman of the Committee on the Peaceful Uses of Outer Space, transmitting a communication dated 5 March 1962 from Permanent Representative of the United States of America, 7 March 1962 UN Doc. A/AC. 105/INF. 2, Letter dated 24 March 1962 from the Acting Permanent Representative of the Union of Soviet Socialist Republics addressed to the Acting Secretary-General, 24 March 1962 UN Doc. A/AC. 105/L. 3, USSR: Draft International Agreement on the Rescue of Astronauts and Spaceships Making Emergency Landing, 10 September 1962 UN Doc. A/AC. 105/L. 4, United States of America: Draft Proposal on Assistance and Return of Space Vehicles and Personnel, Liability for Space Vehicle Accidents, 11 September 1962
1963	UN Doc. A/AC. 105/12, Report of the Legal Subcommittee on the work of its second Session (16 April-3 May 1963), 6 May 1963
1964	UN Doc. A/AC. 105/21, Report of the Legal Sub-Committee on the Work of the Second Part of its Third Session (5-23 October 1964) to the Committee on the Peaceful Uses of Outer Space, Annex I, Proposals and amendments relating to assistance to and return of astronauts and space vehicles, 23 October 1964 UN Doc. A/AC. 105/21, Report of the Legal Sub-Committee on the Work of the Second Part of its Third Session (5-23 October 1964) to the Committee on the Peaceful Uses of Outer Space, Annex IV, Summary of Views Expressed in Working Groups I and II, 23 October 1964 UN Doc. A/AC. 105/21, Report of the Legal Sub-Committee on the work of the Second Part of its Third Session (5-23 October 1964) to the Committee on the Peaceful Uses of Outer Space, Annex Ⅲ, Text of Certain Provisions of a Draft Agreement on Assistance to and Return of Personnel and Spacecraft, on which Preliminary Agreement was reached by the Informal Working-Party of the Sub-Committee, 23 October 1964 UN Doc. A/AC. 105/21, Report of the Legal Sub-Committee on the Work of the Second Part of its Third Session (5-23 October 1964), 23 October 1964
1965	UN Doc. A/AC. 105/21/Add. 2, Report of the Legal Sub-Committee on the Work of the Second Part of its Third Session (5-23 October 1964) to the Committee on the Peaceful Uses of Outer Space, Addendum to Annex IV, Summary of views expressed in Working Groups I and II, Note by the Secretariat, 21 May 1965 UN Doc. A/AC. 105/29, Report of the Legal Sub-Committee on the Work of its Fourth Session (20 September-1 October 1965), 1 October 1965
1966	UN Doc. A/AC. 105/32, Draft Treaty Governing the Exploration of the Moon and Other Celestial Bodies: Letter dated 16 June 1966 from the Permanent Representative of the United States of America addressed to the Chairman of the Committee on the Peaceful Uses of Outer Space, Annex, 17 June 1966 UN Doc. A/AC. 105/35, Report of the Legal Sub-Committee on the Work of its Fifth Session (12 July-4 August and 12-16 September 1966), Annex I, 16 September 1966 UN Doc. A/AC. 105/35, Report of the Legal Sub-Committee on the Work of its Fifth Session (12 July-4 August and 12-16 September 1966), 16 September 1966
1967	UN Doc. A/AC. 105/L. 203, Assistance to and Return of Astronauts and Space Objects, Revised Australian-Canadian proposal submitted as a Working Paper, 21 June 1967 UN Doc. A/AC. 105/37, Report of the Legal Sub-Committee on the Work of its Sixth Session (19 June-14 July 1967), 14 July 1967

续表

1967	UN Doc. A/AC. 105/PV. 49, Provisional Verbatim Record of its Forty-Ninth Session, held 13 December 1967, 13 September 1967 UN Doc. A/AC. 105/INF. 180, Letter dated 1 December 1967 from the Permanent Representative of Australia addressed to the Secretary-General, 5 December 1967
1968	UN Doc. A/AC. 105/PV. 52, Provisional Verbatim Record of the Fifty-Second Meeting, held 16 December 1967, 12 February 1968 UN Doc. A/AC. 105/PV. 52, Committee on the Peaceful Uses of Outer Space, Provisional Verbatim Record of the Fifty-Second Meeting, held 16 December 1967, 12 February 1968 UN Doc. A/AC. 105/45, Report of the Legal Sub-Committee on the Work of its Seventh Session (4-28 June 1968), 11 July 1968
1969	UN Do. A/AC. 105/L. 40/Rev. 1, Working Paper submitted by the Italian delegation-Draft Convention Concerning Liability for Damage Caused by the Launching of Objects Into Outer Space, in: A/AC. 105/58, Report of the Legal Sub-Committee on the Work of Eighth Session (9 June-4 July 1969), Annex II, Proposals and Other Documents Relating to Liability for Damage Caused by the Launching of Objects into Outer Space, 4 July 1969 UN Doc. A/AC. 105/58, Report of the Legal Sub-Committee on the Work of its Eighth Session (9 June-4 July 1969) to the Committee on the Peaceful Uses of Outer Space, Annex I, 4 July 1969 UN Doc. A/AC. 105/58 Annex I, Report of the Legal Sub-Committee on the Work of its Eighth Session (9 June-4 July 1969), Annex I, Proposals Concerning Questions Relative to the Definition of Outer Space and the Utilization of Outer Space and Celestial Bodies, Including the Various Implications of Space Communications, 4 July 1969 UN Doc. A/AC. 105/58, Report of the Legal Sub-Committee on the Work of Eighth Session (9 June-4 July 1969), 4 July 1969
1970	UN Doc. A/AC. 105/INF. 215, Letter dated 12 February 1970 from the Permanent Representative of Japan addressed to the Secretary-General, 16 February 1970 UN Doc. A/AC. 105/82, 1 May 1970 UN Doc. A/AC. 105/INF. 220, Letter dated 17 April 1970 from the Permanent Representative of the United States of America addressed to the Secretary-General, 11 May 1970 UN Doc. A/AC. 105/85, Report of the Legal Sub-Committee on the Work of its Ninth Session (8 June-3 July 1970), Annex II, Proposals Concerning Questions Relative to the Definition of Outer Space and the Utilization of Outer Space and Celestial Bodies, Including the Various Implications of Space Communications, 3 July 1970 UN Doc. A/AC. 105/85, Report of the Legal Sub-Committee on the Work of its Ninth Session (8 June-3 July 1970), 3 July 1970
1971	UN Doc. A/AC. 105/94, Report of the Legal Sub-Committee on the Work of its Tenth Session (7 June-2 July 1971), 8 July 1971 UN Doc. A/AC/105/INF. 240, Letter dated 3 November 1971 from the Permanent Representative of the United Kingdom to the United Nations addressed to the Secretary-General, 3 November 1971
1972	UN Doc. A/AC. 105/101, Report of the Legal Sub-Committee on the Work of its Eleventh Session (10 April-5 May 1972), Annex I, Proposals and Other Documents Relating to Agenda Item 3 (Questions Relating to the Moon), 11 May 1972

续表

1973	UN Doc. A/AC. 105/115, Report of the Legal Sub-Committee on the Work of its Twelfth Session (26 March-20 April 1973), Annex II, Documents Relating to the Draft Convention on Registration of Objects Launched into Space for the Exploration or Use of Outer Space, Argentina: Working Paper, 20 April 1973 UN Doc. A/AC. 105/115, Report of the Legal Sub-Committee on the Work of its Twelfth Session (26 March-20 April 1973), Annex I, Documents Relating to Agenda Item 2 (Draft Treaty Relating to the Moon), 27 April 1973 UN Doc. A/AC. 105/INF. 284, Letter dated 21 December 1973 from the Permanent Representative of Canada addressed to the Secretary-General, 31 December 1973
1974	UN Doc. A/AC. 105/133, Report of the Legal Sub-Committee of its 13th session (6-31 May 1974), 6 June 1974
1975	UN Doc. A/AC. 105/INF. 305, Letter dated 24 January 1975 from the Acting Permanent Representative of the Federal Republic of Germany addressed to the Secretary-General, 24 January 1975 UN Doc. A/AC. 105/INF. 325, Note Verbale dated 3 October 1975 from the Permanent Mission of France addressed to the Secretary-General, 16 October 1975 UN Doc. A/AC. 105/INF. 329, Letter dated 14 November 1975 from the Permanent Representative of the Federal Republic of Germany to the United Nations addressed to the Secretary-General, 14 November 1975
1976	UN Doc. A/AC. 105/PV. 164, Verbatim Record of the Hundred and Sixty-Fourth Meeting (25 June 1976), 25 June 1976
1977	UN Doc. A/AC. 105/INF. 358, Note Verbale dated 7 April 1977 from the Permanent Representative of Japan to the Secretary-General, 18 April 1977 UN Doc. A/AC. 105/PV. 175, Verbatim Record of the One Hundred and Seventy-First Meeting (28 June 1977), 25 July 1977 UN Doc. A/AC. 105/INF. 366, Note Verbale dated 13 September 1977 from the Acting Permanent Representative of Japan addressed to the Secretary-General, 28 September 1977
1978	UN Doc. A/AC. 105/INF. 371, Note Verbale dated 31 March 1978 from the Permanent Representative of Japan to the Secretary-General, 14 April 1978 UN Doc. A/AC. 105/INF. 380, Note Verbale dated 16 November 1978 from the Permanent Mission of the Federal Republic of Germany to the United Nations addressed to the Secretary-General, 29 November 1978
1979	UN Doc. A/AC. 105/240, Report of the Legal Sub-Committee on the Work of its Eighteenth Session (12 March-6 April 1979), 10 April 1979 UN Doc. A/AC. 105/240, Report of the Legal Sub-Committee on the Work of its Eighteenth Session (12 March-6 April 1979), Annex Ⅲ, Report of the Chairman of Working Group I, Appendix A, 10 April 1979 UN Doc. A/AC/105/INF. 384, Note Verbale dated 10 October 1979 from the Permanent Mission of the United Kingdom of Great Britain and Northern Ireland to the United Nations addressed to the Secretary-General, 19 October 1979
1987	UN Doc. A/AC. 105/382, UN Study on the Application of the Convention on Registration of Objects Launched into Outer Space, 2 March 1987
1993	UN Doc. A/AC/105/INF. 397, Note Verbale dated 24 February 1993 from the Permanent Representative of Brazil to the United Nations addressed to the Secretary-General, 8 March 1993

续表

1998	UN Doc. A/AC. 105/698, Report of the Legal Subcommittee on the Work of Its Thirty-Seventh Session (23-31 March 1998), 6 April 1998
1999	UN Doc. A/AC/105/INF. 404, Note Verbale dated 14 December 1999 from the Permanent Mission of Brazil to the United Nations (Vienna) addressed to the Secretary-General, 27 January 2000
2000	UN Doc. A/AC. 105/735, Note verbale dated 20 January 2000 from the Permanent Mission of Japan (Vienna) addressed to the Secretary-General, 2 February 2000 UN Doc. A/AC. 105/737, Note verbale dated 13 March 2000 from the Permanent Mission of the United States of America to the United Nations (Vienna) addressed to the Secretary General, 24 March 2000 UN Doc. A/AC. 105/740, Note verbale dated 3 July 2000 from the Permanent Mission of the Republic of South Africa to the United Nations (Vienna) addressed to the Secretary General, 11 July 2000
2001	UN Doc. A/AC. 105/762, Note verbale dated 8 March 2001 from the Permanent Mission of Saudi Arabia to the United Nations (Vienna) addressed to the Secretary-General, 3 April 2001 UN Doc. A/56/10, Report of the International Law Commission on the work of its fifty-third session (23 April-1 June and 2 July-10 August 2001), Official Records of the General Assembly, Fifty-Sixth Session, Supplement No. 10, New York and Geneva 2007
2003	UN Doc. A/AC. 105/806, Note Verbale dated 29 July 2003 from the Permanent Mission of the Netherlands to the United Nations (Vienna) addressed to the Secretary-General, 22 August 2003
2004	UN Doc. A/AC. 105/824, Note Verbale dated 18 February 2004 from the Permanent Mission of the Netherlands to the United Nations (Vienna) addressed to the Secretary-General, 16 March 2004 UN Doc. A/AC. 105/826, Report of the Legal Subcommittee on the work of its forty-third session, held in Vienna from 29 March-8 April 2004, 16 April 2004 UN Doc. A/AC. 105/824/Corr. 1, Note Verbale dated 18 February 2004 from the Permanent Mission of the Netherlands to the United Nations (Vienna) addressed to the Secretary-General, Corrigendum, 1August 2008
2006	UN Doc. A/AC. 105/871, Report of the Legal Subcommittee on its Forty-Fifth Session (3-13 April 2006), Annex I, Report of the Chairman of the Working Group on the Status and Application of the Five United Nations Treaties on Outer Space, Appendix, Advantages of adherence to the Convention on International Liability for Damage Caused by Space Objects, 24 April 2006
2007	UN Doc. A/AC. 105/891, Report of the Legal Subcommittee on its Forty-Sixth Session (26 March-5 April 2007), Annex I, Report of the Chairman of the Working Group on the Status and Application of the Five United Nations Treaties on Outer Space, 2 May 2007
2008	UN Doc. A/AC. 105/912, Information on national legislation relevant to the peaceful exploration and use of outer space, 29 January 2008 UN Doc. A/AC. 105/917, Report of the Legal Subcommittee on its Forty-Seventh Session, (31 March-11 April 2008), 18 April 2008 UN Doc. A/AC/105/INF. 417, Note Verbale dated 31 December 2008 from the Permanent Mission of Venezuela to the United Nations (Vienna) addressed to the Secretary-General, 10 March 2009
2009	UN Doc. A/AC. 105/932, Information on national legislation relevant to the peaceful exploration and use of outer space, 2 February 2009 UN Doc. A/AC. 105/935, Report of the Legal Subcommittee on its Forty-Eighth Session (23 March-3 April 2009), 20 April 2009

续表

2009	UN Doc. A/AC. 105/965, Note Verbale dated 3 November 2009 from the Permanent Mission of the United Kingdom of Great Britain and Northern Ireland to the United Nations (Vienna) addressed to the Secretary-General, 3 November 2009 UN Doc. A/AC. 105/1002, Note Verbale dated 3 June 2009 from the Permanent Mission of the Netherlands to the United Nations (Vienna) addressed to the Secretary-General, 22 November 2010
2010	UN Doc. A/AC. 105/957, Information on national legislation relevant to the peaceful exploration and use of outer space, 15 January 2010 UN Doc. A/AC. 105/942, Report of the Legal Subcommittee on its Forty-Ninth Session (22 March-1 April 2010), 16 April 2010
2011	UN Doc. A/AC. 105/990, Report of the Legal Subcommittee on its fiftieth session (28 March-8 April 2011), 20 April 2011 UN Doc. A/AC. 105/1004/Rev. 1, Note Verbale dated 26 April 2011 from the Permanent Mission of the Netherlands to the United Nations (Vienna) addressed to the Secretary-General, 13 September 2011
2012	UN Doc. A/AC. 105/1001, Report of the Scientific and Technical Subcommittee on its forty-ninth session (6-17 February 2012), 28 February 2012 UN Doc. A/AC. 105/1003, Report of the Legal Subcommittee on its fifty-first session (19-30 March 2012), 10 April 2012
Series A/AC. 105/C. 2/	
1962	UN Doc. A/AC. 105/C. 2/L. 4, USA: Proposal-Liability for Space Vehicle Accidents, 4 June 1962, in: UN Doc. A/AC. 105/6, Report of the Legal Sub-Committee on the Work of its First Session (28 May-20 June 1962), 9 July 1962 UN Doc. A/AC. 105/C. 2/L. 2, International Agreement on the Rescue of Astronauts and Spaceships Making Emergency Landings, USSR Proposal, 6 June 1962 UN Doc. A/AC. 105/C. 2/L. 1, Declaration of Basic Principles Governing the Activities of States Pertaining to the Exploration and Use of Outer Space, USSR Proposal, 6 June 1962 UN Doc. A/AC. 105/C. 2/L. 3, Draft Proposal on Assistance to and Return of Space Vehicles and Personnel, United States Proposal, 8 June 1962
1963	UN Doc. A/AC. 105/C. 2/L. 7, Working Paper Submitted by the Belgian Delegation on the Unification of Certain Rules Governing Liability for Damage Caused by Space Devices, 29 April 1963, in: UN Doc. A/AC. 105/12, Report of the Legal Sub-Committee on the Work of its Second Session (16 April-3 May 1963), Annex I, C, 6 May 1963
1964	UN Doc. A/AC. 105/C. 2/L. 2/Rev. 1, International Agreement on the Rescue of Astronauts and Spaceships Making Emergency Landings, USSR Revised Draft, 9 March 1964 UN Doc. A/AC. 105/C. 2/L. 9, International Agreement on Assistance to and Return of Astronauts and Objects Launched into Outer Space, United States Proposal, 9 March 1964 UN Doc. A/AC. 105/C. 2/L. 8, United States: Proposal-Convention concerning liability for damage caused by the launching of objects into outer space, 9 March 1964, in: UN Doc. A/AC. 105/19, Report of the Legal Sub-Committee on the Work of its Third Session (9-26 March 1964), Annex II, Proposals and amendments relating to liability for damage caused by objects launched into outer space, 26 March 1964

续表

1964	UN Doc. A/AC. 105/C. 2/L. 10, Hungary: Proposed draft agreement-Agreement concerning liability for damage caused by the launching of objects into outer space, 16 March 1964, in: UN Doc. A/AC. 105/19, Report of the Legal Sub-Committee on the Work of its Third Session (9-26 March 1964), Annex II, Proposals and amendments relating to liability for damage caused by objects launched into outer space, 26 March 1964 UN Doc. A/AC. 105/C. 2/L. 7/Rev. 1, Belgium: Proposal for a Convention on the Unification of Certain Rules Governing Liability for Damage Caused by Space Devices, 1 October 1964, in: UN Doc. A/AC. 105/21, Report of the Legal Sub-Committee on the Work of the Second Part of its Third Session (5-23 October 1964), Annex II, Proposals and amendments relating to liability for damage caused by objects launched into outer space, 23 October 1964 UN Doc. A/AC. 105/C. 2/L. 7/Rev. 2, Belgium: Proposal for a Convention on the Unification of Certain Rules Governing Liability for Damage Caused by Space Devices, 14 October 1964, in: UN Doc. A/AC. 105/21, Report of the Legal Sub-Committee on the Work of the Second Part of its Third Session (5-23 October 1964), Annex II, Proposals and amendments relating to liability for damage caused by objects launched into outer space, 23 October 1964 UN Doc. A/AC. 105/C. 2/L. 8/Rev. 2, United States: Revised Proposal-Convention concerning liability for damage caused by the launching of objects into outer space, 20 October 1964, in: UN Doc. A/AC. 105/21, Report of the Legal Sub-Committee on the Work of the Second Part of its Third Session (5-23 October 1964), Annex II, Proposals and amendments relating to liability for damage caused by objects launched into outer space, 23 October 1964 UN Doc. A/AC. 105/C. 2/L. 8/Rev. 1, United States: Proposal-Convention concerning liability for damage caused by the launching of objects into outer space, in: UN Doc. A/AC. 105/21, Report of the Legal Sub-Committee on the Work of the Second Part of its Third Session (5-23 October 1964), Annex II, Proposals and amendments relating to liability for damage caused by objects launched into outer space, 23 October 1964 UN Doc. A/AC. 105/C. 2/L. 2/Rev. 2, International Agreement on the Rescue of Astronauts and Spaceships Making Emergency Landings, USSR Revised Draft, 26 October 1964
1965	UN Doc. A/AC. 105/C. 2/L. 10/Rev. 1, Hungary: Revised draft Convention concerning Liability for Damages caused by the Launching of Objects into Outer Space, 24 September 1965, in: UN Doc. A/AC. 105/29, Report of the Legal Sub-Committee on the Work of its Fourth Session (20 September-1 October 1965), Annex II, Proposals and amendments relating to liability for damage caused by objects launched into outer space, 1 October 1965 UN Doc. A/AC. 105/C. 2/L. 8/Rev. 3, United States: Revised Proposal-Convention concerning liability for damage caused by the launching of objects into outer space, 24 September 1965, in: UN Doc. A/AC. 105/29, Report of the Legal Sub-Committee on the Work of its Fourth Session (20 September-1 October 1965), Annex II, Proposals and amendments relating to liability for damage caused by objects launched into outer space, 1 October 1965
1966	UN Doc. A/AC. 105/C. 2/L. 12, Draft Treaty Governing the Exploration of the Moon and Other Celestial Bodies, Proposal United States of America, 11 July 1966
1967	UN Doc. A/AC. 105/C. 2/L. 18, Agreement on the Rescue of Astronauts in the Event of Accidents or Emergency Landing, USSR Revised Draft, 19 June 1967 UN Doc. A/AC. 105/C. 2/L. 20, Assistance to and Return of Astronauts and Space Objects, Revised Australian-Canadian proposal submitted as a working paper, 21 June 1967

续表

1967	UN Doc. A/AC. 105/C. 2/L. 19, United States of America: Proposal-Convention concerning liability for damage caused by the launching of objects into outer space, 21 June 1967, in: UN Doc. A/AC. 105/37, Report of the Legal Sub-Committee on the Work of its Sixth Session (19 June-14 July 1967), Annex II, Proposals, amendments and other documents relating to liability for damage caused by the launching of objects into outer space, 14 July 1967 UN Doc. A/AC. 105/C. 2/L. 23, Agreement on Assistance to, and Rescue and Return of Astronauts, 23 June 1967 UN Doc. A/AC. 105/C. 2/L. 7/Rev. 3, Belgium: Proposal for a Convention on the Unification of Certain Rules Governing Liability for Damage Caused by Space Devices to Third Parties on the Surface of the Earth and Aircraft in Flight, 26 June 1967, in: UN Doc. A/AC. 105/37, Report of the Legal Sub-Committee on the Work of its Sixth Session (19 June-14 July 1967), Annex II, Proposals, amendments and other documents relating to liability for damage caused by the launching of objects into outer space, 14 July 1967 UN Doc. A/AC. 105/C. 2/L. 24 and Add. 1, Hungary: Proposal, 26 and 28 June 1967, in: UN Doc. A/AC. 105/37, Report of the Legal Sub-Committee on the Work of its Sixth Session (19 June-14 July 1967), Annex II, Proposals, amendments and other documents relating to liability for damage caused by the launching of objects into outer space, 14 July 1967 UN Doc. A/AC. 105/C. 2/L. 22, Proposal by Argentina, in: A/AC. 105/37, Report of the Legal Sub-Committee on the Work of Its Sixth Session (19 June-14 July 1967), Annex II, Proposals, amendments and other documents relating to liability for damage caused by the launching objects into outer space, 14 July 1967 UN Doc. A/AC. 105/C. 2/L. 25, Argentina: proposal-Arbitration Commission, in: UN Doc. A/AC. 105/37, Report of the Legal Sub-Committee on the Work of its Sixth Session (19 June-14 July 1967), Annex II, Proposals, amendments and other documents relating to liability for damage caused by the launching of objects into outer space, 14 July 1967 UN Doc. A/AC. 105/C. 2/L. 26, India: Draft Agreement on Liability-Proposal, 30 June 1967, in: UN Doc. A/AC. 105/37, Report of the Legal Sub-Committee on the Work of its Sixth Session (19 June-14 July 1967), Annex II, Proposals, amendments and other documents relating to liability for damage caused by the launching of objects into outer space, 14 July 1967 UN Doc. A/AC. 105/C. 2/L. 28, Draft agreement on the rescue of astronauts, the return of astronauts and the return of objects launched into outer space, 12 December 1967 UN Doc. A/AC. 105/C. 2/L. 28/Rev. 1, Draft agreement on the rescue of astronauts, the return of astronauts and the return of objects launched into outer space, 14 December 1967
1968	UN Doc. A/AC. 105/C. 2/L. 36, France: proposal concerning the state liable and joint and several liability, 10 June 1968 UN Doc. A/AC. 105/C. 2/L. 36/Rev. 1, France: revised proposal concerning the state liable and joint and several liability, 12 June 1968, in: UN Doc. A/AC. 105/45, Report of the Legal Sub-Committee on the Work of its Seventh Session (4-28 June 1968), Annex I, Proposals, amendments and other documents relating to liability for damage caused by the launching of objects into outer space, 11 July 1968 UN Doc. A/AC. 105/C. 2/L. 40, Working Paper submitted by the Italian delegation-Draft convention concerning liability for damage caused by the launching of objects into outer space, 13 June 1986, in: UN Doc. A/AC. 105/45, Report of the Legal Sub-Committee on the Work of its Seventh Session (4-28 June 1968), Annex I, Proposals, amendments and other documents relating to liability for damage caused by the launching of objects into outer space, 11 July 1968

续表

1968	UN Doc. A/AC. 105/C. 2/L. 45, French Proposal, Draft Convention Concerning the Registration of Objects Launched into Space for the Exploration or Use of Outer Space, 18 June 1968 UN Doc. A/AC. 105/C. 2/L. 47, Australia/United Kingdom: Working Paper-Applicable Law for Determination of Compensation, 19 June 1968, in: UN Doc. A/AC. 105/45, Report of the Legal Sub-Committee on the Work of its Seventh Session (4-28 June 1968), Annex I, Proposals, amendments and other documents relating to liability for damage caused by the launching of objects into outer space, 11 July 1968 UN Doc. A/AC. 105/C. 2/L. 32, India: proposal-Convention concerning liability for damage caused by the launching of objects into outer space, 2 June 1968, in: UN Doc. A/AC. 105/45, Report of the Legal Sub-Committee on the Work of its Seventh Session (4-28 June 1968), Annex I, Proposals, amendments and other documents relating to liability for damage caused by the launching of objects into outer space, 11 July 1968 UN Doc. A/AC. 105/C. 2/L. 32/Rev. 1, India: proposal-Convention concerning liability for damage caused by the launching of objects into outer space, in: UN Doc. A/AC. 105/45, Report of the Legal Sub-Committee on the Work of its Seventh Session (4-28 June 1968), Annex I, Proposals, amendments and other documents relating to liability for damage caused by the launching of objects into outer space, 11 July 1968 UN Doc. A/AC. 105/C. 2/L. 39, Australia: proposal, in: UN Doc. A/AC. 105/45, Report of the Legal Sub-Committee on the Work of its Seventh Session (4-28 June 1968), Annex I, Proposals, amendments and other documents relating to liability for damage caused by the launching of objects into outer space, 11 July 1968 UN Doc. A/AC. 105/C. 2/L. 37/Rev. 1, United Kingdom: revised proposal-Field of Application, 14 June 1968, in: UN Doc. A/AC. 105/45, Report of the Legal Sub-Committee on the Work of its Seventh Session (4-28 June 1968), Annex I, Proposals, amendments and other documents relating to liability for damage caused by the launching of objects into outer space, 11 July 1968
1969	UN Doc. A/AC. 105/C. 2/L. 53, Poland: Working Paper, 13 June 1969 UN Doc. A/AC. 105/C. 2/L. 54, Argentina: Proposal, 13 June 1969 UN Doc. A/AC. 105/C. 2/L. 59, Argentina: Proposal-Law applicable for the determination of compensation, 20 June 1969, in: UN Doc. A/AC. 105/58, Report Of The Legal Sub-Committee on the Work of its Eighth Session (9 June-4 July 1969), Annex II, Proposals and other documents relating to liability for damage caused by the launching of objects into outer space, 4 July 1969 UN Doc. A/AC. 105/C. 2/L. 66, Argentina and Poland: Proposal, 27 June 1969 UN Doc. A/AC. 105/C. 2/L. 69, Argentina, France and Poland: Proposal, 1 July 1969 UN Doc. A/AC. 105/C. 2/L. 32/Rev. 2, India: proposal-Convention concerning liability for damage caused by the launching of objects into outer space, 3 July 1969, in: UN Doc. A/AC. 105/58, Report of the Legal Sub-Committee on the Work of its Eighth Session (9 June-4 July 1969), Annex II, Proposals and other documents relating to liability for damage caused by the launching of objects into outer space, 4 July 1969 UN Doc. A/AC. 105/C. 2/L. 58, United States of America: Proposal-Convention concerning liability for damage caused by the launching of objects into outer space, in: UN Doc. A/AC. 105/58, Report Of The Legal Sub-Committee on the Work of its Eighth Session (9 June-4 July 1969), Annex II, Proposals and other documents relating to liability for damage caused by the launching of objects into outer space, 4 July 1969 UN Doc. A/AC. 105/C. 2/L. 55 and Rev. 1, Canadian Proposal, 13 June 1969, reproduced in: UN Doc. A/AC. 105/58 Annex I, Proposals Concerning Questions Relative to the Definition of Outer Space and the Utilization of Outer Space and Celestial Bodies, Including the Various Implications of Space Communications, 4 July 1969

续表

1969	UN Doc. PUOS/C. 2/69/WG. I/CRP. 12, USSR: Proposal, in: UN Doc. A/AC. 105/58, Report Of The Legal Sub-Committee on the Work of its Eighth Session (9 June-4 July 1969), Annex II, Proposals and other documents relating to liability for damage caused by the launching of objects into outer space, 4 July 1969 UN Doc. PUOS/C. 2/69/WG. I/CRP. 9, France: Proposal-Question of joint liability, in: UN Doc. A/AC. 105/58, Report Of The Legal Sub-Committee on the Work of its Eighth Session (9 June-4 July 1969), Annex II, Proposals and other documents relating to liability for damage caused by the launching of objects into outer space, 4 July 1969 UN Doc. A/AC. 105/C. 2/L. 60 and Add. 1, Belgium, France, Italy, Sweden and United Kingdom: proposal-International Organizations, in: UN Doc. A/AC. 105/58, Report Of The Legal Sub-Committee on the Work of its Eighth Session (9 June-4 July 1969), Annex II, Proposals and other documents relating to liability for damage caused by the launching of objects into outer space, 4 July 1969 UN Doc. PUOS/C. 2/69/WG. 1/CRP. 2/Rev. 1, Austria: Working paper-Field of application and exemptions from provisions of agreement; Question of absolute liability and exoneration from liability, in: UN Doc. A/AC. 105/58, Report Of The Legal Sub-Committee on the Work of its Eighth Session (9 June-4 July 1969), Annex II, Proposals and other documents relating to liability for damage caused by the launching of objects into outer space, 4 July 1969 UN Doc. PUOS/C. 2/69/WG. I/CRP. 13, Belgium: Proposal, in: UN Doc. A/AC. 105/58, Report Of The Legal Sub-Committee on the Work of its Eighth Session (9 June-4 July 1969), Annex II, Proposals and other documents relating to liability for damage caused by the launching of objects into outer space, 4 July 1969 UN Doc. PUOS/C. 2/69/WG. I/CRP. 17, United Kingdom and United States: Working Paper, in: UN Doc. A/AC. 105/58, Report Of The Legal Sub-Committee on the Work of its Eighth Session (9 June-4 July 1969), Annex II, Proposals and other documents relating to liability for damage caused by the launching of objects into outer space, 4 July 1969
1970	UN Doc. A/AC. 105/C. 2/L. 77, Text approved by the Working Group on 1 July 1970-Draft Convention on International Liability for Damage Caused by Space Objects, 1 July 1970, in: UN Doc. A/AC. 105/85, Report Of The Legal Sub-Committee on the Work of its Ninth Session (8 June-3 July 1970), Annex I, Proposals And Other Documents Relating To Liability For Damage Caused By The Launching Of Objects Into Outer Space (Agenda item 2), 3 July 1970 UN Doc. A/AC. 105/C. 2/WG(IX)/L. 5, Text approved by the Working Group at its meeting on 10 June 1970-Pursuit of remedies available in Respondent State or under other international agreements, 10 June 1970, in: UN Doc. A/AC. 105/85, Report Of The Legal Sub-Committee on the Work of its Ninth Session (8 June-3 July 1970), Annex I, Proposals And Other Documents Relating To Liability For Damage Caused By The Launching Of Objects Into Outer Space (Agenda item 2), 3 July 1970 UN Doc. A/AC. 105/C. 2/L. 71 and Corr. 1, Argentina: Draft Agreement on the Principles Governing Activities in the Use of the Natural Resources of the Moon and other Celestial Bodies, 23 June 1970, reproduced in: UN Doc. A/AC. 105/85, Report of the Legal Sub-Committee on the Work of its Ninth Session (8 June-3 July 1970), Annex II, Proposals Concerning Questions Relative to the Definition of Outer Space and the Utilization of Outer Space and Celestial Bodies, Including the Various Implications of Space Communications, 3 July 1970

续表

1970	UN Doc. PUOS/C. 2/DG (IX)/1, Working Paper prepared by the Secretariat in accordance with the tentative agreement reached by the Drafting Group on 27 June 1970, 3 July 1970, in: UN Doc. A/AC. 105/85, Report Of The Legal Sub-Committee on the Work of its Ninth Session (8 June-3 July 1970), Annex I, Proposals And Other Documents Relating To Liability For Damage Caused By The Launching Of Objects Into Outer Space (Agenda item 2), 3 July 1970 UN Doc. A/AC. 105/C. 2/L. 74 and Adds. 1 and 2, Argentina, Australia, Belgium, Canada, Italy, Japan, Sweden, United Kingdom: Proposal-Measure of Compensation and Competence of the Claims Commission, 29 June 1970, in: UN Doc. A/AC. 105/85, Report Of The Legal Sub-Committee on the Work of its Ninth Session (8 June-3 July 1970), Annex I, Proposals And Other Documents Relating To Liability For Damage Caused By The Launching Of Objects Into Outer Space (Agenda item 2), 3July 1970 UN Doc. A/AC. 105/C. 2/L. 76, Bulgaria, Hungary, USSR: Proposal-Settlement of Disputes, 30 June 1970, in: UN Doc. A/AC. 105/85, Report Of The Legal Sub-Committee on the Work of its Ninth Session (8 June-3 July 1970), Annex I, Proposals And Other Documents Relating To Liability For Damage Caused By The Launching Of Objects Into Outer Space (Agenda item 2), 3 July 1970 UN Doc. A/AC. 105/C. 2/L. 75, Bulgaria, Hungary, USSR: Proposal-Applicable Law, in: UN Doc. A/AC. 105/85, Report Of The Legal Sub-Committee on the Work of its Ninth Session (8 June-3 July 1970), Annex I, Proposals And Other Documents Relating To Liability For Damage Caused By The Launching Of Objects Into Outer Space (Agenda item 2), 3 July 1970 UN Doc. PUOS/C. 2/70/WG. I/CRP. 15, India: Amendment (PUOS/C. 2/70/WG. I/CRP. 15) to the proposal by Belgium, France, Italy, Sweden and United Kingdom on International Organizations (PUOS/C. 2/WG. I/CRP. 11), in: UN Doc. A/AC. 105/85, Report Of The Legal Sub-Committee on the Work of its Ninth Session (8 June-3 July 1970), Annex I, Proposals And Other Documents Relating To Liability For Damage Caused By The Launching Of Objects Into Outer Space (Agenda item 2), 3 July 1970 UN Doc. PUOS/C. 2/70/WG. I/CRP. 16, Argentina, Belgium, France: Working Paper, in: A/AC. 105/85, Report of the Legal Sub-Committee on the Work of Its Ninth Session (8 June-3 July 1970), Annex I, Proposals and Other Documents Relating to Liability For Damage Caused by the Launching of Objects into Outer Space (Agenda Item 2), 3 July 1970 UN Doc. PUOS/C. 2/70/WG. I/CRP. 2 and Corr. 1, Bulgaria: Working Paper, in: UN Doc. A/AC. 105/85, Report Of The Legal Sub-Committee on the Work of its Ninth Session (8 June-3 July 1970), Annex I, Proposals And Other Documents Relating To Liability For Damage Caused By The Launching Of Objects Into Outer Space (Agenda item 2), 3 July 1970 UN Doc. PUOS/C. 2/70/WG. I/CRP. 8, Mexico: Working Paper-International organizations, in: UN Doc. A/AC. 105/85, Report Of The Legal Sub-Committee on the Work of its Ninth Session (8 June-3 July 1970), Annex I, Proposals And Other Documents Relating To Liability For Damage Caused By The Launching Of Objects Into Outer Space (Agenda item 2), 3 July 1970 UN Doc. PUOS/C. 2/WG (IX)/L. 10, Text approved by the Drafting Group-Draft convention on international liability for damage caused by space objects, in: UN Doc. A/AC. 105/85, Report Of The Legal Sub-Committee on the Work of its Ninth Session (8 June-3 July 1970), Annex I, Proposals And Other Documents Relating To Liability For Damage Caused By The Launching Of Objects Into Outer Space (Agenda item 2), 3 July 1970

续表

1971	UN Doc. PUOS/C. 2/DG(X)/1, Final clauses-text approved by the Drafting Group on 17 June 1971, 17 June 1971, in: UN Doc. A/AC. 105/94, Report Of The Legal Sub-Committee on the Work of its Tenth Session (7 June-2 July 1971), Annex I, Proposals and Other Documents Relating to Agenda Item 2 (Draft Convention on Liability for Damage Caused by Objects Launched into Outer Space), 8 July 1971 UN Doc. PUOS/C. 2/DG(X)/WP. I, Final clauses-Argentina, Austria, Brazil, and Mexico: proposal, 18 June 1971, in: UN Doc. A/AC. 105/94, Report Of The Legal Sub-Committee on the Work of its Tenth Session (7 June-2 July 1971), Annex I, Proposals and Other Documents Relating to Agenda Item 2 (Draft Convention on Liability for Damage Caused by Objects Launched into Outer Space), 8 July 1971 UN Doc. A/AC. 105/C. 2/L. 79, Belgium, Brazil and Hungary: proposal, 21 June 1971, in: UN Doc. A/AC. 105/94, Report Of The Legal Sub-Committee on the Work of its Tenth Session (7 June-2 July 1971), Annex I, Proposals and Other Documents Relating to Agenda Item 2 (Draft Convention on Liability for Damage Caused by Objects Launched into Outer Space), 8 July 1971 UN Doc. PUOS/C. 2/WG(X)/1, Draft Convention on International Liability for Damage Caused by Space Objects: texts approved by the Working Group at its meetings on 22 and 23 June 1971, 23 June 1971, in: UN Doc. A/AC. 105/94, Report Of The Legal Sub-Committee on the Work of its Tenth Session (7 June-2 July 1971), Annex I, Proposals and Other Documents Relating to Agenda Item 2 (Draft Convention on Liability for Damage Caused by Objects Launched into Outer Space), 8 July 1971 UN Doc. PUOS/C. 2/WG(X)/L. 2/Rev. 1, Australia: proposal, India: proposal, 24 June 1971, in: UN Doc. A/AC. 105/94, Report Of The Legal Sub-Committee on the Work of its Tenth Session (7 June-2 July 1971), Annex I, Proposals and Other Documents Relating to Agenda Item 2 (Draft Convention on Liability for Damage Caused by Objects Launched into Outer Space), 8 July 1971 UN Doc. PUOS/C. 2/WG (X)/L. 4/Rev. 1, Morocco: Proposal, 25 June 1971, in: UN Doc. A/AC. 105/94, Report Of The Legal Sub-Committee on the Work of its Tenth Session (7 June-2 July 1971), Annex I, Proposals and Other Documents Relating to Agenda Item 2 (Draft Convention on Liability for Damage Caused by Objects Launched into Outer Space), 8 July 1971 UN Doc. PUOS/C. 2/DG(X)/2, Draft Convention on International Liability for Damage Caused by Space Objects, text approved by the Drafting Group on 28 June 1971, 28 June 1971, in: UN Doc. A/AC. 105/94, Report Of The Legal Sub-Committee on the Work of its Tenth Session (7 June-2 July 1971), Annex I, Proposals and Other Documents Relating to Agenda Item 2 (Draft Convention on Liability for Damage Caused by Objects Launched into Outer Space), 8 July 1971 UN Doc. A/AC. 105/C. 2/10, Legal Sub-Committee -Draft Convention on International Liability for Damage Caused by Space Objects, 29 June 1971, in: UN Doc. A/AC. 105/94, Report Of The Legal Sub-Committee on the Work of its Tenth Session (7 June-2 July 1971), 8 July 1971
1972	UN Doc. PUOS/C. 2/WG. 2/XI/5 and Corr. 1 and Add. 1, Legal Subcommittee Working Group Proposal, 1972 UN Doc. A/AC. 105/C. 2/L. 82, Canadian Proposal, 4 April 1972 UN Doc. A/AC. 105/C. 2(XI)/WP. 1, United States of America: Working Paper (Article I), 11 April 1972, reproduced in: UN Doc. A/AC. 105/101, Report of the Legal Sub-Committee on the Work of its Eleventh Session (10 April-5 May 1972), Annex I, Proposals and other Documents relating to Agenda Item 3 (Questions relating to the Moon), 11 May 1972

续表

1972	UN Doc. A/AC. 105/C. 2(XI)/WP. 4, United States of America: Working Paper (Article IV), 11 April 1972, reproduced in UN Doc. A/AC. 105/101, Report of the Legal Sub-Committee on the Work of its Eleventh Session (10 April-5 May 1972), Annex I, Proposals and other Documents relating to Agenda Item 3 (Questions relating to the Moon), 11 May 1972 UN Doc. A/AC. 105/C. 2(XI)/WP. 3, United States of America: Working Paper, 11 April 1972, in: UN Doc. A/AC. 105/101, Report of the Legal Sub-Committee on the Work of its Eleventh Session (10 April-5 May 1972), Annex I, Proposals and Other Documents Relating to Agenda Item 3 (Questions relating to the Moon), 11 May 1972 UN Doc. A/AC. 105/C. 2(XI)/WP. 9, United States of America: Working Paper, 12 April 1972, is reproduced in: A/AC. 105/101, Report of the Legal Sub-Committee on the Work of its Eleventh Session (10 April-5 May 1972), Annex I, Proposals and other Documents relating to Agenda Item 3 (Questions relating to the Moon), 11 May 1972 UN Doc. A/AC. 105/C. 2(XI)/WP. 10, Sweden and United Kingdom: Working Paper, 12 April 1972, reproduced in: UN Doc. A/AC. 105/101, Report of the Legal Sub-Committee on the Work of its Eleventh Session (10 April-5 May 1972), Annex I, Proposals and Other Documents Relating to Agenda Item 3 (Questions Relating to the Moon), 11 May 1972 UN Doc. A/AC. 105/C. 2(XI)/WP. 12, United States of America: Working Paper, 13 April 1972, reproduced in: A/AC. 105/101, Report of the Legal Sub-Committee on the Work of its Eleventh Session (10 April-5 May 1972), Annex I, Proposals and other Documents relating to Agenda Item 3 (Questions relating to the Moon), 11 May 1972 UN Doc. A/AC. 105/C. 2(XI)/WP. 10/Rev. 1, Sweden and United Kingdom: revised Working Paper, 13 April 1972, reproduced in: UN Doc. A/AC. 105/101, Report of the Legal Sub-Committee on the Work of its Eleventh Session (10 April-5 May 1972), Annex I, Proposals and Other Documents Relating to Agenda Item 3 (Questions Relating to the Moon), 11 May 1972 UN Doc. A/AC. 105/C. 2(XI)/WP. 11, Australia: Working Paper, 13 April 1972, reproduced in: UN Doc. A/AC. 105/101, Report of the Legal Sub-Committee on the Work of its Eleventh Session (10 April-5 May 1972), Annex I, Proposals and Other Documents Relating to Agenda Item 3 (Questions Relating to the Moon), 11 May 1972 UN Doc. A/AC. 105/C. 2(XI)/WP. 13, Australia: Working Paper, 13 April 1972, reproduced in: UN Doc. A/AC. 105/101, Report of the Legal Sub-Committee on the Work of its Eleventh Session (10 April-5 May 1972), Annex I, Proposals and Other Documents Relating to Agenda Item 3 (Questions Relating to the Moon), 11 May 1972 UN Doc. A/AC. 105/C. 2(XI)/WP. 14, United States of America: Working Paper, 13 April 1972, in: UN Doc. A/AC. 105/101, Report of the Legal Sub-Committee on the Work of its Eleventh Session (10 April-5 May 1972), 11 May 1972, Annex I, Proposals and other Documents relating to Agenda Item3 (Questions relating to the Moon), p. 14, Doc. no. 18 UN Doc. A/AC. 105/C. 2(XI)/WP, Egypt and India: Working Paper, 14 April 1972, in: UN Doc. A/AC. 105/101, Report of the Legal Sub-Committee on the Work of its Eleventh Session (10 April-5 May 1972), Annex I, Proposals and Other Documents Relating to Agenda Item 3 (Questions Relating to the Moon), 11 May 1972

续表

1972	UN Doc. A/AC. 105/C. 2 (XI)/WP. 12/Rev. 1, United States of America: Working Paper, 17 April 1972, reproduced in: A/AC. 105/101, Report of the Legal Sub-Committee on the Work of its Eleventh Session (10 April-5 May 1972), Annex I, Proposals and other Documents relating to Agenda Item 3 (Questions relating to the Moon), 11 May 1972 UN Doc. PUOS/C. 2/WG (XI)/9, Text formulated by the Working Group, 18 April 1972, in: UN Doc. A/AC. 105/101, Report of the Legal Sub-Committee on the Work of its Eleventh Session (10 April-5 May 1972), 11 May 1972, Annex I, Proposals and other Documents relating to Agenda Item 3 (Questions relating to the Moon), p. 24, Doc. no. 39 UN Doc. A/AC. 105/C. 2/L. 83, Canadian/French Proposal, 20 April 1972 UN Doc. A/AC. 105/C. 2 (XI)/WP. 24, United Kingdom: Working Paper, 20 April 1972, in: A/AC. 105/101, Report of the Legal Sub-Committee on the Work of its Eleventh Session (10 April-5 May 1972), Annex I, Proposals and other Documents relating to Agenda Item 3 (Questions relating to the Moon), 11 May 1972 UN Doc. A/AC. 105/C. 2/L. 83/Corr. 1, 25 April 1972 UN Doc. A/AC. 105/C. 2(XI), Bulgaria: Working Paper, 27 April 1972, reproduced in: UN Doc. A/AC. 105/101, Report of the Legal Sub-Committee on the Work of its Eleventh Session (10 April-5 May 1972), Annex I, Proposals and Other Documents Relating to Agenda Item 3 (Questions Relating to the Moon), 11 May 1972 UN Doc. PUOS/C. 2/WG (XI)/15, Text formulated by the Working Group, 27 April 1972, in: UN Doc. A/AC. 105/101, Report of the Legal Sub-Committee on the Work of its Eleventh Session (10 April-5 May 1972), 11 May 1972, para. 21 UN Doc. A/AC. 105/C. 2(XI)/WP. 26, United States of America: Working Paper, 28 April 1972, in: UN Doc. A/AC. 105/101, Report of the Legal Sub-Committee on the Work of its Eleventh Session (10 April-5 May 1972), 11 May 1972, Annex I, Proposals and other Documents relating to Agenda Item 3 (Questions relating to the Moon), p. 20, Doc. no. 30 UN Doc. PUOS/C. 2/WG(XI)/15/Rev. 1, Draft Treaty Concerning the Moon: Text formulated by the Working Group, 4 May 1972, in: UN Doc. A/AC. 105/101, Report of the Legal Sub-Committee on the Work of its Eleventh Session (10 April-5 May 1972), 11 May 1972, para. 21
1973	UN Doc. A/AC. 105/C. 2/L. 85, US Proposal, 19 March 1973 UN Doc A/AC. 105/C. 2/L. 86, Canadian/French Proposal, 27 March 1973 UN Doc. A/AC. 105/C. 2/L. 87, Argentina, 11 April 1973
1974	UN Doc. A/AC. 105/C. 2/L. 91 and Corr. 1, United States of America: Working Paper, 6 May 1974, reproduced in: UN Doc. A/AC. 105/133, Report of the Legal Sub-Committee on the Work of its Thirteenth Session (6-31 May 1974), Annex I, Documents Relating to Agenda Item 2, 6 June 1974 UN Doc. A/AC. 105/C. 2/L. 92, 7 May 1974 UN Doc. A/AC. 150/C. 2/L. 93, Bulgaria: Working Paper-Draft Treaty Relating to the Moon, 8 May 1974, reproduced in: UN Doc. A/AC. 105/133, Report of the Legal Sub-Committee on the Work of its Thirteenth Session (6-31 May 1974), Annex I, Documents Relating to Agenda Item 2, 6 June 1974 UN Doc. A/AC. 105/C. 2/L. 94, 10 May 1974 UN Doc. A/AC. 105/C. 2/L. 96, India: Working Paper, 13 May 1974, reproduced in: UN Doc. A/AC. 105/133, Report of the Legal Sub-Committee on the Work of its Thirteenth Session (6-31 May 1974, Annex I, Documents Relating to Agenda Item 2, 6 June 1974

续表

1974	UN Doc. A/AC. 105/C. 2/L. 95, Egypt and India: Working Paper, 13 May 1974, reproduced in: UN Doc. A/AC. 105/133, Report of the Legal Sub-Committee on the Work of its Thirteenth Session (6-31 May 1974, Annex I, Documents Relating to Agenda Item 2, 6 June 1974 UN Doc. A/AC. 105/C. 2/L. 97, Egypt, India and Nigeria: Working Paper, 13 May 1974, reproduced in:UN Doc. A/AC. 105/133, Report of the Legal Sub-Committee on the Work of its Thirteenth Session (6-31 May 1974, Annex I, Documents Relating to Agenda Item 2, 6 June 1974 UN Doc. A/AC. 105/C. 2/L. 98/Rev. 1, Mongolia: Working Paper, 20 May 1974, reproduced in: UN Doc. A/AC. 105/133, Report of the Legal Sub-Committee on the Work of its Thirteenth Session (6-31 May 1974, Annex I, Documents Relating to Agenda Item 2, 6 June 1974 UN Doc. A/AC. 105/C. 2/13, 28 May 1974
1997	UN Doc. A/AC. 105/C. 2/L. 206, Working paper submitted by Mexico, 4 April 1997, in: UN Doc. A/AC. 105/674, Report of the Legal Subcommittee on the Work of Its Thirty-Sixth Session (1-8 April 1997), 14 April 1997, Annex II, Documents Annexed To The Report, Part B, Open-Ended Informal Consultations On New Agenda Items: Review Of The Status Of The Five International Legal Instruments Governing Outer Space
2004	UN Doc. A/AC. 105/C. 2/L. 250/Add. 1, Practice of registration of space objects by states and international organizations: replies from Member states. Note by the Secretariat. Addendum, 9 March 2004
2005	UN Doc. A/AC. 105/C. 2/L. 255, Practice of States and international organizations in registering space objects, Background paper by the Secretariat, 25 January 2005
2008	UN Doc. A/AC. 105/C. 2/L. 272, Joint statement on the benefits of adherence to the Agreement Governing the Activities of States on the Moon and Other Celestial Bodies by States parties to the Agreement, Annex, 3 April 2008
2010	UN Doc. A/AC. 105/C. 2/2010/CRP. 11, Information on national legislation relevant to the peaceful exploration and use of outer space: reply of the Netherlands, 23 March 2010
2011	UN Doc. A/AC. 105/C. 2/2011/CRP. 4, Draft Report of the Working Group on National Legislation Relevant to the Peaceful Exploration and Use of Outer Space, 24 March 2011 UN Doc. A/AC. 105/C. 2/2011/CRP. 7, Information on national legislation relevant to the peaceful exploration and use of outer space, 29 March 2011
2012	UN Doc. A/AC. 105/C. 2/2012/CRP. 3, Status of International Agreements relating to activities in outer space as at 1 January 2012, 12 March 2012
Series A/AC. 105/C. 2/SR.	
1962	UN Doc. A/AC. 105/C. 2/SR. 1, Legal Sub-Committee, Summary Record of the First Meeting, held on 28 May 1962 UN Doc. A/AC. 105/C. 2/SR. 7, Legal Sub-Committee, First Session, Summary Record of the Seventh Meeting, held 7 June 1962, 21 August 1962 UN Doc. A/AC. 105/C. 2/SR. 9, Legal Sub-Committee, First Session, Summary Record of the Ninth Meeting, held 12 June 1962, 21 August 1962 UN Doc. A/AC. 105/C. 2/SR. 14, Legal Sub-Committee, Summary Record of the Fourteenth Meeting, held on 19 June 1962, 22 August 1962

续表

1963	UN Doc. A/AC. 105/C. 2/SR. 25, Legal Sub-Committee, Second Session, Summary Record of the Twenty-Fifth Meeting, 30 April 1963
1964	UN Doc. A/AC. 105/C. 2/SR. 35, Legal Sub-Committee, Summary Record of the Thirty-Fifth Meeting, held on 16 March 1964, in: UN Doc. A/AC. 105/C. 2/SR. 29-37, Summary records of the 29th to 37th meetings held from 9 to 26 March 1964, 24 August 1964 UN Doc. A/AC. 105/C. 2/SR. 29-37, Legal Sub-Committee, Third Session (1st Part), Summary Record of the Twenty-Ninth to Thirty-Seventh Meetings, held from 9-26 March 1964, 24 August 1964
1965	UN Doc. A/AC. 105/C. 2/SR. 42, Legal Sub-Committee, Fourth Session, Summary Record of the Forty-Second Meeting, held 21 September 1965, 30 November 1965 UN Doc. A/AC. 105/C. 2/SR. 46, Legal Sub-Committee, Fourth Session, Summary Record of the Forty-Sixth Meeting, held 23 September 1965, 30 November 1965 UN Doc. A/AC. 105/C. 2/SR. 47, Legal Sub-Committee, Fourth Session, Summary Record of the Forty-Sixth Meeting, held 23 September 1965, 30 November 1965 UN Doc. A/AC. 105/C. 2/SR. 48, Legal Sub-Committee, Summary Record of the Forty-Eighth Meeting, held on 27 September 1965, 30 November 1965 UN Doc. A/AC. 105/C. 2/SR. 49, Legal Sub-Committee, Summary Record of the Forty-Ninth Meeting, held on 28 September 1965, 30 November 1965 UN Doc. A/AC. 105/C. 2/SR. 50, Legal Sub-Committee, Summary Record of the Fiftieth Meeting, held on 28 September 1965, 30 November 1965 UN Doc. A/AC. 105/C. 2/SR. 52 Legal Sub-Committee, Summary Record of the Fifty-Second Meeting, held on 29 September 1965, 19 January 1966
1967	UN Doc. A/AC. 105/C. 2/SR. 77, Legal Sub-Committee, Summary Record of the Seventy-Seventh Meeting, held on 23 June 1967, 14 November 1967 UN Doc. A/AC. 105/C. 2/SR. 75, Legal Sub-Committee Sixth Session, Summary Record of the Seventy-Fifth (Opening) Meeting, held on 19 June 1967, 13 November 1967 UN Doc. A/AC. 105/C. 2/SR. 76, Legal Sub-Committee Sixth Session, Summary Record of the Seventy-Sixth Meeting, held 20 June 1967, 13 November 1967 UN Doc. A/AC. 105/C. 2/SR. 85, Legal Sub-Committee Sixth Session, Summary Record of the Eighty-Fifth (Closing) Meeting, held 14 July 1967, 14 November 1967
1968	UN Doc. A/AC. 105/C. 2/SR. 86, Summary Record of the Eighty-Sixth Meeting, held on 14 December 1967, 9 February 1968 UN Doc. A/AC. 105/C. 2/SR. 87, Summary Record of the Eighty-Seventh Meeting, held on 15 December 1967, 2 February 1968 UN Doc. A/AC. 105/C. 2/SR. 89, Summary Record of the Eighty-Ninth Meeting, held on 15 December 1967, 2 February 1968 UN Doc. A/AC. 105/C. 2/SR. 92, Legal Sub-Committee, Summary Record of the Ninety-Second Meeting, held on 6 June 1968, in: UN Doc. A/AC. 105/C. 2/SR. 90-101, Summary records of the Ninetieth to One Hundred and First meetings held from 4 to 18 June 1968, 22 July 1968 UN Doc. A/AC. 105/C. 2/SR. 93, Legal Sub-Committee, Summary Record of the Ninety-Third Meeting, held on 7 June 1968, in: UN Doc. A/AC. 105/C. 2/SR. 90-101, Summary records of the Ninetieth to One Hundred and First meetings held from 4 to 18 June 1968, 22 July 1968

续表

1968	UN Doc. A/AC. 105/C. 2/SR. 95, Legal Sub-Committee, Summary Record of the Ninety-Fifth Meeting, held on 11 June 1968, in: UN Doc. A/AC. 105/C. 2/SR. 90-101, Summary records of the Ninetieth to One Hundred and First meetings held from 4 to 18 June 1968, 22 July 1968
1969	UN Doc. A/AC. 105/C. 2/SR. 120, Draft Agreement on Liability for Damage Caused by Space Objects Launched into Outer Space, 19 June 1969 UN Doc. A/AC. 105/C. 2/SR. 121, Legal Sub-Committee, Summary Record of the One Hundred and Twenty-First Meeting, held on 20 June 1969
1970	UN Doc. A/AC. 105/C. 2/SR. 132-151, Summary Records of the One Hundred and Thirty-Second to the One Hundred and Fifty-First Meetings (8 June-3 July 1970), 29 July 1970
1971	UN Doc. A/AC. 105/C. 2/SR. 162, Legal Sub-Committee, Summary Record of the One Hundred and Sixty-Second Meeting, held on 22 June 1971, in: UN Doc. A/AC. 105/C. 2/SR. 152-169, Summaryrecords of the One Hundred and Fifty-Second to the One Hundred and Sixty-Ninth Meetings held from 6 June to 2 July 1971, 25 August 1971 UN Doc. A/AC. 105/C. 2/SR. 167, Legal Sub-Committee, Summary Record of the One Hundred and Sixty-Seventh Meeting, held on 29 June 1971, in: UN Doc. A/AC. 105/C. 2/SR. 152-169, Summary records of the One Hundred and Fifty-Second to the One Hundred and Sixty-Ninth Meetings held from 6 June to 2 July 1971, 25 August 1971
1972	UN Doc. A/AC. 105/C. 2/SR. 187-191, Legal Sub-Committee, Eleventh Session, Summary Record of the One Hundred and Eighty-Seventh to the One Hundred and Ninety-First and Meetings (2-5 May 1972), 12 July 1972
Series ST/SG/SER. E/	
1977	UN Doc. ST/SG/SER. E/001, Letter dated 31 March 1977 From the Permanent Representative of the United States addressed to the Secretary-General, 14 April 1977
1979	UN Doc. ST/SG/SER. E/021, Note Verbale dated 29 May 1979 from the Permanent Representative of the United States of America to the United Nations addressed to the Secretary-General, 6 June 1979 UN Doc. ST/SG/SER. E/022, Note Verbale dated 13 June 1979 from the Permanent Representative of Czechoslovakia to the United Nations addressed to the Secretary-General, 11 July 1979 UN Doc. ST/SG/SER. E/024, Note Verbale dated 25 June 1979 from the Permanent Representative of Canada to the United Nations addressed to the Secretary-General, 11 July 1979
1983	UN Doc. ST/SG/SER. E/72/Add. 4, Note Verbale dated 7 February 1983 from the Permanent Mission of the Union of Soviet Socialist Republics to the United Nations addressed to the Secretary-General, 9 February 1983
1984	UN Doc. ST/SG/SER. E/096, Information Furnished in Conformity with the Convention on Registration of Objects Launched into Outer Space, 5 March 1984 UN Doc. ST/SG/SER. E/103, Note Verbale dated 27 April 1984 from the Permanent Representative of Japan to the United Nations addressed to the Secretary-General, 15 May 1984
1985	UN Doc. ST/SG/SER. E/129, Note Verbale dated 8 May 1985 from the Permanent Representative of the United Kingdom of Great Britain and Northern Ireland to the United Nations addressed to the Secretary-General, 21 August 1985

续表

1986	UN Doc. ST/SG/SER. E/145, Note Verbale dated 4 June 1986 from the Permanent Mission of Sweden to the United Nations addressed to the Secretary-General, 11 June 1986 UN Doc. ST/SG/SER. E/184, Note Verbale dated 14 November 1986 from the Permanent Mission of Mexico to the United Nations addressed to the Secretary-General, 4 August 1988
1987	UN Doc. ST/SG/SER. E/167, Note Verbale dated 3 August 1987 from the Permanent Mission of Sweden to the United Nations addressed to the Secretary-General, 13 August 1987
1988	UN Doc. ST/SG/SER. E/176/Add. 2, Additional information furnished in conformity with the Convention on Registration of Objects Launched into Outer Space, Note Verbale dated 14 June 1988 from the Permanent Mission of the Union of Soviet Socialist Republics to the United Nations addressed to the Secretary-General, 15 June 1988
1989	UN Doc. ST/SG/SER. E/199, Note Verbale dated 3 May 1989 from the Permanent Mission of Australia to the United Nations addressed to the Secretary-General, 11 May 1989 UN Doc. ST/SG/SER. E/210, Note Verbale dated 8 December 1989 from the Permanent Representative of the United Kingdom of Great Britain and Northern Ireland to the United Nations addressed to the Secretary-General, 19 December 1989
1990	UN Doc. ST/SG/SER. E/213, Note Verbale dated 20 December 1989 from the Permanent Representative of Czechoslovakia to the United Nations addressed to the Secretary-General, 3 January 1990 UN Doc. ST/SG/SER. E/215, Note Verbale dated 31 January 1990 from the Permanent Mission of the Union of Soviet Socialist Republics to the United Nations addressed to the Secretary-General, 2 February 1990 UN Doc. ST/SG/SER. E/215/Add. 1, Note Verbale dated 16 July 1990 from the Permanent Mission of the Union of Soviet Socialist Republics to the United Nations addressed to the Secretary-General, 24 August 1990
1992	UN Doc. ST/SG/SER. E/251, Note Verbale dated 14 February 1992 from the Permanent Representative of Czechoslovakia to the United Nations addressed to the Secretary-General, 26 February 1992
1994	UN Doc. ST/SG/SER. E/275, Note Verbale dated 14 June 1994 from the Permanent Mission of the Russian Federation to the United Nations addressed to the Secretary-General, 13 June 1994
1995	UN Doc. ST/SG/SER. E/291, Note Verbale dated 22 September 1995 from the Permanent Mission of Ukraine to the United Nations addressed to the Secretary-General, 12 October 1995 UN Doc. ST/SG/SER. E/296, Note Verbale dated 7 December 1995 from the Permanent Representative of Spain to the United Nations Office at Vienna addressed to the Secretary-General, 14 December 1995
1996	UN Doc. ST/SG/SER. E/305, Note Verbale dated 27 March 1996 from the Permanent Mission of Spain to the United Nations (Vienna) addressed to the Secretary-General, 3 April 1996 UN Doc. ST/SG/SER. E/311, Note Verbale dated 12 June 1996 from the Permanent Mission of Sweden to the United Nations (Vienna) addressed to the Secretary-General, 28 June 1996 UN Doc. ST/SG/SER. E/314, Note Verbale dated 12 July 1996 from the Permanent Mission of the Czech Republic to the United Nations (Vienna) addressed to the Secretary-General, 5 August 1996

续表

1997	UN Doc. ST/SG/SER. E/317, Note Verbale dated 30 December 1996 from the Permanent Mission of Argentina to the United Nations (Vienna) addressed to the Secretary-General, 15 January 1997 UN Doc. ST/SG/SER. E/318, Note Verbale dated 10 January 1997 from the Permanent Mission of Sweden to the United Nations (Vienna) addressed to the Secretary-General, 21 January 1997 UN Doc. ST/SG/SER. E/323, Note Verbale dated 10 July 1997 from the Permanent Mission of Argentina to the United Nations (Vienna) addressed to the Secretary-General, 29 July 1997 UN Doc. ST/SG/SER. E/322, Note Verbale dated 30 June 1997 from the Permanent Mission of the United States of America to the United Nations (Vienna) addressed to the Secretary-General, 31 July 1997 UN Doc. ST/SG/SER. E/326, Note Verbale dated 9 October 1997 from the Permanent Mission of Spain to the United Nations (Vienna) addressed to the Secretary-General, 20 October 1997
1998	UN Doc. ST/SG/SER. E/327, Note Verbale dated 10 November 1997 from the Permanent Mission of the Russian Federation to the United Nations (Vienna) addressed to the Secretary-General, 30 January 1998 UN Doc. ST/SG/SER. E/329, Note Verbale dated 22 December 1997 from the Permanent Mission of the United States of America to the United Nations (Vienna) addressed to the Secretary-General, 19 January 1998 UN Doc. ST/SG/SER. E/332, Note Verbale dated 4 March 1998 from the Permanent Mission of the Russian Federation to the United Nations (Vienna) addressed to the Secretary-General, 19 March 1998 UN Doc. ST/SG/SER. E/335, Note Verbale dated 6 April 1998 from the Permanent Mission of Sweden to the United Nations (Vienna) addressed to the Secretary-General, 28 April 1998 UN Doc. ST/SG/SER. E/339, Note Verbale dated 12 June 1998 from the Permanent Mission of the United States of America to the United Nations (Vienna) addressed to the Secretary-General, 24 June 1998 UN Doc. ST/SG/SER. E/341, Note Verbale dated 22 July 1998 from the Permanent Mission of the United States of America to the United Nations (Vienna) addressed to the Secretary-General, 4 August 1998 UN Doc. ST/SG/SER. E/342, Note Verbale dated 31 July 1998 from the Permanent Mission of Chile to the United Nations (Vienna) addressed to the Secretary-General, 11 August 1998 UN Doc. ST/SG/SER. E/343, Note Verbale dated 6 August 1998 from the Permanent Mission of the Russian Federation to the United Nations (Vienna) addressed to the Secretary-General, 13 August 1998 UN Doc. ST/SG/SER. E/344, Note Verbale dated 17 August 1998 from the Permanent Mission of the United States of America to the United Nations (Vienna) addressed to the Secretary-General, 26 August 1998 UN Doc. ST/SG/SER. E/351, Note Verbale dated 23 December 1998 from the Permanent Mission of Argentina to the United Nations (Vienna) addressed to the Secretary-General, 1 February 1999
1999	UN Doc. ST/SG/SER. E/352 and Note Verbale dated 1 February 1999 from the Permanent Mission of Sweden to the United Nations (Vienna) addressed to the Secretary-General, 19 February 1999 UN Doc. ST/SG/SER. E/361, Note Verbale dated 20 September 1999 from the Permanent Mission of the Czech Republic to the United Nations (Vienna) addressed to the Secretary-General, 29 September 1999 UN Doc. ST/SG/SER. E/364, Note Verbale dated 3 November 1999 from the Permanent Mission of Sweden to the United Nations (Vienna) addressed to the Secretary-General, 3 November 1999 UN Doc. ST/SG/SER. E/365, Note Verbale dated 11 November 1999 from the Permanent Mission of China to the United Nations (Vienna) addressed to the Secretary-General, 30 November 1999

续表

2000	UN Doc. ST/SG/SER. E/382, Note Verbale dated 7 December 2000 from the Permanent Mission of Argentina to the United Nations (Vienna) addressed to the Secretary-General, 7 December 2000 UN Doc. ST/SG/SER. E/380, Note Verbale dated 28 November 2000 from the Permanent Mission of Sweden to the United Nations (Vienna) addressed to the Secretary-General, 12 December 2000 UN Doc. ST/SG/SER. E/384, Note Verbale dated 29 December 2000 from the Permanent Mission of the Russian Federation to the United Nations (Vienna) addressed to the Secretary-General, 20 March 2001
2001	UN Doc. ST/SG/SER. E/393, Note Verbale dated 25 May 2001 from the Permanent Mission of the Russian Federation to the United Nations (Vienna) addressed to the Secretary-General, 21 June 2001 UN Doc. ST/SG/SER. E/396, Note Verbale dated 5 September 2001 from the Permanent Representative of Germany to the United Nations (Vienna) addressed to the Secretary-General, 14 September 2001
2002	UN Doc. ST/SG/SER. E/413, Note Verbale dated 5 June 2002 from the Permanent Mission of India to the United Nations (Vienna) addressed to the Secretary-General, 19 June 2002 UN Doc. ST/SG/SER. E/417/Rev. 1, Note Verbale dated 9 September 2002 from the Permanent Mission of the United Kingdom of Great Britain and Northern Ireland to the United Nations (Vienna) addressed to the Secretary-General, 3 December 2002
2003	UN Doc. ST/SG/SER. E/433, Note Verbale dated 21 August 2003 from the Permanent Mission of the Czech Republic to the United Nations (Vienna) addressed to the Secretary-General, 9 September 2003 UN Doc. ST/SG/SER. E/439, Note Verbale dated 24 November 2003 from the Permanent Mission of the Czech Republic to the United Nations (Vienna) addressed to the Secretary-General, 3 December 2003
2004	UN Doc. ST/SG/SER. E/445, Note Verbale dated 28 January 2004 from the Permanent Mission of France to the United Nations (Vienna) addressed to the Secretary-General, 2 March 2004 UN Doc. ST/SG/SER. E/446, Note Verbale dated 25 March 2004 from the Permanent Mission of Greece to the United Nations addressed to the Secretary-General, 29 March 2004 UN Doc. ST/SG/SER. E/460, Note Verbale dated 16 November 2004 from the Permanent Mission of the Russian Federation to the United Nations (Vienna) addressed to the Secretary-General, 17 December 2004
2005	UN Doc. ST/SG/SER. E/466, Note Verbale dated 24 January 2005 from the Permanent Mission of Ukraine to the United Nations (Vienna) addressed to the Secretary-General to the United Nations addressed to the Secretary-General, 7 February 2005 UN Doc. ST/SG/SER. E/468, Note Verbale dated 29 March 2005 from the Permanent Mission of France to the United Nations (Vienna) addressed to the Secretary-General, 21 April 2005 UN Doc. ST/SG/SER. E/475, Note Verbale dated 8 June 2005 from the Permanent Mission of China to the United Nations (Vienna) addressed to the Secretary-General, 16 November 2005
2006	UN Doc. ST/SG/SER. E/498, Note Verbale dated 18 August 2006 from the Permanent Mission of Brazil to the United Nations (Vienna) addressed to the Secretary-General, 25 August 2006 UN Doc. ST/SG/SER. E/499, Note Verbale dated 20 September 2006 from the Permanent Mission of France to the United Nations (Vienna) addressed to the Secretary-General, 7 November 2006
2007	UN Doc. ST/SG/SER. E/509, Note Verbale dated 9 March 2007 from the Permanent Mission of Kazakhstan to the United Nations addressed to the Secretary-General, 28 March 2007 UN Doc. ST/SG/SER. E/527, Note Verbale dated 10 December 2007 from the Permanent Mission of Australia to the United Nations (Vienna) addressed to the Secretary-General, 19 December 2007

续表

2008	UN Doc. ST/SG/SER. E/533, Note Verbale dated 31 January 2008 from the Permanent Mission of Japan to the United Nations (Vienna) addressed to the Secretary-General, 5 March 2008 UN Doc. ST/SG/SER. E/540, Note Verbale dated 8 April 2008 from the Permanent Mission of Canada to the United Nations (Vienna) addressed to the Secretary-General, 11 April 2008 UN Doc. ST/SG/SER. E/538, Note Verbale dated 11 March 2008 from the Permanent Mission of Italy to the United Nations (Vienna) addressed to the Secretary-General, 29 May 2008 UN Doc. ST/SG/SER. E/542, Note Verbale dated 5 May 2008 from the Permanent Mission of the Russian Federation to the United Nations (Vienna) addressed to the Secretary-General, 3 July 2008 UN Doc. ST/SG/SER. E/531, Note Verbale dated 28 July 2008 from the Permanent Mission of Spain to the United Nations (Vienna) addressed to the Secretary-General, 17 September 2008 UN Doc. ST/SG/SER. E/552, Note Verbale dated 5 September 2008 from the Permanent Mission of Japan to the United Nations (Vienna) addressed to the Secretary-General, 19 September 2008 UN Doc. ST/SG/SER. E/545, Note Verbale dated 21 May 2008 from the Permanent Mission of India to the United Nations (Vienna) addressed to the Secretary-General, 12 November 2008 UN Doc. ST/SG/SER. E/555, Note Verbale dated 6 October 2008 Permanent Mission of the United Kingdom of Great Britain and Northern Ireland to the United Nations (Vienna) addressed to the Secretary-General, 24 November 2009
2009	UN Doc. ST/SG/SER. E/563, Note Verbale dated 11 February 2009 from the Permanent Mission of France to the United Nations (Vienna) addressed to the Secretary-General, 21 May 2009 UN Doc. ST/SG/SER. E/576, Note Verbale dated 9 September 2009 from the Permanent Mission of the United States of America to the United Nations (Vienna) addressed to the Secretary-General, 14 September 2009 UN Doc. ST/SG/SER. E/575, Note Verbale dated 6 August 2009 from the Permanent Mission of the United Kingdom of Great Britain and Northern Ireland to the United Nations (Vienna) addressed to the Secretary-General, 4 November 2009 UN Doc. ST/SG/SER. E/570, Note Verbale dated 13 October 2009 from the Permanent Mission of India to the United Nations (Vienna) addressed to the Secretary-General, 10 November 2009
2010	UN Doc. ST/SG/SER. E/584, Note Verbale dated 30 November 2009 from the Permanent Mission of Australia to the United Nations (Vienna) addressed to the Secretary-General, 18 January 2010 UN Doc. ST/SG/SER. E/590, Note Verbale dated 22 February 2010 from the Permanent Mission of the United States of America to the United Nations (Vienna) addressed to the Secretary-General, 5 March 2010 UN Doc. ST/SG/SER. E/598/Corr. 1, Note Verbale dated 3 June 2010 from the Permanent Mission of the Russian Federation to the United Nations (Vienna) addressed to the Secretary-General: Corrigendum, 3 June 2010 UN Doc. ST/SG/SER. E/597, Note Verbale dated 30 June 2010 from the Permanent Mission of Canada to the United Nations (Vienna) addressed to the Secretary-General, 6 July 2010 UN Doc. ST/SG/SER. E/592, Note Verbale dated 20 April 2010 from the Permanent Mission of Germany to the United Nations (Vienna) addressed to the Secretary-General, 22 June 2010 UN Doc. ST/SG/SER. E/588, Note Verbale dated 22 January 2010 from the Permanent Mission of France to the United Nations (Vienna) addressed to the Secretary-General, 30 June 2010 UN Doc. ST/SG/SER. E/593, Note Verbale dated 10 May 2010 from the Permanent Mission of the Russian Federation to the United Nations (Vienna) addressed to the Secretary-General, 6 July 2010

续表

2010	UN Doc. ST/SG/SER. E/596, Note Verbale dated 10 May 2010 from the Permanent Mission of the Russian Federation to the United Nations (Vienna) addressed to the Secretary-General, 19 October 2010 UN Doc. ST/SG/SER. E/606, Note Verbale dated 1 September 2010 from the Permanent Mission of Italy to the United Nations (Vienna) addressed to the Secretary-General, 21 October 2010 UN Doc. ST/SG/SER. E/604, Note Verbale dated 15 September 2010 from the Permanent Mission of Japan to the United Nations (Vienna) addressed to the Secretary-General, 22 November 2010 UN Doc. ST/SG/SER. E/607, Note Verbale dated 13 September 2010 from the Permanent Mission of Germany to the United Nations (Vienna) addressed to the Secretary-General, 30 November 2010
2011	UN Doc. ST/SG/SER. E/615, Note Verbale dated 17 February 2011 from the Permanent Mission of Italy to the United Nations (Vienna) addressed to the Secretary-General, 27 July 2011 UN Doc. ST/SG/SER. E/616, Note Verbale dated 23 February 2011 from the Permanent Mission of France to the United Nations (Vienna) addressed to the Secretary-General, 16 August 2011 UN Doc. ST/SG/SER. E/626, Note Verbale dated 11 August 2011 from the Permanent Mission of the Russian Federation to the United Nations (Vienna) addressed to the Secretary-General, 18 November 2011 UN Doc. ST/SG/SER. E/634, Note Verbale dated 24 November 2011 from the Permanent Mission of Italy to the United Nations (Vienna) addressed to the Secretary-General, 24 November 2011 UN Doc. ST/SG/SER. E/632, Note Verbale dated 14 November 2011 from the Permanent Mission of the United States of America to the United Nations (Vienna) addressed to the Secretary-General, 12 December 2011
2012	UN Doc. ST/SG/SER. E/641, Note Verbale dated 27 January 2012 from the Permanent Mission of the Russian Federation to the United Nations (Vienna) addressed to the Secretary-General, 27 January 2012 UN Doc. ST/SG/SER. E/637, Note Verbale dated 26 December 2011 from the Permanent Mission of Kazakhstan to the United Nations (Vienna) addressed to the Secretary-General, 13 January 2012
Series ST/SG/SER. E/INF.	
1976	UN Doc. ST/SG/SER. E/INF. 2, Note Verbale dated 24 August 1976 from the Permanent Mission of Canada to the United Nations addressed to the Secretary-General, 16 November 1976
1977	UN Doc. ST/SG/SER. E/INF. 3, Letter dated 9 February 1977 from the Deputy Representative of the United States in the Security Council addressed to the Secretary-General, 17 February 1977
1978	UN Doc. ST/SG/SER. E/INF. 4, Information furnished by the Permanent Mission of the Union of Soviet Socialist Republics to the United Nations in Note Verbale dated 13 January 1978 addressed to the Secretary-General, 18 January 1978
1979	UN Doc. ST/SG/SER. E/INF. 5, Note Verbale dated 13 June 1979 from the Permanent Representative of Czechoslovakia to the United Nations addressed to the Secretary-General, 11 July 1979
1983	UN Doc. ST/SG/SER. E/INF. 6, Information furnished by the European Space Agency to the United Nations in a letter dated 2 June 1983, 23 June 1983 UN Doc. ST/SG/SER. E/INF. 7, Note Verbale dated 19 December 1983 from the Permanent Mission of Japan to the United Nations addressed to the Secretary-General, 12 November 1986

续表

1987	UN Doc. ST/SG/SER. E/INF. 8, Information furnished by the Permanent Mission of India to the United Nations in a letter dated 11 February 1987, 4 March 1987
1988	UN Doc. ST/SG/SER. E/INF. 9, Note Verbale dated 7 April 1988 from the Permanent Mission of the Federal Republic of Germany to the United Nations addressed to the Secretary-General, 27 April 1988
1995	UN Doc. ST/SG/SER. E/INF. 10, Note Verbale dated 23 March 1995 from the Permanent Mission of Spain to the United Nations (New York) addressed to the Secretary-General, 31 May 1995 UN Doc. ST/SG/SER:E/INF. 11, Note Verbale dated 22 September 1995 from the Permanent Mission of Ukraine to the United Nations addressed to the Secretary-General, 12 October 1995
1996	UN Doc. ST/SG/SER. E/INF. 12, Note Verbale dated 12 July 1996 from the Permanent Representative of Czech Republic to the United Nations (Vienna) addressed to the Secretary-General, 5 August 1996 UN Doc. ST/SG/SER. E/INF. 13, Note Verbale dated 30 December 1996 from the Permanent Mission of Argentina to the United Nations (Vienna) addressed to the Secretary-General, 15 January 1997
1998	UN Doc. ST/SG/SER. E/INF. 14, Letter dated 6 May 1998 from the European Organisation for the Exploitation of Meteorological Satellites addressed to the Secretary-General, 27 May 1998
2003	UN Doc. ST/SG/SER. E/INF. 15, Note Verbale dated 1 October 2003 from the Permanent Mission of Australia to the United Nations (Vienna) addressed to the Secretary-General, 6 October 2003
2004	UN Doc. ST/SG/SER. E/INF. 16, Note Verbale dated 28 January 2004 from the Permanent Mission of France to the United Nations (Vienna) addressed to the Secretary-General, 6 February 2004
2005	UN Doc. ST/SG/SER. E/INF. 17, Note Verbale dated 8 June 2005 from the Permanent Mission of China to the United Nations (Vienna) addressed to the Secretary-General, 21 June 2005
2006	UN Doc. ST/SG/SER. E/INF. 18, Note Verbale dated 12 July 2006 from the Permanent Mission of Belarus to the United Nations (Vienna) addressed to the Secretary-General, 13 July 2006
2007	UN Doc. ST/SG/SER. E/INF. 19, Note Verbale dated 27 March 2007 from the Permanent Mission of Brazil to the United Nations (Vienna) addressed to the Secretary-General, 27 March 2007
2008	UN Doc. ST/SG/SER. E/INF. 20, Note Verbale dated 14 May 2008 from the Permanent Mission of Greece to the United Nations (Vienna) addressed to the Secretary-General, 15 May 2008 UN Doc. ST/SG/SER. E/INF. 21, Note Verbale dated 3 June 2008 from the Permanent Mission of Belgium to the United Nations (Vienna) addressed to the Secretary-General, 2 July 2008 UN Doc. ST/SG/SER. E/INF. 22, Note Verbale dated 13 November 2008 from the Permanent Mission of Pakistan to the United Nations (Vienna) addressed to the Secretary-General, 14 November 2008
2009	UN Doc. ST/SG/SER. E/INF. 23, Note Verbale dated 15 January 2009 from the Permanent Mission of the Republic of Korea to the United Nations (Vienna) addressed to the Secretary-General, 16 April 2009 UN Doc. ST/SG/SER. E/INF. 24, Note Verbale dated 3 June 2009 from the Permanent Mission of the Netherlands to the United Nations (Vienna) addressed to the Secretary-General, 20 August 2009 UN Doc. ST/SG/SER. E/INF. 25, Note Verbale dated 14 July 2009 from the Permanent Mission of the Czech Republic to the United Nations (Vienna) addressed to the Secretary-General, 20 August 2009

续表

2012	UN Doc. ST/SG/SER. E/INF. 26, Note Verbale dated 20 February 2012 from the Permanent Mission of Kazakhstan to the United Nations (Vienna) addressed to the Secretary-General, 28 February 2012 UN Doc. ST/SG/SER. E/INF. 27, Note Verbale dated 11 July 2012 from the Permanent Mission of South Africa to the United Nations (Vienna) addressed to the Secretary-General, 16 July 2012
其他与联合国和平利用外层空间委员会有关的文件	
1964	UN Doc. WG. I/12, USSR: Amendment, in: UN Doc. A/AC. 105/19, Report of the Legal Sub-Committee on the Work of its Third Session (9-26 March 1964) to the Committee on the Peaceful Uses of Outer Space, Annex I, Proposals and Amendments Relating to Assistance to and Return of Astronauts and Space Vehicles, 26 March 1964 UN Doc. PUOS/WG. II/7, Japan: Amendment to Article I lit. (ii) of USA draft, reproduced in: UN Doc. A/AC. 105/19, Report of the Legal Sub-Committee on the Work of its Third Session (9-26 March 1964), Annex II, Proposals and amendments relating to liability for damage caused by objects launched into outer space, 26 March 1964 UN Doc. PUOS/WG. II/9, Italy: Proposal, in: UN Doc. A/AC. 105/19, Report of the Legal Sub-Committee on the Work of its Third Session (9-26 March 1964), Annex II, Proposals and amendments relating to liability for damage caused by objects launched into outer space, 26 March 1964 UN Doc. WG. I/30, Australia and Canada: Proposal, in: UN Doc. A/AC. 105/21, Report of the Legal Sub-Committee on the Work of the Second Part of its Third Session (5-23 October 1964) to theCommittee on the Peaceful Uses of Outer Space, Annex I, Proposals and Amendments Relating to Assistance to and Return of Astronauts and Space Vehicles, 23 October 1964 UN Doc. WG. I/27, United States' proposed modification of Art. 4 Australian-Canadian Draft Agreement on Assistance and Return, in: UN Doc. A/AC. 105/21, Report of the Legal Sub-Committee on the work of the Second Part of its Third Session (5-23 October 1964) to the Committee on the Peaceful Uses of Outer Space, Annex I, Proposals and Amendments Relating to Assistance to and Return of Astronauts and Space Vehicles, 23 October 1964 UN Doc. PUOS/WG. II/20, India: Amendments to definitions, in: A/AC. 105/21, Report of the Legal Sub-Committee on the Work of the Second Part of its Third Session (5-23 October 1964), Annex II, Proposals and amendments relating to liability for damage caused by objects launched into outer space, 23 October 1964 UN Doc. PUOS/WG. II/19, Italy: Amendments to Article 1 of the United States draft (A/AC. 105/C. 2/L. 8/Rev. 1), in: UN Doc. A/AC. 105/21, Report of the Legal Sub-Committee on the Work of the Second Part of its Third Session (5-23 October 1964), Annex II, Proposals and amendments relating to liability for damage caused by objects launched into outer space, 23 October 1964
1965	UN Doc. WG. I/33, USA: Proposal, in: UN Doc. A/AC. 105/29, Report of the Legal Sub-Committee on the work of its Fourth Session (20 September-1 October 1965) to the Committee on the Peaceful Uses of Outer Space, Annex I, Proposals and Amendments Relating to Assistance to and Return of Astronauts and Space Vehicles, 1 October 1965
1968	UN Doc. A/AC. 105/C. 2/L. 34, United States of America: Proposal-Field of application and exemptions from provisions of agreement, 10 June 1968, in: UN Doc. A/AC. 105/45, Report of the Legal Sub-Committee on the Work of its Seventh Session (4-28 June 1968), Annex I, Proposals, amendments and other documents relating to liability for damage caused by the launching of objects into outer space, 11 July 1968

续表

1978	UN Doc. WG. I(1978)/WP. 2 Austria: Working Paper, Agreement Governing the Activities of States on the Moon and other Celestial Bodies, 3 April 1978
2006	UN Doc. COPUOS/LEGAL/T. 741, Committee on the Peaceful Uses of Outer Space, Legal Subcommittee, Unedited Transcript of the 741st Meeting, 10 April 2006
2008	UN Doc. COPUOS/LEGAL/T. 769, Committee on the Peaceful Uses of Outer Space, Legal Subcommittee, Unedited Transcript of the 769th Meeting, 2 April 2008
其他联合国文件	
1953	UN Doc. A/CN. 4/8ER. A/1953, Yearbook of the International Law Commission 1953, Volume I
1966	UN Doc. A/6309/Rev. 1, Reports of the Commission to the General Assembly, Part II, Report of the International Law Commission on the work of its eighteenth session, Geneva 4 May-19 July 1966
1967	UN Doc. A/C. 1/PV. 1515, UNGA Official Records, Twenty-Second Session, Agenda Item 92, 1 November 1967
1969	UN Doc. A/7610/Rev. 1, Report of the International Law Commission on the work of its twenty-first session 2 June-8 August 1969
1972	Stockholm Declaration of the United Nations Conference on the Human Environment of 16 June 1972, 11 ILM 1416 UN Doc. A/CONF. 48/14/Rev. 1, Report of the United Nations Conference on the Human Environment, Stockholm 5-16 June 1972
1997	UN Doc. A/CN. 4/SER. A/1997/Add. 1 (Part. 2), Yearbook of the International Law Commission 1997, Vol. II, Part II, Chapter Ⅷ-Diplomatic Protection
2007	UN Doc. A/56/10, Report of the International Law Commission on the work of its fifty-third session (23 April-1 June and 2 July-10 August 2001), Official Records of the General Assembly, Fifty-Sixth Session, Supplement No. 10, New York and Geneva 2007 UN Doc. A/61/10, Report of the International Law Commission, 58th session, GA Official Records, Sixty-first Session, Supplement No. 10, p. 16, Draft articles on Diplomatic Protection, 21 September 2007
国内立法	
Argentina	National Decree No. 125/95 On Establishment of the National Registry of Space Objects Launched into Outer Space (25 July 1995)
Australia	Space Activities Act No. 123 (1998)
Austria	Federal Law on the Licensing of Space Activities and the Establishment of a Space Registry (6 December 2011)
Belarus	Decree of the Presidium of the Supreme Council of the Byelorussian SSR No. 1359-IX On ratification of the Convention on Registration of Objects Launched into Outer Space (20 July 1977)
Belgium	Law on the Activities of Launching, Flight Operations or Guidance of Space Objects (17 September 2005)
China	Order No. 6 of the Commission for Science, Technology, Industry and National Defense and the Ministry of Foreign Affairs of the People's Republic of China (8 February 2001)

续表

France	Act No. 61-1382 (19 December 1961) Decree No. 84-510 Regarding the Centre National d'Etudes Spatiales (CNES) (28 June 1984) (modified by Decree No. 2009-644, 9 June 2009) Space Operation Act, Law No. 2008-518 (3 June 2008) Decree No. 2009-426 (16 April 2009)
Italy	Law No. 153 On Accession of the Republic of Italy to the Convention on Objects Launched into Outer Space (12 July 2005)
Japan	Law No. 161 Concerning Japan Aerospace Exploration Agency (JAXA) (13 December 2002) Law No. 43 Fundamental Act of Outer Space (enacted 21 May 2008, entered into force 27 August 2008)
Kazakhstan	Law of the Republic of Kazakhstan No. 108-1 On the Accession of the Republic of Kazakhstan to the Convention on Registration of Objects Launched into Outer Space (15 May 1997) Agreement between the Russian Federation and the Republic of Kazakhstan on the Development of Cooperation Concerning the Effective Utilization of the Baikonur Cosmodrome (9 January 2004) Order of the Minister of Defense and Aerospace Industry No. 1/NK On Approval of Regulations of the Aerospace Committee of the Ministry of Defense and Aerospace Industry of the Republic of Kazakhstan (16 November 2016) Law of the Republic of Kazakhstan on Space Activity No. 528-IV (6 January 2012)
Netherlands	Rules Concerning Space Activities and the Establishment of a Registry of Space Objects (Space Activities Act) (24 January 2007) Decree Containing Rules with Regard to a Registry of Information Concerning Space Objects (Space Objects Registry Decree) (13 November 2007) Order Concerning Licence Applications for the Performance of Space Activities and the Registration of Space Objects (7 February 2008) (as amended by Order of 16 April 2010)
Russia	Law of the Russian Federation On Space Activity No. 5663-1 (20 August 1993) (as amended 7 March 2018) Federal Law No. 215-FZ On State Space Corporation "Roscosmos" (13 July 2015) (as amended 23 April 2018) Law of the Russian Federation No. 5485-1 On State Secret (21 July 1993) (as amended 8 November 2011) Decree of the Government of the Russian Federation No. 30 On Model Regulation of Interaction between Federal Executive Authorities (19 January 2005) The Administrative Regulation of the Russian Federal Space Agency on the Implementation of the State Function of Maintaining the Registry of Space Objects Launched in Outer Space by the Russian Federation (approved by Order of the Federal Space Agency dated 22 March 2010 No. 44, registered in the Ministry of Justice of the Russian Federation on 22 September 2010 No. 18508)
Spain	Royal Decree No. 278/1995 Establishing in the Kingdom of Spain the registry foreseen in the Convention adopted by the United Nations General Assembly on 2 November 1974 (24 February 1995)
Ukraine	Law of the Ukraine On Space Activity (15 November 1996) Decree of the Cabinet of Ministers of Ukraine No. 1722 On Provision on the National Space Agency of Ukraine (13 December 2006)

续表

United Kingdom	United Kingdom Outer Space Act (1986)
United States of America	Commercial Space Launch Activities Act, 49 USC 701, as revised by the Commercial Space Launch Amendments Act 2004, Public Law 108-492, 23 December 2004
Sweden	Decree No. 1069 On Space Activities (25 November 1982)
其他文件	
1977	ESA/C/XXII/Res. 3, Resolution of the Council of the European Space Agency on the Agency´s Legal Liability, 13 December 1977
1979	Canada: Claim Against The Union Of Soviet Socialist Republics For Damage Caused By Soviet Cosmos 954, International Legal Materials (18) 1979, pp. 907 ff
1981	Canada-Union of Soviet Socialist Republics: Protocol on Settlement of Canada´s Claim for Damages Caused by "Cosmos 954", International Legal Materials (20) 1981, p. 689
2001	UNESCO Universal Declaration on Cultural Diversity (adopted at the 31st Session of the General Conference of UNESCO in Paris, 2 November 2001)
2002	COSPAR Planetary Protection Policy (adopted 20 October 2002, amended 24 March 2005), <http://cosparhq. cnes. fr/Scistr/Pppolicy. htm> accessed 1 October 2012
2004	Council Regulation (EC) No 1321/2004 of 12 July 2004 on the establishment of structures for the management of the European satellite radio-navigation programmes [2004] OJ L246/1
2007	Inter-Agency Space Debris Coordination Committee, Space Debris Mitigation Guidelines Revision 1, September 2007, <http://www. iadc-online. org/index. cgi? item=docs_pub> accessed 1 October 2012 Regulation (EC) 864/2007 of the European Parliament and of the Council of 11 July 2007 on the law applicable to non-contractual obligations (Rome II), [2007] OJ L199/40
2008	European Council Doc. 17175/08, Council Conclusions and Draft Code of Conduct for Outer Space Activities, 17 December 2008, Annex II
2009	NASA Procedural Requirements for Limiting Orbital Debris, NPR 8715. 6 A, 14 May 2009, <http://orbitaldebris. jsc. nasa. gov/library/NPR_8715_006 A. pdf> accessed 1 October 2012
2011	ISO standard 24113:2011, Space systems-Space debris mitigation requirements

案例目录

常设国际法院（PCIJ）

1925 年霍茹夫工厂案（德国诉波兰）

国际法院（ICJ）

1949 年科孚海峡案

1949 年为联合国服务遭受伤害的赔偿案（咨询意见）

1952 年摩洛哥美国国民权利案（法国诉美国）

1955 年诺特鲍姆案（列支敦士登诉危地马拉）

1970 年巴塞罗那电车、电灯和电力公司案（第二阶段）（比利时诉西班牙）

1986 年在尼加拉瓜境内和针对尼加拉瓜的军事和准军事活动案（尼加拉瓜诉美国）

1994 年领土争端案（利比亚诉乍得）

1995 年海洋划界和领土问题案（卡塔尔诉巴林）

1996 年使用或威胁使用核武器合法性案（咨询意见）

2004 年在被占领的巴勒斯坦领土建隔离墙的法律后果案（咨询意见）

国际仲裁裁决

1928 年帕尔马斯岛案（荷兰诉美国）

1931 年克利柏顿岛案（法国诉墨西哥）

1957 年兰诺湖仲裁案（法国诉西班牙）

国内案件

1987 年麦克莱·瓦特森公司诉英格兰贸易与工业部案

缩略语

Add.	补遗
AIAA	美国航空和航天学会
ARABSAT	阿拉伯卫星通信组织
ARRA	《关于营救宇航员、送回宇航员和归还射入外层空间的物体的协定》
Art. /Arts.	条/条款
ASI	意大利航天局
BELSPO	比利时科学政策办公室
BGBl.	联邦法律公报
BNSC	英国国家航天中心
BUSTIND	国防科技工业局(中国)
Byelorussian SSR	白俄罗斯苏维埃社会主义共和国
CFR	《联邦法规汇编》(美国)
CIS	独立国家联合体
CHM	人类共同遗产
CNES	国家空间研究中心(法国)
CNSA	中国国家航天局
CoCoSL	《科隆空间法评注》
CONAE	阿根廷国家空间活动委员会
COPUOS	和平利用外层空间委员会

续表

Corr.	订正
COSPAR	空间研究委员会
COSPAR INFO. BULL.	空间研究委员会信息公告
COSTIND	国防科工委(中国)
CRAMRA	《南极矿物资源活动管理公约》
CSG	圭亚那空间中心
CSSTEAP	亚太空间科技教育中心
DLR	德国宇航中心
Doc./Docs.	文件
DoD	国防部(美国)
DOS	空间部(印度)
e. g.	例如
ECSL	欧洲空间法中心
ed./eds.	编者/编辑
edn.	版本
ELDO	欧洲运载火箭发展组织
ESA	欧洲空间局
ESPI	欧洲空间政策研究所
ESRO	欧洲空间研究组织
etc.	诸如此类
EUMETSAT	欧洲气象卫星应用组织
EUTELSAT	欧洲通信卫星组织
f./ff.	下一页/以下页面
FAA	联邦航空管理局(美国)
Fed. Reg.	《联邦登记》(美国)

续表

GA	联合国大会
GKKO	空间物体主要目录
GNSS	全球卫星导航系统
GPS	全球定位系统
i. a.	特别是
IAU	国际天文学联合会
i. e.	即
IADC	机构间空间碎片协调委员会
ibid.	同上
ICAO	国际民航组织
ICC	国际商会
ICDSD	国际数据存储和传播中心
ICJ	国际法院
ICJ Rep.	国际法院判决书、咨询意见和命令汇编
IGA	政府间协议
IISL	国际空间法学会
ILC	国际法委员会
ILM	《国际法律资料》
ILR	《国际法报告》
IMSO	国际移动卫星组织
Inc.	股份有限公司
INTERSPUTNIK	国际宇宙通信组织
ISAS	宇宙科学研究所(日本)
ISRO	印度空间研究组织
ISS	国际空间站

续表

ITU	国际电信联盟
JAXA	日本宇宙航空研究开发机构
Kazakh SSR	哈萨克苏维埃社会主义共和国
LCROSS	月球陨石坑观测和传感卫星
LEO	低地球轨道
LIAB	《空间物体所造成损害的国际责任公约》
lit.	文献
Ltd.	有限责任公司
mn	页码
MOON	《关于各国在月球和其他天体上活动的协定》
MOU	谅解备忘录
Mr.	先生
NASA	国家航空航天局(美国)
NASDA	国家空间发展局(美国)
NATO	北大西洋公约组织
no.	编号
NORAD	北美防空司令部
NPS	核动力源
NSSDC	国家空间科学数据中心(美国)
OST	《关于各国探索和利用包括月球和其他天体在内的外层空间活动的原则条约》
p. /pp.	页
para. /paras.	段
PCA	常设仲裁法院
REG	《关于登记射入外层空间物体的公约》

续表

Rep.	报告
Res.	决议
Rev.	修正
RF	俄罗斯联邦
RLV	可重复使用的运载火箭
ROSCOSMOS	俄罗斯联邦航天局
sec.	节
SES	欧洲卫星公司
SKKP	外层空间管制系统
SLASO	空间许可证和安全办公室
SNSB	瑞典国家航天局
SSA	空间态势感知
SSC	瑞典的空间合作
STM	空间交通管理
STS	空间运输系统
tr.	翻译
TSKKP	外层空间控制中心
TSUP	任务控制中心
UARS	高层大气研究卫星
UCS	《美国法典》
UK	英国
UN	联合国
UNCLOS	《联合国海洋法公约》
UNCOPOUS	联合国和平利用外层空间委员会
UNESCO	联合国教育、科学及文化组织

续表

UNGA	联合国大会
UNIDROIT	国际统一私法协会
UNOOSA	联合国外层空间事务处
UNTS	《联合国条约汇编》
US	美国
USA	美国
US GAO	美国审计署
USSR	苏联
v.	诉
VCLT	维也纳条约法公约
WG	工作小组
WP	工作文件

空间法的发展

1. 空间法的发展概述

空间条约/决议的发展		
第1721(XVI)号决议《和平利用外层空间中的国际合作》,1961年12月20日	第1962(XVI)号决议《各国探索和利用外空活动的法律原则宣言》,1963年12月13日	《外空条约》
A. 外层空间的探索和利用 —根据国际法/联合国宪章的规定 —所有国家都有探索和使用的自由/不得据为己有 授权联合国和平利用外层空间委员会	人类共同利益 自由探索与利用 不得据为己有 遵守国际法	《外空条约》第一至三条
B. 联合国作为国际合作的协调中心 呼吁各国……迅速向联合国和平利用外层空间委员会/秘书长提供信息,以便对发射进行登记 请秘书长……维持一个公共登记册	登记原则	《外空条约》第八条
请联合国和平利用外层空间委员会……利用秘书处与政府和非政府组织保持密切联系/交流信息/协助开展国际合作	国际合作/共同协助	《外空条约》第九条

空间条约/决议的发展				
第1721(XVI)B号决议,1961年12月20日	第1962(XVI)号决议,1963年12月13日	《外空条约》,1967年12月10日	实施协议,1968至1984年	关于主题事项的决议 2004/2007
	《外空条约》第五条纲要九	援助/归还,《外空条约》第五条	1968年12月3日,《营救协定》生效	
	《外空条约》第七条纲要八	国家责任(《外空条约》第七条)	《责任公约》,1972年9月1日生效	2004年12月10日第59/115号决议——“发射国”

续表

空间条约/决议的发展				
发射登记/联合国公共“登记处”	《外空条约》第八条纲要七	登记原则(《外空条约》第八条)	《登记公约》,1976年9月15日生效	
	月球制度(《外空条约》第四条/第十二条)	《月球协定》,1984年7月11日生效		

第1721（XVI）B号决议,1961年12月20日	第1962(XVI)号决议《各国探索和利用外空活动的法律原则宣言》,1963年12月13日	在《外空条约》中的转变
A部分	人类共同利益	《外空条约》第一条
	自由探索与利用	《外空条约》第一条
	不得据为己有	《外空条约》第二条
	遵守国际法	《外空条约》第三条
	国家对国家活动的责任/成员国的责任与政府间组织的责任并行	《外空条约》第六条
(B部分3.)	合作与互助	《外空条约》第九条
(B部分1/2.)	国家登记/管辖和控制权/所有权	《外空条约》第八条
	发射国/责任	《外空条约》第七条
	宇航员/人类使者	《外空条约》第五条

2. 非官方的条款标题

五个国际空间条约的非官方条款标题提供了关于相应条款的监管内容的概述。此外,它们使人们更容易理解和比较这些条约的系统结构。	
1967年《关于各国探索和利用包括月球和其他天体在内的外层空间活动的原则条约》(OST)	
序言	
第一条	自由探索与利用和利益条款
第二条	国家不得据为己有条款
第三条	国际法的适用
第四条	外层空间的军事用途
第五条	航天员和空间物体的救援和归还
第六条	国际责任
第七条	赔偿责任
第八条	登记、管辖和控制、所有权
第九条	顾及和保护空间环境的原则

续表

第十条	外空物体的飞行观测
第十一条	信息的提供
第十二条	他国对空间站的访问
第十三条	政府间国际组织
第十四至十七条	其他条款（签署、批准、退出）
1968年《关于营救宇航员、送回宇航员和归还射入外层空间的物体的协定》	
第一条	事故/危难/紧急情况或意外着陆的通知
第二条	救援和协助/缔约国管辖范围内的领土
第三条	协助和救援/不属于缔约方管辖的地区
第四条	人员的及时归还
第五条	空间物体的通知、回收和归还
第六条	发射机构
第七条	签署/批准/加入/生效
第八条	拟议修正案
第九至十条	最终条款
1972年《空间物体所造成损害的国际责任公约》	
序言	
第一条	定义
第二条	绝对责任
第三条	过错责任
第四条	两个或更多空间物体共同造成的损害/第三方责任
第五条	联合发射/连带责任
第六条	免除绝对责任
第七条	对发射国的国民和外国参与者不适用
第八条	索赔国的资格
第九条	外交渠道
第十条	索赔的期限
第十一条	与国家管辖权的关系
第十二条	赔偿的确定
第十三条	赔偿的货币
第十四条	缺少解决/索赔委员会
第十五条	索赔委员会的组成
第十六条	缺少任命/空额/程序

续表

第十七条	联合和集体任命
第十八条	决定的内容
第十九条	最终和有约束力的决定
第二十条	费用
第二十一条	大规模的危险
第二十二条	政府间国际组织
第二十三条	与国际协定的关系
第二十四条	签署/批准/加入/生效
第二十五条	拟议修正案
第二十六条	审查/修订
第二十七条	最终条款
1975 年《关于登记射入外层空间物体的公约》	
序言	
第一条	定义
第二条	国家登记处/登记义务
第三条	联合国登记册/登记义务
第四条	各登记国的信息
第五条	指定人或登记号
第六条	要求查证/协助
第七条	政府间国际组织
第八条	签署/批准/加入/生效
第九条	拟议修正案
第十条	审查/修订
第十一至十二条	最终条款
1979 年《关于各国在月球和其他天体上活动的协定》	
序言	
第一条	适用范围
第二条	国际法/合作
第三条	和平目的/非军事化
第四条	全人类的范围
第五条	任务信息/科学界
第六条	科学考察/样品/矿物
第七条	环境/放射性材料

续表

第八条	勘探和使用/咨询
第九条	科考站/自由出入
第十条	保障生命和健康
第十一条	人类的共同遗产/国际制度
第十二条	管辖权和控制权/所有权/紧急情况
第十三条	坠毁、被迫或意外着陆
第十四条	国际责任/赔偿责任
第十五条	核查/准入/协商/争端解决
第十六条	政府间国际组织
第十七条	拟议修正案
第十八条	审查/修订
第十九条	签署/批准/加入/生效
第二十至二十一条	最终条款

1968年《关于营救宇航员、送回宇航员和归还射入外层空间的物体的协定》

联合国大会通过：1967年12月19日
开放供签署：1968年4月22日
生效：1968年12月3日
来源：672 UNTS 119

《营救协定》文本

各缔约国，

鉴于关于各国探测及使用外空包括月球与其他天体之活动所应遵守原则之条约至关重要，该约规定遇宇航员有意外事故，危难或紧急降落之情形，应给予一切可能协助，迅速并安全送回宇航员，及送回射入外空之物体，

亟欲发展并进一步具体表示此种义务，

深愿促进外空和平探测及[1] 使用之国际合作，

益以人道精神驱使，

兹议定条款如下：

第一条

缔约国于获悉或发现航天器人员遭遇意外事故，或正遭受危难情况，或已在缔约

国管辖领域内，在公海上，或在不属任何国家管辖之任何其他地点作紧急或非出于本意之降落时，应立即：

（甲）通知发射当局，或在不能查明发射当局并立即与之通讯时，缔约国需立即以可以使用的一切适当通讯工具公开宣告此情况；

（乙）通知联合国秘书长，由秘书长以其可以使用的一切适当通讯工具传播此项消息。

第二条

航天器人员因意外事故、危难、紧急或非出于本意降落，在一缔约国管辖领域内，该缔约国应立即采取一切可能措施开展援救，并提供一切必要协助。该缔约国应将所采取措施及其进展情况通知发射当局及联合国秘书长。如发射当局的协助有助于实现迅速援救，或对搜寻及援救行动大有贡献，发射当局应与该缔约国合作，以求有效进行搜寻及援救行动。此项行动应受该缔约国指挥管制，该缔约国应与发射当局密切磋商行事。

第三条

如获悉或发现航天器人员已迫降于公海上或不属任何国家管辖的任何其他地点，能提供协助的各缔约国应于必要时对搜寻及援救行动提供协助，以确保航天器人员迅速获救。各该国应将其所采措施及其进展情形通知发射当局及联合国秘书长。

第四条

如航天器人员因意外事故、危难、紧急或非出于本意在一缔约国管辖领域内降落，或在公海上或不属任何国家管辖的任何其他地点被发现，应确保其安全并迅速送交发射当局代表。

第五条

一、缔约国在获悉或发现空间物体或其组成部分已于其管辖领域内，或在公海上，或在不属任何国家管辖之任何其他地点返回地球时，应通知发射当局及联合国秘书长。

二、缔约国发现空间物体或其组成部分在其管辖范围内，如经发射当局请求同时该当局提供协助，缔约国应采取其认为可行的措施，寻获该物体或其组成部分。

三、如经发射当局请求，在发射当局领域范围以外发现的射入空间物体或其组成部分应送还发射当局代表或留待发射当局代表处置；如经请求，在送还之前，该当局应先提供证明资料。

四、虽有本条第二项及第三项的规定，缔约国有理由相信在其管辖领域内发现或其于他处寻获的空间物体或其组成部分具为危险或毒害性质时，应将此情形通知发射当局，发射当局应立即采取有效措施，于该缔约国指挥及管制下，消除可能的损害危险。

五、为履行本条第二项及第三项下履行寻获及送还空间物体或其组成部分的义务所产生的费用应由发射当局承担。

第六条

本协定称“发射当局”是指负有发射责任的国家或指负有发射责任的政府间国际组织，但该组织必须宣布接受本协定所规定的权利与义务，且该组织的多数会员国为本协定及关于各国探测及使用外空包括月球与其他天体之活动所应遵守原则的条约的缔约国。

第七条

一、本协定应开放供所有国家签署。凡在本协定依照本条第三项发生效力前尚未签署的任何国家可随时加入本协定。

二、本协定须经签署国批准，批准书及加入书应送交美利坚合众国、大不列颠及北爱尔兰联合王国及苏维埃社会主义共和国联盟政府存放，该三国政府为指定各保存政府。

三、本协定应于包括指定为保存政府的三国政府在内的五国政府，交存批准书后发生效力。

四、对于在本协定发生效力后交存批准书或加入书的国家，本协定应于其交存批准书或加入书之日起生效。

五、保存政府应将每一签署的日期，每一份批准书及加入书的交存日期，本协定发生效力日期及其他通知事项，迅速告知所有签署及加入国家。

六、本协定应由保存政府遵照《联合国宪章》第一百零二条规定办理登记。

第八条

本协定任何缔约国可对本协定提出修正案。修正案应自本条约多数缔约国接受之日起，对接受修正案的各缔约国生效。嗣后对于其余各缔约国应于其接受之日起生效。

第九条

本协定任何缔约国在本协定生效一年后书面通知保存政府退出协定。退出应自接到通知之日起一年后发生效力。

第十条

本协定应存放保存政府档库，其英文、俄文、法文、西班牙文及中文五种文本具有同等法律效力。保存政府应将本协定正式核正的副本分送各签署及加入国政府。

为此，下列经正式授权代表在本条约签字，以昭信守。

本条约一式三份，于公历1968年4月22日订于华盛顿、伦敦及莫斯科。

目录

第一章　历史背景和上下文

一、引言

二、历史背景

三、政治背景

四、实践背景

文件精选

Convention on International Civil Aviation (signed 7 December 1944, entered into force 4 April 1947) 15 UNTS 295 (Chicago Convention)

Treaty on Principles Governing the Activities of States in the Exploration and Use of Outer Space, including the Moon and Other Celestial Bodies (done 27 January 1967, entered into force 10 October 1967) 610 UNTS 250 (OST)

UN Doc. A/AC. 105/C. 2/L. 2, International Agreement on the Rescue of Astronauts and Spaceships making Emergency Landings, USSR Proposal, 6 June 1962

UN Doc. A/AC. 105/C. 2/L. 3, Draft Proposal on Assistance to and Return of Space Vehicles and Personnel, United States Proposal, 8 June 1962

UN Doc. A/AC. 105/C. 2/L. 2/Rev. 1, Agreement on the rescue of astronauts and spaceships in the event of accident or emergency landing, USSR Revised Draft, 9 March 1964

UN Doc. A/AC. 105/C. 2/L. 9, International Agreement on Assistance to and Return of Astronauts and Objects Launched into Outer Space, United States Proposal, 9 March 1964

UN Doc. WG. I/30, Australia and Canada: Proposal, in: UN Doc. A/AC. 105/21, Report of the Legal Sub-Committee on the Work of the Second Part of its Third Session (5-23 October 1964) to the Committee on the Peaceful Uses of Outer Space, Annex I, Proposals and Amendments Relating to Assistance to and Return of Astronauts and Space Vehicles, 23 October 1964

UN Doc. A/AC. 105/C. 2/L. 2/Rev. 2, Agreement on the rescue of astronauts and spaceships in the event of accident or emergency landing, USSR Revised Draft, 26 October 1964

UN Doc. A/AC. 105/C. 2/L. 18, Agreement On the Rescue of Astronauts In The Event Of Accident Or Emergency Landing, USSR Revised Draft, 19 June 1967

UN Doc. A/AC. 105/C. 2/L. 20, Assistance to and Return of Astronauts and Space Objects, Revised Australian-Canadian proposal submitted as a working paper, 21 June 1967

UN Doc. A/AC. 105/C. 2/L. 28, Draft agreement on the rescue of astronauts, the return of astronauts and the return of objects launched into outer space, 12 December 1967

UN Doc. A/AC. 105/C. 2/L. 28/Rev. 1, Draft agreement on the rescue of astronauts, the return of astronauts and the return of objects launched into outer space, 14 December 1967

第一章　历史背景和上下文

一、引言

《关于营救宇航员、送回宇航员和归还射入外层空间的物体的协定》（以下简称《营救协定》）[①] 是在缔结《关于各国探索和利用外层空间包括月球与其他天体活动所应遵守原则条约》（以下简称《外空条约》）[②] 后一年批准的。考虑到《营救协定》的协商在《外空条约》制定的过程中已经开展，因此，这样的高效是可能的。两项条约谈判过程中的密切联系体现在《外空条约》第五条和第八条[③]，以及《营救协定》的各项规定中。两者均以联合国大会于 1963 年 12 月 13 日经第 1962（XⅧ）号决议通过的《关于各国探索和利用外层空间活动的法律原则宣言》（以下简称 1963 年《外空宣言》）[④] 的第七项和第九项原则为基础。通过这一点，可以勾勒出从 1963 年的两项原则，到 1967 年的两项条款，最后到 1968 年的具体协议的脉络。据此，《营救协定》是对先前一些规定的进一步发展，具有更精确和更广泛的规定[⑤]。

《营救协定》的内容回应了当时美国和苏联这两个航天大国的迫切需要，即以人道主义方式处理涉及宇航员的事故。在人道主义理由背后（如序言所述），存在政治上的担忧，即对宇航员采取与其他冷战做法不相上下的虐待或扣押的隐忧。20 世纪

① Agreement on the Rescue of Astronauts, the Return of Astr onauts and the Return of Objects Launched into Outer Space (done 22 April 1968, entered into force 3 December 1968) 672 UNTS 119 (ARRA).

② Treaty on Principles Governing the Activities of States in the Exploration and Use of Outer Space, including the Moon and Other Celestial Bodies (done 27 January 1967, entered into force 10 October 1967) 610 UNTS 205 (OST).

③ See von der Dunk, Frans/Goh, Gérardine M., *Article V*, in: Hobe, Stephan/Schmidt-Tedd, Bernhard/Schrogl, Kai-Uwe (eds.), Cologne Commentary on Space Law, Volume I, Heymanns, Cologne 2009, pp. 94-102.

④ UNGA Res. 1962 (XⅧ), Declaration of Legal Principles Governing the Activities of States in the Exploration and Uses of Outer Space, 13 December 1963.

⑤ See van Bogaert, Eric R. C., *Aspects of Space Law*, Kluwer, Deventer 1986, p. 100.

60 年代，两个超级大国发生的一些意外事故加速了《营救协定》的谈判和通过。自那时起，《营救协定》为宇航员提供了特殊的地位，并包含了一些对从事载人航天飞行的国家的特殊而深远的义务（然而，《营救协定》并没有提及《外空条约》第五条所使用的“全人类的使者”这一概念）。

虽然《营救协定》与《外空条约》的联系显而易见，但它与空间法发展的另一种联系只能通过研究谈判历史来追溯，即《营救协定》和《空间物体造成损害的国际责任公约》（以下简称《责任公约》）[①] 的起草和通过之间的联系。尽管可以理解的是，两个航天大国在政治上倾向于《营救协定》，但其他国家却对《责任公约》表现出特别的兴趣。虽然《责任公约》直到 1971 年才达成协议[②]，但双方的利益诉求最终都得到了满足。

《营救协定》中关于营救宇航员和返回宇航员的规定（包含在第一至四条中）在实践中被视为没有什么实际意义的规定。自《协定》生效以来，从未进行过救援、援助或送回。然而，除了营救和送回宇航员之外，《协定》还有第三个义务，即返还发射进入外层空间的物体。这项义务在第五条（单独的一条）中明确规定，并采用了与前几条不同的格式，其来源于 1963 年《外空宣言》（原则七）和《外空条约》（第八条）。自《营救协定》通过以来，有许多实践案例涉及该义务。

《营救协定》还为空间法引入了一些新的特征，例如，政府间国际组织可以宣布接受《营救协定》规定的权利和义务（第六条）。这一规定虽然没有体现在《外空条约》中，但却由此延伸至《责任公约》《关于登记发射进入外层空间物体的公约》（以下简称《登记公约》）[③] 和《关于各国在月球和其他天体上活动的协定》（以下简称《月球协定》）[④]。虽然《营救协定》由于在营救和送回宇航员方面的实际意义不大而被忽视，但它为空间法明确了重要的规则和发展趋势。当前，“太空旅游”的出现引发了一个问题，即在冷战背景下为顺应人类宇航活动的早期实践而诞生的《营救

① Convention on International Liability for Damage Caused by Space Objects (done 29 March 1972, entered into force 1 September 1972) 961 UNTS 187 (LIAB).

② See UNGA Res. 2777 (XXVI), Convention on International Liability for Damage Caused by Space Objects, 29 November 1971.

③ Convention on Registration of Objects Launched into Outer Space (done 14 January 1975, entered into force 15 September 1976) 1023 UNTS 15 (REG).

④ Agreement Governing the Activities of States on the Moon and Other Celestial Bodies (done 18 December 1979, entered into force 11 July 1984) 1363 UNTS 3 (MOON).

协定》，在私人载人航天时代是否仍然切实可行，毕竟在后一语境下的参与人很难被视为“全人类的使者”。

二、历史背景

1967年12月19日，联合国大会以115票赞成、0票反对的结果通过了《营救协定》①，这标志着近十年为达成一项广泛的国际协议的所有努力的一个巅峰，以确保在营救遇险宇航员、送回宇航员和返还空间物体时，实现人道主义和科学的目标②。《营救协定》是1962年成立的联合国和平利用外层空间委员会法律小组委员会的产物。1958年，联合国大会成立了一个和平利用外层空间特设委员会，并于1959年转变为一个常设委员会③，目的是报告“在执行外层空间探索计划过程中可能出现的法律问题的性质④”。法律小组委员会在其第一份报告中确定了一些需要优先处理的问题，其中包括“将缔结关于重返和着陆的多边协议，这些协议包含关于合作的适当承诺和关于程序的适当规定。”⑤ 这些协议应涵盖“将航天器返还其发射国，以及（载人情况下）对人员快速送回的规定。”⑥ 然而，通常形成一份可以提交联合国大会审阅的文本需要耗费数年时间。

究其延迟的原因，在于法律小组委员会还必须就其他一些优先于《营救协定》的问题开展工作，尤其是制定有关探索和利用外层空间的一般原则的工作。这些一般原

① UNGA Res. 2345（XXⅡ），Agreement on the Rescue of Astronauts, the Return of Astronauts and the Return of Objects Launched into Outer Space, 19 December 1967.

② See Dembling, Paul G./Arons, Daniel M., The Treaty on Rescue and Return of Astronauts and Space Objects, William and Mary Law Review (9) 1968, p. 630.

③ See UNGA Res. 1472（XⅣ），International co-operation on the peaceful uses of outer space, 12 December 1959.

④ UNGA Res. 1348（XⅢ），Question of the peaceful use of outer space, 13 December 1958.

⑤ UN Doc. A/AC. 98/2, Report of the Legal Committee, 12 June 1959, p. 7. The Report of the Legal Subcommittee became Part Ⅲ of the Report of the full Ad Hoc Committee to the General Assembly, UN Doc. A/4141, Report of the Ad Hoc Committee on the Peaceful Uses of Outer Space, 14 July 1959; as for the problems listed in the report see Dembling, Paul G./Arons, Daniel M., *Space Law and the United Nations: The Work of the Legal Subcommittee on the Peaceful Uses of Outer Space*, Journal of Air Law and Commerce (32) 1966, pp. 329-330.

⑥ UN Doc. A/AC. 98/2, Report of the Legal Committee, 12 June 1959, p. 7. The Report of the Legal Subcommittee became Part Ⅲ of the Report of the full Ad Hoc Committee to the General Assembly: UN Doc. A/4141, Report of the Ad Hoc Committee on the Peaceful Uses of Outer Space, 14 July 1959.

则首先由联合国大会的第1962（XⅧ）号决议通过，即1963年12月13日《关于各国探索和利用外层空间活动的法律原则宣言》①，后来成为《外空条约》的主体，并由大会于1966年12月19日通过②。

《外空条约》通过后，关于《营救协定》的讨论重新恢复。1967年，法律小组委员会在其第六届会议期间处理了两个空间大国的若干修订草案。然而，法律小组委员会无法结束相关的辩论。直到1967年深秋，在第二十二届联合国大会于纽约举办期间，两个超级大国进行了密集的双边谈判，为法律小组委员会以及随后的和平利用外层空间委员会达成共识铺平了道路，进而实现了这一目标③。随后，《营救协定》草案直接提交到了联合国大会，并经一致表决获得通过。1968年4月22日，43个国家分别在华盛顿特区、伦敦和莫斯科签署了该协定。1968年12月3日，在五个必要的国家批准后，《营救协定》生效④。

三、政治背景

（一）空间大国的兴趣

作为当时仅有的两个空间大国，美国和苏联寻求制定营救宇航员和返还空间物体的相关规则。这表现在一次换文中，两国之间讨论了可能的合作领域⑤。赫鲁晓夫主席在1962年3月20日给肯尼迪总统的一封信中强调，需要"一项国际协议，以协助搜救因事故降落到地球的宇宙飞船、人造卫星和太空舱。这一协议十分必要，因为它

① UNGA Res. 1962（XⅧ）, Declaration of Legal Principles Governing the Activities of States in the Exploration and Use of Outer Space, 13 December 1963.

② UNGA Res. 2222（XXI）, Treaty on Principles Governing the Activities of States in the Exploration and Use of Outer Space, Including the Moon and Other Celestial Bodies, 19 December 1966.

③ See Hall, Cargil, *Rescue and Return of Astronauts on Earth and in Outer Space*, American Journal of International Law（63）1969, p. 204; Cheng, Bin, *The* 1968 *Astronauts Agreement or How not to make a Treaty*, The Yearbook of World Affairs（23）1969, p. 194; Houben, Piet-Hein, A New Chapter of Space Law: The Agreement on the Rescue and Return of Astronauts and Space Objects, Netherlands International Law Review（15）1968, p. 121.

④ See Historical Background and Context, mn. 56.

⑤ See Dembling, Paul G./Arons, Daniel M., The Treaty on Rescue and Return of Astronauts and Space Objects, William and Mary Law Review（9）1968, pp. 633-634; van Bogaert, Eric R. C., *Aspects of Space Law*, Kluwer, Deventer 1986, p. 98.

关涉拯救宇航员的生命……”[①]。

因为在接回宇航员和空间物体方面相对不利，苏联更有意达成协议。美国拥有大西洋和太平洋海岸、众多岛屿和世界各地的军事基地，拥有全球跟踪网络和其他设施。因此，它有更好的可能性将宇航员和空间物体带到公海[②]。此外，它还与亚洲、非洲、拉丁美洲和欧洲国家缔结了许多双边协议，允许其使用专门设施，并允许美国技术人员在这些国家任职。相比之下，苏联通常将宇航员返回至自己的领土上，也没有可与之相比的网络。因此，苏联可能更需要第三国的援助[③]。

对美国来说，就援助和返还问题达成国际协议并不是那么紧迫。然而，它需要的是确保宇航员能够无条件和不受限制地送回。尽管发生了越南战争，但美国也寻求与苏联在太空探索方面的进一步合作[④]。与此同时，美国不想错过在 1963 年 8 月 5 日于莫斯科签署《禁止核试验条约》后，缔结另一项国际条约的机会[⑤]。

法律小组委员会的其他成员国对缔结一项关于营救和返还的协议不太感兴趣，而是关注空间物体造成损害的责任和保证无辜受害者得到适当赔偿的法律问题[⑥]。因此，关于援助和返还的谈判与关于赔偿责任的谈判同时进行。然而，这两个问题仍然是分开的[⑦]。他国营救或返还宇航员和空间物体的义务不以发射国承担相应的损害赔偿义

---

① Khrushchev Letter on Space Cooperation, New York Times, 22 March 1962, p. 18, cited in: Hall, Cargil, *Rescue and Return of Astronauts on Earth and in Outer Space*, American Journal of International Law (63) 1969, p. 202.

② See Cheng, Bin, The 1968 Astronauts Agreement or How Not to make a Treaty, The Yearbook of World Affairs (23) 1969, pp. 186f.; Houben, Piet-Hein, *A New Chapter of Space Law: The Agreement on the Rescue and Return of Astronauts and Space Objects*, Netherlands International Law Review (15) 1968, p. 122.

③ See ibid.

④ See Cheng, Bin, The 1968 Astronauts Agreement or How Not to make a Treaty, The Yearbook of World Affairs (23) 1969, p. 188; Houben, Piet-Hein, A New Chapter of Space Law: The Agreement on the Rescue and Return of Astronauts and Space Objects, Netherlands International Law Review (15) 1968, p. 122.

⑤ See ibid.; Cheng, Bin, The 1968 Astronauts Agreement or How Not to make a Treaty, The Yearbook of World Affairs (23) 1969, p. 188.

⑥ See van Bogaert, Eric R. C., Aspects of Space Law, Kluwer, Deventer 1986, p. 99; Cheng, Bin, The 1968 Astronauts Agreement or How Not to make a Treaty, The Yearbook of World Affairs (23) 1969, p. 197; Dembling, Paul G./Arons, Daniel M., *Space Law and the United Nations: The Work of the Legal Subcommittee on the Peaceful Uses of Outer Space*, Journal of Air Law and Commerce (32) 1966, p. 342; Lee, Roy S. K., Assistance to and Return of Astronauts and Space Objects, in: Jasentuliyana, Nandasiri/Lee, Roy S. K. (eds.), Manual on Space Law, Volume I, Oceana, New York 1979, p. 55.

⑦ See Dembling, Paul G./Arons, Daniel M., Space Law and the United Nations: The Work of the Legal Subcommittee on the Peaceful Uses of Outer Space, Journal of Air Law and Commerce (32) 1966, p. 337.

务为条件[①]。所有参与国都赞同营救和返还的基本理由，即人道主义援助和保护科学成果的利益[②]。

（二）空间大国之间的争议问题

在法律小组委员会就营救和返还问题进行谈判的同时，两个空间大国之间也存在一些争议。在 1962 年法律小组委员会第一届会议上，对文本的约束力上有不同看法[③]。苏联提交了一份草案，以期达成具有约束力的国际条约[④]；但是，美国则倾向于通过一项联合国大会决议[⑤]。苏联和社会主义国家强调需要一项具有约束力的国际协定，认为根据既有的国际实践，向遇险人员提供援助应由条约规定。有人指出，鉴于与飞往外层空间有关的法律问题很可能不受航空法或海洋法的管辖，似乎有必要制定一项条约，界定各国在营救宇航员方面的权利和义务。最后，苏联质疑联合国大会决议是否可以作为一项有法律效力的文件，来确保宇航员不会被逮捕或视为罪犯，以及紧急着陆的航天器不会被扣押[⑥]。

美国则辩称，人道主义和科学是国际社会的共同利益，各国当然愿意遵守大会的决议[⑦]。它认为，相关原则已经非常简单明确，不需要起草正式的法律文书，通过一

---

① Only at an early date, it was urged that the return of a space object from the territory should be condi-tioned upon payment of compensation for any damage caused by the landing. Such a condition was put forward, amongst others, by Loftus Becker, Legal Adviser to the Department of State, in the late 1950s. See Dembling, Paul G./Arons, Daniel M., *The Treaty on Rescue and Return of Astronauts and Space Objects*, William and Mary Law Review (9) 1968, pp. 631f. with further references.

② See ibid.

③ See Cheng, Bin, *The 1968 Astronauts Agreement or How Not to Make a Treaty*, The Yearbook of World Affairs (23) 1969, pp. 188f.; van Bogaert, Eric R. C., Aspects of Space Law, Kluwer, Deventer 1986, p. 98.

④ UN Doc. A/AC. 105/C. 2/L. 2, International Agreement on the Rescue of Astronauts and Spaceships making Emergency Landings, USSR Proposal, 6 June 1962.

⑤ UN Doc. A/AC. 105/C. 2/L. 3, Draft Proposal on Assistance to and Return of Space Vehicles and Personnel, United States Proposal, 8 June 1962.

⑥ See UN Doc. A/AC. 105/C. 2/SR. 7, Legal Sub-Committee, First Session, Summary Record of the Seventh Meeting, held 7 June 1962, 21 August 1962, p. 6.

⑦ See, e. g., UN Doc. A/AC. 105/C. 2/SR. 1, Legal Sub-Committee, First Session, Summary Record of the First Meeting, held 28 May 1962. The United States position was shared by Canada and the United Kingdom. France, however, expressed doubts on the legal effectiveness of General Assembly resolutions; see UN Doc. A/AC. 105/C. 2/SR. 9, Legal Sub-Committee, First Session, Summary Record of the Ninth Meeting, held 12 June 1962, 21 August 1962, p. 2; Cheng, Bin, The 1968 Astronauts Agreement or How Not to Make a Treaty, The Yearbook of World Affairs (23) 1969, p. 188..

项决议可以避免条约拟订和批准的冗长过程①；相反，责任问题则需要由一项国际协议来解决②。苏联在这一问题上持不同意见，认为“赔偿无疑是应该支付的”③。直到一年后，各方才达成一致意见，即应就各个议题分别制定一项条约④。

另一个有争议的问题涉及航天器返还的附加条件⑤。苏联的立场是，外国航天器只有在有识别标志且发射已正式宣布的情况下，才应立即归还⑥。此外，苏联在其初稿中提议，运载“用于在另一国境内收集情报信息”⑦ 的装置的航天器不应归还。后来，这一规定被改为一项条件，即该空间物体的发射必须是为了“和平探索和利用外层空间的目的⑧”，或“根据1963年《外空宣言》发射”⑨。然而，美国和许多其他西方国家不接受这些条件，他们认为在没有仲裁条款的情况下，这些条件很容易在实践中产生严重困难⑩。最后，根据1963年《外空宣言》第七原则和第九原则，以及1967年《外空条约》第五条和第八条，一致认为返还空间物体的义务应是无条件的。

---

① See UN Doc. A/AC. 105/C. 2/3, Report of the Legal Sub-Committee on the Work of its First Session (28 May-20 June 1962) to the Committee on the Peaceful Uses of Outer Space, para. 39.

② UN Doc. A/AC. 105/C. 2/L. 4, Liability for Space Vehicle Accidents, USA Proposal, 4 June 1962.

③ UN Doc. A/AC. 105/C. 2/SR. 14, Legal Sub-Committee, First Session, Summary Record of the Fourteenth Meeting, held 19 June 1962, 22 August 1962, p. 3.

④ UN Doc. A/AC. 105/C. 2/SR. 14, Legal Sub-Committee, First Session, Summary Record of the Fourteenth Meeting, held 19 June 1962, 22 August 1962, p. 3.

⑤ See van Bogaert, Eric R. C., Aspects of Space Law, Kluwer, Deventer 1986, p. 98; Hall, Cargil, *Rescue and Return of Astronauts on Earth and in Outer Space*, American Journal of International Law (63) 1969, p. 203; Dembling, Paul G. /Arons, Daniel M., Space Law and the United Nations: The Work of the Legal Subcommittee on the Peaceful Uses of Outer Space, Journal of Air Law and Commerce (32) 1966, pp. 338-349; Cheng, Bin, The 1968 Astronauts Agreement or How Not to Make a Treaty, The Yearbook of World Affairs (23) 1969, p. 191; Kopal, Vladimir, The Agreement on Rescue of Astronauts and Return of Space Objects, in: McWhinney, Edward/Bradley, Martin A., New Frontiers in Space Law, Sijthoff, Leyden 1969, pp. 112-115. .

⑥ See UN Doc. A/AC. 105/C. 2/L. 2/Rev. 1, Agreement on the rescue of astronauts and spaceships in the event of accident or emergency landing, USSR Revised Draft, 9 March 1964, Art. 9; UN Doc. A/AC. 105/C. 2/SR. 29-37, Legal Sub-Committee, Third Session (1st Part), Summary Record of the Twenty-Ninth to Thirty-Seventh Meetings, held from 9-26 March 1964, 24 August 1964, pp. 31 50.

⑦ UN Doc. A/AC. 105/C. /L. 2, International Agreement on the Rescue of Astronauts and Spaceships making Emergency Landings, USSR Proposal, 6 June 1962, Art. 7.

⑧ UN Doc. A/AC. 105/C. 2/L. 2/Rev. 1, Agreement on the rescue of astronauts and spaceships in the event of accident or emergency landing, USSR Revised Draft, 9 March 1964, Art. 9.

⑨ UN Doc. A/AC. 105/C. 2/L. 2/Rev. 2, Agreement on the rescue of astronauts and spaceships in the event of accident or emergency landing, USSR Revised Draft, 26 October 1964, Art. 6 para. 2.

⑩ See Cheng, Bin, The 1968 Astronauts Agreement or How Not to Make a Treaty, The Yearbook of World Affairs (23) 1969, p. 191; van Bogaert, Eric R. C., Aspects of Space Law, Kluwer, Deventer 1986, p. 111.

政府间国际组织的作用是空间大国之间的又一场持续争议。虽然美国和大多数其他西方国家赞成将从事空间活动的国际组织与国家同等对待，但苏联出于政治和司法原因拒绝了这一想法①。最终，达成了一项折衷方案，使《营救协定》适用于国际组织，但条件是，该组织已接受《营救协定》规定的权利和义务，且该国际组织的大多数成员国已批准《营救协定》和《外空条约》（参见第六条）。

四、实践背景

（一）宇航员的事故

当在谈判阶段发生悲惨的事故和事件后，达成关于营救宇航员和返还空间物体的国际规则的必要性就变得明显和紧迫。

在《营救协定》谈判的最后阶段，谈判人员回忆起两起悲惨的事故。1967 年 1 月 27 日，美国宇航员罗杰·B. 查菲（Roger B. Chaffee）、维吉尔·格里松（Virgil Grissom）和爱德华·H·怀特（Edward H. White）在阿波罗 1 号宇宙飞船的地面试验中死于火灾②。1967 年 4 月 24 日，苏联宇航员弗拉基米尔·M. 科马罗夫（Vladimir M. Komarov）在联盟 1 号（Soyuz-1）宇宙飞船着陆过程中因降落伞功能缺陷而死亡③。一些其他事件，例如，1966 年尼尔·阿姆斯特朗（Neil Armstrong）搭载的双子座 8 号在太平洋而不是大西洋过早降落④，提高了人们对国际援助和返还义务必要性的认识。

---

① The Soviet Union perceived the European Launcher Development Organization ELDO as too closely related to the North Atlantic Treaty Organisation (NATO). From a juridical point of view, the Soviet Union was reluctant to regard international organizations as legal subjects under international law. Cheng, Bin, Le Traité de 1967 sur l'espace, Journal du Droit International (95) 1968, pp. 588f.; Cheng, Bin, The 1968 Astronauts Agreement or How Not to Make a Treaty, The Yearbook of World Affairs (23) 1969, p. 191; van Bogaert, Eric R. C., Aspects of Space Law, Kluwer, Deventer 1986, p. 106; Hall, Cargil, *Rescue and Return of Astronauts on Earth and in Outer Space*, American Journal of International Law (63) 1969, pp. 129f.

② See Gál, Gyula, Observations on the Rescue Agreement, in: Jasentuliyana, Nandasiri (ed.), Maintaining Outer Space for Peaceful Purposes, The United Nations University, Tokyo 1984, p. 93; Cheng, Bin, The 1968 Astronauts Agreement or How Not to Make a Treaty, The Yearbook of World Affairs (23) 1969, p. 186.

③ See ibid.; Gál, Gyula, Observations on the Rescue Agreement, in: Jasentuliyana, Nandasiri (ed.), Maintaining Outer Space for Peaceful Purposes, The United Nations University, Tokyo 1984, p. 93; the Soviet representative referred to both accidents during the 6th session of the Legal Subcommittee, see UN Doc. A/AC. 105/C. 2/SR. 75, Legal Sub-Committee, Sixth Session, Summary Record of the Seventy-Fifth (Opening) Meeting, held 19 June 1967, 13 November 1967.

④ See van Bogaert, Eric R. C., Aspects of Space Law, Kluwer, Deventer 1986, p. 99.

应该指出的是，截至本卷出版时，还未发生根据《营救协定》的规定送回宇航员的情况。

（二）空间物体的事故

非载人空间物体的一些事故表明，需要制定关于回收和返还的法律规则。1967 年 9 月 7 日，美国发射了生物卫星 2 号。最初的设想是三天后将其回收。然而，由于通信故障和太平洋回收区即将发生热带风暴，美国决定提前 24 小时终止飞行。然而，该卫星没有对美国地面站的命令作出反应，最终只能在澳大利亚设施的帮助下，根据先前制定的应急计划，安全地回收①。

在空间物体再入的情况下，发生了许多导致此类空间物体返还其登记国的事故②。

五、起草历史

（一）谈判的第一阶段

1962 年 5 月 28 日至 6 月 20 日在日内瓦举行的联合国外空委法律小组委员会第一次会议，开始了关于援助和送回宇航员和空间物体的文件的谈判。在那次会议上，美国和苏联各自提出了关于拯救和送回宇航员和空间物体的国际文书的提案。

---

① See Cheng, Bin, The 1968 Astronauts Agreement or How Not to Make a Treaty, The Yearbook of World Affairs (23) 1969, p. 187.

② See the notifications made by States in the series UN Docs. ST/SG/SER. E. Recent incidents concern, for example, the return of space objects by Japan (UN Doc. A/AC. 105/735, Note Verbale dated 20 January 2000 from the Permanent Mission of Japan (Vienna) addressed to the Secretary-General, 2 February 2000); by the United States (UN Doc. A/AC. 105/737, Note Verbale dated 13 March 2000 from the Permanent Mission of the United States of America to the United Nations (Vienna) addressed to the Secretary General, 24 March2000); by South Africa (UN Doc. A/AC. 105/740 Note Verbale dated 3 July 2000 from the Permanent Mission of the Republic of South Africa to the United Nations (Vienna) addressed to the Secretary General, 11 July 2000); by Saudi Arabia (UN Doc. A/AC. 105/762, Note Verbale dated 8 March 2001 from the Permanent Mission of Saudi Arabia to the United Nations (Vienna) addressed to the Secretary-General, 3 April 2001). See Hodgkins, Ken, Procedures for Return of Space Objects Under the Agreement on the Rescue of Astronauts, the Return of Astronauts and the Return of Objects Launched into Outer Space, in: Proceedings United Nations/International Institute of Air and Space Law Workshop on Capacity Building in Space Law, United Nations, New York 2003, pp. 61f.; see also the report about the return of a space object by Brazil to the United States by dos Santos, Alvaro Fabricio, Analysis of the Legal Instrument Signed between Brazil and the United States of America Regarding the Return of a Space Object, in: IISL, Proceedings of the 53rd Colloquium on the Law of Outer Space 27 September-1 October 2010 Prague (Czech Republic), AIAA, 2011, pp. 227-233.

苏联提出了一项《关于救援紧急着陆的宇航员和宇宙飞船的国际协议》①。其中包括序言和九项条款。其中，第一条规定了各国的一般义务，即“向发生事故的宇宙飞船的船员提供援助，并采取措施营救紧急着陆的宇航员”。此外，它还规定了毫不拖延地通知发射国的义务（第二条和第三条）；在紧急降落于公海的情况下，应由发射国可能向其提出申请的所有国家进行联合搜寻（第四条）；各国应为任何宇航员尽早返回另一国提供便利（第六条）。关于宇宙飞船、卫星和太空舱的归还，苏联的提案规定，如果飞船、卫星和太空舱有识别标志，且发射国已正式宣布发射了被发现的装置，那么，应毫不拖延地将其归还；然而，在另一国境内发现的载有情报收集设备的航天器不应归还（第七条）。此外，发射国应偿还履行这些义务所产生的费用（第八条）。该协议应向世界所有国家开放加入（第九条）。

美国提出了一项大会决议草案，包含了关于“航天器和人员的援助和返还”的三项原则②。根据第一项原则，“应向事故对象，或经历遇险状况，或因事故、遇险、错误或其他原因着陆的航天器人员提供一切可能的帮助。”第二项原则确立了将未按计划着陆的航天器及其人员安全、迅速地送回负责发射的一国、多国或国际组织的义务。第三项原则规定，负责发射的国家或国际组织应承担为航天器及其人员提供援助或返还所产生的任何费用。

关于文件形式的争论，即苏联提出的国际条约与美国提出的联合国大会决议，是法律小组委员会第一次会议讨论的绝对主题③。尽管对文件的形式存在争议，但法律小组委员会达成了一项共识，即就援助和返还问题达成一项协议既可行又可取④。1962 年 12 月的联合国大会要求联合国外空委“继续加紧开展援助和返还宇航员和航天器的工作”⑤。

---

① UN Doc. A/AC. 105/C. 2/L. 2, International Agreement on the Rescue of Astronauts and Spaceships making Emergency Landings, USSR Proposal, 6 June 1962.

② UN Doc. A/AC. 105/C. 2/L. 3, Assistance and Return of Space Vehicles and Personnel, United States Proposal, 8 June 1962. 9.

③ See UN Doc. A/AC. 105/C. 2/3, Report of the Legal Subcommittee on the Work of its First Session (28 May-20 June 1962) to the Committee on the Peaceful Uses of Outer Space, para. 39. See already His-torical Background and Context, mn. 13f.

④ See Dembling, Paul G./Arons, Daniel M., Space Law and the United Nations: The Work of the Legal Subcommittee on the Peaceful Uses of Outer Space, Journal of Air Law and Commerce (32) 1966, p. 332.

⑤ UNGA Res. 1802 (XVII), International co-operation in the peaceful uses of outer space, 14 December 1962.

法律小组委员会于1963年4月16日至5月3日在纽约举行的第二次会议上，解决了有关文件形式的争议，并就有关文书应采取国际协定的形式达成了一致意见①。在1963年会议的剩余时间里，法律小组委员会不再处理这个议题，而是集中起草了一份关于各国探索和利用外层空间活动的一般法律原则宣言的草案②。

（二）1963年《外空宣言》

1963年《外空宣言》的一致通过表明联合国大会就适用于开展外层空间活动的若干基本原则达成了共识③。《外空宣言》的第七项和第九项原则涉及宇航员的营救和空间物体的返还。

1963年《外空宣言》第七项原则涉及空间物体的返还。它规定："在登记国国境以外发现的这些物体或其组成部分，应返还登记国，但在返还前，登记国应当根据要求提供识别数据。"应当指出，返还空间物体的义务不受任何条件限制。然而，苏联并不认为这是达成协议的障碍④。

1963年《外空宣言》第九项原则涉及宇航员的营救和送回。它规定："各国应将宇航员视为人类在外层空间的使者，并在发生事故、遇险，或在外国领土或公海上紧急降落时，向其提供一切可能的援助。进行此类降落的宇航员应被安全并迅速地送回其航天器的登记国。"

（三）1963年《外空宣言》的谈判

在就1963年《外空宣言》达成协议后，法律小组委员会再次将注意力转向起草一份关于援助和返还的条约。1964年的第三届会议分为两部分。第一次于1964年3

① See UN Doc. A/AC. 105/C. 2/SR. 25, Legal Sub-Committee, Second Session, Summary Record of the Twenty-Fifth Meeting, 30 April 1963, p. 15; Cheng, Bin, The 1968 Astronauts Agreement or How Not to Make a Treaty, The Yearbook of World Affairs (23) 1969, p. 189.

② See Dembling, Paul G. /Arons, Daniel M., Space Law and the United Nations: The Work of the Legal Subcommittee on the Peaceful Uses of Outer Space, Journal of Air Law and Commerce (32) 1966, pp. 334-336.

③ See Dembling, Paul G. /Arons, Daniel M., *The Treaty on Rescue and Return of Astronauts and Space Objects*, William and Mary Law Review (9) 1968, p. 635.

④ The revised USSR Draft of 1964 contained the condition that the space object must have been launched for peaceful purposes and that the State has officially announced the launch and its purpose; UN Doc. A/AC. 105/C. 2/L. 2/Rev. 1 Agreement on the rescue of astronauts and spaceships in the event of accident or emergency landing, USSR Revised Draft, 9 March 1964, Art. 9. The revised version of this Draft explicitly demanded the space object being launched in accordance with the 1963 Principles Declaration as a condition for the return; UN Doc. A/AC. 105/C. 2/L. 2/Rev. 2, Agreement on the rescue of astronauts and spaceships in the event of accident or emergency landing, USSR Revised Draft, 26 October 1964, Art. 6 para. 2. 9.

月 9 日至 26 日在日内瓦举行，第二次于 1964 年 10 月 5 日至 23 日在纽约举行。大约一年后，法律小组委员会第四届会议于 1965 年 9 月 20 日至 10 月 1 日在纽约举行。

法律小组委员会的这两次会议几乎专门讨论关于“援助和返还”以及“责任”的公约草案。

1964 年和 1965 年，苏联未能成功说服其他代表团应同时就一般空间条约进行辩论，并且法律小组委员会应该考虑除了这两个具体主题之外的“一般原则”作为第三项议题和工作①。然而，在 1966 年，优先事项发生了变化。法律小组委员会将大部分时间用于就一项关于一般原则的条约进行辩论，于是，《外空条约》的文本得以在同年年底提交联合国大会通过②。在这次之后，法律小组委员会于 1967 年再次就“援助和返还”以及“责任”的公约草案进行辩论。

（1）1964 年和 1965 年的草案和初步协议

1964 年和 1965 年法律小组委员第三和第四届会议收到了关于援助和返还问题的若干草案③。苏联提交了基于其早期提案作了修订的两份草案。美国提交了一份新起草的关于援助和返还的国际协议提案，该提案比其早先的大会决议提案更加详细和广泛④。澳大利亚和加拿大也提交了单独的草案文本⑤。一些代表团建议对这些草案进

---

① See Dembling, Paul G./Arons, Daniel M., Space Law and the United Nations: The Work of the Legal Subcommittee on the Peaceful Uses of Outer Space, Journal of Air Law and Commerce (32) 1966, p. 337.

② See Lee, Roy S. K., Assistance to and Return of Astronauts and Space Objects, in: Jasentuliyana, Nandasiri/Lee, Roy S. K. (eds.), Manual on Space Law, Volume I, Oceana, New York 1979, p. 55; van Bogaert, Eric R. C., Aspects of Space Law, Kluwer, Deventer 1986, p. 99; Hall, Cargil, *Rescue and Return of Astronauts on Earth and in Outer Space*, American Journal of International Law (63) 1969, p. 203.

③ See UN Doc. A/AC. 105/C. 2/L. 2/Rev. 1, Agreement on the rescue of astronauts and spaceships in the event of accident or emergency landing, USSR Revised Draft, 9 March 1964; UN Doc. A/AC. 105/C. 2/L. 2/Rev. 2, Agreement on the rescue of astronauts and spaceships in the event of accident or emergency landing, USSR Revised Draft, 26 October 1964. The Soviet Revised Draft 1 of March 1964 is longer and more detailed than the earlier draft of 1962. It contains 15 articles and several new specifications which were not all met with approval by the member of the Legal Subcommittee. The Revised Draft 1 of October 1964 consisting of 12 articles took a number of concerns by members of the Legal Subcommittee into consideration.

④ It contained eleven articles and contained also a dispute settlement clause as well as provisions on amendments, signatories, entering into force etc.; see UN Doc. A/AC. 105/C. 2/L. 9, International Agreement on Assistance to and Return of Astronauts and Objects Launched into Outer Space, United States Proposal, 9 March 1964.

⑤ The joint Australia and Canada proposal consists of a preamble and seven articles; UN Doc. WG. I/30, Australia and Canada: Proposal, in: UN Doc. A/AC. 105/21, Report of the Legal Sub-Committee on the Work of the Second Part of its Third Session (5-23 October 1964) to the Committee on the Peaceful Uses of Outer Space, Annex I, Proposals and Amendments Relating to Assistance to and Return of Astronauts and Space Vehicles, 23 October 1964, pp. 8-12.

行修改①。

到 1964 年法律小组委员会第三届会议结束时，就序言和三个条款的内容已达成了一致。随后，向联合国大会提交了由法律小组委员会非正式工作组就“机组人员和航天器援助和返还协议草案的某些条款文本”所达成的初步协议②。然而，谈判中的这一过渡并没有产生持久的影响。该文本并没有成为协议最终版本的一部分。

（2）讨论中的问题

尽管 1963 年的《外空宣言》已经明确了关于无条件返还空间物体的原则，苏联仍然坚持认为，返还的义务应限于为“和平目的”③ 或是“根据 1963 年《外空宣言》所发射的空间物体”④。西方代表团则坚持认为，1963 年《外空宣言》的措辞可以理解为强加了无条件的义务，因此不应当依赖任何特定国家对发射目的的主观判断⑤。苏联、罗马尼亚和保加利亚代表辩称，应将符合 1963 年《外空宣言》视为送回宇航员的条件，因为若发射违悖《外空宣言》，那么就是具有敌对性的，这意味着相关宇

① See Hall, Cargil, *Rescue and Return of Astronauts on Earth and in Outer Space*, American Journal of International Law (63) 1969, p. 203; UN Doc. A/AC. 105/19, Report of the Legal Sub-Committee on the Work of its Third Session (9-26 March 1964) to the Committee on the Peaceful Uses of Outer Space, 26 March 1964, p. 3; UN Doc. A/AC. 105/19, Report of the Legal Sub-Committee on the Work of its Third Session (9-26 March 1964) to the Committee on the Peaceful Uses of Outer Space, Annex I, Proposals and Amendments Relating to Assistance to and Return of Astronauts and Space Vehicles, 26 March 1964, pp. 12-24; UN Doc. A/AC. 105/21, Report of the Legal Sub-Committee on the Work of the Second Part of its Third Session (5-23 October 1964) to the Committee on the Peaceful Uses of Outer Space, Annex I, Proposals and amendments relating to assistance to and return of astronauts and space vehicles, 23 October 1964, pp. 6-8, 13-14.

② Ibid.

③ UN Doc. A/AC. 105/C. 2/L. 2/Rev. 1, Agreement on the rescue of astronauts and spaceships in the event of accident or emergency landing, USSR Revised Draft, 9 March 1964, Art. 9.

④ UN Doc. A/AC. 105/C. 2/L. 2/Rev. 2, Agreement on the rescue of astronauts and spaceships in the event of accident or emergency landing, USSR Revised Draft, 26 October 1964, Art. 6 para. 2.

⑤ This view of the United States was shared by the Canadian and the Australian delegation. See UN Doc. A/AC. 105/C. 2/SR. 46, Legal Sub-Committee, Fourth Session, Summary Record of the Forty-Sixth Meet-ing, held 23 September 1965, 30 November 1965, pp. 3f.; UN Doc. A/AC. 105/C. 2/SR. 47, Legal Sub-Committee, Fourth Session, Summary Record of the Forty-Seventh Meeting, held 24 September 1965, 30 November 1965, pp. 3, 6f.; see also Dembling, Paul G. /Arons, Daniel M., Space Law and the United Nations: The Work of the Legal Subcommittee on the Peaceful Uses of Outer Space, Journal of Air Law and Commerce (32) 1966, p. 345.

航员应被视为间谍，甚至应被视为战俘①。墨西哥代表团建议采取折衷办法，引入争端解决程序，以避免对此事作出单方面判决②。在接下来的几年里，没有就这一点达成协议③。

讨论的另一个问题是费用偿付的程度。虽然开始时一致认为，向宇航员提供援助是一项人道主义义务，不应要求偿付，但一些代表团后来辩称，营救宇航员只对少数国家有利④。

至于如果航天器降落的国家无法提供必要的援助时，所应遵循的程序问题存在一些意见分歧。美国⑤和苏联⑥似乎都同意，在这种情况下，该国必须向发射国请求援助。然而，其他代表团强调，每个国家都有权拒绝外国代表进入具有军事重要性或对国家安全至关重要的地区⑦。

关于在公海或国家管辖或控制领土以外的其他地方（例如：南极洲）进行救援的规定进行了很多讨论。苏联的草案允许发射当局保留进行搜救行动的专属权利，且由

---

① See UN Doc. A/AC. 105/C. 2/SR. 46, Legal Sub-Committee, Fourth Session, Summary Record of the Forty-Sixth Meeting, held 23 September 1965, 30 November 1965, pp. 3f.; UN Doc. A/AC. 105/C. 2/SR. 47, Legal Sub-Committee, Fourth Session, Summary Record of the Forty-Seventh Meeting, held 24 September 1965, 30 November 1965, pp. 5f.

② See UN Doc. A/AC. 105/C. 2/SR. 46, Legal Sub-Committee, Fourth Session, Summary Record of the Forty-Sixth Meeting, held 23 September 1965, 30 November 1965, p. 5.

③ See Cheng, Bin, The 1968 Astronauts Agreement or How Not to make a Treaty, The Yearbook of World Affairs (23) 1969, p. 191; Hall, Cargil, *Rescue and Return of Astronauts on Earth and in Outer Space*, American Journal of International Law (63) 1969, p. 203.

④ See UN Doc. A/AC. 105/21, Report of the Legal Sub-Committee on the Work of the Second Part of its Third Session (5-23 October 1964) to the Committee on the Peaceful Uses of Outer Space, Annex I, Proposals and amendments relating to assistance to and return of astronauts and space vehicles, p. 342.

⑤ The United States Proposal provided that "each Contracting Party shall permit, subject to the control by its own authorities, the authorities of the State of registry or international organizations responsible for launching to provide measures of assistance as my be necessitated by the circumstances," UN Doc. A/AC. 105/C. 2/L. 9, United States: Proposal, International Agreement on Assistance to and Return of Astronauts and Objects Launched into Outer Space, 9 March 1964.

⑥ According to the USSR Revised Draft 1, if a "State in whose territory the astronauts have landed is unable to carry out the necessary rescue operations unaided it shall request assistance from the launching State", UN Doc. A/AC. 105/C. 2/L. 2/Rev. 1, Agreement on the rescue of astronauts and spaceships in the event of accident or emergency landing, USSR Revised Draft, 9 March 1964, Art. 3.

⑦ See the statement of the Italian delegate, UN Doc. A/AC. 105/C. 2/SR. 29-37, Legal Sub-Committee, Third Session (1st Part), Summary Record of the Twenty-Ninth to Thirty-Seventh Meetings, held from 9-26 March 1964, 24 August 1964, p. 56; see Dembling, Paul G. /Arons, Daniel M., Space Law and the United Nations: The Work of the Legal Subcommittee on the Peaceful Uses of Outer Space, Journal of Air Law and Commerce (32) 1966, p. 338.

其决定[1]。这被批评为不符合尽快提供援助的人道主义愿望[2]。

关于争端解决问题，美国草案规定，任何缔约方均应提交国际法院[3]。苏联草案则没有包含争端解决的条款，并建议在美国草案中添加“经争端各方同意”的字样[4]。

法律小组委员会第二届和第三届会议还讨论了是否应允许国际组织独立于这些组织的成员国享有《营救协定》规定的权利和义务的问题，但这一问题仍未解决[5]。

对于有资格成为《营救协定》签署国的国家，公约生效所需的批准或加入的国家数量，以及《营救协定》的修正程序等问题也存在不同意见。美国希望将有权进行签署的国家限制在联合国成员国或大会明确邀请成为缔约国的国家[6]，而苏联则提到“所有国家”[7]，包括例如德意志民主共和国[8]。关于生效所需的国家数量，美国的提

① Art. 4 provided that “［r］escue operations on the high seas shall be directed by the launching State or by such State as the launching State may request to take charge thereof.” Art. 5 went even further and maintained that “［t］he launching State may reserve the exclusive right to carry out, by its own means and with its own personnel, operations for the finding and rescue of astronauts and spaceships in a zone of the high seas designated by itself”. UN Doc. A/AC. 105/C. 2/L. 2/Rev. 1, Agreement on the rescue of astronauts and spaceships in the event of accident or emergency landing, USSR Revised Draft, 19 March 1964.

② See UN Doc. A/AC. 105/C. 2/SR. 29-37, Legal Sub-Committee, Third Session（1st Part）, Summary Record of the Twenty-Ninth to Thirty-Seventh Meetings, held from 9-26 March 1964, 24 August 1964, p. 68; Dembling, Paul G. /Arons, Daniel M., Space Law and the United Nations: The Work of the Legal Subcommittee on the Peaceful Uses of Outer Space, Journal of Air Law and Commerce（32）1966, pp. 338f.

③ See UN Doc. A/AC. 105/C. 2/L. 9, International Agreement on Assistance to and Return of Astronauts and Objects Launched into Outer Space, United States Proposal, 9 March 1964, Art. 4. Such a clause would confer jurisdiction to the International Court of Justice in accordance with the provision of Art. 36 para. 1 Statute of the Statute of the International Court of Justice（26 June 1945）1 UNTS 16（ICJ Statute）.

④ UN Doc. WG. I/12, USSR: Amendment, in: UN Doc. A/AC. 105/19, Report of the Legal Sub-Committee on the Work of its Third Session（9-26 March 1964）to the Committee on the Peaceful Uses of Outer Space, Annex I, Proposals and Amendments Relating to Assistance to and Return of Astronauts and Space Vehicles, 26 March 1964, p. 22; see Dembling, Paul G. /Arons, Daniel M., Space Law and the United Nations: The Work of the Legal Subcommittee on the Peaceful Uses of Outer Space, Journal of Air Law and Commerce（32）1966, p. 340.

⑤ See ibid., p. 342; Dembling, Paul G. /Arons, Daniel M., *The Treaty on Rescue and Return of Astronauts and Space Objects*, William and Mary Law Review（9）1968, p. 636.

⑥ See UN Doc. A/AC. 105/C. 2/L. 9, International Agreement on Assistance to and Return of Astronauts and Objects Launched into Outer Space, United States Proposal, 9 March 1964, Art. 7.

⑦ UN Doc. A/AC. 105/C. 2/L. 2/Rev. 2, Agreement on the rescue of astronauts and spaceships in the event of accident or emergency landing, USSR Revised Draft, 26 October 1964, Art. 7.

⑧ See Cheng, Bin, *The* 1968 *Astronauts Agreement or How Not to make a Treaty*, The Yearbook of World Affairs（23）1969, p. 191; Hall, Cargil, *Rescue and Return of Astronauts on Earth and in Outer Space*, American Journal of International Law（63）1969, p. 131.

案表示只需要 2 个①。苏联的第一份草案则表示需要 15 个国家的批准②，但后来的草案也将其减少到了 2 个③。

（四）《外空条约》中的援助与返还

1966 年，法律小组委员会第五届会议几乎完全致力于就一项条约达成协议，以确定各国在探索和利用外层空间方面的一般法律义务。在《外空条约》文本达成一致意见之前，法律小组委员会分别于 7 月和 9 月，在日内瓦和纽约举行了两次会议。《外空条约》于 1966 年 12 月 19 日经联合国大会通过④，于 1967 年 1 月 27 日开放签署⑤，并于 1967 年 10 月 10 日生效。《外空条约》第五条和第八条包含关于援助宇航员、送回宇航员和返还空间物体的规定。

《外空条约》第五条规定："本条约各缔约国应把宇航员视为人类在外层空间的使者，宇航员如遇意外事故、危难或在另一缔约国领土上或公海上紧急降落时，应给予他们一切可能的协助。宇航员降落后，应将他们安全和迅速地送回航天器的登记国。在外层空间及天体上进行活动时，任一缔约国的宇航员应给予其他缔约国的宇航员一切可能的协助。本条约各缔约国如发现在包括月球与其他天体在内的外层空间有对宇航员的生命活健康可能构成危险的任何现象，应立即通知本条约其他缔约国或联合国秘书长。"⑥

《外空条约》第八条规定："凡本条约缔约国为射入外层空间物体的登记国者，对于该空间物体及其所载人员，当其在外层空间或某一天体上时，应保有管辖权和控制权。"对于空间物体返还的义务，它规定："空间物体或其组成部分在其所登记的缔约

---

① See UN Doc. A/AC. 105/C. 2/L. 9, International Agreement on Assistance to and Return of Astronauts and Objects Launched into Outer Space, United States Proposal, 9 March 1964, Art. 7.

② See UN Doc. A/AC. 105/C. 2/L. 2/Rev. 1, Agreement on the rescue of astronauts and spaceships in the event of accident or emergency landing, USSR Revised Draft, 9 March 1964, Art. 13. .

③ See UN Doc. A/AC. 105/C. 2/L. 2/Rev. 2, Agreement on the rescue of astronauts and spaceships in the event of accident or emergency landing, USSR Revised Draft, 26 October 1964, Art. 9.

④ UNGA Res. 2222 (XXI), Treaty on Principles Governing the Activities of States in the Exploration and Use of Outer Space, Including the Moon and Other Celestial Bodies, 19 December 1966.

⑤ For the Drafting History of the Outer Space Treaty see Hobe, Stephan, *Historical Background*, in: Hobe, Stephan/Schmidt-Tedd, Bernhard/Schrogl, Kai-Uwe (eds.), Cologne Commentary on Space Law, Volume I, Heymanns, Cologne 2009, pp. 1, 12-14.

⑥ For a commentary on this provision, see von der Dunk, Frans/Goh, Gérardine M., *Article V*, in: Hobe, Stephan/Schmidt-Tedd, Bernhard/Schrogl, Kai-Uwe (eds.), Cologne Commentary on Space Law, Volume I, Heymanns, Cologne 2009, pp. 94-102.

国境外发现，应返还该缔约国，如经请求，该缔约国应在返还前提供认证资料。”[①]

虽然《外空条约》已有相关规定，许多国家仍认为，有必要就援助和返还问题达成具体的协议。尤其是苏联，其主张应达成更为具体的协议。这归因于苏联计划开展一项全面的太空计划，使得苏联宇航员和空间物体处在苏联领土之外的可能性增加[②]。对于制定一项更为具体的协议的总体共识，在联合国大会就确认《外空条约》签署所达成的同一份决议中也有体现。在该决议中，联合国大会要求联合国外空委“继续努力拟订……一项关于协助宇航员和空间物体返回的协定。”[③]

（五）1967 年《外空条约》达成协议后的谈判

1966 年《外空条约》通过后，拟订有关援助和营救宇航员，以及返还空间物体的协议的工作重新恢复。在 1967 年 6 月 19 日至 7 月 14 日于日内瓦举行的第六届会议上，法律小组委员会讨论了第四届会议上美国的提案[④]，苏联修订后的提案[⑤]，以及澳大利亚和加拿大联合提交的一份修订后的工作文件[⑥]。

苏联提交的经修订的简要提案只涉及救援和援助宇航员的标准，而没有提及航天器甚至宇航员的送回[⑦]。提案没有涉及之前有争议的问题，即送回是有条件的还是无

---

① For a commentary to this provision, see Schmidt-Tedd, Bernhard/Mick, Stephan, *Article* Ⅷ, in: Hobe, Stephan/Schmidt-Tedd, Bernhard/Schrogl, Kai-Uwe (eds.), Cologne Commentary on Space Law, Volume I, Heymanns, Cologne 2009, pp. 146-168.

② Piradov, Head of the Soviet delegation pointed to the vital nature and importance of the problem in view of the tragic incidents which occurred to Soviet and US astronauts in 1967; Houben, Piet-Hein, *A New Chapter of Space Law: The Agreement on the Rescue and Return of Astronauts and Space Objects*, Netherlands International Law Review (15) 1968, p. 122; see also Christol, Carl Q., *The Modern International Law of Outer Space*, Pergamon Press, New York 1982, p. 168.

③ UNGA Res. 2222 (XXI), Treaty on Principles Governing the Activities of States in the Exploration and Use of Outer Space, Including the Moon and Other Celestial Bodies, 19 December 1966; see Dembling, Paul G./Arons, Daniel M., *The Treaty on Rescue and Return of Astronauts and Space Objects*, William and Mary Law Review (9) 1968, pp. 637f.

④ UN Doc. A/AC. 105/C. 2/L. 9, International Agreement on Assistance to and Return of Astronauts and Objects Launched into Outer Space, United States Proposal, 9 March 1964.

⑤ UN Doc. A/AC. 105/C. 2/L. 18, Agreement On The Rescue Of Astronauts In The Event Of Accident Or Emergency Landing, USSR Revised Draft, 19 June 1967.

⑥ UN Doc. A/AC. 105/C. 2/L. 20, Assistance to and Return of Astronauts and Space Objects, Revised Australian-Canadian proposal submitted as a working paper, 21 June 1967; Hall, Cargil, *Rescue and Return of Astronauts on Earth and in Outer Space*, American Journal of International Law (63) 1969, p. 204.

⑦ See Hall, Cargil, *Rescue and Return of Astronauts on Earth and in Outer Space*, American Journal of International Law (63) 1969, p. 204; Cheng, Bin, *The 1968 Astronauts Agreement or How not to make a Treaty*, The Yearbook of World Affairs (23) 1969, p. 193.

条件[①]。另一方面，美国、澳大利亚和加拿大的草案涵盖了宇航员的送回和发射到外层空间的物体的送还。这种范围上的差异在第六届会议期间引发了很大程度的分歧，结果进展甚微[②]。

苏联代表团试图为其提案的有限范围辩护，理由是美国和苏联宇航员在 1967 年 1 月和 3 月的事故中死亡，显然迫切需要尽早就宇航员救援达成协议。它认为，排除关于送回宇航员和返还空间物体的规定将加快这一进度，而有关援助的协议是现阶段外空活动可以实现的绝对最低限度[③]。

然而，美国并不愿意放弃其提案中涉及返还的部分，并表示在联合国大会规定的任务中，包括有义务就宇航员和空间物体的归还以及宇航员的营救达成协议[④]。其他国家也表示，将援助宇航员、宇航员送回和空间物体返还这三个事项结合起来，是满足所有有关国家的要求，同时为人类利益服务的唯一途径[⑤]。

尽管在协议的范围上存在着根本性的意见分歧，但对涉及在缔约国领土上通知事故和向宇航员提供援助的部分案文，各国则达成了临时协议[⑥]。然而，维兹内尔（Wyzner）主席提请注意：1964 年就序言和三个条款已达成的共识并没有得到重申[⑦]。因此，第六届会议在达成一项有关援助和返还方面的协议上，没有取得多大进展，反

---

① See ibid.

② See Dembling, Paul G./Arons, Daniel M., *The Treaty on Rescue and Return of Astronauts and Space Objects*, William and Mary Law Review (9) 1968, p. 638. As no agreement on assistance was in sight, the Subcommittee turned its attention to further work on the Draft Convention on Liability; see Hall, Cargil, *Rescue and Return of Astronauts on Earth and in Outer Space*, American Journal of International Law (63) 1969, p. 204.

③ UN Doc. A/AC. 105/C. 2/SR. 76, Legal Sub-Committee, Sixth Session, Summary Record of the Seventy-Sixth Meeting, held 20 June 1967, 13 November 1967, pp. 4f.; Dembling, Paul G./Arons, Daniel M., *The Treaty on Rescue and Return of Astronauts and Space Objects*, William and Mary Law Review (9) 1968, p. 638.

④ UN Doc. A/AC. 105/C. 2/SR. 85, Legal Sub-Committee, Sixth Session, Summary Record of the Eighty-Fifth (Closing) Meeting, held 14 July 1967, 14 November 1967, pp. 5f.; see Dembling, Paul G./Arons, Daniel M., *The Treaty on Rescue and Return of Astronauts and Space Objects*, William and Mary Law Review (9) 1968, p. 639.

⑤ See ibid.; UN Doc. A/AC. 105/C. 2/SR. 85, Legal Sub-Committee, Sixth Session, Summary Record of the Eighty-Fifth (Closing) Meeting, held 14 July 1967, 14 November 1967, p. 7.

⑥ UN Doc. A/AC. 105/37, Report of the Legal Subcommittee on the Work of its Sixth Session (19 June-14 July 1967), 14 July 1967, pp. 3f.

⑦ See UN Doc. A/AC. 105/C. 2/SR. 76, Legal Sub-Committee Sixth Session, Summary Record of the Seventy-Sixth Meeting, held 20 June 1967, 13 November 1967, p. 4.

而标志着谈判进程倒退了一步[①]。

（2）1967 年 9 月后的双边会议

9 月，当联合国外空委在纽约召开会议时，苏联改变了立场[②]，表示愿意讨论宇航员和航天器的返还问题[③]，这令美国和其他代表团大吃一惊。随后，美国和苏联代表在大会第二十二届会议期间举行了 15 次双边会议[④]。这些非正式会谈就援助和送回宇航员以及返还航天器的协定的一些条款达成了一致，并通过与其他感兴趣的代表团进行磋商，以期迅速就最后案文达成一致意见[⑤]。

1967 年 11 月 3 日，联合国大会全体会议请联合国外空委“以更为紧迫之势，继续开展工作，拟订一项关于协助宇航员和航天器返还的协定”[⑥]。

（3）1967 年 12 月最后阶段

1967 年 12 月 14 日，法律小组委员会召开了一次特别会议。对“关于营救宇航员、送回宇航员和返还射入外层空间物体的协定草案”[⑦] 进行了讨论，并作了少许修改[⑧]。会谈中航天大国与其他国家之间存在着分歧。后者指出，协议所规定的义务主

---

① See Dembling, Paul G. /Arons, Daniel M. , *The Treaty on Rescue and Return of Astronauts and Space Objects*, William and Mary Law Review (9) 1968, p. 639.

② The Deputy Soviet Ambassador declared that his delegation had no objection to completing the draft presented by the Soviet Union with provisions concerning the return of astronauts and space vehicles, in conformity with the OST. This should make it unnecessary to criticize his delegation further and hold it responsible for the protracted negotiations in the Legal Subcommittee; see Dembling, Paul G. /Arons, Daniel M. , *The Treaty on Rescue and Return of Astronauts and Space Objects*, William and Mary Law Review (9) 1968, p. 640.

③ See UN Doc. A/AC. 105/PV. 49, Provisional Verbatim Record of its Forty-Ninth Session, held 13 December 1967, 13 September 1967, p. 61; Hall, Cargil, *Rescue and Return of Astronauts on Earth and in Outer Space*, American Journal of International Law (63) 1969, p. 204; Houben, Piet-Hein, *A New Chapter of Space Law: The Agreement on the Rescue and Return of Astronauts and Space Objects*, Netherlands International Law Review (15) 1968, p. 121.

④ See Hall, Cargil, *Rescue and Return of Astronauts on Earth and in Outer Space*, American Journal of International Law (63) 1969, p. 204; Dembling, Paul G. /Arons, Daniel M. , *The Treaty on Rescue and Return of Astronauts and Space Objects*, William and Mary Law Review (9) 1968, p. 640.

⑤ See ibid.

⑥ UNGA Res. 2260 (XXII), Report of the Committee on the Peaceful Uses of Outer Space, 3 November 1967.

⑦ UN Doc. A/AC. 105/C. 2/L. 28, Draft agreement on the rescue of astronauts, the return of astronauts and the return of objects launched into outer space, 12 December 1967.

⑧ UN Doc. A/AC. 105/C. 2/L. 28/Rev. 1, Draft agreement on the rescue of astronauts, the return of astronauts and the return of objects launched into outer space, 14 December 1967; see also UN Doc. A/AC. 105/C. 2/SR. 86, Legal Sub-Committee, Special Session, Summary Record of the Eighty-Sixth Meeting, held 14 December 1967, 9 February 1968, p. 3; Cheng, Bin, *The 1968 Astronauts Agreement or How Not to make a Treaty*, The Yearbook of World Affairs (23) 1969, p. 185.

要为航天大国服务①。他们虽然欢迎关于援助和送回的协议，但强调拟订一项有关责任的公约的重要性，并认为从法律和实践的角度来看，这两个专题是相辅相成且相互关联的，并对没有同时拟订这两项协议感到遗憾②。许多代表批评没有时间详细审议协定草案③，最终，他们代表本国政府对草案表示了保留立场④。

1967年12月15日举行了三次会议，对苏联和美国就包括国际组织在内的许多问题提交的草案进行了修改之后⑤，该草案被转交给了全体委员会，委员会于1967年12月16日进行了一些修改后予以批准，并决定将其提交联合国大会审议⑥。然而，不同寻常的是，该草案并没有提交至第一委员会，该委员会通常负责审查裁军和国际安全

---

① See ibid., p. 197; emphasized by the delegate of India, UN Doc. A/AC. 105/C. 2/SR. 86, Legal Sub-Committee, Special Session, Summary Record of the Eighty-Sixth Meeting, held 14 December 1967, 9 February 1968, p. 12.

② See United Kingdom, UN Doc. A/AC. 105/PV. 52, Provisional Verbatim Record of the Fifty-Second Meeting, held 16 December 1967, 12 February 1968, p. 22; Sierra Leone, ibid., pp. 27f., 30; Australia, ibid., p. 46; Belgium, ibid., pp. 55f.; Austria, ibid., p. 58; United Arab Republic, ibid., 66; Iran, UN Doc. A/AC. 105/C. 2/SR. 86, Legal Sub-Committee, Special Session, Summary Record of the Eighty-Sixth Meeting, held 14 December 1967, 9 February 1968, pp. 9f.; Brazil, ibid., p. 14; United Arab Republic, ibid., p. 15; India, ibid., p. 11f.; Australia, UN Doc. A/AC. 105/C. 2/SR. 87, Legal Sub-Committee, Special Session, Summary Record of the Eighty-Seventh Meeting, held 15 December 1967, 2 February 1968, p. 3; Sierra Leone, ibid., p. 5; Italy, ibid., p. 6; Belgium, ibid., p. 8; Austria, ibid., p. 9; United Kingdom, ibid., p. 5; Houben, Piet-Hein, *A New Chapter of Space Law: The Agreement on the Rescue and Return of Astronauts and Space Objects*, Netherlands International Law Review (15) 1968, p. 132.

③ See Sierra Leone, UN Doc. A/AC. 105/C. 2/SR. 87, Legal Sub-Committee, Special Session, Summary Record of the Eighty-Seventh Meeting, held 15 December 1967, 2 February 1968, p. 5; Belgium, ibid., p. 9; Japan, ibid., p. 6.

④ See Cheng, Bin, *The 1968 Astronauts Agreement or How Not to make a Treaty*, The Yearbook of World Affairs (23) 1969, p. 196; India, UN Doc. A/AC. 105/PV. 52, Provisional Verbatim Record of the Fifty-Second Meeting, held 16 December 1967, 12 February 1968, pp. 38ff.; Italy, ibid., pp. 41f.; Japan, ibid., p. 52.

⑤ See Cheng, Bin, *The 1968 Astronauts Agreement or How Not to make a Treaty*, The Yearbook of World Affairs (23) 1969, p. 195.

⑥ Commentators emphasize the crucial role of the bilateral negotiations between the two space powers in the final phase of the negotiations. See, for example, Hall, Cargil, *Rescue and Return of Astronauts on Earth and in Outer Space*, American Journal of International Law (63) 1969, p. 204; Cheng, Bin, *The 1968 Astronauts Agreement orHow Not to make a Treaty*, The Yearbook of World Affairs (23) 1969, p. 195. Some maintain that the agreement, although many of its particular provisions had their origins in discussions in the Committee for the Peaceful Uses of Outer Space, "was a bilateral draft which was rushed through the multilateral arena"; see Houben, Piet-Hein, *A New Chapter of Space Law: The Agreement on the Rescue and Return of Astronauts and Space Objects*, Netherlands International Law Review (15) 1968, p. 121.

领域的草案，而外空事务历来归该委员会审查[1]。

1967 年 12 月 19 日，大会一致通过了该草案[2]。然而，一些代表抱怨时间不够，并强调，不应让大会审议未经其主要委员会审查且未按照议事规则列入议程的决议成为先例[3]。

（六）批准程序

大会 1967 年 12 月 19 日第 2345 号决议请保存国政府“尽早开放《营救协定》供签署和批准”[4]，并表示希望“《营救协定》能够得到尽可能广泛地加入”[5]。1968 年 4 月 22 日，43 个国家在华盛顿特区、伦敦和莫斯科签署了该协议。根据《协定》第七条第三款的规定，需要有 5 个国家批准，《营救协定》才能生效。继白俄罗斯、爱尔兰和尼泊尔之后，三个保存国即美国、英国和苏联也批准了，《营救协定》于 1968 年 12 月 3 日生效[6]。

截至 2019 年 1 月 1 日，已有 96 个国家批准了《营救协定》，另有 23 个国家签署了《协定》。两个政府间国际组织——欧洲宇航局和欧洲气象卫星组织宣布接受《营救协定》规定的权利和义务[7]。

---

① See Cheng, Bin, *The* 1968 *Astronauts Agreement or How Not to make a Treaty*, The Yearbook of World Affairs (23) 1969, p. 188.

② See ibid., p. 196.

③ See Japan, UN Doc. A/AC. 105/C. 2/SR. 86, Legal Sub-Committee, Special Session, Summary Record of the Eighty-Sixth Meeting, held 14 December 1967, 9 February 1968, p. 10; India, ibid., p. 12; Brazil, ibid., p. 14; Sierra Leone, UN Doc. A/AC. 105/C. 2/SR. 87, Legal Sub-Committee, Special Session, Summary Record of the Eighty-Seventh Meeting, held 15 December 1967, 2 February 1968, p. 5; Japan, UN Doc. A/AC. 105/C. 2/SR. 89, Legal Sub-Committee, Special Session, Summary Record of the Eighty-Ninth Meeting, held 15 December 1967, 2 February 1968, p. 6; France, UN Doc. A/AC. 105/PV. 52, Provisional Verbatim Record of the Fifty-Second Meeting, held 16 December 1967, 12 February 1968, p. 32; France, UN Doc. A/PV. 1640, United Nations General Assembly, Twenty-Second Session, Official Records 1640th Plenary Meeting, 19 December 1967, p. 7; Iran, ibid., p. 10; Burma, ibid., p. 10; see also Cheng, Bin, *The* 1968 *Astronauts Agreement or How Not to make a Treaty*, The Yearbook of World Affairs (23) 1969, p. 196.

④ UNGA Res. 2345 (XXII), Agreement on the Rescue of Astronauts, the Return of Astronauts and the Return of Objects Launched into Outer Space, 19 December 1967, para. 2.

⑤ Ibid., para. 3; see Houben, Piet-Hein, *A New Chapter of Space Law: The Agreement on the Rescue and Return of Astronauts and Space Objects*, Netherlands International Law Review (15) 1968, p. 132.

⑥ See Cheng, Bin, *The* 1968 *Astronauts Agreement or How Not to make a Treaty*, The Yearbook of World Affairs (23) 1969, p. 186.

⑦ UN Doc. A/AC. 105/C. 2/2018/CRP. 3, Status of International Agreements relating to activities in outer space as at 1 January 2018, 9 April 2019 with regular updates published on http://www.unoosa.org/documents/pdf/spacelaw/treatystatus/AC105_ C2_ 2018_ CRP03E. pdf.

六、与其他条约的关系

关于《月球协定》的谈判与关于责任问题和制定一般原则的讨论是同时开展的。起初，对于哪一个问题应该优先考虑是不明确的。苏联赞成从一开始就同时讨论援助和送回问题，以及一般原则问题，并在 1962 年法律小组委员会第一届会议上，除了提出关于援助和送回的提案外，还提出了“关于各国探索和利用外层空间活动的基本原则的拟议宣言”①。然而，美国和西方国家认为关于一般原则的讨论为时过早，倾向于集中精力就援助和送回问题，以及责任问题等更具体和实际的问题进行谈判。因此，一般原则在会议开幕时仅作了简要讨论，而在 1962 年法律小组委员会第一届会议期间，更广泛的辩论集中在援助和送回，以及赔偿责任问题上。相比之下，1963 年的第二届会议几乎完全讨论了一般原则，并以 1963 年《外空宣言》的通过宣告结束。1964 年和 1965 年，讨论集中在关于援助和送回，以及赔偿责任的两项特别条约上②。1966 年，一般原则和关于《外空条约》的辩论再次成为优先事项，并将其他两个专题优先级降低。因此，《营救协定》是以《外空条约》的讨论所取得的结果为基础的。关于援助和送回的一些一般原则已纳入《外空条约》第五条和第八条，而《营救协定》对这些一般原则进行了进一步细化。

此外，应指出《营救协定》与《责任公约》的密切联系。这主要是由于航天国家和非航天国家的利益冲突。虽然《营救协定》主要服务于航天大国的利益，但《责任公约》主要服务于非航天国家的利益。大会第 1962（XVIII）号决议同样处理了送回和赔偿责任问题，即将其列为各国探索和利用外层空间的同等重要原则③。法律小组委员会第一工作组后来于 1964 年采用了这种做法，强调关于营救的协议和有关责任

---

① UN Doc. A/AC. 105/C. 2/L. 1, Declaration of Basic Principles Governing the Activities of States Pertaining to the Exploration and Use of Outer Space, USSR Proposal, 6 June 1962. It included in its Art. 9 a duty to render all possible assistance to spaceships and their crews which make emergency landings on the territory of a foreign State or on the high seas, and the return of space objects found beyond the limits of the launching State.

② However, the Soviet Union kept insisting on the continuation of the debate on general principles and a corresponding treaty. See Cheng, Bin, *The 1968 Astronauts Agreement or How Not to make a Treaty*, The Yearbook of World Affairs (23) 1969, p. 190.

③ UNGA Res. 1962 (XVIII), Declaration of Legal Principles Governing the Activities of States in the Exploration and Uses of Outer Space, 13 December 1963, Principles 7 and 8.

的条约应同时拟定，因为它们涉及同一问题的两个方面[①]。然而，援助和送回义务与进行损害赔偿的责任之间没有直接关联[②]。这两项条约的谈判虽是同时进行的，却是分别达成的。

七、遗漏的问题

（一）争端解决

在谈判过程中，争端解决问题是十分重要的。然而，《营救协定》草案几乎没有关于解决争端的规定。1962 年苏联和美国的提案中均没有此类条款。1963 年《外空宣言》和 1967 年《外空条约》对此问题也保持了沉默。美国 1964 年提出的《援助和送回宇航员的国际协议》提案首次明确提到了争端解决问题。根据该提案第四条："因本协定的解释或适用而产生的任何争端，可由本协定的任何缔约方提交国际法院裁决"[③]。

在讨论中，西方国家代表支持制定有关争端解决的条款。然而，一些代表认为，争端解决机制应是一个为解决更广泛的问题且更具区别性的制度；此外，还应包括其他和平解决争端的手段。也有提议认为，可以建立类似于《责任公约》草案中的仲裁程序[④]。一些代表团则支持在提交国际法院之前，以非正式的方式解决争端的想法[⑤]。西方代表普遍支持通过司法解决争端，但承认一些代表团可能难以接受国际法院。因此，有人提议考虑其他选择，如按照《南极条约》第十一条所规定的方式[⑥]，或通过

① See UN Doc. A/AC. 105/21/Add. 2, Report of the Legal Sub-Committee on the Work of the Second Part of its Third Session (5-23 October 1964) to the Committee on the Peaceful Uses of Outer Space, Addendum to Annex IV, Summary of views expressed in Working Groups I and II, Note by the Secretariat, 21 May 1965, p. 4.

② See Dembling, Paul G. /Arons, Daniel M. , *The Treaty on Rescue and Return of Astronauts and Space Objects*, William and Mary Law Review (9) 1968, p. 631.

③ UN Doc. A/AC. 105/C. 2/L. 9, International Agreement on Assistance to and Return of Astronauts and Objects Launched into Outer Space, United States Proposal, 9 March 1964.

④ See the statement of the Canadian delegate, UN Doc. A/AC. 105/C. 2/SR. 29-37, Legal Sub-Committee, Third Session (1st Part), Summary Record of the Twenty-Ninth to Thirty-Seventh Meetings, held from 9-26 March 1964, 24 August 1964, p. 26.

⑤ See ibid. ; Statement of the delegate of the United Kingdom, p. 52.

⑥ The Antarctic Treaty (done 1 December 1959, entered into force 23 June 1961) 402 UNTS 71.

强制解决争端的任择议定书的方式①。

一些共产主义国家以及亚洲和非洲国家对在国际法院解决争端持强烈保留意见②。蒙古代表回顾说，在大会第十八届会议上，当时只有 38 个国家承认其管辖权是强制性的，许多非洲和亚洲国家在第六委员会的代表曾警告不要夸大国际法院的重要性，并反对扩大其权力③。美国代表后来解释说，拟议条款将根据《国际法院规约》第三十六条第一款的规定，在《联合国宪章》明确规定的地方④，以及在“现行条约和公约中……特别规定的事项”⑤ 上拥有管辖权。

此外，亚洲和非洲国家不愿意仅有诉诸司法程序的一种方式，倾向于在《联合国宪章》第三十三条提到的所有“和平手段”中自由选择。更重要的是，法院的地域代表性严重偏向于西方法学家及其司法系统⑥。

苏联的提案并没有涉及争端解决条款。然而，在谈判期间，苏联代表团没有将该问题视为一项原则问题而反对，并在讨论中多次提到这一条款⑦。苏联建议在美国的提案中加入“经争端各方同意”一词⑧。然而，由于其他有争议的问题主导了谈判，且由于缺乏时间，在最后阶段没能再次讨论解决争端的问题，因此，最终没有在《营

① See the statement of the delegate of the Sweden, UN Doc. A/AC. 105/C. 2/SR. 29-37, Legal Sub-Committee, Third Session (1st Part), Summary Record of the Twenty-Ninth to Thirty-Seventh Meetings, held from 9-26 March 1964, 24 August 1964, p. 56.

② See the statement of the delegate of Czechoslovakia, ibid., p. 60.

③ See ibid.

④ Charter of the United Nations (done 26 June 1945, entered into force 24 October 1945) 1 UNTS 16 (UN Charter).

⑤ UN Doc. A/AC. 105/C. 2/SR. 29-37, Legal Sub-Committee, Third Session (1st Part), Summary Record of the Twenty-Ninth to Thirty-Seventh Meetings, held from 9-26 March 1964, 24 August 1964, pp. 91f.

⑥ See ibid. the statement of the delegate of Mongolia, p. 60.

⑦ See the statements of the delegate of the Soviet Union, UN Doc. A/AC. 105/C. 2/SR. 42, Legal Sub-Committee, Fourth Session, Summary Record of the Forty-Second Meeting, held 21 September 1965, 30 November 1965, p. 5; UN Doc. A/AC. 105/C. 2/SR. 46, Legal Sub-Committee, Fourth Session, Summary Record of the Forty-Sixth Meeting, held 23 September 1965, p. 7; see also Dembling, Paul G./Arons, Daniel M., *Space Law and the United Nations: The Work of the Legal Subcommittee on the Peaceful Uses of Outer Space*, Journal of Air Law and Commerce (32) 1966, p. 340.

⑧ UN Doc. WG. I/12, USSR: Amendment, in: UN Doc. A/AC. 105/19, Report of the Legal Sub-Committee on the Work of its Third Session (9-26 March 1964) to the Committee on the Peaceful Uses of Outer Space, Annex I, Proposals and Amendments Relating to Assistance to and Return of Astronauts and Space Vehicles, 26 March 1964, p. 22; see also Dembling, Paul G./Arons, Daniel M., *Space Law and the United Nations: The Work of the Legal Subcommittee on the Peaceful Uses of Outer Space*, Journal of Air Law and Commerce (32) 1966, p. 340.

救协定》中涉及该条款。但是，这并不意味着国际法院或其他司法手段不能处理《营救协定》的适用和解释问题的争端解决。缔约国可依据《国际法院规约》第三十六条下国际法院的管辖权，或国际仲裁法庭的管辖权，解决《营救协定》中缔约方之间的争端。

（二）时间框架

《营救协定》未规定或未准确定义的其他事项，是适用于缔约方履行各种职责的时间问题。关于通知、援助、返还或支付收回和返还空间物体的费用的义务必须在什么期限内完成，只有相当模糊的规定。大多数义务必须“立即”或“即刻”履行，这留下了很大的余地，各国在这方面的做法差别很大①。

（三）宇航员援助和送回的费用

《营救协定》没有规定由谁承担履行援助和送回宇航员的义务所产生的费用。然而，根据第五条第五款，为履行收回和返还空间物体或其组成部分的义务而发生的费用应由发射当局承担。

起初，人们普遍认为，救援宇航员产生的费用不应要求偿还，因为这被视为一项人道主义义务，类似于救助遇险船员的情况，即便没有收回救援费用的权利，他们也必须援救。然而，在法律小组委员会随后的讨论中，一些国家辩称，应偿还搜寻宇航员的费用，原因是，与所有航海国都可能有遇险人员的海上救援不同，对宇航员的救援将只对少数国家有利②。

美国在其第一份提案中没有对这两种情况加以区分，并提议“为航天器及其人员提供援助或返回所发生的任何费用应由负责发射的一个或多个国家或国际组织承担。”③ 苏联的草案没有包括这样的义务，而是规定了发射国直接协助救援行动的权利

① See von der Dunk, Frans, *A Sleeping Beauty Awakens*: *The* 1968 *Rescue Agreement after Forty Years*, Journal of Space Law (34) 2008, pp. 411, 425-431; Sundahl, Mark, *The Duty to Rescue Space Tourists and Return Private Space Craft*, Journal of Space Law (35) 2009, pp. 163, 179-180.

② See UN Doc. A/AC. 105/21, Report of the Legal Sub-Committee on the Work of the Second Part of its Third Session (5-23 October 1964), Annex IV, Summary of Views Expressed in Working Groups I and II, 23 October 1964; see also Dembling, Paul G./Arons, Daniel M., *Space Law and the United Nations*: *The Work of the Legal Subcommittee on the Peaceful Uses of Outer Space*, Journal of Air Law and Commerce (32) 1966, p. 342.

③ UN Doc. A/AC. 105/C. 2/L. 3, Assistance and Return of Space Vehicles and Personnel, United States Proposal, 8 June 1962, Principle 3.

和义务①。同样，澳大利亚和加拿大的草案侧重于发射国进行直接援助的可能性，没有规定有义务偿还援助和送回航天器人员所产生的费用②。因此，法律小组委员会将回收和返还空间物体的费用与援助和送回航天器人员的费用加以区分，只有前者可以得到偿付③。

八、小结

《营救协定》的历史背景已经表明，该条约涉及两个主题：航天器上的人员和空间物体及其组成部分。这一区别在《营救协定》的最终版本中进行了明确的描述，其中，有关航天器人员的规定集中在《营救协定》第一至四条；而有关空间物体及其组成部分的规定，则在第五条。

关于航天器上的人员，第一至四条主要规定了三个方面，即：（1）关于事故、紧急情况或意外着陆的信息，（2）援助在登记国境外着陆的人员，（3）人员的送回。

关于空间物体，第五条包括：（1）关于返还至地球的空间物体的信息，（2）回收发现的物体，（3）将物体归还发射当局，（4）消除可能的危险，（5）费用偿还。

《营救协定》第六条包含“发射当局”一词的定义，这是整个协议中唯一的一项定义。最后《协定》第七至十条，包含关于签署、批准和退出的一些其他条款。

---

① See, for example, UN Doc. A/AC. 105/C. 2/L. 2/Rev. 2, Agreement on the rescue of astronauts and spaceships in the event of accident or emergency landing, USSR Revised Draft, 26 October 1964, Art. 3.

② See Art. 3 of the Australian-Canadian proposals of 1964 and 1967, UN Doc. WG. I/30, Australia and Canada: Proposal, in: UN Doc. A/AC. 105/21, Report of the Legal Sub-Committee on the Work of the Second Part of its Third Session (5-23 October 1964), Annex I, Proposals and Amendments Relating to Assistance to and Return of Astronauts and Space Vehicles, 23 October; and UN Doc. A/AC. 105/C. 2/L. 20, Assistance to and Return of Astronauts and Space Objects, Revised Australian-Canadian proposal submitted as a working paper, 21 June 1967.

③ UN Doc. A/AC. 105/C. 2/L. 28, Draft agreement on the rescue of astronauts, the return of astronauts and the return of objects launched into outer space, 12 December 1967, Art. 5; and UN Doc. A/AC. 105/C. 2/L. 28/Rev. 1, Draft agreement on the rescue of astronauts, the return of astronauts and the return of objects launched into outer space, 14 December 1967, Art. 5.

第二章 《营救协定》评注

一、序言

各缔约国，

鉴于关于各国探测及使用外空包括月球与其他天体之活动所应遵守原则之条约至关重要，该约规定遇宇航员有意外事故，危难或紧急降落之情形，应给予一切可能协助，迅速并安全送回宇航员，及送回射入外空之物体，

亟欲发展并进一步具体表示此种义务，

深愿促进外空和平探测及使用之国际合作，

益以人道精神驱使，

兹议定条款如下：

（一）谈判和起草历史

序言明确提到了《外空条约》，它是在《营救协定》通过的前一年商定的。通过强调《外空条约》中所载的原则应当得到发展并得到进一步的具体表达，《营救协定》与一般性的《外空条约》相比，代表了“后法”（lex posterior）和特别法（lex specialis）。然而，在缔结更为专门和具体的有关营救和送回的条约前，起初并不清楚会制定更为一般性的《外空条约》①。虽然苏联赞成这样一种做法，或者至少与更为具体的救援和送回条约一起，同时讨论一般性条约的制定；但是，一些西方国家当时认为讨论一般性条约为时过早，宁愿首先集中讨论更实际和具体的问题②。最终，一

① See Historical Background and Context, mn. 30.

② See ibid.

般性条约——《外空条约》，以及在此之前的 1963 年《外空宣言》，获得了相比更为专门问题进行讨论的优先级，而《营救协定》也因此成为了“后法”和“特别法”。

1962 年苏联初稿的序言提到“人类在促进和平利用外层空间方面的共同利益”，并提到各国政府“将尽最大努力援助可能发生事故的宇宙飞船船员”①。在 1964 年的苏联修订草案中，序言中增加了“征服外层空间的国际合作”和“人道情感”的内容，作为该条约的目的②。1964 年的美国草案还包含“人类在促进和平利用外层空间方面的共同利益”以及“各国的行动应以共同的人道主义关切为指导，并适当考虑科学需要”的理念③。澳大利亚和加拿大提案的序言则明确提到 1963 年的《外空宣言》，并据此拟定，例如“各国应将宇航员视为人类在外层空间的使者”，宇航员“应安全迅速地返回其航天器的登记国”，发射到外层空间的物体“在登记国之外发现的，应归还该国”④。

1964 年就序言达成的初步协议反映了上述提法，并明确提及 1963 年《外空宣言》⑤。此外，它强调，缔约方寻求“制定关于援助和送回航天器上的人员、航天器和其他空间物体人员的国际规则”⑥。《外空条约》制定后，修订后的苏联草案仅明确提及该条约，认为该条约应得到“发展和具体表达”，只补充提及了“人道情感”⑦。

---

① UN Doc. A/AC. 105/C. 2/L. 2, International Agreement on the Rescue of Astronauts and Spaceships mak-ing Emergency Landings, USSR Proposal, 6 June 1962.

② See UN Doc. A/AC. 105/C. 2/L. 2/Rev. 1, Agreement on the rescue of astronauts and spaceships in the event of accident or emergency landing, USSR Revised Draft, 9 March 1964; and UN Doc. A/AC. 105/C. 2/L. 2/Rev. 2, Agreement on the rescue of astronauts and spaceships in the event of accident or emergency landing, USSR Revised Draft, 26 October 1964.

③ UN Doc. A/AC. 105/C. 2/L. 9, International Agreement on Assistance to and Return of Astronauts and Objects Launched into Outer Space, United States Proposal, 9 March 1964.

④ UN Doc. WG. I/30, Australia and Canada: Proposal, in: UN Doc. A/AC. 105/21, Report of the Legal Sub-Committee on the Work of the Second Part of its Third Session (5-23 October 1964) to the Committee on the Peaceful Uses of Outer Space, Annex I, Proposals and Amendments Relating to Assistance to and Return of Astronauts and Space Vehicles, 23 October 1964.

⑤ See UN Doc. A/AC. 105/21, Report of the Legal Sub-Committee on the Work of the Second Part of its Third Session (5-23 October 1964), Annex Ⅲ, Text of Certain Provisions of a Draft Agreement on Assistance to and Return of Personnel and Spacecraft, on which Preliminary Agreement was Reached by the Informal Working-Party of the Sub-Committee, 23 October 1964.

⑥ Ibid.

⑦ UN Doc. A/AC. 105/C. 2/L. 18, Agreement On The Rescue of Astronauts In The Event Of Accident Or Emergency Landing, USSR Revised Draft, 19 June 1967.

修订后的澳大利亚和加拿大提案比原始版本更加紧凑[①]。序言的最终版本以其相当简短和紧凑的形式反映了这一趋势。对《外空条约》的提及是全面的，并明确了《营救协定》是密切地基于该条约规定的援助和送回宇航员以及归还空间物体的一般原则；新条约的首要目标是发展和进一步具体表达这些义务。它只是增加了促进“和平探索和利用外层空间方面的国际合作”和“人道情感”的内容，这在以前的大多数草案中都有体现。

（二）评注

序言表明，《营救协定》是《外空条约》第五条和第八条规定的义务的结晶，应加强和平探索和利用外层空间的国际合作[②]。此外，它明确提到人道主义情感是达成协议的动机。

1. 特别法

序言部分指出，缔约国希望“发展并进一步具体体现”《外空条约》中所载的义务，即在发生事故、遇险或紧急着陆时向宇航员提供一切可能的援助、宇航员迅速送回以及射入外层空间的物体返还。这是一个明确的澄清，即《营救协定》是《外空条约》的特别法。没有其他后续条约以这种明确的方式对此作出规定[③]。《营救协定》是在《外空条约》一年后缔结的，显然也是“后法”。

然而，《外空条约》第五条所载义务与《营救协定》之间的关系并不完全清楚。通常，如果《外空条约》第五条所规定的义务与《营救协定》不一致，则必须以后者为准。“特别法优于一般法”（lex specialis derogate legi generali）和“后法优于前法”（lex posterior derogate legi priori）原则都确立了《营救协定》的优先适用。在某些方面，《营救协定》扩大了营救和送回的责任范围，适用于意外降落在天体和南极

① See UN Doc. A/AC. 105/C. 2/L. 20, Assistance to and Return of Astronauts and Space Objects, Revised Australian-Canadian proposal submitted as a working paper, 21 June 1967.

② See Art. Ⅳ OST; see also Schrogl, Kai-Uwe/Neumann, Julia, Article IV, in: Hobe, Stephan/Schmidt-Tedd, Bernhard/Schrogl, Kai-Uwe (eds.), Cologne Commentary on Space Law, Volume I, Heymanns, Cologne 2009, pp. 70-93.

③ The LIAB only speaks of ‘recalling’ the OST in its Preamble, the REG of ‘recalling’ several specific obligations contained in the OST. The State Parties of the Moon Agreement were ‘recalling’ not only the OST, but also the other three UN Treaties on outer space, thus not indicating any lex specialis relation with regard to the OST.

洲的情况[①]。此外，由于《营救协定》在其有效条款中未提及“宇航员”，而是采用“航天器人员”，因此，《营救协定》可被视为比《外空条约》第五条更适用于“太空游客”，然而，鉴于有义务在其上下文中解释条约条款（《维也纳条约法公约》第三十一条，以下简称《维也纳公约》[②]），不能保证“航天器人员”的单独解释[③]。

2. “宇航员”的定义

序言提及了《外空条约》第五条的义务，并使用了“宇航员”一词。序言中使用“宇航员”一词是值得注意的，因为在条约的有效条款中，只使用了“航天器人员”一词。

苏联在其初稿的序言中使用了“宇宙飞船船员”（crews of spaceships）一词[④]。然而，“宇航员”或“宇宙航行员”（космонавт）[⑤]一词出现在条约草案的标题及其一些条款中（第一、三、四和六条）。在 1964 年的苏联修订草案中，序言部分使用了“宇航员”，而具体条款中则同时使用了“宇航员”和“宇宙飞船船员”[⑥]。这就引发了一个问题，正如秘书处在一份说明中所述，即协议是否应包含“宇宙飞船船员”和“宇航员”两种不同的表述，或者说“宇宙飞船的全体船员［都是］宇航员”[⑦]。然而，这个问题并没有得到解决，1967 年的苏联修订草案在序言和执行条款中还是同时

① See Sundhal, Mark, The Duty to Rescue Space Tourists and Return Private Spacecraft, Journal of Space Law (35) 2009, pp. 177-178.

② Vienna Convention on the Law of Treaties (done 23 May 1969, entered into force 27 January 1980) 1155 UNTS 331 (VCLT).

③ As regards the interpretation of the term ‘astronaut’ see Commentary ARRA, Preamble, mn. 79ff.; as regards the interpretation of the term ‘personnel of a spacecraft’ see Commentary ARRA, Article 1, mn. 99ff.

④ See UN Doc. A/AC. 105/C. 2/L. 2, International Agreement on the Rescue of Astronauts and Spaceships making Emergency Landings, USSR Proposal, 6 June 1962.

⑤ The Russian term ‘космонавт’ [kosmonavt, cosmonaut] is used in the equally authentic Russian text of the OST and the later space treaties. Thus, ‘astronaut’ as a legal concept includes ‘cosmonaut’ and also ‘taikonauts’ later used to decribe the Chinese astronaut. See also von der Dunk, Frans/Goh, Gérardine M., Article V, in: Hobe, Stephan/Schmidt-Tedd, Bernhard/Schrogl, Kai-Uwe (eds.), Cologne Commentary on Space Law, Volume I, Heymanns, Cologne 2009, p. 96, mn. 7.

⑥ See UN Doc. A/AC. 105/C. 2/L. 2/Rev. 1, Agreement on the rescue of astronauts and spaceships in the event of accident or emergency landing, USSR Revised Draft, 9 March 1964; and UN Doc. A/AC. 105/C. 2/L. 2/Rev. 2, Agreement on the rescue of astronauts and spaceships in the event of accident or emergency landing, USSR Revised Draft, 26 October 1964.

⑦ UN Doc. A/AC. 105/21, Report of the Legal Sub-Committee on the Work of the Second Part of its Third Session (5-23 October 1964), Annex IV, Note by the Secretariat, 23 October 1964, p. 4.

使用了“宇航员”和“航天器人员”（personnel of a spacecraft）[①]。

美国在“宇航员”和“航天器人员”之间也没有明确的偏好。1964 年的第一份草案在序言和具体条款中采用了“航天器人员”一词[②]。然而，在一份修订后的提案第一条中，美国的文本又使用了“宇航员”一词[③]。

1964 年澳大利亚和加拿大的提案在序言中引用了 1963 年的《外空宣言》，包括“宇航员”一词。但在其具体条款中，却始终使用“航天器人员”一词[④]。在 1967 年修订文本中，序言删除了“宇航员”一词，整个文件中仅使用了“航天器人员”一词[⑤]。值得注意的是，与苏联和美国的提案不同，澳大利亚和加拿大的提案包含了一套“定义”，但“宇航员”或“航天器人员”不在定义的术语之列。这促使阿根廷提议收录“宇航员”的定义，并将其认定为“在外层空间，包括月球和其他天体履行其作为人类代表的职责，专为和平目的的民用探险家[⑥]”。然而，这项建议并没有得到采纳。

法律小组委员会非正式工作组关于序言和某些条款的初步协议案文在序言的草案中同时提到了“宇航员”和“航天器人员”。它提到“所有国家都有义务援助宇航员”，并指出有必要“制定关于援助和返还航天器人员、航天器和其他空间物体的国

① See UN Doc. A/AC. 105/C. 2/L. 18, Agreement On The Rescue Of Astronauts In The Event Of Accident Or Emergency Landing, USSR Revised Draft, 19 June 1967.

② UN Doc. A/AC. 105/C. 2/L. 9, International Agreement on Assistance to and Return of Astronauts and Objects Launched into Outer Space, United States Proposal, 9 March 1964.

③ See UN Doc. WG. I/33, USA: Proposal, in: UN Doc. A/AC. 105/29, Report of the Legal Sub-Committee on the Work of its Fourth Session (20 September-1 October 1965), Annex I, Proposals and Amendments Relating to Assistance to and Return of Astronauts and Space Vehicles, 1 October 1965, p. 2.

④ See UN Doc. WG. I/30, Australia and Canada: Proposal, in: UN Doc. A/AC. 105/21, Report of the Legal Sub-Committee on the Work of the Second Part of its Third Session (5-23 October 1964) to the Committee on the Peaceful Uses of Outer Space, Annex I, Proposals and Amendments Relating to Assistance to and Return of Astronauts and Space Vehicles, 23 October 1964.

⑤ See UN Doc. WG. I/30, Australia and Canada: Proposal, in: UN Doc. A/AC. 105/21, Report of the Legal Sub-Committee on the Work of the Second Part of its Third Session (5-23 October 1964) to the Committee on the Peaceful Uses of Outer Space, Annex I, Proposals and Amendments Relating to Assistance to and Return of Astronauts and Space Vehicles, 23 October 1964.

⑥ UN Doc. A/AC. 105/C. 2/L. 20, Assistance to and Return of Astronauts and Space Objects, Revised Australian-Canadian Proposal Submitted as a Working Paper, 21 June 1967.

际规则”①。草案中的具体条款一直采用的是“航天器人员”②。

因此，序言和具体条款的起草历史表明，“宇航员”一词逐渐被“航天器人员”一词所取代。“宇航员”仅用于早期的文件和一般原则，如《外空宣言》或《外空条约》。这就解释了为什么《营救协定》的序言中保留了“宇航员”一词，而在其具体条款中却没有。序言部分强调了《外空条约》中规定的援助和送回的一般义务。在具体条款中涉及各国更为细化的义务时，航天大国的关注主要集中在“航天器人员”的生命安全上，当时这些人员通常是执行国家任务。然而，联合国外空委及其法律小组委员会没有就此问题进行广泛辩论。它们主要关注的是整个协议中术语的一致性，各代表团显然倾向于使用“航天器人员”一词。《营救协定》中的“航天器人员”一词基本上被认为与《外空条约》中使用的“宇航员”一词相同③。

值得注意的是，《外空条约》第五条规定，宇航员应被视为“人类在外层空间的使者”④。然而，这一表述在《营救协定》的序言中没有被明确重复。

近年来，“宇航员”一词的定义变得越来越重要，特别是在“太空旅游”的背景下，即非政府和非军事人员参与太空飞行。“太空游客”能被称为“宇航员”吗？这个问题的答案对《营救协定》的适用有着重要的影响，尤其是协议的第一至四条。《营救协定》本身没有提供定义。根据条约的解释规则（《维也纳条约法公约》第三十一和三十二条），必须根据条约的一般含义、上下文以及条约的目的和宗旨来解释条约的术语。该术语的一般含义可能是在条约签署时赋予它的含义⑤，这意味着“宇航员”必须是受过专业训练的国家雇佣的专业人员⑥。然而，鉴于条约的背景以及目

---

① UN Doc. A/AC. 105/C. 2/L. 23, Agreement on Assistance to, and Rescue and Return of Astronauts, 23 June 1967.

② See ibid., Art. 2 and 3.

③ For an account of the term ‘personnel of a spacecraft’, see Commentary ARRA, Article 1, mn. 99ff.

④ See Art. V OST. For a recent account of astronauts as ‘envoys of mankind’ see Hobe, Stephan, Space tourism as a challenge to the astronaut concept, in: Lafferranderie, Gabriel/Marchisio, Sergio (eds.), The Astronauts and Rescue Agreement-Lessons Learned, The European Centre for Space Law, Paris 2011, p. 71.

⑤ See Fitzmaurice, Malgosia, Treaties, in: Wolfrum, Rüdiger (ed.), Max Planck Encyclopedia of Pulic International Law, Volume IX, Oxford University Press, Oxford 2012, p. 1075, para. 86. See Historical Background and Context, mn. 18. See Sundhal, Mark, The Duty to Rescue Space Tourists and Return Private Spacecraft, Journal of Space Law (35) 2009, p. 187.

⑥ See Lyall, Francis, Who is an astronaut? The inadequacy of current international law, Acta Astronautica (6) 2009, p. 1613.

的和宗旨，这种狭隘的解释不一定是有道理的。序言中提到了促使缔约方就《营救协定》达成一致的“人道情感”。营救和送回的义务可以被视为是出于对人类福祉的关切，因而其概念的外延应更为宽泛①。然而，营救和送回的义务在其他很多方面也有约束，因此，《营救协定》的条款对“太空游客”的适用仍然是法律理论和实践中讨论的一个问题②。

“宇航员”一词也出现在《月球协定》中。该协议在第十条第一款中确实载有相关解释，即缔约国视“月球上的任何人为《外空条约》第五条所指的宇航员”，并责成所有缔约国“采取一切切实可行的措施，保障月球上人员的生命和健康。”《月球协定》上述条款的适用范围是广泛的，包括任何登上月球的人，无论是专业人员还是个人③。

3. 国际合作

序言强调促进“探索和利用外层空间方面的国际合作”，以此作为制定《营救协定》的动机。在航天器发生事故、遇险或紧急着陆，以及空间物体返回的情况下，国际合作主要符合航天大国的利益。然而，还应提醒其他国家，基于人道主义考虑，在救援和送回行动中进行合作的精神和义务。

在《外空条约》中可以找到国际合作的渊源，但是在不同的背景下。《外空条约》第三条将其与“维护国际和平与安全的利益”联系起来。《外空条约》第九条在“适当顾及所有其他条约缔约国的相应利益”的背景下提及“国际合作”，这通常是

---

① See Sundhal, Mark, The Duty to Rescue Space Tourists and Return Private Spacecraft, Journal of Space Law (35) 2009, p. 167.

② See Lyall, Francis, Who is an astronaut? The inadequacy of current international law, Acta Astronautica (6) 2009, p. 1617; Sundhal, Mark, The Duty to Rescue Space Tourists and Return Private Spacecraft, Journal of Space Law (35) 2009, p. 189; von der Dunk, Frans, A Sleeping Beauty awakens: the 1968 Rescue Agreement After Forty Years, Journal of Space Law (34) 2008, p. 434; Hobe, Stephan, Space tourism as a challenge to the astronaut concept, in: Lafferranderie, Gabriel/Marchisio, Sergio (eds.), The Astronauts and Rescue Agreement-Lessons Learned, The European Centre for Space Law, Paris 2011, pp. 74f.; see also below, Commentary ARRA, Article 1, mn. 99ff.

③ Accordingly, the early Soviet draft for the MOON clarified that Art. V OST applies to any person on the Moon "irrespective of the duration of the stay of such person on the Moon, the place where he is situated on the Moon, his formal membership of the crew of a spacecraft and other similar circumstances." UN Doc. A/8391, Request for the Inclusion of an Item in the Provisional Agenda of the Twenty-Sixth Session, Preparation of a Treaty Concerning the Moon, Letter dated 27 May 1971 from the Minister for Foreign Affairs of Soviet Socialist Republics addressed to the Secretary-General, Annex, Treaty Concerning the Moon, 4 June 1971, Art. Ⅶ.

考虑到尽量减少对其他国家和地球环境的损害[1]。《外空条约》第十一条提到“国际合作”与“通知联合国秘书长”此类活动的性质、行为、地点和结果的义务之间的关系。有趣的是，在《外空条约》第五条关于营救和送回宇航员的条款中，并没有出现“国际合作”这一术语。

4. “人道情感”术语

序言中提到“人道情感”似乎不同寻常。首先，因为缔约国通常不被视为具有“情感”能力的生物；其次，因为与“人道主义理由”或“人道主义考量”相比，“人道”是一个更具哲学意义的术语，例如，“人道主义理由”或“人道主义考量”是一个更具法律意义的术语。在外层空间条约的其他地方找不到“人道”一词。

美国早期的《营救协定》草案提到了“人道主义关切”[2]，而其他草案则在早期就采用了“人道情感”一词[3]。这种用词方式背后的主要原因尚不清楚。宇航员事故的悲剧事件震撼了谈判者们[4]，直到1967年才加速了谈判最后阶段的进程，而当时“人道情感”一词已经出现在了《营救协定》的草案中。

一般而言，提及“人道情感”被视为强调人道主义的本质，这是《营救协定》中规定营救和送回宇航员或“航天器人员”的义务的基础[5]。

---

① See Marchisio, Sergio, Article IX, in: Hobe, Stephan/Schmidt-Tedd, Bernhard/Schrogl, Kai-Uwe (eds.), Cologne Commentary on Space Law, Volume I, Heymanns, Cologne 2009, p. 175, mn. 23-25.

② See the US drafts: UN Doc. A/AC. 105/L. 4, United States of America: Draft Proposal on Assistance and Return of Space Vehicles and Personnel, Liability for Space Vehicle Accidents, 11 September 1962; and UN Doc. A/AC. 105/C. 2/L. 9, International Agreement on Assistance to and Return of Astronauts and Objects Launched into Outer Space, United States Proposal, 9 March 1964.

③ See UN Doc. A/AC. 105/C. 2/L. 2/Rev. 1, Agreement on the rescue of astronauts and spaceships in the event of accident or emergency landing, USSR Revised Draft, 9 March 1964; and UN Doc. WG. I/30, Australia and Canada: Proposal, in: UN Doc. A/AC. 105/21, Report of the Legal Sub-Committee on the Work of the Second Part of its Third Session (5-23 October 1964), Annex I, Proposals and Amendments Relating to Assistance to and Return of Astronauts and Space Vehicles, 23 October 1964.

④ See Historical Background and Context, mn. 18.

⑤ See Sundhal, Mark, The Duty to Rescue Space Tourists and Return Private Spacecraft, Journal of Space Law (35) 2009, p. 187.

二、第一条　事故、遇险、紧急或意外降落的通知

缔约国于获悉或发现航天器人员遭遇意外事故，或正遭受危难情况，或已在缔约国管辖领域内，在公海上，或在不属任何国家管辖之任何其他地点作紧急或非出于本意之降落时，应立即：

（甲）通知发射当局，或在不能查明发射当局并立即与之通讯时，缔约国需立即以可以使用的一切适当通讯工具公开宣告此情况；

（乙）通知联合国秘书长，由秘书长以其可以使用的一切适当通讯工具传播此项消息。

（一）谈判和起草历史

1962 年，苏联的第一份草案中规定了通知“宇航员”“宇宙飞船船员”或“航天器人员”[①] 任何事故或紧急着陆的义务。根据该草案，发现宇宙飞船船员遭遇事故的国家应“尽最大努力毫不拖延地通知发射国”[②]。然而，美国关于援助和送回的联合国决议提案的草案并不包含这样的义务[③]。同样，1963 年的《外空宣言》也没有提到通知宇航员发生事故、遇险或紧急着陆的义务。尽管 1963 年《外空宣言》对此未作规定，但 1964 年和 1965 年法律小组委员会的所有草案和辩论都涉及事故和紧急着陆的通知。1964 年底，苏联修订草案将“发射国”相关的通知义务修改为“正式宣布发射的国家”，并增加了“立即通知联合国秘书长”的义务[④]。美国在其草案的第一

① As regards the use of the terms ‘astronauts’, ‘the crew of a spaceship’, or ‘the personnel of a spacecraft’, see Commentary ARRA, mn. 99ff.

② Art. 2 stipulated: “A Contracting State which discovers that the crew of a spaceship of another Contracting State has met with an accident shall do its utmost to notify the launching State without delay”. UN Doc. A/AC. 105/L. 3, USSR: Draft International Agreement on the Rescue of Astronauts and Spaceships Making Emergency Landing, 10 September 1962.

③ The draft UNGA Resolution only contained three principles which concentrated on the duty to render assistance, the return of space vehicles and their personnel, and the covering of expenses incurred; UN Doc. A/AC. 105/L. 4, USA: Draft Proposal on Assistance and Return of Space Vehicles and Personnel, 11 September 1962; see Historical Background and Context, mn. 22ff.

④ UN Doc. A/AC. 105/C. 2/L. 2/Rev. 2, Agreement on the rescue of astronauts and spaceships in the event of accident or emergency landing, USSR Revised Draft, 26 October 1964.

条提到有义务“毫不拖延地通知登记国或负责发射的国际组织或联合国秘书长”①，且该义务应由“缔约方”承担，而不是像苏联提案中那样由“缔约国”承担。原因是美国的提案将国际组织视为可能负责发射的实体。他们应在发生事故、遇险或紧急着陆时得到通知，并应能够接受协议规定的权利和义务。关于通知所针对的实体，美国没有提及“发射国”，而是提及“登记国”。有人提到通知联合国秘书长是另一种选择，而不是对登记国或负责发射的国际组织的通知的补充。根据美国的提议，通知义务还包括射入外层空间或部分返回地球的物体②。这项义务没有得到其他代表团的一致同意，因此也没有列入《营救协定》的最终版本。

1964年的澳大利亚和加拿大提案载有向发射国通知航天器人员发生事故、遇险或紧急着陆的义务，但也表达了在确认发射国方面可能出现的困难③。“立即通知联合国秘书长”的义务补充了通知发射国的义务。通知义务是“缔约方”的义务。1964年，就各“缔约方”向“宣布发射的国家”和联合国秘书长通报事故、遇险或紧急着陆的义务达成了初步协议④。

1967年的《外空条约》不包含通知宇航员发生事故、遇险或紧急着陆的义务。《外空条约》第五条仅规定，缔约国应在发生事故、遇险或紧急着陆时向其提供一切可能的援助，并应安全、迅速地将其送回航天器登记国。关于通知义务，《外空条约》第五条仅提及“在外层空间，包括月球和其他天体中发现的可能对宇航员的生命或健

---

① UN Doc. A/AC. 105/C. 2/L. 9, International Agreement on Assistance to and Return of Astronauts and Objects Launched into Outer Space, United States Proposal, 9 March 1964.

② Ibid., Art. 1 para. 2 reads: “A Contracting Party which discovers that an object launched into outer space or parts thereof have returned to Earth shall notify without delay the State of registry or international organization responsible for launching, or the Secretary-General of the United Nations.”.

③ According to Art 2 lit. (a), lit. (b), the Contracting Party “shall do its utmost immediately to ascertain and notify the Launching State”, but “if it cannot readily ascertain the Launching State, [it] shall forwith notify the State it presumes to be the Launching State”; UN Doc. A/AC. 105/21, Report of the Legal Sub-Committee on the Work of the Second Part of its Third Session (5-23 October 1964), Annex Ⅲ, Text of Certain Provisions of a Draft Agreement on Assistance to and Return of Personnel and Spacecraft, on which Preliminary Agreement was reached by the Informal Working-Party of the Sub-Committee, 23 October 1964.

④ The text summarized the preliminary agreement reached by the informal working party of the Legal Subcommittee on the issue of notification. According to this preliminary Art. 2, each ‘Contracting Party’ should “do its utmost immediately to notify the State which announced the launching” as well as “immediately notify the Secretary-General of the United Nations”. UN Doc. A/AC. 105/L. 3, USSR: Draft International Agreement on the Rescue of Astronauts and Spaceships Making Emergency Landing, 10 September 1962.

康构成危险的任何情形”[1]，有关此类情形的信息应立即发送给“条约其他缔约国或联合国秘书长”。因此，如果宇航员在地球上发生事故、遇险或紧急着陆，没有义务通知任何人[2]。

尽管《外空条约》中存在这一缺陷，但法律小组委员会在其1967年的会议上继续讨论通知义务。苏联修订后的条约草案将相应条款从第二条改为第一条[3]。值得注意的是，新的文本涉及“缔约方”——正如《营救协定》的最终版本一样——而不再是“缔约国”，因此，它承认了国际组织加入的可能性。这项义务包括通知“宣布发射航天器的国家”和联合国秘书长，以及“立即通过无线电或其所掌握的其他通信手段发布公告”[4]。澳大利亚和加拿大重新提交了其草案的早期版本，未作任何更改[5]。

苏联就国际组织的地位作出的让步，为《营救协定》第一条所载通知义务的最终版本铺平了道路，即通知义务应归于“发射当局”，而不是“发射国”。相比之下，美国提出的还应通知“负责发射的国际组织”的建议没有得到采纳。最终版本没有像草案那样规定通知“发射国[6]”或“登记国[7]”，但它规定了通知“发射当局”的义务。这一解决方式受到其他代表团的欢迎[8]。

（二）评注

第一条规定了有关影响航天器人员的事故和类似情况的通知义务。协议中未定义

---

① For a commentary on this provision, see von der Dunk, Frans/Goh, Gérardine M., Article V, in: Hobe, Stephan/Schmidt-Tedd, Bernhard/Schrogl, Kai-Uwe (eds.), Cologne Commentary on Space Law, Vol-ume I, Heymanns, Cologne 2009, pp. 94-102.

② See ibid.

③ See UN Doc. A/AC. 105/C. 2/L. 18, Agreement On The Rescue Of Astronauts In The Event Of Accident Or Emergency Landing, USSR Revised Draft, 19 June 1967.

④ Ibid.

⑤ The draft thus still referred to the ‘launching State’ which should be ascertained and notified immediately, in addition to the Secretary-General of the United Nations; see UN Doc. A/AC. 105/L. 203, Assistance to and Return of Astronauts and Space Objects, Revised Australian-Canadian proposal submitted as a Working Paper, 21 June 1967.

⑥ This was the case in the Soviet and the Australian-Canadian drafts. See Commentary ARRA, Article 1, mn. 94.

⑦ This was the proposal by the US. See UN Doc. A/AC. 105/C. 2/L. 9, International Agreement on Assis-tance to and Return of Astronauts and Objects Launched into Outer Space, United States Proposal, 9 March 1964; and Commentary ARRA, Article 1, mn. 93.

⑧ See the statement of the representative of Australia, UN Doc. A/AC. 105/C. 2/SR. 87, Legal Sub-Committee, Special Session, Summary Record of the Eighty-Seventh Meeting, held 15 December 1967, 2 February 1968, p. 6.

条款中的任何术语。

1. “航天器人员” 术语

空间法条约对外空的人类使用了不同的术语[1]，如“宇航员”[2]、“人员”[3]、“自然人”[4]、“军事人员”[5]、“国民”[6]、“外国人”[7]、“科学人员和其他人员”[8]、“条约其他缔约国的代表”[9] 或 “人类”[10]。在某些条款中，宇航员被视为 “人类的使者”[11]。条约文本中没有对这些术语的任何定义。

（1）与“宇航员” 的关系

一方面，可以认为，《营救协定》中使用的“航天器人员” 基本上与《外空条约》第五条和《营救协定》序言（非具体条款）中使用的“宇航员” 一词具有相同的含义。“航天器人员” 和“宇航员” 具有相同的含义，这可以从《营救协定》的标题和序言提及“宇航员” 这一事实中得出。如果协议的其余部分提到“航天器人员” 的含义有所不同，那么这样的措辞几乎没有意义。这种理解似乎也得到了《营救协定》起草历史的支持[12]。

另一方面，有人认为，《月球协定》第十条第一款表明，航天器上的某些人员可能不是宇航员，因为该条规定，所有登上月球的人都应被视为《外空条约》第五条意义上的宇航员，以及《营救协定》框架下的航天器人员的一部分[13]。然而，《月球协定》第十条第一款也可以理解为简单地确保所有登上月球的人都将同时受益于《外空

① See Achilléas, Philippe, L' astronaute en droit international, in: ECSL and others, Proceedings of the Symposium on the Legal and Ethical Framework for Astronauts in Space Sojourns, 29 October 2004 Paris (France), UNESCO, 2004, pp. 14-15.

② Art. Ⅴ para. 1-3 OST; Title and Preamble of the ARRA; Art. 10 no. 1 MOON.

③ Art. Ⅷ OST; Art. Ⅰ-Ⅳ LIAB; Art. Ⅱ para. 2 REG; Art. 3 no. 2, Art. 8 no. 2, Art. 9 no. 2, Art. 10 no. 1, Art. 11 no. 3, Art. 12 no. 1 MOON.

④ Art. Ⅶ OST; Art. 1 lit. (a), Art. Ⅳ para. 1, Art. Ⅷ para. 1-2 LIAB; Art. Ⅵ, sentence 1 REG.

⑤ Art. Ⅳ para. 2 sentence 3 OST; Art. 3 no. 4 sentence 2 MOON.

⑥ Art. Ⅸ sentence 3 OST; Art. Ⅶ lit. (a) LIAB.

⑦ Art. Ⅶ lit. (b) LIAB.

⑧ Art. 6 no. 3 MOON.

⑨ Art. Ⅻ OST.

⑩ Art. Ⅰ OST; Art. 4 no. 1, Art. 11 no. 1 MOON.

⑪ Art. Ⅴ para. 1 no. 1 OST; Art. 10 no. 1 sentence 2 MOON.

⑫ See Commentary ARRA, Preamble, mn. 73ff.

⑬ See Lyall, Francis, Who is an astronaut? The inadequacy of current international law, Acta Astronautica (6) 2009, p. 1614.

条约》第五条和《营救协定》的规定，尽管两者使用的措辞不同。

（2）与“航天飞行参与者”的关系

自从非政府和非军事人员越来越多地参与太空飞行以来，“航天器人员”和“宇航员”的含义引起了争论。因此，在确定“航天器人员”的含义时，主要问题是“太空旅游者”或“航天飞行参与者”是否属于《营救协定》的定义范围，是否可以受益于《营救协定》的规定。

虽然在起草《营救协定》时，在外层空间中的人类仅仅是直接参与飞行任务的人员，但后来参与科学任务的人员也前往外层空间。最近，一些私人乘坐航天飞机（或联盟号）前往国际空间站，在那里履行次要职责①。对于这些私人，美国国家航空航天局（NASA）和俄罗斯联邦航天局（ROSCOSMOS）于 2003 年商定了“航天飞行参与者”一词，以便将这些太空旅行者与这两个机构执行任务的人员区分开来。此外，在不久的将来，私人将能够参与亚轨道飞行，而无需在此类飞行任务中执行任何积极的任务②。

在此背景下，可以确定外层空间的三大类人：（1）直接参与任务、在航天器运行中执行任务的人；（2）直接参与专业活动的人员，例如执行任务的科学家；（3）作为太空游客登上航天器的个人，在任务中只有次要任务或没有任何任务。

虽然对于前两类人在《营救协定》下的“航天器人员”身份似乎有着共识，但对于第三类的太空游客身份，无法得出最终结论。

在一般意义上，“人员”是指具有官方职责和责任的人员，类似于船舶或飞机的

① Dennis Tito was the first officially acclaimed space tourist, travelling to outer space in 2001; he was followed in 2002 by Mark Shuttleworth, in 2005 by Gregory Olsen, in 2006 by Anousheh Ansari, in 2007 and 2009 by Charles Simonyi, in October 2007 by Sheikh Muszaphar Shukor (who performed scientific tasks aboard), in October 2008 by Richard Garriott and in 2009 by Guy Laliberté, see e. g. Hobe, Stephan, Space tourism as a challenge to the astronaut concept, in: Lafferranderie, Gabriel/Marchisio, Sergio (eds.), The Astronauts and Rescue Agreement-Lessons Learned, The European Centre for Space Law, Paris 2011, p. 71. After a break in space tourist flights, Space Adventures and the Russian Federal Space Agency announced on 12 January 2011, that orbital space tourism would resume in 2013 with the increase of manned Soyuz launches to the ISS from four to five per year, see Denise Chow, Multimillion-Dollar Space Tourist Trips to Resume in 2013, Space. com, 12 January 2011 <http: //www. space. com/10611-space-adventures-space-station-tourist-trips. html> accessed 26 April 2019.

② E. g. Virgin Galatic with its SpaceShipTwo, see the Virgin Galactic website <http: //www. virgingalactic. com> accessed 26 April 2019.

机组人员[①]。在起草《营救协定》时，没有明确规定将机组人员的范围扩大到包括不直接参与航天器驾驶的成员。1973年8月14日生效的《太空实验室协议》从法律角度提出了延伸，该协议预见了航天飞机上的科学人员在执行特定项目任务期间的存在[②]。因此，"航天器人员"一词可以理解为包括在航天器上从事与完成任务有关的活动的所有人员[③]。

然而，学术界的大多数观点认为，"人员"一词不包括航天飞机或任何其他航天器上的私人乘客[④]。然而，也有人强调，"从道德角度来看，他们必须能够指望可以得到类似的保护，而这种保护必须……得到登记国的保证。"[⑤]

可以进一步区分购买国际空间站旅行的"太空游客"，他们在飞船上接受了大量培训并履行（有限的）职责，以及那些在不久的将来将参与商业短途亚轨道飞行的付费乘客。后者不会执行任何特定任务，且仅接受侧重于健康检查的一些基本培训。虽然一些作者认为前者是"航天器人员"或"宇航员"，但后者似乎普遍被认为不是上述人员[⑥]。从《营救协定》的措辞中可以清楚地看出，它仅适用于乘坐"航天器"的人，而对于亚轨道飞行，仍在讨论其飞行器或航天器的分类，并可能取决于任务的设计[⑦]。

《外空条约》第八条中也使用了"人员"一词。在这方面，有人争论该术语是否包括空间物体中的所有自然人，以及该术语是否仅包含参与其运行或履行任务职能的

---

① See Lyall, Francis, Who is an astronaut? The inadequacy of current international law, Acta Astronautica (6) 2009, p. 1614.

② See van Bogaert, Eric R. C., Aspects of Space Law, Kluwer, Deventer 1986, p. 101.

③ See ibid.

④ See ibid.; Lyall, Francis, Who is an astronaut? The inadequacy of current international law, Acta Astronautica (6) 2009, pp. 1613-1617; with regard to the term 'astronaut', see von der Dunk, Frans/Goh, Gérardine M., Article V, in: Hobe, Stephan/Schmidt-Tedd, Bernhard/Schrogl, Kai-Uwe (eds.), Cologne Commentary on Space Law, Volume I, Heymanns, Cologne 2009, p. 97, mn. 11.

⑤ van Bogaert, Eric R. C., Aspects of Space Law, Kluwer, Deventer 1986, p. 101.

⑥ See Lyall, Francis, Who is an astronaut? The inadequacy of current international law, Acta Astronautica (6) 2009, p. 1614; the Virgin Galactic website employs the term 'astronaut' and 'passengers' <http://www.virgingalactic.com> accessed 26 April 2019.

⑦ For an account of the legal issues of suborbital flights with regard to the air and space law regimes, see Farand, André, Space tourism: legal considerations pertaining to suborbital flights, in: Lafferranderie, Gabriel/Marchisio, Sergio (eds.), The Astronauts and Rescue Agreement-Lessons Learned, The European Centre for Space Law, Paris 2011, p. 55.

自然人[①]。空间法条约中术语的前后一致地使用可能有利于对该术语有更广泛的理解[②]。然而，《外空条约》第八条与《营救协定》的目的不同，因为它规定了登记国对空间物体的任何人员（即航天器上的所有自然人）的管辖权和控制权。这可能需要更广泛的理解，而《营救协定》不一定具有如此广泛的适用范围。

尽管国家法在解释国际公法条约方面的权限有限，但值得注意的是，《美国法典》第49章是包含“航天飞行参与者”定义的第一部国家空间立法，它明确区分了“机组人员”和“航天飞行参与者”[③]。在《美国法典》第49章中，“机组人员”包括执行“与运载人类的运载火箭或再入飞行器的发射、再入或其他操作直接相关的活动……的人员”[④]；而“航天飞行参与者”被定义为“运载火箭或再入飞行器上的非机组人员”[⑤]。“航天飞行参与者”被要求放弃所有索赔，并承担其参与飞行的个人责任（14 CFR § 440 附录 E；2006；71 Fed. Reg. 75642-3）。基本上，“旅游飞行”机组人员的要求是严格的，而“参与者”的要求仅仅是良好的健康加上安全和逃生程序的基本培训（《美国联邦法规》第14卷第460. 51节：（2006）71 Fed. Reg. 75645）[⑥]。因此，美国立法也拒绝将太空飞行参与者归为“航天飞行人员”或“宇航员”，由于其独特性，它可能会影响未来对这些术语的理解。

即使航天飞行参与者不被视为“航天器人员”，根据国际习惯的一般人道主义原则，他们在遇险时仍应获得援助[⑦]。此外，当涉及亚轨道飞行的参与者时，国际航空

① See Bittlinger, Horst, Menschen im Weltraum, in: Böckstiegel, Karl-Heinz (ed.), Handbuch des Weltraumrechts, Heymanns, Cologne 1991, p. 210. In the case described by Bittlinger, visitors, injured persons, delinquents or stowaways would not be included.

② A detailed discussion of this matter is provided in footnote 34 in Bittlinger, Horst, Menschen im Weltraum, in: Böckstiegel, Karl-Heinz (ed.), Handbuch des Weltraumrechts, Heymanns, Cologne 1991, p. 211.

③ Commercial Space Launch Activities, 49 USC 701, as revised by the Commercial Space Launch Amendments Act 2004, Public Law 108-492, 23 December 2004. The establishment of such regulatory framework in the US takes account of the private sector investment in these activities, see Farand, André, Space tourism: legal considerations pertaining to suborbital flights, in: Lafferranderie, Gabriel/Marchisio, Sergio (eds.), The Astronauts and Rescue Agreement-Lessons Learned, The European Centre for Space Law, Paris 2011, p. 61.

④ 49 USC 70102 para. 1.

⑤ 40 USC 70102 para. 17.

⑥ See Lyall, Francis, Who is an astronaut? The inadequacy of current international law, Acta Astronautica (6) 2009, p. 1614.

⑦ See Hobe, Stephan, Space tourism as a challenge to the astronaut concept, in: Lafferranderie, Gabriel/Marchisio, Sergio (eds.), The Astronauts and Rescue Agreement-Lessons Learned, The European Centre for Space Law, Paris 2011, pp. 73f., with further reference.

法，特别是 1944 年《芝加哥国际民用航空公约》[①] 及其附件十二和十三是否适用尚未解决[②]。

2. 术语“事故”“遇险情况”“紧急或意外降落”

《营救协定》关于航天器人员的规定基于某些情况，即仅在发生第一条所述事件之一时适用。然而，应当注意的是，所有合理的需要外部帮助的情况都应该包括在内[③]。

上述情形也可在航空法中找到，例如 1944 年《芝加哥公约》第二十五条就涉及遇险飞机，其附件十二和十三涉及对在外国领土上发生事故、紧急或意外着陆的飞机机组人员的援助。关于公海的多边条约也有类似的规定，例如 1910 年《统一海上救助某些规则的布鲁塞尔公约》（以下简称《布鲁塞尔公约》）第十一条[④]，以及 1982 年《联合国海洋法公约》（以下简称《海洋法公约》）第九十八条[⑤]。

（1）术语“事故”

“事故”是高度安全敏感类操作（如航空）中的一个相当常见的术语”[⑥]。“事故”一词的一般含义来自拉丁语动词 accidere，意指“意外和不可预见的伤害发生，是在通常的事件过程中没有发生或无法合理预期的事情”[⑦]，即“任何没有预见或预期的事情；由未知原因引起的异常事件，或已知原因的异常影响，伤亡，意外事件”[⑧]。在航空中，它通常指对相关飞行器造成物理损坏的事件，其结果也可能导致机上人员受

① Convention on International Civil Aviation (done 7 December 1944, entered into force 4 April 1947) 15 UNTS 295 (Chicago Convention).

② Annex 12-Search and Rescue, ICAO Doc. AN 12; and Annex 13-Aircraft Accident Investigation, ICAO Doc. AN 13.

③ See van Bogaert, Eric R. C., Aspects of Space Law, Kluwer, Deventer 1986, p. 101.

④ International Convention for the Unification of certain Rules of Law relating to Assistance and Salvage at Sea of 23 September 1910 (done 23 September 1910, entered into force 1 March 1913) <http://www.admiraltylawguide.com/conven/salvage1910.html> accessed 26 April 2019.

⑤ See United Nations Convention on the Law of the Sea (done 10 December 1982, entered into force 16 November 1994) 1833 UNTS 396 (UNCLOS).

⑥ von der Dunk, Frans/Goh, Gérardine M., Article V, in: Hobe, Stephan/Schmidt-Tedd, Bernhard/Schrogl, Kai-Uwe (eds.), Cologne Commentary on Space Law, Volume I, Heymanns, Cologne 2009, p. 100, mn. 21.

⑦ Garner, Bryan A. (ed.), Black's Law Dictionary, 9th edn., West, St. Paul 2009, at 'accident', p. 13.

⑧ Stevenson, Angus (ed.), Oxford Dictionary of English, 3rd edn., Oxford University Press, Oxford 2010, at 'accident'.

伤或死亡[①]。鉴于没有任何国际空间条约包含“事故”一词的定义，1998 年《澳大利亚空间活动法》第八十五条规定，“涉及空间物体的事故发生的条件是：（a）一个人因空间物体的运行而死亡或受重伤；或（b）该空间物体遭到破坏或严重损坏或造成财产损坏。”尽管国家法律无法对国际条约作出权威性解释，但这种释意在一定程度上表明了“事故”一词在空间活动中的含义。

（2）术语“遇险”

“遇险”一词的一般含义是指紧张、压力的情况，以及某种不利力量的压倒性压力，如恶劣天气、(天气等的）压力[②]。因此，“遇险”似乎是《营救协定》第一条所述三种情况中最广泛的一种，即尚未发生任何事故，但相关人员处于“困境中”，事故可能会威胁到，或至少不能排除，并且可能发生遇险情况，即使在该事件中没有发生任何事故[③]。

（3）术语“紧急或意外降落”

“紧急”是指意外发生并要求立即采取行动的严重情况或状态[④]。因此，“紧急降落”一词指的是积极应对实际威胁，努力防止事故发生，或至少将其严重性降至最低的情况[⑤]。尽管紧急降落可能意味着仍有降落的意图，但意外降落指的是降落不是其计划遵循的行动路线的情况[⑥]。

（4）“在其管辖的领土或公海或任何其他不受任何国家管辖的地方”的表述

第一条的义务仅适用于事件发生在各国领土、公海或不受任何国家管辖的任何其他地方的情况。这意味着该义务仅适用于《营救协定》的缔约国，且事件发生在该国

① See e. g. Art. 26 Chicago Convention; von der Dunk, Frans/Goh, Gérardine M., Article V, in: Hobe, Stephan/Schmidt-Tedd, Bernhard/Schrogl, Kai-Uwe (eds.), Cologne Commentary on Space Law, Vol-ume I, Heymanns, Cologne 2009, p. 100, mn. 21.

② See Stevenson, Angus (ed.), *Oxford Dictionary of English*, 3rd edn., Oxford University Press, Oxford 2010, at ‘distress’.

③ von der Dunk, Frans/Goh, Gérardine M., Article V, in: Hobe, Stephan/Schmidt-Tedd, Bernhard/Schrogl, Kai-Uwe (eds.), Cologne Commentary on Space Law, Volume I, Heymanns, Cologne 2009, p. 100, mn. 22.

④ See Stevenson, Angus (ed.), *Oxford Dictionary of English*, 3rd edn., Oxford University Press, Oxford 2010, at ‘emergency’.

⑤ See von der Dunk, Frans/Goh, Gérardine M., *Article V*, in: Hobe, Stephan/Schmidt-Tedd, Bernhard/Schrogl, Kai-Uwe (eds.), Cologne Commentary on Space Law, Volume I, Heymanns, Cologne 2009, p. 100, mn. 22.

⑥ See Gorove, Stephen, *Legal Problems of the Rescue and Return of Astronauts*, The International Lawyer (3) 1969, p. 900.

领土。如果事件发生在不受本协定约束的国家管辖的地方，则不适用本协定[1]。

3. 术语“缔约方”

第一条的通知义务适用于每个“缔约方”。

鉴于第七条至九条使用“国家”和“缔约国”一词，并规定《营救协定》开放给所有国家签署，缔约国可提出修正并退出《营救协定》。因此采用“缔约方”的一词让人难以理解。由于只有国家才能成为《营救协定》的缔约国，因此可以说只有那些国家才能被视为缔约方。

“缔约方”，而不是“缔约国”或“发射国”的术语，是由美国有关协议的提案的第一条引入的[2]。在就国际组织的地位进行了艰难的谈判之后，就允许国际组织接受《营救协定》的权利和义务达成了共识，使国际组织处于与“协议各方”类似的地位[3]，而在正式意义上，他们仍然不是缔约方。

4. “获悉或发现情况”的表述

使用“获悉或发现”这一表述方式表明以下这两种情况都包括在内：一国被动地了解事故、遇险或意外降落的情况，以及一国主动了解这种情况。

5. 缔约方的义务

第一条包含必须“立即”通知的义务，这意味着缔约方必须毫不延迟地发送信息，以便在可能危及生命的情况下快速采取行动[4]。

（1）通知发射当局或发布公告

相关方必须将事件通知发射当局。如果无法确定发射当局并立即与之沟通，则必须立即通过各自国家可使用的一切适当通信手段发布公告。这就为所发布的公告类型留下了自由裁量权。

第六条将“发射当局”一词定义为负责发射的国家或国际组织。它仅在 1967 年底的最后谈判阶段才被纳入《营救协定》文本，是航天大国之间双边会议的结果。这是《营救协定》独用的一个术语，之后的《责任公约》和《登记公约》都使用“发

① See van Bogaert, Eric R. C. , *Aspects of Space Law*, Kluwer, Deventer 1986, p. 102.

② See Commentary ARRA, Article 1, mn. 93.

③ See Dembling, Paul G. /Arons, Daniel M. , *Space Law and the United Nations: The Work of the Legal Subcommittee on the Peaceful Uses of Outer Space*, Journal of Air Law and Commerce (32) 1966, p. 349; as regards the role and obligations of international organizations see Commentary, Article 6, mn. 195ff.

④ See van Bogaert, Eric R. C. , *Aspects of Space Law*, Kluwer, Deventer 1986, p. 102.

射国”这个术语，并分别在其第一条给予了同样的定义①。相比之下，《营救协定》第六条的“发射当局”一词的定义有所不同，即其包括了国际组织。第六条赋予该术语的“特殊含义”对于根据《维也纳公约》第三十一条第一款解释本协定具有决定性意义②。关于“发射当局”定义的详细情况载于第六条的评注③。

（2）“通知联合国秘书长”的表述

此外，必须通知联合国秘书长。反之，联合国秘书长应立即通过其掌握的一切适当通信手段传播信息。然而，联合国秘书长无权对有关国家提出要求④。

三、第二条　缔约方管辖区域内的营救和援助

航天器人员因意外事故、危难、紧急或非出于本意降落，在一缔约国管辖领域内，该缔约国应立即采取一切可能措施开展援救，并提供一切必要协助。该缔约国应将所采取措施及其进展情况通知发射当局及联合国秘书长。如发射当局的协助有助于实现迅速援救，或对搜寻及援救行动大有贡献，发射当局应与该缔约国合作，以求有效进行搜寻及援救行动。此项行动应受该缔约国指挥管制，该缔约国应与发射当局密切磋商行事。

（一）谈判和起草历史

从谈判开始到最后阶段，联合国外空委及其法律小组委员会一直在对航天器人员降落的缔约方的权利和义务进行广泛辩论。缔约方的援助手段是若干草案和修正案的主题。此外，尚不清楚如果缔约方无法提供所需的援助时，援助该如何进行。关于人

① The definition of Art. 6 reads：“For the purpose of this Agreement, the term ‘launching authority’ shall refer to the State responsible for launching, or, where an international intergovernmental organization is responsible for launching, that organization, provided that organization declares its acceptance of the rights and obligations provided for in this Agreement and a majority of the States members of that organization are Contracting Parties to this Agreement and to the Treaty on Principles Governing the Activities of States in the Exploration and Use of Outer Space, including the Moon and Other Celestial Bodies.” See in more detail Commentary, Article 6, mn. 195 ff.

② Art. 31 para. 4 VCLT：“A special meaning shall be given to a term if it is established that the parties so intended.”.

③ See Commentary ARRA, Article 6, mn. 199ff.

④ See van Bogaert, Eric R. C., Aspects of Space Law, Kluwer, Deventer 1986, p. 102, with further reference.

道主义原则，应寻求一切可能的援助，但另一方面，也应维护相关缔约方的领土主权。

1. 援助的手段和方式

1962 年的苏联初稿规定，缔约国应“利用其所掌握的一切手段，包括电子和光学设备、通信手段和各种救援设施”①，并且其所提供的援助应“与可向本国宇航员提供的援助没有任何区别”②。另一方面，美国在其 1962 年的草案中，仅表述为“一切可能的援助”③。有人批评苏联草案列举了各国提供援助的手段，认为这将具有约束性，意味着对援助的一般原则的否定④。苏联代表辩称，这一列举完全是为了举例说明⑤。在讨论中，有人表示，可能没有必要列举各项手段，因为“一切可能的援助”一词足以涵盖⑥。此外，1963 年的《外空宣言》只提到“一切可能的援助”，没有进一步说明⑦。

1964 年的美国草案要求缔约方“采取一切可能的措施，迅速援助或营救航天器人员”，并规定“这些措施应包括可能进行搜救行动的缔约方的联合活动”⑧。1964 年的苏联修订草案重申了其早期的具体内容，并增加了一些额外的义务，例如有义务向正

① UN Doc. A/AC. 105/C. 2/L. 2, International Agreement on the Rescue of Astronauts and Spaceships mak-ing Emergency Landings, USSR Proposal, 6 June 1962, Art. 1.

② UN Doc. A/AC. 105/C. 2/L. 2, International Agreement on the Rescue of Astronauts and Spaceships mak-ing Emergency Landings, USSR Proposal, 6 June 1962, Art. 5.

③ UN Doc. A/AC. 105/C. 2/L. 3, Assistance and Return of Space Vehicles and Personnel, United States Proposal, 8 June 1962.

④ See the statement of the Argentinian, Mexican, Brazilian, French and Belgian delegates, UN Doc. A/AC. 105/C. 2/SR. 42, Legal Sub-Committee, Fourth Session, Summary Record of the Forty-Second Meeting, held 21 September 1965, 30 November 1965, pp. 7-11; see also Dembling, Paul G. /Arons, Daniel M. , *Space Law and the United Nations: The Work of the Legal Subcommittee on the Peaceful Uses of Outer Space*, Journal of Air Law and Commerce (32) 1966, p. 343.

⑤ See the statement of the Soviet delegate, UN Doc. A/AC. 105/SR. 42, Legal Sub-Committee, Fourth Session, Summary Record of the Forty-Second Meeting, held 21 September 1965, 30 November 1965, p. 5.

⑥ See UN Doc. A/AC. 105/21, Report of the Legal Sub-Committee on the Work of the Second Part of its Third Session (5-23 October 1964), Annex IV, Summary of views expressed in Working Groups I and II, 23 October 1964.

⑦ UNGA Res. 1962 (XVIII), Declaration of Legal Principles Governing the Activities of States in the Exploration and Uses of Outer Space, 13 December 1963, Principle 9.

⑧ UN Doc. A/AC. 105/C. 2/L. 9, International Agreement on Assistance to and Return of Astronauts and Objects Launched into Outer Space, United States Proposal, 9 March 1964, Art. 2.

式宣布发射有关宇宙飞船的国家以及联合国秘书长通报所采取的措施及其结果①。澳大利亚和加拿大的提案载有同样的通知义务，但只要求缔约方“迅速采取一切可行的措施，搜寻、营救和援助这些人员”②。到1964年法律小组委员会第三届会议结束时，已达成初步协议，即缔约方“应在力所能及的范围内，立即采取一切可能的措施，营救这些人员并向他们提供必要的援助”，同时“应随时向宣布发射的国家和联合国秘书长通报所采取的措施及所取得的结果”③。

将《营救协定》的草案和最终文本与《外空条约》的谈判及其第五条的最终文本进行比较，很明显，《营救协定》第二条的义务不适用于各自的航天人员本身。《外空条约》第五条规定，有义务“在另一缔约国领土或公海发生事故、遇险或紧急降落时，向他们提供一切可能的协助。”此外，《外空条约》第五条呼吁在外层空间和天体上的其他宇航员提供帮助。它明确规定，“一个缔约国的宇航员应向其他缔约国的宇航员提供一切可能的协助。”《营救协定》的草案和最终文本均未包含此类义务。

苏联在1967年修订的草案中没有列举营救宇航员的具体方式和方法，只提到了“营救宇航员和向他们提供必要援助的所有可能措施”④。1967年大会第二十二届会议期间，两个空间大国进行了双边谈判，1967年12月14日向法律小组委员会特别会议提交了一份提案，其中第二条规定，缔约方有义务“立即采取一切可能的措施营救他

① See UN Doc. A/AC. 105/C. 2/L. 2/Rev. 1, Agreement on the rescue of astronauts and spaceships in the event of accident or emergency landing, USSR Revised Draft, 9 March 1964; and UN Doc. A/AC. 105/C. 2/L. 2/Rev. 2, Agreement on the rescue of astronauts and spaceships in the event of accident or emergency landing, USSR Revised Draft, 26 October 1964.

② UN Doc. WG. I/30, Australia and Canada: Proposal, in: UN Doc. A/AC. 105/21, Report of the Legal Sub-Committee on the Work of the Second Part of its Third Session (5-23 October 1964), Annex I, Proposals and Amendments Relating to Assistance to and Return of Astronauts and Space Vehicles, 23 October 1964, Art. 3 (emphasis added). This formulation remained unchanged in the revised draft Art. 3, UN Doc. A/AC. 105/C. 2/L. 20, Assistance to and Return of Astronauts and Space Objects, Revised Australian-Canadian proposal submitted as a working paper, 21 June 1967, Art. 3.

③ Art. 3 of the "Text of certain provisions of a draft agreement on assistance to and return of personnel and spacecraft, on which preliminary agreement was reached by the informal working party of the Sub-Committee", reproduced in UN Doc. A/AC. 105/21, Report of the Legal Sub-Committee on the Work of the Second Part of its Third Session (5-23 October 1964), Annex Ⅲ, Text of Certain Provisions of a Draft Agreement on Assistance to and Return of Personnel and Spacecraft, on which Preliminary Agreement was reached by the Informal Working-Party of the Sub-Committee, 23 October 1964.

④ UN Doc. A/AC. 105/C. 2/L. 18, Agreement On The Rescue Of Astronauts In The Event Of Accident Or Emergency Landing, USSR Revised Draft, 19 June 1967.

们，并向他们提供一切必要的援助”，以及“将发射当局正在采取的措施及其进展情况通知发射当局和联合国秘书长。”① 在1967年12月16日联合国外空委会议的最后讨论中，第二条的这一部分保持不变，并成为最终文本。

2. 在缔约方领土上的援助

发射当局和其他缔约方在发生事故或意外降落的缔约方领土内协助救援行动，这一点颇有争议。对人道主义、航天大国的利益限度的考量必须兼顾该国的主权保护。美国和苏联在各自的草案中明确地强调了发射当局的利益限度。美国草案第二条规定，每个缔约国应采取一切可能的措施，“除非登记国或负责发射的国际组织另有要求”②，“并应允许登记国或负责发射的国际组织在其主管部门的控制下，根据情况提供必要的协助措施。”③ 同样，苏联草案规定，“如果宇航员在其领土上着陆的缔约国无法在没有帮助的情况下进行必要的救援行动，则应请求发射国提供协助。”④ 这就提出了一个问题，即由谁来确定“一个国家不能在没有帮助的情况下开展救援行动?”⑤

澳大利亚和加拿大则从不同的角度来解决这个问题。其草案规定，“如果缔约国认为发射国的援助将大大有助于搜救行动的有效进行，则应请求发射国在缔约国的指导和控制下，在此类行动中与其合作⑥。” 这一提法在法律小组委员会获得批准，并于

---

① UN Doc. A/AC. 105/C. 2/L. 28, Draft agreement on the rescue of astronauts, the return of astronauts and the return of objects launched into outer space, 12 December 1967; and UN Doc. A/AC. 105/C. 2/L. 28/Rev. 1, Draft agreement on the rescue of astronauts, the return of astronauts and the return of objects launched into outer space, 14 December 1967.

② UN Doc. A/AC. 105/C. 2/L. 9, International Agreement on Assistance to and Return of Astronauts and Objects Launched into Outer Space, United States Proposal, 9 March 1964, Art. 2 para. 1.

③ Ibid., para. 2.

④ UN Doc. A/AC. 105/C. 2/L. 2/Rev. 1, Agreement on the rescue of astronauts and spaceships in the event of accident or emergency landing, USSR Revised Draft, 9 March 1964.

⑤ UN Doc. A/AC. 105/21, Report of the Legal Sub-Committee on the Work of the Second Part of its Third Session (5-23 October 1964), Annex IV, Summary of views expressed in Working Groups I and II, 23 October 1964.

⑥ UN Doc. WG. I/30, Australia and Canada: Proposal, in: UN Doc. A/AC. 105/21, Report of the Legal Sub-Committee on the Work of the Second Part of its Third Session (5-23 October 1964), Annex I, Proposals and Amendments Relating to Assistance to and Return of Astronauts and Space Vehicles, 23 October 1964. This formulation remained unchanged in the revised draft Art. 3, UN Doc. A/AC. 105/C. 2/L. 20, Assistance to and Return of Astronauts and Space Objects, Revised Australian-Canadian proposal submitted as a working paper, 21 June 1967, Art. 3.

1964 年第三届会议结束时作为暂定的初步协定条款提出[①]。然而，缔约国“应请求”合作的措辞被视为意味着一项义务，因此有人建议使用“可以请求”一词来代替[②]。

1967 年，在谈判的最后阶段，这个问题一直摆在桌面上，直到最后一刻。苏联重新拟订了其提案，并提出了一项修订后的条款草案，其中规定“各缔约方应向本协定另一缔约方提供一切援助，若该缔约方已请求提供援助，以确保在发生事故、遇险或紧急降落时尽快发现和营救宇航员。这种援助可以包括允许宣布发射航天器的国家使用必要的手段和人员，对降落在该缔约国领土上的宇航员进行搜救。”[③]

然而，航天大国之间的双边谈判产生了一个全新的草案，该草案强调有效地开展搜救行动，同时也强调搜救行动所在的缔约方的指导和控制。新草案规定，“如果发射当局的协助将有助于迅速实施救援或对搜救行动的有效性作出重大贡献，缔约方应与发射当局合作，以有效开展搜救行动。这类行动应服从缔约方的指示和控制，缔约方应与发射当局密切和持续协商[④]。”法律小组委员会商定了该条款，并将其转交联合国外空委核准。外空委讨论了该条款并决定对其进行修改，“缔约方应与发射当局合作，以有效开展搜救行动”的表述被认为意味着事故发生地所在的国家或紧急降落的国家负有义务。相反，发射当局有义务帮助开展有效的搜索和救援行动[⑤]。因此，最终版本被修改为“发射当局应与缔约方合作，以有效开展搜救行动”。这满足了非航天国家对其主权可能受到限制的关切。

（二）评注

《营救协定》第二条规定了在缔约方领土内降落时对航天器人员进行营救或提供一切必要援助的义务。从这个角度来说，该条规定类似于《芝加哥公约》第二十

① See UN Doc. A/AC. 105/21, Report of the Legal Sub-Committee on the Work of the Second Part of its Third Session (5-23 October 1964), Annex Ⅲ, Text of Certain Provisions of a Draft Agreement on Assistance to and Return of Personnel and Spacecraft, on which Preliminary Agreement was reached by the Informal Working-Party of the Sub-Committee, 23 October 1964.

② UN Doc. A/AC. 105/21, Report of the Legal Sub-Committee on the Work of the Second Part of its Third Session (5-23 October 1964), Annex IV, Summary of views expressed in Working Groups I and II, 23 October 1964.

③ UN Doc. A/AC. 105/C. 2/L. 18, Agreement On The Rescue Of Astronauts In The Event Of Accident Or Emergency Landing, USSR Revised Draft, 19 June 1967.

④ UN Doc. A/AC. 105/C. 2/L. 28, Draft agreement on the rescue of astronauts, the return of astronauts and the return of objects launched into outer space, 12 December 1967, Art. 2.

⑤ On the discussion of this matter see Cheng, Bin, *The* 1968 *Astronauts Agreement or How Not to make a Treaty*, The Yearbook of World Affairs (23) 1969, pp. 198-199.

五条。

1. “在缔约方管辖的领土内降落”的表述

如果由于第一条所述事件，航天器人员降落在缔约方管辖的领土上①，则适用第二条规定的义务。

2. 缔约方的义务

（1）营救和提供援助（第一句）

在其领土内发生降落的缔约方必须立即采取一切可能的措施营救航天器人员，并向他们提供一切必要的援助。“一切可能的措施”一语表明，将采取的措施仍由缔约方裁量，并有选择的自由。然而，谈判历史表明，在起草时，所有可能的手段都包括在内，即缔约方可以使用的一切可以利用的手段，包括电子和光学设备、通信手段和各种救援设施②。

然而，《营救协定》不要求缔约方超越其能力的限度③。《营救协定》第二条“立即采取一切可能的措施进行救援”的义务并不意味着救援程度高于 1944 年《芝加哥公约》对航空器的规定。《芝加哥公约》第二十五条规定，对遇险航空器采取的援助措施应尽可能地由该国确定④。航空器所有人或航空器注册地当局可根据情况需要并在领土国当局的控制下提供协助。在法律小组委员会关于《营救协定》的辩论中，各国代表们发表了一些意见⑤，最终各代表团对《营救协定》第二条的解释达成了一致意见，即一国将尽其所能提供帮助，但无需作出超出其能力限度的努力。然而，尽管《芝加哥公约》在制定调查规则时，明确了“切实可行”一词的适用范围不会太广，但空间法并不包含精确规范的程序内容。

此外，缔约方应在其可采取的所有可能措施的限度内，向航天器人员提供“一切

---

① See Commentary ARRA, Article 1, mn. 112ff.

② See Commentary ARRA, Article 2, mn. 127ff.

③ See van Bogaert, Eric R. C. , Aspects of Space Law, Kluwer, Deventer 1986, p. 108.

④ Art. 25 Chicago Convention: “Each contracting State undertakes to provide such measures of assistance to aircraft in distress in its territory as it may find practicable, and to permit, subject to control by its own authorities, the owners of the aircraft or authorities of the State in which the aircraft is registered to provide such measures of assistance as may be necessitated by the circumstances. Each contracting State, when undertaking search for missing aircraft, will collaborate in coordinated measures which may be recommended from time to time pursuant to this Convention. ”.

⑤ See Commentary ARRA, Article 2, mn. 127ff.

必要的援助”①。

（2）通知发射当局和联合国秘书长（第二句）

缔约方必须将其正在采取的措施及其进展情况通知发射当局和联合国秘书长。第二条没有规定提供信息的时间节点。虽然这给缔约方留下了酌情处置权，但从“进度”的措辞以及第二条前后表述的系统联系中可以清楚地看出，缔约方必须在营救和援助行动过程中提供信息。这符合该条款的目标，即确保缔约方采取“所有可能的措施”的透明度，从而使发射当局有可能提供进一步的援助，并使联合国秘书长在必要时协调任何进一步的援助。

（3）与发射当局协商搜救行动（第四句）

由于被着陆的缔约方有义务与发射当局密切、持续地进行协调，发射当局的利益因而得到维护。缔约方保留对行动的指导和控制权，且接受发射当局的帮助并非缔约方的义务。当发射当局能够帮助救援的有效进行时，可以在发射当局的帮助下进行。因此，第二条规定明确地尊重了各国的领土主权②。

（4）缔约方对行动的指挥和控制（第四句）

第二条第四句阐明了参与搜救行动的各方的地位和责任，尽管它要求缔约方与发射当局持续进行磋商，但行动本身应受缔约方的指挥和控制。因此，缔约方在这类行动中处于领导地位。

3. 发射当局的义务（第三句）

第二条第三句规定了如果发射当局的协助有助于迅速实施救援或将极大地有助于搜救行动的有效性，发射当局有义务与缔约方合作，以期有效开展联合搜救行动。

这或可被认为是赋予了发射当局在规定的情况下参与搜救行动的权利，正如苏联在 1978 年宇宙-954 号卫星在加拿大领土上坠毁后根据《营救协定》第二条所主张的那样。为了限制损失，加拿大政府拒绝苏联当局参与搜救行动，后来苏联以该条款的规定为依据，主张支付低于索赔金额的赔偿③。最终，苏联只支付了不足加拿大政府

---

① See van Bogaert, Eric R. C., Aspects of Space Law, Kluwer, Deventer 1986, p. 108.

② See ibid. with further references.

③ See Diederiks-Verschoor, I. H. Philepina/Kopal, Vladimir, An Introduction to Space Law, 3rd rev. edn., Kluwer Law International, The Netherlands 2008, p. 32.

的索赔账单一半的金额①。然而，第二条第四句很明确地表示，发射当局参与搜救行动不得干扰缔约方指挥和控制这一行动的权利。

四、第三条　在不受缔约方管辖的区域的援助和营救

如获悉或发现航天器人员已迫降于公海上或不属任何国家管辖的任何其他地点，能提供协助的各缔约国应于必要时对搜寻及援救行动提供协助，以确保航天器人员迅速获救。各该国应将其所采措施及其进展情形通知发射当局及联合国秘书长。

（一）谈判和起草历史

在公海和不受任何国家管辖的地方向宇航员提供援助的问题有一些不同的看法。谈判过程中的讨论主要集中于缔约方在搜救行动中的地位和责任。

苏联在其第一份草案中提议，“如有必要，发射国应与缔约国进行联合搜救，前提是发射国向缔约国提出这一申请。”② 后来，苏联重新拟订了该条款，并提议发射国“可保留在其指定的公海区域内，以自己的方式和人员进行宇航员和宇宙飞船搜救的专属权利。”③ 出于人道主义考虑，这种做法被认为是有问题的，因为它将宇航员的营救置于发射国的主动权之下，并可能“阻止某一组织或国家对宇宙飞船进行搜救”④。此外，不可接受的是，该提案将允许发射国为自己保留在不受任何国家管辖的区域内

① See Andem, Maurice N., The 1968 Rescue Agreement and the Commercialisation of Outer Space Activities During the 21st Century-Some Reflections, in: IISL, Proceedings of the 41st Colloquium on the Law of Outer Space, 28 September-2 October 1998 Melbourne (Australia), AIAA, 1998, p. 78, according to this source, $ 15 million.

② UN Doc. A/AC. 105/C. 2/L. 2, International Agreement on the Rescue of Astronauts and Spaceships mak-ing Emergency Landings, USSR Proposal, 6 June 1962.

③ UN Doc. A/AC. 105/C. 2/L. 2/Rev. 1, Agreement on the rescue of astronauts and spaceships in the event of accident or emergency landing, USSR Revised Draft, 9 March 1964, Art. 5.

④ Statement of the Italian delegate, UN Doc. A/AC. 105/C. 2/SR. 29-37, Legal Sub-Committee, Third Session (1st Part), Summary Record of the Twenty-Ninth to Thirty-Seventh Meetings, held from 9-26 March 1964, 24 August 1964, p. 68; see also Dembling, Paul G./Arons, Daniel M., *Space Law and the United Nations: The Work of the Legal Subcommittee on the Peaceful Uses of Outer Space*, Journal of Air Law and Commerce (32) 1966, pp. 338-339.

进行搜救行动的专属权利[①]。苏联考虑到了这些意见，随后修改了其表述，提出“搜救行动应由有能力进行这些行动的缔约国进行。这些行动应由正式宣布发射有关航天器的国家或其他可能要求负责的国家进行指挥。”[②] 排他性的主张被取消，但正式宣布发射的国家的主导地位被保留下来。

1964 年的美国草案还包含了负责发射的登记国或国际组织的特权地位。然而，它规定“每一缔约方应采取一切可能的措施，迅速协助或营救航天器人员；除非登记国或负责发射的国际组织另有要求”[③]。关于公海或南极洲的具体情况，美国的草案规定“在航天器人员在公海或南极洲紧急降落时，由可能有能力进行搜救行动的缔约方联合开展”[④]。

澳大利亚和加拿大的提案还规定了发射国的优先权，但同时指出，如果该国无法立即进行有效的搜救行动，“此类行动应由有能力的缔约方在与发射国密切和持续合作的情况下进行。”[⑤]

在这个问题上，直至法律小组委员会第三次会议结束时，未能达成初步协议[⑥]。

然而，《外空条约》谈判的结果证实了 1963 年《外空宣言》第九项原则中已经包含的一般原则[⑦]，即“条约缔约国应将宇航员视为人类在外层空间的使者，并当他

① See ibid. , p. 338.

② UN Doc. A/AC. 105/C. 2/L. 2/Rev. 2, Agreement on the rescue of astronauts and spaceships in the event of accident or emergency landing, USSR Revised Draft, 26 October 1964.

③ UN Doc. A/AC. 105/C. 2/L. 9, International Agreement on Assistance to and Return of Astronauts and Objects Launched into Outer Space, United States Proposal, 9 March 1964, Art. 2 para. 1 sentence 2 (emphasis added).

④ Ibid.

⑤ UN Doc. WG. I/30, Australia and Canada: Proposal, in: UN Doc. A/AC. 105/21, Report of the Legal Sub-Committee on the Work of the Second Part of its Third Session (5-23 October 1964), Annex I, Proposals and Amendments Relating to Assistance to and Return of Astronauts and Space Vehicles, 23 October 1964, Art. 4. This formulation remained unchanged in the revised draft Art. 4, UN Doc. A/AC. 105/C. 2/L. 20, Assistance to and Return of Astronauts and Space Objects, Revised Australian-Canadian proposal submitted as a working paper, 21 June 1967, Art. 4.

⑥ Such tentative preliminary agreement could be reached on the Preamble and three other operative articles. See UN Doc. A/AC. 105/21, Report of the Legal Sub-Committee on the Work of the Second Part of its Third Session (5-23 October 1964), Annex Ⅲ, Text of Certain Provisions of a Draft Agreement on Assistance to and Return of Personnel and Spacecraft, on which Preliminary Agreement was reached by the Informal Working-Party of the Sub-Committee, 23 October 1964; and Historical Background and Context, mn. 33f.

⑦ UNGA Res. 1962 (XⅧ), Declaration of Legal Principles Governing the Activities of States in the Exploration and Use of Outer Space, 13 December 1963.

们在另一缔约国领土或公海上发生事故、遇险或紧急降落时，应提供一切可能的援助。”① 苏联 1967 年修正后的提案完全取消了“宣布发射了有关航天器的国家”的主导地位，只提议“有能力这样做的缔约国应向［该国］提供援助，开展宇航员搜救行动②”。这为两个航天大国在 1967 年第 22 届联合国大会期间的双边谈判中，就这一问题达成协议铺平了道路。一份新的草案完成制定，其中包含了苏联上次提议的大部分内容。但是，增加了一项额外的义务，即“将他们正在采取的措施和进展情况通知发射当局和联合国秘书长”③。该条款的表述在随后的讨论中没有改动，并成为第三条的最终版本。

（二）评注

第三条规定了航天器人员在公海或不受任何国家管辖的地方降落时，缔约方协助救援行动的义务（第一句），并载有通知联合国秘书长的义务（第二句）。与第二条的义务相比，第三条的义务只适用于在任何国家管辖范围以外的情况。第三条第一句所规定的义务是在起草《外空条约》过程中经过大量谈判取得的结果。

1. 在搜救行动中提供援助

根据该条款的谈判历史背景，第三条第一句“在搜救行动中提供援助”的义务可以理解为：

当获悉或发现航天器人员已在公海或不属于任何国家管辖的地方降落时，必要时凡有能力的缔约方，均应协助搜救行动，以确保迅速营救这些人员。

第二条的义务必须毫不拖延地履行，与此相反，第三条的义务只需由“有相应能力”的缔约方履行，而且只需“在必要时”履行。因此，有关国家在决定是否采取主动措施方面拥有宽泛的裁量权，并可自由决定参与援助和营救行动中的哪一部分④。

---

① Art. V para. 1 sentence 1 OST; for a detailed discussion see von der Dunk, Frans/Goh, Gérardine M., Article V, in: Hobe, Stephan/Schmidt-Tedd, Bernhard/Schrogl, Kai-Uwe (eds.), Cologne Commentary on Space Law, Volume I, Heymanns, Cologne 2009, pp. 94-102.

② UN Doc. A/AC. 105/C. 2/L. 18, Agreement On The Rescue Of Astronauts In The Event Of Accident Or Emergency Landing, USSR Revised Draft, 19 June 1967, Art. 4.

③ UN Doc. A/AC. 105/C. 2/L. 28, Draft agreement on the rescue of astronauts, the return of astronauts and the return of objects launched into outer space, 12 December 1967, Art. 3; and UN Doc. A/AC. 105/C. 2/L. 28/Rev. 1, Draft agreement on the rescue of astronauts, the return of astronauts and the return of objects launched into outer space, 14 December 1967, Art. 3.

④ See van Bogaert, Eric R. C., Aspects of Space Law, Kluwer, Deventer 1986, p. 109.

发射当局和登记国在搜救行动中都没有特殊地位。

第三条仅适用于在公海或不受任何国家管辖的地方着陆的情况。因此，第三条的条款涵盖了不受一国管辖的任何着陆地点。这包括南极洲和天体，尽管后者在月球上有更具体的规则。由于航天器人员必须在公海或不受任何其他国家管辖的任何地方“降落”，因此不包括在外层空间移动的航天器人员，也不包括在轨道上的危险情况①。这些情况仅适用于《外空条约》第五条第二款的规定。然而，除非备用的救援飞行器能够及时到达并提供援助，否则无论如何在外层空间都不可能实施营救行动②。

2. 通知发射当局和联合国秘书长

在第三条所述情形中（在公海或不受任何国家管辖的地方着陆），凡有能力参与搜救行动的缔约方③，必须将他们正在采取的措施和进展情况通知发射当局和联合国秘书长。在第二条第二句中，没有规定必须提供信息的时间节点，但显然应在行动过程中提供④。

五、第四条　人员的即刻送回

如航天器人员因意外事故、危难、紧急或非出于本意在一缔约国管辖领域内降落，或在公海上或不属任何国家管辖的任何其他地点被发现，应确保其安全并迅速送交发射当局代表。

（一）谈判和起草历史

在《营救协定》的谈判期间，航天器人员的送回与营救义务是区分开来的。这些义务与返还空间物体的义务也是区分开的。这表现在送回航天器人员的义务是单独列

---

① See ibid.

② See Diederiks-Verschoor, I. H. Philepina/Kopal, Vladimir, An Introduction to Space Law, 3rd rev. edn., Kluwer Law International, The Netherlands 2008, p. 32.

③ See Commentary ARRA, Article 3, mn. 154.

④ See ibid., mn. 140.

为一项条款的。相比之下，《外空宣言》[①] 和《外空条约》[②] 均将宇航员的援助和送回义务规定在一个条款中。1963 年《外空宣言》在其第九项原则中规定了“在另一缔约国领土或公海发生事故、遇险或紧急降落时”[③] 送回的义务，“进行上述降落的宇航员应被安全迅速地送回其航天器的登记国”[④]。1967 年《外空条约》第五条也有同样的规定。然而，苏联、美国的提案以及澳大利亚与加拿大的提案都分别在单独的条款中规定了送回宇航员的义务。

虽然美国一直建议“迅速和安全地”无条件送回[⑤]，苏联的提案只要求每个缔约国“尽其最大努力促使尽早送回”[⑥]。在 1964 年的草案中，苏联甚至增加了一个条件，即宇宙飞船应该是按照 1963 年《外空宣言》发射的[⑦]。在讨论中，法国代表表示，宇航员可以被拘留，以便对他们提起刑事指控[⑧]。一些国家认为，第四条的规定不应优先于国内法有关庇护的规定。奥地利表示，希望能够按照其“对外国人的传统政策”

---

① See UNGA Res. 1962 (XVIII), Declaration of Legal Principles Governing the Activities of States in the Exploration and Use of Outer Space, 13 December 1963, Art. 9.

② See Art. V OST; see also von der Dunk, Frans/Goh, Gérardine M., Article V, in: Hobe, Stephan/Schmidt-Tedd, Bernhard/Schrogl, Kai-Uwe (eds.), Cologne Commentary on Space Law, Volume I, Heymanns, Cologne 2009, pp. 94-102.

③ UNGA Res. 1962 (XVIII), Declaration of Legal Principles Governing the Activities of States in the Exploration and Use of Outer Space, 13 December 1963, Art. 9.

④ Ibid.

⑤ This was the case from the first proposal on a General Assembly resolution, in its operative para. 2. UN Doc. A/AC. 105/C. 2/L. 3, Assistance and Return of Space Vehicles and Personnel, United States Proposal, 8 June 1962. In its subsequent draft for a treaty, the same obligation is contained in Art. 3 para. 1, UN Doc. A/AC. 105/C. 2/L. 9, International Agreement on Assistance to and Return of Astronauts and Objects Launched into Outer Space, United States Proposal, 9 March 1964.

⑥ UN Doc. A/AC. 105/C. 2/L. 2, International Agreement on the Rescue of Astronauts and Spaceships mak-ing Emergency Landings, USSR Proposal, 6 June 1962, Art. 6; UN Doc. A/AC. 105/C. 2/L. 2/Rev. 1, Agreement on the rescue of astronauts and spaceships in the event of accident or emergency landing, USSR Revised Draft, 9 March 1964, Art. 8.

⑦ See UN Doc. A/AC. 105/C. 2/L. 2/Rev. 2, Agreement on the rescue of astronauts and spaceships in the event of accident or emergency landing, USSR Revised Draft, 26 October 1964, Art. 5.

⑧ See UN Doc. WG. I/21, France: Amendment to Art. 5 of the proposal by Australia and Canada, in: UN Doc. A/AC. 105/19, Report of the Legal Sub-Committee on the Work of its Third Session (9-26 March 1964) to the Committee on the Peaceful Uses of Outer Space, Annex I, Proposals and Amendments Relating to Assistance to and Return of Astronauts and Space Vehicles, 26 March 1964, p. 24; see Dembling, Paul G./Arons, Daniel M., *Space Law and the United Nations: The Work of the Legal Subcommittee on the Peaceful Uses of Outer Space*, Journal of Air Law and Commerce (32) 1966, p. 339.

继续提供庇护[1]。法国支持这一解释[2]。然而，航天器人员可能会向他降落的缔约方寻求庇护，这仅仅是一个理论问题，人们普遍认为，企图叛逃的宇航员得找到一种更方便的方式[3]。1967年的苏联草案[4]根本没有提到送回航天器人员的义务，只包含了援助条款[5]。1967年两个航天大国进行双边谈判后，拟定了一份新的草案，其中载有无条件送回航天器人员的义务，并规定应"安全、迅速"地进行送回[6]。在联合国大会最后通过草案之前，这一提法没有改动。

此外，还就宇航员应交还给谁的问题展开了一些讨论。

1962年苏联的提案提到"任何宇航员都应送回他们自己的国家"[7]。1964年，它将这一表述改为"他们自己的国家，即人类在外层空间的使者——另一个国家的宇航员"[8]。后来它规定，"根据1963年《外空宣言》，宇航员应送回发射宇宙飞船的船员的本国"[9]。美国首先提出"负责发射的一个或多个国家或国际组织"[10]，在后来的草案中，他们将这一提法改为"登记国或负责发射的国际组织"[11]。澳大利亚和加拿大

① UN Doc. A/AC. 105/C. 2/SR. 87, Legal Sub-Committee, Special Session, Summary Record of the Eighty-Seventh Meeting, held 15 December 1967, 2 February 1968, p. 10; see also Christol, Carl Q., The Modern International Law of Outer Space, Pergamon Press, New York 1982, pp. 175, 193.

② See UN Doc. A/AC. 105/C. 2/SR. 86, Legal Sub-Committee, Special Session, Summary Record of the Eighty-Sixth Meeting, held 14 December 1967, 9 February 1968, Art. 5.

③ See Dembling, Paul G. /Arons, Daniel M., *The Treaty on Rescue and Return of Astronauts and Space Objects*, William and Mary Law Review (9) 1968, p. 653.

④ See UN Doc. A/AC. 105/C. 2/L. 18, Agreement On The Rescue Of Astronauts In The Event Of Accident Or Emergency Landing, USSR Revised Draft, 19 June 1967.

⑤ See ibid.; see Dembling, Paul G. /Arons, Daniel M., *The Treaty on Rescue and Return of Astronauts and Space Objects*, William and Mary Law Review (9) 1968, pp. 630-663; Cheng, Bin, *The* 1968 *Astronauts Agreement or How Not to make a Treaty*, The Yearbook of World Affairs (23) 1969, pp. 185-208.

⑥ UN Doc. A/AC. 105/C. 2/L. 28, Draft agreement on the rescue of astronauts, the return of astronauts and the return of objects launched into outer space, 12 December 1967, Art. 4.

⑦ UN Doc. A/AC. 105/C. 2/L. 2, International Agreement on the Rescue of Astronauts and Spaceships mak-ing Emergency Landings, USSR Proposal, 6 June 1962, Art. 6.

⑧ UN Doc. A/AC. 105/C. 2/L. 2/Rev. 1, Agreement on the rescue of astronauts and spaceships in the event of accident or emergency landing, USSR Revised Draft, 9 March 1964, Art. 8.

⑨ UN Doc. A/AC. 105/C. 2/L. 2/Rev. 2, Agreement on the rescue of astronauts and spaceships in the event of accident or emergency landing, USSR Revised Draft, 26 October 1964, Art. 5.

⑩ UN Doc. A/AC. 105/C. 2/L. 3, Assistance and Return of Space Vehicles and Personnel, United States Proposal, 8 June 1962, operative para. 2.

⑪ UN Doc. A/AC. 105/C. 2/L. 9, International Agreement on Assistance to and Return of Astronauts and Objects Launched into Outer Space, United States Proposal, 9 March 1964, Art. 3 para. 1.

提议将航天器人员送回“发射国”①。

与之相对,《外空宣言》第九项原则和《外空条约》第五条规定，宇航员应送回“其航天器的登记国”②。作为接收实体的“发射当局的代表”仅在 1967 年末苏联和美国就《营救协定》进行双边谈判后才出现在草案中③。“发射当局”是指负责发射的国家，或在政府间国际组织负责发射的情况下指该组织④。这一表述反映了两个航天大国在国际组织地位上的妥协⑤。

（二）评注

第四条规定了将航天器人员送回发射当局的代表的义务。

该条款规定，缔约国有绝对的义务当航天器人员在其领土，或在公海，或在不属于一国管辖的地方被发现时将其送回。该条款的表述没有为缔约方的自由裁量权留下余地。

第四条中的义务既指第二条所述的事件（在缔约国管辖的领土内发生意外、遇险、紧急或意外降落），也指第三条所述的事件（在公海或不属于任何国家管辖范围内的区域降落或被发现）。因此,《营救协定》涵盖了缔约方与航天器人员有关的任何情况下的义务。

航天器人员必须送回至《营救协定》第六条意义下的发射当局的代表。从第四条的谈判和起草历史可以看出，送回的义务是无条件的。无条件的送回义务被视为美国在谈判过程中取得的重大胜利。苏联提出的以航天器人员遵守 1963 年《外空宣言》为返回条件的建议，使得有可能出现如果人员被指控从事鼓动战争或被指控从事侵略

---

① UN Doc. WG. I/30, Australia and Canada: Proposal, in: UN Doc. A/AC. 105/21, Report of the Legal Sub-Committee on the Work of the Second Part of its Third Session (5-23 October 1964), Annex I, Proposals and Amendments Relating to Assistance to and Return of Astronauts and Space Vehicles, 23 October 1964, Art. 5. The ‘launching State’ remained also in the revised version of 1967; see UN Doc. A/AC. 105/C. 2/L. 20, Assistance to and Return of Astronauts and Space Objects, Revised Australian-Canadian proposal submitted as a working paper, 21 June 1967, Art. 5.

② UNGA Res. 1962 (XVIII), Declaration of Legal Principles Governing the Activities of States in the Exploration and Use of Outer Space, 13 December 1963, Art. 9. ; Art. 5 OST.

③ UN Doc. A/AC. 105/C. 2/L. 28, Draft agreement on the rescue of astronauts, the return of astronauts and the return of objects launched into outer space, 12 December 1967, Art. 4.

④ Provided that organization declares its acceptance of the rights and obligations provided for in the ARRA and that a majority of the States members of that organization are Contracting Parties to the ARRA and to the OST. See Art. 6 ARRA; and the corresponding Commentary ARRA, Article 6, mn. 198.

⑤ See already Historical Background and Context, mn. 40; and Commentary ARRA, Article 1, mn. 97.

性军事活动或间谍活动，则无需返回的情况①。显然最终苏联更关心的是人道主义问题②。应当指出的是，《营救协定》没有提到这些人员的军事或民事属性③，因此航天器人员是否在发射当局的军事部门工作无关紧要。

第四条还解决了航天器人员若犯下罪行，或请求政治庇护，是否应予以遣返的问题④。然而，在这种情况下，各缔约方可能辩称降落并非不是有意的⑤。

必须指出，航天器人员的送回并不以偿还任何费用为条件。

六、第五条　通知、收回和返还空间物体

一、缔约国在获悉或发现空间物体或其组成部分已于其管辖领域内，或在公海上，或在不属任何国家管辖之任何其他地点返回地球时，应通知发射当局及联合国秘书长。

二、缔约国发现空间物体或其组成部分在其管辖范围内，如经发射当局请求同时该当局提供协助，缔约国应采取其认为可行的措施，寻获该物体或其组成部分。

三、如经发射当局请求，在发射当局领域范围以外发现的射入空间物体或其组成部分应送还发射当局代表或留待发射当局代表处置；如经请求，在送还之前，该当局应先提供证明资料。

四、虽有本条第二项及第三项的规定，缔约国有理由相信在其管辖领域内发现或其于他处寻获的空间物体或其组成部分具为危险或毒害性质时，应将此情形通知发射当局，发射当局应立即采取有效措施，于该缔约国指挥及管制下，消除可能的损害危险。

---

① See Christol, Carl Q., The Modern International Law of Outer Space, Pergamon Press, New York 1982, p. 193.

② See UN Doc. A/AC. 105/C. 2/SR. 86, Legal Sub-Committee, Special Session, Summary Record of the Eighty-Sixth Meeting, held 14 December 1967, 9 February 1968, p. 2; see also Piradov, Aleksandr S. (ed.) /Belitsky, Boris (tr.), International Space Law, Progress Publications, Moscow 1976, p. 155; Chris-tol, Carl Q., The Modern International Law of Outer Space, Pergamon Press, New York 1982, p. 194.

③ See ibid., p. 652.

④ See Commentary ARRA, Article 4, mn. 158.

⑤ See Christol, Carl Q., The Modern International Law of Outer Space, Pergamon Press, New York 1982, p. 193; See Dembling, Paul G. /Arons, Daniel M., *The Treaty on Rescue and Return of Astronauts and Space Objects*, William and Mary Law Review (9) 1968, p. 652.

五、为履行本条第二项及第三项下履行寻获及送还空间物体或其组成部分的义务所产生的费用应由发射当局承担。

（一）谈判和起草历史

与空间物体的收回和返还有关的法律义务在起草和谈判过程中受到了各种关切。与宇航员的援助和送回义务不同，空间物体的收回和返还不仅涉及人道主义方面，而且涉及科学和商业利益以及政治、安全和安保方面。讨论中的问题包括：应在何种条件下返还空间物体、空间物体的潜在危险性质、在收回过程中可能需要援助、应将空间物体返还给哪个实体以及回收和返还的费用。

美国提议，“发射到外层空间的物体或其组成部分已返回地球的”，只应当“应登记国或负责发射的国际组织的请求”予以返还[①]。但是，如果有这样的请求，并且在按要求提供了证明材料的情况下，缔约方应有义务返还该物体。苏联对返还的义务附加了更多的条件。根据其提议，只有在外国航天器有识别标志并且发射已正式宣布的情况下，才应毫不拖延地将其归还[②]。此外，苏联提议，运载“用于在另一国境内收集情报信息”的装置的航天器[③]不应返还。后来，这一规定被改为条件，即该空间物体必须是为“和平探索和利用外层空间的目的”发射的[④]，或是“根据 1963 年《外空宣言》发射的”[⑤]。然而，这些条件并不为美国和其他西方国家所接受，因为特别是在没有争端解决条款的情况下，这些条件在实践中容易造成无尽的困难[⑥]。针对这些条件提出的主要争论是，《外空宣言》第七项原则和《外空条约》第八条并不包含此类条件。关于返还条件的争论结果是，苏联在 1967 年的草案中最终没有规定有

---

① UN Doc. A/AC. 105/C. 2/L. 9, International Agreement on Assistance to and Return of Astronauts and Objects Launched into Outer Space, United States Proposal, 9 March 1964, Art. 3 para. 2.

② UN Doc. A/AC. 105/C. 2/L. 2, International Agreement on the Rescue of Astronauts and Spaceships making Emergency Landings, USSR Proposal, 6 June 1962, Art. 7.

③ Ibid.

④ UN Doc. A/AC. 105/C. 2/L. 2/Rev. 1, Agreement on the rescue of astronauts and spaceships in the event of accident or emergency landing, USSR Revised Draft, 9 March 1964, Art. 9.

⑤ UN Doc. A/AC. 105/C. 2/L. 2/Rev. 2, Agreement on the rescue of astronauts and spaceships in the event of accident or emergency landing, USSR Revised Draft, 26 October 1964, Art. 6 para. 2.

⑥ See Cheng, Bin, *The* 1968 *Astronauts Agreement or How Not to make a Treaty*, The Yearbook of World Affairs (23) 1969, p. 191.

关返还的义务，而是将协议的范围限制在营救宇航员。直到 1967 年底，苏联改变了这一立场，并与美国进行了密集的双边谈判，随后向法律小组委员会提出的新草案再次载有返还的义务，并规定只有在被要求时才有义务提供证明材料。

澳大利亚和加拿大的提案为讨论增添了另一个焦点，即空间物体的潜在危险属性和在收回中可能需要的援助。据此，其建议发射国有义务“在缔约方的领导和监督下，迅速采取有效措施，将物体追回，并将其从缔约方主权、管辖或控制的领土上移走，或以其他方式消除危险或损害。”① 这一提议被批准，进而就空间物体返还问题达成了初步协议，其中绝大部分采纳了澳大利亚和加拿大的提案②。非航天国家的关切还包括发射当局在收回进程中的地位③。提交大会的最后草案肯定了面临空间物体潜在危险的非航天国家的关切④。

在大多数谈判过程中，空间物体应归还给谁仍然存在争议。苏联提出了“发射国”⑤，后来又提出了“正式宣布发射的国家”⑥；美国提出“负责发射的登记国或国际组织”⑦；澳大利亚和加拿大建议为“发射国”⑧。《外空宣言》第七项原则和《外

---

① UN Doc. WG. I/30, Australia and Canada: Proposal, Art. 5, in: UN Doc. A/AC. 105/21, Report of the Legal Sub-Committee on the Work of the Second Part of its Third Session (5-23 October 1964), Annex I, Proposals and amendments relating to assistance to and return of astronauts and space vehicles, 23 October 1964; similarly, draft Art. 6 of the revised proposal of 1967, UN Doc. A/AC. 105/C. 2/L. 20, Assistance to and Return of Astronauts and Space Objects, Revised Australian-Canadian proposal submitted as a working paper, 21 June 1967.

② UN Doc. A/AC. 105/21, Legal Sub-Committee on the Work of the Second Part of its Third Session (5-23 October 1964), Annex Ⅲ, Text of Certain Provisions of a Draft Agreement on Assistance to and Return of Personnel and Spacecraft, on which Preliminary Agreement was reached by the Informal Working-Party of the Sub-Committee, 23 October 1964, Art. 6.

③ See Historical Background and Context, mn. 59.

④ See UN Doc. A/AC. 105/C. 2/L. 28/Rev. 1, Draft agreement on the rescue of astronauts, the return of astronauts and the return of objects launched into outer space, 14 December 1967, Art. 5.

⑤ See UN Doc. A/AC. 105/C. 2/L. 2, International Agreement on the Rescue of Astronauts and Spaceships making Emergency Landings, USSR Proposal, 6 June 1962, Art. 7.

⑥ UN Doc. A/AC. 105/C. 2/L. 2/Rev. 2, Agreement on the rescue of astronauts and spaceships in the event of accident or emergency landing, USSR Revised Draft, 26 October 1964, Art. 6.

⑦ UN Doc. A/AC. 105/C. 2/L. 9, International Agreement on Assistance to and Return of Astronauts and Objects Launched into Outer Space, United States Proposal, 9 March 1964, Art. 3.

⑧ UN Doc. WG. I/30, Australia and Canada: Proposal, Art. 5, in: UN Doc. A/AC. 105/21, Report of the Legal Sub-Committee on the Work of the Second Part of its Third Session (5-23 October 1964), Annex I, Proposals and Amendments Relating to Assistance to and Return of Astronauts and Space Vehicles, 23 October 1964; similarly, UN Doc. A/AC. 105/C. 2/L. 20, Assistance to and Return of Astronauts and Space Objects, Revised Australian-Canadian proposal submitted as a working paper, 21 June 1967, Art. 6.

空条约》第八条提到了“登记国”。直到在谈判的最后阶段，在 1967 年联合国大会第二十二届会议期间，航天大国之间进行了深入磋商之后，“发射当局的代表”才被列入最后版本①。

从一开始，收回该空间物体的费用就没有争议。美国和苏联在其初稿中都规定了负责发射的国家支付收回和返还的费用的义务②。令人惊讶的是，1964 年的美国草案中竟然没有这样一项义务③。然而，在谈判过程中，补偿收回空间物体的费用通常被视为负责发射的国家的义务。这与各国代表关于营救宇航员的费用的意见形成了鲜明对比，因为营救宇航员的费用被视为人道主义援助，因此通常在国家之间是无偿的。与此相反，人们普遍认为，救援空间物体的费用应由发射当局承担。

（二）评注

第五条涉及空间物体或其组成部分的收回和返还。经过一些修改后，该条款载有与营救和送回航天器人员类似的权利和义务。然而，虽然有关人员的规定分布在《营救协定》的四个条款中，但有关空间物体的规定仅包含在这一条中。

1. 关于空间物体返回地球的通知（第一款）

（1）术语“空间物体或其组成部分”

与该协议的其他条款一样，“空间物体或其组成部分”在《营救协定》中没有定义。

“空间物体”一词已在《外空条约》中使用④，后来被《责任公约》采用，并出现在该公约和《登记公约》的标题中。这两项协议都在一定程度上对该术语进行了定义，明确指出“‘空间物体’一词包括空间物体的组成部分及其运载工具和部件”⑤。

尽管《营救协定》中缺乏对该术语的准确定义，但根据《维也纳公约》第三十

① UN Doc. A/AC. 105/C. 2/L. 28, Draft agreement on the rescue of astronauts, the return of astronauts and the return of objects launched into outer space, 12 December 1967, Art. 5; UN Doc. A/AC. 105/C. 2/L. 28/Rev. 1, Draft agreement on the rescue of astronauts, the return of astronauts and the return of objects launched into outer space, 14 December 1967, Art. 5.

② UN Doc. A/AC. 105/C. 2/L. 2, International Agreement on the Rescue of Astronauts and Spaceships making Emergency Landings, USSR Proposal, 6 June 1962, Art. 8; UN Doc. A/AC. 105/C. 2/L. 3, Assistance and Return of Space Vehicles and Personnel, United States Proposal, 8 June 1962, Principle 3.

③ UN Doc. A/AC. 105/C. 2/L. 9, International Agreement on Assistance to and Return of Astronauts and Objects Launched into Outer Space, United States Proposal, 9 March 1964.

④ Other provisions also speak of ‘objects’ in outer space etc.

⑤ Art. 1 lit. (d) LIAB; Art. 1 lit. (b) REG.

一至三十三条的规定，这一公认的条约解释方法对其进行解释有助于阐明其含义：

“物体”一词的一般含义是一个事物、存在或概念，在给定的上下文中，它是有形的，且在感官的掌握范围内。“空间”一词表明，必须是在外层空间使用的有形物。而且，在《营救协定》的背景下，探索、开发和其他具体利用外层空间、月球和其他天体的目的是决定性的。此外，该术语同时包含“载人”和“无人”的空间物体，这从其在这方面明显缺乏区分可以看出①。

然而，一个物体可以被视为空间物体的时间点的问题仍未得到解决。一些人认为，空间物体的定义应涵盖该物体从在地球上或任何其他地方制造或组装到返回并降落或坠落在地球上的时间②。在这种情况下，有必要牢记《登记公约》并深入审视该任务的属性③。

只有借助《营救协定》的谈判和起草历史，才能在有限的程度上澄清“空间物体”一词的含义。虽然在《营救协定》的整个谈判和起草过程中，几乎没有就“空间物体”的定义提交任何提案，但其中一项包含这一定义的提案后来被纳入了《责任公约》和《登记公约》。

苏联和美国的早期草案中都没有提出“空间物体”的定义，取而代之的是“宇宙飞船”④ 或“太空运载工具”⑤ 一词。后来，双方均在其关于返还的拟议条款中使用

① See Abdurrasyid, Priyatna, Certain Views on the Agreement on Rescue of Astronauts, the Return of Astronauts and the Return of Objects Launched into Outer Space, in: Jasentuliyana, Nandasiri (ed.), Maintaining Outer Space for Peaceful Purposes-Proceedings of a Symposium held in The Hague, March 1984, The United Nations University, Tokyo 1984, p. 100.

② See ibid.

③ See ibid.

④ See UN Doc. A/AC. 105/C. 2/L. 2, International Agreement on the Rescue of Astronauts and Spaceships making Emergency Landings, USSR Proposal, 6 June 1962; UN Doc. A/AC. 105/C. 2/L. 3, Draft Proposal on Assistance to and Return of Space Vehicles and Personnel, United States Proposal, 8 June 1962; UN Doc. A/AC. 105/C. 2/L. 2/Rev. 1, Agreement on the rescue of astronauts and spaceships in the event of accident or emergency landing, USSR Revised Draft, 9 March 1964.

⑤ See UN Doc. A/AC. 105/C. 2/L. 3, Draft Proposal on Assistance to and Return of Space Vehicles and Personnel, USA Proposal, 8 June 1962; and UN Doc. A/AC. 105/C. 2/L. 2/Rev. 1, Agreement on the rescue of astronauts and spaceships in the event of accident or emergency landing, USSR Revised Draft, 9 March 1964.

了“射入外层空间的物体”一词①。而澳大利亚和加拿大的草案文本是唯一包含“定义条款”的，它规定“‘空间物体’是指发射国已发射或试图发射到外层空间的物体或其任何组成部分。”② 然而，这一定义没有得到法律小组委员会的批准。1964 年关于规定返还空间物体的义务的初步协定仅使用了“空间物体或其任何组成部分”一词③，其序言中提到“返还航天器和其他空间物体”④。然而，《营救协定》草案的后续版本不再使用“航天器”一词，取而代之的是“空间物体或其组成部分”一词⑤。这不同于 1963 年《外空宣言》，该宣言在第七项原则中提到“射入外层空间的物体及其组成部分”；《外空条约》延续了这一解释，并在其第八条中提到“射入外层空间的物体，包括降落或建造在天体上的物体及其组成部分”。但是《营救协定》的最终文本没有采用这一解释。

考虑到《营救协定》的目的和宗旨，有人建议对“空间物体”一词的解释应得出这样的结论，即如果一个物体被发射或试图发射到外层空间，那么它将成为一个空

① See UN Doc. A/AC. 105/C. 2/L. 9, International Agreement on Assistance to and Return of Astronauts and Objects Launched into Outer Space, United States Proposal, 9 March 1964, Art. 3 para. 2; see UN Doc. A/AC. 105/C. 2/L. 2/Rev. 2, Agreement on the rescue of astronauts and spaceships in the event of accident or emergency landing, USSR Revised Draft, 26 October 1964, Art. 6.

② UN Doc. WG. I/30, Australia and Canada: Proposal, in: UN Doc. A/AC. 105/21, Report of the Legal Sub-Committee on the Work of the Second Part of its Third Session (5-23 October 1964), Annex I, Proposals and amendments relating to assistance to and return of astronauts and space vehicles, 23 October 1964. This formulation remained unchanged in the revised Australian-Canadian draft of 1967, UN Doc. A/AC. 105/C. 2/L. 20, Assistance to and Return of Astronauts and Space Objects, Revised Australian-Canadian proposal submitted as a working paper, 21 June 1967.

③ UN Doc. A/AC. 105/21, Report of the Legal Sub-Committee on the Work of the Second Part of its Third Session (5-23 October 1964) to the Committee on the Peaceful Uses of Outer Space, Annex Ⅲ, Text of Certain Provisions of a Draft Agreement on Assistance to and Return of Personnel and Spacecraft, on which Preliminary Agreement was Reached by the Informal Working-Party of the Sub-Committee, 23 October 1964, draft Art. 3.

④ Ibid., draft Preamble.

⑤ UN Doc. A/AC. 105/C. 2/L. 28, Draft agreement on the rescue of astronauts, the return of astronauts and the return of objects launched into outer space, 12 December 1967, Art. 5; UN Doc. A/AC. 105/C. 2/L. 28/Rev. 1, Draft agreement on the rescue of astronauts, the return of astronauts and the return of objects launched into outer space, 14 December 1967, Art. 5.

间物体[①]。

（2）“在其管辖的领土内或公海或不受任何国家管辖的地方返回地球”的表述

第一款的通知义务仅适用于在缔约国的领土、公海或不受任何国家管辖的地方返回地球的此类空间物体。由于该条款的内容为“返回地球”，因此显然不包括在外层空间丢失的物体[②]。然而，对于《月球协定》的缔约方，该《协定》的第十二条第二款将其第五条的规定扩展到在月球上预定位置以外的地方发现的运载工具、装置和设备或其组成部分。

依据《营救协定》第五条第一款的通知义务发表在标号为 ST/SG/SER. E 的联合国文件系列中。

2. 空间物体或其组成部分的收回（第二款）

第二款规定，在其境内发现空间物体或其组成部分的缔约方有义务收回该物体或组成部分。然而，缔约方只需采取其认为可行的措施来收回该物体，这就给缔约方留下了相当大的自由裁量权。与《营救协定》第二条关于营救和援助航天器人员的规定不同，第五条不要求缔约方通知联合国秘书长在空间物体收回行动中采取的措施。此外，《营救协定》第五条第二款的义务[③]仅适用于发射当局要求缔约方进行收回的情况，且不应要求缔约方在第二条和第三条要求的范围内调动资源和紧急行事[④]。如果

① See Kopal, Vladimir, Some Remarks on Issues Relating to Legal Definitions of “Space Object”, “Space Debris” and “Astronaut”, in: IISL Proceedings of the 37th Colloquium on the Law of Outer Space, 9-14 October 1994 Jerusalem, (Israel), AIAA, 1995, p. 101; Gorove, Stephen, Definitional Issues Pertaining To “Space Object”, in: IISL Proceedings of the 37th Colloquium on the Law of Outer Space, 9-14 October 1994 Jerusalem (Israel) AIAA, 1995, pp. 90f.; Gorove, Stephen, Toward a Clarification of the Terms “Space Object” -An International Legal and Policy Imperative?, Journal of Space Law (21) 1993, p. 20; the question was also discussed in the context of liability for damages caused by space objects, see Kerrest, Armel/Smith, Lesley Jane, Article Ⅶ, in: Hobe, Stephan/Schmidt-Tedd, Bernhard/Schrogl, Kai-Uwe (eds.), Cologne Commentary on Space Law, Volume I, Heymanns, Cologne 2009, pp. 139f. with further references.

② See Abdurrasyid, Priyatna, Certain Views on the Agreement on Rescue of Astronauts, the Return of Astronauts and the Return of Objects Launched into Outer Space, in: Jasentuliyana, Nandasiri (ed.), Maintaining Outer Space for Peaceful Purposes-Proceedings of a Symposium held in The Hague, March 1984, The United Nations University, Tokyo 1984, p. 100.

③ See Commentary ARRA, Article 6, mn. 195ff.

④ See Dembling, Paul G./Arons, Daniel M., *The Treaty on Rescue and Return of Astronauts and Space Objects*, William and Mary Law Review (9) 1968, p. 654.

缔约方提出要求，发射当局应协助其收回空间物体[①]。发射当局的行动应在缔约方的领导和监督下进行[②]。这是对太空运载工具所降落的国家无法提供必要援助时应遵循的程序进行讨论的结果。虽然美国和苏联似乎同意在这种情况下一个国家必须请求发射国提供援助，但其他代表团强调，每个国家都有权拒绝外国代表进入具有军事重要性或对国家安全至关重要的区域[③]。

3. 返还空间物体或其组成部分并提交证明材料（第三款）

第三款补充了第二款所载的收回的义务，因为该款规定缔约方有义务将空间物体或其组成部分返还发射当局[④]，或由发射当局的代表处置。这项义务适用于在发射当局领土范围以外发现的此类物体，而无论这些物体是在缔约方领土内还是在任何国家管辖范围以外的地方发现的。

这一义务还以发射当局的请求为条件。如果缔约方提出要求，发射当局的代表必须在返还空间物体或其组成部分之前提供证明材料。《营救协定》中没有定义应由发射当局提供的证明材料的属性和特征。该术语的一般含义意味着它必须是毫无疑问能够识别该物体的数据。尽管与《营救协定》的目的和宗旨不同，“证明材料”可以是根据《外空条约》第十一条和（或）《登记公约》第四条必须提交给联合国秘书长的材料。《外空条约》第十一条和《登记公约》制定了识别在轨空间物体的规则，但《营救协定》第五条的目的是在该物体坠落到地球上后将其返还。然而，根据《登记公约》第四条提供的一些信息可被用于在《营救协定》第五条所规定的范围内进行识别，例如，空间物体的一般功能及其标志或注册号。尽管可用于识别空间物体的轨道参数并不总是与《营救协定》的目的相关，无论如何，除了根据《登记公约》第四条的规定提交的数据外，还需要其他资料来证明发射当局的身份。

---

① At the request of the Swedish delegation as well as others, a formulation was chosen that provided the Contracting Party with the option of obtaining assistance from the launching authority in the recovery operation; see also Dembling, Paul G./Arons, Daniel M., *The Treaty on Rescue and Return of Astronauts and Space Objects*, William and Mary Law Review (9) 1968, p. 654.

② See ibid., p. 655.

③ See Historical Background and Context, mn. 37.

④ See Commentary ARRA, Article 6, mn. 195ff.

4. 通知空间物体或其组成部件的危险或有害性，并消除可能造成损害的危险（第四款）

如果缔约方有理由相信在其管辖领土内发现的或在其他地方收回的空间物体或其组成部分具有危险性或有害性，则第四款允许其免除第二款和第三款所规定的收回和返还空间物体及其组成部分的义务。在这种情况下，缔约方可通知发射当局，发射当局应在该缔约方的领导和监督下立即采取有效措施，以消除可能造成损害的危险。

《营救协定》没有定义术语“危害的”或“有害的”。这些术语的通常被定义为：“有风险的；有危险的”①，以及“（1）有毒的（有害毒素）。（2）不健康的；对心理或身体有害的（有害影响）”②。国际法委员会在关于预防危险活动的跨界损害的条款草案中没有定义“危害的”一词，而是提出“造成重大跨界损害的风险”的活动，这些活动会对人类健康、工业、财产、环境、农业等产生实实在在的有害影响③。

发射当局需要采取的措施取决于该物体的属性。发射当局可能需要受过培训的人员将该物体从缔约方领土上移走，或使其免受烟火或有毒燃料的损害④。

缔约方请求发射当局协助的权利取决于对该空间物体的占有，而无论该物体首先降落在何处。缔约方可能在本国领土上发现该物体，或在另一国领土、公海或任何国家管辖范围以外的其他地方发现该物体。在后一种情况下，发射当局将有义务使该物体无害化，但不一定受缔约方的领导和监督。根据《外空条约》第八条，发射当局仍然是该空间物体的所有人，即使另一国的代表可能占有该空间物体⑤。

5. 费用（第五款）

第五款规定，为履行第二款和第三款规定的收回和返还空间物体或其组成部分的义务而发生的费用应由发射当局承担。

---

① Garner, Bryan A. (ed.), Black's Law Dictionary, 9th edn., West, St. Paul 2009, at 'hazardous', p. 618.

② Garner, Bryan A. (ed.), Black's Law Dictionary, 9th edn., West, St. Paul 2009, at 'deleterious', p. 386.

③ For the text of the ILC Articles on Prevention of transboundary harm from hazardous activities see UNGA Res. 62/68, Consideration of prevention of transboundary harm from hazardous activities and allocation of loss in the case of such harm, Annex, 6 December 2007. The ILC's commentary to the articles is contained in UN Doc. A/56/10, Report of the International Law Commission on the work of its fifty-third session (23 April-1 June and 2 July-10 August 2001), Official Records of the General Assembly, Fifty-Sixth Session, Supplement No. 10, New York and Geneva 2007.

④ See Dembling, Paul G./Arons, Daniel M., *The Treaty on Rescue and Return of Astronauts and Space Objects*, William and Mary Law Review (9) 1968, p. 656.

⑤ See ibid., pp. 656-657.

1978 年发生的宇宙-954 号事件[①]是适用《营救协定》第五条第五款的首个重要实践案例。另一个案例是 1996 年德国快车号（EXPRESS）科学返回舱的意外降落，该舱原计划在澳大利亚着陆，但最终落在了加纳[②]。从加纳收回并返还德国的工作最终是在两国政府的一致意见下进行的，并没有出现任何问题。而宇宙-954 号事件，由于卫星上有核动力源，引发了起草 1992 年《联合国关于在外层空间使用核动力源的原则》的规则（特别是第九项原则）[③]。

鉴于现行的公海上的搜救传统，有关营救和送回宇航员的费用没有进行规定[④]。同样，在海商法中，1910 年《布鲁塞尔公约》只规定了抢救出的财产的费用补偿，但对营救这些人员也没有类似规定[⑤]。这一区分可以用这些文件的人道主义性质来解释，这一点在《营救协定》序言的第四段中加以明确，它表示《营救协定》“由人道主义情感推动”。这与根据《外空条约》第五条的规定[⑥]，将宇航员视为“人类在外层空间的使者”，进而《营救协定》没有规定有关营救航天器人员的费用条款是相一致的。然而，与营救宇航员不同，收回和返还空间物体主要是为了发射当局的利益，因此，此类行动产生的费用应由发射当局承担[⑦]。

如上所述，在《营救协定》谈判和起草的历史中采纳了这一解释，列入了一项关于偿还收回和返还空间物体相关费用的规定，但其中不包括航天器人员的费用[⑧]。

---

① See Commentary ARRA, Article 2, mn. 144.

② The governments of Germany and Australia concluded a specific agreement that pertained to the landing and recovery of the EXPRESS capsule. See Australia and Germany-Agreement Concerning the Landing and Recovery of a Space Capsule in Australia (entered into force 4 January 1995) 1889 UNTS 219; and Autorenkollektiv, Express-Raumkapsel gefunden, Flieger Revue (44) 1996.

③ Principle 9 reads: “For the purpose of this principle, compensation shall include reimbursement of the duly substantiated expenses for search, recovery and clean-up operations, including expenses for assistance received from third parties”, see UNGA Res. 47/68, Principles Relevant to the Use of Nuclear Power Sources in Outer Space, 14 December 1992.

④ See with further reference van Bogaert, Eric R. C., Aspects of Space Law, Kluwer, Deventer 1986, p. 108.

⑤ See Kopal, Vladimir, The Agreement on Rescue of Astronauts and Return of Space Objects, in: McWhinney, Edward/Bradley, Martin A., New Frontiers in Space Law, Sijthoff, Leyden 1969, p. 106.

⑥ See ibid., pp. 119, 122; Diederiks-Verschoor, I. H. Philepina/Kopal, Vladimir, An Introduction to Space Law, 3rd rev. edn. Kluwer Law International, The Netherlands 2008, p. 33.

⑦ See Kopal, Vladimir, The Agreement on Rescue of Astronauts and Return of Space Objects, in: McWhinney, Edward/Bradley, Martin A., New Frontiers in Space Law, Sijthoff, Leyden 1969, pp. 119, 122.

⑧ See Historical Background and Context, mn. 36.

七、第六条　发射当局

本协定称“发射当局”是指负有发射责任的国家或指负有发射责任的政府间国际组织，但该组织必须宣布接受本协定所规定的权利与义务，且该组织的多数会员国为本协定及关于各国探测及使用外空包括月球与其他天体之活动所应遵守原则的条约的缔约国。

（一）谈判和起草历史

《营救协定》的各个草案在宇航员和空间物体应返还至哪个主体上存在着很大的分歧。最终采用“发射当局”的表述是在谈判的后期阶段才出现的。直到 1967 年秋，两个航天大国才试图在双边谈判中就一些悬而未决的问题达成妥协[①]。在此之前，苏联在其草案中一直使用的是“发射国”[②]；美国曾采用“负责发射的一个或多个国家或国际组织”[③]，后来又使用“负责发射的登记国或国际组织”[④]。1964 年和 1967 年的

① See Cheng, Bin, *The* 1968 *Astronauts Agreement or How Not to make a Treaty*, The Yearbook of World Affairs (23) 1969, pp. 185-208.

② See UN Doc. A/AC. 105/C. 2/L. 2, International Agreement on the Rescue of Astronauts and Spaceships making Emergency Landings, USSR Proposal, 6 June 1962; UN Doc. A/AC. 105/C. 2/L. 3, Draft Proposal on Assistance to and Return of Space Vehicles and Personnel, United States Proposal, 8 June 1962; UN Doc. A/AC. 105/C. 2/L. 2/Rev. 2, Agreement on the rescue of astronauts and spaceships in the event of accident or emergency landing, USSR Revised Draft, 26 October 1964.

③ See Principle 2 and 3 of the United States proposal for a General Assembly resolution: UN Doc. A/AC. 105/C. 2/L. 3, Draft Proposal on Assistance to and Return of Space Vehicles and Personnel, United States Proposal, 8 June 1962.

④ See UN Doc. A/AC. 105/C. 2/L. 9, International Agreement on Assistance to and Return of Astronauts and Objects Launched into Outer Space, United States Proposal, 9 March 1964, Art. 3; see also UN Doc. WG. I/27, United States' proposed modification of Art. 4, Australian-Canadian Draft Agreement on Assistance and Return, in: UN Doc. A/AC. 105/21, Report of the Legal Sub-Committee on the Work of the Second Part of its Third Session (5-23 October 1964), Annex I, Proposals and Amendments Relating to Assistance to and Return of Astronauts and Space Vehicles, 23 October 1964, p. 7.

澳大利亚和加拿大草案采用的是“发射国”①。

相反，1963年的《外空宣言》提到了登记国。它在第七项原则中规定，射入外层空间的物体“或其组成部分在登记国范围以外发现的应归还该国”；第九项原则规定，紧急降落的宇航员应安全迅速地送回“其航天器的登记国”。《外空条约》在有关援助和返还的条款中也使用了登记国。根据《外空条约》第五条的规定，宇航员应安全、迅速地“送回其航天器的登记国”。《外空条约》第八条规定，如果这类物体或其组成部分在“其所登记的缔约国”境外发现的，应返还给该缔约国。

在谈判期间，空间物体或宇航员应返还的实体是一个重要而有争议的问题②。虽然美国和其他大多数西方国家赞成将从事空间活动的国际组织与国家同等对待，但苏联和东欧国家出于政治和司法原因拒绝了这一想法③。他们反对将国际组织包括在内，理由是这些组织并不拥有领土，因此不具有适用《营救协定》第一条的所载义务的适格条件④。这一主张背后的政治动机是，他们认为，欧洲运载火箭发展组织（ELDO，欧洲航天局的前身之一，是支持北约的一个政治实体）是这一条款的潜在第一受益人。另一方面，许多国家表示，它们只能通过国际组织参与空间活动⑤。

最终，在谈判的最后阶段，苏联同意了英国关于国际组织的提议⑥。因此，找到了一种折衷办法，即如果该国际组织的大多数成员国都批准了《营救协定》和《外空

① UN Doc. WG. I/30, Australia and Canada: Proposal, in: UN Doc. A/AC. 105/21, Report of the Legal Sub-Committee on the Work of the Second Part of its Third Session (5-23 October 1964), Annex I, Proposals and Amendments Relating to Assistance to and Return of Astronauts and Space Vehicles, 23 October 1964, pp. 8-12; and UN Doc. A/AC. 105/C. 2/L. 20, Assistance to and Return of Astronauts and Space Objects, Revised Australian-Canadian proposal submitted as a working paper, 21 June 1967.

② See already Historical Background and Context, mn. 16.

③ See Cheng, Bin, Le Traité de 1967 sur l'espace, Journal du Droit International (95) 1968, pp. 588-598; Cheng, Bin, *The* 1968 *Astronauts Agreement or How Not to make a Treaty*, The Yearbook of World Affairs (23) 1969, p. 191; van Bogaert, Eric R. C., Aspects of Space Law, Kluwer, Deventer 1986, p. 106; Hall, Cargil, *Rescue and Return of Astronauts on Earth and in Outer Space*, American Journal of International Law (63) 1969, pp. 129f.

④ See van Bogaert, Eric R. C., Aspects of Space Law, Kluwer, Deventer 1986, p. 106.

⑤ See Cheng, Bin, The 1968 Astronauts Agreement or How not to make a Treaty, The Yearbook of World Affairs (23) 1969, p. 191.

⑥ UN Doc. A/AC. 105/C. 2/SR. 86, Legal Sub-Committee, Special Session, Summary Record of the Eighty-Sixth Meeting, held 14 December 1967, 9 February 1968, p. 13; supported by France, ibid., p. 13; Canada, ibid., p. 18; Sweden, ibid., pp. 19-20.

条约》，则该国际组织就可以接受《营救协定》中规定的权利和义务①。从而，《营救协定》第六条中采用“发射当局”这一术语及其定义，与其他条约中的发射国的概念和地位形成了鲜明对比②。

（二）评注

第六条表达了在本条款的艰难谈判中最终达成的妥协。它包含了《营救协定》中仅有的一个定义，即“发射当局”。《营救协定》使用“发射当局”一词，而不是如《责任公约》第一条第三款和《登记公约》第一条第一款所使用的“发射国”的概念。与《责任公约》中所使用的术语一样，“发射当局”一词指的是发射国，但在某些情况下也包括国际组织。在起草《营救协定》的谈判中，将国际组织纳入《营救协定》的范围困难重重③。

“发射当局”一词包括国际组织，前提是它们宣布接受《营救协定》的权利和义务，并且其大多数成员国同时是《营救协定》和《外空条约》的缔约方。第六条是《外空条约》第六条和第十三条的延伸，该条为国际组织开展空间活动提供了规范④。《外空条约》第六条规定，当此类活动由国际组织进行时，“遵守条约的责任应由国际组织和参与该组织的条约缔约国共同承担”。第十三条规定，《外空条约》适用于各国在政府间国际组织框架内开展空间活动的情况，任何实际问题都应与适当的国际组织或该国际组织的一个或多个成员国共同解决。随后，《责任公约》第二十二条⑤和《登记公约》第七条⑥进一步明确了国际组织的地位，详细地规定了其接受权利和义务的声明。

值得注意的是，国际组织并不能成为缔约方，而只能声明“接受本协定所规定的

---

① UN Doc. A/AC. 105/C. 2/L. 28, Draft agreement on the rescue of astronauts, the return of astronauts and the return of objects launched into outer space, 12 December 1967; and UN Doc. A/AC. 105/C. 2/L. 28/Rev. 1, Draft agreement on the rescue of astronauts, the return of astronauts and the return of objects launched into outer space, 14 December 1967.

② See Cheng, Bin, The 1968 Astronauts Agreement or How not to make a Treaty, The Yearbook of World Affairs (23) 1969, p. 202.

③ See van Bogaert, Eric R. C., Aspects of Space Law, Kluwer, Deventer 1986, p. 106.

④ See Christol, Carl Q., The Modern International Law of Outer Space, Pergamon Press, New York 1982, p. 201.

⑤ See chapter on LIAB in this volume, Commentary LIAB, Article XXII, mn. 377ff.

⑥ See chapter on REG in this volume, Commentary REG, Article Ⅶ, mn. 243ff.

权利和义务”。据此有人由此得出结论说，其权利和义务仅限于发射当局的权利和义务[①]。因此，国际组织有义务协助安全返还空间物体，而缔约方则同时有通知和援助航天器人员的义务[②]。相反地，另一些人指出《营救协定》首次承认了国际组织本身可以接受《营救协议》所规定的权利和义务[③]。通过其接受的声明，国际组织将有权主张所有权利，并有履行《营救协定》所规定的所有义务，但与个别国家的领土基础及其作为《营救协定》缔约方的地位有关的义务除外[④]。这意味着承认这些国际组织有能力使其作出的声明对自己具有约束力，并可能影响国际组织在其他协议中的地位[⑤]。

反对者认为，由于《营救协定》中的大多数义务只能由拥有领土的主体（即国家）履行，国际组织将免除所有此类义务，并且有鉴于“大多数”该组织的成员必须同时是《营救协定》和《外空条约》的缔约方，那么所有非成员虽然不是《营救协定》的缔约方并受其约束，却将从《营救协定》中受益。然而，这一反对意见在这里并不完全适用，因为《营救协定》不具有双务属性，但正如序言所说，它是由“人道主义的情感”推动的，各方相互承诺帮助营救和收回航天器的人员和空间物体，而无论发射当局是否处于条约缔约方的领土内[⑥]。

接受国际组织作为发射当局是空间法的一项重要创新，新的国际法律主体能够在未来的空间活动中发挥重要作用[⑦]。

发射当局可以要求在外国领土上发现空间物体或其组成部分时予以归还（第三至五条）。如果发射当局的援助将有助于迅速实施救援，或将极大地有助于搜救行动的有效实施，那么发射当局还应与该缔约方合作（第二条）。

---

① See Cheng, Bin, The 1968 Astronauts Agreement or How not to make a Treaty, The Yearbook of World Affairs (23) 1969, p. 204.

② See van Bogaert, Eric R. C. , Aspects of Space Law, Kluwer, Deventer 1986, p. 107.

③ See Houben, Piet-Hein, A New Chapter of Space Law: The Agreement on the Rescue and Return of Astronauts and Space Objects, Netherlands International Law Review (15) 1968, p. 201.

④ See Kopal, Vladimir, The Agreement on Rescue of Astronauts and Return of Space Objects, in: McWhinney, Edward/Bradley, Martin A. , New Frontiers in Space Law, Sijthoff, Leyden 1969, p. 123.

⑤ See Houben, Piet-Hein, A New Chapter of Space Law: The Agreement on the Rescue and Return of Astronauts and Space Objects, Netherlands International Law Review (15) 1968, p. 131.

⑥ See Cheng, Bin, The 1968 Astronauts Agreement or How not to make a Treaty, The Yearbook of World Affairs (23) 1969, p. 204.

⑦ See van Bogaert, Eric R. C. , Aspects of Space Law, Kluwer, Deventer 1986, p. 107.

迄今为止，欧洲气象卫星应用组织（EUMETSAT）和欧洲航天局这两个国际组织已在第六条的规定下宣布接受《营救协定》规定的权利和义务①。这些组织还就其接受《责任公约》和《登记公约》的权利和义务发表了声明②。

八、第七条　签署、批准、加入和生效

一、本协定应开放供所有国家签署。凡在本协定依照本条第三项发生效力前尚未签署的任何国家可随时加入本协定。

二、本协定须经签署国批准，批准书及加入书应送交美利坚合众国、大不列颠及北爱尔兰联合王国及苏维埃社会主义共和国联盟政府存放，该三国政府为指定各保存政府。

三、本协定应于包括指定为保存政府的三国政府在内的五国政府，交存批准书后发生效力。

四、对于在本协定发生效力后交存批准书或加入书的国家，本协定应于其交存批准书或加入书之日起生效。

五、保存政府应将每一签署的日期，每一份批准书及加入书的交存日期，本协定发生效力日期及其他通知事项，迅速告知所有签署及加入国家。

六、本协定应由保存政府遵照《联合国宪章》第一百零二条规定办理登记。

（一）谈判和起草历史

自谈判开始以来，对于有可能成为协议授权签署方的国家、交存方和《营救协定》生效所需的批准数量存在意见分歧。苏联提议，《营救协定》应开放给世界上

① UN Doc. A/AC. 105/C. 2/2018/CRP. 3, Status of International Agreements relating to activities in outer space as at 1 January 2018, 9 April 2019 with regular updates published on http://www.unoosa.org/documents/pdf/spacelaw/treatystatus/AC105_ C2_ 2018_ CRP03E. pdf.

② Ibid.

"所有国家"① 加入。另一方面，美国建议《营救协定》应开放供"联合国成员国或任何专门机构或《国际法院规约》的缔约方，以及联合国大会邀请成为缔约国的任何其他国"②。这一做法将减少"联合国大家庭"的成员，特别是将排除德意志民主共和国③。1967年底，两个航天大国进行了双边审议，最终文本规定，《营救协定》应向"所有国家"开放④。

关于协定生效所需的批准数量，苏联最初提议为15份⑤，随后改为仅需要2份⑥，最后提议5份，包括指定为交存国政府的批准⑦。美国的草案表示，只需要2份批准书就足够了⑧。这些分歧在双边谈判中得到了解决，随后达成了需要五个国家批准的一致意见，包括三个交存国政府，即美国、英国和苏联的批准⑨。

---

① UN Doc. A/AC. 105/C. 2/L. 2, International Agreement on the Rescue of Astronauts and Spaceships mak-ing Emergency Landings, USSR Proposal, 6 June 1962, Art. 9; UN Doc. A/AC. 105/C. 2/L. 2/Rev. 1, Agreement on the rescue of astronauts and spaceships in the event of accident or emergency landing, USSR Revised Draft, 9 March 1964, Art. 12; UN Doc. A/AC. 105/C. 2/L. 2/Rev. 2, Agreement on the rescue of astronauts and spaceships in the event of accident or emergency landing, USSR Revised Draft, 26 October 1964, Art. 7; UN Doc. A/AC. 105/C. 2/L. 18, Agreement On The Rescue Of Astronauts In The Event Of Accident Or Emergency Landing, USSR Revised Draft, 19 June 1967.

② UN Doc. A/AC. 105/C. 2/L. 9, International Agreement on Assistance to and Return of Astronauts and Objects Launched into Outer Space, United States Proposal, 9 March 1964, Art. 7.

③ See Cheng, Bin, The 1968 Astronauts Agreement or How not to make a Treaty, The Yearbook of World Affairs (23) 1969, p. 191.

④ UN Doc. A/AC. 105/C. 2/L. 28, Draft agreement on the rescue of astronauts, the return of astronauts and the return of objects launched into outer space, 12 December 1967; and UN Doc. A/AC. 105/C. 2/L. 28/Rev. 1, Draft agreement on the rescue of astronauts, the return of astronauts and the return of objects launched into outer space, 14 December 1967.

⑤ See UN Doc. A/AC. 105/C. 2/L. 2/Rev. 1, Agreement on the rescue of astronauts and spaceships in the event of accident or emergency landing, USSR Revised Draft, 9 March 1964, Art. 13.

⑥ See UN Doc. A/AC. 105/C. 2/L. 2/Rev. 2, Agreement on the rescue of astronauts and spaceships in the event of accident or emergency landing, USSR Revised Draft, 26 October 1964, Art. 9.

⑦ See UN Doc. A/AC. 105/C. 2/L. 18, Agreement On The Rescue Of Astronauts In The Event Of Accident Or Emergency Landing, USSR Revised Draft, 19 June 1967, Art. 6.

⑧ See UN Doc. A/AC. 105/C. 2/L. 9, International Agreement on Assistance to and Return of Astronauts and Objects Launched into Outer Space, United States Proposal, 9 March 1964, Art. 9.

⑨ See UN Doc. A/AC. 105/C. 2/L. 28, Draft agreement on the rescue of astronauts, the return of astronauts and the return of objects launched into outer space, 12 December 1967, Art. 7; and UN Doc. A/AC. 105/C. 2/L. 28/Rev. 1, Draft agreement on the rescue of astronauts, the return of astronauts and the return of objects launched into outer space, 14 December 1967, Art. 7.

指定交存方也是各草案和谈判的主题。美国提议交存方应是联合国秘书长①。苏联最初也提议联合国秘书长②。然而，在一份修订草案中，它提出了由苏联和美国政府作为交存方的建议③。随后苏联的一项提案提到了“交存方政府”，但对候选国名单持开放态度④。1967年底双边谈判后达成的妥协是，应该有交存方政府，但这些政府不应该仅仅是苏联和美国，还应包括英国⑤。

（二）评注

《营救协定》仅对国家开放签署。各国可以随时加入（第七条第一款）。《营救协定》须经签署国批准，并由苏联、英国和美国政府作为交存国政府（第七条第二款）。《营救协定》由五个国家的政府批准交存后生效（第7条第三款）。《营救协定》于1968年4月22日开放签署，当时在华盛顿有43个国家的代表签署，莫斯科有25个，伦敦有24个；其中一些代表在所有的三个城市分别进行了签署，一些代表仅在两个城市进行了签署⑥。《营救协定》于1968年12月3日在第五份批准文件交存后生效。对于此后加入《营救协定》的每个国家，《营救协定》于其交存批准书或加入书之日起生效（第七条第四款）。交存国政府根据第七条第五款有义务将每一签署的日期、每一批准书或加入书的交存日期、其生效日期和其他事项，立即通知所有签署国和加入国。《营救协定》的登记依据《联合国宪章》第一百零二条（第七条第六款）。

第三方国家不受《营救协定》的约束⑦。这一具体规定超出了1963年《外空宣

---

① See UN Doc. A/AC. 105/C. 2/L. 9, International Agreement on Assistance to and Return of Astronauts and Objects Launched into Outer Space, United States Proposal, 9 March 1964, Art. 8.

② See UN Doc. A/AC. 105/C. 2/L. 2/Rev. 1, Agreement on the rescue of astronauts and spaceships in the event of accident or emergency landing, USSR Revised Draft, 9 March 1964, Art. 11.

③ See UN Doc. A/AC. 105/C. 2/L. 2/Rev. 2, Agreement on the rescue of astronauts and spaceships in the event of accident or emergency landing, USSR Revised Draft, 26 October 1964, Art. 8.

④ See UN Doc. A/AC. 105/C. 2/L. 18, Agreement On The Rescue Of Astronauts In The Event Of Accident Or Emergency Landing, USSR Revised Draft, 19 June 1967, Art. 6.

⑤ See UN Doc. A/AC. 105/C. 2/L. 28, Draft agreement on the rescue of astronauts, the return of astronauts and the return of objects launched into outer space, 12 December 1967, Art. 7; and UN Doc. A/AC. 105/C. 2/L. 28/Rev. 1, Draft agreement on the rescue of astronauts, the return of astronauts and the return of objects launched into outer space, 14 December 1967, Art. 7.

⑥ See Kopal, Vladimir, The 1968 Rescue Agreement-History of Negotiations and their Outcome, in: -Lafferranderie, Gabriel/Marchisio, Sergio (eds.), The Astronauts and Rescue Agreement-Lessons Learned, The European Centre for Space Law, Paris 2011, p. 109.

⑦ See Gál, Gyula, Observations on the Rescue Agreement, in: Jasentuliyana, Nandasiri (ed.), Maintaining Outer Space for Peaceful Purposes, The United Nations University, Tokyo 1984, p. 98.

言》第七和第九项原则所规定的一般义务，不构成习惯国际法，因为这不能被视为是建立习惯国际法规则所必需的法律确信（opinio iuris）。

国际组织不能成为《营救协定》的签署方，但是它们可以根据第六条宣布接受《营救协定》的权利和义务①。

除了两个国际组织宣布接受《营救协定》的权利和义务外②，《营救协定》已被 96 个国家批准，并有 23 个国家签署③。

九、第八条　提出修正

本协定任何缔约国可对本协定提出修正案。修正案应自本条约多数缔约国接受之日起，对接受修正案的各缔约国生效。嗣后对于其余各缔约国应于其接受之日起生效。

（一）谈判和起草历史

美国在 1964 年的草案中提议，《营救协定》的任何缔约方均可对其提出修正，这些修正案应“对接受修正案的每一缔约方来说，修正案在多数缔约方接受后生效；此后，对其余缔约方来说，自其接受之日起生效”④。苏联在其初稿中没有包括任何关于修正案的规定。然而，在其后来的 1967 年草案中，它提议《营救协定》的每一缔约方都应当可以提出修正，并且这些修正案应得到大多数缔约国的接受⑤。这一提法与

① See Commentary ARRA, Article 6, mn. 200ff.

② See ibid.

③ UN Doc. A/AC. 105/C. 2/2018/CRP. 3, Status of International Agreements relating to activities in outer space as at 1 January 2018, 9 April 2019 with regular updates published on http://www. unoosa. org/documents/pdf/spacelaw/treatystatus/AC105_ C2_ 2018_ CRP03E. pdf.

④ UN Doc. A/AC. 105/C. 2/L. 9, International Agreement on Assistance to and Return of Astronauts and Objects Launched into Outer Space, United States Proposal, 9 March 1964, Art. 5.

⑤ See UN Doc. A/AC. 105/C. 2/L. 18, Agreement On The Rescue Of Astronauts In The Event Of Accident Or Emergency Landing, USSR Revised Draft, 19 June 1967, Art. 6.

美国的提案几乎相同，这使得在草案的最后版本中列入该条款成为可能①。

（二）评注

《营救协定》的任何缔约国均可提出对《营救协定》的修正（第八条）。修正案在多数缔约国接受后，对接受修正案的每个国家生效；并对其余缔约国，在其接受之日生效。

十、第九条和第十条　最后的条款

第九条

本协定任何缔约国在本协定生效一年后书面通知保存政府退出协定。退出应自接到通知之日起一年后发生效力。

第十条

本协定应存放保存政府档库，其英文、俄文、法文、西班牙文及中文五种文本具有同等法律效力。保存政府应将本协定正式核正的副本分送各签署及加入国政府。

为此，下列经正式授权代表在本条约签字，以昭信守。

本条约一式三份，于公历 1968 年 4 月 22 日订于华盛顿、伦敦及莫斯科。

（一）谈判和起草历史

1. 第九条　退出

美国在其 1964 年草案中提议，协定一方可在协定生效两年后，以书面形式通知联合国秘书长退出协定，退出将自秘书长收到通知之日起一年后生效②。另一方面，

---

① UN Doc. A/AC. 105/C. 2/L. 28, Draft agreement on the rescue of astronauts, the return of astronauts and the return of objects launched into outer space, 12 December 1967, Art. 8; UN Doc. A/AC. 105/C. 2/L. 28/Rev. 1, Draft agreement on the rescue of astronauts, the return of astronauts and the return of objects launched into outer space, 14 December 1967.

② UN Doc. A/AC. 105/C. 2/L. 9, International Agreement on Assistance to and Return of Astronauts and Objects Launched into Outer Space, United States Proposal, 9 March 1964, Art. 6.

苏联在其草案中没有包括任何关于退出的规定。然而，这并不妨碍将退出协定的权利列入草案的最终版本①。与美国草案中的两年期限不同的是，最终版版规定在协定生效后的一年即可退出。

2. 第十条 官方语言和《营救协定》的交存

美国在其第一份草案中提议，《营救协定》的官方语言应为中文、英文、法文、俄文和西班牙文②。苏联仅在后期 1967 年提出的一项提案中提到了官方语言，并做了相同规定③。这为在草案的最后版本中列入这一条款铺平了道路④。

关于交存方的义务，美国草案建议联合国秘书长应向所有签署方送交核证副本⑤。苏联的草案指定交存国政府向签署国和加入国送交经正式核证的协定副本⑥。最终的案文取自苏联的草案，并加入了法律小组委员会讨论和批准的最后案文⑦。

（二）评注

第九条和第十条包含关于退出的技术规定以及协定的官方语言。《营救协定》没有规定任何争端解决问题，尤其是它没有提到国际法院解决争端的问题⑧。

---

① UN Doc. A/AC. 105/C. 2/L. 28, Draft agreement on the rescue of astronauts, the return of astronauts and the return of objects launched into outer space, 12 December 1967, Art. 9; and UN Doc. A/AC. 105/C. 2/L. 28/Rev. 1, Draft agreement on the rescue of astronauts, the return of astronauts and the return of objects launched into outer space, 14 December 1967.

② UN Doc. A/AC. 105/C. 2/L. 9, International Agreement on Assistance to and Return of Astronauts and Objects Launched into Outer Space, United States Proposal, 9 March 1964, Art. 11.

③ UN Doc. A/AC. 105/C. 2/L. 18, Agreement On The Rescue Of Astronauts In The Event Of Accident Or Emergency Landing, USSR Revised Draft, 19 June 1967, Art. 8.

④ UN Doc. A/AC. 105/C. 2/L. 28, Draft agreement on the rescue of astronauts, the return of astronauts and the return of objects launched into outer space, 12 December 1967, Art. 10; and UN Doc. A/AC. 105/C. 2/L. 28/Rev. 1, Draft agreement on the rescue of astronauts, the return of astronauts and the return of objects launched into outer space, 14 December 1967.

⑤ UN Doc. A/AC. 105/C. 2/L. 9, International Agreement on Assistance to and Return of Astronauts and Objects Launched into Outer Space, United States Proposal, 9 March 1964, Art. 11.

⑥ UN Doc. A/AC. 105/C. 2/L. 18, Agreement On The Rescue Of Astronauts In The Event Of Accident Or Emergency Landing, USSR Revised Draft, 19 June 1967, Art. 8.

⑦ UN Doc. A/AC. 105/C. 2/L. 28, Draft agreement on the rescue of astronauts, the return of astronauts and the return of objects launched into outer space, 12 December 1967, Art. 10; and UN Doc. A/AC. 105/C. 2/L. 28/Rev. 1, Draft agreement on the rescue of astronauts, the return of astronauts and the return of objects launched into outer space, 14 December 1967.

⑧ See Cheng, Bin, The 1968 Astronauts Agreement or How not to make a Treaty, The Yearbook of World Affairs (23) 1969, p. 191.

1. 第九条　退出

各国可以书面通知退出《营救协定》。退出通知只能在《营救协定》生效后的一年发出，退出在交存国政府收到通知后的一年生效（第九条）。到本卷出版时为止，还没有收到任何退出的通知。

2. 第十条　官方语言和《协定》的交存

《营救协议》的中文、英文、法文、俄文和西班牙文具有同等效力。均由交存国政府存档。交存国政府必须向签署国和加入国政府提供经核证的协定副本（第十条）。

第三章　前景展望

《营救协定》的两大要素——航天器人员的营救和送回，以及空间物体的收回和返还，都有各自的未来前景。

一、送回宇航员

随着商业和私营载人航天（太空旅游）的出现，宇航员的送回问题变得越来越重要。

然而，“太空游客”或“航天飞行参与者”最终是否可以包含在“航天器人员”的定义中，仍有待解决。如前所述，该术语的一般含义、起草历史和背景有利于将其视为在外层空间的自然人的一个单独类别①。他们越来越多地参与外层空间活动，这可能使得为这类参与者量身定制的国际公共法律条款不仅可行，而且必要。

此外，私人更多地参与太空飞行不仅会引起国际公法问题，还会引起合同法的问题，例如，若发生事故、遇险、紧急情况或意外着陆并造成损害的，谁将承担相关费用等问题。这也提出了这样一个问题：此类私人航天飞行的商业运营商是否也需要建设救援设施。

二、空间物体的返还

每年都有数吨物质落到地球上，其中大部分都是很小的碎片。无论发射到轨道上的空间活动怎样保持稳定，或是在数量和质量上都有增长，这类情况都将持续下去，因为围绕地球轨道的大量空间碎片，其中的少量碎片不断进入大气层。在极少数的情

① See Commentary ARRA, Article 1, mn. 102ff.

况下，空间碎片会无法完全燃烧，进而其较大的部分进入地球。这些碎片可以重达数百公斤。俄罗斯和平号空间站就是这样一个例子，此外，美国于 1991 年发射的高层大气研究卫星（UARS），于 2011 年在未知地点部分解体坠落。

此外，2007 年由联合国外空委批准的《空间碎片缓减指南》① 预计空间物体将在其寿命结束时主动脱离轨道，这也可能引发撞击地面的额外情况，尽管我们的想法是，尽可能地使这些物体的组成部分在大气中燃烧殆尽。发现较大的组件并向联合国秘书长报告的罕见事件的规定载于联合国系列文件编号：ST/SG/SER. E. 。

将空间物体（及其组成部分）送回地球也与此类空间物体造成的损害的赔偿责任有关。然而，这将适用《责任公约》的有关规定②。从现实的角度来看，考虑到空间物体返回地球的影响（以及《责任公约》所载之后果）及其作为空间碎片的影响，最终目标应该是找到一种解决方法，以最大限度地减少从空间返回任何组件或相当重量的危险物。对于需要返回空间物体的情况，例如载人航天任务中的返回舱，或未来用于紧急着陆的可重复使用运载火箭，以及空间实验，《营救协定》的规定似乎足以保障此类空间物体的收回和返还。

① UNGA Res 62/217, International cooperation in the peaceful uses of outer space, 22 December 2007, 1 February 2008.

② For a commentary on the LIAB, see chapter on the LIAB in this Volume.

1972年《空间物体所造成损害的国际责任公约》

Lesley Jane Smith, Armel Kerrest and Fabio Tronchetti

《责任公约》文本

本公约当事国，

确认在推进为了和平目的探索和利用外层空间的全人类共同利益，

回顾了《关于各国探索和利用包括月球与其他天体在内外层空间活动原则的条约》，

考虑到从事发射空间物体的国家和政府间国际组织虽将采取预防性措施，但仍存在空间物体可能造成损害的情形，

确认需要详细制定关于空间物体造成损害赔偿责任的有效的国际规则和程序，特别需要确保此类损害的受害人按本公约规定尽速得到充分公正的赔偿，

深信确立这些规则与程序，有助于强化为和平目的探索和利用外层空间方面的国际合作，

兹议定条款如下：

第一条

就适用本公约而言：

1. “损害”，是指生命丧失，身体受伤或其他健康损害；国家、自然人、法人的

财产，或政府间国际组织的财产受损失或损害；

2. “发射”包括发射未成功在内；

3. “发射国”是指：

(1) 发射或促使发射空间物体的国家；

(2) 从其领土或设施发射空间物体的国家；

4. “空间物体”，包括空间物体的组成部分、物体的运载工具和运载工具的组件。

第二条

发射国对其空间物体在地球表面，或给飞行中的飞机造成损害，应负有赔偿的绝对责任。

第三条

任一发射国的空间物体在地球表面以外的其他地方，对另一发射国的空间物体，或其所载人员或财产造成损害时，只有当损害是因前者的过失或所属负责人的过失造成的，该国才对损害负有赔偿责任。

第四条

1. 任一发射国的空间物体在地球表面以外的其他地方，对另一发射国的空间物体，或其所载人员或财产造成损害，并因此对第三国或第三国的自然人或法人造成损害时，前两国应在下述范围内对第三国承担连带赔偿责任：

(1) 若对第三国的地面表面或飞行中的飞机造成损害，前两国应对第三国应负绝对赔偿责任；

(2) 若在地球表面以外的其他地方，对第三国的空间物体，或其所载人员或财产造成损害，前两国对第三国所负的赔偿责任，应依据它们的过失或所属负责人员的过失而定。

2. 在本条第 1 款提及的所有连带赔偿责任案件中，赔偿义务应按前两国过失程度分摊；若前两国的过失程度无法断定，两国应均摊赔偿义务。但赔偿义务分担不得妨碍第三国向连带责任发射国的任何一国或全体，索取根据本公约规定应予偿付的全部赔偿的权利。

第五条

1. 两个或两个以上国家共同发射空间物体时，对所造成的任何损害应承担连带责任。

2. 发射国在赔偿损失后，有权向共同参与发射的其他国家要求补偿。参加共同发射的国家可缔结协定，依据各自所负的连带责任分摊财政义务。但此种协定，不得妨碍受害国向承担连带责任发射国的任何一国或全体，索求根据本公约规定应予偿付的全部赔偿的权利。

3. 从其领土或设施上发射空间物体的国家，应视为参与共同发射的国家。

第六条

1. 除本条第二款另有规定外，发射国若证明，全部或部分是因为要求赔偿国，或其代表的自然人或法人的重大疏忽，或因作为或不作为蓄意造成损害时，该发射国对损害的绝对责任，应依证明的程度予以免除。

2. 发射国如果因为从事不符合国际法，特别是不符合《联合国宪章》和《关于各国探索和利用包括月球与其他天体在内外层空间活动原则的条约》的活动造成损害，其赔偿责任不得免除。

第七条

本公约之规定不适用于发射国的空间物体对下列人员造成的损失：

1. 该发射国的国民；

2. 在空间物体从发射至降落的任何阶段参与操作，或在空间物体从发射至降落的任何阶段内，应发射国的邀请而留在紧邻计划发射或回收区域的外国国民。

第八条

1. 遭受损害的国家，或其自然人或法人，可向发射国提出损害赔偿的要求。

2. 如果遭受损害的自然人或法人的国籍国没有提出赔偿要求，该自然人或法人的所在国可就其在本国境内遭受的损害，向发射国提出赔偿要求。

3. 如果永久居民的国籍国或损害发生的所在地国，都没有提出赔偿要求，或通知有意提出赔偿要求，永久居民的居住地国可就其遭受的损害，向发射国提出赔偿要求。

第九条

损害赔偿要求，应通过外交途径向发射国提出。求偿国如果和发射国没有外交关系，可请另一国代其向发射国提出赔偿要求，或以其他方式代表其在本公约项下的利益。求偿国也可通过联合国秘书长提出赔偿要求，前提是求偿国和发射国都是联合国成员国。

第十条

1. 损害赔偿要求，须于损害发生之日起，或判明应负责任的发射国之日起一年内向发射国提出。

2. 如一国不知损害业已发生，或未能判明应付责任的发射国，应于获悉上述事实之日起一年内，提出赔偿要求；如有理由认为，求偿国由于行使尽职调查，已获悉上述事实，则提出赔偿要求的时间从知悉之日起，不论如何不得超过一年。

3. 即使不完全了解损害的程度，也应当适用本条第一款和第二款规定的时间限制。在这种情况下，求偿国应当有权自该时限期满至全面了解损害程度后一年止，修改其要求，提交补充文件。

第十一条

1. 根据本公约向发射国提出损害赔偿要求，无须求偿国或其代表的自然人或法人用尽当地救济。

2. 本公约不妨碍一国，或其可能代表的自然人或法人在发射国的法院、行政法庭或机构提起赔偿要求。若一国已在发射国的法院、行政法庭或机构提起了赔偿要求，则不得根据公约或其他对有关国家有约束力的国际协定，就同一损害提出赔偿要求。

第十二条

发射国在本公约项下有责任支付的赔偿金，应依照国际法以及公平合理的原则确定，以使对损害所做的赔偿，能确保提出赔偿要求的自然人或法人、国家或国际组织恢复到未发生损害前的状态。

第十三条

除非求偿国与依照本公约应当赔偿的国家就赔偿方式另行达成协议，应以求偿国货币支付赔偿金；如果该国有相应的请求，赔偿金可以赔偿国的货币支付。

第十四条

若求偿国通知发射国已提出赔偿要求文件之日起一年内，通过第九条规定的外交谈判无法解决赔偿要求，有关各方应于任一方提出请求时，成立赔偿委员会。

第十五条

1. 赔偿委员会应由三人组成：一人由求偿国指派，一人由发射国指派，第三人由两方共同指派，并担任主席。每一方应于请求成立赔偿委员会之日起两个月指派出其人员。

2. 如果指派主席未能于请求成立委员会之日起 4 个月内达成协议，任一方均可请求联合国秘书长于另两个月内指派。

第十六条

1. 如果一方未于规定期限内指派出其人员，主席应当应另一方的要求，组成仅有一个成员的赔偿委员会。

2. 无论任何原因造成委员会成员空缺，应当按照原定的指派程序进行补派。

3. 委员会应自行决定其工作程序。

4. 委员会应选定一个或数个工作地点，并确定其他一些行政事项。

5. 除单一成员的委员会作出的决定和裁定外，委员会的一切决定和裁定均应以多数票表决通过。

第十七条

赔偿委员会的成员人数，不得因由两个或两个以上求偿国或发射国共同参加委员会任一工作程序，而有所增加。共同参加的求偿国，应按照与一个求偿国相同的方式和条件，共同指派一名委员会的成员。两个或两个以上发射国参加时，应按同样方式共同指派一名委员会的成员。如果求偿国或发射国未能在规定期限内指派出人选，主席应组成单一成员委员会。

第十八条

赔偿委员会应当决定赔偿要求是否成立，并在需要赔偿的情况下，确定应付赔偿金的总额。

第十九条

1. 赔偿委员会应当按照第 12 条的规定行事。

2. 若各方同意，委员会的决定应当是终局的，并具有约束力；否则，委员会应做出最终的建议性裁定，交由各方善意考量。委员会应表明其决定或裁定的理由。

3. 委员会应尽速做出决定或裁定，至迟在委员会成立之日起一年内做出，除非委员会认为有必要将此期限延长。

4. 委员会应公布其决定或裁定。委员会应将决定或裁定的正式副本送交各方和联合国秘书长。

第二十条

除非委员会另有规定，赔偿委员会的费用应当由各方平等分担。

第二十一条

如果空间物体造成的损害严重危及人类生命，或严重干扰人们的生活条件或重要中心的功能，各当事国，特别是发射国，在受害国请求时应审查提供适当与快速援助的可能性。但本条规定不影响各当事国在本公约项下的权利和义务。

第二十二条

1. 如果任何从事外空活动的政府间国际组织声明接受本公约所规定的权利和义务，其多数成员国系本公约和《关于各国探索和利用包括月球与其他天体在内外层空间活动原则条约》的当事国，本公约，除第二十四条至第二十七条外，对所称国家的一定规定，均应适用于该组织。

2. 凡既是此类组织的成员国，又是本公约当事国的国家，应采取一切适当行动，确保该组织按照前款规定做出声明。

3. 如果政府间国际组织根据本公约规定对损害负有责任，该组织及其成员国中的本公约当事国，应承担连带责任；但：

（1）对于这种损害的任何赔偿要求，应首先向该组织提出；

（2）唯有在该组织于 6 个月内，未支付经协商一致或决定的损害赔偿金，求偿国才得要求该组织成员国中的本公约当事国支付该款项。

4. 凡按本条第一款规定发表了声明的组织，受到损害时，应由该组织内的本公约当事国根据本公约的规定，提出赔偿要求。

第二十三条

1. 本公约规定，对当事国之间现行其他国际协定的关系，不发生影响。

2. 本公约规定，不妨碍各国缔结国际协定，重申、补充或推广本公约各条款。

第二十四条

1. 本公约应开放供一切国家签署。在本公约依据本条第 3 款生效之前，没有签署本公约的任何国家可随时加入本公约。

2. 本公约应由签署国批准。批准书和加入文件应交由苏维埃社会主义共和国联盟、大不列颠及北爱尔兰联合国王国和美利坚合众国政府存放，为此指定这三国政府为交存国政府。

3. 本公约应于第五个批准书交存时生效。

4. 对于在本公约生效后，交存批准书或加入文件的国家，本公约应于其交存批准书或加入文件之日生效。

5. 交存国政府应将每次签署日期、每次批准书和加入文件交存日期、公约生效日期以及其他事项，尽速通知所有签署国和加入国。

6. 本公约应由交存国政府遵照《联合国宪章》第一百零二条予以登记。

第二十五条

本公约的任何当事国均可提议修正本公约。对每个当事国来说，每项修正在其获得多数当事国接受后即可生效，对此后每个加入国来说，修正应于其接受之日起生效。

第二十六条

本公约生效十年后，应将审查本公约议题纳入联合国大会临时议程，以便参照本公约的实施情况，审议是否须做修正。但公约在生效五年后的任何时间，根据三分之一公约当事国请求并经多数当事国同意，应召开本公约当事国大会审议本公约。

第二十七条

本公约任何当事国在公约生效一年后，可书面通知交存国政府，退出公约。退出公约应自收悉通知之日起一年后生效。

第二十八条

本公约的中文、英文、法文、俄文以及西班牙文文本具有同等效力，均交交存国政府存档。交存国政府应把本公约之正式副本送交各签署国和加入国政府。

为此，下列全权代表在本公约上签字，以昭信守。

一九七二年三月二十九日订于伦敦、莫斯科和华盛顿，一式三份。

目录

一、前言
二、第一条（定义）
三、第二条（绝对责任）
四、第三条（过失责任）
五、第四条（两个或多个空间物体联合造成损害/第三方责任）
六、第五条（共同发射/连带责任）
七、第六条（绝对责任的免除）
八、第七条（不适用于发射国本国国民或参与发射的外国国民）
九、第八条（求偿国的适格性）
十、第九条（外交途径）
十一、第十条（提出损害赔偿要求的期限）
十二、第十一条（与本国管辖权的关系）
十三、第十二条（损害赔偿金数额的确定）
十四、第十三条（损害赔偿金的货币）
十五、第十四条（未解决的赔偿要求/赔偿委员会）
十六、第十五条（赔偿委员会的构成）
十七、第十六条（未指派/空缺/工作程序）
十八、第十七条（共同指派）
十九、第十八条（赔偿委员会决定内容）
二十、第十九条（终局和有约束力的决定）
二十一、第二十条（赔偿委员会的费用分担）
二十二、第二十一条（大规模危险）
二十三、第二十二条（政府间国际组织）
二十四、第二十三条（与其他国际协定的关系）
二十五、第二十四条（签署/批准/加入/生效）
二十六、第二十五条（修正提案）
二十七、第二十六条（修正/审查）
二十八、第二十七至二十八条（最终条款）
第三章　前景展望

文件精选

–Convention on International Liability for Damage Caused by Space Objects (opened for signature 29 March 1972, came into force 1 September 1972) 961 UNTS 187 (LIAB)

–UN Doc. A/AC. 105/C. 2/L. 7, Working Paper Submitted by the Belgian Delegation on the Unification of Certain Rules Governing Liability for Damage Caused by Space Devices, 29 April 1963, in: UN Doc. A/AC. 105/12, Report of the Legal Sub-Committee on the Work of its Second Session (16 April-3 May 1963), Annex I, C, 6 May 1963

– UN Doc. A/AC. 105/C. 2/L. 8, United States: Proposal-Convention concerning liability for damage caused by the launching of objects into outer space, 9 March 1964, in: UN Doc. A/AC. 105/19, Report of the Legal Sub-Committee on the Work of its Third Session (9-26 March 1964), Annex II, Proposals and amendments relating to liability for damage caused by objects launched into outer space, 26 March 1964

– UN Doc. A/AC. 105/C. 2/L. 19, United States of America: Proposal-Convention concerning liability for damage caused by the launching of objects into outer space, 21 June 1967, in: UN Doc. A/AC. 105/37, Report of the Legal Sub-Committee on the Work of its Sixth Session (19 June-14 July 1967), Annex II, Proposals, amendments and other documents relating to liability for damage caused by the launching of objects into outer space, 14 July 1967

–UN Doc. A/AC. 105/C. 2/L. 32, India: proposal-Convention concerning liability for damage caused by the launching of objects into outer space, 2 June 1968, in: UN Doc. A/AC. 105/45, Report of the Legal Sub-Committee on the Work of its Seventh Session (4-28 June 1968), Annex I, Proposals, amendments and other documents relating to liability for damage caused by the launching of objects into outer space, 11 July 1968

–UN Doc. A/AC. 105/C. 2/L. 40, Working Paper submitted by the Italian delegation-Draft convention concerning liability for damage caused by the launching of objects into outer space, 13 June 1986, in: UN Doc. A/AC. 105/45, Report of the Legal Sub-Committee on the Work of its Seventh Session (4-28 June 1968), Annex I, Proposals, amendments and other documents relating to liability for damage caused by the launching of objects into outer space, 11 July 1968

–UN Doc. A/AC. 105/C. 2/L. 79, Belgium, Brazil and Hungary: proposal, 21 June 1971, in: UN Doc. A/AC. 105/94, Report Of The Legal Sub-Committee on the Work of its Tenth Session (7 June-2 July 1971), Annex I, Proposals and Other Documents Relating to Agenda Item 2 (Draft Convention on Liability for Damage Caused by Objects Launched into Outer Space), 8 July 1971

参考文献精选

–Berridge, Geoff R., *Diplomacy: Theory and Practice*, 4th edn., Palgrave Macmillan, Basingstoke 2010

–Böckstiegel, Karl-Heinz, *Settlement of Disputes Regarding Space Activities*, Journal of Space Law (21) 1993, pp. 1-10

–Cheng, Bin, *International Liability for Damage Caused by Space Objects*, in: Jasentuliyana, Nandasiri/Lee, Roy S. K. (eds.), Manual on Space Law Volume I, Oceana Publications, New York 1979, pp. 83-172

–Diederiks-Verschoor, I. H. Philepina/Kopal, Vladimir, *An Introduction to Space Law*, 3rd edn., Kluwer Law International, The Hague 2008, pp. 34-44

–Ersfeld, Herrmann, *Empfehlungen für eine nationale deutsche Weltraumgesetzgebung aus Industriesicht*, Zeitschrift für Luft- und Weltraumrecht (59) 2010, pp. 241-251

–Goh, Gérardine M., *Dispute Settlement in International Space Law-A Multi-Door Courthouse for Outer Space*, Brill Academic Publishers, Leiden 2007

–Gorove, Stephen, *Some Comments on the Convention on International Liability for Damage Caused by Space Objects*, in: IISL, Proceedings of the 16th Colloquium on the Law of Outer Space, 7-13 October 1973 Baku (USSR), AIAA, 1974, pp. 253-255

–Gummer, W. K./Campbell, F. R./Knight, G. B./Ricard, J. L., *Cosmos 954-The Occurrence and Nature of Recovered Debris*, Canadian Government Publishing Center, Sipply and Services Canada, Hull, Quebec 1980

–Haanappel, Peter P. C., *Enforcing the Liability Convention: Ensuring the Binding Force of the Award of the Claims Commission*, in: Benkö, Marietta/Schrogl, Kai-Uwe

(eds.), Space Law-Current Problems and Perspectives For Future Regulation, Eleven, Utrecht 2005, pp. 113-120

– Hobe, Stephan, *The Permanent Court of Arbitration Adopts Optional Rules for Arbitration of Disputes Relating to Outer Space Activities*, Zeitschrift für Luft- und Weltraumrecht (61) 2012, pp. 4-25

–Kayser, Valérie, *Launching Space Objects*: *Issues of Liability and Future Prospects*, Kluwer Academic Publishers, Dordrecht 2001

–Kerrest, Armel, *Liability for Damage Caused by Space Activities*, in: Benkö, Marietta/Schrogl, Kai-Uwe (eds.), Space Law: Current Problems and Perspectives For Future Regulation, Eleven, Utrecht 2005, pp. 91-111

–Kerrest, Armel, *La responsabilité des Etats du fait de la destruction de satellites dans l'espace*, in: Groupement Français pour la Recherche en Droit International (ed.), Annuaire Français de Droit International 2009, CNRS, Paris 2010, pp. 615-626

– Mejia-Kaiser, Martha, *Collision course*: 2009 *Iridium-Cosmos crash*, in: IISL, Proceedings of the 52nd Colloquium on the Law of Outer Space, 12-16 October 2009 Daejeon (Republic of Korea), AIAA, 2010, pp. 274-285

– Montpert, Phillippe, *Space Insurance*, in: Smith, Lesley J./Baumann, Ingo, Contracting for Space, Contract Practice in the European Space Sector, Ashgate, Surrey 2011, pp. 283-289.

– Lyall, Francis/Larsen, Paul B., *Space Law a Treatise*, Ashgate, Burlington/Surrey 2009

–Smith, Lesley J./Doldirina, Catherine, *Jurisdiction and applicable law in cases of damage from space in Europe-The advent of the most suitable choice-Rome II*, Acta Astronautica (66) 2010, pp. 239-244

–Smith, Lesley J./Kerrest, Armel, *Article* Ⅶ, in: Hobe, Stephan/Schmidt-Tedd, Bernhard/Schrogl Kai-Uwe (eds.), Cologne Commentary on Space Law Volume I, Carl Heymanns, Cologne 2009, pp. 127-145

– Wolfrum, Rüdiger/Langenfeld, Christine, *Umweltschutz durch internationales Haftungsrecht*, Erich Schmidt, Berlin 1999

第一章　历史背景和上下文

目录

一、最初启动和发展

对《空间物体所造成损害的国际责任公约》（以下简称《责任公约》）[①] 条款的理解必须放在联合国和平利用外层空间委员会（以下简称外空委）早年谈判的背景中。作为临时机构，外空委是联合国大会在 1958 年设立的[②]，其起初的几份报告中将“航天器造成的伤亡和损害责任”问题作为“容许优先考量的法律问题”[③]。1962 年，联合国大会明确指示外空委研究航天器事故责任问题的提案[④]。当时担心高度危险的

① Convention on International Liability for Damage Caused by Space Objects (opened for signature 29 March 1972, entered into force 1 September 1972) 961 UNTS 187 (LIAB).

② See UNGA Res. 1348 (XIII), Question of the peaceful use of outer space, 13 December 1958.

③ See UN Doc. A/4141, Report of the Ad Hoc Committee on the Peaceful Uses of Outer Space, 14 July 1959, GA Official Records, Fourteenth Session, Agenda Item 25, Annexes, p. 23.

④ See UNGA Res. 1802 (XVII), International co-operation in the peaceful uses of outer space, 14 December 1962, Art. I para. 3.

外空活动发生意外会给人类社会带来迫近的安全威胁，需要充分的规制[①]。然而，直到1963年，外空委起草《各国探索和利用外层空间活动的法律原则宣言》（以下简称1963年《外空宣言》）的时候，才第一次正式关注责任问题[②]。这些原则是国际探索和利用外空目标和精神的奠基石[③]。《外空宣言》第八段是发射国国际责任规范，包括促使发射国以及利用其国土或设施向外空发射物体的国家。但当时，外空活动的国家责任并没有成为争端事项，有关责任形式等的详细讨论留存了。[④]

外空委面临的下一个任务是为在外空可能从事的活动提供清晰的法律框架[⑤]。当时对于国家需要遵守的、获得国际认可的外空活动制度有不同角度的担忧。一些担心外空活动的安全，特别是宇航员的重返，迫切需要规则[⑥]。联合国外空委法律小组委员会[⑦]讨论的首要关注点都涵盖在《关于各国探索和利用包括月球和其他天体在内的外层空间活动原则的条约》（以下简称《外空条约》）草案的主要规范事项中[⑧]。在纳入1963年《外空宣言》后，该草案也认可责任是需要进一步关注的话题。但是，外空活动的特殊风险和发射国作为首要责任人在面对外空有关事故的受害人及其国家提出赔偿要求的风险，后期才被纳入法律小组委员会的议事日程。

《责任公约》和《关于营救宇航员、送回宇航员和归还射入外层空间的物体的协

---

① See Smith, Lesley J./Kerrest, Armel, *Article* Ⅶ, in: Hobe, Stephan/Schmidt-Tedd, Bernhard/Schrogl Kai-Uwe (eds.), Cologne Commentary on Space Law, Volume I, Carl Heymanns, Cologne 2009, p. 130, mn. 7.

② UNGA Res. 1962 (ⅩⅧ), Declaration of Legal Principles Governing the Activities of States in the Exploration and Uses of Outer Space, 13 December 1963.

③ The terms of the Declaration were thereafter effectively fully imported into the OST. For a discussion of the other Declarations relating to outer space passed at that stage, see Lyall, Francis/Larsen, Paul B., *Space Law a Treatise*, Ashgate, Burlington/Surrey 2009, pp. 43ff.

④ See Smith, Lesley J./Kerrest, Armel, *Article* Ⅶ, in: Hobe, Stephan/Schmidt-Tedd, Bernhard/Schrogl, Kai-Uwe (eds.), Cologne Commentary on Space Law, Volume I, Carl Heymanns, Cologne 2009, p. 133, mn. 22.

⑤ A full chronology of the discussions and documents can be found in Jasentuliyana, Nandasiri/Lee, Roy S. K., *Manual on Space Law, Volume* Ⅲ, Oceana Publications, New York 1981, pp. 209ff.

⑥ See UN Doc. A/AC. 105/C. 2/SR. 92, Legal Sub-Committee, Summary Record of the Ninety-Second Meeting, held on 6 June 1968, in: UN Doc. A/AC. 105/C. 2/SR. 90-101, Summary records of the Ninetieth to One Hundred and First meetings held from 4 to 18 June 1968, 22 July 1986, Mr. Donovan (Australia).

⑦ 法律小组委员会成立于1962年，见 Smith, Lesley J./Kerrest, Armel, *Article* Ⅶ, in: Hobe, Stephan/Schmidt-Tedd, Bernhard/Schrogl, Kai-Uwe (eds.), Cologne Commentary on Space Law, Volume I, Carl Heymanns, Cologne 2009, p. 131, mn. 9.

⑧ Treaty on Principles Governing the Activities of States in the Exploration and Use of Outer Space, including the Moon and Other Celestial Bodies (opened for signature 27 January 1967, entered into force 10 October 1967) 610 UNTS 205 (OST).

定》（以下简称《营救协定》）的谈判平行进行[①]，非航天国家以接受《营救协定》换取《责任公约》的谈判[②]。

二、不同的草案文本

联合国外空委磋商外空活动法律框架的起初几年中，收到了几部《外空活动损害赔偿责任的条约》草案。在确定《责任公约》最终文本前，这样的讨论仍在进行。1962年6月，美国提交确立国际责任制度提案是最早的文本[③]。这个标题为“航天器事故责任”的文本在1963年《外空宣言》达成一致前就提交给了联合国外空委。美国草案并不是国际层面关于责任制度的唯一提案。比利时、美国、匈牙利分别向外空委提交了共三份草案，此后又提交了修改初始文本的进一步提案。这些草案文本的容量和差异增加了责任问题的复杂性。美国1962年提交最初草案，比利时1963年提交草案，[④] 美国此后提交了几份修订和补充文本[⑤]，匈牙利1964年提交草案[⑥]。这三个国家提交了草案的修改版本，其他国家提交了修改意见[⑦]。

《责任公约》文本的谈判拖延且冗长，主要原因有五个，即国际组织的地位、损

① Agreement on the Rescue of Astronauts, the Return of Astronauts and the Return of Objects Launched into Outer Space (done 22 April 1968, entered into force 3 December 1968) 672 UNTS 119 (ARRA).

② See chapter on ARRA in this volume, Historical Background and Context ARRA, mn. 3, 12.

③ See UN Doc. A/AC. 105/C. 2/L. 4, USA: Proposal-Liability for Space Vehicle Accidents, 4 June 1962, in: UN Doc. A/AC. 105/6, Report of the Legal Sub-Committee on the Work of its First Session (28 May-20 June 1962), 9 July 1962, p. 6.

④ UN Doc. A/AC. 105/C. 2/L. 7, Working Paper Submitted by the Belgian Delegation on the Unification of Certain Rules Governing Liability for Damage Caused by Space Devices, 29 April 1963, in: UN Doc. A/AC. 105/12, Report of the Legal Sub-Committee on the Work of its Second Session (16 April-3 May 1963), 6 May 1963, Annex I, C, p. 10.

⑤ UN Doc. A/AC. 105/C. 2/L. 8, United States: Proposal-Convention concerning liability for damage caused by the launching of objects into outer space, 9 March 1964, in: UN Doc. A/AC. 105/19, Report of the Legal Sub-Committee on the Work of its Third Session (9-26 March 1964), 26 March 1964, Annex II, Proposals and amendments relating to liability for damage caused by objects launched into outer space, p. 2.

⑥ UN Doc. A/AC. 105/C. 2/L. 10, Hungary: Proposed draft agreement-Agreement concerning liability for damage caused by the launching of objects into outer space, 16 March 1964, in: UN Doc. A/AC. 105/19, Report of the Legal Sub-Committee on the Work of its Third Session (9-26 March 1964), Annex II, Proposals and amendments relating to liability for damage caused by objects launched into outer space, 26 March 1964, p. 7.

⑦ See Jasentuliyana, Nandasiri/Lee, Roy S. K., *Manual on Space Law, Volume* Ⅲ, Oceana Publications, New York 1981, pp. 209ff., for the chronology of the documents submitted with regard to the drafting of the LIAB.

害、确定空间物体造成损害赔偿额适用的法律、责任限制以及强制性第三方仲裁。

到1966年，法律小组委员会主要致力于《外空条约》的起草和谈判。因此，航天器事故责任的谈判推迟到1967年①。

自1964年开始，各国提交的草案文本成为外空损害国家责任的谈判基础。② 这些草案中的很多条款最终纳入了1972年《责任公约》。这些条款反映了1963年《外空宣言》的一般原则。

三、法律小组委员会工作小组

法律小组委员会为确保《责任公约》谈判进程成立的工作小组是起草责任制度细则的机构。除了国家责任和国家的国际损害赔偿责任，其他考量主要是损害赔偿责任对仅有的几个提供发射服务国家的影响。一方面，损害赔偿责任规则应当为给第三方提供发射服务（涵盖促使发射的损害赔偿责任）的仅有的几个国家提供某些形式的激励；另一方面，有必要通过粗泛的损害赔偿制度培育探索和利用外层空间的国际合作的持续发展。没有一个清晰的法律框架，外空活动将处于危险之中。

1964年以后，其他代表团向工作小组提交提案供讨论，特别是印度③、阿根廷和加拿大④。意大利和印度提交了损害赔偿制度的单独提案，印度提交了修改版本，英国、苏联、墨西哥和奥地利随后加入讨论。1968~1969年以后，还有一些国家的提案

① See UN Doc. A/AC. 105/35, Report of the Legal Sub-Committee on the Work of its Fifth Session (12 July-4 August and 12-16 September 1966), 16 September 1966, p. 2.

② For a compiled and edited collection of the *travaux préparatoires* and related documents, see Jasentuliyana, Nandasiri/Lee, Roy S. K., *Manual on Space Law*, *Volume* Ⅲ, Oceana Publications, New York 1981, pp. 209ff.

③ See UN Doc. A/AC. 105/C. 2/L. 26, India: Draft Agreement on Liability-Proposal, 30 June 1967, in: UN Doc. A/AC. 105/37, Report of the Legal Sub-Committee on the Work of its Sixth Session (19 June-14 July 1967), Annex II, Proposals, amendments and other documents relating to liability for damage caused by the launching of objects into outer space, 14 July 1967, p. 20.

④ Jasentuliyana, Nandasiri/Lee, Roy S. K., *Manual on Space Law*, *Volume* Ⅲ, Oceana Publications, New York 1981, p. 210.

得到了工作小组的修订意见，特别是法国和英国。[①]

为了便利法律小组委员会的最终讨论，1969 年联合国外空委届会前，在新德里组织了非正式协商。此次会议的目的是促进在委员会层面就不同议题达成一致，方便工作小组继续讨论剩余提案。法律小组委员会为此设立了起草小组，到 1971 年，完成了条约标题、前言和 27 条规则的起草，随后在法律小组委员会通过[②]。该草案建立在此前有关国家和国际组织损害赔偿责任、航天器造成损失或损害等讨论的基础上。

最初，对《责任公约》能否适用于“国家之外的其他实体”存在担忧[③]，主要是为确保政府间国际组织[④]能够接受在草案文本项下国际损害赔偿责任的国际义务。将《责任公约》延伸适用到国际组织的原因是，如果不这么做，国际组织的某一成员国作为发射国将承担全部损害赔偿责任，而不是由国际组织代表所有成员国承担相应责任。[⑤]

四、从《外空条约》到《责任公约》的谈判

总体上，有关损害赔偿责任的谈判持续了将近十年[⑥]。从 1963 年《外空宣言》最初的一致意见开始，到 1967 年《外空条约》，此后又持续了四年，直到应联合国外空

① See UN Doc. A/AC. 105/C. 2/L. 36/Rev. 1, France: revised proposal concerning the state liable and joint and several liability, 12 June 1968, in: UN Doc. A/AC. 105/45, Report of the Legal Sub-Committee on the Work of its Seventh Session (4-28 June 1968), Annex I, Proposals, amendments and other documents relating to liability for damage caused by the launching of objects into outer space, 11 July 1968, p. 41; and UN Doc. A/AC. 105/C. 2/L. 37/Rev. 1, United Kingdom: revised proposal-Field of Application, 14 June 1968, in: UN Doc. A/AC. 105/45, Report of the Legal Sub-Committee on the Work of its Seventh Session (4-28 June 1968), Annex I, Proposals, amendments and other documents relating to liability for damage caused by the launching of objects into outer space, 11 July 1968, p. 41.

② See UN Doc. A/AC. 105/94, Report of the Legal Sub-Committee on the Work of its Tenth Session (7 June-2 July 1971), 8 July 1971, pp. 5-13.

③ Lyall, Francis/Larsen, Paul B., *Space Law a Treatise*, Ashgate, Burlington/Surrey 2009, p. 106.

④ 偶尔也表述为“国际组织”。在没有特别原因的情况下，谈判《责任公约》过程中两种表述是可以互换的。尽管《外空条约》第六条用的是“国际组织”，此后条约都使用“政府间国际组织”（见《营救协定》第六条，《责任公约》第二十二条，《登记公约》第七条和《月球协定》第十六条）。两种表述都指的是国家之间的常设机构性合作，并不包括跨国私人公司，这一点是没有争议的。

⑤ See UN Doc. A/AC. 105/C. 2/SR. 52, Legal Sub-Committee, Summary Record of the Fifty-Second Meeting, held on 29 September 1965, 19 January 1966, Mr. Darwin (United Kingdom).

⑥ 从 1962 年 6 月第一份提案（UN Doc. A/AC. 105/C. 2/L. 4）到 1971 年 11 月联合国大会通过《责任公约》(UNGA Res. 2777 (XXVI)).

委提交给联合国大会报告的建议[①]，1971 年 11 月 29 日联合国大会通过了《空间物体所造成损害的国际责任公约》。[②]

谈判过程中，1969 到 1970 年完全处于僵局状态，期间法国和英国代表团号召法律小组委员会将注意力转到其他日程上。联合国大会对缔结损害赔偿责任公约推延了六年深表不满[③]。

联合国外空委对待和讨论外空活动法律规则的顺序直接影响了《责任公约》的最终内容。早在起草《外空条约》第七条的时候，就意识到关于损害赔偿责任需要起草一个单独的文件，以增加准确性[④]。《外空条约》第一条第 2 款规定外空活动必须“依照国际法”进行，《外空条约》第三条确立了同样的义务[⑤]。这些规则都承认了国际责任规则在外空的有效性[⑥]。《外空条约》第六条明确当事国对本国外空活动应负国际责任，《外空条约》第七条规定了空间物体造成损害的国际赔偿责任。这些都是进一步详细制定空间活动国际损害赔偿责任新公约的基础。换言之，自 1967 年开始，已经有了谈判确立空间活动责任综合性条约作为《外空条约》特别法的需求[⑦]。

五、实质性争议

《责任公约》的谈判过程的主要特点是不同代表团在方法上的诸多分歧，其中有原则性问题。例如，有观点认为应当将《责任公约》的适用范围局限在空间物体之间

---

① See UN Doc. A/8420, Report of the Committee on the Peaceful Uses of Outer Space, General Assembly Official Records, Twenty-Sixth Session, Supplement No. 20, 1971, p. 8.

② See UNGA Res. 2777 (XXVI), Convention on International Liability for Damage Caused by Space Objects, 29 November 1971.

③ See UNGA Res. 2601 (XXIV) B, International co-operation in outer space, 16 December 1969.

④ Smith, Lesley J. /Kerrest, Armel, *Article VII*, in: Hobe, Stephan/Schmidt-Tedd, Bernhard/Schrogl, Kai-Uwe (eds.), Cologne Commentary on Space Law, Volume I, Carl Heymanns, Cologne 2009, p. 134, mn. 27.

⑤ Lyall, Francis/Larsen, Paul B., *Space Law a Treatise*, Ashgate, Burlington/Surrey 2009, p. 104.

⑥ Ibid.

⑦ Smith, Lesley J. /Kerrest, Armel, *Article VII*, in: Hobe, Stephan/Schmidt-Tedd, Bernhard/Schrogl, Kai-Uwe (eds.), Cologne Commentary on Space Law, Volume I, Carl Heymanns, Cologne 2009, p. 134, mn. 27.

的碰撞，进而避免空气空间和外层空间的区分和划界[1]。同样地，绝对责任和过失责任问题也争论了许久。谈判各国认可证明过失的难度，所以日本等代表团赞同绝对责任，特别是两个空间物体相撞给第三方造成的损害。争端解决是另一个在代表团中引发很大分歧的核心问题。

这些争议在谈判中持续了九年多，直到就《责任公约》文本最终达成一致，1971 年 11 月 29 日，联合国大会 2777 号决议通过了《空间物体所造成损害的国际责任公约》。[2]

---

① 例如，英国的修改意见支持匈牙利的草案，“发射空间物体的国家以及积极或实质性参与发射空间物体的另一国应当为本公约规定的损害承担赔偿责任，不论损害发生的地点”。UN Doc. A/AC. 105/C. 2/SR. 95, Legal Sub-Committee, Summary Record of the Ninety-Fifth Meeting, held on 11 June 1968, in：UNDoc. A/AC. 105/C. 2/SR. 90-101, Summary records of the Ninetieth to One Hundred and First meetings held from 4 to 18 June 1968, 22 July 1968.

② UNGA Res. 2777（XXVI）, Convention on International Liability for Damage Caused by Space Objects, 29 November 1971；1972 年 3 月 29 日，《公约》开放签署，1972 年 9 月 1 日生效。

第二章 《责任公约》评注

一、前言

Smith and Kerrest

本公约当事国，

确认在推进为了和平目的探索和利用外层空间的全人类共同利益，

回顾了《关于各国探索和利用包括月球与其他天体在内外层空间活动原则的条约》，

考虑到从事发射空间物体的国家和政府间国际组织虽将采取预防性措施，但仍存在空间物体可能造成损害的情形，

确认需要详细制定关于空间物体造成损害赔偿责任的有效的国际规则和程序，特别需要确保此类损害的受害人按本公约规定尽速得到充分公正的赔偿，

深信确立这些规则与程序，有助于强化为和平目的探索和利用外层空间方面的国际合作，

兹议定条款如下：

目录

4. 尽速赔偿

5. 强化国际合作

(一) 谈判和起草过程

前言的起草谨记《责任公约》的主要目的，即为空间运营活动引发的损害确立受害人导向的赔偿制度。这将确保受害人无需付出不成比例的努力，就能获取恰当的赔偿。这个聚焦是为了在外空活动国家损害赔偿责任概念下创设国际赔偿制度。

认可需要详细制定关于空间物体造成损害赔偿责任的有效的国际规则和程序，前言表明了《责任公约》旨在补充《外空条约》第七条确立的空间损害国际赔偿责任制度。该条留下了几个核心事项的空白，即损害的界定、赔偿责任的类型（绝对还是过失）、适用于地面和外空损害的赔偿责任类型、连带责任和快速获取应支付的损害赔偿的程序。

联合国外空委耗时九年才对《责任公约》文本达成一致①，期间积累了冗长的立法准备性文件，这些文件中的前言内容都有所不同。《责任公约》的目的是，通过为代表受害人的国家确立有效的国际程序和规则，即使存在潜在的危险，仍能确保外空活动继续进行。空间国家数量的有限性凸显了确保有效国际合作的必要性，规范责任和风险有助于支撑外空探索领域的协作。与 1963 年《外空宣言》《外空条约》和《营救协定》等现有空间法文件的术语和方法保持一致的需要也影响了谈判。谈判各方认可《责任公约》应当符合 1963 年《外空宣言》②。

政府间国际组织的损害赔偿责任引发了一些担忧。在前言中提及国际组织表明《责任公约》文本将涵盖与此相关的内容③。国际组织的损害赔偿责任详见下文第二

---

① 联合国外空委 1971 年 6 月向联合国大会提交《责任公约》草案，1962 年 6 月美国最初提出草案（UN Doc. A/AC. 105/C. 2/L. 4），期间共历时九年。

② 这是苏联当时的强烈倡议，见 UN Doc. A/AC. 105/C. 2/SR. 48, Legal Sub-Committee, Summary Record of the Forty-Eighth Meeting, held on 27 September 1965, 30 November 1965, Mr. Rybakov (Soviet Union).

③ The imposition of a duty and the ability of international organizations to compensate victims were dependent on the organizations themselves and the subsidiary role of their State members. The details of liability of international organizations were discussed in the context of joint and several liability, 见 UN Doc. A/AC. 105/21, Report of the Legal Sub-Committee on the Work of the Second Part of its Third Session (5-23 October 1964), 23 October 1964, Annex IV, Summary of views expressed in Working Groups I and II, Summary of points raised in discussions of Working Group II, Part I, Points raised in general discussion, p. 9.

十二条的有关内容①。

前言的最终文本内容少于印度代表团在《责任公约》早期工作中提交的草案②。在那个草案中，印度“希望详细确立国际社会对于外空活动的期许”③，为此应当重复联合国大会有关外空活动原则和决议的一些前言内容④。《责任公约》的前言没有引用1963年《外空宣言》文本和《营救协定》序言的内容，未强调人类和平探索和利用外层空间的共同利益，这让某些代表团有些失望⑤。因而，《责任公约》前言的最终版本比印度草案简洁。即便如此，也反映了起草《责任公约》的主要动机。

（二）评注

《责任公约》前言共包括五个实效段落，涉及起草《责任公约》的主要动机。

1. 一般性目的

尽管前言中没有明确提及联合国大会1884号决议⑥，也没有提及1963年《外空宣言》，《责任公约》前言的第一个实效段落确认了推进为和平目的探索和利用外层空间的全人类的共同利益，基本逐字重复了《外空条约》前言的有关内容。《外空条约》前言确认了为和平目的探索和利用外层空间的进展关系到全人类的共同利益。

2. 引用《外空条约》

前言的第二个实效段落是向《外空条约》的重要作用致敬，《外空条约》为外空活动确立了恰当的法律制度。这表明《责任公约》将进一步详细制定《外空条约》第七条确立的一般性损害赔偿责任规则。

但是，前言只引用了《外空条约》，并没有提及《营救协定》。有趣的是，《关于登记射入外层空间物体的公约》（以下简称《登记公约》）⑦ 和《关于各国在月球和

① See Commentary LIAB, Article XXII, mn. 384f.

② UN Doc. A/AC. 105/C. 2/SR. 92, Legal Sub-Committee, Summary Record of the Ninety-Second Meeting, held on 6 June 1968, in: UN Doc. A/AC. 105/C. 2/SR. 90-101, Summary records of the Ninetieth to One Hundred and First meetings held from 4 to 18 June 1968, 22 July 1986, Mr. Rao (India).

③ Ibid.

④ Ibid.

⑤ Ibid.

⑥ UNGA Res. 1884 (XVIII), Question of general and complete disarmament, 17 October 1963.

⑦ Convention on Registration of Objects Launched into Outer Space (done 14 January 1975, entered into force 15 September 1976) 1023 UNTS 15 (REG).

其他天体上活动的协定》（以下简称《月球协定》）[①] 的前言都提及了在它们之前的所有外空条约。

3. 预防措施和仍旧存在的风险

前言的第三个实效段落直接点明了与外空活动有关的内在危险，特别是在发射过程中。这要求各国采取预防性安全措施，以确保这些操作和运营的最大安全。同时强调一个事实，即使采取了预防措施，发射过程中仍可能发生意外和损害。换言之，外空活动的内生危险性，经常被描述为高度危险，要求获得国际认可的外空活动责任制度必须考虑这些活动蕴含着不可避免的风险，必须通过提供充分的赔偿来保护潜在的受害人。

4. 尽速赔偿

在前言的第四个实效段落中，《责任公约》宣告了为空间物体造成的损害确立独立于现有的国内和国际损害赔偿制度的、有效的国际机制的必要性。现有的国内和国际制度无法满足外空这种高度危险活动的损害赔偿需要。

新的机制应当确保“尽速赔偿”，这种赔偿应当确保“此类损害的受害人得到充分公正的赔偿”。这强调了《责任公约》受害人导向的特征。

5. 强化国际合作

最后，在第五个实效段落中，前言强调了这些国际规则和程序确立的国际赔偿机制，目的是服务和强化“为和平目的探索和利用外层空间方面的国际合作”。总体上，一个粗泛高效的赔偿制度比耗时长久的、需要详细证据证明过错的国内诉讼更有利于国际合作。

二、第一条（定义）

Smith and Kerrest

就适用本公约而言：

1. “损害”，是指生命丧失，身体受伤或其他健康损害；国家、自然人、法人的

① Agreement Governing the Activities of States on the Moon and Other Celestial Bodies (done 18 December 1979, entered into force 11 July 1984) 1363 UNTS 3 (MOON).

财产，或政府间国际组织的财产受损失或损害；

2. “发射”包括发射未成功在内；

3. “发射国”是指：

（1）发射或促使发射空间物体的国家；

（2）从其领土或设施发射空间物体的国家；

4. “空间物体”，包括空间物体的组成部分、物体的运载工具和运载工具的组件。

目录

（一）谈判和起草过程

1. 一般性谈判

第一条涵盖了贯穿《责任公约》全文的关键词界定。其一般性谈判主要是关于《责任公约》第一条是否应当界定关键词和术语，还是整个条约仅包含空间物体造成损害责任的原则[1]。最终达成的一致意见是第一条应该是定义。

第一条的定义和其他外空条约采用的方法有明显不同。《外空条约》没有定义，《营救协定》仅在第六条中简单界定了“发射当局”。在谈判过程中，阿根廷代表特别提到，“1968年《营救协定》连宇航员都没有界定，避免同样的错误是极其重要的”[2]。谈判各国认可需要界定的关键词如下：“损害”“空间物体”“发射”和“发射国”。与此相比，国际法中已经比较清晰的术语则不需要定义，包括“人”“财产”和“领土”[3]。

源于定义的重要性，在就条约文本达成最终一致之前，在法律小组委员会的讨论和谈判中，定义得到了专门的关注。

2. 定义的谈判

（1）“损害”

工作小组意识到，就外空活动可能造成的所有种类的损害达成一个穷尽式列举定义是很困难的[4]；最初几份草案中有关定义的提案已经与最终文本第1款中的措辞类似，提及了身体损害（包括生命丧失和身体受伤）和财产性损害[5]。只有比利时草案

---

① See e. g. UN Do. A/AC. 105/L. 40/Rev. 1, Working Paper submitted by the Italian delegation-Draft Convention Concerning Liability for Damage Caused by the Launching of Objects Into Outer Space, in: A/AC. 105/58, Report of the Legal Sub-Committee on the Work of Eighth Session (9 June-4 July 1969), Annex II, Proposals and Other Documents Relating to Liability for Damage Caused by the Launching of Objects into Outer Space, 4 July 1969, pp. 12, 18.

② UN Doc. A/AC. 105/C. 2/SR. 132-151, Summary Records of the One Hundred and Thirty-Second to the One Hundred and Fifty-First Meetings (8 June-3 July 1970), 29 July 1970, p. 25.

③ See UN Doc. A/AC. 105/21, Report of the Legal Sub-Committee on the Work of the Second Part of its Third Session (5-23 October 1964), 23 October 1964, Annex IV, Summary of views expressed in Working Groups I and II, Summary of points raised in discussions of Working Group II, Part II, Points raised in discussion of specific Articles, p. 17.

④ Ibid.

⑤ See UN Doc. A/AC. 105/C. 2/L. 8, United States: Proposal-Convention concerning liability for damage caused by the launching of objects into outer space, 9 March 1964, in: UN Doc. A/AC. 105/19, Report of the Legal Sub-Committee on the Work of its Third Session (9-26 March 1964), 26 March 1964, Annex II, p. 2; UN Doc. A/AC. 105/C. 2/L. 10, Hungary: Proposed draft agreement-Agreement concerning liability for damage caused by the launching of objects into outer space, Art. XII (1), in: UN Doc. A/AC. 105/19, Report of the Legal Sub-Committee on the Work of its Third Session (9-26 March 1964), Annex II, 26 March 1964, p. 7; and UN Doc. PUOS/WG. II/20, India: Amendments to definitions, in; A/AC. 105/21, Report of the Legal Sub-Committee on the Work of the Second Part of its Third Session (5-23 October 1964), Annex II, Proposals and amendments relating to liability for damage caused by objects launched into outer space, 23 October 1964, p. 28.

建议用“受伤人的本国法”[①] 或“损害发生地法”[②] 决定损害的范围[③]。这个提议后来遭到否决，理由是《责任公约》不应当规定确立损害计算方法的规则，重点应放在依据国际法而非国内法应当支付的损害[④]。有建议扩大美国的提案以在损害的定义中包含所有折损健康的情形，也被否决。尽管细节上有出入，当时占优势的观点是“损害赔偿的首要原则必须是尽可能排除不法行为的所有结果”[⑤]。一些国家有意明确是否包括间接损害，但多数国家认为这是因果关系是否充分的问题，没必要在《责任公约》中加以界定[⑥]。

---

① UN Doc. A/AC. 105/C. 2/L. 7, Working Paper Submitted by the Belgian Delegation on the Unification of Certain Rules Governing Liability for Damage Caused by Space Devices, 29 April 1963, in: UN Doc. A/AC. 105/12, Report of the Legal Sub-Committee on the Work of its Second Session (16 April-3 May 1963), 6 May 1963, Annex I, C, p. 10; and UN Doc. A/AC. 105/C. 2/L. 7/Rev. 1, Belgium: Proposal for a Convention on the Unification of Certain Rules Governing Liability for Damage Caused by Space Devices, 1 October 1964, in: UN Doc. A/AC. 105/21, Report of the Legal Sub-Committee on the Work of the Second Part of its Third Session (5-23 October 1964), Annex II, Proposals and amendments relating to liability for damage caused by objects launched into outer space, 23 October 1964, p. 18.

② See UN Doc. A/AC. 105/C. 2/L. 7/Rev. 2, Belgium: Proposal for a Convention on the Unification of Certain Rules Governing Liability for Damage Caused by Space Devices, 14 October 1964, in: UN Doc. A/AC. 105/21, Report of the Legal Sub-Committee on the Work of the Second Part of its Third Session (5-23 October 1964), Annex II, Proposals and amendments relating to liability for damage caused by objects launched into outer space, 23 October 1964, p. 22.

③ UN Doc. A/AC. 105/C. 2/L. 7, Working Paper Submitted by the Belgian Delegation on the Unification of Certain Rules Governing Liability for Damage Caused by Space Devices, 29 April 1963, in: UN Doc. A/AC. 105/12, Report of the Legal Sub-Committee on the Work of its Second Session (16 April-3 May 1963), 6 May 1963, Annex I, C, p. 10; UN Doc. A/AC. 105/C. 2/L. 7/Rev. 1, Belgium: Proposal for a Convention on the Unification of Certain Rules Governing Liability for Damage Caused by Space Devices, 1 October 1964, in: UN Doc. A/AC. 105/21, Report of the Legal Sub-Committee on the Work of the Second Part of its Third Session (5-23 October 1964), Annex II, Proposals and amendments relating to liability for damage caused by objects launched into outer space, 23 October 1964, p. 18; and UN Doc. A/AC. 105/C. 2/L. 7/Rev. 2, Belgium: Proposal for a Convention on the Unification of Certain Rules Governing Liability for Damage Caused by Space Devices, 14 October 1964, in: UN Doc. A/AC. 105/21, Report of the Legal Sub-Committee on the Work of the Second Part of its Third Session (5-23 October 1964), Annex II, Proposals and amendments relating to liability for damage caused by objects launched into outer space, 23 October 1964, p. 22.

④ See Commentary LIAB, Article XII, mn. 292.

⑤ 损害赔偿应恢复原状的原则和具体做法可追溯到国际常设法院的霍茹夫工厂案，谈判中比利时、美国和匈牙利草案中表达了类似观点。见 UN Doc. A/AC. 105/21, Report of the Legal Sub-Committee on the Work of the Second Part of its Third Session (5-23 October 1964), 23 October 1964, Annex IV, Summary of views expressed in Working Groups I and II, Summary of points raised in discussions of Working Group II, Part II, Points raised in discussion of specific Articles, p. 18.

⑥ Cheng, Bin, *International Liability for Damage Caused by Space Objects*, in: Jasentuliyana, Nandasiri/Lee, Roy S. K. (eds.), Manual on Space Law, Volume I, Oceana Publications, New York 1979, p. 115.

在工作小组提案的基础上，1969 年法律小组委员会就损害的最终措辞达成一致。①

（2）“发射”

从谈判早期开始就有一致的观点，即不成功的发射以及进入外空但没有效用的空间物体造成损害亦应承担责任。美国第一份草案已经明确，“发射行为、单数的发射和复数的发射等都应当包括不成功的发射”②。匈牙利草案对此与美国立场一致，即不管发射成功与否，即使空间物体没有进入外空，发射国都应当承担损害赔偿责任③。比利时第一份草案没有提及失败的发射，但后来的修改版本纳入了类似规定④。

1965 年，《责任公约》采纳了美国关于“发射”定义的提案⑤。

（3）“发射国”

1964 年，美国草案中第一次提到“发射国”概念，并将“发射国”定义为“发射或促使发射物体进入外空，或将其领土或设施用于上述发射的当事国或国际组织”⑥。可见当时在谈判中已经提出了如今认定发射国的四个标准。美国第一份草案已

① See UN Doc. A/AC. 105/58, Report of the Legal Sub-Committee on the Work of Eighth Session (9 June-4 July 1969), 4 July 1969, p. 8.

② See UN Doc. A/AC. 105/C. 2/L. 8, United States: Proposal-Convention concerning liability for damage caused by the launching of objects into outer space, 9 March 1964, Art. I lit. (b).

③ UN Doc. A/AC. 105/C. 2/L. 10, Hungary: Proposed draft agreement-Agreement concerning liability for damage caused by the launching of objects into outer space, Art. I.

④ See UN Doc. A/AC. 105/C. 2/L. 7, Working Paper Submitted by the Belgian Delegation on the Unification of Certain Rules Governing Liability for Damage Caused by Space Devices, 29 April 1963, in: UN Doc. A/AC. 105/12, Report of the Legal Sub-Committee on the Work of its Second Session (16 April-3 May 1963), 6 May 1963, Annex I, C, p. 10; and UN Doc. A/AC. 105/C. 2/L. 7/Rev. 1, Belgium: Proposal for a Convention on the Unification of Certain Rules Governing Liability for Damage Caused by Space Devices, 1 October 1964, in: UN Doc. A/AC. 105/21, Report of the Legal Sub-Committee on the Work of the Second Part of its Third Session (5-23 October 1964), Annex II, Proposals and amendments relating to liability for damage caused by objects launched into outer space, 23 October 1964, p. 18.

⑤ UN Doc. A/AC. 105/C. 2/L. 8/Rev. 3, United States: Revised Proposal-Convention concerning liability for damage caused by the launching of objects into outer space, 24 September 1965, in: UN Doc. A/AC. 105/29, Report of the Legal Sub-Committee on the Work of its Fourth Session (20 September-1 October 1965), 1 October 1965, Annex II, Proposals and amendments relating to liability for damage caused by objects launched into outer space, p. 7.

⑥ UN Doc. A/AC. 105/C. 2/L. 8/Rev. 1, United States: Proposal-Convention concerning liability for damage caused by the launching of objects into outer space, in: UN Doc. A/AC. 105/21, Report of the Legal Sub-Committee on the Work of the Second Part of its Third Session (5-23 October 1964), Annex II, Proposals and amendments relating to liability for damage caused by objects launched into outer space, 23 October 1964, p. 6, Art. I lit. (c).

经明确了促使发射以外的三个标准，当时促使发射的表述是“参与发射”①。这份草案将损害赔偿责任分派给了登记国，“发射国”定义是因为在空间物体没有登记情况下，将发射国作为认定承担责任的补充方式②。

其他草案没有明确提及“发射国”，但认定标准类似，大多界定为发射空间物体或自其领土发射空间物体的国家③。也有观点主张，发射国应当是将发射通知给联合国秘书长，并向联合国登记册提交识别空间物体所需信息的国家。当时美国草案第九条和其他草案中有限制赔偿责任的规定，没有在联合国登记空间物体的发射国不得享有限制赔偿责任的惠益④。美国还提议发射国包括拥有和控制空间物体的国家，不论该国是否参与发射⑤。

起草《责任公约》的一个关键点是认定发射国的四个标准中是否有分派损害赔偿

① See UN Doc. A/AC. 105/C. 2/L. 8, United States: Proposal-Convention concerning liability for damage caused by the launching of objects into outer space, 9 March 1964, in: UN Doc. A/AC. 105/19, Report of the Legal Sub-Committee on the Work of its Third Session (9-26 March 1964), 26 March 1964, Annex II, Proposals and amendments relating to liability for damage caused by objects launched into outer space, p. 2, Art. I lit. (e).

② Ibid.

③ See e. g. UN Doc. A/AC. 105/C. 2/L. 7, Working Paper Submitted by the Belgian Delegation on the Unification of Certain Rules Governing Liability for Damage Caused by Space Devices, 29 April 1963, in: UN Doc. A/AC. 105/12, Report of the Legal Sub-Committee on the Work of its Second Session (16 April-3 May 1963), 6 May 1963, Annex I, C, p. 10, Art. I lit. (b); UN Doc. A/AC. 105/C. 2/L. 10, Hungary: Proposed draft agreement-Agreement concerning liability for damage caused by the launching of objects into outer space, 16 March 1964, in: UN Doc. A/AC. 105/19, Report of the Legal Sub-Committee on the Work of its Third Session (9-26 March 1964), Annex II, Proposals and amendments relating to liability for damage caused by objects launched into outer space, 26 March 1964, p. 7, Art. Ⅶ; and UN Doc. A/AC. 105/C. 2/L. 7/Rev. 1, Belgium: Proposal for a Convention on the Unification of Certain Rules Governing Liability for Damage Caused by Space Devices, 1 October 1964, in: UN Doc. A/AC. 105/21, Report of the Legal Sub-Committee on the Work of the Second Part of its Third Session (5-23 October 1964), Annex II, Proposals and amendments relating to liability for damage caused by objects launched into outer space, 23 October 1964, p. 18.

④ UN Doc. A/AC. 105/C. 2/L. 8, United States: Proposal-Convention concerning liability for damage caused by the launching of objects into outer space, 9 March 1964, in: UN Doc. A/AC. 105/19, Report of the Legal Sub-Committee on the Work of its Third Session (9-26 March 1964), 26 March 1964, Annex II, Proposals and amendments relating to liability for damage caused by objects launched into outer space, p. 2.

⑤ See UN Doc. A/AC. 105/C. 2/L. 19, United States of America: Proposal-Convention concerning liability for damage caused by the launching of objects into outer space, 21 June 1967, in: UN Doc. A/AC. 105/37, Report of the Legal Sub-Committee on the Work of its Sixth Session (19 June-14 July 1967), Annex II, Proposals, amendments and other documents relating to liability for damage caused by the launching of objects into outer space, 14 July 1967, p. 6, Art. I lit. (c); and UN Doc. A/AC. 105/C. 2/L. 19 and 58, United States of America: proposal-Convention concerning liability for damage caused by the launching of objects into outer space, in: UN Doc. A/AC. 105/58, Report of the Legal Sub-Committee on the Work of Eighth Session (9 June-4 July 1969), Annex II, Proposals and other documents relating to liability for damage caused by the launching of objects into outer space, 4 July 1969, p. 4.

责任的层级顺序①。一些国家认为“领土”和“设备”标准具有附属性②，或者说此种情况下发射必须获得该国同意③。他们主张发射国或促使发射国是损害赔偿责任的

① See UN Doc. A/AC. 105/C. 2/L. 7, Working Paper Submitted by the Belgian Delegation on the Unification of Certain Rules Governing Liability for Damage Caused by Space Devices, 29 April 1963, in: UN Doc. A/AC. 105/12, Report of the Legal Sub-Committee on the Work of its Second Session (16 April-3 May 1963), 6 May 1963, Annex I, C, p. 10, Art. 2; UN Doc. A/AC. 105/C. 2/L. 8, United States: Proposal-Convention concerning liability for damage caused by the launching of objects into outer space, 9 March 1964, in: UN Doc. A/AC. 105/19, Report of the Legal Sub-Committee on the Work of its Third Session (9-26 March 1964), 26 March 1964, Annex II, Proposals and amendments relating to liability for damage caused by objects launched into outer space, p. 2, Art. I lit. (e) (ii); UN Doc. A/AC. 105/C. 2/L. 10, Hungary: Proposed draft agreement-Agreement concerning liability for damage caused by the launching of objects into outer space, 16 March 1964, in: UN Doc. A/AC. 105/19, Report of the Legal Sub-Committee on the Work of its Third Session (9-26 March 1964), Annex II, Proposals and amendments relating to liability for damage caused by objects launched into outer space, 26 March 1964, p. 7, Art. Ⅶ; UN Doc. PUOS/WG. II/19, Italy: Amendments to Article 1 of the United States draft (A/AC. 105/C. 2/L. 8/Rev. 1), in: UN Doc. A/AC. 105/21, Report of the Legal Sub-Committee on the Work of the Second Part of its Third Session (5-23 October 1964), Annex II, Proposals and amendments relating to liability for damage caused by objects launched into outer space, 23 October1964, p. 18; UN Doc. A/AC. 105/29, Report of the Legal Sub-Committee on the Work of its Fourth Session (20 September-1 October 1965), 1 October 1965, pp. 4, 5; and UN Doc. A/AC. 105/37, Report of the Legal Sub-Committee on the Work of its Sixth Session (19 June-14 July 1967), 14 July 1967, p. 6.

② See UN Doc. A/AC. 105/C. 2/L. 7/Rev. 3, Belgium: Proposal for a Convention on the Unification of Certain Rules Governing Liability for Damage Caused by Space Devices to Third Parties on the Surface of the Earth and Aircraft in Flight, 26 June 1967, in: UN Doc. A/AC. 105/37, Report of the Legal Sub-Committee on the Work of its Sixth Session (19 June-14 July 1967), Annex II, Proposals, amendments and other documents relating to liability for damage caused by the launching of objects into outer space, 14 July 1967, p. 1; and UN Doc. A/AC. 105/C. 2/L. 39, Australia: proposal, in: UN Doc. A/AC. 105/45, Report of the Legal Sub-Committee on the Work of its Seventh Session (4-28 June 1968), Annex I, Proposals, amendments and other documents relating to liability for damage caused by the launching of objects into outer space, 11 July 1968.

③ See e. g. UN Doc. PUOS/WG. II/7, Japan: Amendment to Article I lit. (ii) of USA draft, reproduced in: UN Doc. A/AC. 105/19, Report of the Legal Sub-Committee on the Work of its Third Session (9-26 March 1964), Annex II, Proposals and amendments relating to liability for damage caused by objects launched into outer space, 26 March 1964, p. 19.

首要承担国家，只有在这两类国家无法识别的情况下才用领土和设备标准确定责任国[①]。这种观点最终未被采纳；当下，第一条第3款规定的四种类别发射国承担同样的损害赔偿责任[②]。

值得注意的是，美国和苏联是当时提供发射服务的主要国家，因此也是主要责任国，两国草案自始至终都赞成广泛界定发射国。

（4）“空间物体”

1963年比利时第一份草案第一条第2款中包含了“空间物体”定义，该定义与《国际民用航空公约》[③] 附件七中“航空器”[④] 定义类似，“航天器是指任何旨在外空中移动，且不靠空气反作用力停留在外空的机器。”[⑤] 匈牙利也采用这种方法，并列举

① See UN Doc. A/AC. 105/C. 2/L. 7/Rev. 3, Belgium: Proposal for a Convention on the Unification of Certain Rules Governing Liability for Damage Caused by Space Devices to Third Parties on the Surface of the Earth and Aircraft in Flight, 26 June 1967, in: UN Doc. A/AC. 105/37, Report of the Legal Sub-Committee on the Work of its Sixth Session (19 June-14 July 1967), Annex II, Proposals, amendments and other documents relating to liability for damage caused by the launching of objects into outer space, 14 July 1967, p. 1, Art. 2; UN Doc. A/AC. 105/C. 2/L. 40, Working Paper submitted by the Italian delegation-Draft convention concerning liability for damage caused by the launching of objects into outer space, 13 June 1986, in: UN Doc. A/AC. 105/45, Report of the Legal Sub-Committee on the Work of its Seventh Session (4-28 June 1968), Annex I, Proposals, amendments and other documents relating to liability for damage caused by the launching of objects into outer space, 11 July 1968, p. 30, Art. 2 para. 2; UN Doc. A/AC. 105/C. 2/L. 36/Rev. 1, France: revised proposal concerning the State liable and joint and several liability, para. 3, in: UN Doc. A/AC. 105/45, Report of the Legal Sub-Committee on the Work of its Seventh Session (4-28 June 1968), Annex I, Proposals, amendments and other documents relating to liability for damage caused by the launching of objects into outer space, 11 July 1968, p. 41; and UN Doc. A/AC. 105/C. 2/L. 39, Australia: proposal, in: UN Doc. A/AC. 105/45, Report of the Legal Sub-Committee on the Work of its Seventh Session (4-28 June 1968), Annex I, Proposals, amendments and other documents relating to liability for damage caused by the launching of objects into outer space, 11 July 1968, p. 42.

② 与《责任公约》第五条第3款规定相比，“从其领土或设施上发射空间物体的国家，应视为参与共同发射的国家”。

③ Convention on International Civil Aviation (done 7 December 1944, entered into force 4 April 1947) 15 UNTS 295 (Chicago Convention).

④ 航空器，指在大气中靠空气的反作用力而不是靠空气对地面的反作用力获得支撑力的任何机器。

⑤ UN Doc. A/AC. 105/C. 2/L. 7, Working Paper Submitted by the Belgian Delegation on the Unification of Certain Rules Governing Liability for Damage Caused by Space Devices, 29 April 1963, in: UN Doc. A/AC. 105/12, Report of the Legal Sub-Committee on the Work of its Second Session (16 April-3 May 1963), 6 May 1963, Annex I, C, p. 10, Art. 1 lit. (b) final literal.

了当时已知的空间物体①。美国的所有草案中都没有界定空间物体②。阿根廷一度建议仅包含专用于和平目的的物体③。

值得注意的是，阿根廷、比利时和法国联合提案中有一个被否决的空间物体的定义。该定义如下："空间物体指任何制造以用于空间活动的物体。就适用本《责任公约》而言，空间物体还包括运载工具及其组件，包括空间物体的所有组成部分，不论是否已从空间物体脱落或剥离"④。不同草案、提案及其修订、修改意见中空间物体的定义颇为不同，最终并没有就空间物体的内涵达成一致，而更像是对空间物体一词所指范围的说明⑤。

① UN Doc. A/AC. 105/C. 2/L. 10, Hungary: Proposed draft agreement-Agreement concerning liability for damage caused by the launching of objects into outer space, 16 March 1964, in: UN Doc. A/AC. 105/19, Report of the Legal Sub-Committee on the Work of its Third Session (9-26 March 1964), Annex II, Proposals and amendments relating to liability for damage caused by objects launched into outer space, 26 March 1964, p. 7.

② See e. g. See UN Doc. A/AC. 105/C. 2/L. 8, United States: Proposal-Convention concerning liability for damage caused by the launching of objects into outer space, 9 March 1964, in: UN Doc. A/AC. 105/19, Report of the Legal Sub-Committee on the Work of its Third Session (9-26 March 1964), 26 March 1964, Annex II, Proposals and amendments relating to liability for damage caused by objects launched into outer space, p. 2; UN Doc. A/AC. 105/C. 2/L. 8/Rev. 1, United States: Proposal-Convention concerning liability for damage caused by the launching of objects into outer space, in: UN Doc. A/AC. 105/21, Report of the Legal Sub-Committee on the Work of the Second Part of its Third Session (5-23 October 1964), Annex II, Proposals and amendments relating to liability for damage caused by objects launched into outer space, 23 October 1964, p. 6; UN Doc. A/AC. 105/C. 2/L. 19, United States of America: Proposal-Convention concerning liability for damage caused by the launching of objects into outer space, 21 June 1967, in: UN Doc. A/AC. 105/37, Report of the Legal Sub-Committee on the Work of its Sixth Session (19 June-14 July 1967), Annex II, Proposals, amendments and other documents relating to liability for damage caused by the launching of objects into outer space, 14 July 1967, p. 6; and UN Doc. A/AC. 105/C. 2/L. 19 and L. 58, United States of America: Proposal-Convention concerning liability for damage caused by the launching of objects into outer space, in: UN Doc. A/AC. 105/58, Report Of The Legal Sub-Committee on the Work of its Eighth Session (9 June-4 July 1969), Annex II, Proposals and other documents relating to liability for damage caused by the launching of objects into outer space, 4 July 1969, p. 4.

③ See UN Doc. A/AC. 105/C. 2/L. 22, Proposal by Argentina, in: UN Doc. A/AC. 105/37, Report of the Legal Sub-Committee on the Work of Its Sixth Session (19 June-14 July 1967), Annex II, Proposals, amendments and other documents relating to liability for damage caused by the launching objects into outer space, 14 July 1967, p. 18.

④ UN Doc. PUOS/C. 2/70/WG. I/CRP. 16, Argentina, Belgium, France: Working Paper, in: UN Doc. A/AC. 105/85, Report of the Legal Sub-Committee on the Work of Its Ninth Session (8 June-3 July 1970), Annex I, Proposals and Other Documents Relating to Liability For Damage Caused by the Launching of Objects into Outer Space (Agenda Item 2), 3 July 1970, p. 16.

⑤ See Smith, Lesley J./Kerrest, Armel, *Article* Ⅶ, in: Hobe, Stephan/Schmidt-Tedd, Bernhard/Schrogl, Kai-Uwe (eds.), Cologne Commentary on Space Law, Volume I, Carl Heymanns, Cologne 2009, p. 139, mn. 50.

（二）评注

1. 上下文和规则的解释

第一条是《责任公约》的定义条款。它包含了四个对公约的适用范围和解释适用至关重要的关键定义：第一条第 1 款的“损害”；第一条第 2 款的“发射”；第一条第 3 款的“发射国”和第一条第 4 款的空间物体；第 3 款下有两项，确立了“发射国”的四种类型。

四个定义中的前两个，第一条第 1 款和第一条第 2 款确立了《责任公约》的“损害”和“发射”概念。第一条第 3 款和第一条第 4 款的其余两个定义分别是“发射国”和“空间物体”。后两个定义并不是《责任公约》独有的，《登记公约》第一条第 1 款和第一条第 2 款中也有发射国和空间物体的定义。

《责任公约》前言明确，缔结该公约的首要宗旨是确立损害赔偿责任的统一规则和以及简单、快捷的赔偿程序。《责任公约》第一条聚焦于国家为其空间物体所造成的损害在国际层面承担赔偿责任的关键定义要素和要求。

第一条第 1 款界定了发射国提供赔偿的损害类型。具体为“生命丧失，身体受伤或其他健康损害；国家、自然人、法人的财产，或政府间国际组织的财产受损失或损害”。第一条第 2 款将不成功的发射纳入发射活动范畴，进而可能产生损害赔偿责任。第一条第 3 款下两项规定了可能为本国空间物体承担损害赔偿责任的发射国的定义。第一条第 4 款将空间物体扩展至其组成部分、运载工具及其组件。

《责任公约》的最终解释须依从国际法的解释规则①。《维也纳条约法公约》② 第三十一条允许依据通常含义、目的宗旨和结合上下文等解释《责任公约》③，并没有迹象表明需要狭义性解释《责任公约》。在没有任何限制的情况下，广义的解释似乎更符合《责任公约》的目的和宗旨，即创设有效的措施，确保高度危险的外空活动造

① See Brownlie, Ian, *Principles of Public International Law*, 7th edn., Oxford University Press, Oxford 2008, pp. 630ff.

② Vienna Convention on the Law of Treaties (done 23 May 1969, entered into force 27 January 1980) 1155 UNTS 331 (VCLT).

③ See Art. 31 para. 1 VCLT: “A treaty shall be interpreted in good faith in accordance with the ordinary meaning to be given to the terms of the treaty in their context and in the light of its object and purpose.”.

成损害的受害人获取赔偿[①]。

2. 定义

（1）“损害”

《责任公约》第一条第 1 款列举的损害种类容易产生足够具体的印象，但在实践中，这样的列举还是过于宽泛。有趣的是，第一条第 1 款中损害的定义不包括对外空环境直接和间接的损害，而利用外空与确保外空环境质量之间的平衡已经持续引发关注[②]。谈判时，澳大利亚代表团曾建议将所有种类的、可合理预见的直接损害纳入到《责任公约》中[③]。求偿国需要证明遭受的损害是直接源自空间物体或者是空间物体活动的自然结果。条约标题《空间物体所造成损害的责任公约》说明损害必须是由空间物体造成的，而不是空间物体运行产生的产品或应用。

空间物体碰撞或在地球表面的事故可能导致不同种类的损害。第一条第 1 款中的财产损失通常认为涵盖直接和间接损失。另外，第一条中没有区分物质和非物质损失；实践中，这个问题留待个案中处理。谈判早期的一些草案和提案中区分了上述两种不同种类的损失，都被否决了[④]。考虑到《责任公约》的目的和宗旨，应当包括物质和非物质两类财产，是否赔偿取决于造成损害的因果关系。

尽管谈判中对健康进行分类的提议被否决了，健康损害应当包括生理和精神健康[⑤]。如果出现精神损害，需要证明造成损害的事件和精神损害的因果关系。曾有一

---

① 考虑到现代科技的固有风险，自由使用财产或国土（看是在民法还是国际法语境中—译者注）原则，甚至适度注意的要求已经显得荒谬和落伍。见 Lachs, Manfred, The Law of Outer Space-An Experience in Contemporary Law-Making, Nijhoff, Leiden, 2010, p. 116.

② See Gorove, Stephen, *Some Comments on the Convention on International Liability for Damage Caused by Space Objects*, in: IISL, Proceedings of the 16th Colloquium on the Law of Outer Space, 7-13 October 1973 Baku (USSR), AIAA, 1974, p. 255.

③ UN Doc. A/AC. 105/C. 2/SR. 92, Legal Sub-Committee, Summary Record of the Ninety-Second Meeting, held on 6 June 1968, in: UN Doc. A/AC. 105/C. 2/SR. 90-101, Summary records of the Ninetieth to One Hundred and First meetings held from 4 to 18 June 1968, 22 July 1986, Mr. O'Donovan (Australia).

④ 郑斌认为谈判代表们将此事认定为因果关系是否充分的问题，见 Cheng, Bin, International Liability for Damage Caused by Space Objects, in Jasentuliyana, Nandasiri/Lee, Roy S. K. (eds.), Manual on Space Law, Volume I, Oceana Publications, New York 1979, p. 115. 一方面是直接损失及其与可预见性的联系，一方面是间接损失与不可预见结果的联系，在二者之间划定严格界限是不会产生什么结果的。Christol, Carl, Q., Space Law-Past, Present and Future, Kluwer Law Publishers, Deventer 1991, p. 222.

⑤ 《责任公约》前言第四段明确，对此种损害的受害人迅速给予充分公正的赔偿。

个草案的条款中包含了精神损害赔偿的内容①。

经济损失是财产损失解释范畴内的另一种损害。经济损失求偿请求是否成立取决于损失和因果关系的证据，损失必须在空间物体造成损害的范畴中。损害是否过于远离事故或和事故不沾边，进而不在损害赔偿责任范围内，视乎个案情况②。

损害的概念需要考虑在外空活动中使用核动力源及其对发射国损害赔偿责任的影响。《核损害民事责任维也纳公约》③ 并不适用于外空活动的核损害④。《外空条约》第七条规定没有排除核动力损害，因而《责任公约》也没有将其排除在外。

在不同的条约草案和提案中，有过一些限制发射国赔偿责任的建议，后来均被否决⑤。因此，外空活动造成损失的赔偿责任是没有限制的。这在国际法中并不常见，甚至是独一无二的。

起草《责任公约》的目的是达成受害人导向的、无上限的损害赔偿制度。这意味着充分赔偿足以重建到损害事故发生之前的情势。在此方面，国际法院及其前身常设国际法院在有关案例中对此有经典解释，比如科孚海峡案⑥和霍茹夫工厂案⑦遵循的充分赔偿原则。在依据《责任公约》确定损害的类型和承担损害赔偿责任的前提条件中应当遵循两案中有关的逻辑链条。

损害赔偿责任问题会产生更为困难的解释问题，特别是空间物体导致的环境恶化或破坏环境的损害问题。法律的问题不仅在于空间物体是否给环境造成损害，当然这

① UN Doc. A/AC. 105/C. 2/L. 10, Hungary: Proposed draft agreement-Agreement concerning liability for damage caused by the launching of objects into outer space, 16 March 1964, in: UN Doc. A/AC. 105/19, Report of the Legal Sub-Committee on the Work of its Third Session (9-26 March 1964), Annex II, Proposals and amendments relating to liability for damage caused by objects launched into outer space, 26 March 1964, p. 7, Art. II para. 2.

② 印度草案（UN Doc. A/AC. 105/C. 2/L. 26）中涵盖了延误损害和间接损害，但谈判中对此没有达成一致意见，见 UN Doc. A/AC. 105/C. 2/L. 26, India: Draft Agreement on Liability-Proposal, 30 June 1967, in: UN Doc. A/AC. 105/37, Report of the Legal Sub-Committee on the Work of its Sixth Session (19 June-14 July 1967), 14 July 1967, Annex II, Proposals, amendments and other documents relating to liability for damage caused by the launching of objects into outer space, p. 20.

③ Vienna Convention on Civil Liability for Nuclear Damage (opened for signature 21 May 1963, entered into force 12 November 1977) 1063 UNTS 266.

④ UN Doc. A/AC. 105/C. 2/SR. 92, Legal Sub-Committee, Summary Record of the Ninety-Second Meeting, held on 6 June 1968, in: UN Doc. A/AC. 105/C. 2/SR. 90-101, Summary records of the Ninetieth to One Hundred and First meetings held from 4 to 18 June 1968, 22 July 1986, Ms. Gutteridge (United Kingdom).

⑤ Ibid.

⑥ *Corfu Channel Case* (United Kingdom v. Albania), (Merits, Judgement) [1949] ICJ Rep. 4.

⑦ *Case concerning the Factoy at Chorzów* (Germany v. Poland) (Merits) PCIJ Rep. Series A No 17.

是前提，还在于环境的特定损害是否影响了某个群体或个人的法律利益。如果缺少具体的权利和法律利益，共有物区域中更难确定和评定赔偿责任和赔偿金额。在外空损害中，外空环境财产性权益的缺失加重了求偿的困难。此类问题或许不应在《责任公约》框架内而是在《外空条约》框架内讨论，因为《责任公约》的“损害”概念不包括对外空环境的损害①。在一国领土内空间物体造成的环境损害，存在受损的法律权利或财产性利益，这种情况属于《责任公约》覆盖范畴。如果不存在可识别的受害人或财产权，换言之，在法律的意义上没有具体指向性，也无法适用《责任公约》，这是该公约覆盖范畴的另一个限制②。

《责任公约》中的损害定义是非常宽泛的，决定了其宽泛的适用范围③。核动力源损害始终在《责任公约》规范的范畴中④。《责任公约》没有排除特定种类的损害，但留下了难题，即如何最终评定什么是空间物体造成的损害以及空间物体和损害之间的直接关联。

（2）“发射”

发射的定义包括不成功的发射或发射未遂⑤。法律工作小组特别关注将外空活动最危险时刻纳入《责任公约》中，即发射阶段⑥。发射是最危险的时刻，特别是对第三方。

发射定义与不返回概念有内在联系，自发射那一刻起，空间运行就是不可阻挡或不可逆的。自此刻起应当认定航天器已经被发射，外空活动开始。只有将该阶段纳入

① See Commentary LIAB, Article I, mn. 48; Art. Ⅲ LIAB, only applies to damage caused by space object to other space objects.

② Lachs, Manfred, The Law of Outer Space- An Experience in Contemporary Law-Making, Nijhoff, Leiden 2010, p. 46.

③ See Commentary LIAB, Article Ⅲ, mn. 352; and UN Doc. A/AC. 105/C. 2/SR. 93, Legal Sub-Committee, Summary Record of the Ninety-Third Meeting, held on 7 June 1968, in: UN Doc. A/AC. 105/C. 2/SR. 90-101, Summary records of the Ninetieth to One Hundred and First meetings held from 4 to 18 June 1968, 22 July 1986, Mr. Riha (Czechoslovakia).

④ UN Doc. A/AC. 105/C. 2/SR. 92, Legal Sub-Committee, Summary Record of the Ninety-Second Meeting, held on 6 June 1968, in: UN Doc. A/AC. 105/C. 2/SR. 90-101, Summary records of the Ninetieth to One Hundred and First meetings held from 4 to 18 June 1968, 22 July 1986, Ms. Gutteridge (United Kingdom).

⑤ See Art. I lit. (b) LIAB.

⑥ 很多国内法现将责任保险作为发射的条件之一。如法国外空法第十五条 No. 2008-518 of 3 June 2008；见 Schmidt-Tedd, Bernhard/Arnold, Isabelle, The French Act relating to space activities-From international law idealism to national industrial pragmatism, ESPI Perspectives (11) 2008，该书中有法国外空法的原文纲要和非官方英文版本。

《责任公约》第一条第2款才合乎逻辑。

（3）“发射国”

一直以来，发射国概念是向受益于发射行为的国家施加损害赔偿责任的关键。当时可以预想到的利益有两类：该国受益于空间物体成功的轨道运行；该国作为发射服务提供者获得商业利益。1968年底的谈判中，法国代表团强调了这一点[①]。损害赔偿责任确定施加给以领土和设施用于发射的国家。求偿程序允许只向一国提出赔偿要求，这有助于追索有责任的当事国，确保其无法逃避其损害赔偿责任[②]。

《责任公约》中对发射国的定义重提了《外空条约》第七条的四个标准。此后的《登记公约》第一条延续了这个标准。发射国包括发射空间物体的国家（第一条第三款第（1）项）和促使发射的国家（第一条第三款第（2）项）。

“促使”显然给不同的解释留下了空间[③]。美国提案中，将“促使”描述为掌控发射方向的能力[④]。“促使”与一国发射空间物体的命令或合同有关。《责任公约》法语版本使用的是“促使”的反身动词。《牛津英文词典》中“促使”的解释是导致某事完成或取得某种事务。“促使”源自法语动词procurer和拉丁文procurare。考虑到“促使”的一般含义，其解释应当包括一国下令发射的情形。一些国内空间法在规范私人外空活动规则中使用“促使”概念，引发了有关国内法符合国际法重要性的争论[⑤]。

（4）“空间物体”

“空间物体”一词通常指发射或意在发射进入外空的人造物体[⑥]。《责任公约》谈

---

① UN Doc. A/AC. 105/C. 2/SR. 92, Legal Sub-Committee, Summary Record of the Ninety-Seventh Meeting, held on 13 June 1968, in: UN Doc. A/AC. 105/C. 2/SR. 90-101, Summary records of the Ninetieth to One Hundred and First meetings held from 4 to 18 June 1968, 22 July 1986, Mr. Deleau (France).

② Ibid.

③ See UN Doc. A/AC. 105/21, Report of the Legal Sub-Committee on the Work of the Second Part of its Third Session (5-23 October 1964), 23 October 1964, Annex IV, Summary of views expressed in Working Groups I and II, Summary of points raised in discussions of Working Group II, Part II, Points raised in discussion of specific Articles, p. 20.

④ Ibid.

⑤ 外空活动活跃国家国内立法的总体论述，见Jakhu, Ram S. (ed.), National Regulation of Space Activities, Spring, Dordrecht 2010.

⑥ Cheng, Bin, International Responsibility and Liability for Launch Activities, Annals of Air and Space Law (XX) 1995, p. 297.

判过程中，似乎隐含着空间物体及其造成的损害具有的特性是有形的物质①。在某种程度上其本质更接近解释而不是法律定义。第一条第四款明确空间物体包括其组成部分、物体的运载工具和运载工具的组件，这为广义解释提供了基础，确保囊括空间物体相关硬件的每个组成部分②。发射国不能在有价值的物体（如有效载荷）和相对不那么有价值的物体（如发射中的解体碎片）中任意作出选择。将发射中的所有组件囊括在空间物体概念中，包括无意进入外空的部分（如一级火箭）符合《责任公约》受害人导向的理念。

区分功能性、非功能性空间物体和空间碎片对认定空间物体是否具有价值，是有争议的。每个射入外空的功能性物体在其运行周期末的某个时间点都会成为非功能性物体。一些组件和运载工具只在一定高度内发挥作用，超越设计高度或进入轨道后很快变成非功能性物体。这些物体的危险性不低于功能性有效载荷。这同样适用于自始丧失功能的有效载荷。为确立受害人导向的保护机制，《责任公约》在发射国和空间物体间确立的联系，在此框架内没有必要区分发射成功的和旨在发射进入外空的人造物体。唯一有必要的区分是人造物体和自然（有害的）物体。外空监视网络对这些物体的处置方式可能是类似的③，但这和空间物体的法律界定无关。

空间物体概念的广泛性，特别是包括空间物体产生的空间碎片，提升了空间物体有效期和此后运行风险的敏感度。降低轨道碰撞风险提升了国内规范需求，以落实预防和减缓空间碎片措施。尽管在《责任公约》文本中，区分“功能性”和“非功能性”对空间物体的定义意义不大，识别仍旧是关键事项，不论空间碎片的大小，识别发射国是确定责任的重要步骤。人造碎片给外空活动的安全持续带来严重威胁。现有关于人造碎片数字和位置的数据引发了在轨碰撞风险提升的切实担忧，特别是空间物体造成的损害以及给空间物体带来的损害④。外空活动的可持续性因此成为热议主题，此间见证了致力于减少和补救这一局势的国际指导性规范的发展。目前，这是科技小

---

① Smith, Lesley J. /Kerrest, Armel, *Article* Ⅶ, in: Hobe, Stephan/Schmidt-Tedd, Bernhard/Schrogl, Kai-Uwe (eds.), Cologne Commentary on Space Law, Volume I, Carl Heymanns, Cologne 2009, p. 139, mn. 51.

② See chapter on REG in this volume, Commentary REG, Article I, mn. 27.

③ 隶属于美国军方的空间监视网络和其他机构一起追踪空间碎片。有关报告见 http://celestrak.com 和 https://www.space-track.org/perl/login.pl，最后访问时间：2019 年 4 月 26 日。

④ See UN Doc. A/AC. 105/990, Report of the Legal Subcommittee on its fiftieth session (28 March-8 April 2011), 20 April 2011, p. 19.

组委员会[1]和外空委的正式工作议题[2]。

三、第二条（绝对责任）

Smith and Kerrest

发射国对其空间物体在地球表面，或给飞行中的飞机造成损害，应负有赔偿的绝对责任。

目录

① 该工作议程的正式标题是“外空活动的长期可持续性”。见如 UN Doc. A/AC. 105/1001, Report of the Scientific and Technical Subcommittee on its forty-ninth session (6-17 February 2012), 28 February 2012, paras. 183-210.

② 见 UN Doc. A/67/20, Report of the Committee on the Peaceful Uses of Outer Space, General Assembly Official Records, Supplement No. 20, 29 June 2012, para. 346. 关于空间碎片，法律小组委员会的工作日程上的有关议题是交换关于空间碎片减缓措施的国内机制信息。见如 UN Doc. A/AC. 105/1003, Report of the Legal Subcommittee on its fifty-first session (19-30 March 2012), 10 April 2012, paras. 136-158.

(1) 因果关系

(2) 宇宙 954 号

(3) 外空信号导致的损害赔偿责任

4. 通过强制保险规范损害赔偿责任

5.《外空条约》和《责任公约》项下得不到赔偿的损害

(一) 谈判和起草过程

1. 背景

第二条事关损害赔偿责任的范畴和发射国的作用，有关讨论横跨了《责任公约》的整个谈判期。基本一致的意见是空间物体在地球表面造成的损害，发射国应当承担损害赔偿责任。

《责任公约》的宗旨，即确保潜在受害者得到充分赔偿，是整个谈判过程的核心焦点。不过，谈判也体现了当时的地缘政治关切，即保护非航天国家，避免其承担没有参与的外空活动造成损害的赔偿责任。

当时的法律小组委员会届会中首要关切有三个：第一，《责任公约》中地面损害概念的构成要素；第二，《责任公约》覆盖损害的性质；第三，受《责任公约》条款保护的法人和自然人以及利益。

谈判中各国代表团反复提及第二条的两个重要原则。第一，绝对责任的概念；第二，发射国与其导致损害的空间物体的关联①。损害地点与可适用法律的关系是进一步的考量。应当注意的是，当时还没有充分界定损害，并且美国 1964 年草案文本将损害赔偿责任施加给登记国②。

2. 绝对责任

美国 1962 年草案已提出，空间物体在地球表面造成的损害应适用绝对赔偿责任③。这意味着起草的国际条约中须包含五个原则，1963 年比利时草案也包含了这五

① Art. II LIAB："A launching State shall be absolutely liable to pay compensation for damage caused by its space object.".

② 见 Commentary LIAB, Article I, mn. 37；根据该草案，登记缺位的情况下，才适用“发射国”概念。

③ 见 UN Doc. A/AC. 105/C. 2/L. 4, USA：Proposal-Liability for Space Vehicle Accidents, 4 June 1962, in：UN Doc. A/AC. 105/6, Report of the Legal Sub-Committee on the Work of its First Session (28 May-20 June 1962), 9 July 1962, p. 6, para. 3 lit. (b)：空间物体造成损害的求偿不需要提供过错证据。

个原则[①]。这两份草案都不要求过错。美国第一份草案第三条第一次明确提及“绝对赔偿责任”[②]。这份草案第三条第一款有关“绝对赔偿责任”的表述为，“第二条所指的损害赔偿责任是绝对的；但是，如果要求赔偿的国家或个人存在重大疏忽，应依过错程度减少或免除给予赔偿的义务。”[③]

有趣的是，美国草案第三条第2款排除了射入外空后空间物体碰撞的损害赔偿责任[④]。似乎当时占据主导的是外空活动的固有危险，互惠分担类似危险以及每个空间系统自担损失等观念，当然最后议定的是各国对外空中的活动承担过错责任。就地球表面的损失而言，绝对赔偿责任原则与1952年《关于外空航空器对地（水）面上第三人造成损害的公约》（以下简称1952年《罗马公约》）保持一致[⑤]。

尽管1963年《外空宣言》第8段仅明确外空活动损害赔偿责任的一般原则，仍为引入地面损害绝对赔偿责任提供了基础[⑥]。非航天国家担心在大多数外空意外事故中只能承受损失。绝对赔偿责任将给航天国家施加更多的义务（当时只有两个航天大

① 见 UN Doc. A/AC. 105/C. 2/L. 7, Working Paper Submitted by the Belgian Delegation on the Unification of Certain Rules Governing Liability for Damage Caused by Space Devices, 29 April 1963, in: UN Doc. A/AC. 105/12, Report of the Legal Sub-Committee on the Work of its Second Session (16 April-3 May 1963), 6 May 1963, Annex I, C, p. 10, Art. 3：一旦提交证明损害和空间物体因果关系的证据，就有给予赔偿的义务。因此，只要求因果关系，无需过错。

② See UN Doc. A/AC. 105/C. 2/L. 8, United States: Proposal-Convention concerning liability for damage caused by the launching of objects into outer space, 9 March 1964, in: UN Doc. A/AC. 105/19, Report of the Legal Sub-Committee on the Work of its Third Session (9-26 March 1964), 26 March 1964, Annex II, Proposals and amendments relating to liability for damage caused by objects launched into outer space, p. 2.

③ Ibid.

④ 该款内容如下，“如果射入外空的物体碰撞，参与发射该物体的登记国或国际组织之间不存在损害赔偿责任”。UN Doc. A/AC. 105/C. 2/L. 8, United States: Proposal-Convention concerning liability for damage caused by the launching of objects into outer space, 9 March 1964, in: UN Doc. A/AC. 105/19, Report of the Legal Sub-Committee on the Work of its Third Session (9-26 March 1964), 26 March 1964, Annex II, p. 2, Art. Ⅲ para. 2.

⑤ Convention on Damage Caused by Foreign Aircraft to Third Parties on the Surface, (signed on 7 October 1952, entry into force 4 February 1958) 310 UNTS 181 (1952 Rome Convention); Art. 1 para. 1 reads as follows: “Any person who suffers damage on the surface shall, upon proof only that the damage was caused by an aircraft in flight or by any person or thing falling therefrom, be entitled to compensation as provided by this Convention. Nevertheless there shall be no right to compensation if the damage is not a direct consequence of the incident giving rise thereto, or if the damage results from the mere fact of passage of the aircraft through the airspace in conformity with existing air traffic regulations.”.

⑥ Para. 8 1963 Principles Declaration: “Each State which launches or procures the launching of an object into outer space, and each State from whose territory or facility an object is launched, is internationally liable for damage to a foreign State or to its natural or juridical persons by such object or its component parts on the Earth, in air space, or in outer space.”.

国)，并为主要是发展中国家的非航天国家提供保护。苏联代表赫列斯托弗先生在法律小组委员会强调国家责任的义务内容时，特别是依据 1963 年《外空宣言》第 5 段和第 8 段，对这个立场有清晰的表述，“必须强调国家不得允许私人公司或国际组织以损害人类生命、健康或财产的方式从事外空活动，《外空宣言》已经明确了起草责任协议时法律小组委员会应当采取的方向”①。工作小组在起草其他有关法律原则的时候承继了这个方向。

3. 不同的草案文本

在漫长的谈判过程中，外空活动损害赔偿责任采用哪种形式最为恰当的争论接连不断。早期，匈牙利草案中曾“为解决损害赔偿责任背后格外复杂的原则问题提出了一个令人满意的解决办法”②。1964 年匈牙利草案首次区分了绝对责任和过错责任。该草案涵盖了充分赔偿原则，区分直接和间接地面损害③。没有充分讨论两种损害赔偿责任并存的原因是，当时压倒一切的担忧是为地面损害创设赔偿制度。匈牙利草案第五条的外空损害有赖于过错，即“如果受损国提交了证据，证明在外空的损害是另一国过错造成的，后者应当对该损害承担赔偿责任”④。

考虑到缺少外空领域的经验，寻求解决办法有必要依赖常识和逻辑⑤。匈牙利草案第四条给非法活动施加了充分赔偿义务。美国第一份修改版草案第二条第 1 款没有

① See UN Doc. A/AC. 105/C. 2/SR. 35, Legal Sub-Committee, Summary Record of the Thirty-Fifth Meeting, held on 16 March 1964, in: UN Doc. A/AC. 105/C. 2/SR. 29-37, Summary records of the 29th to 37th meetings held from 9 to 26 March 1964, 24 August 1964.

② Ibid. Mr. Khlestov (Union of Soviet Socialist Republics).

③ See UN Doc. A/AC. 105/C. 2/L. 10, Hungary: Proposed draft agreement-Agreement concerning liability for damage caused by the launching of objects into outer space, 16 March 1964, in: UN Doc. A/AC. 105/19, Report of the Legal Sub-Committee on the Work of its Third Session (9-26 March 1964), Annex II, Proposals and amendments relating to liability for damage caused by objects launched into outer space, 26 March 1964, p. 7, Art. IV.

④ UN Doc. A/AC. 105/C. 2/L. 10, Hungary: Proposed draft agreement-Agreement concerning liability for damage caused by the launching of objects into outer space, 16 March 1964, in: UN Doc. A/AC. 105/19, Report of the Legal Sub-Committee on the Work of its Third Session (9-26 March 1964), Annex II, Proposals and amendments relating to liability for damage caused by objects launched into outer space, 26 March 1964, p. 7, Art. V.

⑤ See UN Doc. A/AC. 105/C. 2/SR. 35, Legal Sub-Committee, Summary Record of the Thirty-Fifth Meeting, held on 16 March 1964, in: UN Doc. A/AC. 105/C. 2/SR. 29-37, Summary records of the 29th to 37th meetings held from 9 to 26 March 1964, 24 August 1964, Mr. Khlestov (Union of Soviet Socialist Republics).

区分绝对责任和过错责任[1]，“发射国应当对赔偿负有绝对责任，并依据《责任公约》的条款，对发射进入外空物体在地面、空气空间和外层空间造成的损害向受害人代表国支付赔偿金”。对于在外空的损害，也曾有建议将其纳入到绝对责任规则项下，尽管当时还没有明确损害赔偿责任应当是无限制的。无论发生地，为损害确立单一损害赔偿责任的建议没有获得支持，且原因不详。捷克斯洛伐克代表团同意，只有遵循1963年《外空宣言》才能解决损害赔偿问题。这需要明确损害的定义、损害赔偿责任的程度、损害责任承担方和赔偿求偿方[2]。

但是，绝对责任和过错责任并用在知名国际法学者群体中获得广泛的支持，比如美国的Cooper，英国的Jenks和德国的Wimmer，谈判中一些代表引用学者著作作为本国意见的支撑[3]。谈判中，苏联代表团认为绝对赔偿责任是最切实可行的解决办法，能将未进入外空的物体纳入到发射国赔偿责任范畴中。如苏联代表雷巴科夫先生所说，“当下最重要的是确立损害赔偿责任的原则，在《责任公约》中为外空活动引发的具体问题提供可行的解决方案”[4]。

是否应当确立连带赔偿责任等进一步的问题，当时并不如确立公正、可行的程序那般重要。

4.《外空条约》和《责任公约》的关系

《外空条约》和《责任公约》之间关系是《责任公约》谈判的一部分。起草《责任公约》是为了补充和扩展《外空条约》有关条款确立的规则。有些国家是《外空条约》当事国但不是《责任公约》当事国，只能应用《外空条约》第七条向这些国

① See UN Doc. A/AC. 105/C. 2/L. 8/Rev. 1, United States: Proposal-Convention concerning liability for damage caused by the launching of objects into outer space, in: UN Doc. A/AC. 105/21, Report of the Legal Sub-Committee on the Work of the Second Part of its Third Session (5-23 October 1964), Annex II, Proposals and amendments relating to liability for damage caused by objects launched into outer space, 23 October 1964, p. 6.

② See UN Doc. A/AC. 105/C. 2/SR. 35, Legal Sub-Committee, Summary Record of the Thirty-Fifth Meeting, held on 16 March 1964, in: UN Doc. A/AC. 105/C. 2/SR. 29-37, Summary records of the 29th to 37th meetings held from 9 to 26 March 1964, 24 August 1964, Mr. Zak (Czechoslovakia).

③ See UN Doc. A/AC. 105/C. 2/SR. 35, Legal Sub-Committee, Summary Record of the Thirty-Fifth Meeting, held on 16 March 1964, in: UN Doc. A/AC. 105/C. 2/SR. 29-37, Summary records of the 29th to 37th meetings held from 9 to 26 March 1964, 24 August 1964, Mr. Khlestov (Union of Soviet Socialist Republics).

④ See UN Doc. A/AC. 105/C. 2/SR. 49, Legal Sub-Committee, Summary Record of the Forty-Ninth Meeting, held on 28 September 1965, 30 November 1965, Mr. Rybakov (Soviet Union).

家求偿，该条规定当事国为本国外空活动承担责任①，这可以作为赔偿要求的基础。

同样地，非《外空条约》当事国可能加入《责任公约》。美国代表团雷斯先生认为，《责任公约》不得影响在发射国管辖下受到伤害个人的权利，即便该国可能既不是《外空条约》的当事国，也不是《责任公约》的当事国②。这个观点与其后将发射国本国国民排除适用范围之外的《责任公约》条款有关，即《责任公约》第七条。这有悖于国际法的传统立场，即条约对缔约方有约束力。但这是对《责任公约》赔偿机制普适性的认可，据此可预言《责任公约》可能演进成为具有国际习惯法地位的赔偿制度。

5. 发射国和空间物体

《营救协定》第六条是向界定“发射国”迈出的第一步③。在谈判起草《责任公约》的过程中，各国认可“发射国”一词应当将不同种类的发射国囊括其中。因此，花费了一些时间就最终定义达成一致。赔偿责任施加给与空间物体有关的国家，尽管这些国家并不一定拥有自己的发射设施。各国认可和鼓励发射国继续提供发射服务的重要性，以及设立确保外空事故受害人能追踪不止一个发射国机制的必要性。

在这个背景下，发射国概念和“本国空间物体”之间的连接引发了基于促使发射国视角的争论，包括提供航天器的国家，以及与非政府实体之间的关系。谈判中各国都强调《外空条约》第六条的重要性，即本国外空活动和国家责任之间的关系。但是，起草《责任公约》的目的是确立独立的、有争端解决机制的赔偿制度，这仍旧是谈判的焦点。

6. 损害地点及其意义

自1964年起，一些草案中就存在关于损害发生地的争论。美国代表团强调在确定损害赔偿金标准中不适用任何国内法的重要性。赔偿数额应当依据国际法有关原则

---

① 外空法的一个明显特征是向非政府实体从事的活动施加责任的理论基础，偏离了国际责任法中有关归因的一般原则，见 Lachs, Manfred, The Law of Outer Space- An Experience in Contemporary Law-Making, Nijhoff, Leiden 2010, p. 114：“接纳这个原则打消了所有关于归因的疑虑”。

② See UN Doc. A/AC. 105/C. 2/SR. 52 Legal Sub-Committee, Summary Record of the Fifty-Second Meeting, held on 29 September 1965, 19 Januar 1966, Mr. Reis (United States), who stated that “[…] the rights available to an injured person in jurisdictions of the launching State remained unaffected even if his country were neither a party to the Treaty on Outer Space nor to the convention on liability.”.

③ Art. 6 ARRA reads as follows: “For the purposes of this Agreement, the term ‚launching authority’ shall refer to the State responsible for launching […]”.

确立，即公正和公平[①]。此后，匈牙利草案没有提及损害发生的地点。1964 年 10 月，比利时草案的焦点是第一条，即创设证明因果关系的损害赔偿制度的必要性。该草案第二条列举了依据发生地法给船舶、航空器和空间设施造成损害的清单[②]。

直到 1968 年，意大利代表团提交的工作文件中才出现了地面损害概念[③]。该文件意在适用于空间物体造成的所有损害，其第三条对不同损害做了区分：第一款是地面损害；第二款是空气空间的损害；第三款是在外空包括天体的损害。这个草案排除了在发射国境内的发射、过境和降落过程中发生的损害和赔偿责任。

1967 年，工作小组第六届会议原则上同意并通过了第二条的文本[④]。“发射国应当为其空间物体在地球表面和给飞行中的飞机造成的损害，应负有赔偿损失的绝对责任”[⑤]。到 1970 年 6 月 30 日，《责任公约》第二条达成了最终文本，包括了损害赔偿责任可能施加给一个或多个发射国的含义。

（二）评注

第二条只有一段话，该条将损害赔偿责任加诸发射国，发射国对其空间物体造成的损害负有赔偿责任，无论是给地球表面还是飞行中的飞机造成的损害。考虑到现代技术带来的巨大风险，且这些风险量级大多仍不为人所知，当时的立法者采用了无过

---

① See UN Doc. A/AC. 105/C. 2/SR. 77, Legal Sub-Committee, Summary Record of the Seventy-Seventh Meeting, held on 23 June 1967, 14 November 1967, Mr. Reis (United States).

② See UN Doc. A/AC. 105/C. 2/L. 7/Rev. 1, Belgium: Proposal for a Convention on the Unification of Certain Rules Governing Liability for Damage Caused by Space Devices, 1 October 1964, in: UN Doc. A/AC. 105/21, Report of the Legal Sub-Committee on the Work of the Second Part of its Third Session (5-23 October 1964), Annex II, Proposals and amendments relating to liability for damage caused by objects launched into outer space, 23 October 1964, p. 18.

③ See UN Doc. A/AC. 105/C. 2/L. 40, Working Paper submitted by the Italian delegation-Draft convention concerning liability for damage caused by the launching of objects into outer space, 13 June 1986, in: UN Doc. A/AC. 105/45, Report of the Legal Sub-Committee on the Work of its Seventh Session (4-28 June 1968), Annex I, Proposals, amendments and other documents relating to liability for damage caused by the launching of objects into outer space, 11 July 1968, p. 30.

④ Working Group II was established for the Liability Convention, Working Group I on the Rescue Agreement, see Report of the 3rd Meeting of the Legal Subcommittee, point 7.

⑤ See UN Doc. PUOS/C. 2/69/WG. 1/CRP. 2/Rev. 1, Austria: Working paper-Field of application and exemptions from provisions of agreement; Question of absolute liability and exoneration from liability, in: UN Doc. A/AC. 105/58, Report Of The Legal Sub-Committee on the Work of its Eighth Session (9 June-4 July 1969), Annex II, Proposals and other documents relating to liability for damage caused by the launching of objects into outer space, 4 July 1969, p. 36.

错要求的、绝对（或曰客观）赔偿受害人的责任制度[①]。正如（Manfred Lachs）法官所说，“此间跨越了很长的一段路，即从最初此类活动不承担任何责任的建议到承担绝对责任”[②]。

国际法不断发展进步，国家面对损害赔偿要求时，从要求过错或过失，到认可在某些情形下，国家批准或支持合法活动可能存在内生性危险，有关救济赔偿需要不同的责任规则[③]。在《责任公约》框架内，国家的绝对国际赔偿责任完全独立于国家责任。换言之，国际空间法引入绝对或客观赔偿责任是为了应对外空活动具有高度危险的特殊性质。绝对责任的概念超越了其他现有国际损害赔偿责任，特别是不要求过错和过失的严格损害赔偿责任。严格责任同样有助于确保特定风险造成损害的赔偿，通常和限制赔偿责任的能力联系密切。这赋予了某些设备和运输系统的运营者以特殊的优势[④]。绝对责任作为责任类别不同于严格责任。绝对责任中，损害赔偿责任是自动的和无限的，且如果有也只有非常严格的豁免。而严格责任是有限的，且有很多特别类别的适用例外。《责任公约》是第一个确立不同于有限严格责任形式的条约。

过去五十年的外空活动只见证了有限次数与外空有关的意外，但是空间物体仍然可能坠入城区带来灾难性的损害[⑤]。以过错为基础的制度不适宜确保潜在受害者受偿，

---

① See Lachs, Manfred, The Law of Outer Space- An Experience in Contemporary Law-Making, Nijhoff, Leiden 2010, pp. 115ff.

② Ibid.

③ Ibid.

④ 以下条约涉及国际和运营者损害赔偿责任。如 the Convention on Third Party Liability in the Field of Nuclear Energy (opened for signature 29 July 1960, entered into force 1 April 1968) 956 UNTS 251; the Convention Supplementary to the Paris Convention of 29th July 1960 on Third Party Liability in the Field of Nuclear Energy (opened for signature 31 January 1963, entered into force on 4 December 1974); and the Vienna Convention on Civil Liability for Nuclear Damage (opened for signature 21 May 1963, entered into force 12 November 1977) 1063 UNTS 266.

⑤ 1978 年，苏联宇宙 954 号卫星坠入加拿大北部境内，见 Gummer, W. K. /Campbell, F. R. /Knight, G. B. / Ricard, J. L., Cosmos 954-The Occurrence and Nature of Recovered Debris, Canadian Government Publishing Center, Supply and Services Canada, Hull, Quebec 1980, passim; 1979 年，天空实验号空间站组成部分落入澳大利亚，珀斯城东的沙漠中，没有造成损害，见 Lyall, Francis/Larsen, Paul B., Space Law a Treatise, Ashgate, Burlington/ Surrey 2009, p. 117; 2012 年 2 月，一个空间碎片坠入某村庄，见 Space. com, Space Junk Falls on Brazilian Village: Reports, Space. com, 24 February 2012 <http: //www. space. com/14672-space-junk-crashes-brazil-village-rocket. html> accessed 26 April 2019; 2011 年 12 月 23 日，子午线通讯卫星坠入西伯利亚，见 RiaNovosti, Russian communication satellite crashes shortly after launch, RiaNovosti, 23 December 2011 <http: //en. rian. ru/russia/ 20111223/170448359. html> accessed 26 April 2019, and BBC News, Russian satellite debris lands in Cosmonaut Street, BBC, 24 December 2011 <http: //www. bbc. co. uk/news/world-europe-16326942> accessed 26 April 2019.

特别是损害是由活动本身的危险性质引发的，和违反义务或过错无关。

《责任公约》第二条没有进一步解释或提及什么构成绝对责任，这与第三条形成对比，后者提及了过错责任。联系《责任公约》上下文，将责任和“绝对”一同使用，毫无疑问，发射国承担了充分和无限赔偿损害赔偿金的义务。而且，《责任公约》第二条引入了《外空条约》第七条所没有的区分，即赔偿责任的形式取决于空间物体造成损害的地点。不同于《外空条约》第七条“发射进入外层空间物体”的表达，《责任公约》第二条在指向损害来源时使用的表述是“空间物体”。对这些词汇的通常阅读和解释要求该物体至少是在发射阶段。但是表述的区别不应当导致不同的法律涵义，因为两组表述都需要广泛的界定①。

《责任公约》第二条的绝对责任原则只适用于空间物体在地球表面或给飞行中的飞机造成的损害，第三条覆盖在其他地方造成的损害。两条的区分通常简化表述为《责任公约》第二条覆盖“地球表面损害”，第三条规范“在外空的损害”。第二条涵盖了“空间物体给飞行中的飞机造成的损害”确认各方认可发射和返回阶段，包括离轨是外空活动最为危险的阶段。值得说明的是，《责任公约》第二条涵盖的“空间物体给飞行中的飞机造成的损害”并不是发生在地球表面，而是空气空间。与此相比，一个空间物体在空气空间给另一空间物体造成的损害由《责任公约》第三条规范。这个区别表面看起来简单，但应当谨慎对待，因为二者损害赔偿责任基础不同。《责任公约》谈判后期才划分了这个界限，详见前文②。

只有当地面损害中出现了绝对责任的概念，谈判中的航天大国才开始认真考量发射国与该国造成损害的空间物体之间的关系。

1. 区分责任和损害赔偿责任

在起草为了外空条约做准备的 1963 年《外空宣言》第五段和第八段时，外空法中第一次区分责任和损害赔偿责任。这两段细微修改后纳入了《外空条约》，前者是《外空条约》第六条，即一国为本国以及非政府实体的外空活动承担责任，后者是关

① See Smith, Lesley J./Kerrest, Armel, *Article* Ⅶ, in: Hobe, Stephan/Schmidt-Tedd, Bernhard/Schrogl Kai-Uwe (eds.), Cologne Commentary on Space Law, Volume I, Carl Heymanns, Cologne 2009, p. 139, mn. 50.

② See Commentary LIAB, Article II, mn. 80f.

于损害赔偿责任的第七条[①]。《责任公约》条款并没有直接涉及国家责任[②]。这是因为《责任公约》将损害赔偿责任施加给发射国，包括领土发射国，并确立了连带责任，且不考虑一国的国际责任。在追究责任的情况下，只有某个行为违反法律规则的结果导致了损害，才会引起损害赔偿义务[③]；而外空活动绝对责任的构成确保任何主体遭受的损失都得到赔偿，不论该损失的发生是否是违反法定义务的结果。因此，《责任公约》第二条只规范国家承担的损害赔偿责任。

国际不法行为的概念含有违反国际义务的因素，这与《责任公约》是不相干的；《外空条约》已经将外空活动合法化。《责任公约》通过向某个空间物体从事合法活动造成损害的受害人提供赔偿，确立了国家之间的具体风险分担。

（1）责任

国家责任是国际不法行为的结果，即某种作为或不作为违反了国际义务，且可归因于某国[④]。其法律后果包括赔偿该不法行为造成的损害[⑤]。

国际法委员会的工作对划分责任和损害赔偿责任起到了关键作用，特别是在外空活动背景下。国际法委员会有关规范国家责任的工作始于 1953 年。该工作最终于 2001 年通过了国际法委员会《国家责任条款草案》[⑥]。今天，该草案被视为国际习惯法法典化的代表[⑦]。1977 年，联合国大会邀请国际法委员会承担有关国际法不禁止行为造成损害后果的国际责任的工作[⑧]。长久以来，人们认为这个主题不同于责任[⑨]。

---

① See Smith, Lesley J. /Kerrest, Armel, *Article* Ⅶ, in: Hobe, Stephan/Schmidt-Tedd, Bernhard/Schrogl, Kai-Uwe (eds.), Cologne Commentary on Space Law, Volume I, Carl Heymanns, Cologne 2009, pp. 128ff., mn. 2ff.

② See Cheng, Bin, International Liability for Damage Caused by Space Objects, in: Jasentuliyana, Nandasiri/Lee, Roy S. K. (eds.), Manual on Space Law, Volume I, Oceana Publications, New York 1979, p. 120.

③ See Cheng, Bin, International Responsibility and Liability for Launch Activities, Annals of Air and Space Law (XX) 1995, p. 300.

④ 见联合国国际法委员会《国家责任条款草案》第一条和第二条。该草案文本纳入了联合国 56/83 号决议，见 Responsibility of States for Internationally Wrongful Acts, Annex, 28 January 2002（以下简称国际法委员会《国家责任条款草案》）。

⑤ See Art. 31 and 34-39 ILC Draft Articles on State Responsibility.

⑥ See UNGA Res. 56/83, Responsibility of States for internationally wrongful acts, Annex, 28 January 2002.

⑦ See Wolfrum, Rüdiger/Langenfeld, Christine, Umweltschutz durch internationales Haftungsrecht, Erich Schmidt, Berlin 1999, p. 112; and Rosenstock, Robert, The ILC and State Responsibility, American Journal of International Law (96) 2002, p. 792.

⑧ See UNGA Res. 32/151, Report of the International Law Commission, 19 December 1977, para. 7.

⑨ See, for example, UN Doc. A/7610/Rev. 1, Report of the International Law Commission on the work of its twenty-first session 2 June-8 August 1969, para. 83.

国际法委员会的起草工作最终通过了两个草案，分别是 2001 年《预防危险活动跨境损害条款草案》[①] 和 2006 年《关于危险活动跨境损害案件中损失分配的原则草案》[②]。

在外空，《外空条约》第六条确立了本国外空活动国家责任规则。该条和《责任公约》一样，规范的外空活动都包含非政府实体从事的活动，包括自然人和法人。这种直接归因于一国是国家责任一般规则的例外，因为公民的行为只有在少数例外情形下才归因于国家[③]。

（2）损害赔偿责任

《责任公约》中没有损害赔偿责任的定义，其内涵必须在各国共同认可的概念中加以解读[④]，即损害赔偿责任是法律施加的，特定主体在某个事件发生造成特定损失或损害支付赔偿金的义务。在国际法中，国家损害赔偿责任这个表述是与国际法不禁止行为的损害性后果有关联的[⑤]。在外空，《外空条约》第七条与《责任公约》第二条和第三条共同确立了一个制度，即在特定条件下国际法允许甚至鼓励的外空活动造成的损害，国家要为此承担损害赔偿责任。

《责任公约》的基本逻辑是为外空活动造成的损害结果施加国家赔偿责任。其条款中不包含国家责任的概念，参与外空活动是国家从事的合法活动。《责任公约》通过给国家施加损害赔偿责任创设了一种特定的法律义务，即为特定事件支付损害赔偿金的义务。该义务的引发是自动的，即有害空间活动或空间物体造成损害的结果。这将风险公正地归咎于从事极度危险活动的发射国。

在《责任公约》第二条的范围内，对地球表面和飞行中的飞机造成损害的救济与

---

① See UN Doc. A/56/10, Report of the International Law Commission on the work of its fifty-third session (23 April-1 June and 2 July-10 August 2001), Official Records of the General Assembly, Fifty-Sixth Session, Supplement No. 10, New York and Geneva 2007, Chapter V, para. 97.

② 两个草案的内容是互补的。前者关注预防危险活动损害的发生和合作，即便采取了所有预防措施，损害仍然可能发生，后者为损失分配提供了一种模式。见 UNGA Res. 61/36, Allocation of loss in the case of transboundary harm arising out of hazardous activities, Annex, 4 December 2006 (Draft Principle on Allocation of Loss).

③ See Chapter II, Art. 4-Art. 11 ILC Draft Articles on State Responsibility.

④ "文明"一词的使用是依从了《国际法院规约》第三十八条第 1 款第 3 项的措辞，即"一般法律原则为文明各国所承认者"。

⑤ See Köck, Heribert F., Staatenverantwortlichkeit und Staatenhaftung im Völkerrecht, in: Köck, Heribert F./Lengauer, Alina M./Ress, Georg (eds.), Europarecht im Zeitalter der Globalisierung-Festschrift für Peter Fischer, Linde, Wien 2004, pp. 193f. In a more narrow sense, the duty to make reparation is occasionally described as liability. See Bedjaoui, Mohammed, Responsibility of States: Fault and Strict Liability, in Bernhardt, Rudolf (ed.), Encyclopedia of Public International Law, Volume Four, North-Holland, Amsterdam 2000, p. 212.

过错无关。但是外空中的损害，取决于过错。《责任公约》第三条中没有过错规则的具体规定，须由主张国证实。详见下文《责任公约》第三条的内容。

绝对责任只能经由有效的法律规则或规范才能确立。被求偿方是发射国。由于国际法中总体性的国家损害赔偿责任制度缺位，《责任公约》确立的损害赔偿责任不能从国际习惯法的一般规则中演进而来。正如 Manfred Lachs 法官指出，“实际上，我们抵达了一个有必要确立新解决办法的转折点：让技术发展的利用者承担由该发展的风险引发的特定责任”①。

尽管《责任公约》作为特别法，确立了空间物体造成损害赔偿的机制，但并不排除可用于寻求损害赔偿的其他法律规则的适用性。《外空条约》第七条与《责任公约》第二条和第三条一道为空间物体造成损害的求偿确立了法律基础。但是，《外空条约》第六条仍旧是一国外空活动涉及国际不法行为造成损害的求偿基础。在满足上述《责任公约》规则规定的有关前提下，该条具有实际应用价值。

第二条有关绝对责任的条款也覆盖了不可抗力造成的情势②。

2. 地球表面损害的绝对责任③

《责任公约》第二条为空间物体在地球表面造成的损害规定了绝对责任，即数额无限制，也不论具体位置。最初，匈牙利草案中将自然灾害情况作为绝对责任原则的例外。但是，1968 年夏天，匈牙利撤回了这个例外。

《责任公约》确立了提出损害赔偿要求的一年时限④。一年的时限影响就《责任公约》提起的请求，但不影响依据国内法在国内法院提出的请求⑤。

作为国际法一般规则的例外，《责任公约》项下的无限责任的原则是在极端危险情势下确保充分赔偿。国际法的其他损害赔偿责任制度一般均规定了赔偿限制，作为

---

① Lachs, Manfred, The Law of Outer Space- An Experience in Contemporary Law-Making, Nijhoff, Leiden 2010, p. 116.

② Diederiks-Verschoor, I. H. Philepina/Kopal, Vladimir, An Introduction to Space Law, 3rd edn., Kluwer Law International, The Hague 2008, p. 39.

③ “地球表面”作为简化短语包括《责任公约》第二条对飞行中飞机造成的损害。

④ 根据《责任公约》第十条第 1 款，提出损害赔偿要求的时限是一年，自损害发生之日起或判明应付责任的发射国之日起。如果是在国内法院提起诉讼请求，时限由具有管辖权的国家或地区有关规范该损害行为国内程序规则决定。此类诉讼请求可能包含依据国际私法确立适用法的问题，即行为地法。

⑤ Kerrest, Armel, Liability for Damage Caused by Space Activities, in: Benkö, Marietta/Schrogl, Kai-Uwe (eds.), Space Law: Current Problems and Perspectives For Future Regulation, Eleven, Utrecht 2005, p. 101.

接受严格赔偿责任制度的回馈[1]。作出不限制赔偿责任决定的可能原因是《责任公约》规定的赔偿责任主体是国家而不是私人实体。国家通常有自保机制，参与外空活动的国家有能力承担外空有关事故的金钱赔偿后果。

在第2条的谈判中曾讨论过核损害的赔偿责任，特别是有关核的国际条约的适用范围并不涵盖外空活动损害。最终决定将核动力源损害纳入到《责任公约》适用范围，其逻辑是以赔偿受害人为主导的有效制度设计。

考虑到在地球表面发生的外空事故可能引发损害的严重程度，《责任公约》没有任何免除责任的规定。受害人的过错也不可能免除发射国的责任[2]。但是，《责任公约》第六条规定了绝对责任规则的例外，即求偿国的重大疏忽或蓄意造成损害。[3]

3. 空间物体造成的损害

《责任公约》第一条第1款界定的损害与“恢复原状”原则有关。这意味着必须将受害人的状态重置到损害事故发生之前。“恢复原状”概念是决定损害赔偿估量的基础，反映了广为人知的常设国际法院在“霍茹夫工厂案”[4]和国际法院在“科孚海峡案”[5]判决中认可的国际法原则。

（1）因果关系

因果关系是损害赔偿责任的必要条件。《责任公约》仅适用于空间物体造成的损害。这样的损害可能是通过撞击直接引发，也可能是最初损害事故的间接后果。《外空条约》第七条和《责任公约》第二条都没有提及因果关系，无论如何，因果关系是要求损害赔偿金的关键，因为求偿国必须证明其遭受的损害来自空间物体。在知晓发射国的地面损害中，易于适用《责任公约》的条款。在宇宙-954号案件[6]中，一颗苏

---

① 规定运营者对核设施损害赔偿责任限制的主要公约有：the Convention on Third Party Liability in the Field of Nuclear Energy（opened for signature 29 July 1960, entered into force 1 April 1968）956 UNTS 251；the Convention Supplementary to the Paris Convention of 29th July 1960 on Third Party Liability in the Field of Nuclear Energy（opened for signature 31 January 1963, entered into force on 04 December 1974）；and the Vienna Convention on Civil Liability for Nuclear Damage（opened for signature 21 May 1963, entered into force 12 November 1977）1063 UNTS 266.

② Art. VI LIAB.

③ See Commentary LIAB, Article VI, mn. 197ff.

④ Case concerning the Factoy at Chorzów（Germany v. Poland）（Merits）PCIJ Rep. Series A No 17.

⑤ Corfu Channel Case（United Kingdom v. Albania），（Merits, Judgement）［1949］ICJ Rep. 4.

⑥ See Canada：Claim Against The Union Of Soviet Socialist Republics For Damage Caused By Soviet Cosmos 954, International Legal Materials（18）1979, pp. 907ff.

联卫星的残骸落入加拿大境内。如果是“直接撞击”损害，空间物体的接近程度或其残骸就是造成损害的明显标志①。在第三条规定的轨道中发生损害的过错责任制度下，求偿方需要适用与证据法有关的程序规则，如实自证②。无论如何，损害赔偿责任都取决于发射国空间物体造成损害的发生。

不是所有源自空间物体的损害都是在本地或立刻发生的。损害可能是由空间物体引发的一系列事件造成，但并不能立即或在同一地点呈现出来。本质上，这些损害可能发生在地球表面，也可能发生在轨道中。损害可能是空间物体直接碰撞的结果，也可能是一段时间间隔后、某个中介事件或最初碰撞引发的事件再造成的间接损害。主张《责任公约》项下赔偿的一年时限考虑到了损害可能不是立即显现③。如果空间物体造成了最初的损害，能够纳入空间物体造成损害的范畴，该间接损害必须是除此不会发生的。该损害必须符合临近规则，即损害必须是空间物体引发事故的结果，且并非遥不相及④。如果空间物体和损害结果之间的因果关系链条被打断［causa interveniens（妨碍诉因——译者注）］、或断裂或不相关的事件发生［causa nova（新介入原因——译者注）］，则损害不再属于空间物体直接损害结果。不同的法律概念用于了界定造成的损害是否属于事故结果范围。通常，损失必须是可预见的，且不是遥不可及。损害必须是最初损害事故的结果或可归因于该事故。尽管适用法和损害的程度可由国际法规则确定和估量，仍有很多观点认为必须符合侵权法中与直接和间接损害有关的传统测试方法⑤。在普通法中，这些测试通常表述为可预见的和临近的⑥。这两个标准是确立赔偿或“恢复原状”的工具，这也适用于《责任公约》规定的赔偿金。

---

① 在地面损害情况下，《责任公约》预知确立了绝对责任，没有必要证明过错。但是，仍需要通过发射国登记空间物体的机制识别空间物体。对此的建设性批评，见 Diederiks-Verschoor，I. H. Philepina/Kopal，Vladimir，An Introduction to Space Law，3rd edn.，Kluwer Law International，The Hague 2008，pp. 44-4.

② See Commentary LIAB，Article Ⅲ，mn. 131ff.

③ See Commentary LIAB，Article X，mn. 255.

④ See Christol，Carl Q.，Space Law-Past，Present and Future，Kluwer Law Publishers，Deventer 1991，pp. 219ff.，who makes reference to Prosser's law of Torts.

⑤ Ibid.，pp. 221-223.

⑥ 立法准备性文件中提到了不同国家和地区的侵权法形式，Haanappel 认为宇宙 954 号案件中的净化费用是间接或从属损害。见 Haanappel，Peter P. C.，Enforcing the Liability Convention：Ensuring the Binding Force of the Award of the Claims Commission，in：Benkö，Marietta/Schrogl，Kai-Uwe（eds.），Space Law-Current Problems and Perspectives For Future Regulation，Eleven，Utrecht 2005，p. 116.

（2）宇宙-954 号

依据《责任公约》，加拿大政府向苏联提出的要求得到了广泛的研究①。该案对适用《责任公约》具有重要价值。1978 年 1 月 24 日，宇宙-954 号核动力卫星坠入加拿大境内北部地区，1979 年，加拿大就有关损害向苏联提出赔偿要求。尽管最终不是赔偿委员会确立的赔偿金，本案还是启动了《责任公约》的实体和程序规则②。首先，两国都是《责任公约》的当事国，加拿大的赔偿要求中，详细讨论了该公约的条款。其次，两国进行了漫长的外交谈判。尽管最终确定的解决方案是以两国政府之间的议定书形式作出的，且没有提及《责任公约》，但求偿声明的法律依据引证并详细论证了《责任公约》的功能和规则③。因此，该案仍旧是《责任公约》规范下的、解决空间物体造成损害赔偿要求的重要和主要案例。赔偿要求的依据既有《责任公约》，也有国际法一般规则。

加拿大赔偿要求包括清理造成其北部某些地区核污染的碎片的赔偿金。加拿大政府的求偿依据是《责任公约》第二条，主张《责任公约》第二条确立的绝对责任原则是国际习惯法。另外，侵犯加拿大主权引发国际法一般原则下的赔偿义务。最终加拿大接受的赔偿金额是 300 万加元，是实际花费和成本的一小部分，依据最终解决方法以无损法定利益的方式支付。但是，以绝对责任为基础计算赔偿金额的法律依据包括上述法律，即卫星坠落导致的合理、临近且有合理程度确定性的费用。《国际法律资料》复印了最终解决方法④。第一条明确“全面和最终解决与 1978 年 1 月宇宙-954 号解体有关的问题”。

---

① See Böckstiegel, Karl-Heinz, Case Law on Space Activities, in: Jasentuliyana, Nandasiri, Space Law-Development and Scope, Praeger, Westport 1992, p. 206; Burke, Joseph A., Convention on International Liability for Damage Caused by Space Objects: Definition and Determination of Damages after the Cosmos 954 Incident, Fordham International Law Journal (8) 1984, pp. 255ff.; Gummer, W. K./Campbell, F. R./Knight, G. B./Ricard, J. L., Cosmos 954-The Occurrence and Nature of Recovered Debris, Canadian Government Publishing Center, Supply and Services Canada, Hull, Quebec 1980, passim; Gorove, Stephen, Cosmos 954 and the Question of Liability, in: IISL Proceedings of the 21st Colloquium on the Law of Outer Space, 11-15 October 1978 Dubrovnik (Yugoslavia), AIAA, 1979, pp. 211-218.

② See Lyall, Francis/Larsen, Paul B., Space Law a Treatise, Ashgate, Burlington/Surrey 2009, p. 117.

③ See Canada: Claim Against The Union Of Soviet Socialist Republics For Damage Caused By Soviet Cosmos 954, International Legal Materials (18) 1979, pp. 907ff.

④ 双方的交换意见上一脚注；最终解决方案复印见 International Legal Materials (20), 1981, p. 689.

（3）外空信号导致的损害赔偿责任

现有外空损害赔偿责任制度是否满足了第三方损害赔偿责任的讨论仍在进行中，即电磁干扰或扰乱卫星无线电信号造成的损失。虽然对此类事故的含义有不同理解，但此类损害在导航卫星和通信卫星运行中是可能发生的。卫星信号失灵或受到干扰可能给其参与的运输或通信服务带来损害。这已经引发了有关空间物体定义的争论，即非实物的、不可见的电磁波和空间物体服务是否是造成损害的空间物体。

几个国际规范机构已经就是否有必要为卫星电磁和无线电波确立专门的损害赔偿责任制度展开协商。主要受到美国法有关 GPS 特殊性质的影响，为航空器确立特别制度的提议已经被否决。国际私法统一协会（International Institute for the Unification of Private Law，UNIDROIT）已将此议题纳入其立法日程中（截至 2011 年）。国际层面有关讨论有助于为此类活动确立专门国际规则的必要性达成最终意见①，其他学者已对这个问题提出了颇有建设性的观点②。

在所有情况中都涉及的问题是如何解释“空间物体造成损害”这个概念。信号和中介性事故带来的损失和损害赔偿责任仍不可避免地需要关注特定情势下所有可能的法律基础，包括大陆法系和普通法系私法中的认定侵权的法律基础③，仍适用前述有关临近损害和因果关系的考量。

有关卫星信号性质的争论还没有达成最终结论。《责任公约》中确切定义的缺位无助于这个问题的澄清。但是，对有关条款基于通常含义的解释支持这样一个观点，即《责任公约》预想的是卫星碰撞造成的损害，而不是因其从事的某种活动而承受的损害，如配套技术和设备传递的卫星信号。“空间物体”这个表述没有给非实物来源

① 国际私法统一协会已经将 GNSS 背景中的第三方损害赔偿责任纳入其研究项目，见 International Institute for the Unification of Private Law（UNIDROIT），Third-Party Liability for Global Navigation Satellite System（GNSS）Services-The Proposed UNIDROIT Project <http：//www. unidroit. org/english/workprogramme/study079/main. htm> accessed 26 April 2019. 初步研究形成了以 GNSS 造成的第三方损害赔偿责任为背景的第一份报告，见 see International Institute for the Unification of Private Law（UNIDROIT），Study LXXIX-Third Party Liability for Global Navigation Satellite System（GNSS），Preliminary Study LXXIX，2010 <http：//www. unidroit. org/english/studies/study79/main. htm> accessed 26 April 2019.

② Bollweg，Hans-Georg，Initial considerations regarding the feasibility of an international Unidroit instrument to cover liability for damage caused by malfunctions in global（navigation）satellite systems，Uniform Law Review（XIII）2008，pp. 1-21.

③ 《外空条约》第 6 条仍有规范作用，例如损害不是空间物体造成的，而是国家违反对本国外空活动的监督义务导致的。

的损害留下空间。

但是，这并不排除根据不同的法律依据确立其他解决办法。欧洲联盟已经在联盟层面，为伽利略全球导航系统运行确立了伽利略 GNSS 损害赔偿的一般规则①。伽利略损害赔偿制度的最终架构仍有待确立，但可能包含某种形式的运行者损害赔偿责任，且有责任限制。

4. 通过强制保险规范损害赔偿责任

《责任公约》第二条确立了损害赔偿责任的要求。这意味着已经决定了赔偿要求的实质性要件，赔偿损害额另有规定。《责任公约》第十二条是关于被求偿国应当支付的损害赔偿额②。

为支持商业部门，一些国内法甚至不仅规定了第三方损害赔偿责任的强制保险，还确立了政府保证制度或第三方赔偿责任强制保险上限③。尽管有专门保险合同覆盖的发射保险和卫星保险④，并不是所有外空风险都是可以投保的，因为保险覆盖范围受限于保险市场。作为商业航天市场的鼓励，国家保证行为让国家可以承担超越强制保险覆盖范围的运行者损害赔偿责任⑤。通过这种方式，发射国在面临损害赔偿要求时，可将一部分风险转移给商业部门。国家是否可以利用一国国内法规则向运营者求

① 2004 年 7 月 12 日，欧盟理事会通过第 1321/2004 号关于设立管理欧洲卫星无线电导航系统结构的规章（［2004］OJ L246/1），第十七条规定了损害赔偿责任条款，该条与《欧盟运行条约》（2007 年 12 月 13 日签署，2009 年 12 月 1 日生效（即通常所指的《里斯本条约》—译者注））第三百四十条第二款确立的欧盟机构契约外责任（即侵权责任，因为有些国家没有侵权责任的提法—译者注）主要规则并行。从其适用范围来看，这些规则主要是用于覆盖行政或管理损害赔偿责任，而不是卫星运行的损害赔偿责任。GNSS 运行产生责任的专门赔偿制度仍有待于确立。

② 《公约》第十八条规范求偿委员会程序，见 Commentary LIAB，Article XII，mn. 292ff.

③ 法国《外空法》第十五条确立了 6 千万欧盟的保险限额。美国法有关强制保险的规定，见《美国统一法典》第 51 编，第 509 章《商业空间发射活动》，第 50194 条（损害赔偿责任保险的要求是 5 亿美金）。

④ 有关效果的系统阐述，见 Kohlhase，Christian/Makiol，Philip，Report of the ‘Project 2001’ Working Group on Launch and Associated Services，in Böckstiegel，Karl-Heinz（ed.），Project 2001，Cologne 2001，pp. 55-143；further，Montpert，Phillippe，Space Insurance，in：Smith，Lesley J./Baumann，Ingo，Contracting for Space，Contract Practice in the European Space Sector，Ashgate，Surrey 2011，pp. 283-289.

⑤ 关于美国，见《美国统一法典》第 50915 条，超越强制保险上限的部分由美国政府承担，其上限是 15 亿美元；关于法国，见法国《外空法》第十五条。

偿取决于该国国内法的详细规定[①]。

除了 1978 年的宇宙-954 号案件，其他案件[②]有助于展示《责任公约》条款的实际运行[③]。尽管一些空间物体再入大气层并影响地面，可能引发《责任公约》项下的求偿，但幸运的是这些物体没有伤到任何人，也没有造成损失。然而，这些案件依然很重要，因为它们证实了《责任公约》得到了广泛接受，特别是考虑到有些国家宣告认可空间物体造成损害的赔偿责任，并广而告之寻找求偿人。

2009 年，美俄宇宙号-铱星轨道相撞事件呈现了更为复杂的场景，因为两颗卫星是同一个发射国在同一个国家境内发射的[④]。这使得两方无法求偿：除了要证明过错，该案中的发射国既是求偿国又是责任国。

5.《外空条约》和《责任公约》项下得不到赔偿的损害

鉴于《责任公约》将损害局限于空间物体造成的，必然存在一些情势无法适用

---

① 不同研究中涉及了欧洲各国为本国私人外空活动限制国家赔偿责任的意图和有关问题。荷兰和比利时立法似乎都未能完全接受为本国私人外空活动承担损害赔偿责任。荷兰立法限制了国家赔偿责任；比利时立法中，承担国家损害赔偿责任的条款受制于国家自由裁量权的行使。英国正在审议第三方损害赔偿责任强制保险的要求，目的是将每个空间物体的赔偿数额限定在 6 千万欧元，并为全部微小卫星移除保险要求，见 UK Space Agency, Reform of the Outer Space Act 1986: Consultation, Department for Business Innovation & Skills, 31 May 2012. <http://www.bis.gov.uk/ukspaceagency/news-and-events/2012/May/reform-of-the-outer-space-act-1986-consultation> accessed 26 April 2019.

② 1978 年，苏联宇宙-954 号卫星坠入加拿大北部境内，见 Gummer, W. K./Campbell, F. R./Knight, G. B./Ricard, J. L., Cosmos 954-The Occurrence and Nature of Recovered Debris, Canadian Government Publishing Center, Supply and Services Canada, Hull, Quebec 1980, passim；2012 年 2 月，一个空间碎片坠入巴西某村庄，见 Space.com, Space Junk Falls on Brazilian Village: Reports, Space.com, 24 February 2012 <http://www.space.com/14672-space-junk-crashes-brazil-village-rocket.html> accessed 26 April 2019；2011 年 12 月 23 日，子午线通信卫星坠入西伯利亚，见 RiaNovosti, Russian communication satellite crashes shortly after launch, RiaNovosti, 23 December 2011 <http://en.rian.ru/russia/20111223/170448359.html> accessed 26 April 2019, and BBC News, Russian satellite debris lands in Cosmonaut Street, BBC, 24 December 2011 <http://www.bbc.co.uk/news/world-europe-16326942> accessed 26 April 2019.

③ 1979 年，天空实验室空间站组成部分落入澳大利亚珀斯城东的沙漠中，没有造成损害。此后，NASA 广而告之寻找求偿人。见 see Lyall, Francis/Larsen, Paul B., Space Law a Treatise, Ashgate, Burlington/Surrey 2009, p. 117；2003 年，意大利—荷兰 BeppoSax 卫星再入大气层，意大利提供了再入信息并邀请可能受影响的国家指定当地联络点，见 Italian Space Agency (ASI), BeppoSAX Reentry, 30 April 2003 <http://www.asdc.asi.it/depposax/reentry/> accessed 26 April 2019.

④ See Kerrest, Armel, La responsabilité des Etats du fait de la destruction de satellites dans l'espace, in: Groupement Français pour la Recherche en Droit International (ed.), Annuaire Français de Droit International 2009, CNRS, Paris 2010, pp. 615-626; and Mejia-Kaiser, Martha, Collision course: 2009 Iridium-Cosmos crash, in: IISL, Proceedings of the 52nd Colloquium on the Law of Outer Space, 12-16 October 2009 Daejeon (Republic of Korea), AIAA, 2010, pp. 274-285.

《责任公约》第二条和第三条的规定。第二条和第三条之外的风险只能由保险或有关当事方自行承担。实践中，这意味着外空活跃的主体必须覆盖或保险有关风险。下文第三条将继续讨论这个话题。在这种情况下，《外空条约》第六条或许能基于国家责任一般规则，提供一个单独的求偿基础。但是，除非存在违反国际义务或不法行为，否则将无法寻求赔偿。此类案件中的受害人只能依据国内法寻求救济[①]。

四、第三条（过失责任）

Smith and Kerrest

任一发射国的空间物体在地球表面以外的其他地方，对另一发射国的空间物体，或其所载人员或财产造成损害时，只有当损害是因前者的过失或所属负责人的过失造成的，该国才对损害负有赔偿责任。

目录

（一）谈判和起草过程

此处，有必要回忆美国提案中的第三条，该条是外空损害绝对赔偿责任规定的起

① Art. XI para. 2 LIAB.

源[①]。在谈判后期，才决定为空间物体在地球表面以外的地方给另一空间物体造成损害确立过错责任。在有一个以上发射国的情况下，所有发射国承担连带责任。

谈判中，意大利代表团曾建议，应当假定在外空发生碰撞的各方之间存在共同过错[②]。意大利的立场反映了外空中活动的风险以及外空系统面对的危险。尽管如此，仍需要继续寻找能够获得国际合意的外空损害赔偿责任的基础。其结果就是各方风险自担的制度，但如果发生碰撞，权衡损害赔偿责任的依据是各发射国是否存在过错。

在为地面损害确立绝对责任达成一致的过程中，对第三条的过失责任基础曾稍有讨论。但谈判中看不出各方是否意识到了实践中证实过失的难度。

《责任公约》将过失责任置于发射国，但并没有规定因另一国过失造成损害的情形。第五条规定的连带责任并没有很好地与过失责任保持一致。这是鼓励发射国之间事前就基于参与和运行风险分担达成协定的又一个原因。

1968 年，第七届会议期间工作小组就第二条的最终文本达成一致。1970 年 1 月，工作小组通过了如今呈现的第三条[③]。

（二）评注

1. 结构和内容

第 3 条是一个整段，规定了确立发射国损害赔偿责任必须满足的不同标准，且这些标准相互联系。必须存在：1）损害；2）且发生在地球表面以外的其他地方；

① See UN Doc. A/AC. 105/C. 2/L. 8, United States: Proposal-Convention concerning liability for damage caused by the launching of objects into outer space, 9 March 1964, in: UN Doc. A/AC. 105/19, Report of the Legal Sub-Committee on the Work of its Third Session (9-26 March 1964), 26 March 1964, Annex II, Proposals and amendments relating to liability for damage caused by objects launched into outer space, p. 2, Art. Ⅲ.

② 见 UN Doc. A/AC. 105/C. 2/L. 40, Working Paper submitted by the Italian delegation-Draft convention concerning liability for damage caused by the launching of objects into outer space, 13 June 1986, in: UN Doc. A/AC. 105/45, Report of the Legal Sub-Committee on the Work of its Seventh Session (4-28 June 1968), Annex I, Proposals, amendments and other documents relating to liability for damage caused by the launching of objects into outer space, 11 July 1968, p. 30, Art. 4 point 2. 这个假定适用于给飞行中的飞机造成的损害，但不适用于地面和外空造成的损害。外空造成损害的责任以过失为基础。

③ See UN Doc. A/AC. 105/C. 2/L. 77, Text approved by the Working Group on 1 July 1970-Draft Convention on International Liability for Damage Caused by Space Objects, 1 July 1970, in: UN Doc. A/AC. 105/85, Report Of The Legal Sub-Committee on the Work of its Ninth Session (8 June-3 July 1970), Annex I, Proposals And Other Documents Relating To Liability For Damage Caused By The Launching Of Objects Into Outer Space (Agenda item 2), 3 July 1970, p. 4.

3）造成该损害的是一个发射国的空间物体；4）损害是给另一发射国的空间物体；5）或其所载的人员或财产造成的。

第3条涉及的损害发生情况是不同发射国的两个空间物体之间，给他国空间物体所载的人员或财产带来损害，损害发生地点是地球表面以外的其他地方。但唯有发射国或其负责人员存有过失的情况下，才产生损害赔偿责任。前文涉及了最初的谈判过程①。实践中，由于《责任公约》第五条给共同发射国规定的连带赔偿责任，可能产生难以认定过失的问题②。

2. 适用范围

《责任公约》第三条的适用领域和《责任公约》第二条逆向相关。《责任公约》第三条没有使用外空或外层空间的一般表述，而是覆盖了《责任公约》第二条适用范围之外的所有情况。这种办法的优势是避免在空气空间和外层空间之间划界。实践中，这意味着《责任公约》第三条也规范了没有到达外层空间的两个空间物体之间的事故，只要该事故不满足《责任公约》第二条规定的条件。另外，《责任公约》第三条这种宽泛的方法避免了该条与《责任公约》第二条之间存在适用缺口。

3. 过失的解释

过失通常指未能遵守或违反了法律施加的义务。不同于《责任公约》第三条，通常认为《外空宣言》和《外空条约》项下的损害赔偿责任基础是绝对责任。③

出于不同原因，特别是需要证明外空损害是由过失造成的，目前广为人知的外空碰撞造成损害的案件都没有引发直接援引《责任公约》的赔偿要求。国际法一般原则以违反国际义务作为衡量过失的基础，除此以外，难以确立个案的外空活动是否存在过失。下文将讨论选取过失责任制度的正当性。

近年来，外空活动管理以及有权限给外空活动施加义务的层级（包括国内和国际）引发了诸多热议。外空环境越发拥挤，特别是近地轨道，增加了航天器碰撞的风

① 见《责任公约》评注第三条，第125段。

② 《责任公约》第五条第一款规定了连带责任原则，《责任公约》第五条第1款规定了损害赔偿责任的事前分派。

（与原文不同：Dembling, Paul G., Treaty on Principles Governing the Activities of States in the Exploration and Use of Outer Space Including the Moon and Other Celestial Bodies, in: Jasentuliyana, Nandasiri/Lee, Roy S. K. (eds.), Manual on Space Law, Volume Ⅲ, Oceana Publications, New York 1979, p. 8.）.

③ See Cheng, Bin, International Liability for Damage Caused by Space Objects, in: Jasentuliyana, Nandasiri/Lee, Roy S. K. (eds.), Manual on Space Law, Volume I, Oceana Publications, New York 1979, p. 116.

险。因此有强化或修改外空过失损害赔偿责任制度的呼声，以及创设管理外空运行活动新规则的建议①。

（1）外空法中过失的概念

《责任公约》第三条中过失的概念在国际法中并不常见；国际法中一般指向的是违反某一国际义务，而不是过失。使用“过失”表述具有重大意义。适用《责任公约》的法官必须检视发射国或发射国负责的个人行为以衡量是否构成过失。为此，法官可能借助知名专家的意见，或者使用获得联合国或机构间空间碎片协调委员会（IADC）等国际组织支持的最相关的行为准则。这些准则并不是强制性的，但结合《外空条约》第九条上下文，法官可能将其作为正确程序和行为规范加以考量②。如果遵行了获得广泛认可的行为准则，则不存在推定过失的空间。在这个意义上，此类准则推荐了一套行为标准，并敦促发射国遵行。

如果发射国或发射国负责的个人没有过失，在轨道中的损害就不能引用《责任公约》。如果另一国家或个人也没有过失，为了获取赔偿，受害人将不得不利用国际和国内层面的其他法律或规则。为此，《责任公约》第十一条第 2 款确保国内机制向受害人开放。

总之，《责任公约》第三条的适用范围决定了，在外空的空间物体碰撞的发射国在过失基础上支付赔偿金，包括空间物体搭载乘客的情形。碰撞造成损害可能是和功能性空间物体碰撞的结果，也可能是和非功能性碎片碰撞的结果。如前所述，《责任公约》第一条项下空间物体的宽泛界定足以涵盖空间碎片③。太空漫步的宇航员实际上有赖于其所属的物体，只是空间物体短暂的外部延伸，因而在《责任公约》第三条的覆盖范围中。

---

① See e. g. Contant-Jorgenson, Corinne/Lála, Petr/Schrogl, Kai-Uwe, Cosmic Study on Space Traffic Management, International Academy of Astronautics（IAA）, Paris 2006.

② See e. g. Inter-Agency Space Debris Coordination Committee-Space Debris Mitigation Guidelines Revision 1, September 2007 <http://www. iadc-online. org/index. cgi? item=docs_ pub> accessed 26 April 2019; UN Doc. A/62/20, Report of the Committee on the Peaceful Uses of Outer Space, GA Official Records, Sixty-second session, Supplement 20, pp. 47ff. , endorsed by UNGA Res. 62/217, International cooperation in the peaceful uses of outer space, 22 December 2007, para. 26; NASA, NASA Procedural Requirements for Limiting Orbital Debris, NPR 8715. 6 A, 14 May 2009 <http://orbitaldebris. jsc. nasa. gov/library/NPR_ 8715_ 006 A. pdf> accessed 26 April 2019; European Council Doc. 17175/08, Council Conclusions and Draft Code of Conduct for Outer Space Activities, 17 December 2008, Annex II; and ISO standard 24113 : 2011, Space systems-Space debris mitigation requirements.

③ See Commentary LIAB, Article I, mn. 63f. .

但是，尚不清楚过失要求是否让该条难以或不可能在实践中适用。过失要求已经引发一些批评，如“将永远无法满意地处置在轨事故”[①]。过失的含义在外空法模糊不清[②]。外空中的过失是难以证明的[③]。基本上，这表明相比外空冒险的参与者，《责任公约》为不参与外空活动的地球表面的人提供了更好的保护[④]。这也彰显了《责任公约》为因外空活动受损的第三方确立受害人导向的损害赔偿责任制度的宗旨，即参与外空活动的主体已经接受了此类活动的风险。

（2）由发射国承担责任的个人

除了采用两种不同的损害赔偿责任制度这个实质性决定，《责任公约》第三条在外空中适用过失赔偿责任的规范还涉及了依据国际外空法，发射国承担责任的个人群体或某类个人的问题[⑤]。

将发射国的损害赔偿责任与发射国承担责任的个人联系起来，《责任公约》第三条实际上是依赖国际法现有规则决定哪类主体的行为适用国家责任，且更进一步。外空法超越了传统国际法中国家承担责任的个人类别[⑥]。外空法中，一国为本国在外空的活动承担责任[⑦]。正是出于这个原因，Manfred Lachs 法官才将这个法律局势明确描述为，“接受这个原则打消所有关于归因问题的疑虑”[⑧]。

《外空条约》第六条为《责任公约》第三条的解释提供了直接帮助：为有关国家

---

① Lyall, Francis/Larsen, Paul B., Space Law a Treatise, Ashgate, Burlington/Surrey 2009, pp. 108f.

② See Cheng, Bin, International Liability for Damage Caused by Space Objects, in: Jasentuliyana, Nandasiri/Lee, Roy S. K. (eds.), Manual on Space Law Volume I, Oceana Publications, New York 1979, p. 116.

③ See Hertzfeld, Henry, National Space Legislation as an Enhancer of Space Policies and Activities, Presentation at the 2010 IISL/ECSL Colloquium "National space legislation-crafting legal engines for the growth of space activities" held on 22 March 2010, Vienna, Austria 2010 <http://www.oosa.unvienna.org/pdf/pres/lsc2010/symp02.pdf> accessed 26 April 2019, at p. 13 he has proposed modifying the convention to change the fault into an absolute liability.

④ 1964年美国草案中，这种损害赔偿责任遭到了否决，“如果发射进入外空的物体碰撞，在参与发射该物体的登记国或国际组织之间应当不存在损害赔偿责任。”.

⑤ See Hertzfeld, Henry, National Space Legislation as an Enhancer of Space Policies and Activities, Presentation at the 2010 IISL/ECSL Colloquium "National space legislation-crafting legal engines for the growth of space activities" held on 22 March 2010, Vienna, Austria 2010 <http://www.oosa.unvienna.org/pdf/pres/lsc2010/symp02.pdf> accessed 26 April 2019.

⑥ See Brownlie, Ian, Principles of Public International Law, 7th edn., Oxford University Press, Oxford 2008, pp. 445ff.; and Maniatis, Dimitri, The Law Governing Liability for Damage caused by Space Objects: From State Responsibility to Private Liability, Annals of Air and Space Law (XXII) 1997, p. 369.

⑦ See Art. VI OST.

⑧ Lachs, Manfred, The Law of Outer Space- An Experience in Contemporary Law-Making, Nijhoff, Leiden 2010, p. 114.

许可的外空活动授予了合法性。谈判中，没有纪录表明指向国际责任具有缩小《责任公约》适用范围的效果。

《责任公约》确立了不同于国家责任一般规范的国家损害赔偿责任制度。但是，其规则符合《外空条约》第六条并与之相呼应。为此，《责任公约》第三条后半句中“发射国承担责任的个人”必须解释为参与发射国依据《外空条约》第六条许可的本国外空活动的所有人。为此，一国是否实际履行了《外空条约》第六条项下的许可义务并不是决定性的。缺少有关国家对本国外空活动的许可并不能改变该国作为特定空间物体发射国参与外空活动的地位。

谈判起草《责任公约》的目的是规范外空活动，确立一个有效的、受害人导向的损害赔偿机制。仅因缺少外空活动责任或归因性的准确解释就主张缩小其适用范围，任何这样的企图都有悖于该公约的宗旨和目标[①]。《责任公约》的目的并不是据此缩小第三条中国家责任概念的解释。必须广义解释第三条，该条包含了《外空条约》第六条覆盖范围中的所有人和所有外空活动，即在国内、政府间或国际层面从事本国或国际外空活动的人，不管这些活动是不是非政府实体从事的。此种解释方法符合《维也纳条约法公约》第三十一条到第三十三条规定的通常含义。

实践中，与责任问题相比，损害赔偿责任问题更多引发的是如何确立至少一个发射国的过失，以及可利用的证明方式。尽管损害赔偿责任法的运行有一定的法律预设，如“事实不言自明”，显示过失的表面证据，认可表面证据过失损害赔偿责任，甚至推定外空活动的过失，但这些都不容易做到。

少见空间物体造成的在轨损害案例，表明此类事故的复杂性。尽管最近有几个碰撞事故，截至本文撰写之时，并没有发生就轨道中的疏忽或其他过失导致的碰撞，依据《责任公约》提出赔偿要求[②]。

尽管如此，仍有必要强调《责任公约》起始于绝对责任。为在轨损害选择不同基础的决定对损害赔偿责任制度及对外空责任的认知有不利影响。有必要为外空事故造

---

① 如荷兰有关外空活动和建立空间物体登记册规范（《外空活动法》），2006年6月13日；比利时外空法，2005年有关发射活动、飞行运行和空间物体指导的法律，见 the National Space Law Database of UNOOSA<http：//unoosa. org/oosa/en/SpaceLaw/national/state-index. html>accessed 26 April 2019.

② See Kerrest，Armel，La responsabilité des Etats du fait de la destruction de satellites dans l’espace，in：Groupement Français pour la Recherche en Droit International（ed.），Annuaire Français de Droit International 2009，CNRS，Paris 2010，pp. 615-626.

成损害确立整体的赔偿机制。

显然，绝对责任法律框架与过错责任不相容。这提升了外空活动第三方责任保险的必要性和重要性。随着航天器尺寸的缩小和小卫星的发展，以及人造空间碎片的增加，预期可获取的外空保险将随之增长。

4. 外空交通管理

如前所述，如果从事外空活动违反国际法有关义务并造成直接结果，将承担《责任公约》第三条项下的在轨外空活动赔偿责任。现有国际法缺少外空活动约束性（如技术类的）标准，个案中可能难以论证或证明过失。但是，国际航天界正在讨论为外空运行确立和施加具体行为规范。这其中包括为了保护外空特殊环境，不同的机构和国际组织发布的减缓空间碎片指导原则①。究其根本，这些指导原则的意义在于确立衡量过失的标准。为达到这个目的，在轨活动的行为程序和标准一般通常为“交通管理”规范，这有赖于国际协议性质在多大程度上能够具有法律约束力。

外空交通管理在和平利用外空委员会科技小组委员会和法律小组委员会的工作日程上，这主要是为了确立有助于实现外空活动可持续性的机制，也有助于进一步领悟外空过失概念的内涵②。

已有确立外空交通管理规则的评议和考量③。为推动外空交通管理的规范进程，

---

① See e. g. Inter-Agency Space Debris Coordination Committee-Space Debris Mitigation Guidelines Revision 1, September 2007 <http：//www. iadc-online. org/index. cgi？ item=docs_ pub> accessed 26 April 2019；UN Doc. A/62/20, Report of the Committee on the Peaceful Uses of Outer Space, GA Official Records, Sixty-second session, Supplement 20, pp. 47ff. , endorsed by UNGA Res. 62/217, International cooperation in the peaceful uses of outer space, 22 December 2007, para. 26；NASA, NASA Procedural Requirements for Limiting Orbital Debris, NPR 8715. 6 A, 14 May 2009 <http：//orbitaldebris. jsc. nasa. gov/library/NPR_ 8715_ 006 A. pdf> accessed 26 April 2019；European Council Doc. 17175/08, Council Conclusions and Draft Code of Conduct for Outer Space Activities, 17 December 2008, Annex II；and ISO standard 24113 ：2011, Space systems-Space debris mitigation requirements.

② Report of Legal Subcommittee on its 50th session, A/AC. 105/990 20 April 2011；The Czech Republic at that stage submitted a working paper to the Subcommittee with a view to transforming the Guidelines on Space Debris Mitigation into a GA Resolution, see Report of Legal Subcommittee, id. , No. 163.

③ See e. g. Inter-Agency Space Debris Coordination Committee-Space Debris Mitigation Guidelines Revision 1, September 2007 <http：//www. iadc-online. org/index. cgi？ item=docs_ pub> accessed 26 April 2019；UN Doc. A/62/20, Report of the Committee on the Peaceful Uses of Outer Space, General Assembly Official Records, Sixty-second session, Supplement No. 20, 2007, pp. 47ff. , endorsed by UNGA Res. 62/217, International cooperation in the peaceful uses of outer space, 22 December 2007, para. 26；NASA, NASA Procedural Requirements for Limiting Orbital Debris, NPR 8715. 6 A, 14 May 2009 <http：//orbitaldebris. jsc. nasa. gov/library/NPR_ 8715_ 006 A. pdf> accessed 26 April 2019；European Council Doc. 17175/08, Council Conclusions and Draft Code of Conduct for Outer Space Activities, 17 December 2008, Annex II；and ISO standard 24113：2011, Space systems-Space debris mitigation requirements.

提出了一些初步建议，但尚未达到具有约束力的层面[①]。

五、第四条（两个或多个空间物体联合造成损害/第三方责任）

Smith and Kerrest

1. 任一发射国的空间物体在地球表面以外的其他地方，对另一发射国的空间物体，或其所载人员或财产造成损害，并因此对第三国或第三国的自然人或法人造成损害时，前两国应在下述范围内对第三国承担连带赔偿责任：

（1）若对第三国的地面表面或飞行中的飞机造成损害，前两国应对第三国应负绝对赔偿责任；

（2）若在地球表面以外的其他地方，对第三国的空间物体，或其所载人员或财产造成损害，前两国对第三国所负的赔偿责任，应依据它们的过失或所属负责人员的过失而定。

2. 在本条第 1 款提及的所有连带赔偿责任案件中，赔偿义务应按前两国过失程度分摊；若前两国的过失程度无法断定，两国应均摊赔偿义务。但赔偿义务分担不得妨碍第三国向连带责任发射国的任何一国或全体，索取根据本公约规定应予偿付的全部赔偿的权利。

目录

① See e. g. Contant-Jorgenson, Corinne/Lála, Petr/Schrogl, Kai-Uwe, Cosmic Study on Space Traffic Management, International Academy of Astronautics (IAA), Paris 2006.

（一）谈判和起草过程

谈判伊始就关注外空活动给第三方造成的损害。两个空间物体在外空相撞并给无辜的第三方造成损害，这涉及每个发射国的赔偿责任。因此有必要在草案中确立规则，并与《责任公约》第二条和第三条类似。首先，这是给第三方造成的损害，其次，与损害的地点有关，确立与《责任公约》内容保持一致且适当的赔偿责任。

在赞成确立第三方损害赔偿责任的赔偿制度的意见中，一个考量是在外空活动中使用的核动力源①。

两个发射国承担连带责任的形式，在航空法中为人所知，1952 年关于航空器给地球表面第三方造成损害的《罗马公约》中有类似规定②。

（二）评注

《责任公约》第四条共两款，第 1 款分成两项。该条涉及三个问题：第一，两个空间物体在外空碰撞给第三方造成损害的赔偿责任形式，损害或发生在地面表面（第四条第 1 款第 1 项），或发生在外空（第四条第 1 款第 2 项）；第二，《责任公约》第四条第 1 款最后一句明确，给第三方造成损害的两个空间物体发射国承担连带责任；第三，《责任公约》第四条第 2 款确立了有关发射国之间的赔偿责任分摊机制。

《责任公约》第四条与赔偿“无辜”第三方有关，前提是给第三方或自然人或法人造成损害。第四条为危险的外空活动造成的损害提供了两种赔偿责任形式。这与《责任公约》第二条和第三条的损害赔偿责任形式保持一致。因此，损害赔偿责任仍取决于损害发生地，并与《责任公约》第二条和第三条联系在一起。

1. 连带责任

（1）前提

《责任公约》第四条第 1 款的起点是将两个发射国的空间物体碰撞给第三方造成损害的赔偿责任施加给该两国。因此，第四条第 1 款覆盖了连带责任和第三方损害赔

① 几年后，与核动力源有关的规则编纂于联合国外层空间使用核动力源的原则中，见 UNGA Res. 47/68, Principles Relevant to the Use of Nuclear Power Sources in Outer Space, 14 December 1992.

② Diederiks-Verschoor, I. H. Philepina/Kopal, Vladimir, An Introduction to Space Law, 3rd edn., Kluwer Law International, The Hague 2008, p. 40.

偿责任两个问题。

施加该损害赔偿责任的要求是：初始损害发生在外空；由两个空间物体在外空碰撞或事故引发；上述碰撞给第三方造成损害；涉及到两个不同的发射国[①]。

《责任公约》第四条第 1 款明确，发生碰撞空间物体的发射国向第三国承担连带责任。在明确连带责任之后，《责任公约》才区分了赔偿责任的类型。

（2）保护第三方

连带责任是确保实现《责任公约》受害人导向宗旨的重要手段。既然是连带责任，受害人向任一发射国都可以索取赔偿。

此后，《责任公约》第四条采用两种不同方法规范给第三方造成损害的赔偿责任形式。第四条设想的情形是，一个发射国的空间物体与另一发射国空间物体在外空相撞并造成损害，并由此给第三国造成进一步损害。在这种情况下，两个发射国向第三国承担连带责任。第三国无需识别造成损害的空间物体，只需明确损害是由卷入初始损害事件的一个空间物体造成即可。这强调了《责任公约》受害人导向的性质。断定两个发射国与初始损害有关，比断定是哪个空间物体给第三方造成损害要简单。

损害赔偿责任的形式取决于损害发生地（简单地说，与《责任公约》第二条和第三条方式相同，第四条第一款确立地球表面的绝对责任，第四条第 2 款确立外空的过失责任）。在第四条第 2 款第一句项下，向第三国赔偿责任的分摊取决于每个发射国的过失程度。如果无法断定每个发射国的过失程度，则赔偿责任在两国之间均摊（《责任公约》第四条第 2 款第一句后半段）。换言之，尽管《责任公约》第三条没有规定共同发射国赔偿责任均摊，《责任公约》第四条第 2 款规定了分摊，但限于给第三方造成损害的情形。

给第三国造成损害的两个发射国之间的初始损害赔偿由《责任公约》第三条规范。

（3）《责任公约》第二条和第三条的差异

就第三方损害赔偿义务，《责任公约》第四条第 1 款区分了两种赔偿责任形式。

① See Kerrest, Armel, La responsabilité des Etats du fait de la destruction de satellites dans l'espace, in: Groupement Français pour la Recherche en Droit International (ed.), Annuaire Français de Droit International 2009, CNRS, Paris 2010, pp. 615-626.

存在如下两种可能性：根据第四条第 1 款第 1 项，如果碰撞给地面带来损害，根据《责任公约》第二条适用绝对责任，即碰撞空间物体的两个发射国向第三国承担连带责任；根据第四条第 1 款第 2 项，如果损害发生在外空，与《责任公约》第三条保持一致，承担过失责任。

《责任公约》第二条为地面和飞行中的飞机造成损害确立了绝对责任，《责任公约》第三条为《责任公约》第二条之外的所有其他损害规定了过失责任。任一发射国的空间物体在轨道中给另一发射国的空间物体造成损害，根据《责任公约》第三条，如果两个发射国均没有过失，则两国都没有赔偿义务。第三条规定，发射国只有损害是因其过失或其负责人员的过失造成的，才对损害负有责任。既然没有赔偿责任，也就不存在两个物体碰撞造成的损害的赔偿均摊。但是，可能在不同地点给不同的第三方造成损害。地面和外空损害可能损害不同的第三方的利益。

随着外空碎片数量的增加，未来在轨碰撞或外空损害的发生可能更加频繁，增加了人类外空活动的危险①。

2. 赔偿义务的内部分摊

与《责任公约》第五条规定不同，第四条第（2）款进一步准确规定了对在轨事件承担连带责任发射国之间赔偿分摊。

《责任公约》第四条预想的事件发生在两个发射国之间。这类事件可能无法事先预见，因此发射前有关国家没有就此订立协议。这与《责任公约》第五条的情形不同，后者规定在发射前，发射国可以也应当就各自的义务缔结协定。《责任公约》第四条第 2 款明确规定不是损害责任的分摊，而是赔偿义务的分担。这意味着受害人不参与该分摊，有关问题应当在向受害国承担责任后，由发射国自行决定。无论损失是发生在地面还是轨道中，不论赔偿责任是绝对还是过失，都适用该规范。

据此，如果能够认定一个或两个发射国存有过失，分摊应遵照下列规则。如果无

---

① 2009 年宇宙号-铱星轨道相撞事件中，俄罗斯和美国两个发射国均决定不起诉对方在《责任公约》项下的损害赔偿责任。由此引发的碎片至今仍在外空中。给第三方造成的潜在损害属于第 4 条规范范畴。See further, Kerrest, Armel, La responsabilité des Etats du fait de la destruction de satellites dans l'espace, in: Groupement Français pour la Recherche en Droit International (ed.), Annuaire Français de Droit International 2009, CNRS, Paris 2010, pp. 615-626; and Chang, Kenneth, Debris Gives Space Station Crew Members a 29, 000-M. P. H. Close Call, New York Times, 28 June 2011 <http://www.nytimes.com/2011/06/29/science/space/29junk.html?_r=0> accessed 26 April 2019.

法断定过失程度，《责任公约》第四条第 2 款项下的赔偿义务应由两个发射国均摊。证明外空过失通常有难度，甚至难到不可能证实的程度。在这种情况下，应当不管两个卫星的内在危险程度，均摊赔偿义务。

如果空间物体载有核动力源，可能造成深远、广泛的损失。根据国际空间法，在外空使用核动力源并不是非法的，核动力推进引发的损害赔偿责任分摊必须考虑其使用是合法的，且不构成过失。在这种情况下，考虑到每颗卫星的风险不同，即使不能证明过失，只有不均摊赔偿义务才是公平合理的。类似考量适用于绝对责任情形，且该活动本身并不非法。

本条规定的是两个或两个以上空间物体碰撞给第三方造成损害的连带责任，而非两个发射国之间的责任，因此《责任公约》第二条和第三条规范不受影响。

六、第五条（共同发射/连带责任）

Smith and Kerrest

1. 两个或两个以上国家共同发射空间物体时，对所造成的任何损害应承担连带责任。

2. 发射国在赔偿损失后，有权向共同参与发射的其他国家要求补偿。参加共同发射的国家可缔结协定，依据各自所负的连带责任分摊财政义务。但此种协定，不得妨碍受害国向承担连带责任发射国的任何一国或全体，索求根据本公约规定应予偿付的全部赔偿的权利。

3. 从其领土或设施上发射空间物体的国家，应视为参与共同发射的国家。

目录

2. 内部分摊/国际协定

（1）内部分摊

（2）可能的协定

3. 领土或设备的相关性

（一）谈判和起草过程

开始谈判《责任公约》的时候，并没有明显的引入发射国承担连带责任原则的决定[①]。为了避免可能阻碍发射服务市场的发展，1964 年的初始谈判聚焦于确保不向发射领土国提交损害赔偿要求。对于区分领土发射国和促使发射国损害赔偿责任，一些代表团表达了反对意见[②]。同时有一些担忧是关于损害赔偿责任对仅在很小范围内参与外空活动国家的冲击[③]。

担心受害国能否识别发射国，“特别考虑到发射是不止一国参与的共同事业”。“对参与共同事业的所有国家而不是单一发射国”施加赔偿责任是达成一致的初始迹象[④]。

有趣的是，特别是事后看来，隐含的假设是存在不止一个发射国。“领土用于发射的国家很可能与空间物体所有国就可能的损害责任达成双边协定”[⑤]。

近年联合国大会通过了关于发射国实践和鼓励就赔偿责任分摊签订协议的决议[⑥]，但发射国之间就风险分担达成安排并未得到切实发展。

直到 1968 年底，法国和美国代表团提议发射国分担损害赔偿责任，连带责任问题才逐渐清晰。美国提案提及了某个发射国的一个空间物体的“个别”和“共同”

① Cheng, Bin, International Liability for Damage Caused by Space Objects, in: Jasentuliyana, Nandasiri/Lee, Roy S. K. (eds.), Manual on Space Law, Volume I, Oceana Publications, New York 1979, p. 119ff.

② See UN Doc. A/AC. 105/21, Report of the Legal Sub-Committee on the Work of the Second Part of its Third Session (5-23 October 1964), 23 October 1964, Annex IV, Summary of views expressed in Working Groups I and II, Summary of points raised in discussions of Working Group II, Part I, Points raised in general discussion, p. 8.

③ See ibid., p. 8.

④ See ibid., p. 8.

⑤ See ibid., p. 7.

⑥ See UNGA Res. 59/115, Application of the concept of the “launching State”, 10 December 2004.

责任[1]，法国代表团使用的表达是“共同”和“单独”责任[2]。实际上这些表述的含义相同。当时美国的草案明确提及个别和共同责任是确保赔偿第三方的工具。尽管法国草案文本在那届会议上经历了小幅改动，仍保留了有关共同和单独责任的条款[3]。

此后，1969 年，在印度提交《责任公约》草案后[4]，不同代表团完善了其构建连带责任的最初建议。法国代表团草案的规定是，“将其领土或设备用于空间物体发射的国家与发射或促使发射国承担同样的责任，前提是不能识别后者，或者后者不是本公约的当事国，或者该国联合参与空间物体发射”[5]。该规定清楚地表明，法国代表团有意识地避免在《责任公约》中出现对受害人不利的第三方赔偿责任制度漏洞。这可能发生在识别发射国有困难的情形中，而发射发生地相对容易识别。另外一个漏洞是，如果发射国不是《责任公约》缔约方，参与发射国也不是该公约缔约方。

与受害人能否利用《外空条约》第六条无关，发射国是否为《责任公约》缔约方是合理的关切。苏联代表团阐明，国际法的传统立场是条约适用于当事国而不是非当事国，“赔偿损失的国家有权向共同发射的其他参与国，且是本公约当事国的国家

① See United States of America: Proposal-Field of application and exemptions from provisions of agreement, 10 June 1968, in: UN Doc. A/AC. 105/45, Report of the Legal Sub-Committee on the Work of its Seventh Session (4-28 June 1968), Annex I, Proposals, amendments and other documents relating to liability for damage caused by the launching of objects into outer space, 11 July 1968, p. 41.

② See UN Doc. A/AC. 105/C. 2/L. 36, France: proposal concerning the state liable and joint and several liability, 10 June 1968, in Jasentuliyana, Nandasiri/Lee, Roy S. K., Manual on Space Law, Volume Ⅲ, Oceana Publications, New York 1981, p. 329.

③ See UN Doc. A/AC. 105/C. 2/L. 36/Rev. 1, France: revised proposal concerning the state liable and joint and several liability, 12 June 1968, in: UN Doc. A/AC. 105/45, Report of the Legal Sub-Committee on the Work of its Seventh Session (4-28 June 1968), Annex I, Proposals, amendments and other documents relating to liability for damage caused by the launching of objects into outer space, 11 July 1968, p. 41.

④ 印度草案中含有关于赔偿制度的重要构想，见 UN Doc. A/AC. 105/C. 2/L. 32/Rev. 2, India: proposal-Convention concerning liability for damage caused by the launching of objects into outer space, 3 July 1969, in: UN Doc. A/AC. 105/58, Report Of The Legal Sub-Committee on the Work of its Eighth Session (9 June-4 July 1969), Annex II, Proposals and other documents relating to liability for damage caused by the launching of objects into outer space, 4 July 1969, p. 23.

⑤ UN Doc. PUOS/C. 2/69/WG. I/CRP. 9, France: Proposal-Question of joint liability, in: UN Doc. A/AC. 105/58, Report Of The Legal Sub-Committee on the Work of its Eighth Session (9 June-4 July 1969), Annex II, Proposals and other documents relating to liability for damage caused by the launching of objects into outer space, 4 July 1969, p. 38.

主张补偿”[①]。有鉴于此，赔偿《责任公约》项下损失的国家向共同发射的其他参与国、但不是该公约当事国的国家主张补偿的权利显然受限[②]。

关于发射国之间的责任分摊，隐含留给了这些国家，是否事前就责任分摊达成双边协定。

第三国受害人的利益在比利时的提案中更加清晰，“本公约不得妨碍两个或两个以上当事国就责任分摊达成协定。但是，此类协定不得向求偿方援引”[③]。与美国提案并行提交的英国工作文件进一步阐释了这个立场，向工作小组提出了连带责任问题[④]。至此，比利时、美国、英国均以准确的表述确认了参与联合发射的国家承担连带责任并不排除任何有关赔偿责任分摊的协定[⑤]。这些提案清楚地表明了所有发射国负有连带责任的原则，且没有先后顺序。这显然取决于发射国之间确立进一步的安排。

但仍有些问题没有得到解答：一是与运行过失和外空损害有关，在只有一个空间物体有过失的情况下；二是与外空中非法活动造成的损害责任有关；最后，不可抗力的后果[⑥]。详见下文。

（二）评注

关于连带责任的《责任公约》第五条有三款。《责任公约》第五条第 1 款表明了

---

① UN Doc. PUOS/C. 2/69/WG. I/CRP. 12, USSR: Proposal, in: UN Doc. A/AC. 105/58, Report Of The Legal Sub-Committee on the Work of its Eighth Session (9 June-4 July 1969), Annex II, Proposals and other documents relating to liability for damage caused by the launching of objects into outer space, 4 July 1969, p. 38.

② 谈判《公约》四十年后，有些观点认为公约如今可能满足了习惯法的标准，因而可确保其适用于非当事国，见 Kerrest, Armel, Liability for Damage Caused by Space Activities, in: Benkö, Marietta/Schrogl, Kai-Uwe (eds.), Space Law: Current Problems and Perspectives For Future Regulation, Eleven, Utrecht 2005, p. 101.

③ UN Doc. PUOS/C. 2/69/WG. I/CRP. 13, Belgium: Proposal, in: UN Doc. A/AC. 105/58, Report Of The Legal Sub-Committee on the Work of its Eighth Session (9 June-4 July 1969), Annex II, Proposals and other documents relating to liability for damage caused by the launching of objects into outer space, 4 July 1969, p. 39.

④ See UN Doc. PUOS/C. 2/69/WG. I/CRP. 17, United Kingdom and United States: Working Paper, in: UN Doc. A/AC. 105/58, Report Of The Legal Sub-Committee on the Work of its Eighth Session (9 June-4 July 1969), Annex II, Proposals and other documents relating to liability for damage caused by the launching of objects into outer space, 4 July 1969, p. 40.

⑤ Ibid.

⑥ 在总结工作小组有关《射入外空空间物体造成损害责任协议草案》考量因素时，法律小组委员会主席宣布了有关绝对责任原则初步一致意见，但没有提及过失问题、自然灾害或不可抗力、两个空间物体碰撞仅给其中一个物体造成损害、以及非法活动问题，见 UN Doc. A/AC. 105/C. 2/SR. 50, Legal Sub-Committee, Summary Record of the Fiftieth Meeting, held on 28 September 1965, 30 November 1965, Mr. Lachs, Chairman (Poland).

连带责任适用于共同发射的一般原则。《责任公约》第五条第 2 款涉及有关发射国之间的补偿权问题。《责任公约》第五条第 3 款规定了将其领土或设施用于发射的国家使得该国成为某个发射的参与者，并进而成为发射国。因此，《责任公约》第五条确认了《外空条约》第七条和《责任公约》第一条第 3 款项下的发射国类别。

1. 连带赔偿责任原则

（1）国家的地位

连带责任是久已确立的法律原则，据此不法行为或者违反法律义务的受害人可向任一可能的不法行为者要求赔偿，不论不法行为者之间的过失或责任分摊。这个技巧广泛使用于私法中，连带不法行为者或侵权行为者对依法承担的赔偿总额承担个别和单独责任。与连带责任制度不同的是，多个债务人通常平等排序和分担法律义务。在国际法中，由于国家为本国非政府实体承担，还意味着国家承担了替代赔偿责任。在国际空间法中，《责任公约》第一条和《登记公约》第一条项下发射国的平行定义支撑了连带责任。

连带责任背后的原理是解除求偿人在寻求赔偿过程中追踪和识别所有潜在责任人的负担；在外空活动背景下，仅向一个负有责任的发射国提出赔偿要求即可。换言之，求偿国代表受害人主张的是外部责任。每个不法行为者之间的任何必要的内部调整与受害人无关；这要么依法由过失程度决定，要么取决于责任方的有关谈判。受害人主张赔偿的权利不能受制于责任国分担责任的主张。

《责任公约》确立了外空法中的连带责任。因此，发射国不得不向受害人承担支付全部赔偿金的风险。法律认定的责任方可能最终承担全部赔偿要求，不需要在共同发射国内部分担经济负担。不能进一步细分赔偿义务可能出于多种原因，例如缺少清偿能力，或者一个发射国无法履行其经济负担份额。也可能是因为无法追踪其他不法行为者。换言之，承担全部赔偿责任的风险仍在不法行为者之间，不影响受害人选择一个不法行为者并主张全部赔偿金的能力。

要求碰撞或坠毁空间物体的发射国自担损失，但如果证明其他某个发射国存在过失，其损失依证明程度予以免除。实践中，发射保险承担了由发射失败直接造成的损害或损失。

（2）国际组织的地位

谈判早期，关于赔偿首要义务是在国际组织还是其成员国问题的探讨曾涉及国际组织豁免权问题[①]。1964年美国草案中提及国际组织，且并非政府间国际组织。匈牙利草案第8条规定赔偿义务应由“国际组织及其成员国”承担。

对此，欧洲空间局有关法律赔偿责任的理事会决议[②]确认了发射国和国际组织的补偿做法，以及赔偿后有关分摊和分担经济负担的特别协议[③]。

2. 内部分摊/国际协定

（1）内部分摊

起草《责任公约》第五条第2款第二句时，商业空间发射市场还没有得到充分发展；但是其规定与当下的局势颇有相关性。《责任公约》第五条第2款第二句对发射前发射国缔结发射协定作了规定[④]。

首先，本规定涉及的发射国数量并不局限在两个，起草《责任公约》第五条的基础是至少有两个发射国。实践中，发射国可能更多。选择向哪个发射国求偿或提起诉讼是一个实用主义问题，这与该国充分满足赔偿要求的能力和意愿有关。如前所述，这个选择权在于求偿国。因此，《责任公约》第五条第2款第二句表明，任何内部分担不得妨碍求偿国向单一国家索取全部赔偿数额。

连带责任法的目的是求偿无需向所有债务人提出，或者在外空活动中，向所有发射国提出。法律上，向一个发射国提出要求即可，且在这种情况下，该国必须全部赔偿。每个发射国对支付全部赔偿负有责任，不论其他发射国的经济状况或清偿能力。因此，不得延误受害国向某个发射国提出的追索，或让该追索受制于连带责任国事前就赔偿金支付份额达成的协定。尽管此前已缔结分摊协定，受害国追索赔偿金的权利优先于连带责任发射国据此寻求补偿的权利[⑤]。这在《责任公约》第五条第2款最后

① 《责任公约》第二十二条第一款确立了有关规则，规定政府间国际组织可以声明受本公约的规定。几个政府间国际组织作出了这样的声明，如欧空局，欧洲气象卫星开发组织，欧洲通讯卫星组织，见<http://www.unoosa.org/oosa/en/SpaceLaw/treatystatus/index.html> accessed 26 April 2019.

② See ESA/C/XXII/Res. 3, Resolution of the Council of the European Space Agency on the Agency's Legal Liability, 13 December 1977.

③ Ibid.

④ 一个可以引用的例子是美国（NASA）和德国（联邦研究与科技部，BMFT）有关Rontgensatellit项目（ROSAT）的谅解备忘录。第十五条责任第二款规定如下：“在他人或其财产造成损害的情况下，且依照国际法或者《空间物体造成损害的国际公约》的原则，”在支付赔偿金或对赔偿金数额达成一致后，NASA和BMFT应立即就公平分担赔偿金进行磋商”。Memorandum of understanding on the Roentgensatellit program (signed 8 August 1982, entered into force 8 August 1982), TIAS 10669; 2000 UNTS 445.

⑤ 第二十三条的目的是便利当事国就其在《责任公约》项下的相互义务缔结协议。

一句中得到了清晰的重申。责任国之间的补偿权与受害国的求偿权相比是次要的。补偿权不具有对外效力。

在外空活动中，这些活动造成的损害可能引发不同寻常的赔偿金，任一发射责任国负有的全部支付义务可能是巨额的。连带责任概念意味着，不管是几个国家参与发射，不管这些国家是否有过失，《责任公约》第一条和《登记公约》第一条项下的发射国地位就足以成为向该国主张赔偿的充分前提条件。

（2）可能的协定

商业外空活动利用外空发射设备的需求凸显了此类协定的重要性，在该领域也取得了一些经验①。由于发射国对有关活动负有责任，建议事先厘清控制外空活动的问题。有关国家必须考虑控制的实际情况。

值得特别注意的是联合国大会 59/115 号决议②，该决议强调并推荐缔结发射和补偿协定的做法③。在操作层面，此类协定越发值得推荐，即便是为应对发射后可能出现的缺少规则的情况。与《责任公约》第四条第 1 款第 2 项不同，其规定的是过失责任国的赔偿分摊；而《责任公约》第五条第 2 款并没有明确分摊风险的方式。此类协定应当依据不同发射阶段考虑风险分担，这与有关国家的特定作用有关（例如，是否自其领土发射，是否促使发射等）。通过缔结此类协定，参与外国发射的国家可以行使有效监督，特别是对其私人部门，并事前规定其损害赔偿责任。实践中，发射国之间缔结的协定寥寥无几。由于发射服务提供者之间的竞争，国内法常不涉及这个问题④。

3. 领土或设备的相关性

《责任公约》第五条第 3 款看起来有些多余，因为重复了《责任公约》第一条第 3 款第（1）项和第（2）项已确立的发射国的标准。但是，该款有助于重申发射国定义，明确参与共同发射被视为发射国⑤。这是因为领土发射国的赔偿责任在谈判中曾

---

① See UNGA Res. 59/115, Application of the concept of the “launching State”, 10 December 2004.

② Ibid.

③ Ibid.

④ 法国起草《外空法》的时候曾讨论过这一点，但考虑到法国是发射服务提供国，最终决定不确立达成此类协定的义务。尽管如此，此类协定的存在便利了发射许可。见 Art. 4 para. 4 French SOA, Law No. 2008-518, see Commentary LIAB, Article I, mn. 59f.

⑤ Lyall, Francis/Larsen, Paul B., Space Law a Treatise, Ashgate, Burlington/Surrey 2009, p. 109.

引发争议。因为《责任公约》第一条第 3 款第（2）项已含有发射国的定义，《责任公约》第五条第 3 款被描述为“要么不完整要么赘述”[①]。总之，《责任公约》第 5 条第 3 款强化了领土发射国作为发射国的地位，且没有增加其他要求。明确了领土发射国在《公约》项下不变的类别。

这进一步确定了与发射地点有关的一个重要方面，即发射可能在国家领土之内或之外。《责任公约》第五条第 3 款不仅确认发射国对本国领土的责任；也避免运行发射设施的国家通过向第三国租赁发射设施协议逃避责任。哈萨克斯坦拜科努尔这样的发射场不能通过和俄罗斯签署长期租赁发射设施的协议解除其作为发射国的地位[②]。

同时，不管发射国是否登记了搭载物，不论发射国是不是该空间物体的登记国，发射国永远是发射国[③]。

七、第六条（绝对责任的免除）

Smith and Kerrest

1. 除本条第二款另有规定外，发射国若证明，全部或部分是因为要求赔偿国，或其代表的自然人或法人的重大疏忽，或因作为或不作为蓄意造成损害时，该发射国对损害的绝对责任，应依证明的程度予以免除。

2. 发射国如果因为从事不符合国际法，特别是不符合《联合国宪章》和《关于各国探索和利用包括月球与其他天体在内外层空间活动原则的条约》的活动造成损害，其赔偿责任不得免除。

---

① Cheng，Bin，International Liability for Damage Caused by Space Objects，in：Jasentuliyana，Nandasiri/Lee，Roy S. K.（eds.），Manual on Space Law，Volume I，Oceana Publications，New York 1979，p. 120.

② 有关协定见哈萨克斯坦空间局 Kazkosmos 网站 <http：//kazcosmos. gov. kz/ru/international/sotrudnichestvo-s-rossijskoj-federacziej. html> accessed 26 April 2019.

③ 根本上，在登记国没有登记的情况下，该国仍可根据《登记公约》第二条第 2 款登记该搭载物，见 chapter on REG in this volume，Commentary REG，Article I，mn. 30.

目录

（一）谈判和起草过程

第六条是《责任公约》中唯一规定排除或豁免损害赔偿责任的条款。

其谈判过程并没有出现任何困难。第七届会议（1968 年）就第六条的表述达成一致，并在 1969 年得到了工作小组的确认①。

第六条不仅是国家依据《责任公约》第二条主张赔偿的障碍；也限制了发射国对责任豁免的利用，如果该国违反国际法或从事不法行为。本条的意义详见下文。

（二）评注

第六条共两款。第六条第 1 款明确发射国对受害人的绝对责任免除；第 2 款给利用责任免除增加了一重限制，即发射国违反国际法规则的情况。

1. 重大疏忽或蓄意损害

第六条规定的是限制性条款，且是发射国空间物体给地球表面造成损害的绝对责任规则的唯一且有限的限制②。此条的基础是罗马法和国内法体系中熟知的法律原则，

---

① See UN Doc. PUOS/C. 2/69/WG. 1/CRP. 2/Rev. 1, Austria: Working paper-Field of application and exemptions from provisions of agreement; Question of absolute liability and exoneration from liability, in: UN Doc. A/AC. 105/58, Report Of The Legal Sub-Committee on the Work of its Eighth Session (9 June-4 July 1969), Annex II, Proposals and other documents relating to liability for damage caused by the launching of objects into outer space, 4 July 1969, p. 36.

② 在工作小组讨论中，意大利提出了拒绝将不可抗力作为免除责任的理由："在给地球表面造成损害的情况中，应当使用绝对责任原则，即使是在不可抗力情况下；（因为受害人的不平等地位，受害人不可能保护自己免于外空活动和发射空间设施的风险）"，见 UN Doc. PUOS/WG. II/9, Italy: Proposal, in: UN Doc. A/AC. 105/19, Report of the Legal Sub-Committee on the Work of its Third Session (9-26 March 1964), Annex II, Proposals and amendments relating to liability for damage caused by objects launched into outer space, 26 March 1964, p. 14.

即任何人不得因其过失获得救济。据此，任何人不应当受益于本人的不法行为（*nemo auditor propriam turpitudinem allegans*）。这个绝对责任例外是符合逻辑的，在国际法的严格或绝对责任制度中比较少见①。

（1）适用范围

求偿国或其代表的自然人或法人的重大疏忽、作为或不作为会导致赔偿责任免除，这是有先例的。这个免除不适用于第三条项下在外空中发生损害的情况。因此，不必在过失责任条款背景下进一步考量重大疏忽或不作为，因为在分派责任时必须考虑具体情形。

《责任公约》第二条绝对责任规则很严格，第六条确立了抵消这个责任的机制。如果适用该条，全部或部分损失将由初始求偿国承担：第六条第 1 款提及“全部或部分”因重大疏忽造成的损失。这实际上将绝对责任规则转变成了损失由所有人承受原则（*casum sentit dominus*），解除了发射国的赔偿责任，部分或全部损失由求偿国承担。据此，《责任公约》为外空活动损害赔偿制度提供了一个例外，条件是求偿国的局部或全部重大疏忽蓄意造成了自身损失。

结果是，因求偿国重大疏忽或蓄意不法行为导致的损害，求偿国无权主张赔偿。发射国可以免除（至少部分）的赔偿责任取决于重大疏忽或恶意争端方造成的损害。第六条并没有排除赔偿要求本身，但是将损害赔偿制度从绝对责任变成了以过失为基础的责任。但这并不是改变《责任公约》第三条原意，只是在损害赔偿分摊的意义上，即赔偿限于不是求偿国行为造成的损害。

（2）自有疏忽或蓄意行为不得获利

本条基于一个根深蒂固的原则，即故意或（因重大疏忽）给本人财产或人身造成损害不能主张赔偿。首先，这需要评估在外空活动中什么构成重大疏忽；其次，在求偿国作为或不作为情况中，需要证明致损的意图。这在实践中可能存在困难。

给发射国承担无限赔偿责任的制度在数量上设立限制符合情理，如果损害是因故意或重大疏忽自己造成的。这条涉及的是《责任公约》第二条项下的责任，前提是因为受害人的重大疏忽或蓄意不法行为导致损害的发生。但适用该条有赖于重大疏忽概

① 目前，严格责任制度主要与其他形式的危险活动有关，例如核电站和核设施。严格责任和绝对责任的区别在于，前者通常允许限制责任，而后者（包括外空法）一般没有责任限制。

念，而《责任公约》中没有重大疏忽概念和注意标准，只有法律体系中众所周知的概念和标准，可能对如何遵守外空法中的技术和安全规则有一定的借鉴价值。

遵守碎片减缓并将其纳入可持续外空活动的长期谈判框架，想知晓这些活动的长远影响，只能待现有外空碎片减缓指南在国际层面的进一步发展①。

2. 违反国际法

虽然《责任公约》第六条第 1 款给绝对赔偿责任规则确立了例外情形，《责任公约》第六条第 2 款马上排除了损害赔偿责任的豁免。

这与发射国从事非法活动的情势有关。尽管该款指向传统的任何人不应当受益于本人的不法行为的规则，却可能产生意想不到的效果。它实际上给对另一国从事非法活动的发射国施加了补偿义务，尽管后者存在重大疏忽或过失。这是否符合该款规则意欲寻求的结果是值得怀疑的。

匈牙利草案的第四条已将非法行为纳入考量②。

3. 需要谨慎解释

因此，对于第六条第 2 款预设的情况应当给予谨慎解释。该款不仅能够排除故意干扰（如离轨或）他国卫星造成损害的赔偿责任，还能覆盖非法活动，例如反卫星导弹试验。

如果一国未能监督本国外空活动或者因疏忽未能回应国际社会在紧急状态下监管本位行为的要求，也可能引发本款的适用。

结合第六条第 2 款和第 1 款中重大疏忽和蓄意不法行为，可能产生出乎意料的后果。如果发射国从事非法活动，即便受害人存在重大疏忽或蓄意不法行为，该国也不能享受责任豁免。这是对该条唯一合乎逻辑的解释。但是，是否是落实不得受益于本人不法行为原则的最好办法存在争议。例如，一国毁损了某个空间物体，参与了不符合国际法的活动，并因此承受损失，但如果该毁损空间物体的活动不符合国际法，该

---

① See Commentary LIAB, Article Ⅲ, mn. 144; Lyall, Francis/Larsen, Paul B., Space Law a Treatise, Ashgate, Burlington/Surrey 2009, pp. 50ff.; and Contant-Jorgenson, Corinne/Lála, Petr/Schrogl, Kai-Uwe, Cosmic Study on Space Traffic Management, International Academy of Astronautics (IAA), Paris 2006.

② See UN Doc. A/AC. 105/C. 2/L. 10, Hungary: Proposed draft agreement-Agreement concerning liability for damage caused by the launching of objects into outer space, 16 March 1964, in: UN Doc. A/AC. 105/19, Report of the Legal Sub-Committee on the Work of its Third Session (9-26 March 1964), Annex II, Proposals and amendments relating to liability for damage caused by objects launched into outer space, 26 March 1964, p. 7, Art. IV.

国仍旧可能获得赔偿。该款的广泛适用可能使得一国因为不法行为获利，如果求偿国无权破坏处于两国争议中的有关空间物体。这个结果将导致悖论。因此，实践中需要谨慎解释该款并进行磋商。

八、第七条（不适用于发射国本国国民或参与发射的外国国民）

Smith and Kerrest

本公约之规定不适用于发射国的空间物体对下列人员造成的损失：

1. 该发射国的国民；

2. 在空间物体从发射至降落的任何阶段参与操作，或在空间物体从发射至降落的任何阶段内，应发射国的邀请而留在紧邻计划发射或回收区域的外国国民。

目录

（一）谈判和起草过程

本条谈判中，对于《责任公约》是否适用于本国国民和外国参与者是有不同观点的，至少在早期会议中对此没有达成一致意见。比利时和美国草案都不仅排除了本国国民，也排除了外国参与者；但匈牙利草案中并没有这样的规则①。

1964 年会议中，苏联代表团发表声明，明确支持排除本国国民和外国参与者，并

① See UN Doc. A/AC. 105/C. 2/L. 10, Hungary: Proposed draft agreement-Agreement concerning liability for damage caused by the launching of objects into outer space, 16 March 1964, in: UN Doc. A/AC. 105/19, Report of the Legal Sub-Committee on the Work of its Third Session (9-26 March 1964), Annex II, Proposals and amendments relating to liability for damage caused by objects launched into outer space, 26 March 1964, p. 7.

提供了解释①。在国际法中，那个年代的认知是位于一国领土中的外国人，“应当享有该国公民的同等待遇”②。苏联不仅在实践中严格遵从，这也是当时国际法立场的真实反映③。

（二）评注

第七条实际上在一个长句子中包含了一款和该款下的两项。

1. 受保护人员的有限性

《责任公约》第七条第 1 款限制了一国本国国民向发射国依据公约提出赔偿要求。同时，第七条第 2 款限制了外国国民在参与空间物体运行时间段内依据公约求偿。这包括自发射到降落，或者应发射国邀请紧邻发射或回收区域。

乍一看，《责任公约》第七条的规定有些让人惊讶：排除了两类在最关键时刻最有可能暴露在外空活动危险中的人的求偿。但是，将外国国民排除在公约之外限于发射和降落这些特定阶段，包括空间物体的回收，并明确必须是应发射国邀请。

尽管看起来很严苛，这个排除是合乎逻辑的。《责任公约》是通过确立一个国际机制，让受害人本国代表受害人，并要求他国赔偿本国国民。第七条限于本国国民和外国参与者。这意味着这两类人群可以利用国内求偿程序而不是国际机制④。而且，国内法通常规定了某种程序或制度，据此可在国内层面赔偿本国国民和参与特定操作的外国人遭受的损失⑤。其目的是确保有关国民通过国内程序而不是国际机制对本国

① See UN Doc. A/AC. 105/C. 2/SR. 49, Legal Sub-Committee, Summary Record of the Forty-Ninth Meeting, held on 28 September 1965, 30 November 1965, Mr. Rybakov (Soviet Union).

② Ibid.

③ Brownlie, Ian, Principles of Public International Law, 7th edn., Oxford University Press, Oxford 2008, p. 524; Cassese, Antonio, International Law, 2nd edn., Oxford University Press, Oxford 2005, pp. 120ff.; and Shaw, Malcolm N., International Law, 6th edn., Cambridge University Press, Cambridge 2008, pp. 824ff.

④ 例如，2011 年 12 月 23 日，子午线通讯卫星落入西伯利亚地区，俄罗斯公民曾就此主张赔偿。见 RiaNovosti, Russian communication satellite crashes shortly after launch, RiaNovosti, 23 December 2011 <http://en.rian.ru/russia/20111223/170448359.html> accessed 26 April 2019, and BBC News, Russian satellite debris lands in Cosmonaut Street, BBC, 24 December 2011, <http://www.bbc.co.uk/news/world-europe-16326942> accessed 26 April 2019.

⑤ 为宇航员在国内层面设立合适经济赔偿机制已经是获得接受的做法，如 NASA 和欧空局。这通常受到内部规范性文件的规范。在有关任务期间，欧空局为宇航员和后备宇航员提供生命和健康保险。如欧空局和荷兰政府之间，关于欧空局宇航员 André Kuipers 作为荷兰资助飞往国际空间站的联盟号飞船飞行工程师的合作安排，第二条第 1 款第 10 项；欧空局和比利时首相科技文化事务办公室，关于欧空局宇航员 Frank De Winne 作为比利时资助飞往国际空间站的联盟号飞船飞行工程师的安排，第三条第 1 款第 9 项和第二条第 1 款第 11 项。

提出赔偿要求。

尽管如此，《责任公约》第七条对参与者的适用前提是“空间物体从发射至降落的任何阶段参与操作，或在空间物体从发射至降落的任何阶段内，应发射国的邀请而留在紧邻计划发射或回收区域”。

2. 在国内层面的落实

国内立法应在各个层面与第七条的严格范围相符。要么将《责任公约》作为处理不参与任务的第三方求偿机制，至少是在符合第二条规定的赔偿要求中。或者，认为《责任公约》规范不足以处理在其境内的本国国民或参与有关操作的外国国民提出的赔偿要求。在后者情况下，一国国内空间法可覆盖该空白。参与操作的外国国民，不论参与是直接的还是间接的，必须作为发射国本国国民对待。国内法中应当有规范本国国民赔偿要求的规定。

因此，通过国内法为这类人群设立强制保险要求，可以减少适用第七条的潜在严重后果①；替代方案是，可以国家“恩典”的形式，向参与发射国有关操作或在临近区域的人提供充分赔偿。尽管如此，这条还是引发了批评，因为未能给特别暴露于危险之中的人群提供最高水准的赔偿②。

实践中，这两类人群要么在强制发射保险的覆盖范围中，要么有国内法明确该类人群在国内赔偿程序的适用范围中。法国国内法（2008 年 6 月 3 日第 2008-518 号法令，《法国空间操作法》，以下简称《法国空间法》）③ 更进一步，《法国空间法》第六条第 3 款规定明确在法律规定范围里，运营者和政府确保承担三类人造成损害的赔偿责任；第一，国家、公共办公室或机构；第二，欧洲空间局及其成员国；运营者和参与空间物体生产和运营的人④。

---

① 多个国家空间法将第三方强制保险作为发放发射等许可的前提条件，见 Sec. 5 para. 2 lit. （f） UK Outer Space Act 1986; for Austria, see Para. 4 subpara. 4, Austrian Space Law; further, Marboe, Irmgard, The New Austrian Outer Space Act, Zeitschrift für Luft- und Weltraumrecht（61）2012, pp. 26-61.

② Diederiks-Verschoor, I. H. Philepina/Kopal, Vladimir, An Introduction to Space Law, 3rd edn. , Kluwer Law International, The Hague 2008, p. 42.

③ 2008 年 6 月 3 日第 2008-518 号法国法，见 Diederiks-Verschoor, I. H. Philepina/Kopal, Vladimir, An Introduction to Space Law, 3rd edn. , Kluwer Law International, The Hague 2008, p. 42. 有法国法及其非官方英文译文的纲要。

④ Art. 6 para. Ⅲ no. 1-3 French SOA.

九、第八条（求偿国的适格性）

Smith and Kerrest

1. 遭受损害的国家，或其自然人或法人，可向发射国提出损害赔偿的要求。

2. 如果遭受损害的自然人或法人的国籍国没有提出赔偿要求，该自然人或法人的所在国可就其在本国境内遭受的损害，向发射国提出赔偿要求。

3. 如果永久居民的国籍国或损害发生的所在地国，都没有提出赔偿要求，或通知有意提出赔偿要求，永久居民的居住地国可就其遭受的损害，向发射国提出赔偿要求。

目录

（一）谈判和起草过程

提交给法律小组委员会的最初草案中已含有依据《责任公约》可提出赔偿要求国家适格性的规定①。谈判过程中，各国对于受损国及其自然人和法人提出赔偿要求没

① See UN Doc. A/AC. /C. 2/L. 7, Working Paper Submitted by the Belgian Delegation on the Unification of Certain Rules Governing Liability for Damage Caused by Space Devices, 29 April 1963, in: UN Doc. A/AC. 105/12, Report of the Legal Sub-Committee on the Work of its Second Session (16 April-3 May 1963), 6 May 1963, Annex I, C, p. 10, Art. 2; UN Doc. A/AC. 105/C. 2/L. 8, United States: Proposal-Convention concerning liability for damage caused by the launching of objects into outer space, 9 March 1964, in: UN Doc. A/AC. 105/19, Report of the Legal Sub-Committee on the Work of its Third Session (9-26 March 1964), 26 March 1964, Annex II, Proposals and amendments relating to liability for damage caused by objects launched into outer space, p. 2, Art. IV; and UN Doc. A/AC. 105/C. 2/L. 10, Hungary: Proposed draft agreement-Agreement concerning liability for damage caused by the launching of objects into outer space, 16 March 1964, in: UN Doc. A/AC. 105/19, Report of the Legal Sub-Committee on the Work of its Third Session (9-26 March 1964), Annex II, Proposals and amendments relating to liability for damage caused by objects launched into outer space, 26 March 1964, p. 7, Art. IX para. 1.

有任何争议①。美国 1964 年草案中甚至包含了双重国籍国民和永久居民②。这是唯一规定双重国籍的草案。法律小组委员会报告中，看不出此后将此类国家从草案条款中移除的原因。

除了匈牙利草案中仅提到受损国及其国民，此后所有草案中都涵盖了美国提议的

① See e. g. UN Doc. A/AC. 105/C. 2/L. 7, Working Paper Submitted by the Belgian Delegation on the Unification of Certain Rules Governing Liability for Damage Caused by Space Devices, 29 April 1963, in: UN Doc. A/AC. 105/12, Report of the Legal Sub-Committee on the Work of its Second Session (16 April-3 May 1963), 6 May 1963, Annex I, C, p. 10, Art. 2; UN Doc. A/AC. 105/C. 2/L. 8, United States: Proposal-Convention concerning liability for damage caused by the launching of objects into outer space, 9 March 1964, in: UN Doc. A/AC. 105/19, Report of the Legal Sub-Committee on the Work of its Third Session (9-26 March 1964), 26 March 1964, Annex II, Proposals and amendments relating to liability for damage caused by objects launched into outer space, p. 2, Art. IV para. 1; UN Doc. A/AC. 105/C. 2/L. 10, Hungary: Proposed draft agreement-Agreement concerning liability for damage caused by the launching of objects into outer space, 16 March 1964, in: UN Doc. A/AC. 105/19, Report of the Legal Sub-Committee on the Work of its Third Session (9-26 March 1964), Annex II, Proposals and amendments relating to liability for damage caused by objects launched into outer space, 26 March 1964, p. 7, Art. IX para. 1; UN Doc. A/AC. 105/C. 2/L. 19, United States of America: Proposal-Convention concerning liability for damage caused by the launching of objects into outer space, 21 June 1967, in: UN Doc. A/AC. 105/37, Report of the Legal Sub-Committee on the Work of its Sixth Session (19 June-14 July 1967), Annex II, Proposals, amendments and other documents relating to liability for damage caused by the launching of objects into outer space, 14 July 1967, p. 6, Art. VI; UN Doc. A/AC. 105/C. 2/L. 32, India: proposal-Convention concerning liability for damage caused by the launching of objects into outer space, 2 June 1968, in: UN Doc. A/AC. 105/45, Report of the Legal Sub-Committee on the Work of its Seventh Session (4-28 June 1968), Annex I, Proposals, amendments and other documents relating to liability for damage caused by the launching of objects into outer space, 11 July 1968, p. 16, Art. V para. 1; UN Doc. A/AC. 105/C. 2/L. 40, Working Paper submitted by the Italian delegation-Draft convention concerning liability for damage caused by the launching of objects into outer space, 13 June 1986, in: UN Doc. A/AC. 105/45, Report of the Legal Sub-Committee on the Work of its Seventh Session (4-28 June 1968), Annex I, Proposals, amendments and other documents relating to liability for damage caused by the launching of objects into outer space, 11 July 1968, p. 30, Art. 9; and UN Doc. A/AC. 105/45, Report of the Legal Sub-Committee on the Work of its Seventh Session (4-28 June 1968), 11 July 1968, p. 7.

② See UN Doc. A/AC. 105/C. 2/L. 8, United States: Proposal-Convention concerning liability for damage caused by the launching of objects into outer space, 9 March 1964, in: UN Doc. A/AC. 105/19, Report of the Legal Sub-Committee on the Work of its Third Session (9-26 March 1964), 26 March 1964, Annex II, Proposals and amendments relating to liability for damage caused by objects launched into outer space, p. 2, Art. IV para. 2.

三类国家（受损国、受害人的国籍国和永久居住地国）[1]。1968 年，法律小组委员会就这三类国家和增加的第四类国家达成一致[2]。可以提出赔偿要求的第四类国家是与国籍或住所无关的损害发生地国。法律小组委员会此后的会议中认可了这四类国家[3]，并最终纳入了 1971 年法律小组委员会通过的《责任公约》草案[4]。

在此，《责任公约》第八条偏离了国际法的一般原则，即只允许国籍国行使外交保护[5]。通常，国家和个人之间必须确立真实联系，在《责任公约》背景下是受害人[6]。

该条说明，保护受害人不仅需要借助广泛界定发射国，也需要受害人——自然人

---

① See UN Doc. A/AC. 105/C. 2/L. 19, United States of America: Proposal-Convention concerning liability for damage caused by the launching of objects into outer space, 21 June 1967, in: UN Doc. A/AC. 105/37, Report of the Legal Sub-Committee on the Work of its Sixth Session (19 June-14 July 1967), Annex II, Proposals, amendments and other documents relating to liability for damage caused by the launching of objects into outer space, 14 July 1967, p. 6, Art. VI; UN Doc. A/AC. 105/C. 2/L. 32, India: proposal-Convention concerning liability for damage caused by the launching of objects into outer space, 2 June 1968, in: UN Doc. A/AC. 105/45, Report of the Legal Sub-Committee on the Work of its Seventh Session (4-28 June 1968), Annex I, Proposals, amendments and other documents relating to liability for damage caused by the launching of objects into outer space, 11 July 1968, p. 16, Art. V; UN Doc. A/AC. 105/C. 2/L. 40, Working Paper submitted by the Italian delegation-Draft convention concerning liability for damage caused by the launching of objects into outer space, 13 June 1986, in: UN Doc. A/AC. 105/45, Report of the Legal Sub-Committee on the Work of its Seventh Session (4-28 June 1968), Annex I, Proposals, amendments and other documents relating to liability for damage caused by the launching of objects into outer space, 11 July 1968, p. 30, Art. 9; and UN Doc. A/AC. 105/45, Report of the Legal Sub-Committee on the Work of its Seventh Session (4-28 June 1968), 11 July 1968, p. 7.

② See UN Doc. A/AC. 105/45, Report of the Legal Sub-Committee on the Work of its Seventh Session (4-28 June 1968), 11 July 1968, p. 7.

③ See UN Doc. A/AC. 105/58, Report of the Legal Sub-Committee on the Work of its Eighth Session (9 June-4 July 1969), 4 July 1969, p. 9; and UN Doc. A/AC. 105/85, Report of the Legal Sub-Committee on the Work of its Ninth Session (8 June-3 July 1970), 3 July 1970, p. 9.

④ See UN Doc. A/AC. 105/94, Report of the Legal Sub-Committee on the Work of its Tenth Session (7 June-2 July 1971), 8 July 1971, p. 8.

⑤ See e. g. UN Doc. A/CN. 4/SER. A/1997/Add. 1 (Part. 2), Yearbook of the International Law Commission 1997, Vol. II, Part II, Chapter Ⅷ-Diplomatic Protection, p. 61.

⑥ See Nottebohm Case, (Liechtenstein v. Guatemala) (Second Phase, Judgement) [1955] ICJ Rep. 4; Case Concerning the Barcelona Traction, Light and Power Company, Limited (New Application 1962), (Belgium v. Spain) (Second Phase, Judgement) [1970] ICJ Rep. 3, for juridical persons; for the rules of diplomatic protection in general see: UN Doc. A/61/10, Report of the International Law Commission, 58th session, GA Official Records, Sixty-first Session, Supplement No. 10, p. 16, Draft articles on Diplomatic Protection; Brownlie, Ian, Principles of Public International Law, 7th edn., Oxford University Press, Oxford 2008, pp. 477ff.; and Shaw, Malcolm N., International Law, 6th edn., Cambridge University Press, Cambridge 2008, pp. 808ff.

和法人——能够寻求一国帮助代表其提出赔偿要求。提供选择国家的不同连接点是为了避免发射国未能回应或隔绝某个受害人追索的情形。与用尽当地救济规则的例外一起，《责任公约》第八条进一步例证了该公约强调受害人导向的性质。

（二）评注

《责任公约》第八条含有三款，每一款都是独立的、连续的基础，据此包括自然人和法人在内的受害人可建立与某一国的联系，进而让后者代其提出赔偿要求。

《责任公约》第八条提供了三个途径，据此空间损害的受害人可以依靠特定的法律或事实与特定国家建立联系。该国可同意代理受害人的不同利益，代表其向发射国提出赔偿要求。该国因此成为受害人在《责任公约》项下赔偿要求的外交代表。通过这种方式，第八条遵行了国际法的要求，即自然人或法人与国家之间的有效或真实联系，特别是启动程序国家不是国籍国的情况下。

通过提供三类适合提出赔偿要求国家的选项，第八条确保了不能以缺少国家利益为由剥夺受害人赔偿主张，无论受害人是自然人还是法人，亦不论这个国家是国籍国、损害发生地国或永久居住地国。

三类国家作为求偿国的情形中，该国有权依据《责任公约》提出赔偿要求。国家最适宜代表受害人利益，可以但不必然是国籍国。

《责任公约》第八条预先避免了不回应或不作为而隔绝赔偿要求的任何企图，特别是在发射国方面。该公约通过确保向发射国提出主张的有效通路，排除了（发射）国不作为妨碍赔偿要求的可能性。

1. 受损国/受害人的国籍国

《责任公约》第八条第一段，即《责任公约》第八条第一款，规定了一般原则，据此一国可在两种情形中向发射国提出赔偿要求。其一，该国或其自然人或法人，统称为人，遭受了空间物体造成的损害。尽管《责任公约》第八条第 1 款没有直接指向受害人的“国籍”状态，但属格词“其”明确了第八条指的是与该国有确定法律关系的人，特别是通过该国国内法确立的国籍关系[①]。这与有关案例和国际法委员会关

① See further Brownlie, Ian, Principles of Public International Law, 7th edn., Oxford University Press, Oxford 2008, pp. 477ff., with reference to the Nottebohm Case, (Liechtenstein v. Guatemala) (Second Phase, Judgement) [1955] ICJ Rep. 4.

于什么构成个人与国家有效联系的观点保持一致[①]。

通常，代表受害人提出赔偿主张的国家可能就是国籍国。但是，其他情况也是有可能的。例如有些国家认可受害人的利益但缺少法定地位，《责任公约》第八条将外空事故的受害人和其他国家的关系或连接正式化，使得国籍国之外的国家可以代表特定种类受害人提出损害赔偿要求。多国代表受害人要求赔偿合法化，《责任公约》第八条强化了受害人导向的方法。

2. 损害发生地国

《责任公约》第八条第 2 款规定了受害人国籍国之外的国家可向发射国提出赔偿要求。在这种情况下，损害必须发生在该国的领土内，并给任何自然人或法人造成了损害。未提及受害人国籍国缺少行动或忽视，第 2 款让其他国家代表在其领土上遭受损失的人提出追索。适用该款的预设前提是，遭受损失的人虽然不是该国国民，但至少在遭受损失时刻，位于该国领土内。《责任公约》第八条第 2 款确保该国可以介入，不管受损人在其境内的期限长短。

如此规定，《责任公约》第八条第 2 款确保了求偿人与其国籍国的首要联系，可作为受害人寻求保护的首选。这是基于《责任公约》第八条第 1 款的一般含义，尽管缺少明确指向。《责任公约》第八条第 2 款确保国籍国之外的，损害发生地国可以为受害人声张正义。

《责任公约》第八条第 2 款为受害人所在的损害发生地国提供了切实的解决办法，如果其国籍国不积极寻求赔偿要求，不管动机为何。

3. 永久居住地国

如果受害人因发生损害时位于其他国家领土而提出赔偿要求受阻，《责任公约》第八条最后一款为受害人提供了另外一个解决方案。如果国籍国和损害发生地国都没有提出要求，第三国可以代表受害人提出赔偿要求。在这种情况下，《责任公约》第八条第 3 款依赖的是国际法熟知的个人和国家之间的联系。此处，追索的国家和受害人的关系取决于后者是否是永久居民。这进一步指向国际法中适用于移民和永久居住

① This has been the subject of controversial discussion within the International Law Commission during its 5th session, particularly in relation to dual nationality, see UN Doc. A/CN. 4/8ER. A/1953, Yearbook of the International Law Commision 1953, Volume I, pp. 170ff.

地的居留意图概念[①]。

十、第九条（外交途径）

Smith and Kerrest

损害赔偿要求，应通过外交途径向发射国提出。求偿国如果和发射国没有外交关系，可请另一国代其向发射国提出赔偿要求，或以其他方式代表其在本公约项下的利益。求偿国也可通过联合国秘书长提出赔偿要求，前提是求偿国和发射国都是联合国成员国。

目录

（一）谈判和起草过程

《责任公约》谈判中对第九条规定并没有什么争议。最初的美国[②]、匈牙利[③]和比利时[④]草案中已经含有和第九条最后规定极为类似的内容。这些草案和第九条最终版

---

① See Brownlie, Ian, Principles of Public International Law, 7th edn., Oxford University Press, Oxford 2008, p. 392.

② UN Doc. A/AC. 105/C. 2/L. 8, United States: Proposal-Convention concerning liability for damage caused by the launching of objects into outer space, 9 March 1964, in: UN Doc. A/AC. 105/19, Report of the Legal Sub-Committee on the Work of its Third Session (9-26 March 1964), 26 March 1964, Annex II, Proposals and amendments relating to liability for damage caused by objects launched into outer space, p. 2, Art. IV.

③ UN Doc. PUOS/C. 2/WG (IX) /L. 10, Text approved by the Drafting Group-Draft convention on international liability for damage caused by space objects, [Date n/a], in: UN Doc. A/AC. 105/85, Report Of The Legal Sub-Committee on the Work of its Ninth Session (8 June-3 July 1970), Annex I, Proposals And Other Documents Relating To Liability For Damage Caused By The Launching Of Objects Into Outer Space (Agenda item 2), 3 July 1970, p. 20, Art. XI.

④ UN Doc. A/AC. 105/C. 2/L. 7/Rev. 2, Belgium: Proposal for a Convention on the Unification of Certain Rules Governing Liability for Damage Caused by Space Devices, 14 October 1964, in: UN Doc. A/AC. 105/21, Report of the Legal Sub-Committee on the Work of the Second Part of its Third Session (5-23 October 1964), Annex II, Proposals and amendments relating to liability for damage caused by objects launched into outer space, 23 October 1964, p. 22.

本的唯一区别是草案中没有通过联合国秘书长提交赔偿要求的内容。这有赖于发射国和求偿国都是《责任公约》的当事国。

1971 年《责任公约》起草小组的谈判后，谈判临近结束才对本条达成一致。《责任公约》起草小组将本条约入 1971 年 6 月 28 日通过的《空间物体所造成损害的国际责任公约》草案中，成为第九条①。同一天，《责任公约》起草小组②通过公约草案确认了该条内容。

（二）评注

《责任公约》第九条是《责任公约》第八条内容的延伸，第八条聚焦于受害人和求偿国之间的关系，第九条则规定了求偿国和发射国之间的关系。《责任公约》项下的赔偿要求需要外交照会形式的国家间外交沟通。本条规定的目的是确保解决因外空活动造成损害国家赔偿责任的国际争端。因此，《责任公约》第九条规定有赖于国家间外交关系的一般法律。这些法律是在长久的国家实践和国内法中发展而来的③。

第九条规定了依据《责任公约》提出赔偿要求背景下，国家间三个层面的沟通。该条只有一段，分成了三句话。第一，如《维也纳外交关系公约》第二条规定的那样，《责任公约》第九条依赖于国家间关系相互同意的一般原则④。第二条规定，“国家间外交关系的确立需要双方同意”。因此，《责任公约》第九条第一句话首先确定基本原则，即《责任公约》项下的赔偿要求应当由求偿国通过外交渠道向发射国提出。如前所述，这个过程开始于外交照会⑤。与赔偿主张有关的国家之间可能没有确立任何外交关系。一般国际法没有规定国家间的外交关系权利，基本原则是双方同意基础上，国家之间通过协议寻求确立关系。

---

① See UN Doc. PUOS/C. 2/DG（X）/2, Draft Convention on International Liability for Damage Caused by Space Objects, text approved by the Drafting Group on 28 June 1971, 28 June 1971, in：UN Doc. A/AC. 105/94, Report Of The Legal Sub-Committee on the Work of its Tenth Session（7 June-2 July 1971）, Annex I, Proposals and Other Documents Relating to Agenda Item 2（Draft Convention on Liability for Damage Caused by Objects Launched into Outer Space）, 8 July 1971, p. 30.

② Ibid.

③ See e. g. US Department of State, Foreign Affairs Handbooks, 5 FAH-1 Correspondence Handbook, 23 September 2005 <http：//www. state. gov/m/a/dir/regs/fah/> accessed 26 April 2019.

④ Vienna Convention on Diplomatic Relations（opened for signature 18 April 1961, entry into force 24 April 1964）, 500 UNTS 95.

⑤ See the examples of Lyall, Francis/Larsen, Paul B. , Space Law a Treatise, Ashgate, Burlington/Surrey 2009, p. 110, mn. 112.

本条第二句适用于一国与有关发射国不存在外交关系的情形。在这种情况下，可请求第三国代为提出赔偿要求。第九条第二句包含了两个选项：在没有外交关系的情况下，一国可请另一国代其向发射国提出赔偿要求，或“其他方式代表”其作为受害国的利益。重要的是，第九条没有如何代表的具体信息。这意味着，代表求偿国的国家可利用已有的做法以及外交特权与豁免，特别是其中与主权国家之间临时沟通有关的①。

最后，《责任公约》第九条第三句，提到了在联合国框架内的替代方式。允许通过联合国秘书长提出赔偿要求。在这种情况下，最重要的是求偿国和发射国都是联合国的成员国。但是，秘书长不能代表求偿国②。不满足上述要求的赔偿要求将被排除在《责任公约》规定的解决争端程序之外。

宇宙-954号坠落案中，在向苏联政府提出赔偿要求时，加拿大政府通过外交照会提出追索③。如前所述④，此后两国政府间达成了远低于加拿大实际承受损失的赔偿方案，且没有依据《责任公约》设立求偿委员会。《国际法律资料》中重印了有关解决方案⑤。

从前文可看出，代表受害国提出赔偿要求的国家至少必须和发射国有外交关系。《责任公约》第九条第二句没有明确规定以其他方式代表求偿国利益应满足什么标准，似乎并不要求代表国一定是《责任公约》的当事国。

十一、第十条（提出损害赔偿要求的期限）

Smith and Kerrest

1. 损害赔偿要求，须于损害发生之日起，或判明应负责任的发射国之日起一年内向发射国提出。

---

① See e. g. Berridge, Geoff R., Diplomacy: Theory and Practice, 4th edn., Palgrave Macmillan, Basingstoke 2010, Part Ⅲ, pp. 207ff.

② 郑斌将此描述为“可疑的效用”。见 Cheng, Bin, International Liability for Damage Caused by Space Objects, in: Jasentuliyana, Nandasiri/Lee, Roy S. K. (eds.), Manual on Space Law, Volume I, Oceana Publications, New York 1979, p. 134.

③ See International Legal Materials (18) 1979, 907ff.

④ See Commentary LIAB, Article II, mn. 108f.

⑤ See International Legal Materials (20) 1981, p. 689.

2. 如一国不知损害业已发生，或未能判明应付责任的发射国，应于获悉上述事实之日起一年内，提出赔偿要求；如有理由认为，求偿国由于行使尽职调查，已获悉上述事实，则提出赔偿要求的时间从知悉之日起，不论如何不得超过一年。

3. 即使不完全了解损害的程度，也应当适用本条第一款和第二款规定的时间限制。在这种情况下，求偿国应当有权自该时限期满至全面了解损害程度后一年止，修改其要求，提交补充文件。

目录

（一）谈判和起草过程

第十条的起草过程很有趣。本条三款在谈判的不同阶段拼凑到一起，而且各国对此并没有一致的观点。

1964 年，美国[1]和匈牙利[2]早期草案中已经有第十条第 1 款的内容，表述与最终版本接近。两个草案均规定，赔偿要求必须在损害发生之日起一年内提出。1965 年比

---

① UN Doc. A/AC. 105/C. 2/L. 8, United States: Proposal-Convention concerning liability for damage caused by the launching of objects into outer space, 9 March 1964, in: UN Doc. A/AC. 105/19, Report of the Legal Sub-Committee on the Work of its Third Session (9-26 March 1964), 26 March 1964, Annex II, Proposals and amendments relating to liability for damage caused by objects launched into outer space, p. 2, Art. IV.

② UN Doc. A/AC. 105/C. 2/L. 10, Hungary: Proposed draft agreement-Agreement concerning liability for damage caused by the launching of objects into outer space, 16 March 1964, in: UN Doc. A/AC. 105/19, Report of the Legal Sub-Committee on the Work of its Third Session (9-26 March 1964), Annex II, Proposals and amendments relating to liability for damage caused by objects launched into outer space, 26 March 1964, p. 7, Art. XI.

利时草案建议将这个时间期限延长到损害发生之日起两年内提出[①]。比利时最终放弃了这个建议，与美国和匈牙利在此问题上结盟。

1965 年美国草案中第一次纳入了第十条第 2 款[②]。匈牙利和比利时接受了这一款，此后纳入两国草案中。

1970 年，《责任公约》起草小组讨论成果作为第 3 款加入第十条。因此，1970 年工作小组通过的《空间物体所造成损害的国际责任公约》草案第一次纳入第十条（当时是第十一条）的现有版本，即三款式结构[③]。

（二）评注

第十条规定的是依据《责任公约》提交赔偿要求的期限或时限问题。该条含有三款，每款设定了《责任公约》期限的时间起点。每款覆盖了与损害发生有关的特定情形，包括发射国的识别、知悉损害和依据《责任公约》提出赔偿要求的时间。

1. 一般规则：一年

第十条第 1 款规定了损害赔偿要求出现并已知发射国的情形，也考虑了稍后才能识别发射国的情形。第一款规定的时限是一年，自损害发生之日起。如果造成损害事故发生时，能够知晓或识别发射国，则时限自这一时刻起算，如果当时不能，只能事后识别发射国，则自识别之日起一年。

第十条第 1 款前半句是两个情形：首先，求偿人因空间物体造成损害；其次，求偿人当时能够识别有关的发射国。

---

① See UN Doc. A/AC. 105/C. 2/L. 7/Rev. 3, Belgium: Proposal for a Convention on the Unification of Certain Rules Governing Liability for Damage Caused by Space Devices to Third Parties on the Surface of the Earth and Aircraft in Flight, 26 June 1967, in: UN Doc. A/AC. 105/37, Report of the Legal Sub-Committee on the Work of its Sixth Session (19 June-14 July 1967), Annex II, Proposals, amendments and other documents relating to liability for damage caused by the launching of objects into outer space, 14 July 1967, p. 1, Art. 4.

② See UN Doc. A/AC. 105/C. 2/L. 8/Rev. 3, United States: Revised Proposal-Convention concerning liability for damage caused by the launching of objects into outer space, 24 September 1965, in: UN Doc. A/AC. 105/29, Report of the Legal Sub-Committee on the Work of its Fourth Session (20 September-1 October 1965), 1 October 1965, Annex II, Proposals and amendments relating to liability for damage caused by objects launched into outer space, p. 7, Art. IV para. 4.

③ See UN Doc. A/AC. 105/C. 2/L. 77, Text approved by the Working Group on 1 July 1970-Draft Convention on International Liability for Damage Caused by Space Objects, 1 July 1970, in: UN Doc. A/AC. 105/85, Report Of The Legal Sub-Committee on the Work of its Ninth Session (8 June-3 July 1970), Annex I, Proposals And Other Documents Relating To Liability For Damage Caused By The Launching Of Objects Into Outer Space (Agenda item 2), 3 July 1970, p. 4.

第十条第 1 款后半句是关于此后才能识别发射国的情形，在这种情况下，提交赔偿要求的时限自受害人能够判明发射国之日起算。该条没有进一步说明多个发射国的可能性，但《责任公约》第五条明确所有发射国都负有赔偿责任。

第十条第 1 款规定的最有趣事项是关于识别发射国的困难。技术上，发射是难以隐藏的活动，因此有关信息应该容易获知。但是，如果事故是由人造空间碎片造成的，就需要仔细的识别，并可能迟延赔偿要求。无法预设在发生损害的地方可以寻获或追踪造成损害的物质碎片。只有经过调查才能确立其与发射国必要的联系。无论如何，多个发射国给识别任务留下了一些空间，因为知晓一个发射国足以。

因此，第十条第 1 款后半句很重要，没有直接回答是否不止一个发射国。如此一来，损害的发生与特定发射的时间和地点无关。

一年的时限似乎是权宜之计。外空事故要么即刻造成损害，要么经过一段时间。对于前者，一般能够判定发射国，一年内提交赔偿要求因而是可行的。第十条第 1 款后半句预计的情形，识别和判明发射国需要不确定长度的时间。因此，虽然可能在事故后一年内求偿，但时限是自明确发射国之日起算。

2. 特定情形中的例外

第十条第 2 款是关于求偿国不知道损害事故业已发生或已遭受损害，抑或无法识别发射国的情形。在这种情况下，一年的时限自该国获悉有关事实起算。

这个规定的适用情形是发射国活动造成的损害发生在偏远的地方，特别是非永久性设施，比如南北极的科考船等，或者是已失踪的公海上的平台、船舶或飞越公海上空的飞机。

第十条第 2 款含有尽职调查条款，意味着《责任公约》要求求偿国有效率地识别发射国或调查损害事故。

将一年时限与应当启动推定日期联系在一起，这意味着《责任公约》确立了合理期待标准。该规定旨在鼓励求偿国提出赔偿要求，以启动争端解决程序，为达成损害赔偿提供有效的办法。

3. 损害的程度

第十条第 3 款为提出赔偿要求时限确立了更加严格的规则。不管是依据第十条第 1 款还是第 2 款提起的，任何赔偿要求不能仅因为求偿人不了解损害程度就迟延提出。换言之，一年时限仅指提出赔偿要求，而无需知晓损害的程度或受损的最终价值。

一年时限是很有必要的，唯一的变量是开始启用的确切时刻。第十条第 3 款第二句允许根据损害程度进一步信息修改赔偿要求，且不受一年时限的限制。第十条第 3 款第二句总结了该条的理论逻辑，即明确必须在一年提交赔偿要求，无论自损害发生或此后的某一时刻起。尽管如此，任何赔偿要求不得仅因不完全了解损害程度而无限延期。一旦全面了解损害程度，将再次启动一年的时限。

在这个上下文中，第十条确认了文明法律制度中的共有规则，即法律行动一般有时限要求，超越时限的赔偿要求将无法获得支持。这是基于法律确定性原则[①]。第十条进一步确认，求偿人不得受制于缺少识别发射国的能力，或不知晓损害程度的事实。第十条的重点是国际争端解决机制背景下的正当程序[②]。

十二、第十一条（与本国管辖权的关系）

Smith and Kerrest

1. 根据本公约向发射国提出损害赔偿要求，无须求偿国或其代表的自然人或法人用尽当地救济。

2. 本公约不妨碍一国，或其可能代表的自然人或法人在发射国的法院、行政法庭或机构提起赔偿要求。若一国已在发射国的法院、行政法庭或机构提起了赔偿要求，则不得根据公约或其他对有关国家有约束力的国际协定，就同一损害提出赔偿要求。

目录

---

① See Brownlie, Ian, Principles of Public International Law, 7th edn., Oxford University Press, Oxford 2008, pp. 501ff.; and Wouters, Jan/Verhoeven, Sten, Prescription, Max Planck Encyclopedia on Public International Law, last updated November 2008 <http://www.mpepil.com> accessed 26 April 2019.

② See Hobe, Stephan, The Permanent Court of Arbitration Adopts Optional Rules for Arbitration of Disputes Relating to Outer Space Activities, Zeitschrift für Luft- und Weltraumrecht (61) 2012, pp. 4-25.

2. 与国内法有关的程序

3. 国内落实

4. 常设仲裁院《与外空活动有关争端的仲裁任择规则》

(1) 与《责任公约》争端解决范围的比较

(2) 常设仲裁院《PCA 规则》的内容

(一) 谈判和起草过程

《责任公约》第十一条起草的核心争议只有一个，即是否纳入用尽当地救济和《责任公约》草案责任国的其他救济。对此，苏联直到谈判后期一直持反对意见。早期的美国①和比利时②草案有关于此事的条款，但作为苏联阵营国家的代表，匈牙利草案中则对此保持沉默。

这个僵局持续到 1970 年，经过《责任公约》工作小组的激烈讨论，苏联阵营国家立场软化，接受了西方国家的提议。

结果是，1970 年 7 月 1 日，工作小组通过了《空间物体所造成损害国际责任公约》草案第十一条（当时的第十二条）的现有内容③，1971 年 6 月 28 日，起草小组认可了《责任公约》最终版本④。

---

① UN Doc. A/AC. 105/C. 2/L. 8, United States: Proposal-Convention concerning liability for damage caused by the launching of objects into outer space, 9 March 1964, in: UN Doc. A/AC. 105/19, Report of the Legal Sub-Committee on the Work of its Third Session (9-26 March 1964), 26 March 1964, Annex II, Proposals and amendments relating to liability for damage caused by objects launched into outer space, p. 2.

② UN Doc. A/AC. 105/C. 2/L. 7/Rev. 3, Belgium: Proposal for a Convention on the Unification of Certain Rules Governing Liability for Damage Caused by Space Devices to Third Parties on the Surface of the Earth and Aircraft in Flight, 26 June 1967, in: UN Doc. A/AC. 105/37, Report of the Legal Sub-Committee on the Work of its Sixth Session (19 June-14 July 1967), Annex II, Proposals, amendments and other documents relating to liability for damage caused by the launching of objects into outer space, 14 July 1967, p. 1.

③ UN Doc. A/AC. 105/C. 2/L. 77, Text approved by the Working Group on 1 July 1970-Draft Convention on International Liability for Damage Caused by Space Objects, 1 July 1970, in: UN Doc. A/AC. 105/85, Report Of The Legal Sub- Committee on the Work of its Ninth Session (8 June-3 July 1970), Annex I, Proposals And Other Documents Relating To Liability For Damage Caused By The Launching Of Objects Into Outer Space (Agenda item 2), 3 July 1970, p. 4.

④ See UN Doc. PUOS/C. 2/DG (X) /2, Draft Convention on International Liability for Damage Caused by Space Objects: text approved by the Drafting Group on 28 June 1971, 28 June 1971, in: UN Doc. A/AC. 105/94, Report Of The Legal Sub-Committee on the Work of its Tenth Session (7 June-2 July 1971), Annex I, Proposals and Other Documents Relating to Agenda Item 2 (Draft Convention on Liability for Damage Caused by Objects Launched into Outer Space), 8 July 1971, p. 30.

（二）评注

第十一条有两款，分别是第十一条第1款和第十一条第2款，第1款是为《责任公约》项下的追索豁免用尽当地救济规则，第二款是关于《责任公约》项下追索与国内层面追索的关系。

1. 豁免当地救济规则

《责任公约》第八条违背了传统国际法有关国籍的一般规则，第十一条违背了国际法要求在诉诸国际管辖权之前穷尽当地救济的传统原则①。

和国际法其他赔偿要求不同，就《责任公约》求偿不需要求偿人首先穷尽其在国内法院要求赔偿的权利②，包括私人外空活动，即《外空条约》第六条所指的“本国外空活动”。尽管第十一条第1款没有界定当地救济，但表述中清晰地认可在国内层面提出的主张或诉讼。就其遭受的损害，国家无须利用当地救济。

这是《责任公约》和赔偿要求程序的重要组成部分。证明公约并不是规范外空事故或碰撞造成损害要求的排他性条款。正如本评注所注意到的，《责任公约》的目的是为国际社会提供独立的国际办法，以解决代表外空活动受害人的国家向发射国提出赔偿要求。对于求偿人可以利用的国内救济类型，《责任公约》不做任何预先评价。该公约规定的是国与国之间的争端解决机制，确保能够在国家层面解决从事外空活动私人和商业部门的赔偿要求。因此，在国内层面还是通过国际外交层面追寻《责任公约》项下的利益，任由当事人选择。

2. 与国内法有关的程序

《责任公约》第十一条第2款是关于赔偿要求的两个独立但有联系的规则。第一句中，将国内法院、行政法庭或机构提出赔偿要求的选择权留给了有关当事方。《责任公约》没有染指各国国内管辖权的细节。

更重要的是，《责任公约》遵循了国际法和国内法关于赔偿的传统规则，即一事不再理。防止求偿国就已经提出赔偿要求的同一法律义务再提起赔偿要求③。这不仅

① See Lyall, Francis/Larsen, Paul B., Space Law a Treatise, Ashgate, Burlington/Surrey 2009, pp. 110f.

② See Brownlie, Ian, Principles of Public International Law, 7th edn., Oxford University Press, Oxford 2008, pp. 492ff.; and Shaw, Malcolm N., International Law, 6th edn., Cambridge University Press, Cambridge 2008, pp. 819ff.

③ See Geiß, Robin, ne bis in idem, Max Planck Encyclopedia on Public International Law, last updated February 2010 <http://www.mpepil.com> accessed 26 April 2019.

排除了就同一损害获得两次赔偿的风险，而且首先，第十一条第2款后一句将一事不再理规则延伸至依据任何其他国际协定提出赔偿要求的权利。第十一条有效确保了不能就同一损失获得多个赔偿。其次，重申了求偿人在国内法院和国际层面保护其利益的自由。第三，求偿人是否在国内寻求救济不影响国际要求。最后，第十一条阻止了依据任何其他国际协定提起求偿的权利，以避免其影响《责任公约》项下的赔偿要求。

因此，《责任公约》为外空活动争端解决确立了独立于国内救济的国际机制。

3. 国内落实

第十一条是诉诸国际管辖权前穷尽国内救济这个国际法一般规则的例外。该条允许有关当事方选择可启动的解决损害赔偿争端的管辖权。求偿人可以但不必需，请求国内或其他法庭审理争端。这个例外用处很大，特别是在非政府实体参与外空活动的情况下。

在有责任支付损害赔偿金情况下，通过国内法规定针对本国非政府实体的赔偿金权利，国家可以“启动或放弃”它在国际层面面对的赔偿要求①。这种做法的预设前提是一国国内和其他国家的损害赔偿法足以处理任何问题。通常来讲，可适用的法律取决于受害人的选择②。

一个替代的实用性路径是不依赖国内法，接受复杂的适用法问题，国际空间法项下赔偿要求依据《责任公约》解决。依从这个路径，只要满足了《责任公约》项下发射国的地位和承担损害赔偿责任的条件，在国内层面权衡赔偿要求和选取解决方案均有利于受害人。如此一来，集中式的损害赔偿解决方案取得了优先地位，淘汰了权衡选取某国法律求偿的做法。

法国《外空法》采纳了这一路径③。根据该法第十三条，所有赔偿要求都仅指向运营者，国家给运营者施加了强制保险要求④。另外，根据一般法免除了参与空间物

① See e. g. Sec. 10 para. 1 United Kingdom Outer Space Act of 18 July 1986.

② See in this context, Regulation (EC) 864/2007 of the European Parliament and of the Council of 11 July 2007 on the law applicable to non-contractual obligations (Rome II), [2007] OJ L199/40; further, Smith, Lesley J./Doldirina, Catherine, Jurisdiction and applicable law in cases of damage from space in Europe-The advent of the most suitable choice-Rome II, Acta Astronautica (66) 2010, p. 239.

③ French Law No. 2008-518 of 3 June 2008 (French SOA).

④ Art. 6 French SOA.

体制造、发射和交付全过程的任何供应商和转包商的所有其他赔偿责任[①]。据此，转包商无须考虑和担忧因为参与空间运营引发的高额赔偿要求。

除了国内层面的上述问题，（外国）第三方也纳入并受益于国家和运营者之间的特殊风险方程式，进而建构了一个简单的、没有冲突的赔偿要求管理架构[②]。

4. 常设仲裁院《与外空活动有关争端的仲裁任择规则》

（1）与《责任公约》争端解决范围的比较

直到最近，除了《责任公约》确立的专门机制，再没有其他专门与外空有关的国际争端解决机制。此类机制的缺位是国际外空法的主要局限之一，诸多学者许久以来呼吁确立相关机制[③]。《责任公约》项下的争端解决程序限于公约条文规定的有关案件，且只有国家可用。确有必要建立其他程序，争端解决机制的缺位意味着在与另一个国际空间运营者发生争端时，私人和商业运营者仅有少数或没有可用的渠道为自己辩护。这阻碍了潜在的私人外空创业者，甚至可能给外空法领域带来一些不确定。

为了解决这些问题，创设满足现有外空活动需要的法律环境，常设仲裁院（PCA）通过了《与外空活动有关争端的仲裁任择规则》。常设仲裁院是政府间国际组织，设立于1899年，目的是为解决争端提供仲裁服务[④]，已经确立了解决特定领域争端的仲裁任择规则，例如《与自然资源有关争端的仲裁任择条款》。这些规则为起草《与外空活动有关争端的仲裁任择规则》（以下简称《PCA规则》）提供了范本[⑤]。

---

① Art. 19 French SOA.

② See Ersfeld, Herrmann, Empfehlungen für eine nationale deutsche Weltraumgesetzgebung aus Industriesicht, Zeitschrift für Luft- und Weltraumrecht（59）2010, pp. 241-251; Smith, Lesley J., Legislating for Outer Space: The Example of Germany: Considerations on a National Space Law, Zeitschrift für Luft- und Weltraumrecht（61）2012, pp. 62-78.

③ See Böckstiegel, Karl-Heinz, Settlement of Disputes Regarding Space Activities, Journal of Space Law（21）1993, p. 1; Diederiks-Verschoor, I. H. Philepina, The Settlement of Disputes in Space: New Developments, Journal of Space Law（26）1998, p. 49; Diederiks-Verschoor, I. H. Philepina, The Settlement of Disputes under Space Law, in: Dupuy, René-Jean（ed.）, The Settlement of Disputes on the New Natural Resources, Martinus Nijhoff Publishers, The Hague 1983, p. 85; Goh, Gérardine M., Dispute Settlement in International Space Law-A Multi-Door Courthouse for Outer Space, Brill Academic Publishers, Leiden 2007.

④ 根据第一次海牙和平会议缔结的1899年《和平解决国际争端公约》设立了常设仲裁院。1907年第二次海牙和平会议修订了1899年《公约》。

⑤ See Hobe, Stephan, The Permanent Court of Arbitration Adopts Optional Rules for Arbitration of Disputes Relating to Outer Space Activities, Zeitschrift für Luft- und Weltraumrecht（61）2012, pp. 4-25; the text of the Optional Rules for Arbitration of Disputes Relating to Outer Space Activities can be accessed at <http://www.pca-cpa.org/showfile.asp?fil_id=1774> accessed 26 April 2019.

（2）常设仲裁院《PAC 规则》的内容

2011 年 12 月 6 日，常设仲裁院（PCA）通过了《与外空活动有关争端的仲裁任择规则》，可以作为第十一条第二款中提及的“其他国际协定”。

该规则的通过标志着外空法领域的重要发展。这是因为该规则确立了解决外空争端的灵活机制，反映了外空活动当下的现实；此外，该规则提供了一个《责任公约》规定之外的解决与外空活动有关国际争端的机制。值得注意的是，《责任公约》的争端解决程序限于与适用该公约规则有关的争端，并不是外空活动的普遍性争端解决机制。

自空间时代伊始，外空活动经历了巨大的变化。传统上，只有国家从事外空活动，且大多为了科学目标，而当下，外空活动主体有政府和非政府两种性质，包括国家、政府间国际组织和私人实体，外空活动更多地用于商业目的。考虑到外空活动不断增加的商业化趋势，以及公共和私人利益的结合，以仲裁方式解决外空活动争端不是不可能的。

《PCA 规则》的最重要特征如下：

第一，该规则本质上是任择性的。与外空活动有关的争端当事方可以选择利用这些规则解决其争端，但他们没有义务这么做。

第二，该规则以 2010 年《联合国国际贸易法委员会仲裁规则》为基础，并根据国际空间法和外空活动特征做了相应修订。

第三，该规则规定了广泛的出庭权（ius standi）。向所有潜在的参与商业利用外空的主体开放，包括国家、政府间国际组织、非政府组织、公司和私人实体。这是与《责任公约》相比的核心区别，后者的争端解决程序仅对国家开放。

第四，《PCA 规则》与《责任公约》的另一个核心区别是，《PCA 规则》可以用于解决与外空活动有关的任何类别的争端，而不仅仅是空间物体损害责任争端。当然，这并不妨碍《责任公约》当事国在寻求解决与空间物体造成损害有关的争端时，不用《责任公约》争端解决程序，而诉诸于《PCA 规则》。该规则也可用于两个或两个以上国家有关解释和适用利用或进入外空多边条约的争端①。这给仲裁庭提供了解释联合国外空条约条款的可能性。这样的解释尽管有意思，却不具有权威法律效力，

① See Introduction of the PCA Rules.

仲裁的效力限于当事人之间，这些解释的相关性限于个案。

第五，与其他争端程序一样，争端当事方可以自由选任由一个、三个或五个仲裁员组成的仲裁庭（第七条）。鉴于外空活动的特殊性，常设仲裁院提供了当事方可以选任仲裁员的外空领域专家名单（第十条第 4 款）。

第六，《PCA 规则》的几个条款旨在避免和限制仲裁程序中不必要的拖延，例如某个当事方没有回应仲裁通知（第四条第 3 款）或指派仲裁员的通知（第九条）。

第七，《PCA 规则》中最重要的内容是，仲裁庭的裁决是书面的，是终局的，且对当事方有约束力。当事方有义务毫不迟延地履行裁决。裁决的终局和约束力是在商业活动领域创设法律确定性氛围的关键因素。

第八，《PCA 规则》附件有合同中的格式仲裁条款，仲裁员独立性声明范本和可能的有关排除追索仲裁裁决的豁免声明。

《PCA 规则》提供了解决与外空活动有关争端的有效依据。鉴于其灵活性和广泛适用性，外空运营者可能乐于接受该规则。

十三、第十二条（损害赔偿金数额的确定）

Smith and Kerrest

发射国在本公约项下有责任支付的赔偿金，应依照国际法以及公平合理的原则确定，以使对损害所做的赔偿，能确保提出赔偿要求的自然人或法人、国家或国际组织恢复到未发生损害前的状态。

目录

（一）谈判和起草过程

有关空间物体造成损害赔偿金的谈判聚焦于赔偿金的作用和目的。谈判主要围绕与外空有关损害赔偿中，确定恢复原状概念标准适用法问题[①]。

谈判开始，比较清晰的是确定损害赔偿金既要适用国际法也要适用国内法。空间物体造成的损害可能发生在一国境内，也可能发生在非国家领土的公共区域，比如公海或外空。在谈判过程中，适用国际法原则明确赔偿金的决定越来越清晰。

损害外空环境是否是法律保护的利益，是否允许就此提出赔偿要求，有关谈判详见下文[②]。

回顾谈判，可以观察到不同的趋势。一些国家主张，空间物体造成损害应当适用国内法；一些国家主张，国内法和国际法应当具有同等地位。阿拉伯联合共和国代表 El Reedy 先生认为，"第十二条和第二十一条，为充分赔偿和援助提供了坚实的基础"[③]。早在 1968 年工作文件中，意大利代表就明确了立场，赔偿金应当依据国际法决定[④]。相比之下，澳大利亚和英国认为国内法应优先适用，只有国内法缺席的时候才适用国际法[⑤]。而阿根廷认为外空活动造成损害的准据法应取决于个案，可选择不同的法律，包括国际法，有关国家选择适用的法律，直至传统的损害发生地法（lex

---

① See e. g. UN Doc. A/AC. 105/C. 2/SR. 162, Legal Sub-Committee, Summary Record of the One Hundred and Sixty-Second Meeting, held on 22 June 1971, in: UN Doc. A/AC. 105/C. 2/SR. 152-169, Summary records of the One Hundred and Fifty-Second to the One Hundred and Sixty-Ninth Meetings held from 6 June to 2 July 1971, 25 August 1971.

② 这个问题涉及到是否以及如何认定国际法主体的问题。国家和国际组织可以就保护全球利益提出权益主张。

③ UN Doc. A/AC. 105/C. 2/SR. 167, Legal Sub-Committee, Summary Record of the One Hundred and Sixty-Seventh Meeting, held on 29 June 1971, in: UN Doc. A/AC. 105/C. 2/SR. 152-169, Summary records of the One Hundred and Fifty-Second to the One Hundred and Sixty-Ninth Meetings held from 6 June to 2 July 1971, 25 August 1971, Mr. El Reedy (United Arab Republic).

④ See UN Doc. A/AC. 105/C. 2/L. 40, Working Paper submitted by the Italian delegation-Draft convention concerning liability for damage caused by the launching of objects into outer space, 13 June 1986, in: UN Doc. A/AC. 105/45, Report of the Legal Sub-Committee on the Work of its Seventh Session (4-28 June 1968), Annex I, Proposals, amendments and other documents relating to liability for damage caused by the launching of objects into outer space, 11 July 1968, p. 30.

⑤ See UN Doc. A/AC. 105/C. 2/L. 47, Australia/United Kingdom: Working Paper-Applicable Law for Determination of Compensation, 19 June 1968, in: UN Doc. A/AC. 105/45, Report of the Legal Sub-Committee on the Work of its Seventh Session (4-28 June 1968), Annex I, Proposals, amendments and other documents relating to liability for damage caused by the launching of objects into outer space, 11 July 1968, p. 45.

loci delicti commissi）[1]。

印度在其最终草案中提出的观点是，应当适用国际法决定一个赔偿要求的理据。[2]据此，该草案第六条规定，“如果求偿人和被求偿人就依据本公约支付赔偿金数额应当适用的法律有协议，则应当适用有关国内法。如果求偿人和被求偿人间无法就适用法达成一致，赔偿金数额应当依据国际法决定，考虑求偿国的法律，也适度考虑责任国的法律。如果二者有冲突，则以国际法为准。”[3]

无论如何，直到 1970 年，阿根廷、加拿大、日本和瑞典提交的《责任公约》草案中都含有确立赔偿金数额的规则，同时明确可适用的法律[4]：“决定发射国在本公约项下有责任支付的赔偿金数额应当确保提出求偿人，无论是自然人还是法人、国家还是国际组织充分恢复到损害未发生之前的状态。为此，应当考虑损害发生地法和国际法的有关原则。”[5] 这是谈判中，第一次清楚地参照了“恢复原状”概念。这个规定也明确了用于确定责任以及损害赔偿金数额的法律。

1970 年 6 月 30 日，在保加利亚、匈牙利和苏联提交的提案中，这些代表团认为，“损害赔偿金应当依据国际法确定，因为《责任公约》目的是确保当事国可就空间物

---

① See UN Doc. A/AC. 105/C. 2/L. 59, Argentina: Proposal-Law applicable for the determination of compensation, 20 June 1969, in: UN Doc. A/AC. 105/58, Report Of The Legal Sub-Committee on the Work of its Eighth Session (9 June-4 July 1969), Annex II, Proposals and other documents relating to liability for damage caused by the launching of objects into outer space, 4 July 1969, p. 30.

② See UN Doc. A/AC. 105/C. 2/L. 32/Rev. 2, India: proposal-Convention concerning liability for damage caused by the launching of objects into outer space, 3 July 1969, in: UN Doc. A/AC. 105/58, Report of the Legal Sub-Committee on the Work of its Eighth Session (9 June-4 July 1969), Annex II, Proposals and other documents relating to liability for damage caused by the launching of objects into outer space, 4 July 1969, p. 23.

③ UN Doc. A/AC. 105/C. 2/L. 32/Rev. 2, India: proposal-Convention concerning liability for damage caused by the launching of objects into outer space, 3 July 1969, in: UN Doc. A/AC. 105/58, Report Of The Legal Sub-Committee on the Work of its Eighth Session (9 June-4 July 1969), Annex II, Proposals and other documents relating to liability for damage caused by the launching of objects into outer space, 4 July 1969, p. 23.

④ UN Doc. A/AC. 105/C. 2/L. 74, Argentina, Australia, Belgium, Canada, Italy, Japan, Sweden, United Kingdom: Proposal-Measure of Compensation and Competence of the Claims Commission, 29 June 1970, in: UN Doc. A/AC. 105/85, Report Of The Legal Sub-Committee on the Work of its Ninth Session (8 June-3 July 1970), 3 July 1970, Annex I, Proposals And Other Documents Relating To Liability For Damage Caused By The Launching Of Objects Into Outer Space (Agenda item 2), p. 3.

⑤ UN Doc. A/AC. 105/C. 2/L. 74, Argentina, Australia, Belgium, Canada, Italy, Japan, Sweden, United Kingdom: Proposal-Measure of Compensation and Competence of the Claims Commission, 29 June 1970, in: UN Doc. A/AC. 105/85, Report Of The Legal Sub-Committee on the Work of its Ninth Session (8 June-3 July 1970), 3 July 1970, Annex I, Proposals And Other Documents Relating To Liability For Damage Caused By The Launching Of Objects Into Outer Space (Agenda item 2), p. 3.

体造成的损害提出赔偿要求，且全面赔偿因此给当事国、自然人或法人造成的损失。”① 此后的工作文件并没有出现该规定，被界定赔偿金和复原赔偿构成要素的条款取代。草案中也有关于如何确定损害赔偿金及其落实程序的单独条款。

认可国际法（而非国内法）的适用最为重要是决定性的：《责任公约》的目的是确立通过外交渠道寻求赔偿的一体化机制。有关纳入国际私法的考量可能分散《责任公约》作为国际赔偿机制的焦点。

（二）评注

第十二条解决了支付赔偿金义务两个主要问题。第一，国际法和公平合理的原则一道作为适用法，决定赔偿要求的理据；第二，损害赔偿或应支付赔偿金的确立标准是，“确保提出赔偿要求的自然人或法人、国家或国际组织恢复到未发生损害前的状态”。

第十二条旨在确保充分赔偿求偿国、及其代表的自然人和法人在《责任公约》规定内造成的损失。因此，制定第十二条的基础是恢复原状原则。

尽管损害赔偿金与损害赔偿或损害利益的概念类似，但还是有区别的，区别在于损害赔偿金超过了恢复原状赔偿的范围，还包括惩罚性赔偿类别或外部因素。在第十二条的规定中这些考量是悬而未决的。确定最终支付赔偿金标准中涵盖公平合理原则，法庭在达致裁决中不能排除此类因素。明确损害赔偿金作用是将受害人状态恢复至损害发生之前。

提出赔偿要求的损害可能是直接的也可能是间接的，视乎空间物体与损害的直接或临近因果关系。《责任公约》文本中，第一条第 1 款有损害的定义。损害可能是由外空损害事故直接或间接造成的，取决于因果关系和地点。在直接因果情况下，特别是损害发生在地面的情况中，评估近因损害相对容易。此处，需要评估的是有关损害是否远离初始事故，换言之，远离空间物体造成的初始损害，进而不属于《责任公约》第二条的范围。但对于外空中的损害，《责任公约》第三条要求损害是“由一国空间物体给另一国空间物体或其所载人员或财产”造成的。在这种情况下，证实间接损害的难度更大。

---

① UN Doc. A/AC. 105/C. 2/L. 75, Bulgaria, Hungary, USSR: Proposal-Applicable Law, in: UN Doc. A/AC. 105/85, Report Of The Legal Sub-Committee on the Work of its Ninth Session (8 June-3 July 1970), Annex I, Proposals And Other Documents Relating To Liability For Damage Caused By The Launching Of Objects Into Outer Space (Agenda item 2), 3 July 1970, p. 4.

与损害程度有关，传统上适用于物质和非物质损失的规则必须由实体法确立。《责任公约》第一条中有损害的定义。这个定义宽泛到足以覆盖所有的物质和非物质损失。国际法和国内法一样，对非物质损害情形格外谨慎。确定损害赔偿金数额要求根据国际法以及公平合理原则仔细考量和权衡个案的具体情形。

外空活动造成的损害可能导致物质花费，如事后清理或修复损害；这种情况下继续适用恢复原状原则[①]。宇宙-954案件中，加拿大和苏联就具体清理措施达成的争端解决方案中包括清理领土和沿岸水域，但这并不等同于与降低环境质量有关的自然环境恶化；后者是指在或穿越外空时，多余的外空技术造成的结果。

对于外空环境损害，《责任公约》是否施加了损害赔偿责任是有争议的。前文提及了《责任公约》第三条中的定义，将损害限于“由一国空间物体给另一国空间物体或其所载人员或财产”造成的，看起来排除了外空环境损害。《责任公约》第一条第1款的损害定义也没有覆盖环境损害。在外空环境损害适用规则缺位的情况下，加上这个领域缺少国家主权、诉讼资格以及法律利益，《责任公约》可能排除了外空环境损害赔偿责任。尽管如此，可否将《外空条约》第九条解释为确立了保护外空环境的义务有待于进一步探讨。因此，与直接污染不同，《责任公约》没有覆盖外空环境恶化的赔偿要求。当然，作为原则，并不妨碍将《外空条约》第九条解释为国家义务。

十四、第十三条（损害赔偿金的货币）

Smith and Kerrest

除非求偿国与依照本公约应当赔偿的国家就赔偿方式另行达成协议，应以求偿国货币支付赔偿金；如果该国有相应的请求，赔偿金可以赔偿国的货币支付。

目录

① See Commentary LIAB, Article II, mn. 109.

(一)谈判和起草过程

1968 年以后，才开始讨论支付公约项下损害赔偿金的货币问题。似乎并没有引发较多讨论[①]。印度代表团较早提出了支付赔偿金货币提案。该提案包含在印度《与发射进入外空物体造成损害有关的赔偿责任公约》草案中[②]。第六条规定“如果求偿人和被求偿人无法就适用的国内法达成一致，支付赔偿金数额应当由国际法决定，并考虑求偿国的国内法”[③]。此前会议中预见到第八条将规定为，“除非双方另有协议，损害赔偿金数额应当依据求偿国货币确定并支付，或可自由兑换货币”，印度马上提交了该提案。

依据《责任公约》规定，不仅有必要确保受害人恢复到此前的状态[④]；还有一个顾虑是确保公约内容与联合国大会关于和平利用外空国际合作的 2733（XXV）B 号决议保持一致，即便不是逐字逐句地一致，也要符合后者的精神[⑤]。

尽管各国认可依据公平合理原则确定损害赔偿金，实践中的重要事项是，确保支付给求偿国的赔偿金可以兑换成需要利用赔偿金恢复到损害前状态国家的货币[⑥]。

当时，与此密切相关两个问题的谈判让损害赔偿金货币问题黯然失色：谈判更多地关注确定支付给受害人损害赔偿金的法律规则和解决赔偿要求的程序。

---

① Cheng, Bin, International Liability for Damage Caused by Space Objects, in: Jasentuliyana, Nandasiri/Lee, Roy S. K. (eds.), Manual on Space Law, Volume I, Oceana Publications, New York 1979, p. 132.

② See UN Doc. A/AC. 105/C. 2/L. 32, India: proposal-Convention concerning liability for damage caused by the launching of objects into outer space, 2 June 1968, in: UN Doc. A/AC. 105/45, Report of the Legal Sub-Committee on the Work of its Seventh Session (4-28 June 1968), Annex I, Proposals, amendments and other documents relating to liability for damage caused by the launching of objects into outer space, 11 July 1968, p. 16.

③ UN Doc. A/AC. 105/C. 2/L. 32/Rev. 1, India: proposal-Convention concerning liability for damage caused by the launching of objects into outer space, in: UN Doc. A/AC. 105/45, Report of the Legal Sub-Committee on the Work of its Seventh Session (4-28 June 1968), Annex I, Proposals, amendments and other documents relating to liability for damage caused by the launching of objects into outer space, 11 July 1968, p. 21.

④ See UN Doc. A/AC. 105/C. 2/SR. 162, Legal Sub-Committee, Summary Record of the One Hundred and Sixty-Second Meeting, held on 22 June 1971, in: UN Doc. A/AC. 105/C. 2/SR. 152-169, Summary records of the One Hundred and Fifty-Second to the One Hundred and Sixty-Ninth Meetings held from 6 June to 2 July 1971, 25 August 1971, Mr. Vranken (Belgium).

⑤ UNGA Resolution 2733 (XXV) B, International cooperation on the peaceful use of outer space, 16 December 1970.

⑥ See UN Doc. A/AC. 105/C. 2/SR. 167, Legal Sub-Committee, Summary Record of the One Hundred and Sixty-Seventh Meeting, held on 29 June 1971, in: UN Doc. A/AC. 105/C. 2/SR. 152-169, Summary records of the One Hundred and Fifty-Second to the One Hundred and Sixty-Ninth Meetings held from 6 June to 2 July 1971, 25 August 1971.

各国代表团在准备最终草案文本前陷入僵局。捷克斯洛伐克代表 Strucka 先生参考了比利时、匈牙利、巴西和印度代表团提案中有关第十三至第二十二条的建议，帮助法律小组委员会打破僵局，完成了联合国大会 2733（XXV）B 号决议授予其的任务[①]。

（二）评注

第十三条规定发射国因其空间物体造成损害支付的赔偿金。只有求偿国和被求偿国没有就支付赔偿金的货币达成协议的情况下，才适用该条，作为缺位规则，赔偿金应以求偿国的货币支付[②]，或者应求偿国的请求，以发射国的货币支付。如果没有协议，支付货币的选择权在求偿国。这是《责任公约》受害人导向特征的标志之一。

十五、第十四条（未解决的赔偿要求/赔偿委员会）

Smith and Kerrest

若求偿国通知发射国已提出赔偿要求文件之日起一年内，通过第九条规定的外交谈判无法解决赔偿要求，有关各方应于任一方提出请求时，成立赔偿委员会。

目录

（一）谈判和起草过程

1971 年 6 月，比利时、巴西和匈牙利提交《责任公约》草案中的有关规定纳入并成为公约最终文本的第十四条和第十五条[③]。1971 年 6 月 22 日和 23 日会议中，工

① Ibid.

② 宇宙 954 号坠入加拿大境内的结果是，1979 年苏联向加拿大支付加拿大元为单位的赔偿金。两国解决方案的正式文本重印于 International Legal Materials（20），1981，见 Commentary LIAB，Article II，mn. 108f.

③ See UN Doc. A/AC. 105/C. 2/L. 79，Belgium，Brazil and Hungary：proposal，21 June 1971，in：UN Doc. A/AC. 105/94，Report Of The Legal Sub-Committee on the Work of its Tenth Session（7 June-2 July 1971），Annex I，Proposals and Other Documents Relating to Agenda Item 2（Draft Convention on Liability for Damage Caused by Objects Launched into Outer Space），8 July 1971，p. 1.

作小组提案确定了第十四条和第十五条的最终内容，包括条文序号①。

公约筹备工作早期，就决定采用两阶段程序解决《责任公约》项下赔偿要求。

早在 1969 年，《责任公约》就清楚地涵盖了赔偿要求解决机制，以应对第九条规定外交谈判失灵的情况。《责任公约》项下争端解决分为两个阶段：第一阶段是依赖传统的外交谈判；第二阶段是在谈判无法达成富有成效的结果时，任命国际赔偿委员会。

《责任公约》定稿前两年，印度建议将争端解决详细规定成强制性议定书，作为公约的附件②。构建赔偿委员会的权力也有不同版本。草案第十二条中曾提及的关于争端解决的议定书，其中规定了任命调查委员会。该委员会应在成立后 6 个月内就解决赔偿要求的程序提出建议。该模式仅规定了要求各方就赔偿要求的解决计划提出建议。

在比利时、匈牙利和苏联提交的有关争端解决条款的建议中，求偿国和被求偿国应成立调解委员会，该委员会有权作出对各方有约束力的终局决定③。

截至 1970 年，各种草案，特别是向工作小组提交的提案，均将国际层面的赔偿要求认定为非排他性救济④。1970 年 6 月 23 日秘书处起草的工作文件第十二条中达成了具有此效果的临时性协议，“公约项下提出的赔偿要求并不要求用尽求偿国或求偿

① See UN Doc. PUOS/C. 2/WG (X) /1, Draft Convention on International Liability for Damage Caused by Space Objects: texts approved by the Working Group at its meetings on 22 and 23 June 1971, 23 June 1971, in: UN Doc. A/AC. 105/94, Report Of The Legal Sub-Committee on the Work of its Tenth Session (7 June-2 July 1971), Annex I, Proposals and Other Documents Relating to Agenda Item 2 (Draft Convention on Liability for Damage Caused by Objects Launched into Outer Space), 8 July 1971, p. 19.

② See UN Doc. A/AC. 105/C. 2/L. 32/Rev. 2, India: proposal-Convention concerning liability for damage caused by the launching of objects into outer space, 3 July 1969, in: UN Doc. A/AC. 105/58, Report Of The Legal Sub-Committee on the Work of its Eighth Session (9 June-4 July 1969), Annex II, Proposals and other documents relating to liability for damage caused by the launching of objects into outer space, 4 July 1969, p. 23, Art. XII.

③ See UN Doc. A/AC. 105/C. 2/L. 75, Bulgary, Hungary, USSR: Proposal-Settlement of Disputes, 30 June 1970, in: UN Doc. A/AC. 105/85, Report Of The Legal Sub-Committee on the Work of its Ninth Session (8 June-3 July 1970), Annex I, Proposals And Other Documents Relating To Liability For Damage Caused By The Launching Of Objects Into Outer Space (Agenda item 2), 3 July 1970, p. 4.

④ See UN Doc. A/AC. 105/C. 2/WG (IX) /L. 5, Text approved by the Working Group at its meeting on 10 June 1970-Pursuit of remedies available in Respondent State or under other international agreements, 10 June 1970, in: UN Doc. A/AC. 105/85, Report Of The Legal Sub-Committee on the Work of its Ninth Session (8 June-3 July 1970), Annex I, Proposals And Other Documents Relating To Liability For Damage Caused By The Launching Of Objects Into Outer Space (Agenda item 2), 3 July 1970, p. 18.

国代表国的当地救济”①。该规定重申了国内层面赔偿要求并不排除《责任公约》条款的引用。

（二）评注

第十四条是有关赔偿委员会任命和程序规则的 7 个条款中的第一条。这一组条款几乎可以单独成章，尽管在《责任公约》文本中并不是单独一组条款。这组条款延续到规定大规模危险的第二十一条之前。这个主题可以视为规范损害的特别情况。第二十二条及以后部分是一般的最终结论性和程序性规定。

第十四条的目的是在外交渠道无法解决争端时，为赔偿委员会的任命确立规范。该委员会任命可能发生在一年时限到期后，如果第九条确立的外交谈判没有达成解决方案。

时限的起点是求偿国向发射国提出赔偿要求之日起②。和国际法中的其他规定不同，《责任公约》项下的赔偿要求并不要求穷尽当地救济③。

第十四条和第九条之间有重要联系。第十四条对一年后外交谈判失败的原因并没有要求。外交层面的失败原因可能是多重的；可能是各方无法就争端达成可接受的解决办法，或者一方未能就外交谈判请求做出回应。既然第九条也允许第三国代表与其他当事国没有外交关系的国家谈判，也不能排除是因为其他国家之间的原因。尽管这些原因可能很重要，它们对于《责任公约》的结构并没有直接相关性。

截至目前，只有一个已知的，由外空活动造成损害引发的外交谈判案例。1978 年加拿大和苏联宇宙-954 号案是关于苏联失效的核动力卫星坠入加拿大境内造成的损失，详见前文第二条评注④。与该案不同，值得特别注意的是 2009 年宇宙号-铱星因

---

① UN Doc. PUOS/C. 2/DG（IX）/1, Working Paper prepared by the Secretariat in accordance with the tentative agreement reached by the Drafting Group on 27 June 1970, 3 July 1970, in: UN Doc. A/AC. 105/85, Report Of The Legal Sub-Committee on the Work of its Ninth Session (8 June-3 July 1970), Annex I, Proposals And Other Documents Relating To Liability For Damage Caused By The Launching Of Objects Into Outer Space (Agenda item 2), 3 July 1970, p. 24.

② Lyall, Francis/Larsen, Paul B., Space Law a Treatise, Ashgate, Burlington/Surrey 2009, p. 112.

③ See Commentary LIAB, Article XI, mn. 267.

④ See Commentary LIAB, Article II, mn. 108f.

为不适用《责任公约》，没有诉诸公约规定的外交谈判规定①

有关赔偿委员会的权力和权限的规定见《责任公约》第十五条到第二十条。

十六、第十五条（赔偿委员会的构成）

Smith and Kerrest

1. 赔偿委员会应由三人组成：一人由求偿国指派，一人由发射国指派，第三人由两方共同指派，并担任主席。每一方应于请求成立赔偿委员会之日起两个月指派出其人员。

2. 如果指派主席未能于请求成立委员会之日起 4 个月内达成协议，任一方均可请求联合国秘书长于另两个月内指派。

目录

（一）谈判和起草过程

与第十四条一起，第十五条来自于 1971 年 6 月比利时、巴西和匈牙利提交《责

① See Kerrest, Armel, La responsabilité des Etats du fait de la destruction de satellites dans l'espace, in: Groupement Français pour la Recherche en Droit International (ed.), Annuaire Français de Droit International 2009, CNRS, Paris 2010, pp. 615-626.

任公约》草案提案[①]。1971年6月22日和23日会议中这两条纳入了工作小组提案[②]。

1971年比利时、巴西和匈牙利提交《责任公约》草案提案第16条规定，赔偿委员会和许多法庭和司法机构一样，寻求确保司法机制的效率，因此由三个人组成。这有助于确保多数票，避免判定过程中出现僵持状态。

尽管对于在《责任公约》框架内设立争端解决委员会有一致意见[③]，对该委员会的构成还是存在不同观点。美国和比利时倾向于三人委员会，因为可确保多数票，[④]

① UN Doc. A/AC. 105/C. 2/L. 79, Belgium, Brazil and Hungary: proposal, 21 June 1971, in: UN Doc. A/AC. 105/94, Report Of The Legal Sub-Committee on the Work of its Tenth Session (7 June-2 July 1971), Annex I, Proposals and Other Documents Relating to Agenda Item 2 (Draft Convention on Liability for Damage Caused by Objects Launched into Outer Space), 8 July 1971, p. 1.

② UN Doc. PUOS/C. 2/WG (X) /1, Draft Convention on International Liability for Damage Caused by Space Objects: texts approved by the Working Group at its meetings on 22 and 23 June 1971, 23 June 1971, in: UN Doc. A/AC. 105/94, Report Of The Legal Sub-Committee on the Work of its Tenth Session (7 June-2 July 1971), Annex I, Proposals and Other Documents Relating to Agenda Item 2 (Draft Convention on Liability for Damage Caused by Objects Launched into Outer Space), 8 July 1971, p. 19.

③ See UN Doc. A/AC. 105/C. 2/L. 8, United States: Proposal-Convention concerning liability for damage caused by the launching of objects into outer space, 9 March 1964, in: UN Doc. A/AC. 105/19, Report of the Legal Sub-Committee on the Work of its Third Session (9-26 March 1964), 26 March 1964, Annex II, Proposals and amendments relating to liability for damage caused by objects launched into outer space, p. 2, Art. Ⅶ; UN Doc. A/AC. 105/C. 2/L. 10, Hungary: Proposed draft agreement-Agreement concerning liability for damage caused by the launching of objects into outer space, 16 March 1964, in: UN Doc. A/AC. 105/19, Report of the Legal Sub-Committee on the Work of its Third Session (9-26 March 1964), Annex II, Proposals and amendments relating to liability for damage caused by objects launched into outer space, 26 March 1964, p. 7, Art. XII; and UN Doc. A/AC. 105/C. 2/L. 7/Rev. 1, Belgium: Proposal for a Convention on the Unification of Certain Rules Governing Liability for Damage Caused by Space Devices, 1 October 1964, in: UN Doc. A/AC. 105/21, Report of the Legal Sub-Committee on the Work of the Second Part of its Third Session (5-23 October 1964), Annex II, Proposals and amendments relating to liability for damage caused by objects launched into outer space, 23 October 1964, p. 18, Art. 6 lit. (c).

④ See UN Doc. A/AC. 105/C. 2/L. 8, United States: Proposal-Convention concerning liability for damage caused by the launching of objects into outer space, 9 March 1964, in: UN Doc. A/AC. 105/19, Report of the Legal Sub-Committee on the Work of its Third Session (9-26 March 1964), 26 March 1964, Annex II, Proposals and amendments relating to liability for damage caused by objects launched into outer space, p. 2, Art. Ⅶ; and UN Doc. A/AC. 105/C. 2/L. 7/Rev. 1, Belgium: Proposal for a Convention on the Unification of Certain Rules Governing Liability for Damage Caused by Space Devices, 1 October 1964, in: UN Doc. A/AC. 105/21, Report of the Legal Sub-Committee on the Work of the Second Part of its Third Session (5-23 October 1964), Annex II, Proposals and amendments relating to liability for damage caused by objects launched into outer space, 23 October 1964, p. 18, Art. 6 lit. (c). Art. 55 ICJ Statute provides that all questions are to be decided by a majority vote of those judges present, with the President or the judge taking his place having the casting vote in cases of equal voting.

而匈牙利则主张委员会决定应建立在平等基础上①。这与前苏联国家不愿意接受强制性第三方争端解决机制有关；他们认为这侵犯了他们解释条约的自主权②。

（二）评注

1. 构成

第十五条关于赔偿委员会构成的规定有两款。争端解决的当事国必须指派本国成员，第三人作为主席由两国联合指派。如果请求成立赔偿委员会之日起四个月，当事国不能就指派主席达成一致，可请求联合国秘书长指派。

第十五条表述反映了允许当事国指派本国委员会成员的重要性，此后两方共同指派委员会主席。每个争端当事方应任命一个成员，这种方法在争端解决或仲裁庭中是很常见的。在这种情况下，如果成员们无法达成一致，独立或中立的主席一般能在其作为主席的职权内保有决定票职能。

第十五条第 1 款规定了选择委员会成员的时限，要求在请求成立赔偿委员会之日起两个月指派成员。

2. 冲突规则

如果当事方在 4 个月内无法就主席的选择达成一致意见，第十五条第 2 款进一步规定了两个月的时限，在此期间，任一方可请求联合国秘书长指派主席。

第十五条规定的指派赔偿委员会成员的程序形式与其他获得国际认可的争端解决机制保持一致③。

① UN Doc. A/AC. 105/C. 2/L. 10, Hungary: Proposed draft agreement-Agreement concerning liability for damage caused by the launching of objects into outer space, 16 March 1964, in: UN Doc. A/AC. 105/19, Report of the Legal Sub-Committee on the Work of its Third Session (9-26 March 1964), Annex II, Proposals and amendments relating to liability for damage caused by objects launched into outer space, 26 March 1964, p. 7, Art. XII.

② Cheng, Bin, International Liability for Damage Caused by Space Objects, in: Jasentuliyana, Nandasiri/Lee, Roy S. K. (eds.), Manual on Space Law, Volume I, Oceana Publications, New York 1979, p. 136.

③ See e. g the Rules of Arbitration of the International Chamber of Commerce <http: //www. iccwbo. org/WorkArea/DownloadAsset. aspx? id = 2147489109> accessed 26 April 2019; and the UNCITRAL Arbitration Rules <http: //www. uncitral. org/pdf/english/texts/arbitration/arb-rules-revised/arb-rules-revised-2010-e. pdf > accessed 26 April 2019, recommend by UNGA Res. 65/22, UNCITRAL Arbitration Rules as revised in 2010, 6 December 2010.

十七、第十六条（未指派/空缺/工作程序）

Smith and Kerrest

1. 如果一方未于规定期限内指派出其人员，主席应当应另一方的要求，组成仅有一个成员的赔偿委员会。

2. 无论任何原因造成委员会成员空缺，应当按照原定的指派程序进行补派。

3. 委员会应自行决定其工作程序。

4. 委员会应选定一个或数个工作地点，并确定其他一些行政事项。

5. 除单一成员的委员会作出的决定和裁定外，委员会的一切决定和裁定均应以多数票表决通过。

目录

（一）谈判和起草过程

《责任公约》第十六条的最终措辞和结构源自1968年印度提交的一份公约草案[①]。该草案引入的条款现在规定在第十六条第2款和第4款中，并重述了第1款、第1款和第5款中的原则。工作小组认可印度提案中的这些条款后[②]，也获得了法律小组委

① See UN Doc. A/AC. 105/C. 2/L. 32, India: proposal-Convention concerning liability for damage caused by the launching of objects into outer space, 2 June 1968, in: UN Doc. A/AC. 105/45, Report of the Legal Sub-Committee on the Work of its Seventh Session (4-28 June 1968), Annex I, Proposals, amendments and other documents relating to liability for damage caused by the launching of objects into outer space, 11 July 1968, p. 16.

② See UN Doc. PUOS/C. 2/WG (X) /1, Draft Convention on International Liability for Damage Caused by Space Objects: texts approved by the Working Group at its meetings on 22 and 23 June 1971, 23 June 1971, in: UN Doc. A/AC. 105/94, Report Of The Legal Sub-Committee on the Work of its Tenth Session (7 June-2 July 1971), Annex I, Proposals and Other Documents Relating to Agenda Item 2 (Draft Convention on Liability for Damage Caused by Objects Launched into Outer Space), 8 July 1971, p. 19.

员会的批准①。

提交给联合国和平利用外空委员会的第二份草案中已经含有第十六条第 1 款的规定，源自美国 1964 年草案②。此前一年，比利时代表提交的第一份草案③的规定是将争端解决交给了国际法院。此后所有草案都采纳了赔偿委员会解决争端的办法。这些草案都没有确立赔偿或仲裁员会的工作程序，也没有对委员会应当自行决定工作程序提出异议④。

美国草案采纳了三人赔偿委员会的多数票投票程序原则⑤，此后各国所有提案中

① See UN Doc. A/AC. 105/94, Report Of The Legal Sub-Committee on the Work of its Tenth Session (7 June-2 July 1971), 8 July 1971.

② See UN Doc. A/AC. 105/C. 2/L. 8, United States: Proposal-Convention concerning liability for damage caused by the launching of objects into outer space, 9 March 1964, in: UN Doc. A/AC. 105/19, Report of the Legal Sub-Committee on the Work of its Third Session (9-26 March 1964), 26 March 1964, Annex II, Proposals and amendments relating to liability for damage caused by objects launched into outer space, p. 2.

③ See UN Doc. A/AC. 105/C. 2/L. 7, Working Paper Submitted by the Belgian Delegation on the Unification of Certain Rules Governing Liability for Damage Caused by Space Devices, 29 April 1963, in: UN Doc. A/AC. 105/12, Report of the Legal Sub-Committee on the Work of its Second Session (16 April-3 May 1963), 6 May 1963, Annex I, C, p. 10.

④ See e. g. UN Doc. A/AC. 105/C. 2/L. 8, United States: Proposal-Convention concerning liability for damage caused by the launching of objects into outer space, 9 March 1964, in: UN Doc. A/AC. 105/19, Report of the Legal Sub-Committee on the Work of its Third Session (9-26 March 1964), 26 March 1964, Annex II, Proposals and amendments relating to liability for damage caused by objects launched into outer space, p. 2; UN Doc. A/AC. 105/C. 2/L. 10, Hungary: Proposed draft agreement-Agreement concerning liability for damage caused by the launching of objects into outer space, 16 March 1964, in: UN Doc. A/AC. 105/19, Report of the Legal Sub-Committee on the Work of its Third Session (9-26 March 1964), Annex II, Proposals and amendments relating to liability for damage caused by objects launched into outer space, 26 March 1964, p. 7; UN Doc. A/AC. 105/C. 2/L. 7/Rev. 1, Belgium: Proposal for a Convention on the Unification of Certain Rules Governing Liability for Damage Caused by Space Devices, 1 October 1964, in: UN Doc. A/AC. 105/21, Report of the Legal Sub-Committee on the Work of the Second Part of its Third Session (5-23 October 1964), Annex II, Proposals and amendments relating to liability for damage caused by objects launched into outer space, 23 October 1964, p. 18; UN Doc. A/AC. 105/C. 2/L. 25, Argentina: proposal-Arbitration Commission, in: UN Doc. A/AC. 105/37, Report of the Legal Sub-Committee on the Work of its Sixth Session (19 June-14 July 1967), Annex II, Proposals, amendments and other documents relating to liability for damage caused by the launching of objects into outer space, 14 July 1967, p. 19; and UN Doc. A/AC. 105/C. 2/L. 40, Working Paper submitted by the Italian delegation-Draft convention concerning liability for damage caused by the launching of objects into outer space, 13 June 1986, in: UN Doc. A/AC. 105/45, Report of the Legal Sub-Committee on the Work of its Seventh Session (4-28 June 1968), Annex I, Proposals, amendments and other documents relating to liability for damage caused by the launching of objects into outer space, 11 July 1968, p. 30.

⑤ See UN Doc. A/AC. 105/C. 2/L. 8/Rev. 1, United States: Proposal-Convention concerning liability for damage caused by the launching of objects into outer space, in: UN Doc. A/AC. 105/21, Report of the Legal Sub-Committee on the Work of the Second Part of its Third Session (5-23 October 1964), Annex II, Proposals and amendments relating to liability for damage caused by objects launched into outer space, 23 October 1964, p. 6.

的相关内容都遵从了这个原则①。

（二）评注

第十六条的目的是为第十五条已规定的指派赔偿员会委员程序提供替代程序。有些情况下，依据第十五条程序组建委员会是不可行或不可能的。因此，第十六条规定了所谓组建程序的替代程序。

第十六条第 1 款首先规定了一方未能在规定期限内指定或任命委员会成员的情形。根据第十五条第 1 款，规定期限是两个月。如果一方未能在该期限内指派，第十六条第 1 款规定了可将赔偿委员会构成从三人委员会改为一人委员会。因此，向一人委员会的转变只能发生在本应指派的两个月期限届满后。

第十六条第 2 款规范的是指派委员会成员出现替代者或继任者的情形。多种原因可能导致需要指派替代者或继任者，例如委员会成员无暇参与此项工作。也可能由某种障碍造成，例如一人没有能力继续留任。争端解决机制本质上要求有关谈判和程序应当无间断地进行。因此有必要规定确保成员在任的、指派替代者或继任者的程序机制。这样机构或法庭才能继续其有关评议。第十六条第 2 款规定指派新成员仍旧使用原定的指派程序。尽管没有重复具体条文，这明确了可以遵循的非此即彼的两个程序。可以遵照第十五条规定的程序：即每一方指派本方成员，两方共同任命主席。或者，遵照第十六条第 1 款规定的程序。如前所述，“任一方不能通过拒绝指派拖延赔偿委员会工作程序。如果任一方在规定时限内未做出指派，应另一方要求，主席可以

① See e. g. UN Doc. A/AC. 105/C. 2/L. 7/Rev. 1, Belgium: Proposal for a Convention on the Unification of Certain Rules Governing Liability for Damage Caused by Space Devices, 1 October 1964, in: UN Doc. A/AC. 105/21, Report of the Legal Sub-Committee on the Work of the Second Part of its Third Session (5-23 October 1964), Annex II, Proposals and amendments relating to liability for damage caused by objects launched into outer space, 23 October 1964, p. 18; UN Doc. A/AC. 105/C. 2/L. 25, Argentina: proposal-Arbitration Commission, in: UN Doc. A/AC. 105/37, Report of the Legal Sub-Committee on the Work of its Sixth Session (19 June-14 July 1967), Annex II, Proposals, amendments and other documents relating to liability for damage caused by the launching of objects into outer space, 14 July 1967, p. 19; UN Doc. A/AC. 105/C. 2/L. 32, India: proposal-Convention concerning liability for damage caused by the launching of objects into outer space, 2 June 1968, in: UN Doc. A/AC. 105/45, Report of the Legal Sub-Committee on the Work of its Seventh Session (4-28 June 1968), Annex I, Proposals, amendments and other documents relating to liability for damage caused by the launching of objects into outer space, 11 July 1968, p. 16; and UN Doc. A/AC. 105/C. 2/L. 40, Working Paper submitted by the Italian delegation-Draft convention concerning liability for damage caused by the launching of objects into outer space, 13 June 1986, in: UN Doc. A/AC. 105/45, Report of the Legal Sub-Committee on the Work of its Seventh Session (4-28 June 1968), Annex I, Proposals, amendments and other documents relating to liability for damage caused by the launching of objects into outer space, 11 July 1968, p. 30.

组成仅有一个成员的赔偿委员会（第十六条第 1 款）”[①]。

第十六条其余规定与赔偿委员会正式工作、经同意确立程序性规则的适用性有关。争端解决机构的规则通常含有一系列关于确立评议案件程序的规定。这特别适合于关于外空损害赔偿的临时性听证会。国家间和商事国际仲裁框架内都有一些广为人知的规范争端解决的程序性规则[②]。

第十六条第 3 款规定赔偿委员会有权自行决定其工作程序。这使得委员会可以决定恰当的流程，用于规范书面赔偿要求文件的提交、口头辩护权和裁定赔偿要求等。关于裁定约束力问题见第十九条第 2 款。

第十六条第 4 款规定了赔偿委员会选定赔偿要求听证地点和其他行政事项的自由裁量权。“其他行政事项”含义宽泛，足以涵盖有关全体成员的管理、口头听证的时间和长度以及进行和确保必要沟通的行政支撑和沟通的流程。这也是国际争端解决规则的常见条款[③]。

最后，只要赔偿委员会不是由单一成员组成，第十六条第 5 款明确，一切决定和裁定均应以多数票表决通过。第 16 条第五款采用的是司法和仲裁机构通常的程序，即依据公平和正当法律程序理论的运行要求，所有决定必须获得多数成员支持。

因此，第十六条既有程序性规定也有实用性规定，使得赔偿委员会可以听取赔偿要求，根据有关规定得出最终决定。

十八、第十七条（共同指派）

Smith and Kerrest

赔偿委员会的成员人数，不得因由两个或两个以上求偿国或发射国共同参加委员会任一工作程序，而有所增加。共同参加的求偿国，应按照与一个求偿国相同的方式和条件，共同指派一名委员会的成员。两个或两个以上发射国参加时，应按同

① Lyall, Francis/Larsen, Paul B., Space Law a Treatise, Ashgate, Burlington/Surrey 2009, p. 112.

② See e. g. the PCA Optional Rules for Arbitration of Disputes Relating to Outer Space Activities <http://www. pca-cpa. org/showfile. asp? fil_ id=1774> accessed 26 April 2019, Art. 7ff.; and Commentary LIAB, Article XI, mn. 277ff.

③ See e. g. Art. 18ff. Rules of Arbitration of the International Chamber of Commerce <http://www. iccwbo. org/WorkArea/DownloadAsset. aspx? id=2147489109> accessed 26 April 2019.

样方式共同指派一名委员会的成员。如果求偿国或发射国未能在规定期限内指派出人选，主席应组成单一成员委员会。

目录

（一）谈判和起草过程

《责任公约》第十七条的最终措辞源自于1971年6月比利时、巴西和匈牙利提交的提案①。隐含的理念在美国1964年提交给联合国外空委第三次届会的提案中已有体现②，该理念的定案出现在1967年美国草案中③。此后所有纳入三人赔偿委员会草案中都采纳了这个规定。这也是为什么匈牙利和苏联草案中对此保持沉默，倾向于“平等表决基础上的”仲裁委员会④。

（二）评注

第十七条规定了赔偿委员会的成员人数是固定的，与参与解决赔偿要求争端的求偿国和发射国数量无关。该条含有关于在此种情形下任命成员的两个原则。

首先，第十七条第一句明确，委员会的成员数量独立于参与有关程序的求偿国的

① See UN Doc. A/AC. 105/C. 2/L. 79, Belgium, Brazil and Hungary: proposal, 21 June 1971, in: UN Doc. A/AC. 105/94, Report Of The Legal Sub-Committee on the Work of its Tenth Session (7 June-2 July 1971), Annex I, Proposals and Other Documents Relating to Agenda Item 2 (Draft Convention on Liability for Damage Caused by Objects Launched into Outer Space), 8 July 1971, p. 1.

② See UN Doc. A/AC. 105/C. 2/L. 8/Rev. 1, United States: Proposal-Convention concerning liability for damage caused by the launching of objects into outer space, in: UN Doc. A/AC. 105/21, Report of the Legal Sub-Committee on the Work of the Second Part of its Third Session (5-23 October 1964), Annex II, Proposals and amendments relating to liability for damage caused by objects launched into outer space, 23 October 1964, p. 6.

③ UN Doc. A/AC. 105/C. 2/L. 19, United States of America: Proposal-Convention concerning liability for damage caused by the launching of objects into outer space, 21 June 1967, in: UN Doc. A/AC. 105/37, Report of the Legal Sub-Committee on the Work of its Sixth Session (19 June-14 July 1967), Annex II, Proposals, amendments and other documents relating to liability for damage caused by the launching of objects into outer space, 14 July 1967, p. 6.

④ E. g. UN Doc. A/AC. 105/C. 2/L. 10, Hungary: Proposed draft agreement-Agreement concerning liability for damage caused by the launching of objects into outer space, 16 March 1964, in: UN Doc. A/AC. 105/19, Report of the Legal Sub-Committee on the Work of its Third Session (9-26 March 1964), Annex II, Proposals and amendments relating to liability for damage caused by objects launched into outer space, 26 March 1964, p. 7.

数量和发射国的数量。这意味着，不管求偿国和发射国的数量有多少，委员会都最多只能由三个成员组成，或者如果一方未能指派出成员，可能成立单一成员委员会。

第十七条第二句明确，“共同参加的求偿国，应按照与一个求偿国相同的方式和条件，共同指派一名委员会的成员”①。在这种情况下，申诉人（共同参加的求偿国）共同指派一名委员会的成员。为此，第十七条明确适用第十五条和第十六条有关指派赔偿委员会成员的规定，尽管参与争端解决的求偿国或发射国数量有增加。

该条第三句继续前述原则，明确适用于求偿国的原则也同样适用于发射国。“两个或两个以上发射国参加时，应按同样方式共同指派一名委员会的成员。”② 同样，所有发射国的集体指派委员会成员应遵照第十五条和第十六条的规定。

《责任公约》的起草考虑到了外空活动的具体情形。航天器造成损害的赔偿过程中，很可能涉及多个求偿国和多个发射国。在多方参与程序的案件中，不可能任命多过三个或少于一个成员的赔偿委员会。

十九、第十八条（赔偿委员会决定内容）

Smith and Kerrest

赔偿委员会应当决定赔偿要求是否成立，并在需要赔偿的情况下，确定应付赔偿金的总额。

目录

① Art. XVII sentence 2 LIAB.
② Art. XVII sentence 3 LIAB.

（一）谈判和起草过程

最后需要决定事项之一是关于外空活动造成损害赔偿金的决定内容。尽管比利时草案自第一次修订版本开始就明确，委员会应当决定被求偿国应当支付的赔偿金数额①，其他草案中并没有涉及此事，直到印度在其修订草案中纳入了与第十八条规定类似的一条②。阿根廷、澳大利亚、比利时、加拿大、意大利、日本和瑞典联合提案建议应决定赔偿要求是否成立和应支付的赔偿金数额③，此后比利时、巴西和匈牙利提议将这些内容规定在单独的一条中④。

（二）评注

第十八条是《责任公约》中最短的条款之一，也是最重要的条款之一。该条规定了赔偿委员会的职能为决定赔偿要求的两个核心要素，即赔偿要求是否成立以及应当支付的赔偿金数额。“在需要支付赔偿的情况”表明《责任公约》项下所有损害案件是否必然导致支付赔偿金是悬而未决的：这个前提条件说明《责任公约》项下的赔偿要求可能有不裁定赔偿金的情形。

1. 赔偿要求是否成立

在赔偿委员会决定是否支付赔偿金之前，它需要根据《责任公约》审议赔偿要求的可受理性。这需要权衡该案是否满足《责任公约》第二条或第三条的规定。换言

---

① Art. 6 lit. (d) states, that “sums due in compensation for damage shall be fixed [···] in the currency of the applicant State”, thus presupposing, that the commission decides on the amount of compensation to be paid. See e. g. UN Doc. A/AC. 105/C. 2/L. 7/Rev. 1, Belgium: Proposal for a Convention on the Unification of Certain Rules Governing Liability for Damage Caused by Space Devices, 1 October 1964, in: UN Doc. A/AC. 105/21, Report of the Legal Sub-Committee on the Work of the Second Part of its Third Session (5-23 October 1964), Annex II, Proposals and amendments relating to liability for damage caused by objects launched into outer space, 23 October 1964, p. 18.

② See UN Doc. A/AC. 105/C. 2/L. 32/Rev. 1, India: proposal-Convention concerning liability for damage caused by the launching of objects into outer space, in: UN Doc. A/AC. 105/45, Report of the Legal Sub-Committee on the Work of its Seventh Session (4-28 June 1968), Annex I, Proposals, amendments and other documents relating to liability for damage caused by the launching of objects into outer space, 11 July 1968, p. 21.

③ See UN Doc. A/AC. 105/C. 2/L. 74, Argentina, Australia, Belgium, Canada, Italy, Japan, Sweden, United Kingdom: Proposal-Measure of Compensation and Competence of the Claims Commission, 29 June 1970, in: UN Doc. A/AC. 105/85, Report Of The Legal Sub-Committee on the Work of its Ninth Session (8 June-3 July 1970), 3 July 1970, Annex I, Proposals And Other Documents Relating To Liability For Damage Caused By The Launching Of Objects Into Outer Space (Agenda item 2), p. 3.

④ See UN Doc. A/AC. 105/C. 2/L. 79, Belgium, Brazil and Hungary: proposal, 21 June 1971, in: UN Doc. A/AC. 105/94, Report Of The Legal Sub-Committee on the Work of its Tenth Session (7 June-2 July 1971), Annex I, Proposals and Other Documents Relating to Agenda Item 2 (Draft Convention on Liability for Damage Caused by Objects Launched into Outer Space), 8 July 1971, p. 1.

之，申诉国必须证明地球表面或飞行中的飞机损害的存在，且是由发射国/被申诉国空间物体直接或间接（但因果关系不能过于遥远）造成的。如果损害是在地球表面之外的其他地方，由一个发射国的空间物体给另一个发射国的空间物体，或其所在人员或财产造成的损害，求偿国必须证明损害是前一发射国的过失造成的。

如果损害发生在地球表面，求偿国必须证明空间物体造成损害的因果关系，必须证明是由被申诉发射国的某个空间物体造成的。如果抗辩方主张适用《责任公约》第六条第 1 款，并证实了求偿国存在重大疏忽或蓄意不法行为，求偿国必须证明该空间物体的外空活动违反了国际法。据此，求偿国可引用《责任公约》第六条第 2 款，该款排除了《责任公约》第六条第 1 款的适用。只要损害包括间接损害，若想成立公约项下的赔偿要求，必须证明其与空间物体的联系和因果关系。

赔偿要求的可受理性必须考虑求偿国的国籍。只要赔偿要求是某个发射国国民提出的，或者第七条规定的参与有关操作的外国国民，就只能认定该赔偿请求不可受理并拒绝。

2. 赔偿金数额

对于空间物体造成损害的赔偿要求，一般赔偿金只覆盖物质损害。和国内案件一样，面对赔偿要求，国际法庭也要裁定在多大程度上覆盖非物质损失①。正如布朗利所说，"如何权衡非物质损失没有简单的答案"②。

在提出赔偿要求时，一国必须展示本国或其所代表的自然人或法人遭受的损失（《责任公约》第八条第 1 款）。如果国籍国不能代表位于外国领土的本国自然人或法人提出赔偿要求，该另一国（外国）可以提出赔偿要求（《责任公约》第八条第 2 款）；最后，如果国籍国和损害发生地国都没提出赔偿要求，或通知有意提出赔偿要求，则永久居民的居住国可以提出赔偿要求。（《责任公约》第八条第 3 款）。

第十八条和第二十一条的区别之一是程度。第十八条规范的是如何界定赔偿要求，此后几条规定了赔偿委员会的工作程序。尽管污染环境属于赔偿范围，《责任公约》并没有预见到基于人道主义援助或救援引发的赔偿要求。有关内容详见第二十一条。

---

① Brownlie, Ian, Principles of Public International Law, 7th edn., Oxford University Press, Oxford 2008, p. 464.

② Ibid.

3. 污染外空环境

本条对于环境损害具有重要意义。第十八条明确规定了，赔偿委员会“在需要赔偿的情况下，确定应付赔偿金的总额。”很多外空活动会给超越国家管辖权或国家领土的区域带来污染。污染也可能发生在地球表面或空气空间，在这些情况下可由承受损害所在领土的国家处理。

发射国给本国领土带来的损害并不在《责任公约》规范范围中；该损害不会引发国际赔偿责任。如前文所述，“如果一国本国领土发射本国卫星，对该领土的污染由该国处理。”①

对于一国领土之外的外空环境恶化，是否适用第十八条规定，国际法并没有清晰的规则。不大可能依据《责任公约》第三条救济外空污染造成的损害：在外空中，《责任公约》的适用范围限于给空间物体或其所载人员或财产造成的损害。环境恶化这个意义上的损害更适合依据国际法中有关国家责任的一般原则来处置。

《外空条约》第九条规定，“本条约各当事国对外层空间，包括月球和其他天体在内进行的研究和探索，应避免使它们受到有害污染以及将地球外物质带入而使地球环境发生不利变化，并应在必要时为此目的采取适当措施”。有观点注意到了该条给国家施加义务有微妙的区别，即“有害污染”外层空间和“将地球外物质带入而使地球环境发生不利变化”。而《责任公约》只规范发射国空间物体给地球表面和外空中的空间物体造成损害的赔偿责任。

污染和损害不同，应当理解为地球或外空环境的恶化。通常有两种类型的污染：将地球物质带入外空的外带式污染；将地球外物质带回地球的返回式污染。为了保护星球，《外空条约》第九条覆盖了两种污染。但是，保护的目的有所不同：返回式污染旨在保护地球环境，即人类的生存；外带式污染旨在保护确保外空未来处于能被所有国家利用的状态②。最初，该条的目的是避免生化污染③。但目前，污染外空的主要是空间碎片带来的威胁。根据《外空条约》第九条的通常含义，加上《外空条约》

① Lyall, Francis/Larsen, Paul B., Space Law a Treatise, Ashgate, Burlington/Surrey 2009, p. 284.

② See ibid., p. 285. The systematic context of the obligation under Art. IX OST to prevent contamination of outer space is to take “due regard to the corresponding interest of all other States Parties to the Treaty.”.

③ See Achilleas, Philippe, Planetary Protection-Legal Issues, in: IISL, Proceedings of the 46th Colloquium on the Law of Outer Space, 29 September-3 October 2003 Bremen (Germany), AIAA, 2004, p. 215.

第三条和第七条，将第九条适用于碎片污染是有一定的正当性依据的[①]。

但是，若想提出赔偿要求，则必须满足《责任公约》的条件，且依据《责任公约》第三条，损害必须是由一个空间物体给另一空间物体直接造成的。除了证明过失，在缺少强制规则的情况下，这样的赔偿要求注定失败。Lyall 和 Larson 以哈萨克斯坦和前苏联/俄罗斯的争端为例，哈萨克斯坦独立后俄罗斯仍旧使用哈萨克斯坦的拜科努尔发射场。该争端与俄罗斯适用领土外的发射场有关。但两国前述的拜科努尔协议覆盖了此后的事故，且支付了赔偿金[②]。

二十、第十九条（终局和有约束力的决定）

Tronchetti, Smith and Kerrest

1. 赔偿委员会应当按照第 12 条的规定行事。

2. 若各方同意，委员会的决定应当是终局的，并具有约束力；否则，委员会应做出最终的建议性裁定，交由各方善意考量。委员会应表明其决定或裁定的理由。

3. 委员会应尽速做出决定或裁定，至迟在委员会成立之日起一年内做出，除非委员会认为有必要将此期限延长。

4. 委员会应公布其决定或裁定。委员会应将决定或裁定的正式副本送交各方和联合国秘书长。

目录

（一）谈判和起草过程

第三方解决赔偿要求可能是导致迟延缔结《责任公约》的最重要原因之一。特别

---

① With regard to Art. IX, see Marchisio, Sergio, Article IX, in: Hobe, Stephan/Schmidt-Tedd, Bernhard/Schrogl, Kai-Uwe (eds.), Cologne Commentary on Space Law, Volume I, Carl Heymanns, Cologne 2009, p. 176, mn. 28f.

② Lyall, Francis/Larsen, Paul B., Space Law a Treatise, Ashgate, Burlington/Surrey 2009, p. 284.

是，第十九条规定的赔偿委员会裁决的法律价值问题，是主要的绊脚石，在谈判的最后阶段才达成一致。

国家间意见分歧的根本在于，前苏联阵营的国家，特别是前苏联，不愿意接受第三方强制争端解决机制，即使接受了争端解决程序，也不愿意接受争端解决机构的决定是具有法律约束力的。在一些国家早期提交的草案意见中这个分歧更加明显：比利时[①]和美国[②]草案都规定如果在一定期限内不能通过谈判解决赔偿要求，就启动强制仲裁程序；而对此匈牙利[③]草案中只涉及了建立在争端双方平等基础上的谈判委员会。

到20世纪60年代末，各方就争端解决程序包含的三个阶段达成一致：第一，外交谈判；第二，平等调解或调查委员会；第三，第三方仲裁委员会。待决问题的难点在于仲裁委员会裁定的效力。尽管西方国家认为，这些决定应当是最终的并具有约束力[④]；苏联阵营的国家仍对约束力持反对意见。1970年法律小组委员会届会期间有了进展，法国代表建议仲裁委员会的裁定是终局的，但不具有约束力，只是公之于众[⑤]。法国提议受到了保加利亚代表的欢迎，后者似乎欣赏裁定的公开和无拘束力性质。但是，第二天早上，保加利亚、匈牙利和苏联的联合提案中删除了仲裁阶段，让争端当

① UN Doc. A/AC. 105/C. 2/L. 7/Rev. 3, Belgium: Proposal for a Convention on the Unification of Certain Rules Governing Liability for Damage Caused by Space Devices to Third Parties on the Surface of the Earth and Aircraft in Flight, 26 June 1967, in: UN Doc. A/AC. 105/37, Report of the Legal Sub-Committee on the Work of its Sixth Session (19 June-14 July 1967), Annex II, Proposals, amendments and other documents relating to liability for damage caused by the launching of objects into outer space, 14 July 1967, p. 1.

② UN Doc. A/AC. 105/C. 2/L. 19, United States of America: Proposal-Convention concerning liability for damage caused by the launching of objects into outer space, 21 June 1967, in: UN Doc. A/AC. 105/37, Report of the Legal Sub-Committee on the Work of its Sixth Session (19 June-14 July 1967), Annex II, Proposals, amendments and other documents relating to liability for damage caused by the launching of objects into outer space, 14 July 1967, p. 6.

③ UN Doc. A/AC. 105/C. 2/L. 24 and Add. 1, Hungary: Proposal, 26 and 28 June 1967, in: UN Doc. A/AC. 105/37, Report of the Legal Sub-Committee on the Work of its Sixth Session (19 June-14 July 1967), Annex II, Proposals, amendments and other documents relating to liability for damage caused by the launching of objects into outer space, 14 July 1967, p. 18.

④ 对此，八个大国向1970年法律小组委员会第9次届会提交了提案，见UN Doc. A/AC. 105/C. 2/L. 74 and Add. 1 and 2, Argentina, Australia, Belgium, Canada, Italy, Japan, Sweden, United Kingdom: Proposal-Measure of Compensation and Competence of the Claims Commission, 29 June 1970, in: UN Doc. A/AC. 105/85, Report Of The Legal Sub-Committee on the Work of its Ninth Session (8 June-3 July 1970), Annex I, Proposals And Other Documents Relating To Liability For Damage Caused By The Launching Of Objects Into Outer Space (Agenda item 2), 3 July 1970, p. 3.

⑤ See UN Doc. A/AC. 105/C. 2/SR. 132-151, Summary Records of the One Hundred and Thirty-Second to the One Hundred and Fifty-First Meetings (8 June-3 July 1970), 29 July 1970, p. 57.

事方自由决定是否接受调解委员会的决定是终局的和具有拘束力的。[①]

一年以后，直到 1971 年 6 月 21 日才打破这个僵局，当时比利时、巴西和匈牙利提交了有关争端解决的提案[②]。依据这个提案，只有当事方同意，仲裁委员会的决定才是终局和具有约束力的。这个提案构成了法律小组委员会《责任公约》工作小组的讨论基础。其后的讨论给联合提案带来了几个变化：第一，去除调查委员会，将争端解决机制变为两阶段程序；第二，在第十九条第 2 款“做出建议性裁决”后加入现有条文中的“交由各方善意考量”；第三，在第十九条中增加现有的第三款，要求赔偿委员会原则上做出裁定的时间不超过委员会成立之日起一年内；第四，增加现有第十九条第 4 款中的第二句，规定联合国秘书长和争端各方收到赔偿委员会达成的任何决定或裁定的副本。工作小组达成的文本是第十九条最终版本的起源，此后工作小组在 1971 年 6 月 28 日通过了上述改动，纳入《空间物体所造成损害的责任公约草案》[③]。

（二）评注

第十九条聚焦于《责任公约》项下第三方争端解决机制的核心问题，即赔偿委员会工作的收尾。其中特别注意了赔偿委员会做出决定的法律价值和达成决定的程序。

第十九条第 1 款开篇明确，赔偿委员会应按照第十二条的规定，发射国在本公约项下有责任支付的赔偿依照国际法以及公平合理的原则确定。

第 2 款是关于委员会裁定的法律，谨记赔偿委员会应当决定损害赔偿金要求是否成立以及在需要赔偿的情况下，应支付赔偿金数额。至于赔偿委员会工作的最终成果效力，法律小组委员会在达成现有妥协过程中经历了种种困难。第十九条第 2 款区分

① See UN Doc. A/AC. 105/C. 2/L. 75, Bulgaria, Hungary, USSR: Proposal-Applicable Law, in: UN Doc. A/AC. 105/85, Report Of The Legal Sub-Committee on the Work of its Ninth Session (8 June-3 July 1970), Annex I, Proposals And Other Documents Relating To Liability For Damage Caused By The Launching Of Objects Into Outer Space (Agenda item 2), 3 July 1970, p. 4.

② See UN Doc. A/AC. 105/C. 2/L. 79, Belgium, Brazil and Hungary: proposal, 21 June 1971, in: UN Doc. A/AC. 105/94, Report Of The Legal Sub-Committee on the Work of its Tenth Session (7 June-2 July 1971), Annex I, Proposals and Other Documents Relating to Agenda Item 2 (Draft Convention on Liability for Damage Caused by Objects Launched into Outer Space), 8 July 1971, p. 1, Art. XIV.

③ See UN Doc. PUOS/C. 2/DG (X) /2, Draft Convention on International Liability for Damage Caused by Space Objects, text approved by the Drafting Group on 28 June 1971, 28 June 1971, in: UN Doc. A/AC. 105/94, Report Of The Legal Sub-Committee on the Work of its Tenth Session (7 June-2 July 1971), Annex I, Proposals and Other Documents Relating to Agenda Item 2 (Draft Convention on Liability for Damage Caused by Objects Launched into Outer Space), 8 July 1971, p. 30.

了“决定”和“裁决”。尽管都是终局的，即不接受上诉，但二者还是有区别：决定对争端当事方具有法律约束力，而“裁决”仅是建议性质。只有当事方同意赔偿委员会的决定才具有拘束力。对此，联合国2777号决议[①]将第十九条第2款解释为类似于《国际法院规约》第三十六条第2款[②]的任择性条款，该第2款规定，“各当事国，应随时声明对于接受同样义务的任何国家，承认法院对有关争端管辖具有约束力”。第十九条没有提及国家做出此类声明应当遵循的形式和程序。对于形式和同意内容，可将国际法院任择条款项下的声明作为例子，至于程序，一般认为有关声明应当交给保存国政府。

很多作者[③]坚持认为赔偿委员会的决定缺少强制性是一个缺陷[④]。这的确弱化了该机制的效用，但应当谨记的是：第一，设立强制性调解委员会在国际法中并不常见；第二，赔偿委员会的决定即使不具有法律约束力，也必然有一定的份量，这是抗辩国无法轻易忽视的。

如果当事方之间就赔偿委员会的裁决缺少一致意见，尽管是终局的，也仅构成“建议性裁定”。该裁定的法律地位仍是有争议的，尽管如此，各方对此应善意考量。

第2款的结尾明确，委员会应当表明做出裁决的理由，无论是决定还是裁定。

第十九条第3款规定的是赔偿委员会作出最终决定或裁定的时间问题。据此，委员会应当尽速做出裁决，且无论如何应当在自其成立之日起一年内。只有在委员会认为有必要的情况下才能延长这个期限。此处需要指出的是，《责任公约》项下的整个争端解决程序，自通知赔偿要求至做出最终决定或裁定，应当不超过两年半，包括根据第十四条的一年，根据第十五条第2款则为4个月外加2个月，以及根据第十九条第3款的一年。如果国际组织以抗辩方参与该程序，时间可能再延长6个月。在整个程序的末期，实际上确保求偿国得到一个权威性判定，即依据《责任公约》赔偿要求是否成立以及赔偿委员会认为抗辩国应当支付的赔偿金额。

---

① UNGA Res. 2777（XXVI），Convention on International Liability for Damage Caused by Space Objects，29 November 1971.

② Statute of the International Court of Justice，26 June 1945，15 UNCIO Document 335.

③ See e. g.，Böckstiegel，Karl-Heinz，Settlement of Disputes Regarding Space Activities，Journal of Space Law（21）1993，p. 1.

④ On this point see Kerrest，Armel，Liability for Damage Caused by Space Activities，in：Benkö，Marietta/Schrogl，Kai-Uwe（eds.），Space Law：Current Problems and Perspectives For Future Regulation，Eleven，Utrecht 2005，pp. 105f.

第十九条最后一款规定委员会有义务将其决定或裁定公布于众。最后，该条要求委员会将决定和裁定的正式副本送交给每个当事方和联合国秘书长。

二十一、第二十条（赔偿委员会的费用分担）

Tronchetti, Smith and Kerrest

除非委员会另有规定，赔偿委员会的费用应当由各方平等分担。

目录

（一）谈判和起草过程

《责任公约》的立法准备性文件中基本没有任何关于赔偿委员会费用谈判的纪录。各国倾向于将谈判注意力聚焦于解决《责任公约》项下争端及其他实质性问题，例如将争端提交给独立第三方争端解决机构的可能性，以及此类机构裁定的法律地位等等。仅在谈判收尾阶段，各国开始讨论赔偿委员会的有关费用问题。

第一次提及此问题的提案是美国 1964 年草案①。有趣的是，该草案第七条仅提议赔偿委员会有关的费用应当在各方之间平等分担，并没有提及如果委员会另有规定。印度 1968 年草案附件中第八条关于争端解决的强制议定书中也含有类似措辞②。与此不同，比利时和匈牙利草案没有涉及赔偿委员会的费用问题。1971 年，当比利时、巴西和匈牙利联合提交有关适用法和争端解决的提案时，局势发生了改变，该提案含有

① See UN Doc. A/AC. 105/C. 2/L. 8/Rev. 2, United States: Revised Proposal-Convention concerning liability for damage caused by the launching of objects into outer space, 20 October 1964, in: UN Doc. A/AC. 105/21, Report of the Legal Sub-Committee on the Work of the Second Part of its Third Session (5-23 October 1964), Annex II, Proposals and amendments relating to liability for damage caused by objects launched into outer space, 23 October 1964, p. 12.

② See UN Doc. A/AC. 105/C. 2/L. 32, India: proposal-Convention concerning liability for damage caused by the launching of objects into outer space, 2 June 1968, in: UN Doc. A/AC. 105/45, Report of the Legal Sub-Committee on the Work of its Seventh Session (4-28 June 1968), Annex I, Proposals, amendments and other documents relating to liability for damage caused by the launching of objects into outer space, 11 July 1968, p. 16.

一条规定，“赔偿委员会的费用应当由各方平等分担”[①]。该联合提案成为法律小组委员会《责任公约》工作小组的讨论基础。此后的讨论为该联合提案带来了几个变化，包括给予赔偿委员会在成员方中做出非均等分担费用的决定权。有关赔偿委员会费用的修改后规定纳入了《责任公约》工作小组于 1971 年 6 月 28 日通过的《空间物体所造成损害的责任公约草案》第二十条中[②]。

（二）评注

第二十条规定完成了《责任公约》确立的第三方争端解决机制法律框架的规范。特别是，该条规定了赔偿委员会的费用问题及其在各方中的分配。

在外交谈判无法解决赔偿要求时，《责任公约》将仲裁作为可取的解决争端的第三方办法[③]。与国际司法解决争端不同，仲裁的特点之一是当事方必须支付仲裁员费用并承担仲裁过程中产生的其他费用[④]。因此，第二十条规定，赔偿委员会的费用由争端当事方分担。一般规则是，各方平等分担这些费用。但是，赔偿委员会可以选择其他不平等的分担比例。该委员会的这个选择权与主要国际仲裁规则保持一致，例如国际商会（ICC）仲裁规则，该规则将费用决定权完全交由仲裁庭自由裁量[⑤]。

① UN Doc. A/AC. 105/C. 2/L. 79, Belgium, Brazil and Hungary: proposal, 21 June 1971, in: UN Doc. A/AC. 105/94, Report Of The Legal Sub-Committee on the Work of its Tenth Session (7 June-2 July 1971), Annex I, Proposals and Other Documents Relating to Agenda Item 2 (Draft Convention on Liability for Damage Caused by Objects Launched into Outer Space), 8 July 1971, p. 1, Art. XXI.

② See UN Doc. PUOS/C. 2/DG (X) /2, Draft Convention on International Liability for Damage Caused by Space Objects: text approved by the Drafting Group on 28 June 1971, 28 June 1971, in: UN Doc. A/AC. 105/94, Report Of The Legal Sub-Committee on the Work of its Tenth Session (7 June-2 July 1971), Annex I, Proposals and Other Documents Relating to Agenda Item 2 (Draft Convention on Liability for Damage Caused by Objects Launched into Outer Space), 8 July 1971, p. 30.

③ See Art. XIV LIAB.

④ 例如，如果争端提交给国际法院，当事国就不需要支付这些费用。国际法院的费用由联合国预算承担。

⑤ For the text of the Rules of Arbitration of the International Chamber of Commerce, see < http: //www. iccwbo. org/WorkArea/DownloadAsset. aspx? id = 2147489109 > accessed 26 April 2019. See also Waincymer, Jeffrey, Procedure and Evidence in International Arbitration, Kluwer Law International, Alphen aan den Rijn 2012.

二十二、第二十一条（大规模危险）

Tronchetti，Smith and Kerrest

如果空间物体造成的损害严重危及人类生命，或严重干扰人们的生活条件或重要中心的功能，各当事国，特别是发射国，在受害国请求时应审查提供适当与快速援助的可能性。但本条规定不影响各当事国在本公约项下的权利和义务。

目录

（一）谈判和起草过程

当事国采取的紧急措施，特别是发射国在空间物体造成大规模损害时采取的措施在《责任公约》谈判收尾阶段才变成重要议题。尽管对“损害”一词的含义讨论贯穿整个谈判过程，直到 1971 年 6 月，在摩洛哥代表团建议下，才在《责任公约》的最终草案中加入了一条明确其具体含义，并就此提出了相关的提案①。该提案得到了其他代表团的正面回应，新条文第二十一条纳入了《责任公约》工作小组于 1971 年 6 月 28 日通过的《空间物体所造成损害的责任公约草案》②。重要的是，第二十一条的最终文本逐字借鉴了摩洛哥提案的内容。

---

① 见 Morocco proposal to insert the following article to UN Doc. A/AC. 105/C. 2/L. 79，“如果空间物体造成的损害给人类生活带来或可能带来严重的大规模危险，或严重干扰人们的生活条件或重要中心的功能，当事国，特别是发射国应当在受害国请求时审查提供适当与快速援助的可能性。但本条规定不影响各当事国在本公约的项下的权利和义务。” UN Doc. PUOS/C. 2/WG（X）/L. 4/Rev. 1，Morocco：Proposal，25 June 1971，in：UN Doc. A/AC. 105/94，Report Of The Legal Sub-Committee on the Work of its Tenth Session（7 June-2 July 1971），Annex I，Proposals and Other Documents Relating to Agenda Item 2（Draft Convention on Liability for Damage Caused by Objects Launched into Outer Space），8 July 1971，p. 19.

② See UN Doc. PUOS/C. 2/DG（X）/2，Draft Convention on International Liability for Damage Caused by Space Objects：text approved by the Drafting Group on 28 June 1971，28 June 1971，in：UN Doc. A/AC. 105/94，Report Of The Legal Sub-Committee on the Work of its Tenth Session（7 June-2 July 1971），Annex I，Proposals and Other Documents Relating to Agenda Item 2（Draft Convention on Liability for Damage Caused by Objects Launched into Outer Space），8 July 1971，p. 30.

（二）评注

第二十一条规定的是可能发生的特定情形，即空间物体及其组成部分撞上地球，并因此造成损害，且该损害给人类生命造成了大规模危险，或严重干扰人们的生活条件或重要中心的功能。在这种情况下，各当事国，特别是发射国，应当考虑否采取紧急措施，向受害国提供适当和快速的援助。

从这个视角出发，《责任公约》第二十一条与《营救协定》第五条第4款密切相关，后者规定如果当事国认为有理由认为在其管辖区域内出现的空间物体及其组成部分，就其性质来说是危险的和有害的时候，可通知发射当局在该当事国的领导和监督下，立即采取有效措施，消除可能的危险或危害。《营救协定》第五条和《责任公约》第二十一条的主要区别是：依据前者，发射国得到通知后，有义务采取有效措施消除危险，且须在请求其帮助的当事国的领导和监督下进行；根据后者，发射国应遭受大规模危险的受害国通知，没有采取行动的义务，而仅考虑采取紧急措施可能性。

分析第二十一条的规定能反映出三个主要问题：第一，值得指出的是，当事国，特别是发射国，仅应受害国请求审查采取紧急措施的可能性。尽管这些国家可能自发地提供帮助，但只有应受害国的正式请求，才有干预的义务。第二，该条规定对于应当采取什么类型的紧急措施有些模糊，例如去除空间物体的组成部分，或者清理受污染区域，以及谁来承担费用。有观点认为此类费用应当由采取措施的当事国承担，但对此是有争议的，如果有清晰的规定就更好了。第三，坠入空间物体是否造成大规模危险及其对特定区域人类生命的负面影响，这个决定权只在受害国还是包括独立第三方也是有不同意见的。实际上，发射国可以拒绝请求其援助的理由是，该损害并没有给人类生命带来大规模危险，也没有严重干扰某类人群的生活条件。

过去曾有几个空间物体给地球环境造成大规模危险的案例，最有名的是1978年1月24日，宇宙-954号苏联卫星坠入加拿大境内，没有造成人员伤亡，但给环境造成了损害①。其他情况中，一些空间物体的碎片落入无人居住区，也没有伤害任何人。

---

① When Cosmos 954 crashed on Canadian territory, it scattered a large amount of debris including radioactive material over 124.000 km south of Great Slave Lake, spilling over into northern Alberta and Saskatchevan. For a description of the Cosmos 954 case and its settlement see Lyall, Francis/Larsen, Paul B., Space Law a Treatise, Ashgate, Burlington/Surrey 2009, p. 117; Diederiks-Verschoor, I. H. Philepina/Kopal, Vladimir, An Introduction to Space Law, 3rd edn., Kluwer Law International, The Hague 2008, p. 42.

例如，1991 年 2 月 7 日，前苏联礼炮七号空间站再入地球轨道，碎片散落在布宜诺斯艾利斯附近的城镇卡皮坦・贝穆德，这次事件中没有人员受伤。

二十三、第二十二条（政府间国际组织）

Tronchetti, Smith and Kerrest

1. 如果任何从事外空活动的政府间国际组织声明接受本公约所规定的权利和义务，其多数成员国系本公约和《关于各国探索和利用包括月球与其他天体在内外层空间活动原则条约》的当事国，本公约，除第二十四条至第二十七条外，对所称国家的一定规定，均应适用于该组织。

2. 凡既是此类组织的成员国，又是本公约当事国的国家，应采取一切适当行动，确保该组织按照前款规定做出声明。

3. 如果政府间国际组织根据本公约规定对损害负有责任，该组织及其成员国中的本公约当事国，应承担连带责任；但：

（1）对于这种损害的任何赔偿要求，应首先向该组织提出；

（2）唯有在该组织于 6 个月内，未支付经协商一致或决定的损害赔偿金，求偿国才得要求该组织成员国中的本公约当事国支付该款项。

4. 凡按本条第一款规定发表了声明的组织，受到损害时，应由该组织内的本公约当事国根据本公约的规定，提出赔偿要求。

目录

（一）谈判和起草过程

政府间国际组织[①]的地位是谈判起草《责任公约》过程中最有争议的主题之一。有关这个问题的谈判进展缓慢，直到1969年才取得重大进展[②]。那一年，联合国外空委法律小组委员会的主席 Haymerle 大使提出一个获得多数代表团赞同的妥协办法。该妥协是在墨西哥[③]、保加利亚[④]、印度[⑤]的提案以及比利时、法国、意大利、瑞典和英国1970年联合提案[⑥]基础上做了细微修改。其结果是，就国际组织参与《责任公约》达成一致意见，第二十二条纳入了《责任公约》工作小组于1971年6月28日通过的《空间物体所造成损害的责任公约草案》[⑦]。

有关国际组织地位的主要问题是这些组织是否具有区别于其成员国的法律人格。

① 有关国际组织在国际法中的地位，见 Shaw，Malcolm N.，International Law，6th edn.，Cambridge University Press，Cambridge 2008，p. 908.

② The status of international organizations was one of the five ‘New Delhi points’. In 1969 informal consultations on the LIAB took place in New Delhi and five key issues to be address were identified：1）status of international organization；2）nuclear damage；3）applicable law；4）limitation of liability；5）compulsory third party arbitration. On this point see Cheng，Bin，International Liability for Damage Caused by Space Objects，in：Jasentuliyana，Nandasiri/Lee，Roy S. K.（eds.），Manual on Space Law，Volume I，Oceana Publications，New York 1979，pp. 87f.

③ See UN Doc. PUOS/C. 2/70/WG. I/CRP. 8，Mexico：Working Paper-International organizations，in：UN Doc. A/AC. 105/85，Report Of The Legal Sub-Committee on the Work of its Ninth Session（8 June-3 July 1970），Annex I，Proposals And Other Documents Relating To Liability For Damage Caused By The Launching Of Objects Into Outer Space（Agenda item 2），3 July 1970，p. 11.

④ See UN Doc. PUOS/C. 2/70/WG. I/CRP. 2 and Corr. 1，Bulgaria：Working Paper，in：UN Doc. A/AC. 105/85，Report Of The Legal Sub-Committee on the Work of its Ninth Session（8 June-3 July 1970），Annex I，Proposals And Other Documents Relating To Liability For Damage Caused By The Launching Of Objects Into Outer Space（Agenda item 2），3 July 1970，p. 9.

⑤ See UN Doc. PUOS/C. 2/70/WG. I/CRP. 15，India：Amendment（PUOS/C. 2/70/WG. I/CRP. 15）to the proposal by Belgium，France，Italy，Sweden and United Kingdom on International Organizations（PUOS/C. 2/WG. I/CRP. 11），in：UN Doc. A/AC. 105/85，Report Of The Legal Sub-Committee on the Work of its Ninth Session（8 June-3 July 1970），Annex I，Proposals And Other Documents Relating To Liability For Damage Caused By The Launching Of Objects Into Outer Space（Agenda item 2），3 July 1970，p. 15.

⑥ See UN Doc. A/AC. 105/C. 2/L. 60 and Add. 1，Belgium，France，Italy，Sweden and United Kingdom：proposal-International Organizations，in：UN Doc. A/AC. 105/58，Report of the Legal Sub-Committee on the Work of its Eighth Session（9 June-4 July 1969），Annex II，Proposals and other documents relating to liability for damage caused by the launching of objects into outer space，4 July 1969，p. 30.

⑦ See UN Doc. PUOS/C. 2/DG（X）/2，Draft Convention on International Liability for Damage Caused by Space Objects：text approved by the Drafting Group on 28 June 1971，28 June 1971，in：UN Doc. A/AC. 105/94，Report Of The Legal Sub-Committee on the Work of its Tenth Session（7 June-2 July 1971），Annex I，Proposals and Other Documents Relating to Agenda Item 2（Draft Convention on Liability for Damage Caused by Objects Launched into Outer Space），8 July 1971，p. 30.

一方面，以英国为首的一群西方空间大国坚持应当认可国际组织的独立法律人格地位，其结果是国际组织不受起草中公约的约束。但作为一定程度上例外，国际组织可以声明接受公约；一旦成为缔约方，国际组织即可受益于该条约。这种情况下，可能其某些成员并不是公约的当事方，不受公约规定的约束①。另一方面，苏联阵营的很多国家否认国际组织是独立于其成员国的存在，坚持认为成员国作为国际组织成员从事外空活动并不能改变其在公约项下的义务②。例如，匈牙利草案不接受国际组织可依据某种行为受制于条约的观点，除非其多数成员是公约的当事国③。

这个问题背后隐含的是较小的航天国家担心它们除非在国际组织框架内集合力量，否则可能没有能力参与外空的利用和探索。如果空间法不承认国际组织，这将让主要的航天大国独立从事外空活动。其他一些国家另外的担心是，某些国家可能利用国际组织作为规避法律义务的屏障，在现有法律框架之外自由地从事外空活动。

（二）评注

1. 前提

第二十二条规定的是在《责任公约》文本中政府间国际组织的地位④。国际组织不是也不可能成为《责任公约》的完全当事方。尽管如此，除了仅适用于国家的规定，包括公约的批准、签署、加入、修订和退出，第二十二条将国际组织和国家彻底同化。《营救协定》第六条在发射当局中给予国际组织操作性地位；但是，《责任公约》第一次明确做了区分，一是《营救协定》中类似于国家的国际组织的操作性地位，二是参与《责任公约》。《责任公约》第二十二条第 1 款和第 2 款中的这个概念后

---

① See UN Doc. A/AC. 105/C. 2/L. 60 and Add. 1, Belgium, France, Italy, Sweden and United Kingdom: proposal-International Organizations, in: UN Doc. A/AC. 105/58, Report Of The Legal Sub-Committee on the Work of its Eighth Session (9 June-4 July 1969), Annex II, Proposals and other documents relating to liability for damage caused by the launching of objects into outer space, 4 July 1969, p. 30.

② See UN Doc. A/AC. 105/C. 2/SR. 121, Legal Sub-Committee, Summary Record of the One Hundred and Twenty-First Meeting, held on 20 June 1969.

③ See UN Doc. A/AC. 105/C. 2/L. 10/Rev. 1, Hungary: Revised draft Convention concerning Liability for Damages caused by the Launching of Objects into Outer Space, 24 September 1965, in: UN Doc. A/AC. 105/29, Report of the Legal Sub-Committee on the Work of its Fourth Session (20 Septemaber-1 October 1965), Annex II, Proposals and amendments relating to liability for damage caused by objects launched into outer space, 1 October 1965, p. 2.

④ On this point see Lyall, Francis/Larsen, Paul B., Space Law a Treatise, Ashgate, Burlington/Surrey 2009, p. 106; Kayser, Valérie, Launching Space Objects: Issues of Liability and Future Prospects, Kluwer Academic Publishers, Dordrecht 2001, pp. 36-40.

来移植到了《登记公约》（见《登记公约》第七条）。第二十二条第 3 款和第 4 款规定的是承担责任的具体问题，既然是责任就没有移植到《登记公约》中。

第二十二条第 1 款为声明接受公约的国际组织在《责任公约》中的地位规定了两个关键条件：第一，该组织必须声明接受公约规定的权利和义务。尽管《责任公约》没有规定做出此类声明的程序，可适用关于批准和加入的有关程序。第二，该组织的多数成员国必须是《责任公约》和《外空条约》的当事国。只要满足了这两个条件，公约的有关规定即可适用于该组织。参与外空活动国际组织的成员国如果是《责任公约》当事国，应当采取措施确保该组织做出第二十二条第 1 款中的声明。目前，只有欧洲空间局（ESA）、欧洲通信卫星组织（EUTELSAT）和欧洲气象卫星应用组织（EUMETSAT）做出了此类声明。

如前所述，《责任公约》并没有将国际组织等同于国家。对国际组织参与方排除适用《责任公约》最终条款的效果是否决了国际组织作为公约当事方的地位。这也产生了一些实际的后果，即：

· 加入、签署和批准仅限于国家（第二十四条）。

· 国际组织不能提议修订《责任公约》，也不能接受或拒绝对公约的修订（第二十五条）。《责任公约》没有规定修订内容适用于国际组织的程序。或许国际组织可能做出类似于接受《责任公约》的声明来接受修订。如果该修订没有获得国际组织所有或多数成员国的接受，可能产生问题。在这种情景中，会出现《责任公约》的不同版本适用于国际组织和某些成员国。

–国际组织没有权利召集会议审查公约（第二十六条）

–退出条款不适用于国际组织（第二十七条）。这意味着国际组织一旦声明接受《责任公约》，就不能退出。接受的命运与接受的条件联系密切，特别是因为该组织的多数成员国必须是《责任公约》和《外空条约》的当事国。如果情况发生变化，接受《责任公约》的前提就消失了。

2. 国际组织成员国的义务

尽管第二十二条第 1 款在一定程度上将成员国等同于国际组织，第二十二条第 2 款明确要求成员国确保国际组织做出接受公约的声明。该款规定后来纳入了《责任公约》。一般来说，这是该组织宪章性文件中的规则，包括费用分摊等。从国际组织成员国的视角来看，做出该声明很重要；通过这个媒介与国际组织对外空活动有关的损害赔偿责任承担连带责任是重大利好，特别是对财力较弱的小国来说。国际组织提供了通过合作深化外空活动的方式。同时，由国际组织优先承担责任可确保充分保护受害人。有助于确保小国参与外空活动，但没有造成额外的麻烦。

3. 国际组织的首要责任

从国际组织的具体案例来看，《责任公约》第二十二条第3款规定了国际组织及其成员国的连带责任制度。这在损害赔偿程序中有明显体现。更为具体的，如果一个国际组织根据《责任公约》规定对损害负有责任，该组织及其成员国中的本公约当事国，在满足下列两个条件基础上承担连带责任：第一，该赔偿要求应首先向该组织提出；第二，只有当该组织在六个月内，未支付经协议确定的损害赔偿金，求偿国才可要求该组织成员国中的《责任公约》当事国支付该款项。

有观点指出①，国际组织参与方负有赔偿责任并没有给受害人的权利增加多少裨益，除非负有责任的国际组织成员国中的《责任公约》当事国要么全部没有清偿能力要么拖欠赔偿。但是这个观点疏忽了一点，即国际组织成员国中的非公约当事国可能热衷于确保公约履行其义务，决心提供必要的资金。根据《责任公约》第五条第1款关于共同发射的有关规定，受害人总能认定某个当事国对整个损害负有赔偿责任，因为根据《责任公约》第二十二条第1款，造成损害的国际组织的多数成员国是《责任公约》和《外空条约》的当事国。

4. 成员国提出的赔偿要求

此外，《责任公约》国际组织参与方在遭受损害时，可以提出赔偿要求。《责任公约》第二十二条第4款规定，赔偿要求必须通过国际组织中的公约当事国提出。

总之，必须注意的是，第二十二条提及了政府间国际组织，但并没有进一步详细规定。在《责任公约》（第十二条和第二十二条）中，“国际组织”和“政府间国际组织”的含义相同。

---

① See Cheng, Bin, International Liability for Damage Caused by Space Objects, in: Jasentuliyana, Nandasiri/Lee, Roy S. K. (eds.), Manual on Space Law Volume I, Oceana Publications, New York 1979, p. 110.

二十四、第二十三条（与其他国际协定的关系）

Tronchetti, Smith and Kerrest

1. 本公约规定，对当事国之间现行其他国际协定的关系，不发生影响。
2. 本公约规定，不妨碍各国缔结国际协定，重申、补充或推广本公约各条款。

目录

（一）谈判和起草过程

在《责任公约》谈判过程中，第二十三条规定并没有成为任何重大讨论的主题。实际上，美国①、匈牙利②和比利时③关于《责任公约》的三大主要草案中，以及

① See UN Doc. A/AC. 105/C. 2/L. 8, United States: Proposal-Convention concerning liability for damage caused by the launching of objects into outer space, 9 March 1964, in: UN Doc. A/AC. 105/19, Report of the Legal Sub-Committee on the Work of its Third Session (9-26 March 1964), 26 March 1964, Annex II, Proposals and amendments relating to liability for damage caused by objects launched into outer space, p. 2.

② See UN Doc. A/AC. 105/C. 2/L. 10, Hungary: Proposed draft agreement-Agreement concerning liability for damage caused by the launching of objects into outer space, 16 March 1964, in: UN Doc. A/AC. 105/19, Report of the Legal Sub-Committee on the Work of its Third Session (9-26 March 1964), Annex II, Proposals and amendments relating to liability for damage caused by objects launched into outer space, 26 March 1964, p. 7.

③ See UN Doc. A/AC. 105/C. 2/L. 7/Rev. 2, Belgium: Proposal for a Convention on the Unification of Certain Rules Governing Liability for Damage Caused by Space Devices, 14 October 1964, in: UN Doc. A/AC. 105/21, Report of the Legal Sub-Committee on the Work of the Second Part of its Third Session (5-23 October 1964), Annex II, Proposals and amendments relating to liability for damage caused by objects launched into outer space, 23 October 1964, p. 22.

1968 年印度提案[①]中都没有涉及《责任公约》条款与其他国际协定规定的关系，也没有提到缔结国际协定是重申或推广《责任公约》的机会。直到 1971 年，在《责任公约》起草小组的工作中，出现了有关这些问题的讨论。各国努力快速达成合意，第二十三条最终文本纳入了《责任公约》起草小组于 1971 年 6 月 28 日通过的《空间物体所造成损害的责任公约草案》，同一天《责任公约》工作小组通过的公约草案[②]中确认了该条。

（二）评注

第二十三条涉及两个问题：首先，《责任公约》条款与当事国之间其他国际协定条款之间的关系（第 1 款）；第二，当事国缔结其他国际协定中确认和补充《责任公约》规定条款的可能性（第 2 款）。

1. 国际协定

第二十三条第 1 款规定，《责任公约》条款不应影响当事国之间基于现行有关国际协定的关系。简言之，这意味着《责任公约》的规定不会减损当事国已加入的其他国际协定的规定。也就是说，如果二者规定有分歧，其他协定的有关条款优先适用。这与《维也纳条约法公约》第三十条第 2 款的规定保持一致，即“遇条约订明须不违反先订或后订条约或不得视为与先订或后订条约不合时，该先订或后订条约之规定应居优先”[③]。

2. 待缔结的国际协定

第二十三条第 2 款明确，当事国有权在缔约其他协定中重申、补充或推广《责任

① See UN Doc. A/AC. 105/C. 2/L. 32, India: proposal-Convention concerning liability for damage caused by the launching of objects into outer space, 2 June 1968, in: UN Doc. A/AC. 105/45, Report of the Legal Sub-Committee on the Work of its Seventh Session (4-28 June 1968), Annex I, Proposals, amendments and other documents relating to liability for damage caused by the launching of objects into outer space, 11 July 1968, p. 16.

② See UN Doc. PUOS/C. 2/DG (X) /2, Draft Convention on International Liability for Damage Caused by Space Objects: text approved by the Drafting Group on 28 June 1971, 28 June 1971, in: UN Doc. A/AC. 105/94, Report Of The Legal Sub-Committee on the Work of its Tenth Session (7 June-2 July 1971), Annex I, Proposals and Other Documents Relating to Agenda Item 2 (Draft Convention on Liability for Damage Caused by Objects Launched into Outer Space), 8 July 1971, p. 30.

③ 类似规定见《国家与国际组织以及国际组织之间的维也纳条约法公约》第三十条（1986 年 3 月 21 日开放签署，并尚未生效），International Legal Materials 1986 (25), p. 543. 关于条约继承的法律问题，见 Fitzmaurice, Malgosia/Elias, Olufemi A., Contemporary Issues in the Law of Treaties, Eleven International Publishing, Utrecht 2005, p. 317.

公约》各条款。但不应当把这个选择权混淆于当事国修订《责任公约》的可能性。《责任公约》第二十五条规定了修订公约的选择权，并确立了具体程序。再者，修订条约意味着修改其内容和法律效果。第二十三条第 2 款只是表达当事国有机会在独立的国际协定中重申、进一步阐释或补充《责任公约》的条款，并不改变《公约》文本内容。

第 59/115 号决议[①]，即寻求便利遵守和适用国际空间条约的规定[②]，因为并非国际协定而是不具有约束力的法律文件，不适用《责任公约》第二十三条第 2 款的规定。尽管如此，该决议阐释了《责任公约》一个关键问题的含义，即“发射国”概念[③]。重要的是，该决议前言第 4 款明确，“本协议任何内容不构成《登记公约》或《责任公约》的权威解释或修订。”

值得注意的是，联合国外空条约中只有《责任公约》含有一条涉及该条约与其他国际协定关系的规定，该公约的起草过程中也没有为此提供明确的解释。一个解释是，考虑到责任问题的高度敏感性以及确立空间物体造成损害国际责任规则的重要性，《责任公约》起草者希望确保其条款的应用不会造成损害当事国关系的风险，特别是在已生效国际条约正式规范下的关系。

二十五、第二十四条（签署/批准/加入/生效）

Tronchetti，Smith and Kerrest

1. 本公约应开放供一切国家签署。在本公约依据本条第 3 款生效之前，没有签署本公约的任何国家可随时加入本公约。

2. 本公约应由签署国批准。批准书和加入文件应交由苏维埃社会主义共和国联盟、大不列颠及北爱尔兰联合国王国和美利坚合众国政府存放，为此指定这三国政府为交存国政府。

3. 本公约应于第五个批准书交存时生效。

① See UNGA Res. 59/115，Application of the concept of the “launching State”，10 December 2004.

② See ibid.，sixth preambular paragraph.

③ See Commentary LIAB，Article I，mn. 59.

4. 对于在本公约生效后，交存批准书或加入文件的国家，本公约应于其交存批准书或加入文件之日生效。

5. 交存国政府应将每次签署日期、每次批准书和加入文件交存日期、公约生效日期以及其他事项，尽速通知所有签署国和加入国。

6. 本公约应由交存国政府遵照《联合国宪章》第一百零二条予以登记。

目录

（一）谈判和起草过程

应联合国外空委提交给联合国大会报告建议[①]，1971 年 11 月 29 日，联合国大会通过了《空间物体所造成损害的国际责任公约》[②]。1972 年 3 月 29 日《责任公约》开放签署，当天有 45 个国家签字。1972 年 9 月 1 日尼日利亚交存第五个批准书，当日《责任公约》生效。值得注意的是，美国和苏联都是在 1972 年 3 月 29 日签署《责任公约》，但 1973 年 10 月 9 日才交存它们的批准书[③]。

第二十四条的起草过程费劲周折。很长时间里，各国对《责任公约》签署和批准的具体立场有分歧，仅在谈判的最后一年才就这些问题达成一致意见。尽管美国[④]和

---

① See UN Doc. A/8420, Report of the Committee on the Peaceful Uses of Outer Space, General Assembly Official Records, Twenty-Sixth Session, Supplement No. 20, 1971, p. 8.

② See UNGA Res. 2777（XXVI）, Convention on International Liability for Damage Caused by Space Objects, 29 November 1971.

③ The dates were retrieved from the Treaty Status Database of UNOOSA, available at <http://www.unoosa.org/oosatdb/showTreatySignatures.do> accessed 26 April 2019.

④ See UN Doc. A/AC. 105/C. 2/L. 8, United States: Proposal-Convention concerning liability for damage caused by the launching of objects into outer space, 9 March 1964, in: UN Doc. A/AC. 105/19, Report of the Legal Sub-Committee on the Work of its Third Session (9-26 March 1964), 26 March 1964, Annex II, Proposals and amendments relating to liability for damage caused by objects launched into outer space, p. 2, Art. XIII. For the text of Art. XIII see infra at page 2.

比利时[①]草案中就签署公约事项采用略带限制的路径，匈牙利草案认为《责任公约》应当向所有国家无差别的开放[②]。这些草案中关于《责任公约》批准问题的不同意见还有公约生效需要交存批准的数量；美国提议五个批准书，匈牙利建议 22 个批准书，而比利时认为只要 3 个。少有的几个聚合点之一是关于交存，三份草案中建议这个任务交给联合国秘书长。

1968 年，当印度提交了一份旨在美国、匈牙利和比利时草案中寻求共同基础的提案时，规范签署、批准、生效和交存的最终条款在迈向最后合意中取得了重大进展[③]。值得注意的是，印度草案第十条文本的措辞稍作修改后，成为《责任公约》第二十四条的最终文本[④]。以印度草案作为基础，在 1971 年《责任公约》起草小组届会期间，参与最终条款谈判的各国在同年 6 月就此达成合意。结果是，这些条款整理为 6 款规

---

① See UN Doc. A/AC. 105/C. 2/L. 7/Rev. 2, Belgium: Proposal for a Convention on the Unification of Certain Rules Governing Liability for Damage Caused by Space Devices, 14 October 1964, in: UN Doc. A/AC. 105/21, Report of the Legal Sub-Committee on the Work of the Second Part of its Third Session (5-23 October 1964), Annex II, Proposals and amendments relating to liability for damage caused by objects launched into outer space, 23 October 1964, p. 22, Art. 5 para. 1.

② See UN Doc. A/AC. 105/C. 2/L. 10, Hungary: Proposed draft agreement-Agreement concerning liability for damage caused by the launching of objects into outer space, 16 March 1964, in: UN Doc. A/AC. 105/19, Report of the Legal Sub-Committee on the Work of its Third Session (9-26 March 1964), Annex II, Proposals and amendments relating to liability for damage caused by objects launched into outer space, 26 March 1964, p. 7, Art. XIII: "This Agreement shall be opened for signature to all States. It shall be subject to ratification. Instruments of ratification shall be deposited with the United Nations Secretary-General".

③ See UN Doc. A/AC. 105/C. 2/L. 32, India: proposal-Convention concerning liability for damage caused by the launching of objects into outer space, 2 June 1968, in: UN Doc. A/AC. 105/45, Report of the Legal Sub-Committee on the Work of its Seventh Session (4-28 June 1968), Annex I, Proposals, amendments and other documents relating to liability for damage caused by the launching of objects into outer space, 11 July 1968, p. 16.

④ 印度草案第十条：

1. 本公约应开放供一切国家签署。在本公约根据本条第四款生效之前，没有签署本公约的国家可随时加入本公约。

2. 本公约应由签署国批准，批准书和加入文件应送交苏维埃社会主义共和国、大不列颠及北爱尔兰联合王国和美利坚合众国政府存放，为此指定这三国政府为交存国政府。

3. （此处插入关于修改国际组织加入公约方式、在《公约》项下的权利义务及其与《公约》当事国关系的规定）

4. 本公约应于第五个政府交存批准书时生效，这五个政府中包括本公约指定的交存国政府。

5. 对于在本公约生效后，交存批准书或加入文件的国家，本公约应于其交存批准书或加入文件之日起生效。

6. 交存国政府应将每次签署日期、每次批准书及加入文件交存日期、本公约生效日期和其他事项，迅速通知所有签署国和加入国。

7. 本公约应由交存国政府依照《联合国宪章》第 102 条予以登记。

定，纳入了 1971 年 6 月 17 日起草小组通过的“最终条款”文件中①。此后，这 6 款规定作为一条纳入了《责任公约》工作小组于 1971 年 6 月 28 日通过的《空间物体所造成损害的责任公约草案》。②

（二）评注

第二十四条规定了签署（第 1 款）、批准（第 2 款和第 4 款）、生效（第 3 款）、交存国政府（第 2 款和第 5 款）以及公约登记（第 6 款）条款。

第二十四条第 1 款明确，所有国家可签署《责任公约》，并根据《责任公约》第二十四条第 3 款生效后的任何时间加入公约。第二十四条第 1 款的措辞来自苏联和印度的《责任公约》草案。这与美国草案第十三条和比利时草案第五条不同，这两个草案规定《责任公约》“应当向联合国成员国或其专门机构，或者《国际法院规约》当事国或者应联合国大会邀请的当事方开放签署。”③ 该措辞背后隐含的意图是排除非联合国成员国。但是，匈牙利、印度和其他代表团坚持《责任公约》不应当歧视任何国家，而应当确保最大可能数量的国家加入。在《责任公约》谈判的最后阶段，美国和比利时被说服接受了这是最佳方案，结果是他们接受了苏联和印度的草案。

第二十四条第 2 款指定美国、苏联和英国政府作为《责任公约》交存国政府。这个表述来自印度草案第十条第 2 款。此前，美国、匈牙利和比利时草案建议将联合国秘书长作为《责任公约》交存方。所有批准书和加入文件交存给交存国政府。而且，第二十四条第 2 款表明，《责任公约》应由签署国批准。这个规定遵循了一般国际法

---

① See UN Doc. PUOS/C. 2/DG（X）/1, Final clauses-text approved by the Drafting Group on 17 June 1971, 17 June 1971, in: UN Doc. A/AC. 105/94, Report Of The Legal Sub-Committee on the Work of its Tenth Session (7 June-2 July 1971), Annex I, Proposals and Other Documents Relating to Agenda Item 2 (Draft Convention on Liability for Damage Caused by Objects Launched into Outer Space), 8 July 1971, p. 29.

② See UN Doc. PUOS/C. 2/DG（X）/2, Draft Convention on International Liability for Damage Caused by Space Objects: text approved by the Drafting Group on 28 June 1971, 28 June 1971, in: UN Doc. A/AC. 105/94, Report Of The Legal Sub-Committee on the Work of its Tenth Session (7 June-2 July 1971), Annex I, Proposals and Other Documents Relating to Agenda Item 2 (Draft Convention on Liability for Damage Caused by Objects Launched into Outer Space), 8 July 1971, p. 30.

③ UN Doc. A/AC. 105/C. 2/L. 7/Rev. 2, Belgium: Proposal for a Convention on the Unification of Certain Rules Governing Liability for Damage Caused by Space Devices, 14 October 1964, in: UN Doc. A/AC. 105/21, Report of the Legal Sub-Committee on the Work of the Second Part of its Third Session (5-23 October 1964), Annex II, Proposals and amendments relating to liability for damage caused by objects launched into outer space, 23 October 1964, p. 22.

长期存在的规则。

第二十四条第3款明确，《责任公约》应当在第五个批准书缴存时生效。和《外空条约》不同[①]，《责任公约》不要求三个交存国政府必须在满足生效条件的五个批准国中。

第二十四条第4款规定了在《责任公约》最初生效日期之后批准或加入国家的生效日期。

第二十四条第5款确立三个交存国的义务。这些政府应当尽速向签署国和加入国通知有关每个签署日期、交存批准书和加入文件日期、《责任公约》生效日期等事项的信息。

第二十四条第6款规定《责任公约》应由交存国政府遵照《联合国宪章》第一百零二条予以登记。其目的是确保透明度和公开外交。而且，根据《联合国宪章》第一百零二条，登记的法律效果是一经登记，《责任公约》就对联合国机关有约束力，且可向其援引[②]。在这个背景下，《联合国宪章》第一百零二条规定了联合国成员国登记公约的绝对义务，不管成员国是否确信有关条约可能向联合国机关援引。

二十六、第二十五条（修正提案）

Tronchetti, Smith and Kerrest

本公约的任何当事国均可提议修正本公约。对每个当事国来说，每项修正在其获得多数当事国接受后即可生效，对此后每个加入国来说，修正应于其接受之日起生效。

目录

---

① See Art. XXIV para. 3 OST.

② See Higgins, Rosalyn, The Development of International Law Through the Political Organs of the United Nations, Oxford University Press, London 1963.

（一）谈判和起草过程

《责任公约》谈判过程中，第二十五条规定并没有引起特别的讨论。美国 1964 年草案首次提出修正程序①。该提案得到了其他代表团的正面回应，为修正问题进一步讨论打下了基础。实际上，1965 年比利时②、1968 年印度③和意大利④提交的公约草案与美国草案关于修正程序的内容大体相似。有趣的是，匈牙利草案（代表苏联阵营国家提交）并没有包含《责任公约》修正程序。尽管如此，考虑到安排修订《责任公约》程序的广泛共识，1971 年《责任公约》起草小组就公约最终条款开始讨论的时候，各国最先达成一致意见之一就是《责任公约》修订规定也就不足为奇了。其结果是，这些规定较早纳入起草小组于 1971 年 6 月 17 日通过的最终条款文本中⑤，此

① See UN Doc. A/AC. 105/C. 2/L. 8, United States: Proposal-Convention concerning liability for damage caused by the launching of objects into outer space, 9 March 1964, in: UN Doc. A/AC. 105/19, Report of the Legal Sub-Committee on the Work of its Third Session (9-26 March 1964), 26 March 1964, Annex II, Proposals and amendments relating to liability for damage caused by objects launched into outer space, p. 2, Art. XI reads as follows: "A Contracting Party may propose amendments to this Convention. Amendments shall come into force for each Contracting Party accepting the amendments on acceptance by a majority of the Contracting Parties and thereafter for each remaining Contracting Party on acceptance by it.".

② See UN Doc. A/AC. 105/C. 2/L. 7/Rev. 2, Belgium: Proposal for a Convention on the Unification of Certain Rules Governing Liability for Damage Caused by Space Devices, 14 October 1964, in: UN Doc. A/AC. 105/21, Report of the Legal Sub-Committee on the Work of the Second Part of its Third Session (5-23 October 1964), Annex II, Proposals and amendments relating to liability for damage caused by objects launched into outer space, 23 October 1964, p. 22, Art. 8 reads as follows: "This Convention may be amended or supplemented at the proposal of one or more Contracting Parties. Such amendments shall take the form of additional protocols which shall be binding on such Contracting Parties as ratify (underlining added), approve or accede to them. Such protocols shall enter into force when the majority of the Contracting Parties to this Convention have thus accepted them.".

③ See UN Doc. A/AC. 105/C. 2/L. 32, India: proposal-Convention concerning liability for damage caused by the launching of objects into outer space, 2 June 1968, in: UN Doc. A/AC. 105/45, Report of the Legal Sub-Committee on the Work of its Seventh Session (4-28 June 1968), Annex I, Proposals, amendments and other documents relating to liability for damage caused by the launching of objects into outer space, 11 July 1968, p. 16, Art. XI.

④ See UN Doc. A/AC. 105/C. 2/L. 40, Working Paper submitted by the Italian delegation-Draft convention concerning liability for damage caused by the launching of objects into outer space, 13 June 1986, in: UN Doc. A/AC. 105/45, Report of the Legal Sub-Committee on the Work of its Seventh Session (4-28 June 1968), 11 July 1968, Annex I, Proposals, amendments and other documents relating to liability for damage caused by the launching of objects into outer space, p. 30, Art. 14.

⑤ See UN Doc. PUOS/C. 2/DG (X) /1, Final clauses-text approved by the Drafting Group on 17 June 1971, 17 June 1971, in: UN Doc. A/AC. 105/94, Report Of The Legal Sub-Committee on the Work of its Tenth Session (7 June-2 July 1971), Annex I, Proposals and Other Documents Relating to Agenda Item 2 (Draft Convention on Liability for Damage Caused by Objects Launched into Outer Space), 8 July 1971, p. 29.

后纳入了《责任公约》工作小组于1971年6月28日通过的《空间物体所造成损害的责任公约草案》①。

（二）评注

第二十五条确立了《责任公约》当事国修正公约的机制以及这些修订生效的程序。任何当事国可建议修正《责任公约》。修正的生效必须获得多数当事国的接受，此后该修正对接受国生效。对其余当事国来说，修正自该国接受之日起生效。这些规定遵循了一般条约法和《维也纳条约法公约》第三十九条至第四十一条。截至目前，没有当事国正式对《责任公约》提出修正案。

有趣的是，鉴于《责任公约》第二十二条的规定，第二十五条不适用于国际组织，第二十二条排除了最终条款对国际组织的适用②。根据第二十二条，接受《责任公约》权利和义务的国际组织并没有权利对公约提出修正案。尽管如此，可以设想的是，任何此类国际组织的成员国可以通过联合提交修正案，克服本条的禁止性规定。

二十七、第二十六条（修正/审查）

Tronchetti, Smith and Kerrest

本公约生效十年后，应将审查本公约议题纳入联合国大会临时议程，以便参照本公约的实施情况，审议是否须做修正。但公约在生效五年后的任何时间，根据三分之一公约当事国请求并经多数当事国同意，应召开本公约当事国大会审议本公约。

目录

① See UN Doc. PUOS/C. 2/DG（X）/2, Draft Convention on International Liability for Damage Caused by Space Objects: text approved by the Drafting Group on 28 June 1971, 28 June 1971, in: UN Doc. A/AC. 105/94, Report Of The Legal Sub-Committee on the Work of its Tenth Session (7 June-2 July 1971), Annex I, Proposals and Other Documents Relating to Agenda Item 2 (Draft Convention on Liability for Damage Caused by Objects Launched into Outer Space), 8 July 1971, p. 30.

② Art. XXII LIAB States that: "In this Convention, with the exception of articles XXIV to XXVII, reference to States shall be deemed to apply to any international organization [···] ".

（一）谈判和起草过程

第二十六条的起草过程比较特别。修正《责任公约》可能性这一话题在谈判后期才成为关注事项。1964 年到 1970 年的立法准备性文件中，几乎没有提及修正《公约》程序。只有美国在 1964 年和 1965 年间提交的三份草案中的第十一条第 2 款均规定，“在本公约生效五年后，应多数当事国邀请可召集修正会议”。[①] 奇怪的是，美国草案的此后版本中删除了该规定。

直到 1971 年，在起草小组关于《责任公约》最终条款一般讨论的背景中，阿根廷、奥地利、巴西和墨西哥联合提案中建议增加关于可能审议或修正公约的最终条款[②]。该建议内容为，“本公约生效十年后，应将审查本公约议题纳入联合国大会临时议程，以便参照本公约的实施情况，审议是否须做修正。但在此前的任何时间，根据三分之一公约当事国请求并经多数缔约国同意，应召开本公约当事国大会审议本公约。”其后，印度修改了该规定，只有《责任公约》生效五年后才能将审查公约提议纳入联合国大会工作日程[③]。经印度修改后，阿根廷、奥地利、巴西和墨西哥的提案建议获得参与《责任公约》谈判其他国家的认可，并成为工作小组于 1971 年 6 月 28 日通过的《空间物体所造成损害的责任公约草案》的第二十六条[④]。第二天，联合国

① UN Doc. A/AC. 105/C. 2/L. 8/Rev. 1, United States: Proposal-Convention concerning liability for damage caused by the launching of objects into outer space, in: UN Doc. A/AC. 105/21, Report of the Legal Sub-Committee on the Work of the Second Part of its Third Session (5-23 October 1964), Annex II, Proposals and amendments relating to liability for damage caused by objects launched into outer space, 23 October 1964, p. 6.

② See UN Doc. PUOS/C. 2/DG (X) /WP. I, Final clauses-Argentina, Austria, Brazil, and Mexico: proposal, 18 June 1971, in: UN Doc. A/AC. 105/94, Report Of The Legal Sub-Committee on the Work of its Tenth Session (7 June-2 July 1971), Annex I, Proposals and Other Documents Relating to Agenda Item 2 (Draft Convention on Liability for Damage Caused by Objects Launched into Outer Space), 8 July 1971, p. 28.

③ See UN Doc. PUOS/C. 2/WG (X) /L. 2/Rev. 1, Australia: proposal, India: proposal, 24 June 1971, in: UN Doc. A/AC. 105/94, Report Of The Legal Sub-Committee on the Work of its Tenth Session (7 June-2 July 1971), Annex I, Proposals and Other Documents Relating to Agenda Item 2 (Draft Convention on Liability for Damage Caused by Objects Launched into Outer Space), 8 July 1971, p. 18.

④ See UN Doc. PUOS/C. 2/DG (X) /2, Draft Convention on International Liability for Damage Caused by Space Objects: text approved by the Drafting Group on 28 June 1971, 28 June 1971, in: UN Doc. A/AC. 105/94, Report Of The Legal Sub-Committee on the Work of its Tenth Session (7 June-2 July 1971), Annex I, Proposals and Other Documents Relating to Agenda Item 2 (Draft Convention on Liability for Damage Caused by Objects Launched into Outer Space), 8 July 1971, p. 30.

外空委法律小组委员会第166次会议期间正式通过了《责任公约》草案。①

（二）评注

第二十六条确立了规范可能修正《责任公约》的程序。根据第二十六条第一句，公约生效十年后，当事国应将审查公约纳入联合国大会临时议程，以便根据实施情况，评估公约是否需要修正。尽管如此，根据第二句，在《责任公约》生效五年后的任何时间，可召开当事国会议审议公约。召开该会议的决定必须是应三分之一当事国请求并得到多数当事国的支持。

《责任公约》1972年生效。依据第二十六条的规定，生效十年后联合国大会审议了《责任公约》②。近二十年后，在联合国外空委法律小组委员会审议联合国外空五大条约倡议背景下，正式讨论了实施《责任公约》的状态和水准。该倡议是墨西哥于1997年发起的③，目的是推动外空五大条约达致最广泛和最充分的遵守，1998年，该议题纳入法律小组委员会议事日程④。2001年，设立了外空五大条约状态工作小组，主席是来自希腊的Vassilios Cassapoglou先生。

在法律小组委员会和工作小组的讨论过程中，一些代表团指出，如果更多国家根据联合国大会2777号决议做出声明⑤，在互惠基础上接受《责任公约》第十四条项下赔偿委员会决定的约束力，将推动实现《责任公约》的更大实践价值⑥。这些代表团还认为此类声明有助于提升公约的效用和可信性，因此号召《责任公约》当事国做出此类声明。

① See UN Doc. A/AC. 105/C. 2/10, Legal Sub-Committee-Draft Convention on International Liability for Damage Caused by Space Objects, 29 June 1971, in: UN Doc. A/AC. 105/94, Report Of The Legal Sub-Committee on the Work of its Tenth Session (7 June-2 July 1971), 8 July 1971, p. 5, para. 22.

② See UNGA Res. 37/91, Question of the review of the Convention on International Liability for Damage Caused by Space Objects, 10 December 1982.

③ See UN Doc. A/AC. 105/C. 2/L. 206, Working paper submitted by Mexico, 4 April 1997, in: UN Doc. A/AC. 105/674, Report of the Legal Subcommittee on the Work of Its Thirty-Sixth Session (1-8 April 1997), 14 April 1997, Annex II, Documents Annexed To The Report, Part B, Open-Ended Informal Consultations On New Agenda Items: Review Of The Status Of The Five International Legal Instruments Governing Outer Space, p. 22.

④ See UN Doc. A/AC. 105/698, Report of the Legal Subcommittee on the Work of Its Thirty-Seventh Session (23-31 March 1998), 6 April 1998, p. 9.

⑤ UNGA Res. 2777 (XXVI), Convention on International Liability for Damage Caused by Space Objects, 29 November 1971.

⑥ See UN Doc. A/AC. 105/698, Report of the Legal Subcommittee on the Work of Its Thirty-Seventh Session (23-31 March 1998), 6 April 1998, p. 10, para. 56.

最重要的进展是，2006 年 4 月 6 日工作小组就遵守《责任公约》益处达成的文本[1]。该文本，尽管强调了批准水平还相对较低，仍旧指出《责任公约》对外空法律秩序的突出重要性，构成外空活动安全和可靠性的基石。遵守《责任公约》的益处为：（1）发射国对其空间物体在地球表面和飞行中的飞机造成的损害承担绝对赔偿责任，据此受害国无需受困于法律程序；（2）受害人的国籍国、损害发生地国、受害人永久居住地国可代表受害人提出赔偿要求；（3）求偿人向发射国提出赔偿要求无需用尽当地救济，且不排除当地救济；（4）依据国际法和公正合理原则决定赔偿金；（5）如果外交谈判无法解决赔偿要求，应任一国请求可要求成立赔偿委员会；（6）《责任公约》当事国，可声明接受赔偿委员会对其和接受同样义务的当事方有关争端做出决定的约束力（联合国大会 2777 号决议[2]）；（7）在严重危及人的生命或严重干扰人类生活条件的情况下，遭受此类损害的国家可以请求发射国和国际社会其他成员的援助。该文本的结论是，遵守《责任公约》对外空活动国家和非外空活动国家均有益处，因为所有国家都可能是空间物体造成事故的潜在受害者。特别是，在对其领土造成损害的情形中，发展中国家将受益于《责任公约》确立的、广泛适用的无过失责任制度，鉴于许多发展中国家拥有广袤的领土，或者位于赤道和亚赤道区域，更容易受到空间物体发射和重返的影响。

尽管很难衡量法律小组委员会的讨论对《责任公约》的落实和遵守是否有实际和直接的影响，不容否认的是公约的批准数量近年来大幅增加。实际上，1997 年，也就是启动审议外空五大条约状态倡议的那一年，《责任公约》当事国的数量是 76 个，2012 年这个数字上升为 90 个。

总之，联合国外空五大条约中，《责任公约》是第一个含有修正条款的条约。1967 年《外空条约》和 1968 年《营救协定》中没有修正规定。此后，《责任公约》

① See UN Doc. A/AC. 105/871, Report of the Legal Subcommittee on its Forty-Fifth Session (3-13 April 2006), 24 April 2006, Annex I, Report of the Chairman of the Working Group on the Status and Application of the Five United Nations Treaties on Outer Space, Appendix, Advantages of adherence to the Convention on International Liability for Damage Caused by Space Objects, p. 27.

② UNGA Res. 2777 (XXVI), Convention on International Liability for Damage Caused by Space Objects, 29 November 1971.

第 26 条用作起草 1975 年《登记公约》[①] 和 1979 年《月球协定》[②] 修正规定的范本。

二十八、第二十七至二十八条（最终条款）

Tronchetti, Smith and Kerrest

第二十七条

本公约任何当事国在公约生效一年后，可书面通知交存国政府，退出公约。退出公约应自收悉通知之日起一年后生效。

第二十八条

本公约的中文、英文、法文、俄文以及西班牙文文本具有同等效力，均交交存国政府存档。交存国政府应把本公约之正式副本送交各签署国和加入国政府。

为此，下列全权代表在本公约上签字，以昭信守。

一九七二年三月二十九日订于伦敦、莫斯科和华盛顿，一式三份。

目录

① Art. X REG.
② Art. 18 MOON.

（一）谈判和起草过程

1. 第二十七条

第二十七条的起草过程略有争议，各国只能在《责任公约》谈判的最后阶段就其规定达成一致意见，即 1971 年 6 月。在将近十年的时间里，美国、苏联和比利时提交的《责任公约》三份主要草案中关于退出公约的时间框架和形式上存有分歧。1964 年美国草案建议，只有在公约生效五年后才可以退出[①]。该草案还有一条规定，退出并不能解除一国在退出生效前对于损害的义务和赔偿责任。和美国建议不同，匈牙利提议没有明确提交退出通知的时限[②]。仅表明，退出在通知联合国秘书长一年后生效。比利时关于退出的提案与美国建议类似[③]。

在 1965 到 1967 年间没有取得重大进展。1968 年，印度提交的《责任公约》草案中有明显的进步[④]。该草案第十二条提议，公约生效一年后才能退出，且退出在通知之日起一年后生效。但没有提及美国的提议，即退出公约并不能解除一国在退出前对于损害的义务和赔偿责任。印度草案第十二条逐字逐句地成为《责任公约》第二十七条。尽管如此，三年后，美国、匈牙利（作为苏联阵营的代表）和比利时才接受印度的提议。最终于 1971 年 6 月达成一致意见，第二十七条的最终版本纳入了《责任公

① See UN Doc. A/AC. 105/C. 2/L. 8, United States: Proposal-Convention concerning liability for damage caused by the launching of objects into outer space, 9 March 1964, in: UN Doc. A/AC. 105/19, Report of the Legal Sub-Committee on the Work of its Third Session (9-26 March 1964), 26 March 1964, Annex II, Proposals and amendments relating to liability for damage caused by objects launched into outer space, p. 2, Art. XII.

② See UN Doc. PUOS/C. 2/WG (IX) /L. 10, Text approved by the Drafting Group-Draft convention on international liability for damage caused by space objects, [Date n/a], in: UN Doc. A/AC. 105/85, Report Of The Legal Sub-Committee on the Work of its Ninth Session (8 June-3 July 1970), Annex I, Proposals And Other Documents Relating To Liability For Damage Caused By The Launching Of Objects Into Outer Space (Agenda item 2), 3 July 1970, p. 20, Art. XVI.

③ See UN Doc. A/AC. 105/C. 2/L. 7/Rev. 2, Belgium: Proposal for a Convention on the Unification of Certain Rules Governing Liability for Damage Caused by Space Devices, 14 October 1964, in: UN Doc. A/AC. 105/21, Report of the Legal Sub-Committee on the Work of the Second Part of its Third Session (5-23 October 1964), Annex II, Proposals and amendments relating to liability for damage caused by objects launched into outer space, 23 October 1964, p. 22, Art. 7.

④ See UN Doc. A/AC. 105/C. 2/L. 32, India: proposal-Convention concerning liability for damage caused by the launching of objects into outer space, 2 June 1968, in: UN Doc. A/AC. 105/45, Report of the Legal Sub-Committee on the Work of its Seventh Session (4-28 June 1968), Annex I, Proposals, amendments and other documents relating to liability for damage caused by the launching of objects into outer space, 11 July 1968, p. 16.

约》起草小组于1971年6月28日通过的《空间物体所造成损害的责任公约草案》[①]。第二天，联合国外空委法律小组委员会通过了该草案[②]。

2. 第二十八条

在《责任公约》谈判过程中，第二十八条没有成为任何讨论的主题。早在1964年，美国[③]和匈牙利[④]（代表苏联阵营）的《责任公约》草案在其第十二条和第十八条分别规定，公约的五种语言文本具有同样效力[⑤]。1967年比利时草案中含有完全同样措辞的规定[⑥]。四年后，这个规定成为《责任公约》草案第二十八条第一句，此后联合国外空委法律小组委员会于1971年6月29日通过[⑦]。

早期美国、苏联和比利时提案和第二十八条最终版本的明显不同是赋予谁公约交存方的职能。在早期条款中，由联合国秘书长担任这个职能，后来这个职能交给了交存国政府。美国、苏联和比利时都采用第一种方法，直到1971年，他们决定改变，由交存国政府承担《责任公约》交存作用。这个变化此后反映在1971年《责任公约》

---

① See UN Doc. PUOS/C. 2/DG（X）/2, Draft Convention on International Liability for Damage Caused by Space Objects: text approved by the Drafting Group on 28 June 1971, 28 June 1971, in: UN Doc. A/AC. 105/94, Report Of The Legal Sub-Committee on the Work of its Tenth Session（7 June-2 July 1971）, Annex I, Proposals and Other Documents Relating to Agenda Item 2 (Draft Convention on Liability for Damage Caused by Objects Launched into Outer Space), 8 July 1971, p. 30.

② See UN Doc. A/AC. 105/C. 2/10, Legal Sub-Committee-Draft Convention on International Liability for Damage Caused by Space Objects 29, June 1971, in: UN Doc. A/AC. 105/94, Report Of The Legal Sub-Committee on the Work of its Tenth Session（7 June-2 July 1971）, 8 July 1971, p. 5, para. 22.

③ See UN Doc. A/AC. 105/C. 2/L. 8, United States: Proposal-Convention concerning liability for damage caused by the launching of objects into outer space, 9 March 1964, in: UN Doc. A/AC. 105/19, Report of the Legal Sub-Committee on the Work of its Third Session（9-26 March 1964）, 26 March 1964, Annex II, Proposals and amendments relating to liability for damage caused by objects launched into outer space, p. 2.

④ See UN Doc. A/AC. 105/C. 2/L. 10, Hungary: Proposed draft agreement-Agreement concerning liability for damage caused by the launching of objects into outer space, 16 March 1964, in: UN Doc. A/AC. 105/19, Report of the Legal Sub-Committee on the Work of its Third Session（9-26 March 1964）, Annex II, Proposals and amendments relating to liability for damage caused by objects launched into outer space, 26 March 1964, p. 7.

⑤ 这五种语言分别是中文、英文、法文、俄文和西班牙文。

⑥ See UN Doc. A/AC. 105/C. 2/L. 7/Rev. 3, Belgium: Proposal for a Convention on the Unification of Certain Rules Governing Liability for Damage Caused by Space Devices to Third Parties on the Surface of the Earth and Aircraft in Flight, 26 June 1967, in: UN Doc. A/AC. 105/37, Report of the Legal Sub-Committee on the Work of its Sixth Session（19 June-14 July 1967）, Annex II, Proposals, amendments and other documents relating to liability for damage caused by the launching of objects into outer space, 14 July 1967, p. 1.

⑦ See UN Doc. A/AC. 105/C. 2/10, Legal Sub-Committee-Draft Convention on International Liability for Damage Caused by Space Objects 29, June 1971, in: UN Doc. A/AC. 105/94, Report Of The Legal Sub-Committee on the Work of its Tenth Session（7 June-2 July 1971）, 8 July 1971, p. 5, para. 22.

草案文本中[①]。将交存职能交给交存国政府而不是联合国秘书长，这个选择并不意外。符合此前各国在《外空条约》[②] 和《营救协定》[③] 就交存国达成的一致意见。

（二）评注

1. 第二十七条

第二十七条确立了缔约国有意退出《责任公约》的程序。据此，只能在公约生效一年后，且必须送交书面通知给交存国政府。退出应自收悉通知之日起一年后生效。截止日前，没有当事国提交退出《责任公约》的通知。

有趣的是，第二十七条不适用于国际组织，因为该条属于《责任公约》中明确排除适用于国际组织的条款。[④] 问题是，国际组织参与方是否有权撤回其依据《责任公约》第二十二条做出的接受公约的声明。如果可以撤回，撤回声明应当遵循的形式和程序也是问题。此外，自什么时间起可以提交撤回声明也有疑问，换言之，要么立即，要么自《责任公约》生效一年后。尽管《责任公约》没有为这些问题提供明确答案，但从第二十七条的立场可以推断，不论出于什么原因，如果某个国际组织不再满足作为《责任公约》参与方的条件，那该组织就不再是公约参与方。

2. 第二十八条

第二十八条第 1 款是关于《责任公约》不同语言文本的效力以及公约交存国的作用。关于第一个问题，第二十八条列举的《责任公约》五种语言文本具有同等效力，即中文、英文、法文、俄文和西班牙文。该规定是此前《外空条约》和《援救协定》的翻版，和后来的《登记公约》和《月球协定》一致，和《联合国宪章》第一百一十一条类似。[⑤]

关于《责任公约》的交存国问题，第二十八条规定进一步确认英国、美国和俄罗斯是《责任公约》的交存国。因此，《公约》的五种文本原件，即中文、英文、法

① Ibid.

② See Art. XⅦ OST.

③ See Art. 10 ARRA.

④ Art. XXII LIAB states that: “In this Convention, with the exception of articles XXIV to XⅩⅦ, reference to States shall be deemed to apply to any international intergovernmental organization […] ”. Consequently, the applicability of Articles XXIV to XⅩⅦ to international organizations is excluded.

⑤ For an analysis of this point see Shelton, Dinah, Reconcilable Differences? The Interpretation of Multilingual Treaties, Hastings International and Comparative Law Review (20) 1997, p. 611; and Tabory, Mala, Multilingualism in International Law and Institutions, Sijthoff and Noordhoff, Alphen aan den Rijn 1980.

文、俄文和西班牙文文本，应交由交存国政府存档。此外，交存国政府有义务将《责任公约》的正式副本送交给各签署国和加入国政府。有趣的是，该规定也和国际组织有关，第二十八条不在《责任公约》的最终条款中，即第二十四条到第二十七条，这些条款不适用于国际组织[①]。因此，值得考虑的是交存国政府对做出第二十二条声明国际组织的义务，是否将其作为签署方或加入国，是否依从第二十八条规定，向其送交《责任公约》的正式副本。

① See Art. XXII LIAB.

第三章 前景展望

Smith and Kerrest

在《责任公约》中为从事外空活动的国家确立国际赔偿责任制度，是规范外空活动国际机制发展过程中的重大成就[①]。在国际外空法律框架中，《责任公约》持续发挥核心作用，是外空活动和技术持续发展和进步的重要侧翼。除了美苏两个大国外，越来越多国家活跃于外空，并参与到围绕《责任公约》文本旷日持久的争论中。眼下，21 世纪的第二个十年，和平利用外空规范性制度的重要性几乎不言自明。

但规范的重点发生了变革。尽管赔偿责任仍旧是关键问题，一些批评意见认为，外空中损害的过失要求是没有效果的。不仅难以证明过失，而且个案中没有注意标准或措施的国际准则。这给实施《责任公约》第三条带来了负面冲击，引发了对该规定长期可行性的疑虑。

自《责任公约》生效以来，外空中仅有几起碰撞导致了大规模、国际性质的损失。其中，只有一起通过外交谈判解决（宇宙-954 号）。2009 年宇宙-铱星轨道相撞事件的解决并没有援引《责任公约》[②]。其余几起外空事故均发生在发射国本国境内，且没有造成损害[③]。

审视《责任公约》的结尾，有必要适度考量其未来发展。正如 Manfred Lachs 法

① Lachs, Manfred, The Law of Outer Space- An Experience in Contemporary Law-Making, Nijhoff, Leiden 2010.

② See Kerrest, Armel, La responsabilité des Etats du fait de la destruction de satellites dans l’espace, in: Groupement Français pour la Recherche en Droit International (ed.), Annuaire Français de Droit International 2009, CNRS, Paris 2010, pp. 615-626; and Commentary LIAB, Article II, mn. 118.

③ E. g. the Chinese Long March Rocket crash in 2007; the failure of the Russian Meridien in 2011, see Lyall, Francis/Larsen, Paul B., Space Law a Treatise, Ashgate, Burlington/Surrey 2009. However the provisions of the LIAB would apply in the case of damage to foreigners who were not involved in the launch.

官指出，《责任公约》“显然仅是起步，不久以后，法律必将对未来发展需求做出回应”[①]。

形式上，《责任公约》并不存在明显的空缺，需要根据第二十六条做出修正。修正程序可能给整个责任制度带来无法接受的挑战。1982 年，联合国大会审议《责任公约》，其 37/91 号决议确认当时国际损害赔偿制度对于外空活动的重要性[②]。随着时间的流逝，为满足清晰规范外空活动的不同需求，也为了管理当下外空活动不同层级的预防性措施，减少外空中人造碎片的数量，外空损害的过失责任制度显得不那么切实可行。

与《责任公约》项下赔偿要求数量较少保持一致，外空活动造成损害的国际损害赔偿要求尚未有诉讼案件。这反映出，国家履行国际义务、接受国际赔偿责任以及在《责任公约》框架内管理外空活动的意愿。

空间物体再入领域的几个案件有助于证明这一点。公开处理航天器再入的风险，特别是在 IADC 对此问题的研究范围内规制再入，已经成为各国接受的实践。这让国际社会得以参与和分享已操作过此类任务空间机构的科学知识和经验[③]。

已有几个案例中，发射国确保了其卫星再入过程的透明。这确认了国际监督和援助的利益所在，以及保障重返安全的重要关切。2011 年 10 月 23 日，德国科研卫星伦琴（ROSAT）在孟加拉湾上空坠落大气层[④]；另一个例子是，2003 年，意大利科研卫星 BeppoSax 由于轨道早衰，提前结束任务离轨。其再入监督得到了美国戈达德太空飞行中心（Goddard Space Flight Centre）的帮助，再入产生的碎片散落于大片区域[⑤]。更为人熟知的案例是美国 Skylab 空间站，1973 年发射，1979 年坠落，碎片散落于（人迹罕至的）西澳大利亚和印度洋的大部分区域，并未做到不为人察觉。碎片散落于广阔的领土之上，此次重返本可以引发诸多因碎片造成损害的赔偿要求。“尽管 NASA

---

① Lachs, Manfred, The Law of Outer Space- An Experience in Contemporary Law-Making, Nijhoff, Leiden 2010, p. 118.

② UNGA Res. 37/91, Question of the review of the Convention on International Liability for Damage Caused by Space Objects, 10 December 1982.

③ 欧空局目前正在审议清除 ENVISAT 卫星碎片的前景，见 ENVISAT Mission Portal <https：//earth. esa. int/web/guest/missions/esa-operational-eo-missions/envisat> accessed 26 April 2019.

④ See German Aerospace Center, ROSAT, 25 October 2011 <http：//www. dlr. de/dlr/en/desktopdefault. aspx/tabid-10424/> accessed 26 April 2019.

⑤ Lyall, Francis/Larsen, Paul B. , Space Law a Treatise, Ashgate, Burlington/Surrey 2009, p. 119.

广而告之，却没有收到一个依据《责任公约》的赔偿要求。”[1]

从外空活动国家承担的国际赔偿责任的大局，有必要进一步精准两个领域的规范，以助益有关法律的进一步发展。

首先，围绕“发射国”类别的讨论已经引发了关于这个概念解释的问题。这些讨论的结果已经体现在联合国大会 59/115 号决议《发射国概念的适用》[2]，该决议重述了发射国和国籍国之间关于损害赔偿责任分担双边协议的重要性。现下仅有少数几个国家，包括运营外国发射基地的国家，缔结了此类协议。

其次，缺少规范的主要领域是在轨外空活动标准，包括生命周期期间和截止。这些标准和规则通常指向的是外空交通管理（STM）。但是，确立《责任公约》第三条项下的过失或不作为尚没有具有约束力的规则。此类参考工具是值得欢迎的，且只能通过一套新的规则确立可执行或严格的外空交通管理规则。只要这些规则处于缺失状态，确立《责任公约》第三条项下的过失就仍旧是整个外空社会面临的挑战。

尽管如此，不能忽视的是依据《责任公约》在国际层面的赔偿要求并不排除国内层面的诉讼或争端解决。会持续出现并不适用《外空条约》规定的案件，或者即便可适用《责任公约》但受害人选择向国内机构提出赔偿要求。国内法院具有某些优势，例如相对容易启动和可能获得更慷慨的赔偿金，取决于法院适用的有关程序法和实体法[3]。这不影响援引国际法中关于国家责任规则和《外空条约》第六条提出赔偿要求；这种情况下，必须证明存在不法行为，或违反了国际法义务。

然而，可以设想在外空委有关持续发展工作基础上发展出来外空交通管理制度。晚近已提出了外空交通管理的蓝本[4]，但是如前所述，目前还没有创设注意标准的、正式的、有约束力的规则体系。

因此，伴随着确保外空活动持续发展的强制性措施，外空中造成损害的过失赔偿的特殊局面已经到了需要国际社会呼吁确立外空交通管理规范性机制的时刻。

目前，在科技小组委员会中设立的外空活动长期可持续性工作小组正在完成这项

---

① Lyall, Francis/Larsen, Paul B., Space Law a Treatise, Ashgate, Burlington/Surrey 2009, p. 117.

② UNGA Res. 59/115, Application of the concept of the “launching State”, 10 December 2004.

③ Smith, Lesley J., Collisions in Space; perspectives on the law applicable to damage arising from space objects, in: IISL, Proceedings of the 55th Colloquium on the Law of Outer Space, 1-5 October 2012 Naples (Italy), AIAA, (forthcoming).

④ See Commentary LIAB, Article Ⅲ, mn. 146.

工作。其工作处于起草阶段，随后进行讨论。工作小组有权确立外空活动规则（外空交通规则），也有助于更好地适用《责任公约》。另外，关于国内空间立法的工作小组的目的是，为更好的衔接联合国条约的核心制度和国内法提出建议[①]。

一个更加迫切的事项是关于新一代更小的航天器，小卫星或微小卫星。与地球同步轨道早期和已有的卫星相比，这些卫星的体积和质量参数极小，这项新技术正在为可预见的近地轨道航天器数量激增铺路。在某些情况中，也给国内空间法带来挑战，国内法对外空活动的许可取决于空间物体的物理轨道参数，而一些小卫星和微小卫星并没有这些参数，而一些法域中没有直接规制新一代航天器的规范[②]。因此，这些航天器给减少空间碎片的持续性努力带来挑战[③]；其有限的生命周期和不可控操作要求更准确的重返和解体编程。

起初，国内许可的规范问题，某些情况下也延展至频率登记。小卫星或微小行为将会影响近地轨道碰撞可能性，即便这可能是微不足道的[④]。此类卫星的大部分不在强制保险要求之列。

执笔之时，空间法的最大挑战与空间碎片减缓技术性指导原则作为有约束力的法律文件的地位和作用有关。截至目前，这些规则还没有被充分认可为法律。而是作为外空活动行为准则的解释方法之一。可在专家评估技术操作标准中发挥作用。被授予“软法”称号，日益成为国际空间法中其他被接受的约束性规则，支持其具有约束力的法律地位的观点持续增长。接受的方式有两种，一是接受其作为外空碰撞中严格注意标准的有效性，二是在国际规范位阶中，给予其国家实践的法定地位。国家实践比较合适，考虑到现有四部在国内层面具有强制力的空间碎片减缓指南均源自于主要的

① See UN Doc. UN Doc. A/73/20, Report of the Committee on the Peaceful Uses of Outer Space, 7 July 2018.

② Palkovitz, Neta/Masson-Zwaan, Tanja, Orbiting under the Radar, Nano-satellites, international obligations and national space laws, in: IISL, Proceedings of the 55th Colloquium on the Law of Outer Space, 1-5 October 2012 Naples (Italy), AIAA, (forthcoming), with reference to both Netherlands and Belgian national space laws.

③ Ibid.

④ UK Space Agency, Impact Assessment of the Review of the "Outer Space Act (1986)", Government Department for Business Innovation and Skills, 18 January 2011 <http://www.bis.gov.uk/assets/ukspaceagency/docs/osa/impact-assessment-reform-of-the-outer-space-act> accessed 26 April 2019.

国际组织或首要政府间机构①。

外空活动仍旧是具有内生风险的活动。尽管技术有长足进步，外空活动的持续发展仍需要确保其可行性和安全性特定环境。过去的半个世纪见证了大量的人造碎片，目前给外空活动持续发展带来严重威胁。尽管这个话题已经引发诸多考量，例如如何减少和移除碎片，但以《责任公约》第三条为基础的外空活动损害赔偿制度仍没有发生决定性变革。

本部分开头提到了《责任公约》第三条中与外空损害赔偿有关的过失概念。其存在并不会阻碍外空活动，但也无助于创设和保持安全的外空环境。对用户群体缺少有效的制裁，对不遵守缺少有效救济。加上过失评估实践发展中的困难，关于可持续和碎片减缓的所谓“软法指导原则”不是完全无用。有必要考虑发射国在维护和保护外空环境方面的义务。尽管利用外空，可依据《外空条约》的不同规定（第三条、第七条和第九条）和国家责任呼吁各国保护外空环境，赔偿责任仍旧是一个单独的考量。

长久以来，始终不时出现创新性解释什么构成“利用”外空，这其中有什么构成滥用的界限，伴随着关于在航天器寿命终止后主动移除的义务争论。这些措施提高了对技术操作标准的依赖程度，目前多体现在国内法中。如果国际损害赔偿责任——与国家责任不同——仍旧是外空活动的重要制度，接受外空活动操作技术标准的软法规则势必成为迫切需要。正如前述提及的《外空条约》原则所示，利用外空需要考虑保护外空。

最后，一个“应然法”（de lege ferenda）立场是，在《责任公约》第三条中赔偿责任形式与国际法中的严格责任制度（和过错责任相对）密切相关。这种制度此前主

① See e. g. Inter-Agency Space Debris Coordination Committee-Space Debris Mitigation Guidelines Revision 1, September 2007 <http://www. iadc-online. org/index. cgi? item=docs_ pub> accessed 26 April 2019; UN Doc. A/62/20, Report of the Committee on the Peaceful Uses of Outer Space, GA Official Records, Sixty-second session, Supplement 20, pp. 47ff. , endorsed by UNGA Res. 62/217, International cooperation in the peaceful uses of outer space, 22 December 2007, para. 26; NASA, NASA Procedural Requirements for Limiting Orbital Debris, NPR 8715. 6 A, 14 May 2009 <http://orbitaldebris. jsc. nasa. gov/library/NPR_ 8715_ 006 A. pdf> accessed 26 April 2019; European Council Doc. 17175/08, Council Conclusions and Draft Code of Conduct for Outer Space Activities, 17 December 2008, Annex II; and ISO standard 24113 : 2011, Space systems-Space debris mitigation requirements.

要用于海洋或其他危险、有害物质和废物运输公约中[①]。鉴于《责任公约》原作者的智慧，以及立法准备性文件见证的当时就赔偿责任达成一致意见的难度，外空活动严格责任制度的新焦点是提升外空运营的可持续性，这是一个符合逻辑要求的前进方向。这不涉及完全的范式改变。正如 Manfred Lachs 所指出，不是所有的国际谈判都必然产生最佳结论；国际谈判过程具有内生的妥协性，在初始阶段通过的一些规则需要进一步详尽阐释[②]。有利于将外空活动花费和投资的经济立场、强制保险要求和第三方赔偿责任结合起来考量，进而确定风险总量，并在国家、产业和保险市场按比例分摊。借鉴现有的海洋油污损害赔偿责任基金，构建类似的基金或征收“外空环境税”。

《责任公约》陪伴外空活动发展超过了五十年；眼下，国际外空社会必须寻找落实现有规范外空活动规则的切实可行、有效的办法。只有这样才能为所有国家提供长久、平等进入和利用外空的机会[③]。

① 几个国际公约旨在减少污染物并提升环境质量，其中有些公约规则比较深入，给处置有关物质或物料的运营者施加了严格责任制度。现列举几个公约以展示已有规范，如 the IMO Convention on Civil Liability for Bunker Oil Pollution Damage（adopted 23 March 2001，entry into force 21 November 2008）. The best known system governing strict operator liability is that of nuclear plants，established under the 1960 OECD Paris Convention on Third Party Liability in the Field of Nuclear Energy（entered into force in 1968），with its 1963 Brussels Supplementary Convention，and the 1963 IAEA Vienna Convention. 这两个公约体系都经历了若干修正，并有补充议定书，且并未全部生效，详情请见<http：//www. world-nuclear. org/info/inf67. html> accessed 26 April 2019.

② Lachs，Manfred，The Law of Outer Space- An Experience in Contemporary Law-Making，Nijhoff，Leiden 2010，p. 130.

③ .

1975年《关于登记射入外层空间物体的公约》

Bernhard Schmidt-Tedd, Ulrike Bohlmann, Natalya Malysheva,
Olga Stelmakhand Leslie Tennen

联合国大会通过：1974年11月12日
开放签署：1975年1月14日
生效：1976年9月15日
来源：1023 UNTS 15

《登记公约》文本

本公约缔约国，

承认全体人类为和平目的而促进探索及利用外层空间的共同利益，

回顾一九六七年一月二十七日的《关于各国探索和利用外层空间包括月球和其他天体在内的活动所应遵守原则的条约》内曾确认各国对其本国在外层空间的活动应负国际责任，并提到射入外层空间的物体登记备案的国家，

又回顾到一九六八年四月二十二日的《关于营救宇航员、送回宇航员及归还射入外层空间物体的协定》规定一个发射当局对于其射入外层空间而在发射当局领域界限之外发现的物体，经请求时，应在交还前提供证明资料，

再回顾到一九七二年三月二十九日的《关于外空物体所造成损害的国际责任公约》确立了关于发射国家对其外空物体造成的损害所负责任的国际规则和程序，

盼望根据各国从事探索和利用外层空间包括月球和其他天体在内的活动所应遵守原则的条约，拟订由发射国登记其射入外层空间物体的规定，

还盼望在强制的基础上设置一个由联合国秘书长保持的射入外层空间物体总登记册，

也盼望为缔约各国提供另外的方法和程序，借以帮助辨认外空物体，

相信一种强制性的登记射入外层空间物体的制度，将特别可以帮助辨认此等物体，并有助于管理探索和利用外层空间的国际法的施行和发展，

兹协议如下：

第一条

为了本公约的目的：

1. “发射国”一词是指

（1）一个发射或促使发射外空物体的国家；

（2）一个从其领土上或设备发射外空物体的国家。

2. “外空物体”一词包括一个外空物体的组成部分以及外空物体的发射载器及其零件。

3. “登记国”一词是指一个依照第二条将外空物体登入其登记册的发射国。

第二条

1. 发射国在发射一个外空物体进入或越出地球轨道时，应以登入其所须保持的适当登记册的方式登记该外空物体。每一发射国应将其设置此种登记册情事通知联合国秘书长。

2. 任何此种外空物体有两个以上的发射国时，各该国应共同决定由其中的那一国依照本条第1款登记该外空物体，同时注意到《关于各国从事探索和利用包括月球和其他天体在内外层空间活动原则的条约》第八条的规定，并且不妨碍各发射国间就外空物体及外空物体上任何人员的管辖和控制问题所缔结的或日后缔结的适当协定。

3. 每一登记册的内容项目和保持登记册的条件应由有关的登记国决定。

第三条

1. 联合国秘书长应保持一份登记册，记录依照第四条所提供的情报。

2. 这份登记册所载情报应充分公开，听任查阅。

第四条

1. 每一登记国应在切实可行的范围内尽速向联合国秘书长供给有关登入其登记册的每一个外空物体的下列情报：

（1）发射国或多数发射国的国名；

（2）外空物体的适当标志或其登记号码；

（3）发射的日期和地域或地点；

（4）基本的轨道参数，包括：

①波节周期，

②倾斜角，

③远地点，

④近地点。

（5）外空物体的一般功能。

2. 每一登记国应随时向联合国秘书长供给有关其登记册内所载外空物体的其他情报。

3. 每一登记国应在切实可行的最大限度内，尽速将其前曾提送情报的原在地球轨道内但现已不复在地球轨道内的外空物体通知联合国秘书长。

第五条

每当发射进入或越出地球轨道的外空物体具有第四条第 1 款第（2）项所述的标志或登记号码，或二者兼有时，登记国在依照第四条提送有关该外空物体的情报时应将此项事实通知秘书长。在此种情形下，联合国秘书长应将此项通知记入登记册。

第六条

本公约各项规定的施行如不能使一个缔约国辨认对该国或对其所辖任何自然人或法人造成损害或可能具有危险性或毒性的外空物体时，其他缔约国，特别包括拥有空间监视和跟踪设备的国家，应在可行的最大限度内响应该缔约国所提出或经由联合国秘书长代其提出，在公允和合理的条件下协助辨认该物体的请求。提出这种请求缔约国应在可行的最大限度内提供关于引起这项请求事件的时间、性质及情况等情报。给予这种协助的安排应由有关各方协议商定。

第七条

1. 除本公约第八条至第十二条［含第八条和第十二条在内］外，凡提及国家时，应视为也适用于从事外空活动的任何政府间国际组织，但该组织须声明接受本公约规定的权利和义务，并且该组织的多数会员国须为本公约和《关于各国探索和利用外层空间包括月球和其他天体在内的活动所应遵守原则的条约》的缔约国。

2. 为本公约缔约国的任何这种国际组织的会员国，应采取一切适当步骤，保证该组织依照本条第一款规定发表声明。

第八条

1. 本公约应听由所有国家在纽约联合国总部签字。凡在本公约按照本条第 3 款生效以前尚未签字于本公约的任何国家得随时加入本公约。

2. 本公约应经各签字国批准。批准书和加入书应交存联合国秘书长。

3. 本公约应于向联合国秘书长交存第五件批准书时在已交存批准书的国家间发生效力。

4. 对于在本公约生效后交存批准书或加入书的国家，本公约应自其交存批准书或加入书之日起开始生效。

5. 秘书长应将每一签字日期、交存本公约的每一批准书和加入书日期、本公约生效日期和其他通知事项，迅速告知所有签字国和加入国。

第九条

本公约任何缔约国得对本公约提出修正案。修正案对于每一接受修正案的缔约国应在过半数缔约国接受该修正案时发生效力，嗣后对于其余每个缔约国应在该缔约国接受修正案之日发生效力。

第十条

本公约生效十年以后，应在联合国大会的临时议程内列入复核本公约的问题，以便按照公约过去施行情形，考虑其是否需要修订。但在本公约生效五年以后的任何时期，如经缔约国三分之一的请求并征得多数缔约国的同意，应即召开缔约国会议复核本公约。此种复核应特别涉及任何相关的技术发展情形，包括有关识别外空物体的技术发展情形。

第十一条

本公约任何缔约国应在本公约生效一年以后以书面通知联合国秘书长退出本公约。退出公约应自接获该通知之日起一年后发生效力。

第十二条

本公约原本应交存联合国秘书长，其阿拉伯文、中文、英文、法文、俄文及西班牙文本同样作准。秘书长应将本公约经证明的副本分送所有签字国和加入国。

为此，下列签字人，经各别政府正式授权，签字于本公约，以昭信守。

本公约于1975年1月14日在纽约由各国签署。

文件精选

Convention on Registration of Objects Launched into Outer Space (done 14 January 1975, came into force 15 September 1976) 1023 UNTS 15 (REG)

UNGA Res. 1721 B (XVI), International co-operation in the peaceful uses of outer space, 20 December 1961

UNGA Res. 1962 (XVIII), Declaration of Legal Principles Governing the Activities of States in the Exploration and Use of Outer Space, 13 December 1963

UNGA Res. 41/66, Question of the review of the Convention on Registration of Objects Launched into Outer Space, 3 December 1986

UNGA Res. 62/101, Recommendations on Enhancing the Practice of States and International Intergovernmental Organizations in Registering Space Objects, 17 December 2007

UN Doc. A/AC. 105/382, UN Study on the Application of the Convention on Registration of Objects Launched into Outer Space, 2 March 1987

UN Doc. A/AC. 105/C. 2/L. 255, Practice of States and International Organizations in Registering Space Objects, Background Paper by the Secretariat, 25 January 2005

参考文献精选

Benkö, Marietta/Schrogl, Kai-Uwe, The 1998 European Initiative in the UNCOPUOS Legal Subcommittee to Improve the Registration Convention, in: IISL, Proceedings of the 41st Colloquium on the Law of Outer Space, 28 September-2 October 1998 Melbourne (Australia), AIAA, 1999, pp. 58-64

Chatzipanagiotis, Michael, Registration of Space Objects and Transfer of Ownership in Orbit, Zeitschrift für Luft-und Weltraumrecht (56) 2007, pp. 229-238

Cheng, Bin, Space Objects and their Various Connecting Factors, in: Lafferanderie, Gabriel/Crowther, Daphné (eds.), Outlook on Space Law over the Next 30 Years: Essays published for the 30th Anniversary of the Outer Space Treaty, Kluwer Law International, The Hague 1997, pp. 203-215

Cocca, Aldo A., Convention on Registration of Objects Launched into Outer Space, in: Jasentuliyana, Nandasiri/Lee, Roy S. K. (eds.), Manual on Space Law, Volume I, Oceana Publications, New York 1979, pp. 173-193

Diederiks-Verschoor, I. H. Philepina, Observations on the Registration Convention, in: Jasentuliyana, Nandasiri (ed.), Maintaining Outer Space for Peaceful Uses-Proceedings of a Symposium held in the Hague, March 1984, United Nations University, Tokyo 1984, pp. 111-116

Diederiks-Verschoor, I. H. Philepina/Kopal, Vladimir, An Introduction to Space Law, 3rd edn., Kluwer Law International, The Hague 2008, pp. 44-48 (The Registration Convention of 1975)

von der Dunk, Frans G., The Registration Convention-Background and Historical Context, in: IISL, Proceedings of the 46th Colloquium on the Law of Outer Space, 29 September-3 October 2003 Bremen (Germany), AIAA, 2004, pp. 450-453

Hintz, Manfred, Weltraumgegenstände-Registrierung, in: Böckstiegel, Karl-Heinz (ed.), Handbuch des Weltraumrechts, Carl Heymanns, Cologne 1991, pp. 179-185

Hobe, Stephan/Schmidt-Tedd, Bernhard/Schrogl, Kai-Uwe (eds.), Proceedings of the Project 2001 Plus-Global and European Challenges for Air and Space Law at the Edge of the 21st Century: Workshop on Current Issues in the Registration of Space Objects, 20-21 January 2005 Berlin, Institute of Air and Space Law/Deutsches Zentrum für Luft- und Raumfahrt, Cologne 2005

Hörl, Kay-Uwe/Hermida, Julian, Change of Ownership, Change of Registry? Which Objects to Register, What data to be Furnished, When, and Until When?, in: IISL, Proceedings of the 46th Colloquium on the Law of Outer Space, 29 September-3 October 2003 Bremen (Germany), AIAA, 2004, pp. 454-463

Kopal, Vladimir, The 1975 Convention on Registration of Objects Launched into Outer Space in View of the Growth of Commercial Space Activities, in: Benkö, Marietta/Kröll, Walter (eds.), Luft- und Weltraumrecht im 21. Jahrhundert (Air and Space Law in the 21st Century) -Liber Amicorum Karl-Heinz Böckstiegel, Carl Heymanns, Cologne 2001, pp. 372-385

Lee, Yoon, Registration of space objects: ESA member states' practice, Space Policy (22) 2006, pp. 42-51

Marchisio, Sergio, International legal regime on outer space: Liability Convention and Registration Convention, in: United Nations Office for Outer Space Affairs, Proceedings of the United Nations/Nigeria Workshop on Space Law-Meeting international responsibilities and addressing domestic needs, 21-24 November 2005 Abuja (Nigeria), United Nations, Vienna 2006, pp. 21-30

Mick, Stephan, Registrierungskonvention und Registrierungspraxis: Aktuelle Rechtsfragen der Registrierung von Weltraumgegenständen, Carl Heymanns, Cologne 2007

Ospina, Sylvia, Revisiting the Registration Convention: A Proposal to Meet the Need to Know "What is up there", in: IISL, Proceedings of the 43rd Colloquium on the Law of Outer Space, 2-6 October 2000 Rio de Janeiro (Brazil), AIAA, 2001, pp. 199-209

Perek, Lubos, The 1976 Registration Convention, in: IISL, Proceedings of the 41st Colloquium on the Law of Outer Space, 28 September-2 October 1998 Melbourne (Australia), AIAA, 1999, pp. 374-384

Qizhi, He, The Registration Convention and Maintenance of the Peaceful Uses of Outer Space, in: Jasentuliyana, Nandasiri (ed.), Maintaining Outer Space for Peaceful Uses: Proceedings of a Symposium held in The Hague, March 1984, United Nations University, Tokyo 1984, pp. 117-120

Schmidt-Tedd, Bernhard/Gerhard, Michael, How to Adapt the Present Regime for Registration of Space Objects to New Developments in Space Applications?, in: IISL, Proceedings of the 48th Colloquium on the Law of Outer Space, 17-21 October 2005 Fukuoka (Japan), AIAA, 2006, pp. 353-363

Schmidt-Tedd, Bernhard/Gerhard, Michael, Registration of Space Objects: Which are the Advantages for States Resulting from Registration?, in: Benkö, Marietta/Schrogl, Kai-Uwe (eds.), Space Law: Current Problems and Perspectives For Future Regulation, Eleven, Utrecht 2005, pp. 121-140

Schmidt-Tedd, Bernhard/Pellander, Erik, From Cape Town to Berlin-a new instrument for financing space assets, The Aviation and Space Journal (11) 2012, pp. 32ff.

Williams, Maureen, The Registration Convention Thirty Years On, in: IISL, Proceedings of the 49th Colloquium on the Law of Outer Space, 2-6 October 2006 Valencia (Spain), AIAA, 2007, pp. 264-269

Williams, Maureen, The "Surprise" Convention on the Registration of Space Objects, Zeitschrift für Luft- und Weltraumrecht (28) 1979, pp. 122-129

Zhukov, Gennady P., Registration and Jurisdiction Aspects of the International Space Station, in: IISL, Proceedings of the 42nd Colloquium on the Law of Outer Space, 4-8

October 1999 Amsterdam (The Netherlands), AIAA, 2000, pp. 75-79

Zhukov, Gennady/Kolosov, Yuri (Belitzky, Boris (tr.)), International Space Law, Praeger, New York 1984, pp. 86-92

目　录

第一章　历史背景和上下文[①]

Schmidt-Tedd and Tennen

目录

一、历史背景

关于火箭和空间物体的特定发射和（或）轨道信息的国际披露程序的建立可以追溯到发射前披露做法，这些做法是1957—1958年国际地球物理年期间采用的。联合国和平利用外层空间特设委员会于1959年提出了发射到外层空间的航天器和物体的登记问题[②]。多个代表团提及了空间物体的识别和登记的必要性问题。联合国外空特设委员会的报告将“航天器的识别和登记以及发射协调”列为可优先处理的法律问题之一[③]。报告建议采用个别呼号和适当的标记来识别物体。报告指出，登记物体将有若干实际用途：有助于跟踪物体，提供通知其他国家的手段；有助于避免空间物体与

① Jasentuliyana, Nandasiri/Lee, Roy S. K. (eds.), Manual on Space Law, Volume II, Oceana Publications, New York 1979, pp. 23ff., 419ff., 469ff. and 531ff.; Diederiks-Verschoor, I. H. Philepina, Observations on the Registration Convention, in: Jasentuliyana, Nandasiri (ed.), Maintaining Outer Space for Peaceful Uses-Proceedings of a Symposium held in The Hague, March 1984, United Nations University, Tokyo 1984, pp. 111ff.

② UN Doc. A/4141, Report of the Ad Hoc Committee on the Peaceful Uses of Outer Space, 14 July 1959, reprinted in: Jasentuliyana, Nandasiri/Lee, Roy S. K. (eds.), Manual on Space Law, Volume IV, Oceana Publications, New York 1981, pp. 703ff.

③ Ibid.

航空器之间的物理干扰；有助于检索返回地球的物体①。

1961年，联合国大会通过了第1721 B（XVI）号决议，呼吁各国“通过秘书长向和平利用外层空间委员会（以下简称联合国外空委）迅速提供信息，用于登记发射”，并请“秘书长保持一份对这些信息的公共登记册”②。1962年，国际空间研究委员会（COSPAR）颁布了关于基础数据发射安排和报告标准化的规则。COSPAR的规则强调及时和完整的报告③。

第1721 B（XVI）号决议建立的登记框架是自愿性质的，而在联合国外空委会内有关缔结一项正式条约意愿的讨论仍在继续，以赋予各国向国际社会披露有关发射到空间的物体的基本数据之义务。包括法国④和加拿大⑤在内的一些国家提交了拟议的条约草案，或以其他方式支持强制性披露的要求。然而，对于是否应要求各国以国际公认的标识对空间物体进行标记，存在着重大分歧⑥。

空间物体的标记将直接服务于登记的主要目的之一，即协助识别一国在地球表面上发现的物体，或可能涉及与另一空间物体碰撞的物体，或可能需要识别该物体的任何其他情况。制定一项有关登记的条约的其他目的还包括空间交通管理和安全⑦。登记条约的首要目的是促进为和平目的探索和利用外层空间。建立和维持公共登记册被认为是确保外层空间完全用于和平目的的不可或缺的条件⑧。一个“井然有序、完整和信息丰富的登记册”将减少大规模毁灭性武器被“偷偷摸摸地”送入轨道的可能

① Cocca, Aldo A., Convention on Registration of Objects Launched into Outer Space, in: Jasentuliyana, Nandasiri/Lee, Roy S. K. (eds.), Manual on Space Law, Volume I, Oceana Publications, New York 1979, pp. 173f.

② There has been a development in the use of the terms 'registry' and 'register'; the terminology is nowadays harmonized in such a way that on national level the term is 'registry' and on the UN level 'register'.

③ Cocca, Aldo A., Convention on Registration of Objects Launched into Outer Space, in: Jasentuliyana, Nandasiri/Lee, Roy S. K. (eds.), Manual on Space Law, Volume I, Oceana Publications, New York 1979, pp. 173f.

④ UN Doc. A/AC/105/C. 2/L. 45, Draft Convention Concerning the Registration of Objects Launched into Space for the Exploration or Use of Outer Space, 18 June 1968.

⑤ UN Doc. A/AC/105/C. 2/L. 83, 20 April 1972.

⑥ Cocca, Aldo A., Convention on Registration of Objects Launched into Outer Space, in: Jasentuliyana, Nandasiri/Lee, Roy S. K. (eds.), Manual on Space Law, Volume I, Oceana Publications, New York 1979, pp. 176-179.

⑦ Ibid, p. 174.

⑧ Qizhi, He, The Registration Convention and Maintenance of Peaceful Uses of Outer Space, in: Jasentuliyana, Nandasiri (ed.), Maintaining Outer Space for Peaceful Uses: Proceedings of a Symposium held in The Hague, March 1984, United Nations University, Tokyo 1984, p. 118.

性，以及由此产生的相关猜疑。[①]

关于该条约的工作始于 1968 年，并最终达成《关于登记射入外层空间物体的公约》（以下简称《登记公约》）[②]。法国向联合国提出了一项关于国际登记协定的具体建议[③]，除其他内容外，包括由每个发射国保持国家空间登记处的设想以及该登记册所载基本资料的清单。然而，在 1968 年和 1969 年举行的第七届和第八届会议上，联合国外空委没有很好地接受法国的建议，主要原因是各国对这种登记制度的实际运行和技术可行性表示关切。因此，1969 年，法律小组委员会首先通过了一项决议，建议联合国外空委邀请科技小组委员会研究登记相关的技术问题[④]。科技小组委员会编写的报告并不十分支持标记问题。其得出的结论是，基于当时的技术水平，一个能够在重返大气层后继续存在的标记系统是不切实际的[⑤]。

1972 年，加拿大提出了第二项提案[⑥]。法国和加拿大的提案随后合并为一个统一文本[⑦]。这项新提案包含序言和十项基本条款。在此基础上，联合国外空委法律小组委员会设立了一个特别工作组，负责拟订一项国际登记公约草案，最终包括序言和九个条款[⑧]。随后，美国提出了一项新的建议[⑨]，并准备参加随后的工作组。加拿大和

① Diederiks-Verschoor, I. H. Philepina/Kopal, Vladimir, An Introduction to Space Law, 3rd edn., Kluwer Law International, The Hague 2008, pp. 44-48 (The Registration Convention of 1975).

② Convention on Registration of Objects Launched into Outer Space (done 14 January 1975, entered into force 15 September 1976) 1023 UNTS 15 (REG).

③ UN Doc. A/AC. 105/C. 2/L. 45, France: Proposal, Draft Convention Concerning the Registration of Objects Launched into Space for the Exploration or Use of Outer Space, 18 June 1968, reproduced in: UN Doc. A/AC. 105/58, Report of the Legal Sub-Committee on the Work of Its Eighth Session (9 June-4 July 1969), Annex I, Proposals Concerning Questions Relative to the Definition of Outer Space and the Utilization of Outer Space and Celestial Bodies, Including the Various Implications of Space Communications, 4 July 1969.

④ UN Doc. A/AC. 105/C. 2/L. 55 and Rev. 1, Canada: Proposal, 13 June 1969, reproduced in: UN Doc. A/AC. 105/58, Report of the Legal Sub-Committee on the Work of Its Eighth Session (9 June-4 July 1969), Annex I, Proposals Concerning Questions Relative to the Definition of Outer Space and the Utilization of Outer Space and Celestial Bodies, Including the Various Implications of Space Communications, 4 July 1969.

⑤ UN Doc. A/AC. 105/82, 1 May 1970.

⑥ UN Doc. A/AC. 105/C. 2/L. 82, 4 April 1972.

⑦ UN Doc. A/AC. 105/C. 2/L. 83, 20 April 1972.

⑧ UN Doc. PUOS/C. 2/WG. 2/XI/5 and Corr. 1 and Add. 1, Legal Subcommittee Working Group Proposal, 1972.

⑨ UN Doc. A/AC. 105/C. 2/L. 85, US Proposal, 19 March 1973.

法国提出了其共同草案的修订版本[①]。阿根廷随后也提出了提案[②]。这些提案的主要差异在于是选择一个中央登记册或是不同的国家登记册。此外，还讨论了数据的传送应是强制性的还是自愿的问题。考虑到这些问题，工作组终于提出了包含序言和 10 个条款的统一文本[③]。除了一些进一步的修订和改变之外，该草案也是最后确定《登记公约》的基础。但是，由于该文本未载有关于对空间物体进行强制性标记的规定，因此被一些国家所拒绝。强制标识问题成为 1974 年第十三届会议的中心议题。加拿大提出了这方面的新提案[④]，阿根廷、巴西、印度、墨西哥、尼日利亚和苏丹也提出了一项联合提案[⑤]。1974 年 5 月 28 日，法律小组委员会通过了《登记公约》的最后草案，其中包含序言以及 12 个条款[⑥]。

《登记公约》与《关于各国探索和利用包括月球和其他天体在内外层空间活动的原则条约》(《以下简称《外空条约》)[⑦]、《营救宇航员、送回宇航员和归还射入外层空间的物体的协定》(以下简称《营救协定》)[⑧] 和《空间物体所造成损害的国际责任公约》(以下简称《责任公约》)[⑨] 有许多联系，特别是在管辖和控制、归还非发射国收回的物体以及空间物体所造成损害的赔偿责任方面[⑩]。然而，这些其他条约并不以登记国作为联系要素。例如，《营救协定》提及“发射当局”，因而认识到可能

---

① UN Doc A/AC. 105/C. 2/L. 86, Canadian/French Proposal, 27 March 1973.

② UN Doc. A/AC. 105/C. 2/L. 87, Argentina, 11 April 1973.

③ UN Doc. A/AC. 105/115, Report of the Legal Sub-Committee on the Work of its Twelfth Session (26 March-20 April 1973), Annex II, Documents Relating to Agenda Item 3 (Draft Convention on Registration of Objects Launched into Space for the Exploration or Use of Outer Space), Argentina: Working Paper, 20 April 1973; Christol, Carl Q., The Modern International Law of Outer Space, Pergamon Press, New York 1982, p. 229.

④ UN Doc. A/AC. 105/C. 2/L. 92, 7 May 1974.

⑤ UN Doc. A/AC. 105/C. 2/L. 94, 10 May 1974.

⑥ UN Doc. A/AC. 105/C. 2/13, Draft Convention on Registration of Objects Launched into Outer Space, 28 May 1974, reproduced in: UN Doc. A/AC. 105/133, Report of the Legal Sub-Committee on the Work of its 13th session (6-31 May 1974), 6 June 1974, para. 24.

⑦ Treaty on Principles Governing the Activities of States in the Exploration and Use of Outer Space, including the Moon and Other Celestial Bodies (done 27 January 1967, entered into force 10 October 1967) 610 UNTS 205 (OST).

⑧ Agreement on the Rescue of Astronauts, the Return of Astronauts and the Return of Objects Launched into Outer Space (done 22 April 1968, entered into force 3 December 1968) 672 UNTS 119 (ARRA).

⑨ Convention on International Liability for Damage Caused by Space Objects (done 29 March 1972, entered into force 1 September 1972) 961 UNTS 187 (LIAB).

⑩ Chatzipanagiotis, Michael, Registration of Space Objects and Transfer of Ownership in Orbit, Zeitschrift für Luft- und Weltraumrecht (56) 2007, p. 235.

有未被任何国家登记的空间物体[①]。同样，《外空条约》和《责任公约》提及“发射国”，这一概念也完全适用，特别是在没有对空间物体进行登记的情况下。

《登记公约》留下了很多未加规定之处，至少有学者批评说，公约推翻了管辖权和控制权应当随登记而转移的最初原则[②]。根据其观点，这种推翻不仅仅是语义或术语方面的，而是实质性的问题，因为《登记公约》允许共同发射的国家就管辖权和控制权作出自己的安排，从而将这些要素与登记分开，而不要求将其记录在登记册中。在（政府间）国际组织登记的情况下，情况会更加复杂，这似乎是《登记公约》第四条和第七条所允许的[③]。虽然该组织的成员可以就管辖权和控制权作出自己的安排，但一个组织，甚至欧洲空间局（欧空局）这样的国际政府组织，由于不是一个国家也无法行使主权管辖权和控制权。只有这些一般性权利和义务的要素可以移交给一个国际政府组织，而绝不是全部内容。因此，该组织有义务指定一个会员国为主管实体，对该目标行使主权权力[④]。根据联合国《外空条约》的总体概念，特别是《外空条约》第六条第3句，填补这一空白以确保将管辖权与控制权清晰地分配给该政府间国际组织中的某一个成员国，将是可取的，尽管该国际组织在登记事项中的作用已被接受。最适当的解决办法是，如果政府间国际组织成员国之间没有特别协定，则将这一职能（管辖和控制）赋予其总部所在地国。

附：1961年12月20日1721B（XVI）号决议

外空和平使用之国际合作

大会，

---

① Cheng, Bin, Space Objects and their Various Connecting Factors, in: Lafferanderie, Gabriel/Crowther, Daphné (eds.), Outlook on Space Law over the Next 30 Years: Essays Published for the 30th Anniversary of the Outer Space Treaty, Kluwer Law International, The Hague 1997, pp. 205f.

② Ibid., pp. 214f.

③ Zhukov, Gennady P., Registration and Jurisdiction Aspects of the International Space Station, in: IISL, Proceedings of the 42nd Colloquium on the Law of Outer Space, 4-8 October 1999 Amsterdam (The Netherlands), AIAA, 2000, p. 77.

④ Zhukov, Gennady P./Kolosov, Yuri (Belitzky, Boris (tr.)), International Space Law, Praeger, New York 1984, p. 88 “[…] member-states have to reach agreement as to which of them shall exercise jurisdiction and control over the space objects by the organization, since the organization itself cannot have such powers.”; von der Dunk, Frans G., Private Enterprise and The Public Interest in the European ‘Spacescape’, IIASL, Leiden 1998, p. 237.

认为联合国应为外空和平探测及使用之国际合作之焦点，

一、请凡发射物体进入轨道或越出轨道之国家迅速经由秘书长向外空和平使用问题委员会提供情报，以便登记；

二、请秘书长设一公开登记册，登录依照上文第一段提供的资料；

三、请和平利用外层空间委员会与秘书长合作并充分利用秘书处的职能与资源，从事下列事项：

1. 与有关外空问题的政府组织及非政府组织保持密切联系；

2. 办理各国政府所自愿供给有关外空活动资料的交换事宜以辅助现有技术及科学交换，而不与之相重复；

3. 协助研究促进外空活动国际合作措施；

四、复请和平利用外层空间委员会将其为执行此等职务所作之安排以及其认为和平使用外空方面之重要发展，向大会具报。

二、上下文

1975 年 1 月 14 日的《登记公约》作为特别法，是对 1967 年 1 月 27 日《外空条约》第八条的进一步发展。《外空条约》第八条的基本规则又是联合国大会 1961 年 12 月 20 日第 1721 B（XVI）号决议的具体化。《外空条约》第八条第 1 句的内容已在 1963 年 12 月 13 日《关于各国探索和利用外层空间活动的法律原则宣言》中规定①。第八条中关于管辖权和控制权的基本原则通过援引的方式纳入了《登记公约》。正如该公约第二条第 2 款所体现的，这是该公约中的固有概念。

相关规则和承诺的顺序如下：联大第 1721 B（XVI）号决议呼吁发射物体进入轨道或轨道以外的外层空间的国家通过秘书长迅速向外空委提供信息，以便登记有关发射。秘书长应维持按照上述程序提供的信息的“公共登记册”②。在这一阶段，联合国登记册被界定为唯一的焦点。此后的《外空条约》第八条意味着出现了国家登记册。这就引入了联合国登记册和国家登记册这两种制度之间的区别。国家登记的法律

① Compare the nearly identical No. 7: “The State on whose registry an object launched in outer space is carried shall retain jurisdiction and control over such object, and any personnel thereon, while in outer space.”

② At that time the wording used on UN level was ‘public registry’, but today it should read ‘public register’.

效力对于保有对外层空间这类物体的管辖权和控制权具有决定性作用。因此，国家登记册在法律上具有一定的优先地位，而联合国登记册具有保存信息和文件的作用，使得国家登记更加透明，并对公众以及特定事实开放，而这一点必须在国际舞台上加以考虑。《登记公约》继续本着这种精神，建立了一个强制性框架。根据《登记公约》第二条第 1 段，发射国有义务登记射入或越出地球轨道的物体，并为此目的建立和维持适当的登记册。在此基础上，发射国应按照《登记公约》的规定通知秘书长。相应地，《登记公约》第三条规定联合国登记册是强制性的，并规定登记册中的信息应对外开放。

区分《外空条约》第八条的现状和《登记公约》中的法律制度在今天仍然具有实际意义。并非所有发射国都是《登记公约》的缔约国，且三个法律文件的约束力各不相同。《登记公约》是一项在本公约缔约国之间具有约束力的国际条约。《外空条约》已超过 100 个缔约国①，包括大多数航天国家，此外在很大程度上已成为国际习惯法。登记空间物体的一般义务是普遍接受的原则之一。此外，这一规则也符合航空器和船舶的类似义务，而不是本公约所特有的概念。1961 年第 1721 B（XVI）号决议属于所谓的“软法”范畴，但实质上是后来的《外空条约》第十一条中国家信息义务的具体化。为了评估不同主体在有关条约遵守的不同地位下的实际义务，这一复杂情况应被考虑在内。

① With its accession on 10 March 2009 it was the Democratic People's Republic of Korea that contributed the 100th ratification to the OST. As of 1 January 2019 the OST had 107 parties to the treaty.

第二章 《登记公约》评注

目录

国家实践在相关条款和段落的背景中都有说明，“第二条第1款”是关于建立登记册以及向联合国提供的国家信息；“第二条第2款”是关于两个或更多发射国的国家实践；“第二条第4款”是关于普遍的国家登记实践；“第四条”是关于向联合国提供空间物体信息的国家实践。

一、序言

本公约缔约国，

承认全体人类为和平目的而促进探索及利用外层空间的共同利益，

回顾一九六七年一月二十七日的《关于各国探索和利用包括月球和其他天体在内外层空间的活动所应遵守原则的条约》内曾确认各国对其本国在外层空间的活动

应负国际责任，并提到射入外层空间的物体登记备案的国家，

又回顾一九六八年四月二十二日的《关于营救宇航员、送回宇航员和归还发射到外层空间的物体的协定》规定，一个发射当局对于其射入外层空间而在发射当局领域界限之外发现的物体，经请求时，应在交还前提供证明资料，

再回顾一九七二年三月二十九日的《关于外空物体所造成损害的国际责任公约》确立了关于发射国家对其外空物体造成的损害所负责任的国际规则和程序，

盼望根据关于各国探索和利用外层空间包括月球与其他天体活动所应遵守原则的条约，拟订由发射国登记其射入外层空间物体的规定，

还盼望在强制的基础上设置一个由联合国秘书长保持的射入外层空间物体总登记册，

也盼望为缔约国提供另外的方法和程序，借以帮助辨认外空物体，相信一种强制性的登记射入外层空间物体的制度，将特别可以帮助辨认此等物体，并有助于管理探索和利用外层空间的国际法的施行和发展，

兹协议如下：

（一）谈判和起草历史

法国提出的最初草案①序言很短，并提及《外空条约》中与登记有关的措辞，以及有关国际登记的共同规则的一般好处。相比之下，后来的加拿大②和加拿大—法国联合草案③包括最终版本的基本要素，即提及前面三项条约——《外空条约》《营救协定》和《责任公约》；正面提及国际登记制度，促进空间物体识别的目标和通过强制性登记制度以改进现有自愿通知制度的愿望。在共同草案④的更正中，对下列要点作了修改："根据请求"，查明《营救协定》相关条款中的数据，《责任公约》相关条

① UN Doc. A/AC. 105/C. 2/L. 45, France: Proposal, Draft Convention Concerning the Registration of Objects Launched into Space for the Exploration or Use of Outer Space, 18 June 1968, reproduced in: UN Doc. A/AC. 105/58, Report of the Legal Sub-Committee on the Work of Its Eighth Session (9 June-4 July 1969), Annex I, Proposals Concerning Questions Relative to the Definition of Outer Space and the Utilization of Outer Space and Celestial Bodies, Including the Various Implications of Space Communications, 4 July 1969.

② UN Doc. A/AC. 105/C. 2/L. 82, 4 April 1972.

③ UN Doc. A/AC. 105/C. 2/L. 83, 20 April 1972.

④ UN Doc. A/AC. 105/C. 2/L. 83/Corr. 1, 25 April 1972.

款中“与赔偿责任相关的规则和程序”，更加接近强制性制度条款方面的最终措辞，并对联合国现有登记册进行了积极反思，但后一版本推翻了这一建议。美国的草案①在序言方面没有根本不同，并采取了当时较为统一的结构，仅措辞略加修改。在提及《外空条约》的段落中其措辞为“指对发射到外层空间的物体的登记”，而不是后来的措辞——“指发射到外层空间的物体登记在册的国家”。

在第二工作组的一份草案和法律小组委员会的公约草案中②，有关于进一步提及正在谈判的《月球协定》③ 的提议。最后，该提议留待联合国外空委作出决定，其最终删除了拟议段落。尽管 1974 年 5 月 28 日法律小组委员会的草案进行了三次正式调整（增加了提及的条约的日期），但其仍然是联合国外空委向联合国大会推荐的文本。

Cocca 承认序言是“公约最值得称赞的部分……因为其明确说明了该文件的宗旨以及为何需要这样一项文件”④。同时，他感到遗憾的是，并非所有实质性条款都完全反映了这一精神。

（二）评注

序言部分分为十段，其主题如下：

1. 缔约国
2. 认识到共同利益
3. 回顾《外空条约》
4. 回顾《营救协定》
5. 回顾《责任公约》
6. 盼望对国家登记作出规定
7. 盼望在强制性基础上维持联合国登记册

---

① UN Doc. A/AC. 105/C. 2/L. 85, 19 March 1973.

② UN Doc. A/AC. 105/115, Report of the Legal Sub-Committee on the Work of its Twelfth Session (26 March-20 April 1973), Annex II, Documents Relating to Agenda Item 3 (Draft Convention on Registration of Objects Launched into Space for the Exploration or Use of Outer Space), Argentina: Working Paper, 20 April 1973; UN Doc. A/AC. 105/C. 2/13, Draft Convention on Registration of Objects Launched into Outer Space, 28 May 1974.

③ The negotiations resulted in the establishment of the Agreement Governing the Activities of States on the Moon and Other Celestial Bodies (done 18 December 1979, entered into force 11 July 1984) 1363 UNTS 3 (hereinafter MOON).

④ Cocca, Aldo A., Convention on Registration of Objects Launched into Outer Space, in: Jasentuliyana, Nandasiri/Lee, Roy S. K. (eds.), Manual on Space Law, Volume I, Oceana Publications, New York 1979, p. 179.

8. 盼望协助识别（空间物体）

9. 相信强制性制度

10. 达成协议

除开头的半句导语和最后的过渡短语外，序言中有 8 段实质性内容。第二段以“承认”开始，与《责任公约》的相应段落相同。以下三段是“回顾”已有空间条约并具体提及登记事项。随后的三段以“盼望“一词引入，反映了公约缔约国的主要动机和规制手段，即规定国家登记、建立和维持强制性的联合国中心登记册以及协助识别空间物体。接下来的段落以“相信”一词开始，总结了关于强制性登记制度的两个基本期望，即加强对空间物体的识别，以及对有关探索和利用外层空间的国际法的适用和发展作出贡献。

序言部分概括了《登记公约》的主要目的，即协助识别空间物体，并对有关探索和利用外层空间的国际法作出贡献。最后一点应该与《外空条约》第六、七和八条相结合看待。正如 Kopal 所得出的结论，《登记公约》的基本方法是“……确定射入外层空间的物体与将该物体登入其登记册的发射国之间的法律联系，以确保对该物体的管辖权和控制权”①。正如 Kopal 进一步阐述的，这是关键的法律要素，不应与其他目标相混淆，如科学和技术数据的分配等。

二、第一条（定义）

为了本公约的目的：

1. “发射国”一词是指

（1）一个发射或促使发射外空物体的国家；

（2）一个从其领土上或设备发射外空物体的国家。

2. “外空物体”一词包括一个外空物体的组成部分以及外空物体的发射载器及其零件。

---

① Kopal, Vladimir, The 1975 Convention on Registration of Objects Launched into Outer Space in View of the Growth of Commercial Space Activities, in: Benkö, Marietta/Kröll, Walter (eds.), Luft- und Weltraumrecht im 21. Jahrhundert (Air and Space Law in the 21st Century) -Liber Amicorum Karl-Heinz Böckstiegel, Carl Heymanns, Cologne 2001, pp. 375f.

3. “登记国”一词是指一个依照第二条将外空物体登入其登记册的发射国。

目录

（一）谈判和起草历史

此定义条款的基本结构是基于最早的加拿大公约草案[①]。在加拿大—法国联合草案中增加了“登记国”的定义[②]。后一草案还做出了以更精确的方式定义“空间物体”这一术语的有趣尝试，即“一个为探索和利用外空，包括月球和其他天体之目的而发射到外空的物体，无论是有人或无人的。本术语包括其发射和运输装置，无论是否可回收，以及将被放置于外空轨道的载荷或人造卫星”。即使此解释未被纳入最终的《登记公约》，该草案也体现了该术语定义背后的涵义。在后续的谈判中仅仅对其作出了细微的修改：“登记国”成为该定义中的第三个术语，该定义中使用了“one whose registry”的表述（而非“register”），以区分联合国登记册和国家登记册。此外，该定义中还增加了“依照第二条”的表述。

（二）评注

《登记公约》包含三个定义，其中两个与《责任公约》的定义相同。《登记公约》第一条第1款第（1）、（2）项中的“发射国”与《责任公约》第一条第3项第（1）、（2）项中的定义相同。“登记国”的定义是在《登记公约》中形成的。

1. 发射国

作为发射国的资格可通过四项标准来满足，即：（1）发射；或（2）促使发射空间物体的国家；以及（3）从其领土；或（4）从其设施发射空间物体的国家。有关空

① UN Doc. A/AC. 105/C. 2/L. 82，4 April 1972.
② UN Doc. A/AC. 105/C. 2/L. 83，20 April 1972.

间物体或发射活动是政府还是非政府的并不重要。在这两种情况下，作为发射国的资格取决于根据《外空条约》第六条对这些活动负责的缔约国。

发射国的四项标准在责任分配中是否应有等级顺序的问题，是起草《责任公约》的关键问题之一①。一些国家主张，发射国或促使发射国相对于在其设施或领土上发射的国家负有首要责任。根据此类草案，只有在无法确定前者的情况下，后一国家才应承担责任②。这一观点最终被放弃了。目前，在第 1（c）（i）项中提到的标准和第

① See UN Doc. A/AC. 105/C. 2/L. 7, Working Paper Submitted by the Belgian Delegation on the Unification of Certain Rules Governing Liability for Damage Caused by Space Devices, 29 April 1963, Art. 2, reproduced in: UN Doc. A/AC. 105/12, Report of the Legal Sub-Committee on the Work of its Second Session (16 April-3 May 1963), 6 May 1963, Annex I, p. 11; UN Doc. A/AC. 105/C. 2/L. 8, United States: Proposal-Convention concerning liability for damage caused by the launching of objects into outer space, 9 March 1964, Art. I lit. (e) (ii), reproduced in: UN Doc. A/AC. 105/19, Report of the Legal Sub-Committee on the Work of its Third Session (9-26 March 1964), 26 March 1964, Annex II, Proposals and amendments relating to liability for damage caused by objects launched into outer space, p. 3; UN Doc. A/AC. 105/C. 2/L. 10, Hungary: Proposed draft agreement-Agreement concerning liability for damage caused by the launching of objects into outer space, [Date n/a], Art. Ⅶ, reproduced in: UN Doc. A/AC. 105/19, Report of the Legal Sub-Committee on the Work of its Third Session (9-26 March 1964), 26 March 1964, Annex II, Proposals and amendments relating to liability for damage caused by objects launched into outer space, p. 8; UN Doc. A/AC. 105/C. 2/L. 8/Rev. 1, WG. II/19, Italy: Amendments to article 1 of the United States draft, reproduced in: UN Doc. A/AC. 105/21, Report of the Legal Sub-Committee on the Work of the Second Part of its Third Session (5-23 October 1964), 23 October 1964, Annex II, Proposals and amendments relating to liability for damage caused by objects launched into outer space, p. 18; UN Doc. A/AC. 105/29, Report of the Legal Sub-Committee on the Work of its Fourth Session (20 September-1 October 1965), 1 October 1965, p. 5; UN Doc. A/AC. 105/37, Report of the Legal Sub-Committee on the Work of its Sixth Session (19 June-14 July 1967), 14 July 1967, p. 6.

② See UN Doc. A/AC. 105/C. 2/L. 7/Rev. 3, Belgium: Proposal for a Convention on the Unification of Certain Rules Governing Liability for Damages caused by Space Devices to Third Parties on the Surface of the Earth and to Aircraft in Flight, Art. 2, reproduced in: UN Doc. A/AC. 105/37, Report of the Legal Sub-Committee on the Work of its Sixth Session (19 June-14 July 1967), 14 July 1967, Annex II, Proposals, amendments and other documents relating to liability for damage caused by the launching of objects into outer space, p. 1; UN Doc. A/AC. 105/C. 2/L. 40, Working Paper submitted by the Italian delegation-Draft convention concerning liability for damage caused by the launching of objects into outer space, [Date n/a], Art. 2 para. 2, reproduced in: UN Doc. A/AC. 105/45, Report of the Legal Sub-Committee on the Work of its Seventh Session (4-28 June 1968), 11 July 1968, Annex I, Proposals, amendments and other documents relating to liability for damage caused by the launching of objects into outer space, p. 30; UN Doc. A/AC. 105/C. 2/L. 36/Rev. 1, France: revised proposal concerning the State liable and joint and several liability, para. 3, in: UN Doc. A/AC. 105/45, Report of the Legal Sub-Committee on the Work of its Seventh Session (4-28 June 1968), 11 July 1968, Annex I, Proposals, amendments and other documents relating to liability for damage caused by the launching of objects into outer space, p. 41; and UN Doc. A/AC. 105/C. 2/L. 39, Australia: Proposal, in: UN Doc. A/AC. 105/45, Report of the Legal Sub-Committee on the Work of its Seventh Session (4-28 June 1968), 11 July 1968, Annex I, Proposals, amendments and other documents relating to liability for damage caused by the launching of objects into outer space, p. 42.

1（c）（ii）项是同等的。[1] 值得注意的是，美国和苏联作为主要的发射服务提供者，因而也是潜在的被告国，却在其第一稿草案中主张采用更广泛的概念[2]。

“发射国”的四项标准中，《登记公约》第一条第1款第（1）项中的两项标准是行动导向和决策导向的。发射或促使发射的行为者背后的国家获得了作为空间物体发射国的责任，因为没有这个国家或负责的行为者，该空间物体就不会被放置在外层空间。相较而言，第一条第1款第（2）项中的两个标准是基于空间物体或领土的，二者与发射场的国籍有关，或为发射设施的国家链接点。任何让别国从其领土进行发射的国家都必然会成为发射国。反之亦然，一国租用发射设施给外国也必然会成为发射国。根据联合国空间法下的定义，租赁合同下的双边安排对发射国的资格没有影响。这是相关国家之间的内部事务。

这方面的一个实际例子是，根据哈萨克斯坦与俄罗斯签订的发射场租赁合同，如何判断位于哈萨克斯坦境内的拜科努尔航天发射场的地位[3]。这两个国家都参与了该发射场的任何发射。俄罗斯联邦政府与哈萨克斯坦共和国政府之间的《拜科努尔建筑

① Compare also the wording of Art. V para. 3 LIAB：“A State from whose territory or facility a space object is launched shall be regarded as participating in a joint launching.”.

② See chapter on LIAB in this volume, Commentary LIAB, Article I, mn. 40.

③ In accordance with a number of bilateral agreements concluded between Russia and Kazakhstan concerning the use of the Baikonur cosmodrome, this space complex is leased to Russia until 2050. See Agreement between the Russian Federation and the Republic of Kazakhstan on the Basic Principles and Conditions of the Utilization of the Baikonur Cosmodrome（done 28 March 1994）; Lease Agreement on the Baikonur Complex between the Government of the Russian Federation and the Government of the Republic of Kazakhstan（done 10 December 1994）; and Agreement between the Russian Federation and the Republic of Kazakhstan on the Development of Cooperation Concerning the Effective Utilization of the Baikonur Cosmodrome（done 9 January 2004）. Under the Agreement between Russia and Kazakhstan dated 23 December 1995 “On the status of the city of Baikonur, order of formation and the status of its executive bodies” the Kazakh city of Baikonur is granted a status corresponding to the status of Russian federal cities, but with a special operation mode of facilities, enterprises and organizations, as well as a special residence regulation for the citizens. The agreements can be accessed on the website of the Kazakh space agency, Kazkosmos: <http://kazcosmos.gov.kz/ru/international/sotrudnichestvo-s-rossijskoj-federacziej.html> accessed 26 April 2019.

群租赁协定》（1994 年 12 月 10 日签订）载有一项在国际公法背景下可能被误解的表述：①

“8. 4. 租赁人承诺：

……

g）对于一项在拜科努尔航天发射场执行俄罗斯空间项目的活动，在造成损害的情况下，根据 1972 年 3 月 29 日《关于空间物体所造成损害的国际责任公约》，俄罗斯作为发射国应承担赔偿责任。因此，哈萨克斯坦共和国不被视为联合发射的参与者，也不被视为发射国。在空间物体的发射是由俄罗斯和哈萨克斯坦共和国共同进行的情况下，损害的赔偿责任根据上述《责任公约》第五条确定。”

该双边租赁协议规定按《责任公约》第五条第 2 款第 2 句提议的方式对风险和赔偿进行了内部分配。这并不改变有关作为发射国资格的国际公法状况。一项从拜科努尔进行的发射即是从哈萨克领土进行的发射②。1936 年，哈萨克斯坦的地位被提升为联盟共和国，即苏联（苏维埃社会主义共和国联盟）内的哈萨克苏维埃社会主义共和国（Kazakh SSR）。1991 年苏联解体后，哈萨克斯坦共和国成为一个独立国家。2012 年 1 月 6 日颁布的新的哈萨克斯坦空间立法③中有一条专门关于拜科努尔航天发射场

---

① Unofficial translation of the original Russian text, as follows：

“8. 4. Арендаторобязуется：

[…]

г）в случае нанесения ущерба，связанного с деятельностью космодрома “Байконур” при выполнении российских космических программ，Россия несет ответственность как запускающее государство в соответствии с Конвенцией о международной ответст венности за ущерб，причиненный космическими объектами от 29 март а 1972 года. При этом Республика Казахстан не рассматривается в качестве участника совместного запуска либо запускающего государст ва.

В случае，когда запуск космического объект а осущест вляет ся Россией совмест но с Республикой Казахстан，ответ ственность за ущерб определяется ст . V указанной Конвенции.”.

② The term ‘territory’ under international law is in so far clear that during the drafting of REG and LIAB it did not seem necessary to define it：See UN Doc. A/AC. 105/21，Report of the Legal Sub-Committee on the work of the second part of its third session（5-23 October 1964），23 October 1964，Annex IV，Summary of views expressed in Working Groups I and II，p. 17.

③ Law of the Republic of Kazakhstan on Space Activity No. 528-IV（6 January 2012），German translation in Schmidt-Tedd，Bernhard/Stelmakh，Olga，Einführung in das Gesetz der Republik Kasachstan über Weltraumaktivitäten，Zeitschrift für Luft- und Weltraumrecht（61）2012，p. 432ff.；English comments in：Schmidt-Tedd，Bernhard/Stelmakh，Olga，Capacity-Building of the National Space Legislation in Post-Soviet Countries：The Recent Contribution of Kazakhstan，in：IISL，Proceedings of the 55th Colloquium on the Law of Outer Space，（IAC-12-E7. 5. 4），1-5 October 2012 Naples（Italy），AIAA，（forthcoming）.

的地位（第二十三条）的特别条款，将其界定为不可私有化的哈萨克战略资产。虽然这一国内法没有改变国际空间法，但其表明了拜科努尔航天发射场的国有性质。

上述平行有效的四项标准[①]形成了对责任进行充分分配的保证，并避免了没有对特定空间物体负责的发射国的情况。登记与发射国相联系，这意味着一个主要责任国的圈子，并将管辖权和控制权分配给该群体中的一个国家；在不止一个发射国的情况下，应通过它们之间的具体协定确定如何分配。在某些情况下，属于“促使发射”的发射国数目可能相当多。就欧洲联盟（以下简称欧盟）的大型伽利略项目而言，发射国数目是欧盟成员国的总数，并可能包含发射场所在国家。如果是可选的欧空局项目，则是所有宣布愿意根据项目声明促成发射的参与国。

2. 空间物体

对“空间物体”一词的解释在某种程度上是一种澄清，而不是真正的定义。空间物体的组成部分及其运载工具和部件都包括在空间物体这一术语中。这就避免了限制性解释的可能性，也避免了在完整纳入相关物体和该物体登记之间的任何空白。

即使“空间物体”这一术语没有定义，但人们普遍认为，空间物体是指发射或意图发射到外层空间的任何人造物体。因此，并非每个空间物体都一定已经到达外层空间。因此，登记的法律义务（《登记公约》第二条第 1 款）不仅与“空间物体”这个术语相关，还与“发射”这个附加标准相关[②]。

对“空间物体”的具有弹性的表述，即一方面包括其组成部分，另一方面包括其发射运载器与零件，对于登记实践而言具有诸多好处。该全面的定义确保了对特定发射事件中的物体的完全责任。共同发射国负有责任决定哪位同伴应当登记哪个物体。在由发射服务提供者进行发射的情况下，大体上，最为充分的解决方案是发射服务提供者登记到达轨道的火箭上面级，而有效载荷客户（或其后的国家）登记该有效载荷。但是，只要有效载荷客户尚未单独登记其有效载荷，该有效载荷在法律意义上仍然是发射运载器登记的一部分（《登记公约》第一条第 2 款）。如未经登记其就不具有对该有效载荷的独立的管辖权和控制权，反之亦然。这意味着如果有效载荷先被登

① Cheng, Bin, Space Objects and their Various Connecting Factors, in: Lafferanderie, Gabriel/Crowther, Daphné (eds.), Outlook on Space Law over the Next 30 Years: Essays Published for the 30th Anniversary of the Outer Space Treaty, Kluwer Law International, The Hague 1975, p. 210: “[…] there can potentially be four different States, or even four different groups of States […]”.

② See Art. II para. 1 REG.

记，而火箭上面级未（按当事方之间达成的协议）登记，那么发射运载器就是所登记的有效载荷的一部分。该定义确保了在发射中没有参与国可以将其责任限制于硬件的某一单独部分，除非是两个或两个以上的发射国达成不同协议并经登记实现。这在单一发射国的情况下也具有非常重要的意义，因为该发射国可能会寻求仅登记发射中功能性的、对其有利的部件。对“空间物体”概念的限制性解释不是《登记公约》所提供的解决不登记和不遵守合同或国际义务的解决方案。相反，该定义方法最大程度地保证了对任一射入轨道的硬件的完全责任，从发射直至离轨，包括其失效的碎片和部件。

一方面，在某一发射中不同的子物体可以被独立登记（不同航程参与者之间的管辖权和控制权的分配）。但另一方面，清楚的是，某一发射中的所有发射国仍然对该发射中的全部硬件承担责任。这表明了有关登记的决定并不改变相关赔偿责任制度，因此可能根据有关管辖权和控制权的客观标准来加以决定。

“空间物体”的相应表述也为双边和多边合作提供了适当的解决办法。“空间物体”一词的灵活性使之能够在一个复杂结构中根据当事方的利益和意愿来分别登记每个国家的贡献并分配管辖权和控制权。例如，在苏联—美国共同运营的“联盟号-阿波罗”（1975 年）任务中，该组合航天器的每个模块都是单独登记的。因此，模块的管辖权和控制权被分配给了提供模块的相应国家①。后来的国际空间站（ISS）可以证明这一点，它是由不同国家提供的部分组成的综合体，不仅是临时性的，而且是一种长期的空间基础设施。

3. 登记国

“登记国”是指根据《登记公约》第二条将空间物体登入其登记册上的发射国。登记国的资格仅限于特定空间物体的发射国②。根据《登记公约》第二条第 2 款，某一特定空间物体仅应由一个国家进行登记。如果有关空间物体有两个或两个以上的发射国，则登记国为该组负有责任的发射国中的一个缔约国。该定义的最后半句澄清，

---

① Ezell, Edward C./Neuman Ezell, Linda, The Partnership: A History of the Apollo-Soyuz Test Project, NASA Special Publication 4209, 1978, online accessible at <http://www.hq.nasa.gov/pao/History/SP-4209/toc.htm> accessed 26 April 2019.

② Hintz, Manfred, Weltraumgegenstände-Registrierung, in: Böckstiegel, Karl-Heinz (ed.), Handbuch des Weltraumrechts, Carl Heymanns, Cologne 1991, pp. 179f. (Registration as the bridge between space object and launching State).

国家登记必须遵照《登记公约》第二条的规定。

三、第二条（国家登记册/登记义务）

1. 发射国在发射一个外空物体进入或越出地球轨道时，应以登入其所须保持的适当登记册的方式登记该外空物体。每一发射国应将其设置此种登记册情事通知联合国秘书长。

2. 任何此种外空物体有两个以上的发射国时，各该国应共同决定由其中的那一国依照本条第 1 款登记该外空物体，同时注意到《关于各国探索和利用包括月球与其他天体在内外层空间活动原则的条约》第八条的规定，并且不妨碍各发射国间就外空物体及外空物体上任何人员的管辖和控制问题所缔结的或日后缔结的适当协定。

3. 每一登记册的内容项目和保持登记册的条件应由有关的登记国决定。

目录

(5) 国内实践案例

3. 每一登记册的内容和条件 (第3款)

4. 后续国家实践 (缔约国和非缔约国)

(1)《登记公约》的缔约国

①俄罗斯联邦、哈萨克斯坦和某些东方国家

②美国/加拿大/英国/澳大利亚

③拉丁美洲 (阿根廷、巴西、智利、墨西哥和委内瑞拉)

④部分欧洲国家 (法国、德国、比利时、荷兰、意大利、西班牙、瑞典、希腊)

⑤亚洲国家 (日本、中国、印度)

(2) 非缔约国

5.《登记公约》之前和之外的通知

(一) 谈判和起草历史

是否应有一个中央登记册或者是缔约国的多个登记册，以及所提供的信息类型应为强制性的或者是由相关缔约国自行决定，是相关讨论中的核心问题。此外，还有第三个复杂的问题，即强制性和可选择性的标识问题。

法国的第一份草案[①]预见到在“一个或多个政府缔约方的监督下”的登记（第一条），并包括了一份强制性信息清单（第二条）。几个国家与一个空间物体相关联的方面体现在不同的“服务”，并朝着运营的方向发展。在随后的加拿大—法国联合提案[②]中，该词被“一个以上的发射国”所取代。它们必须在其中指定“登记国”。这一概念与《登记公约》第二条相一致，并对其进行了有趣的补充，即增加了“就发射的每个空间物体而言”。这清楚地表明，一次发射可能导致不同的登记，这对发射服务提供商来说是一个关键问题。不过，该提案也明确宣布“每个空间物体只应登记一次”（加拿大—法国草案第二条第1款第2句）。

---

① UN Doc. A/AC. 105/C. 2/L. 45, French Proposal, Draft Convention Concerning the Registration of Objects Launched into Space for the Exploration or Use of Outer Space, 18 June 1968, reproduced in: UN Doc. A/AC. 105/58, Report of the Legal Sub-Committee on the Work of Its Eighth Session (9 June-4 July 1969), Annex I, Proposals Concerning Questions Relative to the Definition of Outer Space and the Utilization of Outer Space and Celestial Bodies, Including the Various Implications of Space Communications, 4 July 1969.

② UN Doc. A/AC. 105/C. 2/L. 83, 20 April 1972.

随着“登记国”这一概念的引入，正如在《外空条约》第五条和第八条中所使用的那样，其在于建立“发射国和空间物体之间的正式联系，以促进对在外空公域中的空间物体的控制权、主权和所有权的行使”①。此外，建立空间物体和国家之间关系的意图在于赋予该物体以国籍，并将其与特定的法律体系相连接②。作为登记制度的基石，该问题在相关谈判中一再被其他代表团提起③。

“管辖与控制”（《登记公约》第二条第 2 款）的表述取自于《外空条约》第八条和 1962 年ⅩⅧ号决议，并被加拿大——法国草案（第三条第 3 款）所引入④。最初的法国草案第一条⑤仍然使用了不明确的“监督”一词。

《登记公约》第二条第 2 款的保留，支持较为普遍的发射国之间的协议，起源于阿根廷的一个影响深远的提案⑥。

（二）评注

除非特别指明，本部分有关批准和通知的情况截至 2019 年 1 月 1 日。

1. 国家登记义务/给联合国的信息

（1）强制性的发射国国内登记

具有约束力的国内登记义务是《登记公约》的一个基本要素，并超越了《外空条

① See Mr. Miller (Canada), in the Summary Record of the 113th meeting of the Legal Sub-Committee, held 12 June 1969, reproduced in: Cocca, Aldo A., Convention on Registration of Objects Launched into Outer Space, in: Jasentuliyana, Nandasiri/Lee, Roy S. K. (eds.), Manual on Space Law, Volume Ⅲ, Oceana Publications, New York 1981, p. 647.

② Mr. Charvet (France), in the Summary Record of the 115th meeting of the Legal Sub-Committee, held 13 June 1969, reproduced in: Cocca, Aldo A., Convention on Registration of Objects Launched into Outer Space, in: Jasentuliyana, Nandasiri/Lee, Roy S. K. (eds.), Manual on Space Law, Volume I, Oceana Publications, New York 1981, p. 652.

③ See Mr. Yoshida (Japan), in the Summary Record of the 187th meeting of the Legal Sub-Committee, held 2 May 1972, reproduced in: Cocca, Aldo A., Convention on Registration of Objects Launched into Outer Space, in: Jasentuliyana, Nandasiri/Lee, Roy S. K. (eds.), Manual on Space Law, Volume I, Oceana Publications, New York 1981, p. 674.

④ UN Doc. A/AC. 105/C. 2/L. 83, 20 April 1972.

⑤ UN Doc. A/AC. 105/C. 2/L. 45, French Proposal, Draft Convention Concerning the Registration of Objects Launched into Space for the Exploration or Use of Outer Space, 18 June 1968, reproduced in: UN Doc. A/AC. 105/58, Report of the Legal Sub-Committee on the Work of Its Eighth Session (9 June-4 July 1969), Annex I, Proposals Concerning Questions Relative to the Definition of Outer Space and the Utilization of Outer Space and Celestial Bodies, Including the Various Implications of Space Communications, 4 July 1969.

⑥ UN Doc. A/AC. 105/C. 2/L. 87, 11 April 1973.

约》第八条[①]。首先，根据《登记公约》第二条第 1 款，进行发射活动的相关缔约国应保持适当的空间物体登记册，并将其设置此种登记册之事通知联合国秘书长。发射国在发射一个外空物体进入或越出地球轨道时，应按照该公约第二条的规定以登入其该登记册的方式登记该外空物体。《登记公约》第二条第 2 款规定，当此种外空物体有两个以上的发射国时，它们应共同决定由其中哪一国登记该空间物体 。其次，登记国应当在切实可行的范围内尽速向联合国秘书长提供该公约第四条所列的信息。因此，就空间物体的国内登记而言，登记公约的缔约国若为一个空间物体的“发射国”，其要么必须建立并保持空间物体的国内登记册，对此类物体进行登记并向联合国秘书长提供相关信息，以使其在联合国中央登记册进行登记；要么同意该空间物体的另一个发射国获得登记国的地位，包括进行国内登记和向联合国提供信息的义务。然而，如果缺乏第一步的国内登记，相关空间物体的管辖权和控制权就未进行分配。因此，一个国家可能是特定空间物体的两个或更多发射国团体中的发射国之一，其自身并没有义务对其进行登记，但空间物体的管辖权和控制权总是和登记相关联的。

登记只能由发射国进行。将相关发射中的登记从一个发射国后续转移到另一发射国符合《登记公约》第二条第 1 款的规定。

曾经有提议认为，根据习惯法，可以将空间物体的登记转移给非发射国，只要该发射中的所有发射国一致同意该转移，并且非发射国对相关义务的接受是以书面形式进行的[②]。有人认为，从概念上讲，将“促使发射国”的概念扩大到包括继受国作为发射国，这将使新的发射国能够与其他发射国缔结协定，并通过变更登记而成为登记国[③]。然而，虽然继受国可以同意被视为发射国并自愿承担主要国际赔偿责任相关义务，转让国是否因此而免除其对所转让的空间物体行使管辖权和控制权的国际责任仍然值得怀疑。依据《登记公约》，上述情形是被排除的，因为公约第二条第 1 款建立

---

① See Schmidt-Tedd, Bernhard/Mick, Stephan, *Article* Ⅷ I, in: Hobe, Stephan/Schmidt-Tedd, Bernhard/Schrogl, Kai-Uwe (eds.), Cologne Commentary on Space Law, Volume I, Carl Heymanns, Cologne 2009, p. 148, mn. 8.

② Hörl, Kay-Uwe/Hermida, Julian, Change of Ownership, Change of Registry? Which Objects to Register, What data to be Furnished, When, and Until When?, in: IISL, Proceedings of the 46th Colloquium on the Law of Outer Space, 29 September-3 October 2003 Bremen (Germany), AIAA, 2004, pp. 457f.

③ Chatzipanagiotis, Michael, Registration of Space Objects and Transfer of Ownership in Orbit, Zeitschrift für Luft- und Weltraumrecht (56) 2007, p. 237.

了空间物体和发射国之间的直接联系。“促使发射”一词包括发射服务客户在轨交付载荷，但不包括购买已在轨卫星的决定。《外空条约》第八条更不明确，但其为1721B（XVI）号决议的原则1转化而来，根据该原则，“发射物体进入或越出轨道的国家”和登记之间的关联已经明确建立了。

（2）地球轨道或越出地球轨道

相关问题是，发射失败的物体是否应列入登记册。关于登记义务，《登记公约》提到“地球轨道或越出地球轨道”。因此，没有义务登记亚轨道飞行的物体。即使是与一项外空任务相关的地面发射失败的情况下，也不需要登记。在此情况下不登记对赔偿责任问题没有负面影响，因为有关登记的决定源自于发射国资格的预定标准。管辖权和控制权的确定仅在空间物体存在于无主权区域（地球轨道及以外）的情况下才有意义，在此情况下需要对其进行明确规定。

多个国家在其国内证实了该问题。基于这一事实，一些国家的国内立法提供了此方面的法律规则。相关标准为轨道。

例如，根据《俄罗斯联邦航天局关于实施维持俄罗斯联邦射入外层空间物体的登记册的国家职能的行政法规》（以下简称《俄罗斯联邦行政法规》）[①] 第1.1节第8段，射入地球轨道并且运行至少一周的空间物体或者发射到更远外层空间的物体的信息应被列入登记册。这些规定与上述不包括亚轨道飞行的做法完全一致。《乌克兰航天器登记规则草案》第3节规定了在乌克兰航天器发射进入轨道后的3天登记期。在此期间[②]，该航天器的发射委员会应根据乌克兰国家航天局所提供的模板向后者提交“乌克兰国家航天器登记册登记表”。

（3）登记的时间

登记的确切时间并未在《登记公约》第二条中明确规定。考虑到公约关于通知义务的第四条使用了“在切实可行的范围内尽速”的用语，该非具体时间也可被视为适用于公约第二条。应当注意，《登记公约》第二条下的义务只有在相关国家登记之后

① The Administrative Regulation of the Russian Federal Space Agency on the Implementation of the State Function of Maintaining the Registry of Space Objects Launched in Outer Space by the Russian Federation (approved by Order of the Federal Space Agency dated 22 March 2010 No. 44, registered in the Ministry of Justice of the Russian Federation on 22 September 2010 No. 18508).

② The commission is composed of teams participating in the launch of the spacecraft, which by decision of the government are empowered to organize and realize preparatory works and the immediate launch of a spacecraft itself.

才能履行，因此，公约第二条第 1 款第 1 句规定下的可接受期限，不能长于公约第四条下的最长可接受期限。此外，也应注意 1721 B（XVI）号决议中“迅速提供信息”的更严格提法。

（4）登记册的公开信息

《登记公约》第二条第 1 款第 2 句规定了有义务通知联合国秘书长根据该段第 1 句建立登记册的情况。对现有国家登记册的全面概览是公开披露规则、宣传的要素，因为国家登记也是在国际层面确定管辖权和控制权的法律因素。“会员国和组织关于建立射入外层空间物体国家登记册的通知索引”由联合国外层空间事务办公室（UNOOSA）管理①。2018 年底，它包含了来自 56 个不同成员国，以及两个国际组织（欧空局和欧洲气象卫星应用组织）的通知②。阿根廷、澳大利亚、奥地利、白俄罗斯、比利时、巴西、加拿大、智利、中国、捷克共和国（和前捷克斯洛伐克）、丹麦、芬兰、法国、德国、希腊、印度、印度尼西亚、意大利、日本、哈萨克斯坦、墨西哥、新西兰、朝鲜、挪威、秘鲁、韩国、斯洛伐克、荷兰、巴基斯坦、俄罗斯/苏联、南非、西班牙、乌克兰、英国、乌拉圭和美国已通知了其国家登记册的建立。

（5）登记册通知的国家实践

第一个通知联合国秘书长根据《登记公约》第二条的规定设立登记册的国家是加拿大（1976 年 8 月 24 日通知）③。此后不久，美国于 1977 年 2 月 9 日在其安理会副代表给联合国秘书长的信函中，通知联合国其设立了国家登记册，并由其国务院空间和先进技术办公室保持该登记册④。

第一个通知联合国关于设立登记册的欧洲国家是德国（1988 年 4 月 7 日通知）⑤。

① United Nations Office for Outer Space Affairs, Index of Notifications by Member States and Organizations on the Establishment of National Registries of Objects Launched into Outer Space< http：//www. unoosa. org/oosa/osoindex/search-ng. jspx? lf_ id=> accessed 26 April 2019.

② Apart from former Soviet republics, the Czech Republic and its predecessor-State was the first European State to make such notification and transmitted 3 notifications between 1979 and 2009.

③ UN Doc. ST/SG/SER. E/INF. 2, Note Verbale dated 24 August 1976 from the Permanent Mission of Canada to the United Nations addressed to the Secretary-General, 16 November 1976.

④ UN Doc. ST/SG/SER. E/INF. 3, Letter dated 9 February 1977 from the Deputy Representative of the United States in the Security Council addressed to the Secretary-General, 17 February 1977.

⑤ UN Doc. ST/SG/SER. E/INF. 9, Note Verbale dated 7 April 1988 from the Permanent Mission of the Federal Republic of Germany to the United Nations addressed to the Secretary-General, 27 April 1988.

其他欧洲国家如西班牙（1995 年 3 月 23 日）[①]、法国（2004 年 1 月 28 日）[②]、希腊（2008 年5 月14 日）[③]、比利时（2008 年6 月3 日）[④]、荷兰（2009 年6 月3 日）[⑤]、挪威（2004 年1 月21 日）、意大利（2014 年 11 月 7 日）、英国（2015 年6 月24 日）、丹麦（2016 年12 月9 日）、奥地利（2017 年1 月30 日）和芬兰（2018 年2 月15 日）紧随其后。应当注意的是，不仅各国向联合国秘书长发出了正式的设立登记册通知，而且欧空局（1979 年6 月2 日）[⑥] 和欧洲气象卫星应用组织（1998 年5 月6 日）[⑦] 等机构也发出了此类通知。

苏联于 1978 年 1 月 13 日以普通照会通知联合国秘书长，其根据《登记公约》设立了“苏联射入外层空间物体登记册”[⑧]。新的登记册取代了苏联根据 1961 年 12 月 20 日联大第 1721 B（XVI）号决议自 1962 年至 1977 年所维持的“空间物体登记册”[⑨]。1991 年苏联解体后，有关维持该登记册的工作由俄罗斯联邦继承[⑩]。如前所述，《俄罗斯联邦行政法规》第 1.1 节第 6 段所述，俄罗斯联邦的登记册被认为是“苏联射入外层空间物体登记册”的延续（这也反映在其名称上——“苏联/俄罗斯登记册”），俄罗斯联邦继续对苏联早先发射的空间物体行使完全的管辖权和控制权。苏联的其他继承国也向联合国通报了设立有关国家登记册的情况。这些国家包括乌克

① UN Doc. ST/SG/SER. E/INF. 10, Note Verbale dated 23 March 1995 from the Permanent Mission of Spain to the United Nations (New York) addressed to the Secretary-General, 31 May 1995.

② UN Doc. ST/SG/SER. E/INF. 16, Note Verbale dated 28 January 2004 from the Permanent Mission of France to the United Nations (Vienna) addressed to the Secretary-General, 6 February 2004.

③ UN Doc. ST/SG/SER. E/INF. 20, Note Verbale dated 14 May 2008 from the Permanent Mission of Greece to the United Nations (Vienna) addressed to the Secretary-General, 15 May 2008.

④ UN Doc. ST/SG/SER. E/INF. 21, Note Verbale dated 3 June 2008 from the Permanent Mission of Belgium to the United Nations (Vienna) addressed to the Secretary-General, 2 July 2008.

⑤ UN Doc. ST/SG/SER. E/INF. 24, Note Verbale dated 3 June 2009 from the Permanent Mission of the Netherlands to the United Nations (Vienna) addressed to the Secretary-General, 20 August 2009.

⑥ UN Doc. ST/SG/SER. E/INF. 6, Information furnished by the European Space Agency to the United Nations in a letter dated 2 June 1983, 23 June 1983.

⑦ UN Doc. ST/SG/SER. E/INF. 14, Letter dated 6 May 1998 from the European Organisation for the Exploitation of Meteorological Satellites addressed to the Secretary-General, 27 May 1998.

⑧ UN Doc. ST/SG/SER. E/INF. 4, Information furnished by the Permanent Mission of the Union of Soviet Socialist Republics to the United Nations in Note Verbale dated 13 January 1978 addressed to the Secretary-General, 18 January 1978.

⑨ UN Doc. A/AC. 105/INF. 2, Letter dated 24 March 1962 from the Acting Permanent Representative of the Union of Soviet Socialist Republics addressed to the Acting Secretary-General, 24 March 1962.

⑩ For more details see Commentary REG, Article II, mn. 76ff.

兰（1995 年 9 月 22 日）[①]、白俄罗斯（2012 年 7 月 12 日）[②] 和哈萨克斯坦共和国（2012 年 2 月 20 日）[③]。

1979 年 7 月，捷克斯洛伐克社会主义共和国在国际宇宙计划的框架内建立了“捷克斯洛伐克射入外层空间物体的国家登记册”[④]。捷克斯洛伐克社会主义共和国分裂为两个国家（捷克共和国和斯洛伐克）之后，捷克共和国成为维持该登记册的继承国。斯洛伐克于 2016 年设立了自己的空间物体登记册，并于 2016 年 4 月 2 日通知了联合国。

其他通知联合国其设立了国内登记册的国家包括日本（1983 年 12 月 19 日）[⑤]、印度（1987 年 2 月 11 日）[⑥]、阿根廷（1996 年 12 月 30 日）[⑦]、澳大利亚（2003 年 10 月 1 日）[⑧]、中国（2005 年 6 月 8 日）[⑨]、巴西（2007 年 3 月 27 日）[⑩]、巴基斯坦（2008 年 11 月 13 日）[⑪]、韩国（2009 年 1 月 15 日）[⑫]、南非（2012 年 7 月 11 日）[⑬]、

① UN Doc. ST/SG/SER. E/INF. 11, Note Verbale dated 22 September 1995 from the Permanent Mission of Ukraine to the United Nations addressed to the Secretary-General, 12 October 1995.

② UN Doc. ST/SG/SER. E/INF. 18, Note Verbale dated 12 July 2006 from the Permanent Mission of Belarus to the United Nations (Vienna) addressed to the Secretary-General, 13 July 2006.

③ UN Doc. ST/SG/SER. E/INF. 26, Note Verbale dated 20 February 2012 from the Permanent Mission of Kazakhstan to the United Nations (Vienna) addressed to the Secretary-General, 28 February 2012.

④ UN Doc. ST/SG/SER. E/22, Note Verbale dated 13 June 1979 from Permanent Representative of Czechoslovakia to the United Nations addressed to the Secretary-General.

⑤ UN Doc. ST/SG/SER. E/INF. 7, Note Verbale dated 19 December 1983 from the Permanent Mission of Japan to the United Nations addressed to the Secretary-General, 12 November 1986.

⑥ UN Doc. ST/SG/SER. E/INF. 8, Information furnished by the Permanent Mission of India to the United Nations in a letter dated 11 February 1987, 4 March 1987.

⑦ UN Doc. ST/SG/SER. E/INF. 13, Note Verbale dated 30 December 1996 from the Permanent Mission of Argentina to the United Nations (Vienna) addressed to the Secretary-General, 15 January 1997.

⑧ UN Doc. ST/SG/SER. E/INF. 15, Note Verbale dated 1 October 2003 from the Permanent Mission of Australia to the United Nations (Vienna) addressed to the Secretary-General, 6 October 2003.

⑨ UN Doc. ST/SG/SER. E/INF. 17, Note Verbale dated 8 June 2005 from the Permanent Mission of China to the United Nations (Vienna) addressed to the Secretary-General, 21 June 2005.

⑩ UN Doc. ST/SG/SER. E/INF. 19, Note Verbale dated 27 March 2007 from the Permanent Mission of Brazil to the United Nations (Vienna) addressed to the Secretary-General, 27 March 2007.

⑪ UN Doc. ST/SG/SER. E/INF. 22, Note Verbale dated 13 November 2008 from the PermanentMission of Pakistan to the United Nations (Vienna) addressed to the Secretary-General, 14 November 2008.

⑫ UN Doc. ST/SG/SER. E/INF. 23, Note Verbale dated 15 January 2009 from the Permanent Mission of the Republic of Korea to the United Nations (Vienna) addressed to the Secretary-General, 16 April 2009.

⑬ UN Doc. ST/SG/SER. E/INF. 27, Note Verbale dated 11 July 2012 from the Permanent Mission of South Africa to the United Nations (Vienna) addressed to the Secretary-General, 16 July 2012.

墨西哥（2013 年 10 月 31 日）、智利（2016 年 1 月 18 日）、秘鲁（2016 年 8 月 11 日）、乌拉圭（2017 年 7 月 19 日）、印度尼西亚（2017 年 9 月 18 日）以及最近的新西兰（2018 年 11 月 27 日）。

2. 两个或两个以上发射国的协议

（1）共同决定，无优先次序

《登记公约》第二条第 2 款包含两项关键表述，即（1）在有两个或两个以上发射国时，这些国家“应共同决定由其中哪一个国家登记该物体”；（2）必须在发射国范围内作出决定。此外，还提到了《外空条约》第八条的基本规定以及发射国之间的适当协议。不存在优先规则隐含地导致了每一个发射国的平等排序。某一特定发射的所有发射国均承担同样的国家责任和赔偿责任，并须在协商一致的基础上就登记、管辖权和控制权问题找到共同的解决办法。

尽管《登记公约》第一条第 1 款的四项发射国资格并没有优先次序，但在国家实践中有确定登记国的某些做法和方法。发射服务提供者所在的主要国家一般期望有效载荷客户背后的国家将有效载荷独立于运载火箭进行登记。这种预期的正当性很容易通过反向结果来证明。如果有效载荷客户所在国不进行登记，则该有效载荷将作为已登记的运载火箭的附属物，或可以由发射服务提供者所在国进行登记，这在管辖权和控制权方面显然违背了客户的意图①。

例如，俄罗斯联邦在与其他发射国（通过俄罗斯发射服务采购发射的国家）的关系中采用了客户有效载荷单独登记的方法。法国的阿丽亚娜火箭的发射服务也是如此，因为库鲁在其领土上，则法国是发射设施的国籍国。法国对从其领土发射进入地球轨道或进入外层空间的载荷保持单独的记录（有别于登记）。

达成正式协议的确切时间并没有明确规定。但《登记公约》第四条中“在切实可行的范围内尽速”的用语可间接地作为一种指示。如果有关发射国在空间物体被置于外层空间之前尚未达成协议，则没有依据证明其按时履行了公约第 3 条所规定的义务。此外，出于实际考虑，应在空间物体发射之前达成协议，因为项目计划过程中的任何变动都可能使达成协议更加困难，例如，载荷客户可能在调试阶段失败后失去

---

① Schmidt-Tedd, Bernhard/Mick, Stephan, Article Ⅷ, in: Hobe, Stephan/Schmidt-Tedd, Bernhard/Schrogl, Kai-Uwe (eds.), Cologne Commentary on Space Law, Volume I, Carl Heymanns, Cologne 2009, p. 151, mn. 24.

兴趣。

（2）对《外空条约》第八条和适当协议的提及

《登记公约》第二条第 2 款提及《外空条约》第八条和关于管辖权与控制权的适当协议。该段“不损害［…］”一词后的最后一部分是对发射国之间的当事方间安排的澄清。因此，可以说《登记公约》第二条第 2 款回顾了由于登记而产生的管辖和控制之间的相关性，并为发射国之间达成协议留有余地。最后一点与管辖权和控制权与发射国资格之间的明确联系并不相冲突，因为这些协议是有关发射国之间达成的。

（3）管辖权与控制权

在这一点上，必须再次强调，管辖权和控制权这一用语抽象地描述了关于空间物体的全面性的主要法律立场①。这一法律立场直接来源于登记，并把这一特殊立场专门集中于一个发射国。该术语通常是抽象的，独立于控制中心的实际监督、占有或所有权问题。这一主要法律立场与发射国标准密不可分，也不受空间物体（例如卫星）所有权随后转移的影响。事实上，登记国负有对物体在空间内的整个时间段行使管辖和控制的责任。此种登记和责任只能转移给该发射事件中的另一发射国。因此，如果将空间物体的运营权或所有权转让给一个非发射国，则必须对此作出充分反应，以履行国际责任。如果这种改变是跨界转让，则一般需要与对新的非政府实体负责的国家达成协议。当然，这也适用于外国政府机构的直接收购。基于这样的协议，接受国可以根据当事方之间的内部安排在事实上接手国家责任和赔偿责任，尽管登记国仍然保留其在国际法上的地位。登记国仍然是管辖和控制相关国际义务的准保证人。实际上是将上述法律立场的大部分内容交给第三方，但不能完全剥离其自身由于登记国地位所产生的国际责任。有关管辖权和控制权的综合法律立场并不排除由此产生的权利和义务的这种内部的、基于合同的转移。事实上，这在相当有限的合同努力下也是可行的。但是，只有坚持发射国和登记国之间的持续联系，才能确保推动空间物体发射的缔约国继续全面负责，并从一开始就防止“方便旗”的倾向。

（4）权限的积极或消极冲突

理论上，积极或消极的登记权限冲突可能会发生。要么是发射服务提供者希望单独登记一个有效载荷，但这并未发生（权限的负面冲突），要么是主导项目的合作伙

① Ibid., pp. 156ff., mn. 44ff.

伴希望自己登记其贡献或有效载荷，而与另一航行参与者的利益相反（权限的正面冲突）。在这点上，可回顾第一个国际空间站的不同模块是由项目主导国或所有贡献国/组织进行登记所进行的长期讨论[①]。

商业发射服务提供者在履行合同义务方面存在一种特殊的冲突。正常情况下，根据大多数发射服务协议的约定，买方即有效载荷客户将履行登记的义务。然而，商业发射服务提供者是否会在买方不遵守登记义务的情况下采取行动，是值得怀疑的。在很多情况下，这可能是由于疏忽造成的简单的不遵守，没有任何具体的意图。此问题必须在政府对政府（机构对机构）的层面上解决。发射服务提供者的有力理由是，如果不进行登记，载荷客户所在国将无法获得管辖权和控制权，因此其行动将具有不确定性。

在登记权限正面冲突的特殊情况下，存在一个空间物体被登入两个国家的国家登记册，并在后续得到纠正的情况：在捷克斯洛伐克的 Magion-2 卫星发射时，苏联和前捷克斯洛伐克之间未就登记国问题达成协议。Magion-2 是在国际空间通信组织（INTERSPUTNIK）的一个联合科学项目框架下由苏联和捷克斯洛伐克共同发射。结果该物体进行了两次登记：1989 年 12 月由捷克斯洛伐克登记[②]，1990 年 1 月由苏联登记[③]。后来，为消除与《登记公约》第二条规定的不一致，苏联向联合国秘书长发出照会，通知该空间物体已从苏联国家登记册中撤出，并要求对联合国国际登记册作出调整[④]。同一项目的四颗类似卫星（Magion、Magion-3、Magion-4 和 Magion-5）仅由

① Staudt, Birgitta, Die transatlantische Raumstationskooperation: Der Rechtliche Rahmen einer Langfristigen Multinationalen Zusammenarbeit, Peter Lang, Frankfurt am Main 1992, pp. 76ff.

② UN Doc. ST/SG/SER. E/213, Note Verbale dated 20 December 1989 from the Permanent Representative of Czechoslovakia to the United Nations addressed to the Secretary-General, 3 January 1990.

③ UN Doc. ST/SG/SER. E/215, Note Verbale dated 31 January 1990 from the Permanent Mission of the Union of Soviet Socialist Republics to the United Nations addressed to the Secretary-General, 2 February 1990.

④ UN Doc. ST/SG/SER. E/215/Add. 1, Note Verbale dated 16 July 1990 from the Permanent Mission of the Union of Soviet Socialist Republics to the United Nations addressed to the Secretary-General, 24 August 1990.

捷克斯洛伐克及其继承国捷克共和国进行登记①。

一些积极的事例表明，计划进行共同系列发射的发射国之间一般都达成了关于空间物体登记的协议。这种安排在欧洲通信卫星组织（EUTELSAT）和法国之间尤其明显。根据这些协议，法国应在 EUTELSAT 获得全部登记权限之前，暂时进行后者卫星的登记②。值得一提的是，由此产生的协议已扩展到使用外国运载火箭从其他国家发射的 EUTELSAT 卫星，而不仅是从法国领土上发射的卫星③。

（5）国内实践的案例

在存在多个发射国的情况下，美国的做法可以描述如下：美国国家航空航天局（NASA）和其他国家相关机构的合作协议通常会包含一个章节，以规定哪个机构将要求其政府登记空间物体。美国的一般立场是，各国应登记所有由该国私人或政府实体所拥有或控制并在该国以外发射的有效载荷，除非相关各国另有约定④。例如，《国际空间站政府间协定》规定，每一个主要模块都应单独进行登记，这些模块在附件中被称为“航行要素”⑤。登记国因此将对航行要素及其人员具有管辖权和控制权。此外，

---

① UN Doc. ST/SG/SER. E/022, Note Verbale dated 13 June 1979 from the Permanent Representative of Czechoslovakia to the United Nations addressed to the Secretary-General, 11 July 1979; UN Doc. ST/SG/SER. E/251, Note Verbale dated 14 February 1992 from the Permanent Representative of Czechoslovakia to the United Nations addressed to the Secretary-General, 26 February 1992; UN Doc. ST/SG/SER. E/314, Note Verbale dated 12 July 1996 from the Permanent Mission of the Czech Republic to the United Nations (Vienna) addressed to the Secretary-General, 5 August 1996; UN Doc. ST/SG/SER. E/361, Note Verbale dated 20 September 1999 from the Permanent Mission of the Czech Republic to the United Nations (Vienna) addressed to the Secretary-General, 29 September 1999.

② Trebaol, Jean-Yves, French Policy and Practices for the Registration of Space Objects, in: Danesy, Dorothea, Proceedings of the 4th European Conference on Space Debris, 18-20 April 2005 Darmstadt (Germany), ESA/ESOC, p. 583; see also: UN Doc. COPUOS/LEGAL/T. 769, Committee on the Peaceful Uses of Outer Space, Legal Subcommittee, Unedited Transcript of the 769th Meeting, 2 April 2008, p. 17: "[…] because of a temporary Agreement with the French Ministry of Foreign Affairs, we had this registered on the French Registry under the name of the Organization because EUTELSAT was not able to directly accept and discharge these duties.".

③ UN Doc. A/AC. 105/C. 2/L. 250/Add. 1, Practice of registration of space objects by states and international organizations: replies from Member states. Note by the Secretariat. Addendum, 9 March 2004.

④ UN Doc. COPUOS/LEGAL/T. 741, Committee on the Peaceful Uses of Outer Space, Legal Subcommittee, Unedited transcript of the 741st Meeting on Information on the Activities of International Organizations Relating to Space Law (Agenda Item 7), 10 April 2006, p. 9.

⑤ Art. 5 Agreement among the Government of Canada, Governments of Member States of the European Space Agency, the Government of Japan, the Government of the Russian Federation, and the Government of the United States of America Concerning Cooperation on the Civil International Space Station (done 29 January 1998, entered into force 28 March 2001), 29 January 1998; see also Memoranda of Understandings (MOU's) with Canada, ESA Member States, Japan, and the Russian Federation.

当事方之间还有《登记公约》第二条第2款最后半句意义下的安排，此安排应与《外空条约》第八条第1句中的一般规则相区别。根据这些单独规则，相关国家对其国民的管辖权可与该国联系起来，不论这些人在国际空间站上的任何地方[①]。虽然在发射和运送到国际空间站期间，空间站合作伙伴对空间运输系统（STS）的某一航行要素的管辖权可能存在问题，但各自的管辖权可以根据《政府间协定》确定[②]。然而，在运输过程中发生的任何损害事件都应遵守《空间站机组人员行为守则》以及有关协定中可能包含的任何损害责任交叉豁免规定[③]。

在俄罗斯，《俄罗斯联邦行政法规》规定，发射国应在发射前的最早阶段就空间物体的登记达成协议。该解决方案包含在《俄罗斯联邦行政法规》（第3.4节）中，包含以下内容：由哪个发射国登记空间物体的问题必须在对有关实体或个人提交给俄罗斯航天局（ROSCOSMOS）的下一年发射计划申请进行初步审议时确定。在申请发射外国的空间物体时，应指明建议的登记国。在此情况下，俄罗斯航天局在与俄罗斯国防部和其他相关政府部门达成一致后，向联邦政府提交发射空间物体的命令草案。关于联合发射，《俄罗斯联邦行政法规》第3.4节规定：

"根据国际空间法，空间物体存在包括俄罗斯联邦在内的两个或两个以上的发射国，而未计划在俄罗斯联邦提出登记申请时，俄罗斯航天局……通过签订发射合同的组织获取根据其法律记录空间物体所有权的国家的保证，或从其他相关国家获取该物体在其国家登记册中的信息。"[④]

一些其他国家的国内立法中也有关于两个或两个以上发射国的空间物体登记的特别规定。例如，根据《乌克兰空间活动法》第十三条[⑤]，航天器在乌克兰国家航天器登记册进行登记后，乌克兰即不应承认该航天器先前在其他国家的空间物体登记册所

① See Zhukov, Gennady P., Registration and Jurisdiction Aspects of the International Space Station, in: IISL, Proceedings of the 42nd Colloquium on the Law of Outer Space, 4-8 October 1999 Amsterdam (The Netherlands), AIAA, 2000, p. 76.

② Ibid.

③ Ibid, p. 78.

④ Sec. 3.4 RF Administrative Regulation.

⑤ Law of the Ukraine On Space Activity (15 November 1996) <http://zakon2.rada.gov.ua/laws/show/502/96-%D0%B2%D1%80> accessed 26 April 2019; for the unofficial English translation see: Ordinance Of The Supreme Soviet Of Ukraine, On Space Activity, Law of Ukraine of 15 November 1996 <http://www.unoosa.org/oosa/en/SpaceLaw/national/ukraine/ordinance_on_space_activity_1996E.html> accessed 26 April 2019.

进行的登记记录。如果该物体未从乌克兰国家航天器登记册中移除，则乌克兰不承认该航天器在另一国空间物体登记册的登记。

如果两个或两个以上发射国之间没有明确的初步协议，在发生特殊事件的情况下，如铱星 33/宇宙 2251 号案件，也可能导致不好的法律后果。2009 年 2 月 9 日，一家美国卫星通信公司于 1997 年发射的“铱星 33 号”卫星与俄罗斯 1993 年发射的军用卫星“宇宙-2251 号”发生碰撞，前者仍在正常运行，后者自 1995 年以来已停止运行。关于宇宙-2251 号卫星，俄罗斯已将其登记在其国家登记册，编号为 2846，并于 1994 年 6 月 14 日照会通知联合国秘书长①。铱星 33 号是由俄罗斯质子号火箭为美国摩托罗拉公司发射的，但俄罗斯和美国并未根据《登记公约》第二条第 2 款达成任何协议。与此同时，俄罗斯采取了单方面行动，于 1998 年 3 月 4 日向联合国秘书长发送照会②，指出 1997 年 9 月 14 日由质子号火箭发射的七颗铱星由美国摩托罗拉公司拥有和控制。这些物体尚未在俄罗斯联邦国家登记册登记。美国也没有登记铱 33 卫星。因此，在发生碰撞时，该空间物体并未在任何发射国进行登记。美国只登记了由其德尔它二号火箭发射的铱星③，而未登记属于摩托罗拉公司但由俄罗斯和中国发射的类似卫星④。因此，对于由俄罗斯和中国发射的所有美国铱星，其管辖权和控制权并未被授予操作者背后的国家，这就导致了有关碰撞避免的明确法律基础的缺失。

---

① UN Doc. ST/SG/SER. E/275, Note Verbale dated 14 June 1994 from the Permanent Mission of the Russian Federation to the United Nations addressed to the Secretary-General, 13 June 1994.

② UN Doc. ST/SG/SER. E/332, Note Verbale dated 4 March 1998 from the Permanent Mission of the Russian Federation to the United Nations (Vienna) addressed to the Secretary-General, 19 March 1998, p. 2.

③ See, e. g. UN Doc. ST/SG/SER. E/329, Note Verbale dated 22 December 1997 from the Permanent Mission of the United States of America to the United Nations (Vienna) addressed to the Secretary-General, 19 January 1998; UN Doc. ST/SG/SER. E/339, Note Verbale dated 12 June 1998 from the Permanent Mission of the United States of America to the United Nations (Vienna) addressed to the Secretary-General, 24 June 1998; UN Doc. ST/SG/SER. E/341, Note Verbale dated 22 July 1998 from the Permanent Mission of the United States of America to the United Nations (Vienna) addressed to the Secretary-General, 4 August 1998; UN Doc. ST/SG/SER. E/344, Note Verbale dated 17 August 1998 from the Permanent Mission of the United States of America to the United Nations (Vienna) addressed to the Secretary-General, 26 August 1998.

④ Nevertheless they were mentioned by the Russian Federation in the following Note Verbale: UN Doc. ST/SG/SER. E/327, Note Verbale dated 10 November 1997 from the Permanent Mission of the Russian Federation to the United Nations (Vienna) addressed to the Secretary-General, 30 January 1998, p. 3; UN Doc. ST/SG/SER. E/332, Note Verbale dated 4 March 1998 from the Permanent Mission of the Russian Federation to the United Nations (Vienna) addressed to the Secretary-General, 19 March 1998, p. 2; UN Doc. ST/SG/SER. E/343, Note Verbale dated 6 August 1998 from the Permanent Mission of the Russian Federation to the United Nations (Vienna) addressed to the Secretary-General, 13 August 1998, p. 3.

3. 每一登记册的内容和条件

第 3 款提到国家登记册的内容以及根据《登记公约》维持国家登记册的条件。《外空条约》第八条意味着存在公约缔约国的国家空间物体登记册。《登记公约》规定了建立和维持适当国家登记册的义务。然而，《登记公约》并未规定国家登记册的建立、维持和内容的具体要求[①]，以及登记册中所应登记的信息规定任何国际义务。根据《登记公约》第二条第 3 款，登记国决定其登记册的内容和维持登记册的条件。因此，国家登记册的建立仅由缔约国自己负责。

一些国家建立了双重国家登记册，对《登记公约》所要求的信息和其他信息加以区分。这种做法原则上由各国自行决定且符合本款的规定。然而，这种做法不应导致《登记公约》第二条意义下的国家登记册的官方部分与不具有同等相关性的信息无法区分的情况。应注意的是，国家登记册中的登记信息是在法律意义上[②]确定空间物体的管辖权和控制权的相关条件，因此在处理登记信息时必须考虑其与登记册功能的相关性。

虽然每个国家可以决定其国家登记册的内容，但向联合国提供的信息必须符合《登记公约》的要求，其中包括确认空间物体发射国的信息。因此，如果某一《登记公约》的缔约国宣称该国的法律实体通过在轨交付取得了卫星，这即意味着该国为“促成发射”意义下的发射国，但如果该国同时否认其作为发射国的资质，这就可能导致相关法律后果。此外，如果该国声称其根据《外空条约》第六条对卫星运营负有国际责任，并根据《外空条约》第八条具有管辖权和控制权，那么其对发射国资格的

① This results in a necessary effort to preserve a reasonable uniformity, see Williams, Maureen, The Registration Convention Thirty Years On, in: IISL, Proceedings of the 49th Colloquium on the Law of Outer Space, 2-6 October 2006 Valencia (Spain), AIAA, 2007, pp. 264ff.

② In German terminology ‘rechtskonstitutiv’.

否认似乎是矛盾的[1]。根据《登记公约》第二条第1款，具有发射国资格是登记空间物体的明确前提条件，而国家登记是《外空条约》第八条下的管辖权和控制权的前提条件，并应根据《登记公约》第四条通知联合国秘书长。因此，上述对发射国资格的矛盾否定不能影响《登记公约》下的管辖权和控制权问题。该声明并不妨碍另一发射国根据《外空条约》第八条和《登记公约》对该空间物体进行登记。只要登记不是以与《外空条约》第八条和《登记公约》不同的方式进行的，且如果此次发射中的发射装置已经登记，则有效载荷（卫星）仍然是已登记的发射装置的附属物[2]。

显然，国家登记册内的注释不能推翻国际法——《外空条约》和《登记公约》的法律后果。如果根据《外空条约》第七条和《登记公约》某一国家是发射国，那么其国家登记册中认定其自身不是发射国的注释是没有法律效力的。

4. 后续国家实践（缔约国和非缔约国）[3]

《登记公约》于1975年1月14日完成，于1976年9月15日生效。截至2019年1月，已有67个国家批准了该公约，另有4个国家签署了该公约[4]。

签署和批准《登记公约》的国家总数低于之前其他空间条约的缔约国数目。例

① See UN Doc, A/AC. 105/806, Note Verbale dated 29 July 2003 from the Permanent Mission of the Netherlands to the United Nations (Vienna) addressed to the Secretary-General, 22 August 2003: " [⋯] the Kingdom of the Netherlands is not the ' launching state' [⋯] . The [⋯] space objects were delivered in orbit to New Skies Satellites after they were launched and positioned in orbit by persons that were not subject to the jurisdiction or control of the Kingdom of the Netherlands. New Skies Satellites is a company that is incorporated in the Kingdom of the Netherlands. The Kingdom of the Netherlands is therefore not required to furnish to the Secretary-General of the United Nations information in accordance with article IV of the Registration Convention. Following the transfer in orbit of ownership of the space objects to New Skies Satellites, the Kingdom of the Netherlands is of the opinion that it bears international responsibility for their operation in accordance with article VI and has jurisdiction and control over them in accordance with article Ⅷ of the Treaty on Principles Governing Activities of States in the Exploration and Use of outer Space, including the Moon and Other Celestial Bodies [⋯] ".

② See the definition of ' space object' under Art. I lit. (b) REG.

③ Collection of examples of the early registration practice documents in: Jasentuliyana, Nandasiri/Lee, Roy S. K. (eds.), Manual on Space Law, Volume IV, Oceana Publications, New York 1981, pp. 549ff.

④ UN Doc. A/AC. 105/C. 2/2018/CRP. 3, Status of International Agreements relating to activities in outer space as at 1 January 2018, 9 April 2019 with regular updates published on http://www.unoosa.org/documents/pdf/spacelaw/treatystatus/AC105 _ C2 _ 2018 _ CRP03E.pdf. For a general overview see Mick, Stephan, Registrierungskonvention und Registrierungspraxis: Aktuelle Rechtsfragen der Registrierung von Weltraumgegenständen, Carl Heymanns, Cologne 2007, pp. 7ff.; Lee, Yoon, Registration of space objects: ESA member states' practice, Space Policy (22) 2006, pp. 42ff.

如，已有 107 个国家批准、23 个国家签署了《外空条约》[①]。原因可能是由于国家对空间资产的不处置，但即使在此情况下也有很好的理由批准该公约[②]。一些实质参与了空间物体的发射或操作的空间国家不是《登记公约》的缔约国[③]。这也适用于大多数国际组织：只有三个积极从事空间活动的国际组织已根据《登记公约》第七条正式宣布接受该公约下的权利和义务[④]。

在《登记公约》生效后的前二十年内，不论是根据该公约或联合国大会第 1721（XⅥ）号决议所登记的空间物体总数比例都相当高，约占所有已发射物体总数的 95%，与《登记公约》的批准状态不同[⑤]。这种情况在第三个十年期间发生了变化，此时正值商业外空活动日益增多以及大多数政府间国际卫星组织私有化的时期[⑥]。此外，各国和国际组织在空间物体登记方面的实践表明，由《登记公约》所确立的空间物体登记程序正日益被缔约国和国际组织所忽视[⑦]。由于建立了不同的国内登记程序，为国际登记所提供的数据也不尽相同。为应对该缺陷，联合国大会于 2007 年通过了《关于加强国家和政府间国际组织登记空间物体的做法的建议》（以下简称《登记实

① UN Doc. A/AC. 105/C. 2/2018/CRP. 3, Status of International Agreements relating to activities in outer space as at 1 January 2018, 9 April 2019 with regular updates published on http://www. unoosa. org/documents/pdf/spacelaw/treatystatus/AC105_ C2_ 2018_ CRP03E. pdf.

② See von der Dunk, Frans G. , The Registration Convention-Background and Historical Context, in: IISL, Proceedings of the 46th Colloquium on the Law of Outer Space, 29 September-3 October 2003 Bremen (Germany), AIAA, 2004, p. 452.

③ Countries that have neither signed nor ratified the REG so far are Colombia, Egypt, Israel, Luxembourg, Malaysia, Morocco, Philippines, Portugal, Romania, Saudi Arabia, Thailand and Vietnam.

④ The first international governmental organization was ESA, see Lafferranderie, Gabriel, L'application, par l'Agence Spatiale Européenne, de la Convention sur l'immatriculation des objects lancés dans l'espace extra-atmosphérique, Annals of Air and Space Law (11) 1986, p. 229. The other organization is the European Organisation for the Exploration of Meteorological Satellites (EUMETSAT).

⑤ See Perek, Lubos, The 1976 Registration Convention, Zeitschrift für Luft- und Weltraumrecht (47) 1998, pp. 352f. , with reference to the United Nations Reports: 1976 to 1986 (97, 6 %) and 1986 to 1996 (94, 5 %) as well as the Jonathan McDowell list of April 1998 and an annex of unregistered objects.

⑥ See Schmidt-Tedd, Bernhard/Mick, Stephan, Article Ⅷ, in: Hobe, Stephan/Schmidt-Tedd, Bernhard/Schrogl, Kai-Uwe (eds.), Cologne Commentary on Space Law, Volume I, Carl Heymanns, Cologne 2009, pp. 162f. , mn. 68ff.

⑦ See UN Doc. A/AC. 105/826, Report of the Legal Subcommittee on the work of its forty-third session, held in Vienna from 29 March-8 April 2004, 16 April 2004.

践决议》)[①]。为协调各国做法，该决议建议在向秘书长提供的信息中加入额外的信息，包括国际标识，作为发射日期参考时间的协调世界时间，作为基本轨道参数标准单位的公里、分钟和角度，以及除了《登记公约》所要求的一般功能之外的空间物体的其他功能。此外，该决议还列出了一般性的适当补充信息[②]以及在轨空间物体监管发生变化时的补充信息[③]。

截至 2019 年 1 月，已有 56 个国家和 2 个国际组织（欧空局和欧洲气象卫星应用组织）根据《登记公约》或联合国大会第 1721 B（XVI）号决议提交了关于射入外层空间物体的信息，这些国家包括阿尔及利亚、阿根廷、澳大利亚、奥地利、阿塞拜疆、白俄罗斯、比利时、玻利维亚、巴西、加拿大、智利、中国、捷克共和国（包括前捷克斯洛伐克）、朝鲜、丹麦、埃及、芬兰、法国、德国、希腊、印度、印度尼西亚、以色列、意大利、日本、哈萨克斯坦、立陶宛、卢森堡、马来西亚、墨西哥、蒙古、荷兰、新西兰、尼日利亚、挪威、巴基斯坦、巴布亚新几内亚、秘鲁、菲律宾、波兰、韩国、俄罗斯联邦（包括前苏联）、沙特阿拉伯、斯洛伐克、西班牙、南非、瑞典、泰国、土耳其、乌克兰、阿拉伯联合酋长国、英国、美国、乌拉圭和委内瑞拉。

对于某些实践，如下所述，有效的申报数量也是一个相关的指标。发出通知最多的国家或国际组织[④]包括美国、俄罗斯联邦、日本、印度、法国、英国、欧空局（26 个）、德国、中国和瑞典。第一个根据联合国大会第 1721 B（XVI）号决议所作的通

① UNGA Res. 62/101, Recommendations on Enhancing the Practice of States and International Intergovernmental Organizations in Registering Space Objects, 17 December 2007; for more information on the resolution see Hobe, Stephan/Schmidt-Tedd, Bernhard/Schrogl, Kai-Uwe (eds.), Cologne Commentary on Space Law, Volume III, Carl Heymanns, Cologne (forthcoming).

② UNGA Res. 62/101, Recommendations on Enhancing the Practice of States and International Intergovernmental Organizations in Registering Space Objects, 17 December 2007, p. 3, para. 2 lit. (b).

③ UNGA Res. 62/101, Recommendations on Enhancing the Practice of States and International Intergovernmental Organizations in Registering Space Objects, 17 December 2007, p. 4, para. 4 lit. (a).

④ The number of notifications, however, does not necessarily reflect the number of space objects, of a State Party. One single notification can contain a several number of objects, especially in case of a notification by a State with a high number of launch events.

知是 1962 年 3 月 7 日[①]由美国提交的，而第二个是 1962 年 3 月 24 日[②]由苏联提交的。上述国家完成了前 179 次登记，只有从 1967 年起，其他国家才开始跟进，包括进行第 180 次登记的澳大利亚[③]，第 284 次登记的加拿大[④]和第 325 次为欧空局登记的法国[⑤]。此外，《登记公约》下的前 21 个登记通知均来自美国和苏联[⑥]。

以下关于国家登记实践的概述[⑦]并非按字母顺序排序，而是根据全球区域、各自的共同法律传统并适当考虑到通知提交数量及与一般实践的相关性进行。

（1）《登记公约》的缔约国

①俄罗斯联邦、哈萨克斯坦和某些东方国家

（a）苏维埃社会主义共和国联盟

苏联最高苏维埃主席团于 1977 年 7 月 13 日批准了《登记公约》。该批准书于 1978 年 1 月 13 日由苏联交存联合国秘书长。根据《登记公约》第八条第 4 款，公约于 1978 年 1 月 13 日对苏联生效。由于苏联于 1991 年解体为 15 个新独立的国家，有关前苏联所缔结的国际条约的继承问题值得注意。苏联是 1975 年《登记公约》的最初签署国之一。根据苏联解体后组成独立国家联合体（独联体）[⑧] 的 12 个国家所通过

---

① UN Doc. A/AC. 105/INF. 1, Letter dated 6 March 1962 from the Acting Secretary-General addressed to the Chairman of the Committee on the Peaceful Uses of Outer Space, transmitting a communication dated 5 March 1962 from Permanent Representative of the United States of America, 7 March 1962.

② UN Doc. A/AC. 105/INF. 2, Letter dated 24 March 1962 from the Acting Permanent Representative of the Union of Soviet Socialist Republics addressed to the Acting Secretary-General, 24 March 1962.

③ UN Doc. A/AC. 105/INF. 180, Letter dated 1 December 1967 from the Permanent Representative of Australia addressed to the Secretary-General, 5 December 1967.

④ UN Doc. A/AC. 105/INF. 284, Letter dated 21 December 1973 from the Permanent Representative of Canada addressed to the Secretary-General, 31 December 1973.

⑤ UN Doc. A/AC. 105/INF. 325, Note Verbale dated 3 October 1975 from the Permanent Mission of France addressed to the Secretary-General, 16 October 1975.

⑥ UN Doc. ST/SG/SER. E/001, Letter dated 31 March 1977 From the Permanent Representative of the United States addressed to the Secretary-General, 14 April 1977, up to UN Doc. ST/SG/SER. E/021, Note Verbale dated 29 May 1979 from the Permanent Representative of the United States of America to the United Nations addressed to the Secretary-General, 6 June 1979.

⑦ A comprehensive overview over the first years of registration practice can be found Jasentuliyana, Nandasiri/Lee, Roy S. K. (eds.), Manual on Space Law, Volume IV, Oceana Publications, New York 1981, pp. 551ff.

⑧ CIS was founded on 8 December 1991 between the Republic of Belarus, the Russian Federation and Ukraine. The Founding Agreement was open to all former Soviet Republics, so that on 21 December 1991 eight additional former Soviet Republics joined the CIS by signing the Alma-Ata Protocol. The new structure did not include Latvia, Lithuania and Estonia. Since 2004, these States are members of the European Union.

的协议，俄罗斯联邦继续参加苏联缔结的所有国际条约，并履行苏联在联合国的全部义务，包括所有国际组织的成员资格，此外还宣布俄罗斯联邦继承了苏联的外债和资产[①]。因此，1978 年 1 月 13 日是《登记公约》对俄罗斯联邦开始生效的日期，虽然俄罗斯联邦是 1991 年 12 月才正式成立的国家。

除前苏联整体外，它的两个组成部分（加盟共和国）乌克兰苏维埃社会主义共和国和白俄罗斯苏维埃社会主义共和国也是联合国的创始成员国，自 1945 年以来一直是联合国成员国。上述两个加盟共和国还在苏联时期就签署了《登记公约》。乌克兰苏维埃社会主义共和国于 1975 年 7 月 11 日签署《登记公约》，并于 1977 年 7 月 22 日由乌克兰最高苏维埃主席团批准。公约于 1977 年 9 月 14 日对乌克兰生效。白俄罗斯苏维埃社会主义共和国于 1975 年 6 月 30 日签署《登记公约》，并于 1977 年 7 月 20 日由白俄罗斯最高苏维埃主席团批准[②]。公约于 6 个月后即 1978 年 1 月 26 日对白俄罗斯生效。作为新国家，乌克兰和白俄罗斯共和国正式确认了继承乌克兰苏维埃社会主义共和国和白俄罗斯苏维埃社会主义共和国为当事国的所有国际条约，而不需要确认它们在每项协议中的成员资格。其加入《登记公约》的日期也被保留下来。关于其他后苏联国家，只有哈萨克斯坦共和国加入了《登记公约》[③]。

（b）俄罗斯联邦

在俄罗斯联邦，维持适当登记册的法律依据是：1993 年 8 月 20 日俄罗斯联邦法第 5663-1 号《俄罗斯联邦空间活动法》[④]；2015 年 7 月 21 日联邦法第 215-FZ 号《国

---

① See, in particular, the message from Russian President Boris Yeltsin to UN Secretary-General of 24 December 1991, as well as agreements on the CIS: The statement of 'Twelve' on the future status of Russia and other former Soviet republics (23 December 1991); Agreement on succession to the external public debt and assets of the Union of Soviet Socialist Republic (4 December 1991), Agreement on the supplement to the Treaty on the succession to the external public debt and assets of the Union of Soviet Socialist Republics (13 March 1992), etc.

② Decree of the Presidium of the Supreme Council of the Byelorussian SSR No. 1359-IX On ratification of the Convention on Registration of Objects Launched into Outer Space (20 July 1977).

③ Law of the Republic of Kazakhstan No. 108-1 On the Accession of the Republic of Kazakhstan to the Convention on Registration of Objects Launched into Outer Space (15 May 1997).

④ Law of the Russian Federation About Space Activity No. 5663-1 (20 August 1993) (as amended 7 March 2018). For a German translation see Marenkov, Dmitry, Zum Russischen Weltraumgesetz in seiner aktualisierten Fassung vom 2. Februar 2006, Zeitschrift für Luft- und Weltraumrecht (56) 2007, p. 65ff.; see also: Russian Newspaper, 6 October 1993; Legislation Collection of the Russian Federation, 1996, No. 50, Art. 5609, 2003, No. 2, Art. 167; 2004; No. 10, Art. 834; No. 35, Art. 3607, 2006, No. 6, Art. 636; No. 52, Art. 5497, 2009, No. 1, Art. 17, 21; the English text version in an unofficial translation is accessible through the website of UNOOSA: <http://www.unoosa.org/oosa/SpaceLaw/national/russian_federation/decree_5663-1_E.html>, accessed 26 April 2019.

家航天公司（ROSCOSMOS）[1] 法》和《俄罗斯联邦航天局关于实施维持俄罗斯联邦射入外层空间物体的登记册的国家职能的行政法规》（《俄罗斯联邦行政法规》）[2]。

苏联社会主义共和国联盟常驻联合国代表团于1978年1月13日的照会中通知联合国秘书长，其已建立了射入外层空间物体的国家登记册[3]。

在俄罗斯联邦，国家登记册由国家航天公司（ROSCOSMOS）管理。在管理登记册过程中，俄罗斯国家航天公司和联邦行政机构之间的协作程序由《联邦行政机构相互协作示范条例》所确定，该条例于2005年1月19日由俄罗斯联邦政府第30号令《联邦行政机构相互协作示范条例》批准[4]。

根据《俄罗斯联邦行政法规》附件41，俄罗斯联邦射入外层空间物体的登记册包含以下信息：

（1）空间物体的登记号码；（2）发射国名称；（3）空间物体的名称；（4）发射日期；（5）发射领土或发射地点（发射场、运载火箭）；（6）基本轨道参数：远地点（公里）、近地点（公里）、倾斜角（角度）、转动周期（分钟）；（7）空间物体的通用目的；（8）国际空间研究委员会（COSPAR）标识编号；（9）空间物体操作者；（10）说明/备注（本栏应载有被置于地球轨道的空间物体已不在该轨道上的信息，并在适用的情况下记载空间物体的发射异常信息）。

在执行关于维持苏联/俄罗斯空间物体国家登记册的公共职能时，立法[5]规定了下列行政程序：

（a）初步审查空间物体的下一年度发射计划；（b）俄罗斯国家航天公司接收对发射到外层空间的空间物体的登记申请；（c）核查所收到的关于向外层空间发射空间

---

① Federal Law dated 21 July 2015 No. 215-FZ On State Space Corporation “Roscosmos”.

② The Administrative Regulation of the Russian Federal Space Agency on the Implementation of the State Function of Maintaining the Registry of Space Objects Launched in Outer Space by the Russian Federation (approved by Order of the Federal Space Agency dated 22 March 2010 No. 44, registered in the Ministry of Justice of the Russian Federation on 22 September 2010 No. 18508).

③ UN Doc. ST/SG/SER. E/INF. 4, Information furnished by the Permanent Mission of the Union of Soviet Socialist Republics to the United Nations in Note Verbale dated 13 January 1978 addressed to the Secretary-General, 18 January 1978.

④ Legislation Collection of the Russian Federation, 2005, No. 4, Art. 305; No. 47, Art. 4933; 2007, No. 43, Art. 5202; 2008, No. 9, Art. 852; No. 14, Art. 1413; 2009, No. 12, Art. 1429; No. 25, Art. 3060; No. 41, Art. 4790; No. 49, Art. 5970.

⑤ Para. 3. 2 RF Administrative Regulation.

物体的信息的完整性和准确性；（d）向空间物体分配登记号码，将其发射数据录入登记册；（e）由俄罗斯国家航天公司获取关于被送入地球轨道但已不在轨道上的空间物体的信息；（f）整理登记册上的空间物体信息，并将该信息转交俄罗斯外交部，以提交联合国秘书长；（g）俄罗斯国家航天公司获取该空间物体的国际登记号码及其纳入国际登记册的相关信息；（h）印发登记册摘要。

根据俄罗斯联邦立法（《俄罗斯联邦行政法规》第 3.7 节），空间物体的登记是通过分配单独的登记号码进行的。俄罗斯联邦登记册中的空间物体的登记号包含一组连贯的阿拉伯数字（第 0000-0000-000 号），第一组四个索引数字表示在苏联/俄罗斯登记册中的序列号，从第一颗人造地球卫星的发射开始计数；第二组四个索引数字为登记物体的发射年份；第三组的三个数字表示空间物体在当年发射的序列号。

《俄罗斯联邦行政法规》规定了以下提交登记文件的截止日期：以月为单位，每月 15 日前，俄罗斯国家航天公司确保建立上月发射的空间物体的登记数据，并按照该法规附件 6 所提供的样例，将其发送至俄罗斯外交部以提交联合国秘书长。

根据联合国射入外层空间物体的在线索引，俄罗斯联邦（包括苏联）已经登记了 3532 个空间物体①。

（c）乌克兰

在乌克兰，维持射入外层空间物体登记册的依据②是《乌克兰空间活动法》第十三条和第十四条③，以及 2015 年 5 月 14 日由第 281 号乌克兰内阁法令批准的《乌克兰国家航天局（SSAU）条例》第 4 款第 23-24 项④。

---

① For information on registered/non-registered space objects see the UNOOSA online index of objects launched into outer space on the UNOOSA website <http：//www. unoosa. org/oosa/osoindex/search-ng. jspx？ lf _ id = > accessed 26 April 2019.

② UN Doc. ST/SG/SER. E/INF. 11, Note Verbale dated 22 September 1995 from the Permanent Mission of Ukraine to the United Nations addressed to the Secretary-General, 12 October 1995.

③ Bulletin of Supreme Council of Ukraine. -1997, No. 1. -Art. 2), as amended by Laws No. 1559-Ⅲ dated 16 March 2000; Bulletin of Supreme Council of Ukraine. -2000. -No. 22. -Art. 172. -No. 3370-IV dated 19 January 2006; Bulletin of Supreme Council of Ukraine. -2006. -No. 22. -Art. 184; No. 2186-VI dated 13 May 2010. -Bulletin of Supreme Council of Ukraine. -2010. -No. 30. -Art. 393; Ordinance of the Supreme Soviet of Ukraine, Law of the Ukraine On Space Activity (15 November 1996), online accessible at <http：//www. oosa. unvienna. org/oosa/en/SpaceLaw/national/ukraine/ordinance_ on_ space_ activity_ 1996E. html> accessed 26 April 2019.

④ Decree of the Cabinet of Ministers of Ukraine No. 1722 On Provision on the National Space Agency of Ukraine (13 December 2006), as amended by Regulation of the Cabinet of Ministers of Ukraine No. 101 dated 27 February 2008, No. 281 dated 14 May 2015.

乌克兰常驻联合国代表团于1995年9月22日的照会中通知联合国秘书长，其已建立了发射进入外层空间物体的国家登记册①。

乌克兰《航天器登记规则（草案）》被提交至乌克兰内阁以进行批准。根据该草案，乌克兰国家登记册分别以乌克兰语和英语进行登记。国家登记册所载信息应可公开查阅。乌克兰国家登记册由乌克兰国家航天局管理，该局负责在其网站上提供国家登记册的电子版本。

根据乌克兰《航天器登记规则（草案）》，乌克兰国家航天局向乌克兰外交部提供航天器登记信息，以便后者进一步将其提交给联合国秘书长②。在此方面，从空间物体登入国家登记册到向联合国秘书长提交信息的期间不应超过三个工作日。

根据《登记公约》，只有相关发射国的登记决定才有意义。这个连接标准没有反映航天器的生产和可用性③。因此，尽管乌克兰有大型的发射装置产业，但其登记的空间物体数量有限，共四个空间物体，且只有一个仍在轨运行④。此外，根据联合国在线索引，乌克兰另外三个在轨运行的空间物体尚未进行登记，但却曾被俄罗斯联邦所提及⑤。

(d) 哈萨克斯坦

哈萨克斯坦共和国国防和航空航天工业部航空航天委员会维持其空间物体登记册

① UN Doc. ST/SG/SER. E/INF. 11, Note Verbale dated 22 September 1995 from the Permanent Mission of Ukraine to the United Nations addressed to the Secretary-General, 12 October 1995.

② Para. 9 and para. 10 Draft Rules on Registration of the Ukraine.

③ Schmidt-Tedd, Bernhard/Khalimova, Gulnaz/Teselkin, Sergey, The legal problems of providing the space activity of space objects launching by aerospace launch systems with the participation of several States (Polyot Air Launch Project as an example), in: IISL, Proceedings of the 54th Colloquium on the Law of Outer Space, 27 September-1 October 2011 Prague (Czech Republic), Eleven International Publishing, The Hague 2012, pp. 500-509.

④ Remote sensing satellite 'Sich-1', launched on 31 August 1995 (See UN Doc. ST/SG/SER. E/291, Note Verbale dated 22 September 1995 from the Permanent Mission of Ukraine to the United Nations addressed to the Secretary-General, 12 October 1995); remote sensing satellite 'Sich-1M', and remote sensing satellite 'Mikron', both launched on 24 December 2004 (see UN Doc. ST/SG/SER. E/466, Note Verbale dated 24 January 2005 from the Permanent Mission of Ukraine to the United Nations (Vienna) addressed to the Secretary-General, 7 February 2005), remote sensing satellite 'Sich-2' launched on 17 August 2011 (See UN Doc. ST/SG/SER. E/677, Note verbale dated 3 June 2013 from the Permanent Mission of Ukraine to the United Nations addressed to the Secretary General, 14 August 2013), all four entered in the National Register of Ukraine, as well as in UN Register.

⑤ UN Doc. ST/SG/SER. E/626, Note Verbale dated 11 August 2011 from the Permanent Mission of the Russian Federation to the United Nations (Vienna) addressed to the Secretary-General, 18 November 2011; UN Doc. ST/SG/SER. E/641, Note Verbale dated 27 January 2012 from the Permanent Mission of the Russian Federation to the United Nations (Vienna) addressed to the Secretary-General, 27 January 2012.

方面的权限由 2016 年 11 月 16 日《哈萨克斯坦共和国国防和航空航天工业部航空航天委员会条例》第二条第 14 款第 13、26、30 项进行规定①。

哈萨克斯坦常驻联合国代表团（维也纳）于 2012 年 2 月 20 日的照会中通知联合国秘书长，其已建立了自 2006 年以来射入外层空间物体的国家登记册②。

哈萨克斯坦国家登记册由哈萨克斯坦共和国国防和航空航天工业部航空航天委员会维持。

2012 年 1 月 6 日通过的哈萨克斯坦《空间活动法》③ 包含了其管辖范围内的空间物体国家登记的主要法律规定④。在《空间活动法》第十一条中规定了需要进行国家登记的物体类别。其中两项是关于下列空间物体：（1）属于哈萨克斯坦个人和法律实体的空间物体及其所附权利；（2）属于外国个人和法律实体但是从哈萨克斯坦领土发射到外层空间的空间物体。

由于适用于这两类空间物体的法律制度不同，登记所产生的法律后果也不尽相同。对于第一类物体，根据哈萨克斯坦民法，其登记被视为记录空间物体，以及国家认可和承认该空间物体相关权利的产生、变化和停止的行为。对于第二类物体，国家登记仅意味着在空间物体登记册中进行记录，而不涉及权利的登记。

在国内层面，空间物体的权利产生于其进行国家登记之时，并由获得授权的部门颁发的国家登记证书予以确认⑤。

根据上述法律，哈萨克斯坦管理空间活动的部门（在本领域内行使行政权力，并在哈萨克斯坦立法范围内进行部门协调的中央机构⑥）制订空间物体及其权利的国家

① Order of the Minister of the Defense and Aerospace Industry of the Republic of Kazakhstan of November 17, 2016 "About approval of the Provision of republican public institution "Committee on information security of the Ministry of the defense and aerospace industry of the Republic of Kazakhstan".

② UN Doc. ST/SG/SER. E/INF. 26, Note Verbale dated 20 February 2012 from the Permanent Mission of Kazakhstan to the United Nations (Vienna) addressed to the Secretary-General, 28 February 2012.

③ Law of the Republic of Kazakhstan on Space Activity dated 6 January 2012 No. 528-IV (Law on Space Activity).

④ For more information on the adoption of the law, see Schmidt-Tedd, Bernhard/Stelmakh, Olga, Einführung in das Gesetz der Republik Kasachstan über Weltraumaktivitäten, Zeitschrift für Luft- und Weltraumrecht (61) 2012, pp. 426-450.

⑤ Art. 11 para. 4 Law of the Republic of Kazakhstan on Space Activitydated 6 January 2012 No. 528-IV.

⑥ See the website of the National Space Agency of the Republic of Kazakhstan <http://www.kazcosmos.kz/> accessed 26 April 2019.

登记规则[1]，执行国家登记[2]并维持空间物体登记册[3]。

国家登记应按照空间物体及其权利的国家登记指令进行[4]。2015 年 4 月 30 日，哈萨克斯坦通过了“投资和发展部长关于批准空间物体及其权利的国家登记规则以及空间物体登记册形式的第 534 号指令”。该文件附件 2 是名为“空间物体及其权利的国家登记”的国家服务标准。

登记需要提交的文件在《空间活动法》第十一条第 6 款中列出。该清单包括三项内容：（1）申请；（2）关于空间物体所有权的文件的电子版本；（3）确认支付空间物体及其权利的国家登记费用的文件。上述列举出来的要求与《空间物体及其权利国家登记规则及空间物体登记册形式》第六条中的要求一致。

哈萨克斯坦共和国发射到外层空间的空间物体的名称应采用由主管空间活动的国家机构确定的标识，并应符合国际标准和哈萨克斯坦立法[5]。

截至目前，哈萨克斯坦已向联合国登记了 2 个空间物体[6]。

（e）白俄罗斯

2015 年 5 月 21 日，白俄罗斯共和国国家科学院决定成立国家空间研究局。

白俄罗斯共和国于 2003 年宣布建立国家空间物体登记册，当时白俄罗斯的第一颗卫星 BelKA-1 的发射（使用乌克兰 LV Dnipro）正处于准备阶段。该卫星于 2006 年 7 月底发射，但不幸的是，由于在飞行第 73 秒火箭发动机出现故障而导致发射失败。虽然该物体尚未在相关国家登记册进行登记，但白俄罗斯国家科学院已向联合国秘书长发出关于设立和维持国家登记册的通知[7]。白俄罗斯常驻联合国代表团于 2017 年 1 月 30 日的照会中向联合国秘书长提交了白俄罗斯两个空间物体，即 BKA 和

---

① Art. 9 para. 1 subpara. 11 Law of the Republic of Kazakhstan on Space Activitydated 6 January 2012 No. 528-IV.

② Art. 9 para. 1 subpara. 12 Law of the Republic of Kazakhstan on Space Activitydated 6 January 2012 No. 528-IV.

③ Art. 9 para. 1 subpara. 13 Law of the Republic of Kazakhstan on Space Activitydated 6 January 2012 No. 528-IV.

④ Art. 11 para. 3 Law of the Republic of Kazakhstan on Space Activitydated 6 January 2012 No. 528-IV.

⑤ Art. 24 Law of the Republic of Kazakhstan on Space Activitydated 6 January 2012 No. 528-IV.

⑥ UN Doc. ST/SG/SER. E/509, Note Verbale dated 9 March 2007 from the Permanent Mission of Kazakhstan to the United Nations addressed to the Secretary-General, 28 March 2007; UN Doc. ST/SG/SER. E/637, Note Verbale dated 26 December 2011 from the Permanent Mission of Kazakhstan to the United Nations (Vienna) addressed to the Secretary-General, 13 January 2012.

⑦ UN Doc. ST/SG/SER. E/INF. 18, Note Verbale dated 12 July 2006 from the Permanent Mission of Belarus to the United Nations (Vienna) addressed to the Secretary-General, 13 July 2006.

BELINTERSAT-1 的登记信息[①]。

（f）捷克共和国

1979 年 6 月 13 日，捷克斯洛伐克社会主义共和国常驻代表团通过照会通知联合国秘书长，其已建立捷克斯洛伐克射入外层空间物体的国家登记册[②]。自 1993 年 1 月 1 日起，在捷克斯洛伐克解体以及捷克共和国和斯洛伐克共和国宣布成立之后，维持适当登记册的责任即转移给捷克共和国[③]。

在捷克共和国，维持适当的国家登记册最初是由捷克科学院大气物理研究所负责，后其职能移交给捷克空间办公室[④]。

根据联合国空间物体线上索引，到目前为止捷克共和国（包括捷克斯洛伐克）共登记了 6 个空间物体，其中 3 个仍在轨运行[⑤]。

②美国/加拿大/英国/澳大利亚

（a）美国

1962 年 3 月，美国首次向联合国秘书长提交文件，从而开启了空间物体的国际登记[⑥]。其向联合国秘书长提供了截至 1962 年 2 月 15 日正在持续轨道或穿越外空的 72

① UN Doc. ST/SG/SER. E/790, Note Verbale dated 30 January 2017from the Permanent Mission of Belarus to the United Nations addressed to the Secretary-General, 15 March 2017.

② UN Doc. ST/SG/SER. E/INF. 5, Note Verbale dated 13 June 1979 from the Permanent Representative of Czechoslovakia to the United Nations addressed to the Secretary-General, 11 July 1979.

③ UN Doc. ST/SG/SER. E/INF. 12, Note Verbale dated 12 July 1996 from the Permanent Representative of Czech Republic to the United Nations (Vienna) addressed to the Secretary-General, 5 August 1996.

④ UN Doc. ST/SG/SER. E/INF. 25, Note Verbale dated 14 July 2009 from the Permanent Mission of the Czech Republic to the United Nations (Vienna) addressed to the Secretary-General, 20 August 2009.

⑤ UN Doc. ST/SG/SER. E/022, Note Verbale dated 13 June 1979 from the Permanent Representative of Czechoslovakia to the United Nations addressed to the Secretary-General, 11 July 1979; UN Doc. ST/SG/SER. E/213, Note Verbale dated 20 December 1989 from the Permanent Representative of Czechoslovakia to the United Nations addressed to the Secretary-General, 3 January 1990; UN Doc. ST/SG/SER. E/251, Note Verbale dated 14 February 1992 from the Permanent Representative of Czechoslovakia to the United Nations addressed to the Secretary-General, 26 February 1992; UN Doc. ST/SG/SER. E/314, Note Verbale dated 12 July 1996 from the Permanent Mission of the Czech Republic to the United Nations (Vienna) addressed to the Secretary-General, 5 August 1996; UN Doc. ST/SG/SER. E/361, Note Verbale dated 20 September 1999 from the Permanent Mission of the Czech Republic to the United Nations (Vienna) addressed to the Secretary-General, 29 September 1999; UN Doc. ST/SG/SER. E/433, Note Verbale dated 21 August 2003 from the Permanent Mission of the Czech Republic to the United Nations (Vienna) addressed to the Secretary-General, 9 September 2003.

⑥ UN Doc. A/AC. 105/INF. 1, Letter dated 6 March 1962 from the Acting Secretary-General addressed to the Chairman of the Committee on the Peaceful Uses of Outer Space, transmitting a communication dated 5 March 1962 from Permanent Representative of the United States of America, 7 March 1962.

个空间运载器及相关物体的统计信息（按时间顺序）。此外，美国还提供了每一物体的相关信息，包括国际标识、运载火箭、发射日期、节点周期、倾角、远地点、近地点和卫星种类。空间物体根据其不同目的被划分为四类：①空间飞行技术的发展；②空间研究和探索；③天基技术的实际应用以及④非功能性物体。

美国于 1975 年 1 月 24 日签署《登记公约》，是少数几个在 1976 年该公约生效前根据 1721 B（XVI）号决议在联合国登记空间物体的西方国家之一。然而，《登记公约》的生效使联合国登记册在法律上一分为二，因为《登记公约》并没有使第 1721 B（XVI）号决议下的登记册作废。相反，《登记公约》建立了第二类登记册，适用于公约的缔约国，规定了该登记册至少应包含的具体内容，以及登记册管理的其他细节。第 1721 B（XVI）号决议作为一项联合国大会决议继续适用于所有国家，无需各国进一步正式同意。

美国在《登记公约》生效后定期向联合国秘书长提供关于空间发射的资料。1977 年春的第一份通知提供了“截至 1976 年 12 月 31 日美国在地球轨道或更远外层空间的所有航天器的完整登记”①。美国提供了《登记公约》所要求的基本信息，并列出了：①轨道上的新物体；②以前未报告但自上次报告以来已确认的物体；③已不在轨的物体。

后来，美国修改了通知的格式，以提供关于已不在轨道上的物体的更多信息，并将此类物体分为以下类别：①以前未报告、自上次报告以来已确认但已不在轨道上的物体；②自上次报告以来已进入轨道但现已不在轨道上的物体（例如可重复使用的空间运输系统，如航天飞机）；③先前确认的已不在轨道上的物体。此外，美国的通知模板中还包括已发射但未进入轨道的物体，以及对先前报告数据的任何修改②。

美国驻联合国安理会副代表于 1977 年 2 月 9 日给联合国秘书长的信中向联合国通报了美国国家登记册的情况③。该国家登记册由国务院空间和先进技术办公室设立和

① UN Doc. ST/SG/SER. E/001, Letter dated 31 March 1977 From the Permanent Representative of the United States addressed to the Secretary-General, 14 April 1977, p. 1.

② See, e. g. , UN Doc. ST/SG/SER. E/576, Note Verbale dated 9 September 2009 from the Permanent Mission of the United States of America to the United Nations (Vienna) addressed to the Secretary-General, 14 September 2009; UN Doc. ST/SG/SER. E/590, Note Verbale dated 22 February 2010 from the Permanent Mission of the United States of America to the United Nations (Vienna) addressed to the Secretary-General, 5 March 2010.

③ UN Doc. ST/SG/SER. E/INF. 3, Letter dated 9 February from the Deputy Representative of the United States in the Security Council addressed to the Secretary-General, 17 February 1977.

维持，其中的信息将纳入联合国登记册①。登记册信息每季度根据战略司令部提供的数据加以更新，战略司令部负责维持所有空间物体的目录②。美国的做法是在其向联合国秘书长的通知中不仅提供功能性有效载荷的信息，而且还包括助推器、运载火箭级、护罩和其他非功能性物体。例如，美国确认了用 1973-086 A 号发射的 165 个物体，以及用 1975-004 号发射的 158 个物体③。

美国在实践中将航天飞机的发射，以及由航天飞机运送的美国有效载荷纳入其通知，但不包括非美国的有效载荷。对于非美国的有效载荷，美国的立场是另一相关国家最适合对该物体行使持续管辖和控制，因此也最适合对该物体进行登记。另一方面，如非政府实体通知美国国务院其将从非美国领土上发射有效载荷，美国则会通知相关国家，一旦该有效载荷被发射进入地球轨道，该发射将被记录在美国登记册④。美国法律规定，根据《外空条约》和《登记公约》在美国登记册登记的设计或用于空间航行的航天器应被视为在美国的特殊海洋和领土管辖范围内⑤。这是管辖权和控制权在国际和国家层面的立法连接的一个例子。

从美国政府获得许可的私人发射运营商须向美国联邦航空管理局（FAA）提交具体信息，以协助美国执行《登记公约》第四条。根据规定，一次性运载火箭的发射运营商必须在发射后 30 天内提交《登记公约》第四条第 1 款 2~5 项下的信息⑥。相关规定使用了和《登记公约》第四条第 1 款完全一致的语言，除了关于轨道参数，《登记公约》用的是“基本”轨道，而美国国内规定用的是“最终”轨道。这些强制性披露的例外包括由美国政府所有和登记的物体以及由任何外国实体所有的物体⑦。上

① See the website of the US Space Objects Registry < www. usspaceobjectsregistry. state. gov> accessed 26 April 2019.

② US Delegation Statement to UNCOPUOS on Practice of States and International Organizations in Registering Space Objects, 10 December 2004 <http://www. state. gov/s/l/2004/78104. htm. > accessed 26 April 2019.

③ UN Doc. ST/SG/SER. E/001, Letter dated 31 March 1977 From the Permanent Representative of the United States addressed to the Secretary-General, 14 April 1977, p. 4.

④ US Delegation Statement to UNCOPUOS on Practice of States and International Organizations in Registering Space Objects, 10 December 2004 <http://www. state. gov/s/l/2004/78104. htm. > accessed 26 April 2019.

⑤ US Code 18 U. S. C. Para. 7 subpara. 6.

⑥ 14 C. F. R. Para. 417. 19 lit. (a); 14 C. F. R. Para. 401. 5 defines a launch operator as “a person who conducts or who will conduct the launch of a launch vehicle and any payload.”.

⑦ 14 C. F. R. Para. 417. 19 lit. (a) no. 1 and no. 2.

述披露义务也适用于运营可重复使用运载火箭（RLV）的许可持有人[①]，但有一个额外要求，即被许可人移除其先前放置于外空中的物体时，应通知联邦航空管理局[②]。该规定很大程度上适用于可重复使用运载火箭返回地球的情形，然而，由于其语言非常宽泛，也可能包括有效载荷或其他空间物体被许可持有人从外空移除的情况，不论是否使用同一可重复使用运载火箭，以及是否是在同一任务中发射的物体。

尽管美国提供的信息看起来可能很完整，但就《登记公约》的披露要求而言，仍然包含以下五类不符之处：

①未能登记在美国发射并由美国实体所有的民用卫星；②未能登记美国实体所有但在美国境外发射的民用卫星；③未能登记军用卫星；④提供有关机密军事卫星的错误轨道信息；⑤提供有关机密军事卫星的误导性轨道信息[③]。

上述所指的不符之处，就其性质而言，可能不仅限于美国的做法。无论是公共的还是私营的，民用的还是军用的载荷，也无论是在国内发射还是在国外发射，未能登记或提供错误信息都可能是由于多种原因所造成，并非所有这些原因都是出于恶意，或恶意企图的结果。但是，取决于空间物体的民用或军用性质，某些披露信息的形式和内容存在差异应在意料之中，虽然《登记公约》第四条在披露目的方面并不区分民用和军用有效载荷。然而，似乎可以公正地得出结论，民用和军用地球静止卫星登记的不同做法存在一定的目的性因素。对于民用卫星，一般将登记某次发射中的三个独立物体：在停泊轨道上的第二级运载火箭，在转移轨道上的第三级运载火箭以及在运行轨道上的卫星。相比之下，许多机密卫星仅登记在停泊轨道的这三个物体。

如果考虑转让在轨电信卫星的所有权，美国联邦通信委员会将与接受国进行协商。这些协商将就载荷的监管、许可及与国际电信联盟协调的责任，以及是否在使用寿命结束后将卫星移出轨道等问题达成共识。这些共识将被记录在不具约束力的交换信件中[④]。然而，任何可能达成的协议或共识都不会改变美国是原始发射国的事实，

① 14 C. F. R. Para. 431. 85.

② 14 C. F. R. Para. 431. 85 lit. （c）.

③ See Jonathan McDowell's Statement on United States Non-Compliance with UNGA Res. 1721 B（XVI）<http：//planet4589. org/space/un/untxt. html> accessed 26 April 2019.

④ UN Doc. COPUOS/LEGAL/T. 741，Committee on the Peaceful Uses of Outer Space，Legal Subcommittee，Unedited transcript of the 741st Meeting on Information on the Activities of International Organizations Relating to Space Law（Agenda Item 7），10 April 2006，p. 9.

也不一定会导致美国登记册的变更①。另外，可能引起的问题是，此类不具有约束力的信件协议是否足以为美国提供依据，以便其在此后不再对相关空间物体实施任何持续的监督和控制，特别是在其他国家未能进行有效监督和控制的情况下。国家不仅要对其授权和继续监督的私人实体负责，也要对其疏于实施监督和控制的私人实体负责②。因此，美国将继续在国际层面承担主要赔偿责任，但可能有权得到其他国家的补偿或赔偿。转让国和接受国之间如果有任何协议的话，该协议只对缔约国本身有效，而对其他国家不具有约束力。

如果在轨物体的所有权转让涉及空间物体的两个发射国，情况就有所不同。《登记公约》并未禁止在此情况下转移在轨空间物体的所有管辖权和控制权。由此看来，空间物体登记国在法律上可与该物体的其他发射国订立协议，以转让因登记而产生的部分或全部权利和义务③。

根据联合国空间物体在线索引，美利坚合众国已登记了近 2000 个空间物体④。

（b）加拿大

加拿大于 1975 年 2 月 14 日签署了《登记公约》，是第一个通知联合国秘书长（通过 1976 年 8 月 24 日的照会）设立了《登记公约》第二条所规定的登记册的国家。其登记册由部门间空间委员会设立⑤。

直至现在，加拿大仍缺乏关于登记问题的具体国内法规。尽管如此，加拿大于 1979 年以通知形式登记了其第一颗卫星 ANIK B-1，提供了《登记公约》所要求的信

① See Frankle, Edward A., Once A Launching State, Always The Launching State?, in: IISL, Proceedings of the 44th Colloquium on the Law of Outer Space, 1-5 October 2001 Toulouse (France), AIAA, 2002, pp. 32ff.

② Schmidt-Tedd, Bernhard/Gerhard, Michael, Registration of Space Objects: Which Are the Advantages for States Resulting from Registration?, in: Benkö, Marietta/Schrogl, Kai-Uwe (eds.), Space Law: Current Problems and Perspectives for Future Regulation, Eleven International Publishing, Utrecht 2005, p. 137.

③ Hörl, Kay-Uwe/Hermida, Julian, Change of Ownership, Change of Registry? Which Objects to Register, What data to be Furnished, When, and Until When?, in: IISL, Proceedings of the 46th Colloquium on the Law of Outer Space, 29 September-3 October 2003 Bremen (Germany), AIAA, 2004, p. 457.

④ For information on registered/non-registered space objects see the UNOOSA online index of objects launched into outer space on the UNOOSA website <http://www.unoosa.org/oosa/osoindex/search-ng.jspx?lf_id=> accessed 26 April 2019.

⑤ UN Doc. ST/SG/SER. E/INF. 2, Note Verbale dated 24 August 1976 from the Permanent Mission of Canada to the United Nations addressed to the Secretary-General, 16 November 1976.

息，并指明了该空间物体的运行机构[1]。指明运行机构的做法在加拿大后续的通知中被保留下来。此外，对于地球静止轨道卫星，加拿大还列出了空间物体的频率和发射机功率[2]。

在加拿大，加拿大航天局准备有关信息，并将其发送给外交和国际贸易部，该部随后通过加拿大联合国办事处将有关信息转达给联合国秘书长[3]。截至目前，加拿大已在联合国登记了 28 个空间物体[4]。

（c）英国

英国自 1971 年起开始按照第 1721 B（XⅥ）号决议向联合国秘书长提供信息[5]。这种做法在 1975 年 5 月 6 日英国批准了《登记公约》后仍在继续，最后一次这样的信息传送是关于 1979 年的 Ariel Ⅳ卫星[6]。英国披露的信息通常包括《登记公约》第四条所要求的信息。

英国根据《登记公约》第二条建立了国家空间登记册，并由英国航天中心维护。该登记册对公众开放，但需要支付一定费用[7]。根据英国《外层空间法》第 7 节第 2 段，空间物体的详细情况应按国务大臣认为符合英国国际义务的适当方式列入登记册。2015 年 6 月 24 日，英国向联合国提交了设立国家登记册的正式通知[8]。英国也依

① UN Doc. ST/SG/SER. E/024, Note Verbale dated 25 June 1979 from the Permanent Representative of Canada to the United Nations addressed to the Secretary-General, 11 July 1979.

② See, e. g. , UN Doc. ST/SG/SER. E/540, Note Verbale dated 8 April 2008 from the Permanent Mission of Canada to the United Nations (Vienna) addressed to the Secretary-General, 11 April 2008; UN Doc. ST/SG/SER. E/597, Note Verbale dated 30 June 2010 from the Permanent Mission of Canada to the United Nations (Vienna) addressed to the Secretary-General, 6 July 2010.

③ Hermida, Julian, Legal Basis for a National Space Legislation, Kluwer Academic Publishers, New York 2004, p. 171.

④ For information on registered/non-registered space objects see the UNOOSA online index of objects launched into outer space on the UNOOSA website <http：//www. unoosa. org/oosa/osoindex/search-ng. jspx？lf_id=> accessed 26 April 2019.

⑤ UN Doc. A/AC/105/INF. 240, Letter dated 3 November 1971 from the Permanent Representative of the United Kingdom to the United Nations addressed to the Secretary-General, 3 November 1971.

⑥ UN Doc. A/AC/105/INF. 384, Note Verbale dated 10 October 1979 from the Permanent Mission of the United Kingdom of Great Britain and Northern Ireland to the United Nations addressed to the Secretary-General, 19 October 1979.

⑦ Lyall, Francis/Larsen, Paul B. , Space Law-A Treatise, Ashgate, Burlington 2009, p. 488.

⑧ UN Doc. ST/SG/SER. E/INF/32, Note Verbale dated 24 June 2015 from the Permanent Representative of the United Kingdom of Great Britain and Northern Ireland to the United Nations addressed to the Secretary-General, 30 July 2015.

据《登记公约》提供了发射进入外层空间物体的通知。这些通知的内容仅限于《登记公约》第四条所明确列出的信息①，但对于地球静止轨道卫星，英国还提供了除基本轨道参数外的轨道位置度数②。值得注意的是，英国在一项通知中说明，其仅授权 NSS-9 和 Deimos-1 卫星的发射，荷兰和西班牙将分别登记其在轨运行③。

英国对特定空间物体的状态更新也提供了具体通知。例如，1989 年英国通知称 UOSAT 1 号已损毁并已不再在轨运行。该通知附件中包含一份来自美国国家航空航天局的简报，证实该物体已损毁，并声明该物体已从英国的登记册中删除④。在国际海事卫星组织私有化后，该政府间组织成为一家英国公司。英国通知联合国秘书长其已向国际海事卫星组织公司（Inmarsat Ltd.）颁发了多颗卫星的运营许可证，并提交了包括《登记公约》第四条所要求信息在内的技术数据。此外，该通知还提供了每颗卫星的名称，确认国际海事卫星组织公司为所有者/运营者，并根据 1986 年《外层空间法》注明了标识、目录编号和颁发许可证的日期⑤。通知中包含一项免责声明，即“对于上述空间物体，英国不是《责任公约》《登记公约》及《营救协定》下的‘发射国’‘登记国’或‘发射当局’。⑥”尽管有上述免责声明，英国仍然向联合国秘书长提供了关于 1991-018 A 号卫星（也被称为 Inmarsat 2F2 号卫星）离轨的通知，它是

① See, e. g. , UN Doc. ST/SG/SER. E/129, Note Verbale dated 9 August 1985 from the Permanent Representative of the United Kingdom of Great Britain and Northern Ireland to the United Nations addressed to the Secretary-General, 21 August 1985.

② See, e. g, UN Doc. ST/SG/SER. E/555, Note Verbale dated 6 October 2008 Permanent Mission of the United Kingdom of Great Britain and Northern Ireland to the United Nations (Vienna) addressed to the Secretary-General, 24 November 2009.

③ UN Doc. ST/SG/SER. E/575, Note Verbale dated 6 August 2009 from the Permanent Mission of the United Kingdom of Great Britain and Northern Ireland to the United Nations (Vienna) addressed to the Secretary-General, 4 November 2009.

④ UN Doc. ST/SG/SER. E/210, Note Verbale dated 8 December 1989 from the Permanent Representative of the United Kingdom of Great Britain and Northern Ireland to the United Nations addressed to the Secretary-General, 19 December 1989.

⑤ UN Doc. ST/SG/SER. E/417/Rev. 1, Note Verbale dated 9 September 2002 from the Permanent Mission of the United Kingdom of Great Britain and Northern Ireland to the United Nations (Vienna) addressed to the Secretary-General, 3 December 2002.

⑥ UN Doc. ST/SG/SER. E/417/Rev. 1, Note Verbale dated 9 September 2002 from the Permanent Mission of the United Kingdom of Great Britain and Northern Ireland to the United Nations (Vienna) addressed to the Secretary-General, 3 December 2002.

上述通知中授予国际海事卫星组织的许可中所列的卫星之一①。英国所提交的这一通知表明，其主要是根据《外空条约》第十一条而非《登记公约》第四条第 2 款作出。这些卫星被列入由英国航天局维护的英国外层空间物体补充登记册中，该登记册列出了转让给英国公司后获得许可的卫星②。

（d）澳大利亚

澳大利亚根据第 1721 B（XVI）号决议向联合国秘书长提供了关于从乌默拉发射的 WRESAT 1 号卫星的信息。这些信息包括卫星的名称、发射日期和时间、空间物体的用途、近点周期、轨道倾角、远地点、近地点及其运载火箭③。

澳大利亚于 1986 年 3 月 11 日加入《登记公约》。澳大利亚第一部有关空间事务管理的法律——《空间活动法》④ 于 1998 年 12 月生效。《空间活动法》第 76 节指定工业、科学和资源部长设立一个登记册，并规定了需列入登记册的空间物体的详细信息。此外，关于登记册内信息的获取，《空间活动法》第 79 节规定，登记册必须可供任何人查阅⑤。执行这些规定以及其他任何关于空间发射活动协定的责任由空间许可和安全办公室（SLASO）承担。

澳大利亚在 2003 年 10 月 1 日的照会中通知联合国秘书长，其已设立了国家登记册，并将由位于堪培拉的空间许可和安全办公室维持⑥。然而，澳大利亚政府此前已根据《登记公约》将由法国发射的 AUSSAT 卫星的情况通知联合国秘书长。该正式通知载有《登记公约》第四条所要求的信息，并提供了卫星的位置和经度变化⑦。澳大

① UN Doc. A/AC. 105/965, Note Verbale dated 3 November 2009 from the Permanent Mission of the United Kingdom of Great Britain and Northern Ireland to the United Nations（Vienna）addressed to the Secretary-General, 3 November 2009.

② Lyall, Francis/Larsen, Paul B., Space Law-A Treatise, Ashgate, Burlington 2009, p. 488.

③ UN Doc. A/AC. 105/INF. 180, Letter dated 1 December 1967 from the Permanent Representative of Australia addressed to the Secretary-General, 5 December 1967.

④ Space Activities Act No. 123（1998）. The Act is online accessible on the ComLaw website of the Australian Government <http://www.comlaw.gov.au/Details/C2004C01013> accessed 26 April 2019.

⑤ The registry is accessible online at the Australian Government Space Portal <http://www.space.gov.au/SpaceLicensingSafetyOffice/Documents/Australian_space_object_register_table_14-12-09.pdf> accessed 26 April 2019.

⑥ UN Doc. ST/SG/SER. E/INF. 15, Note Verbale dated 1 October 2003 from the Permanent Mission of Australia to the United Nations（Vienna）addressed to the Secretary-General, 6 October 2003.

⑦ UN Doc. ST/SG/SER. E/199, Note Verbale dated 3 May 1989 from the Permanent Mission of Australia to the United Nations addressed to the Secretary-General, 11 May 1989.

利亚一直保持了其通知的基本格式，但在国际标识、卫星名称或登记号码的使用方面有一些细微的变化。直至 2007 年，澳大利亚开始对发射国的不同种类进行区分，即将澳大利亚认定为《登记公约》第一条第 1 款第（1）项下促成发射的国家，而实际提供发射服务的国家被认定为《登记公约》第一条第 1 款第（2）项下的发射国①。澳大利亚也就其国家登记册上的不同空间物体的状况变化和进入处置轨道的情况进行了单独通知②。澳大利亚总共在联合国登记了 13 个空间物体③。

③拉丁美洲（阿根廷、巴西、智利、墨西哥和委内瑞拉）

（a）阿根廷

阿根廷于 1975 年 3 月 26 日签署了《登记公约》。阿根廷于 1996 年 12 月 30 日的照会中通知联合国秘书长其设立了国家登记册④。该登记册由阿根廷国家空间活动委员会管理⑤。其也向联合国秘书长提供了《登记公约》所要求的卫星信息，以及包括空间物体的标识或名称及登记号码（虽然公约只要求提供其中一项）的正式通知，并注明发射物体的所有人或运营人、运载工具及发射组织⑥。联合国空间物体在线索引

① UN Doc. ST/SG/SER. E/527, Note Verbale dated 10 December 2007 from the Permanent Mission of Australia to the United Nations (Vienna) addressed to the Secretary-General, 19 December 2007.

② UN Doc. ST/SG/SER. E/584, Note Verbale dated 30 November 2009 from the Permanent Mission of Australia to the United Nations (Vienna) addressed to the Secretary-General, 18 January 2010.

③ For information on registered/non-registered space objects see the UNOOSA online index of objects launched into outer space on the UNOOSA website < http://www.unoosa.org/oosa/osoindex/search-ng.jspx? lf_ id = > accessed 26 April 2019.

④ UN Doc. ST/SG/SER. E/INF. 13, Note Verbale dated 30 December 1996 from the Permanent Mission of Argentina to the United Nations (Vienna) addressed to the Secretary-General, 15 January 1997.

⑤ See Art. 1 National Decree No. 125/95 On Establishment of the National Registry of Space Objects Launched into Outer Space (25 July 1995).

⑥ See, e. g., UN Doc. ST/SG/SER. E/317, Note Verbale dated 30 December 1996 from the Permanent Mission of Argentina to the United Nations (Vienna) addressed to the Secretary-General, 15 January 1997; UN Doc. ST/SG/SER. E/382, Note Verbale dated 7 December 2000 from the Permanent Mission of Argentina to the United Nations (Vienna) addressed to the Secretary-General, 7 December 2000; see also Art. 5 National Decree No. 125/95 On Establishment of the National Registry of Space Objects Launched into Outer Space (25 July 1995).

列出了阿根廷的 5 个已登记物体和 4 个未登记物体[①]。

（b）巴西

2007 年 3 月 27 日，巴西通知联合国秘书长其建立了国家登记册，并由巴西航天局管理[②]。在 CBERS-1 和 SACI-1 登记后，巴西直到 2006 年 3 月 17 日才加入《登记公约》，此后提交了 Brasilsat 系列多颗卫星的登记通知。除了公约要求披露的信息外，巴西还提供了每一空间物体的运载火箭及所有者名称的信息。在地球同步卫星 Brasilsat-A-2 的登记中，巴西通报该卫星于 2004 年被重置于近地点为地球同步轨道上方 209 公里的处置轨道，该卫星于 1986 年发射，且在通知时已不再在轨运行[③]。

巴西根据第 1721 B（XVI）号决议又另外登记了两颗卫星，即中巴地球资源一号卫星（CBERS-1）和科学应用一号卫星（SACI-1）。这两颗卫星都由一份通知文件进行登记，其中载有空间物体的名称、发射日期、远地点高度、近地点高度、倾角、节点周期等轨道参数以及空间物体的一般功能[④]。这两颗卫星的登记内容虽然相似，但所载信息与巴西登记其第一个空间物体时所提供的信息有所不同，虽然没有一颗卫星是使用其国际标识进行登记的。

巴西登记了数据收集卫星一号（SCD-1），并明确了卫星的发射国、名称和登记编号（但不包括国际标识）、发射日期和领土、节点周期、倾角、远地点和近地点等基本轨道参数，空间物体的总体描述及其任务，包括其功能、运载火箭和重量[⑤]。

---

① UN Doc. ST/SG/SER. E/317, Note Verbale dated 30 December 1996 from the Permanent Mission of Argentina to the United Nations (Vienna) addressed to the Secretary-General, 15 January 1997; UN Doc. ST/SG/SER. E/323, Note Verbale dated 10 July 1997 from the Permanent Mission of Argentina to the United Nations (Vienna) addressed to the Secretary-General, 29 July 1997; UN Doc. ST/SG/SER. E/351, Note Verbale dated 23 December 1998 from the Permanent Mission of Argentina to the United Nations (Vienna) addressed to the Secretary-General, 1 February 1999; UN Doc. ST/SG/SER. E/382, Note Verbale dated 7 December 2000 from the Permanent Mission of Argentina to the United Nations (Vienna) addressed to the Secretary-General, 7 December 2000.

② UN Doc. ST/SG/SER. E/INF. 19, Note Verbale dated 27 March 2007 from the Permanent Mission of Brazil to the United Nations (Vienna) addressed to the Secretary-General, 27 March 2007.

③ UN Doc. ST/SG/SER. E/498, Note Verbale dated 18 August 2006 from the Permanent Mission of Brazil to the United Nations (Vienna) addressed to the Secretary-General, 25 August 2006.

④ UN Doc. A/AC/105/INF. 404, Note Verbale dated 14 December 1999 from the Permanent Mission of Brazil to the United Nations (Vienna) addressed to the Secretary-General, 27 January 2000.

⑤ UN Doc. A/AC/105/INF. 397, Note Verbale dated 24 February 1993 from the Permanent Representative of Brazil to the United Nations addressed to the Secretary-General, 8 March 1993.

联合国空间物体在线索引列出了巴西的 8 个已登记物体和 6 个未登记物体[①]。

（c）墨西哥、智利和委内瑞拉

墨西哥于 1975 年 12 月 19 日签署了《登记公约》，而智利在 1981 年 9 月 17 日才加入。墨西哥和智利都向联合国秘书长提供了发射进入外层空间物体的登记信息，尽管二者都尚未作出设立国家登记册的正式通知。1986 年，墨西哥提交了关于莫雷洛斯一号和莫雷洛斯二号卫星的资料。根据《登记公约》第 4 条，墨西哥确认了其自身为发射国，并提供了上述空间物体的名称，以及发射的日期和地点、基本轨道特征和一般功能[②]。除此之外墨西哥未提供更多的信息。墨西哥于 2013 年 10 月 31 日通过照会通知联合国其建立了国家空间物体登记册[③]，而智利于 2016 年 1 月 18 日的照会中作出了建立登记册的通知[④]。

同样，智利在 1998 年向联合国秘书长提交了关于 FASAT-BRAVO 卫星的信息。该信息名为“智利航天发射登记数据”，列出了物体的名称、所有者和经营者（智利空军）、目录编号、发射地点和日期、基本轨道参数及一般功能。此外，该通知还提供了智利空军卫星控制站的地址、电话、传真和电子邮件，并说明该物体的预期运行寿命（预计为六年）[⑤]。除了两个已登记的物体外，联合国还列出了墨西哥的五个未登记物体。对于智利，联合国列出了其一个已登记物体和一个未登记物体[⑥]。

作为非缔约国，委内瑞拉登记了 Simon Bolivar 卫星（VENESAT-1）的发射，并提交了包含其国际标识、名称、发射日期、发射地点、发射国、节点周期、倾角、远地

① For information on registered/non-registered space objects see the UNOOSA online index of objects launched into outer space on the UNOOSA website <http：//www. oosa. unvienna. org/oosa/showSearch. do> accessed 26 April 2019.

② UN Doc. ST/SG/SER. E/184, Note Verbale dated 14 November 1986 from the Permanent Mission of Mexico to the United Nations addressed to the Secretary-General, 4 August 1988.

③ UN Doc. ST/SG/SER. E/INF/28, Note Verbale dated 31 October 2013, from the Permanent Mission of Mexico to the United Nations addressed to the Secretary-General, 11 December 2013.

④ UN Doc. ST/SG/SER. E/INF/33, Note Verbale dated 18 January 2016, from the Permanent Mission of Chile to the United Nations addressed to the Secretary-General, 2 March 2016.

⑤ UN Doc. ST/SG/SER. E/342, Note Verbale dated 31 July 1998 from the Permanent Mission of Chile to the United Nations（Vienna）addressed to the Secretary-General, 11 August 1998.

⑥ For the registered object see UN Doc. ST/SG/SER. E/342, Note Verbale dated 31 July 1998 from the Permanent Mission of Chile to the United Nations（Vienna）addressed to the Secretary-General, 11 August 1998.

点、近地点、经度、一般功能、物体所有者以及运营机构的正式通知①。

④部分欧洲国家（法国、德国、比利时、荷兰、意大利、西班牙、瑞典、希腊）

（a）法国

法国自1975年起成为《登记公约》的当事国②。根据其规定，法国建立了一个发射至地球轨道或更远外层空间的物体登记册。其于2004年1月28日的照会中通知联合国秘书长建立了国家登记册③。该登记册由法国航天局（以下简称国家空间研究中心④，CNES）管理。2008年《法国空间活动法》⑤第十二条正式明确了法国国家空间研究中心的权限，以及代表政府维持登记册，并根据《登记公约》第二条及相关国际协议进行登记的义务。其登记始于法国1965年11月26日发射的第一颗卫星Asterix⑥。

《法国空间活动法》第十二条提及了一项将由国务委员会通过的法令。该法令即2009年6月9日的第2009-644号法令，其对1984年6月28日有关法国国家空间研究中心的第84-510号法令进行了修订⑦。该修订（第2009-644号法令第一条）在第84-510号法令第十四条中增加了三个新的章节（第三、第四和第五章）。后者整合了登记信息的要求，除提供基本参数外，还要求提供关于空间物体运营者、所有者和制造商的身份信息，以及关于其运营国家的信息⑧。应当注意的是，根据该法令的现行规定，只有在有关个人或公司初步同意的情况下，才能披露关于空间物体所有者或制造

① UN Doc. A/AC/105/INF. 417, Note Verbale dated 31 December 2008 from the Permanent Mission of Venezuela to the United Nations (Vienna) addressed to the Secretary-General, 10 March 2009.

② Signature 14 January 1975, Ratification 17 December 1975 <http://www.oosa.unvienna.org/oosatdb/showTreatySignatures.do> accessed 26 April 2019.

③ UN Doc. ST/SG/SER. E/INF. 16, Note Verbale dated 28 January 2004 from the Permanent Mission of France to the United Nations (Vienna) addressed to the Secretary-General, 6 February 2004.

④ Founded by Act No. 61-1382 (19 December 1961), JO of 20 December 1961.

⑤ Space Operation Act, Law No. 2008-518 (3 June 2008); see Schmidt-Tedd, Bernhard/Arnold, Isabelle, The French Act relating to space activities-From international law idealism to national industrial pragmatism, ESPI Perspectives (11) 2008, with a synopsis of the French original act and an unofficial English translation.

⑥ Mariez, Julien, Decrees and Technical Regulations on space operations of France (presented at the UNCOPUOS Legal Subcommittee in Vienna on 26 March 2010), <http://www.oosa.unvienna.org/pdf/pres/lsc2010/tech-05.pdf> accessed 26 April 2019.

⑦ Decree No. 84-510 Regarding the Centre National d'Etudes Spatiales (CNES) (28 June 1984) (modified by Decree No. 2009-644, 9 June 2009) <http://www.legifrance.gouv.fr/affichTexte.do?cidTexte=JORFTEXT000020719559&dateTexte=&categorieLien=id> accessed 26 April 2019.

⑧ Ibid.

商的信息（第十四条和第十五条，第 84-510 号法令）。

《法国空间活动法》第十二条为其今后执行《登记公约》要求的立法发展奠定了基础。值得注意的是，它规定了根据《登记公约》第二条的一项明确义务，即在由国家空间研究中心所维持的登记册中登记已发射的空间物体。该法特别援引了将由上述法令所确定的登记规定。该法令包含关于空间物体登记册的规定（第三节），并赋予经营者向法国国家空间研究中心提供识别空间物体所需的一切信息的义务。根据这一要求所应提供的数据应由主管空间活动的部长命令确定。通常使用的措词“在切实可行的情况下尽速”已通过规定明确的期限加以完善。因此，提交所要求信息的期限被限定为发射后的 60 天内。

法国外交部向联合国提供登记所需的数据。除基本数据外，法国还根据《登记公约》第四条第 2 款提交了由其发射的空间物体的其他信息，并根据《登记公约》第四条第 3 款提交了重返地球大气层的空间物体的信息①。因此，法国应会将影响空间物体在轨寿命的任何事件通知联合国秘书长，特别是关于空间物体离轨、任务结束或物体损失的信息。

在过去几年中，法国提交的通知中的信息可分为三个主要部分：（1）关于所发射的空间物体的信息；（2）关于再入地球大气层的空间物体的信息；（3）关于先前发射的空间物体的补充信息②。更新的补充信息以结构化的形式提供：（a）关于仍在运行的法国近地轨道卫星，及其精确的轨道信息；（b）仍在运行的法国地球静止轨道卫星，及其大致轨道位置；（c）仍在轨道中但已不再运行的法国卫星，及其所在轨道的信息③。为了登记的目的，法国对发射到外层空间的两类物体作了区分：“卫星”和“其他空间物体”。④ 最后，作为其通知的组成部分，法国也提供了由其发射但未由其登记，目前由外国卫星运营者运营的空间物体的数据⑤。

法国国家空间研究中心为每一个发射到地球轨道或更远外层空间的物体分配登记号码，并将其列入国家登记册。相关管理框架没有就国际标识号码作出规定。值得特

① UN Doc. ST/SG/SER. E/616, Note Verbale dated 23 February 2011 from the Permanent Mission of France to the United Nations (Vienna) addressed to the Secretary-General, 16 August 2011.

② Ibid.

③ Ibid.

④ Ibid.

⑤ Ibid.

别注意的是，法国在 2004 年发送给联合国的照会[1]中通知了该登记册的组成内容。在该照会中，法国通报了关于法国在 1965 年至 2003 年期间发射的空间物体的全面资料，更新了以前提交的登记数据。在该通知中，所有以前记录的物体都分配了国际标识编号。值得一提的是，从登记所涉及的利益相关方来看，法国登记空间物体的实践较为广泛。在这方面，至少应提及三种不同的情况：法国政府（1）在欧洲空间局宣布接受《登记公约》的权利和义务之前代表欧洲空间研究组织；（2）在欧洲通信卫星组织私有化之前以及目前代表该组织；（3）当从法国领土发射时[2]，就联盟号火箭的上面级和相关部件与俄罗斯联邦政府[3]达成协议。

在统计数据方面，法国于 1966 年至 2018 年期间，总共向联合国提交了 144 份通知（包括代表欧洲空间研究组织和欧洲通信卫星组织等提交的通知）[4]。

（b）德国

在部际协调的基础上，德国在联邦航空办公室设立了一个外层空间登记册。外层空间登记册附属于联邦航空办公室的德国航空器登记册，该办公室位于布伦瑞克。目前仍然缺乏有关私营产业登记义务的正式法律基础。无论是《空中交通法》（第三条和第十四条）还是涉及登记的频率协调管理规则（第 8/2005 号法令），都未包含这样的正式义务[5]。但是，实践中登记所需的全部数据都可以在自愿的基础上从非政府实体获得。然而，这种情况并不是完美的，并导致了一些必要的更新。德国宇航中心负责进行必要的修正。2004 年进行了一次更新，并于 2009、2010 年在联合国外空委法律小组委员会第四十八届会议交换信息之后进行了另一次更新。由于联合国外空事务办公室已制定了登记模板，登记所需的信息由德国航天局以联合国模板的格式传送给

---

① UN Doc. ST/SG/SER. E/445, Note Verbale dated 28 January 2004 from the Permanent Mission of France to the United Nations (Vienna) addressed to the Secretary-General, 2 March 2004.

② Trebaol, Jean-Yves, French Policy and Practices for the Registration of Space Objects, in: Danesy, Dorothea, Proceedings of the 4th European Conference on Space Debris, 18-20 April 2005 Darmstadt (Germany), ESA/ESOC, p. 583 < http://articles. adsabs. harvard. edu//full/2005ESASP. 587. . 583T/0000585. 000. html > accessed 26 April 2019.

③ Decree No. 2009-426 (16 April 2009) < http://www. legifrance. gouv. fr/affichTexte. do? cidTexte = JORFTEXT000020530658> accessed 26 April 2019.

④ United Nations Register of Objects Launched into Outer Space: Notifications from France (Launch Year 1966-present) <http://www. oosa. unvienna. org/oosa/en/Reports/docsfra. html> accessed 26 April 2019.

⑤ Gerhard, Michael, Management von Raumfahrtprojekten: Raumfahrtrecht, in: Ley, Wilfried/Wittmann, Klaus/Hallmann, Willi (eds.), Handbuch der Raumfahrttechnik, 3rd ed., Hanser, Munich 2008, p. 770.

登记员。然而，要使国家登记完全适应联合国模板，就需要制定额外的行政法规，这需要在国家空间法的框架下进行。

德国没有自己的发射场，原则上只涉及“促成发射”的标准。德国的载荷登记并不涉及其性质，即政府的或非政府的、民用的或军用的①。此外，不再运行的物体或调试阶段失败的物体也需要进行登记②。

只有在少数情况下存在对登记必要性的实质怀疑。比如当德国的微纳卫星鲁宾 8 号与其他外国微纳卫星一起被置于外国的火箭上，而未达到独立卫星的地位时，情况尤其如此。③ 该火箭的主要载荷是两颗印度遥感卫星（Cartosat-2-A 和 IMS-1），印度已经将其登记，同时印度也是发射服务提供者，因此从形式上来看，这次发射中的每一件硬件都被包含在该登记中。关于单独额外登记的怀疑和理由主要集中于对所附实验的单独管辖权和控制权的相关性方面，该实验是关于自动海洋识别系统的新接收机的实验。但总体而言，德国有效载荷的独立登记，包括所有非政府和私人有效载荷（除了由发射服务提供者登记的火箭上面级之外），是没有问题的。

德国的第一颗卫星是 Azur 号，1969 年 11 月 8 日在范登堡发射，是在与美国航天局合作项目的框架下发射的。该卫星由美国登记④。在此后的航天飞机任务 STS 7 的合作项目中，美国也登记了一个德国载荷 SPAS-1⑤。1970 年 3 月 10 日发射、1978 年

---

① See e. g. the registration of COMSATBw-1：UN Doc. ST/SG/SER. E/592，Note Verbale dated 20 April 2010 from the Permanent Mission of Germany to the United Nations（Vienna）addressed to the Secretary-General，22 June 2010；as well as the registration of COMSATBw-2：UN Doc. ST/SG/SER. E/607，Note Verbale dated 13 September 2010 from the Permanent Mission of Germany to the United Nations（Vienna）addressed to the Secretary-General，30 November 2010.

② See the case of ABRIXAS，launched 28 April 1999，UN Doc. ST/SG/SER. E/396，Note Verbale dated 5 September 2001 from the Permanent Representative of Germany to the United Nations（Vienna）addressed to the Secretary-General，14 September 2001.

③ The mini-cubesat called Rubin 8 was launched on a Indian PSLV-9 on 28 April 2008，for the registration by India see UN Doc. ST/SG/SER. E/545，Note Verbale dated 21 May 2008 from the Permanent Mission of India to the United Nations（Vienna）addressed to the Secretary-General，12 November 2008.

④ Designator：1969-097 A，UN Doc. A/AC. 105/INF. 220，Letter dated 17 April 1970 from the Permanent Representative of the United States of America addressed to the Secretary-General，11 May 1970. In the Online Index of Objects Launched into Outer Space on the UNOOSA website，the object is listed with the remark “USA（for Germany）” <http：//www. oosa. unvienna. org/oosa/search. do> accessed 26 April 2019.

⑤ Designator：1983-059 F，UN Doc. ST/SG/SER. E/096，Information Furnished in Conformity with the Convention on Registration of Objects Launched into Outer Space，5 March 1984. In the Online Index of Objects Launched into Outer Space on the UNOOSA website，the object is listed with the remark “USA（for Germany）” <http：//www. oosa. unvienna. org/oosa/search. do> accessed 26 April 2019.

10月5日损坏的德国的第二颗卫星 DIAL-WIKA 没有进行登记①。第三颗卫星 HELIOS 1 于 1974 年 12 月 10 日发射，并根据联合国大会第 1721 B（XVI）号决议通知了联合国②。关于接下来的两颗卫星，即基于法、德双边项目所产生的 SYMPHONIE A 和 SYMPHONIE B 卫星，其特别之处在于，这两颗卫星均由法、德两国进行登记③。在此后《登记公约》第二条第 2 款对相关规则进行澄清之后，这样的双重登记应当避免。

有时由于外部原因需要更正联合国外空事务办公室登记网站上的信息。如关于 Cryosat 2 号卫星，提供发射服务的俄罗斯表示该载荷是德国。尽管德国参与了该项目，但它实际上是欧洲航天局的卫星。该更正在联合国外空事务办公室和相关各方之间简要协调后作出④。

德国自 1979 年 10 月 16 日起成为《登记公约》的缔约国⑤。其于 1988 年 4 月 7 日的照会中通知联合国在布伦瑞克的联邦航空办公室设立了德国空间物体登记册⑥。空间物体被登记于国家航空器登记册⑦的附件中。除了《登记公约》要求的其他空间物体和发射数据外，在航空器登记册中“航天器”项下的登记日期也进行了明确。自 2007 年起，除了空间物体名称、国家标识或登记号码等识别标准外，还向联合国外空事务办公室单独提交了所有登记物体的国际空间研究委员会（COSPAR）标识编号。

---

① Designator：1970-017 A，the first on the UNOOSA online index for Germany.

② Designator：1974-097 A，UN Doc. A/AC. 105/INF. 380，Note Verbale dated 16 November 1978 from the Permanent Mission of the Federal Republic of Germany to the United Nations addressed to the Secretary-General，29 November 1978.

③ Designator：1974-101 A and 1975-077 A，launched 18 December 1974 respectively 27 August 1975，UN Doc. A/AC. 105/INF. 305，Letter dated 24 January 1975 from the Acting Permanent Representative of the Federal Republic of Germany addressed to the Secretary-General，24 January 1975 and UN Doc. A/AC. 105/INF. 329，Letter dated 14 November 1975 from the Permanent Representative of the Federal Republic of Germany to the United Nations addressed to the Secretary-General，14 November 1975，with cross-reference to the French registration. See also the French notification UN Doc. ST/SG/SER. E/445，Note Verbale dated 28 January 2004 from the Permanent Mission of France to the United Nations（Vienna）addressed to the Secretary-General，2 March 2004.

④ The Russian Federation corrected their information with the remark to read “European Space Agency's” instead of “German”，see UN Doc. ST/SG/SER. E/598/Corr. 1，Note Verbale dated 3 June 2010 from the Permanent Mission of the Russian Federation to the United Nations（Vienna）addressed to the Secretary-General：Corrigendum，3 June 2010.

⑤ See the UNOOSA Treaty Status Database <http：//www. oosa. unvienna. org/oosatdb/showTreatySignatures. do> accessed 26 April 2019.

⑥ UN Doc. ST/SG/SER. E/INF. 9，Note Verbale dated 7 April 1988 from the Permanent Mission of the Federal Republic of Germany to the United Nations addressed to the Secretary-General，27 April 1988.

⑦ UN Doc. A/AC. 105/912，Information on national legislation relevant to the peaceful exploration and use of outer space，29 January 2008.

目前，德国已经登记了其所有轨道上的空间物体[①]。截至 2011 年底，已登记的空间物体共 47 个。在联合国外空事务办公室网站上，德国所发射的 52 个空间物体中有 47 个已在联合国登记[②]。这种差异是由于在向联合国外空事务办公室更新资料时，有些卫星已经损毁，以及上述 Rubin 8 号微纳卫星的情况[③]。关于过去登记被忽略的情况，在 2010 年的重新评估中，只有那些当时还未返回地球的物体后来被登记。为了明确起见，最好填补这一差距，尽管这些物体所造成的风险和登记册的识别功能并不实际相关。

（c）荷兰

荷兰于 1981 年 1 月 26 日加入《登记公约》。其三项法案为登记由荷兰发射进入外层空间的物体奠定了国家法律基础：2007 年 1 月 24 日的《空间活动法》（Wet ruimtevaartactiviteiten）[④] 为框架性法律，另外两项包括 2007 年 11 月 13 日的《空间物体登记法令》（Besluit register ruimtevoorwerpen）[⑤]，以及 2008 年 2 月 7 日的《关于空间活动许可申请与空间物体登记的命令》（Regeling aanvraag vergunning ruimtevaartactiviteten

① The latest registration was the registration of TET-1, 2012-039D, launched 22 July 2012, UN Doc. ST/SG/SER. E/657, Note Verbale dated 18 October 2012 from the Permanent Mission of Germany to the United Nations (Vienna) addressed to the Secretary-General.

② See the Online Index of Objects Launched into Outer Space on the UNOOSA website <http://www.oosa.unvienna.org/oosa/search.do> accessed 26 April 2019.

③ These objects listed as not registered with the UN are: DIAL-WIKA, 1970-017 A, launched 10 March 1970, decayed 5 October 1978; Oskar 13/Amsat 3 C, 1988-51 B, launched 15 April 1988, decayed 6 December 1996 (Not registered with the United Nations. Reported as no longer in orbit as of 31 December 1996 by USA in UN Doc. ST/SG/SER. E/322, Note Verbale dated 30 June 1997 from the Permanent Mission of the United States of America to the United Nations (Vienna) addressed to the Secretary-General, 31 July 1997); Express-Return-Capsule 1995-002, launched and decayed 15 January 1995; Rubin 1, 2000-039 C (also called Bird-Rubin, but not to confound with BIRD, 2001-049C), launched 15 July 2000, decayed 30 August 2001 (Not registered with the United Nations. Mentioned by Russian Federation in UN Doc. ST/SG/SER. E/384, Note Verbale dated 29 December 2000 from the Permanent Mission of the Russian Federation to the United Nations (Vienna) addressed to the Secretary-General, 20 March 2001) and the case of the attached payload Rubin 8, 2008-021K.

④ Rules Concerning Space Activities and the Establishment of a Registry of Space Objects (Space Activities Act) (24 January 2007) <http://mijnwetten.nl/zoeken/wetsfamilie:: wet-ruimtevaartactiviteiten> accessed 26 April 2019.

⑤ Decree Containing Rules with Regard to a Registry of Information Concerning Space Objects (Space Objects Registry Decree) (13 November 2007) <http://lexius.nl/besluit-register-ruimtevoorwerpen> accessed 26 April 2019.

en registratie)[1]。前两项于2008年1月1日生效，后一项于2008年2月22日生效[2]。

正如荷兰常驻联合国代表团2009年6月3日致联合国秘书长的普通照会所述，荷兰已经建立了一个射入外层空间物体的国家登记册，名为《空间物体登记册》(register ruimtevoorwerpen)[3]。在其体系中包含两个子类别：(1) 根据《登记公约》第二条建立的以联合国为导向的子登记册；(2) 以国家为重点的子登记册，以记录那些荷兰认为国家本身不被视为严格意义上的“发射国”“登记国”或“发射当局”[4]的空间物体（尽管这些物体与《空间活动法》规范的空间活动有关）[5]。

根据《空间活动法》，由荷兰经济事务、农业和创新部部长负责荷兰管辖范围内的空间物体的登记[6]。在实践中，这一职能已被委托给经济事务部中的一个部门——荷兰无线电通信局(Agentschap Telecom)[7][8]。

《空间活动法》规定了在《空间物体登记册》(register ruimtevoorwerpen)中进行登记的一个强制性先决条件——该物体应参与属于其监管范围的空间活动[9]。其他要求涉及从事空间活动的实体的法律性质，例如非政府实体应获得授权/许可，以及应满足的其他相关要求[10]。

---

① Order Concerning Licence Applications for the Performance of Space Activities and the Registration of Space Objects (7 February 2008) (as amended by Order of 16 April 2010) <http://lexius.nl/regeling-aanvraag-vergunning-ruimtevaartactiviteiten-en-registratie> accessed 26 April 2019.

② UN Doc. A/AC.105/C.2/2010/CRP.11, Information on national legislation relevant to the peaceful exploration and use of outer space: reply of the Netherlands, 23 March 2010.

③ UN Doc. ST/SG/SER.E/INF.24, Note Verbale dated 3 June 2009 from the Permanent Mission of the Netherlands to the United Nations (Vienna) addressed to the Secretary-General, 20 August 2009.

④ Art. 2 Space Objects Registry Decree.

⑤ For more information please see UN Doc. ST/SG/SER.E/INF.24, Note Verbale dated 3 June 2009 from the Permanent Mission of the Netherlands to the United Nations (Vienna) addressed to the Secretary-General, 20 August 2009, and Art. 2 Space Objects Registry Decree.

⑥ Sec. 11 para. 1 Space Activities Act.

⑦ For purposes of accessing official information with regard to objects launched into outer space and recorded in the registry of the Netherlands one should refer to their website <http://www.agentschaptelecom.nl/english/Pages/Default.aspx> accessed 26 April 2019.

⑧ UN Doc. A/AC.105/C.2/2010/CRP.11, Information on national legislation relevant to the peaceful exploration and use of outer space: reply of the Netherlands, 23 March 2010.

⑨ See Space Activities Act <http://mijnwetten.nl/zoeken/wetsfamilie::wet-ruimtevaartactiviteiten> accessed 26 April 2019.

⑩ UN Doc. A/AC.105/C.2/2010/CRP.11, Information on national legislation relevant to the peaceful exploration and use of outer space: reply of the Netherlands, 23 March 2010.

需要提供数据的基本项目列举在《空间物体登记法令》第三条中，包括（1）概述和功能；（2）轨道参数；（3）发射国家和地点；（4）预计和实际发射日期；（5）预计和实际运行寿命/离轨日期；（6）许可证持有人的信息；（7）《关于空间活动许可申请与空间物体登记的命令》所预见的与空间物体有关的其他数据。该命令附有登记表模板，应根据该模板提交有关物体的信息。

尽管荷兰有如此发达的国家空间立法，并在 1981 年 1 月 26 日加入了《登记公约》[①]，但迄今为止，荷兰还没有按照联合国第 1721 B（XⅥ）号决议或根据《登记公约》第四条向联合国秘书长提供任何信息。而只是提供了空间物体在线索引中出现的空间物体状况变化的信息。荷兰还依据《外空条约》第十一条提供了有关其射入外层空间物体登记册中国家部分所包括的空间物体的信息[②]。

（d）比利时

比利时于 1975 年 3 月 19 日成为《登记公约》的缔约国。2008 年 6 月 3 日，比利时向秘书长通报了其国家登记册的建立情况[③]。虽然登记册是根据 2008 年 3 月 19 日的皇家法令建立的，但关于建立和维持登记册的管理规则载于 2005 年 9 月 17 日的《空间物体发射、飞行作业或制导活动法》[④]。该法明确规定了比利时国王和负责空间研究及其在国际合作框架内应用的部长之间的责任划分[⑤]。登记表附在该法中，可在

---

① See the UNOOSA Treaty Status Database <http：//www. oosa. unvienna. org/oosatdb/showTreatySignatures. do> accessed 26 April 2019.

② UN Doc. A/AC. 105/806, Note Verbale dated 29 July 2003 from the Permanent Mission of the Netherlands to the United Nations（Vienna）addressed to the Secretary-General, 22 August 2003; UN Doc. A/AC. 105/824, Note Verbale dated 18 February 2004 from the Permanent Mission of the Netherlands to the United Nations（Vienna）addressed to the Secretary-General, 16 March 2004; UN Doc. A/AC. 105/824/Corr. 1, Note Verbale dated 18 February 2004 from the Permanent Mission of the Netherlands to the United Nations（Vienna）addressed to the Secretary-General, Corrigendum, 1 August 2008; UN Doc. A/AC. 105/1002, Note Verbale dated 3 June 2009 from the Permanent Mission of the Netherlands to the United Nations（Vienna）addressed to the Secretary-General, 22 November 2010; UN Doc. A/AC. 105/1004/Rev. 1, Note Verbale dated 26 April 2011 from the Permanent Mission of the Netherlands to the United Nations（Vienna）addressed to the Secretary-General, 13 September 2011.

③ UN Doc. ST/SG/SER. E/INF. 21, Note Verbale dated 3 June 2008 from the Permanent Mission of Belgium to the United Nations（Vienna）addressed to the Secretary-General, 2 July 2008.

④ Law on the Activities of Launching, Flight Operations or Guidance of Space Objects（17 September 2005）<http：//www. belspo. be/belspo/space/doc/beLaw/Loi_ en. pdf> accessed 26 April 2019.

⑤ See Art. 14 para. 1 and Art. 14 para. 3 Law on the Activities of Launching, Flight Operations or Guidance of Space Objects.

比利时科学政策办公室（BELSPO）网站上查阅①。

《空间物体发射、飞行作业或制导活动法》的第十四条可被视为国内登记条例的核心部分，该条表明了比利时处理登记问题的思路。除了《登记公约》第四条所注明的信息外，比利时国内法还要求提供有关空间物体的制造商和运营商的数据，以及星上的主要组成部件和仪器的清单。经营者有义务向国家登记册提交上述数据。值得一提的是，尽管比利时国内法明确要求向国家登记册提交的额外数据的名目，但这其中只有《登记公约》明确要求的数据才会由主管部长进一步转交给联合国秘书长。除此之外，更新以及与空间物体丢失、脱离轨道或结束飞行作业有关的信息也被认为是要通报的。比利时国内法规定，任何数据的修改都要在登记册上进行补充登记，费用由操作者负责，修改需在操作者意识到这种变化后的三十天内完成。如果没有及时通知，部长有权暂停授权。应当注意的是，该登记表中需要包括比利时授予的发射授权/许可证号。这种在空间物体发射时已生效的强制性登记先决条件可被视为一种预先条款。关于标识编号，法律只关注国家登记号码的归属。根据规定，这种编号应由法律要求的要素组成。迄今为止，比利时已根据《登记公约》第四条登记了 32 个空间物体。

（e）意大利

意大利在 2005 年 12 月 8 日才加入《登记公约》。于 2005 年 7 月 12 日颁布的第 153 号法律规定意大利共和国加入《登记公约》（官方公报第 177 号，2005 年 8 月 1 日），② 也为执行国家登记程序的规则奠定了基础。在此之前，意大利政府参照 1961 年联合国大会第 1721 B（XVI）号决议，在自愿的基础上向联合国递交关于发射到外层空间的物体的信息③。至于法律框架的建设，2011 年 3 月，意大利航天局（ASI）通知联合国，关于建立国家登记册和确定登记程序的条例草案已经定稿，计划提交给

① For the registration form which is annexed to it see the BELSPO（Federal Public Planning Service Science Policy）website at <http：//www. belspo. be/belspo/space/doc/beLaw/AnnexForm_ A2_ fr. pdf>.

② Law No. 153 On Accession of the Republic of Italy to the Convention on Objects Launched into Outer Space（12 July 2005）<http：//www. parlamento. it/parlam/leggi/05153 l. htm> accessed 26 April 2019.

③ United Nations Register of Objects Launched into Outer Space：Notifications from Italy（Launch Year 1965-present）<http：//www. oosa. unvienna. org/oosa/en/Reports/docsital. html> accessed 26 April 2019.

外交部、研究部和经济发展部批准。①

意大利国家登记框架的核心内容载于《意大利共和国加入<关于登记射入外层空间物体的公约>法律》的第三条②。该法规定，意大利将建立一个射入外层空间物体的国家登记册，由意大利航天局负责维护。关于需要登记的物体，意大利采取的办法是要求记录两大类物体：（1）由意大利国籍的自然人或法人实施或促成发射的空间物体；（2）由外国自然人或法人从位于意大利境内或意大利管辖和控制下的发射场发射到外层空间的物体③。这些主体应将所进行的发射活动通知意大利航天局，并递交《登记公约》第四条规定的所有信息。他们也有义务提供关于已不在地球轨道的空间物体的信息。

根据该法，意大利航天局承诺将载入登记册的信息递交给意大利研究部、经济发展部和外交部，后者有责任履行《登记公约》的国际义务。到目前为止，联合国已经记录了七份来自意大利的按照《登记公约》提交的通知④。

（f）西班牙

西班牙于 1978 年 12 月 20 日加入了《登记公约》⑤。根据第 278/1995 号皇家法

① UN Doc. A/AC. 105/C. 2/2011/CRP. 7, Information on national legislation relevant to the peaceful exploration and use of outer space, 29 March 2011, p. 3.

② Accession of the Republic of Italy to the Convention on Registration of Objects Launched into Outer Space <http://www. parlamento. it/parlam/leggi/05153 l. htm> accessed 26 April 2019.

③ UN Doc. A/AC. 105/C. 2/2011/CRP. 7, Information on national legislation relevant to the peaceful exploration and use of outer space, Italy, 29 March 2011.

④ UN Doc. ST/SG/SER. E/538, Note Verbale dated 11 March 2008 from the Permanent Mission of Italy to the United Nations (Vienna) addressed to the Secretary-General, 29 May 2008; UN Doc. ST/SG/SER. E/606, Note Verbale dated 1 September 2010 from the Permanent Mission of Italy to the United Nations (Vienna) addressed to the Secretary-General, 21 October 2010; UN Doc. ST/SG/SER. E/615, Note Verbale dated 17 February 2011 from the Permanent Mission of Italy to the United Nations (Vienna) addressed to the Secretary-General, 27 July 2011; UN Doc. ST/SG/SER. E/634, Note Verbale dated 24 November 2011 from the Permanent Mission of Italy to the United Nations (Vienna) addressed to the Secretary-General, 24 November 2011; UN Doc. ST/SG/SER. E/652, Note Verbale dated 28 August 2012 from the Permanent Mission of Italy to the United Nations (Vienna) addressed to the Secretary-General, 18 September 2012; UN Doc. ST/SG/SER. E/734, Note Verbale dated 7 November 2014 from the Permanent Mission of Italy to the United Nations (Vienna) addressed to the Secretary-General, 19 December 2014; UN Doc. ST/SG/SER. E/779, Note Verbale dated 24 October 2016 from the Permanent Mission of Italy to the United Nations (Vienna) addressed to the Secretary-General, 1 November 2016; UN Doc. ST/SG/SER. E/845 Note Verbale dated 25 April 2018 from the Permanent Mission of Italy to the United Nations (Vienna) addressed to the Secretary-General, 18 May 2018.

⑤ Royal Decree No. 278/1995 Establishing in the Kingdom of Spain the registry foreseen in the Convention adopted by the United Nations General Assembly on 2 November 1974 (24 February 1995) <http://www. oosa. unvienna. org/oosaddb/showDocument. do? documentUid=317&country=SPA> accessed 26 April 2019.

令，西班牙为射入外层空间的物体建立了一个国家登记册[①]。该登记册由外交部国际经济关系总局负责管理[②]。关于登记册内信息的获取是完全自由的，但根据该皇家法令中的一个条款，这种获取应依据《关于公共行政法律制度和共同行政程序的第30/1992号法案》第三十七条中的规定以及为执行该法案而通过的相关规章制度进行管理[③]。

该皇家法令概述了登记要求的适用范围。它指出，任何空间物体都应登记，如果（1）已经发射或其发射是由西班牙促成的，或（2）从西班牙发射或从属于西班牙的设施发射的。一般来说，后者与《登记公约》对“发射国”的定义相一致。但根据相关记录，西班牙的卫星一般是从外国领土上的发射场和设施发射的。因此，西班牙一般只有在“促成发射”的标准下才成为“发射国”。

除了列举为登记目的必须提供的基本数据外，（该皇家法令）还可能要求申请人提交对处理登记有用的其他数据。维持登记册的实体有权从申请人那里获得国家和国际登记所需的任何补充资料[④]。通知中还应包括对已登记的空间物体数据的任何修正，即在空间物体已不在地球轨道上的情况下。在实践中，“物体销毁或损坏的日期和原因”这一条目构成了登记表的一个组成部分[⑤]。

根据皇家法令，对于在建立西班牙登记册之前发射的任何空间物体，如果西班牙

① UN Doc. ST/SG/SER. E/INF. 10, Note Verbale dated 23 March 1995 from the Permanent Mission of Spain to the United Nations (New York) addressed to the Secretary-General, 31 May 1995.

② Art. 1 and Art. 2 Royal Decree 278/1995.

③ Art. 3 Royal Decree 278/1995.

④ Art. 7 Royal Decree 278/1995.

⑤ UN Doc. ST/SG/SER. E/531, Note Verbale dated 28 July 2008 from the Permanent Mission of Spain to the United Nations (Vienna) addressed to the Secretary-General, 17 September 2008.

被认为是发射国，则应登记并随后正式通知联合国[①]。到目前为止，联合国已经记录了[②]八份来自西班牙的按照《登记公约》提交的通知[③]。

（g）瑞典

瑞典于 1976 年 6 月 9 日加入了《登记公约》。尽管瑞典没有就建立国家登记册单独发出通知，但在其 1986 年发出的第一份通知，即关于为瑞典的利益而发射的空间物体的通知中列入了这类信息[④]。在 1999 年，瑞典提供了一份最新的汇编表，反映了瑞典发射到外层空间的物体的登记现状[⑤]。值得注意的是，从 1982 年起，瑞典就有了

① See Transitory Provision of the Royal Decree 278/1995.

② Several space objects have not been registered by Spain with the UN, however, information on them was obtained through mentioning in notifications of the Russian Federation: UN Doc. ST/SG/SER. E/460, Note Verbale dated 16 November 2004 from the Permanent Mission of the Russian Federation to the United Nations (Vienna) addressed to the Secretary-General, 17 December 2004; UN Doc. ST/SG/SER. E/593, Note Verbale dated 10 May 2010 from the Permanent Mission of the Russian Federation to the United Nations (Vienna) addressed to the Secretary-General, 6 July 2010; and France: UN Doc. ST/SG/SER. E/468, Note Verbale dated 29 March 2005 from the Permanent Mission of France to the United Nations (Vienna) addressed to the Secretary-General, 21 April 2005; UN Doc. ST/SG/SER. E/499, Note Verbale dated 20 September 2006 from the Permanent Mission of France to the United Nations (Vienna) addressed to the Secretary-General, 7 November 2006; UN Doc. ST/SG/SER. E/588, Note Verbale dated 22 January 2010 from the Permanent Mission of France to the United Nations (Vienna) addressed to the Secretary-General, 30 June 2010; UN Doc. ST/SG/SER. E/616, Note Verbale dated 17 February 2011 from the Permanent Mission of Italy to the United Nations (Vienna) addressed to the Secretary-General, 16 August 2011.

③ UN Doc. ST/SG/SER. E/296, Note Verbale dated 7 December 1995 from the Permanent Representative of Spain to the United Nations Office at Vienna addressed to the Secretary-General, 14 December 1995; UN Doc. ST/SG/SER. E/305, Note Verbale dated 27 March 1996 from the Permanent Mission of Spain to the United Nations (Vienna) addressed to the Secretary-General, 3 April 1996; UN Doc. ST/SG/SER. E/326, Note Verbale dated 9 October 1997 from the Permanent Mission of Spain to the United Nations (Vienna) addressed to the Secretary-General, 20 October 1997; UN Doc. ST/SG/SER. E/376, Letter dated 10 October 2000 from the Permanent Mission of Spain to the United Nations (Vienna) addressed to the Secretary-General, 17 October 2000; UN Doc. ST/SG/SER. E/531, Note Verbale dated 28 July 2008 from the Permanent Mission of Spain to the United Nations (Vienna) addressed to the Secretary-General, 17 September 2008; UN Doc. ST/SG/SER. E/296/Add. 1, Note Verbale dated 14 March 2014 from the Permanent Mission of Spain to the United Nations (Vienna) addressed to the Secretary-General, 17 July 2014; UN Doc. ST/SG/SER. E/829, Note Verbale dated 28 November 2017 from the Permanent Mission of Spain to the United Nations (Vienna) addressed to the Secretary-General, 22 March 2018.

④ UN Doc. ST/SG/SER. E/145, Note Verbale dated 4 June 1986 from the Permanent Mission of Sweden to the United Nations addressed to the Secretary-General, 11 June 1986.

⑤ UN Doc. ST/SG/SER. E/352, Note Verbale dated 1 February 1999 from the Permanent Mission of Sweden to the United Nations (Vienna) addressed to the Secretary-General, 19 February 1999.

与登记问题有关的立法。1982 年 11 月 25 日颁布的关于空间活动的第 1069 号法令[①]第 4 节为将《登记公约》要求转化为国内法要求奠定了基础。该法令规定，国家空间活动委员会（后改名为瑞典国家空间委员会）是负责登记的主管机构。条件是根据《登记公约》第一条，瑞典应被视为这些空间物体的发射国。

与其他国家相比，瑞典外交部向联合国发出的通知的一个显著特点是登记表上“空间物体的概述和任务”项目所通报的信息的格式。通常而言，瑞典将其作为一个综合信息块呈现，极大优于其他国家在信息通报方面的一般做法。此外，瑞典还提供了相关网站的链接，提供了获得更详细数据的途径[②]。另一个重点是，瑞典充分考虑“任务结束”的通知要求并提交相关信息[③]。瑞典发射的其他空间物体在轨道上的存在没有通过官方外交渠道通报给联合国，而是通过与俄罗斯联邦在通知中提到的相同方式进行通报[④]。迄今为止，瑞典已按照《登记公约》的规定向联合国秘书长发出了 21 份通知。

① Decree No. 1069 On Space Activities (25 November 1982), online accessible at the UNOOSA website <http://www.oosa.unvienna.org/oosaddb/showDocument.do? documentUid=319&country=SWE> accessed 26 April 2019.

② UN Doc. ST/SG/SER. E/380, Note Verbale dated 28 November 2000 from the Permanent Mission of Sweden to the United Nations (Vienna) addressed to the Secretary-General, 12 December 2000.

③ UN Doc. ST/SG/SER. E/167, Note Verbale dated 3 August 1987 from the Permanent Mission of Sweden to the United Nations addressed to the Secretary-General, 13 August 1987; UN Doc. ST/SG/SER. E/311, Note Verbale dated 12 June 1996 from the Permanent Mission of Sweden to the United Nations (Vienna) addressed to the Secretary-General, 28 June 1996; UN Doc. ST/SG/SER. E/318, Note Verbale dated 10 January 1997 from the Permanent Mission of Sweden to the United Nations (Vienna) addressed to the Secretary-General, 21 January 1997; UN Doc. ST/SG/SER. E/335, Note Verbale dated 6 April 1998 from the Permanent Mission of Sweden to the United Nations (Vienna) addressed to the Secretary-General, 28 April 1998; UN Doc. ST/SG/SER. E/364, Note Verbale dated 3 November 1999 from the Permanent Mission of Sweden to the United Nations (Vienna) addressed to the Secretary-General, 3 November 1999.

④ UN Doc. ST/SG/SER. E/393, Note Verbale dated 25 May 2001 from the Permanent Mission of the Russian Federation to the United Nations (Vienna) addressed to the Secretary-General, 21 June 2001; UN Doc. ST/SG/SER. E/542, Note Verbale dated 5 May 2008 from the Permanent Mission of the Russian Federation to the United Nations (Vienna) addressed to the Secretary-General, 3 July 2008; UN Doc. ST/SG/SER. E/626, Note Verbale dated 11 August 2011 from the Permanent Mission of the Russian Federation to the United Nations (Vienna) addressed to the Secretary-General, 18 November 2011.

有时，BSB-1 A 号卫星的案例[①]被作为瑞典向非发射国转让登记的例子[②]，它涉及瑞典 1999 年 2 月 1 日发出的普通照会，其中提到该卫星所有权的改变[③]。然而，这份容易被误解的通知并不能促进向非发射国转移登记。考虑到“瑞典于 1996 年在轨道上购买”这一注释的表述以及各代表团提供的信息，这一增补实际上只是根据《登记公约》第四条第 2 款的规定提供的补充信息，而并不能视为是对发射国资格的后续取得。

（h）希腊

希腊于 2003 年 5 月 27 日加入了《登记公约》。希腊在 2008 年 5 月 14 日的普通照会中通知联合国秘书长，希腊外交部中“联合国和其他专门国际组织”D1 部秘书处对发射到外层空间的物体进行了适当登记[④]。在联合国外空事务办公厅网站上可查到的唯一代表希腊的通知是关于地球静止通信卫星 HellasSat-2 的发射[⑤]。其登记表在内容上没有任何明显的特点，但“一般功能”的描述包含了广泛的技术方法。

（i）奥地利

1980 年 3 月 6 日，奥地利承诺履行其在《登记公约》项下的义务[⑥]。由于奥地利自 1987 年以来主要通过其欧空局成员资格参与空间活动[⑦]，因此奥地利最初没有具体的国家立法。这种情况在两个大学卫星项目纳入审议后发生了变化。2011 年 12 月 6

---

① The satellite BSB-1 A, launched by the USA for a British operator, was sold in 1996 by this operator to the Swedish company Nordic Satellite AB（NSAB）and the operation was transferred to the Swedish Space Cooperation（SSC）. Sweden changed the name in Sirius-1 and notified the UN about the acquisition of the Satellite in UN Doc. ST/SG/SER. E/352 Annex II, Note Verbale dated 1 February 1999 from the Permanent Mission of Sweden to the United Nations（Vienna）addressed to the Secretary-General, 19 February 1999：“bought in orbit by Sweden 1996”.

② Mick, Stephan, Registrierungskonvention und Registrierungspraxis：Aktuelle Rechtsfragen der Registrierung von Weltraumgegenständen, Carl Heymanns, Cologne 2007, pp. 141f. Though the author clarifies that this single case neither fulfills the requirements of a consistent State practice（consuetudo）nor a general opinion of law（opinion iuris）and therefore does not constitute international customary law.

③ UN Doc. ST/SG/SER. E/352 Annex II, Note Verbale dated 1 February 1999 from the Permanent Mission of Sweden to the United Nations（Vienna）addressed to the Secretary-General, 19 February 1999.

④ UN Doc. ST/SG/SER. E/INF. 20, Note Verbale dated 14 May 2008 from the Permanent Mission of Greece to the United Nations（Vienna）addressed to the Secretary-General, 15 May 2008.

⑤ UN Doc. ST/SG/SER. E/446, Note Verbale dated 25 March 2004 from the Permanent Mission of Greece to the United Nations addressed to the Secretary-General, 29 March 2004.

⑥ Austrian BGBl. No. 163/1980.

⑦ UN Doc. A/AC. 105/957, Information on national legislation relevant to the peaceful exploration and use of outer space, 15 January 2010.

日，奥地利议会通过了其国内空间法，即《关于授权空间活动和建立空间登记册的联邦法》（Bundesgesetz über die Genehmigung von Welt-raumaktivitäten und die Einrichtung eines Weltraumregisters）[①]。与登记要求有关的条款是第九条和第十条。第九条和第十条包含了要求维护国家登记册的规定和登记所需的信息的规定。根据该法第九条第1款，由运输、创新和技术部长负责维护空间物体的登记册。在奥地利的登记表上，必须填写空间物体的准确名称、登记号和ITU（国际电信联盟）频率分配号[②]。其登记所需信息的要求比《登记公约》的最低标准更宽松。在识别/登记标准下，以下项目被纳入：（第6号）空间物体的制造商及其（第7号）所有者和经营者。值得注意的是，运营商有义务在发射后立即递交相关信息，并提供所有进一步的额外信息，作为初始数据变化的结果。

就《登记公约》下的国际义务而言，关键的执行部门是联邦交通、创新和技术部（负责国内登记）和联邦欧洲和国际事务部（负责涉外及联合国沟通）。

迄今为止，奥地利已向联合国提交了两份文件，与BRITE-A TUGSAT-1、BRITE-U UNIBRITE和PEGASUS等卫星相关[③]。

⑤亚洲国家（日本、中国、印度）

（a）日本

日本的发射活动主要由在2003年之前被称为国家空间发展局（NASDA）的日本宇宙航空研究开发机构（JAXA）以及空间和航空科学研究所（ISAS）进行[④]。鉴于这些组织的法律地位和性质，很明显，发射活动是国家的一种特权。然而，在过去的十年中，除了JAXA之外，在日本还出现了其他的发射组织，例如非政府实体三菱重工有限公司（Mitsubishi Heavy Industries，Ltd.）。[⑤]

---

① Federal Law on the Licensing of Space Activities and the Establishment of a Space Registry (6 December 2011) Austrian BGBl. I No. 132/2011.

② Art. 10 para. 1 No. 2 Federal Law on the Licensing of Space Activities and the Establishment of a Space Register.

③ For more information see http://www.unoosa.org/oosa/en/spaceobjectregister/submissions/austria.html, accessed 26 April 2019 as well as the BRITE-AUSTRIA/TUGSAT-1 project website <http://www.tugsat.at> accessed 26 April 2019.

④ UN Doc. A/AC. 105/957, Information on national legislation relevant to the peaceful exploration and use of outer space, 15 January 2010.

⑤ For more information see theMitsubishi Heavy Industries, Ltd., website <http://www.mhi.co.jp/en> accessed 26 April 2019.

尽管在日本，专门的国家空间立法工作刚刚开始，但日本还是履行了其相关国际义务。与空间登记问题相关的第一部国内法是关于 JAXA 的法律（2002 年 12 月 13 日第 161 号法律；称为 JAXA 法）①。根据其规定，日本政府负责监督 JAXA 履行国际空间条约项下义务的活动。然而，目前只有 JAXA 的活动直接受 JAXA 法的管辖。无论在日本领土之内与否，JAXA 的活动必须在主管部委的授权和持续监督下进行。根据 JAXA 法，教育、文化、体育、科学和技术部以及总务省负责执行各自的职能。此外，值得注意的是，JAXA 有责任保障从日本领土上进行的任何受托发射在每一个发射阶段的安全，不管该发射是由外国还是日本/外国的私人公司促成的②。因此，之前提到的所有发射活动都属于 JAXA 法管辖的范围。

2008 年，日本空间活动相关的国家法律框架得到了《外层空间基本法》（2008 年 8 月 27 日第 43 号法律；在一些资料中被称为《空间基本法》）的补充③。与登记目的最相关的条款被纳入其第三十五条。该条“与空间活动有关立法的颁行”规定了为执行与空间活动有关的条约和其他国际义务而需要颁布的法律。

在联合国外层空间事务办公室的国际登记册中，来自日本的第一份通知可追溯到 1970 年。这份通知是参照大会《关于和平利用外层空间国际合作的第 1721 B（XVI）号决议》提供的④。再次通知发生在 1984 年，当时日本首次提交了符合公约规定的射入外层空间的空间物体的数据⑤，这是因为日本在 1983 年 6 月 20 日才加入该公约⑥。几个月后，准确地说，是 1983 年 12 月 19 日，日本常驻联合国代表团向秘书长发出普通照会，通知日本已建立射入外层空间物体的登记册⑦。从 1984 年开始，日本所有关

① Law No. 161 Concerning Japan Aerospace Exploration Agency（JAXA）（13 December 2002）. For an unofficial provisional translation of the law see <http：//www. jaxa. jp/about/law/law_ e. pdf> accessed 26 April 2019.

② UN Doc. A/AC. 105/957, Information on national legislation relevant to the peaceful exploration and use of outer space, 15 January 2010.

③ Law No. 43 Fundamental Act of Outer Space（enacted 21 May 2008, entered into force 27 August 2008）. For an unofficial translation of that law see <http：//download. esa. int/docs/ECSL/jAP2. pdf> accessed 26 April 2019.

④ UN Doc. A/AC. 105/INF. 215, Letter dated 12 February 1970 from the Permanent Representative of Japan addressed to the Secretary-General, 16 February 1970.

⑤ UN Doc. ST/SG/SER. E/103, Note Verbale dated 27 April 1984 from the Permanent Representative of Japan to the United Nations addressed to the Secretary-General, 15 May 1984.

⑥ See the UNOOSA Treaty Status Database <http：//www. oosa. unvienna. org/oosatdb/showTreatySignatures. do> accessed 26 April 2019.

⑦ UN Doc. ST/SG/SER. E/INF. 7, Note Verbale dated 19 December 1983 from the Permanent Mission of Japan to the United Nations addressed to the Secretary-General, 12 November 1986.

于发射物体的通知都涉及到《登记公约》[1]。

根据 UNOOSA 网站提供的数据，联合国国际登记册记载了日本发射和登记的约 150 个空间物体，其中约 125 个目前仍在太空[2]。然而，直到 2011 年底，仍有 8 个空间物体没有在联合国登记。

数个职能相关的部门合作建立并参与了国家登记册的维护，但最后向联合国秘书长提供信息的义务归属于日本外务省[3]。在这些通知中，日本直接提及应沿用根据联合国大会第 62/101 号决议《关于加强国家和国际政府间组织登记空间物体的做法的建议》制定的表格，该表格后来由秘书处重新编制。

根据《登记公约》第四条被要求递交的所有基本数据都包含在上述表格中。日本政府将上述表格作为国际通知的格式文本。除这些数据外，由日本自行决定提供的额外自愿信息包括：空间物体所有者或经营者、发射载体、空间物体在轨运行的天体、可获得该物体更多详细信息的网站链接、其他信息（发射组织、描述基本轨道参数的日期等）[4]。物体的精确技术特征，如重量、物理配置和尺寸、预期寿命框架的年数（生存概率）/有效寿命期限、姿态控制子系统、用于跟踪和遥测的无线电频率等，也提供给公众使用[5]。进一步的信息还可能包括日本以前登记的空间物体的状态变化、已在轨道上停止存在的空间物体的数据以及衰变/进入/脱离轨道的日期[6]。在某些情

① See United Nations Register of Objects Launched into Outer Space：Notifications from Japan（Launch Year 1970-present）<http：//www. oosa. unvienna. org/oosa/en/Reports/docsjapan. html> accessed 19 September 2012.

② For information on registered/non-registered space objects see the UNOOSA online index of objects launched into outer space on the UNOOSA website <http：//www. oosa. unvienna. org/oosa/showSearch. do> accessed 26 April 2019.

③ UN Doc. A/AC. 105/957, Information on national legislation relevant to the peaceful exploration and use of outer space, 15 January 2010.

④ UN Doc. ST/SG/SER. E/604, Note Verbale dated 15 September 2010 from the Permanent Mission of Japan to the United Nations（Vienna）addressed to the Secretary-General, 22 November 2010.

⑤ UN Doc. A/AC. 105/INF. 358, Note Verbale dated 7 April 1977 from the Permanent Representative of Japan to the Secretary-General, 18 April 1977；UN Doc. A/AC. 105/INF. 366, Note Verbale dated 13 September 1977, from the Acting Permanent Representative of Japan addressed to the Secretary-General, 28 September 1977.

⑥ UN Doc. ST/SG/SER. E/552, Note Verbale dated 5 September 2008 from the Permanent Mission of Japan to the United Nations（Vienna）addressed to the Secretary-General, 19 September 2008；UN Doc. ST/SG/SER. E/533, Note Verbale dated 31 January 2008 from the Permanent Mission of Japan to the United Nations（Vienna）addressed to the Secretary-General, 5 March 2008.

况下，卫星的名称在发射前由一个暂定的名称①、原始名称（日文版）② 和随后的英文翻译（如果名称是用日文提供的）③ 加以补充。如果发射涉及几个国家和/或其各自组织的参与，则在“发射组织”或“一般职能”一节中提供分工结构的概要④。但值得注意的是，后者有时是以非常笼统的方式提出的，例如采用“卫星执行日本政府指定的任务”的措辞⑤。最后，几乎所有日本的国际通知都包含国际标识编号。

由于发射了大量的空间物体，日本在提供相应的信息时采用了“一揽子办法”。这种方法既扩大了关于在一定时期内发射的多个物体的信息提供范围，又在完成上述数据的基础上增加了额外的信息，特别是日本以前登记的空间物体的状态变化。

国际空间站的案例可以作为日本参与国际空间项目合作所产生的登记实践的一个例子。登记义务在法律上规定于《加拿大政府、欧空局成员国政府、日本政府、俄罗斯联邦政府和美利坚合众国政府间关于民用国际空间站合作的协议》（1998年，以下简称“国际空间站政府间协议”）第五条中⑥。根据上述条款和《登记公约》第2条的规定，每个成员国都应登记其在国际空间站上的所有信息。每个成员国应将其提供的附件中所列的组成部件作为空间物体进行登记。每个伙伴对其登记的部件保留管辖权和控制权；这种管辖权和控制权的行使须遵守任何执行安排，包括其中规定的相关程序机制。

（b）中国

中国于1988年12月12日加入了《登记公约》。2001年2月，中国通过了《空间

---

① UN Doc. A/AC. 105/INF. 358, Note Verbale dated 7 April 1977 from the Permanent Representative of Japan to the Secretary-General, 18 April 1977.

② UN Doc. A/AC. 105/INF. 371, Note Verbale dated 31 March 1978 from the Permanent Representative of Japan to the Secretary-General, 14 April 1978.

③ UN Doc. A/AC. 105/INF. 366, Note Verbale dated 13 September 1977 from the Acting Permanent Representative of Japan addressed to the Secretary-General, 28 September 1977.

④ Ibid.

⑤ UN Doc. ST/SG/SER. E/552, Note Verbale dated 5 September 2008 from the Permanent Mission of Japan to the United Nations (Vienna) addressed to the Secretary-General, 19 September 2008.

⑥ Agreement among the Government of Canada, Governments of Member States of the European Space Agency, the Government of Japan, the Government of the Russian Federation, and the Government of the United States of America Concerning Cooperation on the Civil International Space Station (done 29 January 1998, entered into force 28 March 2001), in: Böckstiegel, Karl-Heinz/Benkö, Marietta/Hobe, Stephan (eds.), Space Law-Basic Legal Documents, D. II. 4. 1 (ISS Intergovernmental Agreement). The agreement is accessible online at <http://download. esa. int/docs/ECSL/ISS_ IGA. pdf> accessed 26 April 2019.

物体登记管理办法》[①]（以下简称《办法》），以加强国家对空间活动的管理，建立空间物体登记制度，保护中国作为空间物体发射国的合法权益，切实履行《登记公约》缔约国的义务[②]。

《办法》涉及与空间物体登记有关的若干问题，特别是“空间物体”和“发射国”的定义，确定有义务登记空间物体的一方和应登记的物体，空间物体的国家和国际登记程序，登记程序的时限等等。

中国常驻联合国（维也纳）代表团在2005年6月8日的普通照会中向秘书长通报了2001年建立射入地球轨道或以外的空间物体登记册的情况。根据2001年条例的最初规定，负责国家登记程序和建立国家空间物体登记册的主要机构是中国国防科学技术工业委员会（COSTIND）。然而，由于中国空间活动管理主管机构的调整，自2008年3月起，中国国家国防科技工业局（BUSTIND）成为负责国家空间物体登记和国家登记册维护的主管机构。

根据《办法》第六条，应列入国家登记册的信息包括：登记号码、登记人、空间物体的所有者、空间物体的适当标识、空间物体的基本特征、发射企业、运载火箭的名称、发射领土或发射地点、空间物体的基本轨道参数以及空间物体的发射和运行状况。

空间物体的登记人应向国家国防科技工业局提供相关信息，并在空间物体发射进入轨道后60天内完成登记程序。在空间物体发生重大变化的情况时（如改变轨道、空无法运行、解体或重新进入地球大气层），《办法》第九条规定，登记人应在空间物体的条件发生变化后60天内修改登记信息。

此外，《办法》还对香港特别行政区和澳门特别行政区所有或发射的空间物体的登记作了特别规定[③]。在《办法》第十条中规定，即便在空间物体国家登记册中专设了香港、澳门分册，它们拥有或发射的空间物体的具体登记办法也还需另行制定。

根据《办法》第四条，在全国范围内，所有发射空间物体或促成其发射的政府部

① Order No. 6 of the Commission for Science, Technology, Industry and National Defense and the Ministry of Foreign Affairs of the People's Republic of China (8 February 2001).

② See UN Doc. A/AC. 105/932, Information on national legislation relevant to the peaceful exploration and use of outer space, 2 February 2009; Art. 1 Regulation.

③ UN Doc. A/AC. 105/C. 2/2011/CRP. 4, Draft Report of the Working Group on National Legislation Relevant to the Peaceful Exploration and Use of Outer Space, Note by the Secretariat, 24 March 2011.

门、法人、其他组织和自然人都有义务进行登记。《办法》通过识别法律层面应当进行登记的发射国的方式解决存在多种发射登记选择的问题。第三条规定了《办法》的适用范围，即在中国境内发射的所有空间物体，以及中国作为共同发射国在境外发射的空间物体。《办法》第七条规定，如果有一个以上的所有者，主要所有者应代表所有所有者对空间物体进行登记。《办法》第五条规定，对于涉及其他联合发射国的国家登记，如有必要，国防科技工业局在与外交部协商后决定由其中哪一个国家登记该空间物体。该条例还规定了从中国境内发射的空间物体为中国以外国家的政府、法人、组织或自然人所有的情况。在这种情况下，依照《办法》第八条规定，在国内登记的义务被转移给“提供国际发射服务的公司”。对于除第八条之外的其他情况，根据《办法》第七条第 2 款，发射服务提供者应在该物体的国家登记中提供必要协助。最后，对于中国和其他国家共同发射的空间物体的国际登记，《办法》第十四条规定，登记国将通过官方外交渠道，即通过外交部和有关国家之间的协商来确定。

国防科技工业局应在空间物体进行国家登记后 60 天内通过外交部在联合国秘书处完成国际登记（《办法》第十二条）。根据联合国在线索引中的统计数据，中国在联合国秘书长处共登记了 307 个功能性空间物体，其中 41 个已经被回收或已经损毁①。

从《办法》第六条和第十三条的比较中可以看出，在国际登记时，并非所有在国内登记时需要的数据都被预设为需要提交。《办法》第十二条的规定明显参照了《登记公约》第四条第 1 款的内容，对于国内登记册中某些数据的提交进行了法律限制。关于提交在轨空间物体发生变化的最新信息，一些学者对《办法》第九条第 2 款做了狭义解释②，认为它只包括技术变化的情况，而不包括法律地位的变化（如所有权的转让）。然而，参照前文述及的例子，可以说空间物体条件的重大变化并不限于技术情况，而是可以以更广义的方式来理解。因此，虽然没有明确规定，但法律地位的改变可以被认为是应在登记册上登记的事项。亚太一号卫星和亚洲一号卫星就是这种情

① See the Online Index of Objects Launched into Outer Space on the UNOOSA website < http://www.unoosa.org/oosa/osoindex/search-ng.jspx? lf_ id=> accessed 26 April 2019.

② Ling, Yan, Comments on the Chinese Space Regulations, Chinese Journal of International Law (7) 2008, pp. 681-689.

况，其所有权于 1997 年转让给中国[1]。

中国提交给联合国秘书长的登记数据中所表达的标识编号包含了空间物体发射时的登记年份以及在中国国家航天局（CNSA）登记的空间物体的序列号。如果一个运载火箭发射了两个或更多的空间物体，为了精确和识别的目的，序列号用字母来补充。中国国家航天局空间物体登记表的序列号和中国国家航天局的登记日期也附在后面[2]。中国直到最近才提供这样的标识编号。从 2008 年开始，向联合国登记册发出的通知开始偶尔包括国际空间研究委员会（COSPAR）标识编号。

（c）印度

根据印度常驻联合国代表团于 1987 年 2 月 11 日提供的数据，印度的国家登记册由印度空间部（DOS）——印度空间研究活动的一个枢纽机构负责维护[3]。自 1975 年开始，印度向联合国秘书长提供适当的信息，开始印度根据大会第 1721B（XVI）号决议[4]提供和，之后根据其于 1982 年 1 月 18 日加入的《登记公约》提供[5]。目前，相关义务是印度空间研究组织（ISRO）职能的一部分。[6]

从 1975 年到 2018 年底，联合国秘书长共记录了 48 份来自印度的通知[7]，其中包含了印度发射到外层空间的 88 个物体的信息（因此获得了联合国登记的地位）[8]。正如联合国外层空间事务办公室（UNOOSA）网站所述，印度发射的空间物体数量达到

---

① UN Doc. ST/SG/SER. E/475, Note Verbale dated 8 June 2005 from the Permanent Mission of China to the United Nations (Vienna) addressed to the Secretary-General, 16 November 2005.

② UN Doc. ST/SG/SER. E/365, Note Verbale dated 11 November 1999 from the Permanent Mission of China to the United Nations (Vienna) addressed to the Secretary-General, 30 November 1999.

③ UN Doc. ST/SG/SER. E/INF. 8, Information furnished by the Permanent Mission of India to the United Nations in a letter dated 11 February 1987, 4 March 1987.

④ See United Nations Register of Objects Launched into Outer Space：Notifications from India (Launch Year 1975-present) <http：//www. oosa. unvienna. org/oosa/en/Reports/docsind. html> accessed 26 April 2019.

⑤ See the UNOOSA Treaty Status Database <http：//www. oosa. unvienna. org/oosatdb/showTreatySignatures. do> accessed 26 April 2019.

⑥ Vasudevan, B., Report on Status of Centre for Space Science & Technology Education in Asia Pacific (CSSTEAP) and Capacity Building Efforts in Space Law in India<http：//www. unoosa. org/pdf/pres/lsc2007/symp-09-1E. pdf> accessed 26 April 2019.

⑦ See United Nations Register of Objects Launched into Outer Space：Notifications from India (Launch Year 1975-present) <http：//www. oosa. unvienna. org/oosa/en/Reports/docsind. html> accessed 26 April 2019.

⑧ See the Online Index of Objects Launched into Outer Space on the UNOOSA website < http：//www. unoosa. org/oosa/osoindex/search-ng. jspx？ lf_ id=> accessed 26 April 2019.

60 个[①]。

迄今为止，印度还没有关于空间活动的具体法规，特别是在与空间物体登记相关的问题上相对缺乏。除此之外，印度尚未对现有的国内监管框架进行修正，以便在国家层面将加入国际空间法律文件所产生的义务转化为国内法。[②] 依照印度在转换国际义务方面的法律惯例，需要参照印度宪法第五十一条，它为在国家层面执行具有国际约束力的义务提供了切入点。为此，第五十一条的规定应与印度宪法第五十三条结合起来阅读。宪法第五十三条委托政府通过具体的行政权限来履行印度承担的国际义务。这就意味着制定专门国家立法要求的例外[③]。

通知中包含的登记信息严格意义上限于基本的普遍被接受的数据要求。对通知范围内提交的数据的进一步分析表明，并非所有这些数据都包含射入外层空间物体的标识编号。

（2）非缔约国[④]

《登记公约》第七条第 1 款认为除了公约第八条到第十二条外，公约中适用于国家的部分在某些条件下也可以适用于政府间国际组织[⑤]，从而允许它们参与《登记公约》法律制度。在联合国大会 1974 年 11 月 12 日第 3235（XXIX）号决议通过《登记公约》文本后不久，就讨论了这种参与是否发展到了允许有关组织建立独立的“国家登记册”的问题。在 1975 年 9 月 19 日的一封信中，联合国法律顾问对欧洲空间研究组织（ESRO）负责国际事务的副主任 1975 年 1 月 26 日涉及该问题的一封信作出了肯定的答复[⑥]。只要满足《登记公约》第七条第 1 款规定的条件，有关的政府间国际组织就有与公约缔约国相同的建立和维持适当的“国家登记册”的义务。

在国际空间法的系统性背景下，允许建立载有空间物体的政府间国际组织登记册的后续问题不可避免地出现了。因为《外空条约》第八条的第 1 句申明，如果《外空

---

① Ibid.

② Kaul, Ranjana/Jakhu, Ram S., Regulation of Space Activities in India, in: Jakhu, Ram S. (ed.), National Regulation of Space Activities, Springer, Dordrecht 2010, pp. 155-156.

③ Ibid., pp. 156-158.

④ Chapter by Ulrike Bohlmann.

⑤ See Commentary REG, Article Ⅶ, mn. 245ff.

⑥ Text reproduced in: Proceedings of the 3rd ECSL Colloquium on International Organisations and Space Law, 6-7 May 1999 Perugia, p. 29.

条约》的一缔约国在其登记册上载有射入外层空间的物体，那么该国应保留对该物体的管辖权和控制权，这种管辖与控制权及于在外层空间或天体上的任何人员①。然而，政府间国际组织在《外空条约》的地位相当有限。由于谈判时的政治环境，《外空条约》虽然承认政府间国际组织在探索和利用外层空间方面的作用②，但并未明确预估到政府间国际组织登记册上载有空间物体的情况。虽然早期的法律文献中曾讨论过一个问题，即一个政府间国际组织如果在该组织的登记册载有空间物体，是否会“保留管辖权和控制权”③。虽然成员国可以决定将一些控制职能委托给有关的政府间国际组织，鉴于这一概念固有的主权属性，没有合理的理由认为这样一个组织可以完全地行使管辖权和控制权④。因此，正确的做法是以政府间国际组织的名义进行登记，管辖权和控制权则相反，由国际组织在其成员国的授权范围内代表这些成员国行使⑤。联合国法律顾问在上文提及的书信往来中提出的解决办法是，在政府间国际组织登记空间物体的同时，该国际组织也应考虑其哪个成员国能最适当地对该空间物体及其人员行使管辖权⑥。

到目前为止，只有两个政府间国际组织符合《登记公约》第七条第1款规定的所有条件⑦，即欧空局和欧洲气象卫星应用组织。双方均已根据《登记公约》第二条第

① For a comprehensive analysis of the concept of ‘jurisdiction and control’ see Schmidt-Tedd, Bernhard/Mick, Stephan, Article Ⅷ, in: Hobe, Stephan/Schmidt-Tedd, Bernhard/Schrogl, Kai-Uwe (eds.), Cologne Commentary on Space Law, Volume I, Carl Heymanns, Cologne 2009, pp. 156ff.

② For details see Bohlmann, Ulrike M./Suess, Gisela, Article XⅢ, in: Hobe, Stephan/Schmidt-Tedd, Bernhard/Schrogl Kai-Uwe (eds.), Cologne Commentary on Space Law, Volume I, Carl Heymanns, Cologne 2009, pp. 215-222.

③ For an overview, see Bittlinger, Horst, Hoheitsgewalt und Kontrolle im Weltraum, Carl Heymanns, Cologne 1988, pp. 105ff.; or Hintz, Manfred, Weltraumgegenstände-Registrierung, in: Böckstiegel, Karl-Heinz (ed.), Handbuch des Weltraumrechts, Carl Heymanns, Cologne 1991, pp. 196ff.

④ See Lafferranderie, Gabriel, Jurisdiction and Control of Space Objects and the Case of an International Intergovernmental Organisation (ESA), Zeitschrift für Luft- und Weltraumrecht (54) 2005, pp. 228ff.

⑤ See Schmidt-Tedd, Bernhard/Mick, Stephan, Article Ⅷ, in: Hobe, Stephan/Schmidt-Tedd, Bernhard/Schrogl, Kai-Uwe (eds.), Cologne Commentary on Space Law, Volume I, Carl Heymanns, Cologne 2009, p. 163, mn. 75.

⑥ Letter dated 19 September 1975, reproduced in: Proceedings of the 3rd ECSL Colloquium on International Organisations and Space Law, 6-7 May 1999 Perugia, p. 31.

⑦ See Commentary REG, Article Ⅶ, mn. 246 and 252.

1 款的规定，将各自登记册的设立通知联合国秘书长①。

如果一个政府间国际组织与一个或多个其他发射国联合发射一个空间物体，则适用《登记公约》第二条第 2 款的规定，即该组织和其他有关发射国应共同决定由哪一方登记该物体，并可就空间物体及其任何人员的管辖权和控制权缔结适当的协定。该条款不仅适用于政府间国际组织与非成员国合作发射空间物体的情况。鉴于一个国际组织从来不能成为唯一的“发射国”，因为总是有一个国家从其领土上发射一个空间物体，而一个国际组织显然不能成为此类发射国，因此“共同确定”哪一个“发射国”要登记空间物体的义务实际上不可避免地适用于每一次此类发射。显然，可以在一个通用协议中明确共同确定登记国的义务，并由该协议全面处理特定类别发射的登记问题②。

欧洲空间局在联合国登记了 70 多个空间物体，是在该领域实践最广泛的政府间国际组织。因此，鉴于其在与国际合作伙伴合作方面的丰富经验，仔细研究欧空局的登记实践很有意义。关于联合发射一个被视为欧空局与其国际伙伴之间的合作成果的空间物体，一贯的做法是在各种合作协定中引入一项条款，规定由哪一方登记该空间物体。

关于国际空间站，《国际空间站政府间协议》第五条第 1 款规定：“根据《登记公约》第 2 条，各成员国应将其提供的附件中所列的飞行要素登记为空间物体，欧洲成员国已将这一责任委托给欧空局，以欧空局的名义并代表欧空局行事。”“成员国”一词指比利时王国、丹麦王国、法兰西共和国、德意志联邦共和国、意大利共和国、荷兰王国、挪威王国、西班牙王国、瑞典王国、瑞士联邦和大不列颠及北爱尔兰联合王国的政府，均为欧空局成员国政府。因此，欧空局已代表《国际空间站政府间协议》

① See UN Doc. ST/SG/SER. E/INF. 6, Information furnished by the European Space Agency to the United Nations in a letter dated 2 June 1983, 23 June 1983; and UN Doc. ST/SG/SER. E/INF. 14, Letter dated 6 May 1998 from the European Organisation for the Exploitation of Meteorological Satellites addressed to the Secretary-General, 27 May 1998.

② For example the agreement between ESA and the Government of the French Republic on the Guiana Space Centre and associated services.

缔约方的成员国政府登记了哥伦布轨道设备模块和自动转移飞行器[①]。

阿丽亚娜运载火箭系列和维加运载火箭是根据欧空局的可选方案[②]开发的。因此，欧空局在研发发射中登记了运载火箭的末级。此外，欧空局是位于法属圭亚那库鲁的圭亚那航天中心（CSG）的阿丽亚娜5号、织女星和联盟号发射器的发射基础设施的所有者。圭亚那航天中心由法国国家空间研究中心（CNES）和阿丽亚娜航天公司运营，并得到欧洲工业界的支持。欧空局与法兰西共和国政府之间关于圭亚那空间中心及相关服务的协议[③]第十六条规定，法国政府对于从圭亚那航天中心所发射的阿丽亚娜、维加和联盟号发射器及其部件，应在其利用阶段（而非开发阶段）进行登记。

根据《登记公约》第二条第3款，每个登记册的内容和保存条件由有关登记国自行决定。欧空局和欧洲气象卫星应用组织都决定按照《登记公约》第四条建立其登记册[④]。

5.《登记公约》之前和之外的通知

与射入外层空间的物体有关的通报行为早在《登记公约》生效之前的1962年就开始了，美国根据第1721 B（XVI）号决议提供了第一次登记通知[⑤]。因此，早在依

① Art. 5 para. 2 IGA goes on to specify that pursuant to Art. VIII OST and Art. II REG, each Partner State shall retain jurisdiction and control over the elements it registers in accordance with para. 1 above and over personnel in or on the Space Station who are its nationals. See Commentary REG, Article VII, mn. 253; and Schmidt-Tedd, Bernhard/Mick, Stephan, Article VIII, in: Hobe, Stephan/Schmidt-Tedd, Bernhard/Schrogl Kai-Uwe (eds.), Cologne Commentary on Space Law, Volume I, Carl Heymanns, Cologne 2009, pp. 146-168.

② All ESA Member States participate in certain mandatory activities, including the scientific programme relating to solar system science, astronomy and fundamental physics, as well as future studies, technological research, education and common investments in facilities laboratories and basic infrastructure. In addition, Member States choose their level of participation in so-called optional programmes, such as human spaceflight, telecommunications, earth observation, launchers, navigation, robotic exploration or space situational awareness. For details on the corresponding legal mechanisms see Lafferranderie, Gabriel, European Space Agency, in: Wouters, Jan (ed.), International Encyclopaedia of Laws: Intergovernmental Organizations, Kluwer Law International, The Hague 2005.

③ Signed on 18 December 2008 and concluded for the period from 1 January 2009 to 31 December 2020.

④ See also Bohlmann, Ulrike M., The Registration Policy of the European Space Agency, in: Hobe, Stephan/Schmidt-Tedd, Bernhard/Schrogl, Kai-Uwe (eds.), Current Issues in the registration of Space Objects, Proceedings of the Project 2001 Plus Workshop, 20/21 January 2005 Berlin (Germany), Institute of Air and Space Law and German Aerospace Center, Cologne 2005, pp. 47ff.

⑤ UN Doc. A/AC. 105/INF. 1, Letter dated 6 March 1962 from the Acting Secretary-General addressed to the Chairman of the Committee on the Peaceful Uses of Outer Space, transmitting a communication dated 5 March 1962 from Permanent Representative of the United States of America, 7 March 1962.

照《登记公约》建立登记册之前，与空间物体相关的国际登记册就出现了。基于第1721 B（XVI）号决议的登记册当时也被称为“登记册”，且在《登记公约》生效后并未停止存在。如今，它得到了特别是《登记公约》非缔约国的补充。

截至2018年底，共有56个国家和两个国际组织（欧空局和欧洲气象卫星应用组织）向秘书长提供了射入外层空间物体的登记信息，其中13个国家提供了符合《登记公约》和大会第1721 B（XVI）号决议的信息，即阿尔及利亚、澳大利亚、巴西、法国、德国、印度、意大利、日本、马来西亚、俄罗斯联邦（包括前苏联的信息）、土耳其、大不列颠及北爱尔兰联合王国以及美利坚合众国；然而，9个国家仅根据决议提交了信息，即埃及、以色列、卢森堡、荷兰、尼日利亚、菲律宾、沙特阿拉伯、泰国和委内瑞拉。

例如，卢森堡是两个主要卫星运营商的住所①，不受《登记公约》的约束，该国已根据联合国第1721 B（XVI）号决议提交了若干通知，涉及欧洲卫星公司（Société Européenne des satellites，SES）运营的Astra卫星。除了《登记公约》预计的基本参数外，卢森堡提供的信息还包括发射器的规格和发射物体的所有者。在这些通知中未发现与物体有关的国际标识编号。联合国在线索引列出了卢森堡的25个已登记物体和1个未登记物体。

四、第三条（联合国登记册）

1. 联合国秘书长应保持一份登记册，记录依照第四条所提供的情报。
2. 这份登记册所载情报应充分公开，听任查阅。

Schmidt-Tedd

目录

（一）谈判和起草历史

（二）评注

① SES <http://www.ses.com/4232583/en> and Intelsat <http://www.intelsat.com/> accessed 26 April 2019.

1. 强制性联合国登记册

2. 开放式访问

（一）谈判和起草历史

第1款的基本思想载于加拿大提案第四条[①]。现在通过联合国外层空间事务办公室网站实现的另一个目标是，应“持续有序地记录信息，以便利随时获取此类信息”。第2款是在阿根廷的倡议下提出的，以确保普遍的全面和开放准入。[②] 在最初加拿大的提案中，缔约国保留了完全进入的权利。

加拿大条款草案中有一个关于“关于协助识别空间物体”的部分前置于《登记公约》第三条，该部分现在载于《登记公约》第六条。该条款草案预见到秘书长有权要求提供信息。明确提到了“先进的空间监测和跟踪能力……和相关空间物体的‘在轨’数据以及关于轨道衰减、重返地球时间和地点的预测”的国家能力。考虑到尚未解决的空间交通管理和空间态势感知（SSA）问题，这一早期考虑是一种有趣而深远的方法。美国草案（第五条）[③] 和《登记公约》第六条最终稿中保留了“特别是拥有空间监测和跟踪设施的国家”的简称。

（二）评注

1. 强制性联合国登记册

如联合国大会第1721 B（XVI）号决议所述，《登记公约》第三条第1款规定了联合国登记册的强制性基础，这一点相比《外空条约》第八条更进了一步。第2款包括了保证对相关信息的可进行全面公开的访问的要求[④]。

2. 开放式访问

根据1961年12月20日1721B（XVI）号决议，为通过联合国秘书长分享各国向和平利用外层空间委员会提供的信息，联合国开始编制‘A/AC. 105/INF’系列文件。

---

① UN Doc. A/AC. 105/C. 2/L. 82, 4 April 1972.

② Cocca, Aldo A., Convention on Registration of Objects Launched into Outer Space, in: Jasentuliyana, Nandasiri/Lee, Roy S. K. (eds.), Manual on Space Law, Volume I, Oceana Publications, New York 1979, p. 181; US draft UN Doc. A/AC. 105/C. 2/L. 85, 19 March 1973, Article Ⅲ.

③ UN Doc. A/AC. 105/C. 2/L. 85, 19 March 1973.

④ See Schmidt-Tedd, Bernhard/Mick, Stephan, Article Ⅷ, in: Hobe, Stephan/Schmidt-Tedd, Bernhard/Schrogl, Kai-Uwe (eds.), Cologne Commentary on Space Law, Volume I, Carl Heymanns, Cologne 2009, p. 148, mn. 8.

自 1977 年 4 月 14 日《登记公约》生效后起，‘ST/SG/SER. E/-’名称下引入了一系列新的登记信息。这一系列文件作为一个整体，具象化了《登记公约》第三条表述的联合国登记册。《登记公约》第二条第 1 款所要求的关于建立国家登记册的信息被收集在另一个系列的文件中，名称为‘ST/SG/SER. E/INF/-’。

作为一种快速有效的工作工具，联合国外层空间事务办公室创建了“射入外层空间物体在线索引”，将根据《登记公约》和联合国大会第 1721 B（XⅥ）号决议向联合国提供的信息汇总在一起。除了通过正式通知获得的信息外，它还包含了一些额外的信息，这些信息记录在方括号内并以绿色标出，以便对 1957 年至今的空间物体有一个完整的概述。这些补充信息摘自世界卫星预警机构、空间研究委员会以及官方新闻稿和媒体来源。索引使用公共领域常用的名称和国际标识符。联合国外层空间事务办公室这种积极搜集和完善信息的行为为进行检索提供了便利，同时也有助于成员国履行其义务。

五、第四条（每个登记国提供的信息）

每一登记国应在切实可行的范围内尽速向联合国秘书长供给有关登入其登记册的每一个外空物体的下列信息：

（1）发射国或多数发射国的国名；

（2）外空物体的适当标志或其登记号码；

（3）发射的日期和地域或地点；

（4）基本的轨道参数，包括：

①波节周期，

②倾斜角，

③远地点，

④近地点。

（5）外空物体的一般功能。

2. 每一登记国应随时向联合国秘书长供给有关其登记册内所载外空物体的其他信息。

3. 每一登记国应在切实可行的最大限度内，尽速将其前曾提送信息的原在地球轨道内但现已不复在地球轨道内的外空物体通知联合国秘书长。

Schmidt-Tedd，Malysheva and Stelmakh

目录

（一）谈判和起草历史

强制性登记信息是第一份法国草案的一个要点，载于该草案第二条[①]。加拿大草案[②]第二条将其缩减到当前版本的《登记公约》第四条。美国最新的草案[③]在最终版本中增加了更多的要点，比如基本轨道参数。

关于信息提供的时限，一些具有深远影响的建议在谈判和起草中过程中被提出。这些提议建议通知应在发射之前或至少在发射的同时发出[④]。最后，公约采用了开放的、非特定的时限要求。

（二）评注

1. 需要提供的信息

《登记公约》第四条第1款包含一份向联合国秘书长提交的强制性信息清单，关

① UN Doc. A/AC. 105/C. 2/L. 45，France：Proposal，Draft Convention Concerning the Registration of Objects Launched into Space for the Exploration or Use of Outer Space，18 June 1968，reproduced in：UN Doc. A/AC. 105/58，Report of the Legal Sub-Committee on the Work of Its Eighth Session（9 June-4 July 1969），Annex I，Proposals Concerning Questions Relative to the Definition of Outer Space and the Utilization of Outer Space and Celestial Bodies，Including the Various Implications of Space Communications，4 July 1969.

② UN Doc. A/AC. 105/C. 2/L. 82，4 April 1972.

③ UN Doc. A/AC. 105/C. 2/L. 85，19 March 1973.

④ See Cocca，Aldo A.，Convention on Registration of Objects Launched into Outer Space，in：Jasentuliyana，Nandasiri/Lee，Roy S. K.（eds.），Manual on Space Law，Volume I，Oceana Publications，New York 1979，p. 182.

于登记国必须提供的有关进入其国家登记册的空间物体的信息。此类信息应尽快被递交。可根据国家立法规定的行政或程序规则规定时限。及时进行国家登记是履行本条规定义务的先决条件。

强制提供的信息列表如下：

（1）发射国家或国家们的名称；

作为备选的“国家们”用词使得条约有机会反映发射活动的发射国总数，并指出其他发射国，而不仅仅反映选定为登记国的单一国家。

（2）空间物体的适当标识或其登记号；

提供资料的义务仅限于在登记国的影响和责任下产生的那些标识或登记号码。第三方，例如空间研究委员会，根据其自己的决定指定空间物体的标识，与这方面的义务无关。相反，这并不排除在自愿的基础上传递和引用国际名称。

（3）发射日期和发射领土或地点；

《登记公约》未规定任何发射前通知义务。

有关发射领土或地点的信息是对第（1）项要求的信息的补充，并有助于澄清发射国的总数。

（4）基本轨道参数，包括：

①节点周期，

②倾斜度，

③远地点，

④近地点，

⑤空间物体的一般功能。

在许多情况下，一般功能的描述遵循科学和应用的标准类别，如地球观测、电信或导航。实际上，卫星的军事功能可能以一般的抽象方式描述。在此一般说明下，还必须考虑根据以后的法律文书提供的信息。一项特别重要的文书是联合国大会 1992 年 12 月 14 日第 47/68 号决议通过的《关于在外层空间使用核动力源的原则》的决议[①]。该决议的原则 4 要求发射前通知，包括关于所需安全评估结果的信息。原则 5

① UNGA Res. 47/68, Principles Relevant to the Use of Nuclear Power Sources in Outer Space, 14 December 1992.

还要求就载有核动力源的这类卫星发生故障并有放射性物质重返地球的风险发出通知。

后来的《登记实践决议》为缔约国提供了协调信息传输的标准，特别是在技术标准方面。

2. 额外信息

建议登记国向联合国秘书长转交关于空间物体的补充信息，但这不是一项义务。《登记公约》本身没有规定此类信息的性质和可能的内容。根据《登记公约》，适当、有用信息如何选择由国家自行决定，可以任何形式发送给联合国秘书长，无需设定时间表。然而，《登记实践决议》[①] 提出了一份补充信息清单，应提供这些信息，以改进登记的实践。2010 年，联合国外层空间事务办公室提出了实施这一升级实践的模板[②]，该模板提供了可提供此类额外信息的方向。

有许多实际例子。在某些情况下，相关普通照会中包含的信息有一个特殊的扩展——“附加”。以前，苏联经常不定期地向联合国秘书长转交此类额外信息。特别是，苏联常驻代表团于 1983 年 2 月 7 日（关于核卫星宇宙 1402）[③] 和 1988 年 6 月 14 日（关于核卫星宇宙-1900）[④] 向联合国秘书长转交了此类信息。

例如，法国向秘书长转交了关于其登记册中所列空间物体的补充资料；又如退出轨道的机动、地球静止卫星轨道位置的修正、在墓地轨道上转移非功能卫星的轨道机动[⑤]；例如，2009 年 2 月 11 日，法国常驻联合国代表团向联合国秘书长发出普通照会，介绍了法国早期发射的空间物体以及在倾斜轨道上继续运行的情况[⑥]。

---

① UNGA Res. 62/101, Recommendations on Enhancing the Practice of States and International Intergovernmental Organizations in Registering Space Objects, 17 December 2007; For more information on the resolution see Hobe, Stephan/Schmidt-Tedd, Bernhard/Schrogl, Kai-Uwe (eds.), Cologne Commentary on Space Law, Volume Ⅲ, Carl Heymanns, Cologne (forthcoming).

② See Future Perspectives, mn. 275.

③ UN Doc. ST/SG/SER. E/72/Add. 4, Note Verbale dated 7 February 1983 from the Permanent Mission of the Union of Soviet Socialist Republics to the United Nations addressed to the Secretary-General, 9 February 1983.

④ UN Doc. ST/SG/SER. E/176/Add. 2, Additional information furnished in conformity with the Convention on Registration of Objects Launched into Outer Space, Note Verbale dated 14 June 1988 from the Permanent Mission of the Union of Soviet Socialist Republics to the United Nations addressed to the Secretary-General, 15 June 1988.

⑤ UN Doc. A/AC. 105/C. 2/L. 250/Add. 1, Practice of registration of space objects by states and international organizations: replies from Member states. Note by the Secretariat. Addendum, 9 March 2004.

⑥ UN Doc. ST/SG/SER. E/563, Note Verbale dated 11 February 2009 from the Permanent Mission of France to the United Nations (Vienna) addressed to the Secretary-General, 21 May 2009.

某些国家的做法是，按照《登记公约》第四条第 1 款的规定，向联合国秘书长提交的信息中包含了额外的数据。例如，在“空间物体的一般用途”一栏中，各国通常只提供对该物体功能的一般描述，如，“地球遥感”“通信卫星”“通信卫星”“向国际空间站运送货物”等。但某些国家会提供具体、全面的信息。例如捷克共和国常驻联合国代表团 2003 年 8 月 21 日的普通照会①提供了以下补充资料：“MIMOSA 航天器的设计目的是非常精确地测量大气阻力和其他非重力来源的力（如太阳辐射压力和地面红外辐射压力）干扰人造卫星的运动。这颗总质量为 51.3 公斤的卫星只包含一个科学仪器，即微加速度计，它可以高精度地监测卫星加速度的变化。任务期间预计不会进行轨道机动。利用全向天线进行卫星遥测和遥控有低功耗的技术手段。预期使用寿命为 18 个月。接收到的数据将用于建立高层大气密度及其变化的详细模型。”

捷克共和国常驻联合国代表团 2003 年 11 月 24 日就所有 5 颗 MAGION 卫星的状况给联合国秘书长的普通照会②，这些卫星已登记用于研究磁层和电离层，并已列入捷克国家空间物体登记册，可作为广义补充信息的一个例子。这些补充信息主要是 1978 年至 1996 年发射的 5 颗 MAGION 卫星在收到最后遥测数据和轨道编号之日的汇总数据，最后是在收到通知时卫星的当前状态（特别是其运行终止日期、轨道改变）。

3. 离轨信息

与《登记公约》第四条第 2 款规定的可选择信息不同，关于已登记空间物体不再位于地球轨道的信息必须更新。其中一个方面是明确信息的需要以及保持联合国登记册的最新状态③。另一个方面是获得关于地球轨道上物体的信息的实际意义。发射国必须登记射入地球轨道或更远的空间物体。然而，根据《登记公约》第四条第 3 款，强制性的离轨信息仅限于不再在地球轨道上的物体。因此，关于围绕月球或其他行星的空间物体的离轨信息是自愿的。

《登记公约》第四条第 3 款包含“在最大程度上可行”和“尽快可行”的相关概

① UN Doc. ST/SG/SER. E/433, Note Verbale dated 21 August 2003 from the Permanent Mission of the Czech Republic to the United Nations (Vienna) addressed to the Secretary-General, 9 September 2003.

② UN Doc. ST/SG/SER. E/439, Note Verbale dated 24 November 2003 from the Permanent Mission of the Czech Republic to the United Nations (Vienna) addressed to the Secretary-General, 3 December 2003.

③ van Bogaert, Erik R. C., Aspects of Space Law, Kluwer Law and Taxation, London 1986, p. 121.

念。第一个概念涉及传输信息的范围，第二个概念涉及向联合国提交信息的条款。在这方面缺乏明确的参考点，导致各国采取不同的做法，特别是在提交相关信息的条件方面。一些缔约方每月或每季度提供关于已经不再在地球轨道上的空间物体的信息①，而其他缔约方的通知频率各不相同②。

例如，俄罗斯联邦以“分组”方式通知联合国秘书长其空间物体退出轨道或终止运行，并且提供在某一时期内从轨道上移除的所有物体的汇编信息③。为了统一向联合国秘书长提交有关移除空间物体的信息的方法，无线电频率管理条例中明确规定：“关于放置在绕地球轨道上但截至上月最后一天 24 小时 00 分（莫斯科时间）已不在轨道上的空间物体的信息，由俄罗斯国防部（空间部队）传输根据推荐样品，在下个月的第十天之前发送至国家航天公司”。自收到此类信息之日起 5 天内，俄罗斯联邦国家登记册中标题为“注释”的一栏中添加了关于放置在绕地球轨道上但不再位于该轨道上的空间物体的记录（《俄罗斯联邦行政法规》第 3. 8 节和第 3. 9 节）。国家航天公司向俄罗斯外交部发送“俄罗斯联邦（或苏联）登记的空间物体信息，这些空间物体已被放置在环绕地球的轨道上，并且不再位于该轨道上”，以便进一步提交给联合国秘书长（作为上个月信息的更新）。俄罗斯联邦常驻联合国代表团以一份普通照会的形式提交了这些信息以及俄罗斯联邦在同一时期发射物体的登记数据。

---

① For example the United States, see Registration information for the period July to September 2011, UN Doc. ST/SG/SER. E/632, Note Verbale dated 14 November 2011 from the Permanent Mission of the United States of America to the United Nations (Vienna) addressed to the Secretary-General, 12 December 2011.

② The Russian Federation provides information on space objects which have been but no longer are in earth orbit giving monthly updates on space objects no longer in Earth orbit, e. g. Information on space objects that ceased to exist during March 2010, UN Doc. ST/SG/SER. E/596, Note Verbale dated 10 May 2010 from the Permanent Mission of the Russian Federation to the United Nations (Vienna) addressed to the Secretary-General, 19 October 2010, updates that are collected over a period of several months which are supplied to the UN multiple months after the decay, e. g. Information covering the period from May to December 2010, UN Doc. ST/SG/SER. E/626, Note Verbale dated 11 August 2011 from the Permanent Mission of the Russian Federation to the United Nations (Vienna) addressed to the Secretary-General, 18 November 2011.

③ See, e. g. Information covering the period from May to December 2010, UN Doc. ST/SG/SER. E/626, Note Verbale dated 11 August 2011 from the Permanent Mission of the Russian Federation to the United Nations (Vienna) addressed to the Secretary-General, 18 November 2011.

六、第五条（标识或登记号码）

每当发射进入或越出地球轨道的外空物体具有第四条第 1 款第（2）项所述的标志或登记号码，或二者兼有时，登记国在依照第四条提送有关该外空物体的情报时应将此项事实通知秘书长。在此种情形下，联合国秘书长应将此项通知记入登记册。

Schmidt-Tedd and Tennen

目录

（一）谈判和起草历史

强制在空间物体上标注登记号码的问题是最具争议的起草要点之一，也是法国原始草案中一个极为重要的概念。[①] 第三条是该草案四个实质性条款之一，专门涉及登记号及其组成，该结构设计详细，例如 Cosmos 的字母 C，分配给相关国家的 ITU 无线电呼叫信号符号，一系列罗马大写字母，阿拉伯数字等。该结构规定，应制作和固定至少两块识别牌，以尽可能保证快速识别返回的物体。加拿大—法国的共同草案坚持了这一概念[②]。相反，科学和技术小组委员会编写了一份报告，指出这种标记系统不可行。在给定的技术水平下，这些标记将无法在重返大气层后继续存在[③]。美国的草

---

① UN Doc. A/AC. 105/C. 2/L. 45, France: Proposal, Draft Convention Concerning the Registration of Objects Launched into Space for the Exploration or Use of Outer Space, 18 June 1968, in: UN Doc. A/AC. 105/58, Report of the Legal Sub-Committee on the Work of Its Eighth Session (9 June-4 July 1969), Annex I, Proposals Concerning Questions Relative to the Definition of Outer Space and the Utilization of Outer Space and Celestial Bodies, Including the Various Implications of Space Communications, 4 July 1969.

② UN Doc. A/AC. 105/C. 2/L. 83, 20 April 1972.

③ Cocca, Aldo A., Convention on Registration of Objects Launched into Outer Space, in: Jasentuliyana, Nandasiri/Lee, Roy S. K. (eds.), Manual on Space Law, Volume I, Oceana Publications, New York 1979, p. 178 with reference to UN Doc. A/8020 (1970).

案[①]仍然包括一个国际名称的细节，包括一个适当的序号。

（二）评注

在空间物体上标明标识或登记号码不是国际义务。但是，如果一个空间物体做了相应的标记，则必须告知该标志或登记号，或在适用的情况下两个均须告知。这些指示参见《登记公约》第四条第1款第（2）项。

在国际地球年时国际地球物理学委员会设计了一个用统一标准来指定物体的系统，该系统被称为“哈佛”系统。该系统有四个要素：一个希腊字母、发射年份、一个表示该年内发射顺序的序列号和一个表示一次发射中所有物体的序列号[②]。国际空间研究委员会在1962年修改了哈佛系统[③]，用数字取代了希腊字母，并修改了各个物体的序列号，增加了拉丁字母中最多3个字符的后缀（除I或O外）[④]。后缀采用代码的形式，根据物体的功能表明其类别。[⑤]

空间研究委员会系统被广泛认为是空间物体的国际标识，尽管在美国，该标识系统被称为国家空间科学数据中心（NSSDC）身份。空间研究委员会定期在其官方出版物《空间研究委员会信息公报》（INFO. BULL）上发布发射清单[⑥]。空间研究委员会拥有两个国际数据存储和传播中心（ICDSD）：华盛顿的A中心和莫斯科的B中心。实际上，空间研究委员会汇编的数据通常与联合国登记册中所载的数据一致。然而，某些发射，例如气象和地球物理火箭发射，仅在国内登记，登记数据包括发射年份和日期、火箭类型、发射场坐标和实验目的。相关信息被定期向空间研究委员会的国际

---

① UN Doc. A/AC. 105/C. 2/L. 85, 19 March 1973.

② McDowell, Jonathan, The United Nations Registry of Space Objects, 13th edn., 2011 <http://www. planet4589. org/space/un/un. html> accessed 26 April 2019.

③ Schmidt-Tedd, Bernhard/Gerhard, Michael, Registration of Space Objects: Which Are the Advantages for States Resulting from Registration?, in: Benkö, Marietta/Schrogl, Kai-Uwe (eds.), Space Law: Current Problems and Perspectives for Future Regulation, Eleven International Publishing, Utrecht 2005, pp. 121ff., citing COSPAR Manual of Rockets and Satellites (1962).

④ McDowell, Jonathan, The United Nations Registry of Space Objects, 13th edn., 2011 <http://www. planet4589. org/space/un/un. html> accessed 26 April 2019.

⑤ Zhukov, Gennady/Kolosov, Yuri (Belitzky, Boris (tr.)), International Space Law, Praeger, New York 1984, p. 91.

⑥ Schmidt-Tedd, Bernhard/Gerhard, Michael, Registration of Space Objects: Which Are the Advantages for States Resulting from Registration?, in: Benkö, Marietta/Schrogl, Kai-Uwe (eds.), Space Law: Current Problems and Perspectives for Future Regulation, Eleven International Publishing, Utrecht 2005, p. 135.

数据存储和传播中心报告①。

在目前用于提供信息的表格中，有关登记标识的文本采用以下表述：空间物体的适当标识或其登记号码。事实上，该案文可被视为只是先前称为“空间物体名称”的项目的修改版本。

七、第六条（协助/识别请求）

本公约各项规定的施行如不能使一个缔约国辨认对该国或对其所辖任何自然人或法人造成损害或可能具有危险性或毒性的外空物体时，其他缔约国，特别包括拥有空间监视和跟踪设备的国家，应在可行的最大限度内响应该缔约国所提出或经由联合国秘书长代其提出，在公允和合理的条件下协助辨认该物体的请求。提出这种请求的缔约国应在可行的最大限度内提供关于引起这项请求事件的时间、性质及情况等情报。给予这种协助的安排应由有关各方协议商定。

Schmidt-Tedd, Malysheva and Stelmakh

目录

（一）谈判和起草历史

起草协助识别空间物体这一条款时有一项谅解，即这些程序将支持《责任公约》的实施②。此外，这是支持强制登记系统的代表团建立共识的必要组成部分。罗伯逊先生（加拿大）说：“因此，登记问题和小组委员会目前关于《责任公约》的工作有着直接联系，因为如果没有一个有助于识别损害责任人的有效制度，任何此类公约都

① Zhukov, Gennady/Kolosov, Yuri (Belitzky, Boris (tr.)), International Space Law, Praeger, New York 1984, p. 91.

② Cocca, Aldo A., Convention on Registration of Objects Launched into Outer Space, in: Jasentuliyana, Nandasiri/Lee, Roy S. K. (eds.), Manual on Space Law, Volume I, Oceana Publications, New York 1979, p. 186.

是不完整的。与汽车、船舶、飞机和铁路的情况一样，登记制度对于认定伤害、损失或损害的责任以及确定对特定车辆的管辖权是必要的。”①

（二）评注

《登记公约》第六条要求拥有空间监视和跟踪设备的缔约国提供协助。协助的请求应当在公允和合理的条件下被授予。太空时代的前十几年，只有两个超级大国拥有先进的监视和跟踪设备。过去十年，欧洲为增强自己的空间态势感知（SSA）能力做出了巨大努力。

美国国防部（DoD）和 NASA 依靠美国太空司令部的空间监视网，该网络由空军、海军和陆军太空司令部运营和维护②。自 1957 年人造卫星发射以来，国防部一直维持着一个空间物体目录。为了预测和防止碰撞，大约对 20000 个空间物体进行定期观测③。美国战略司令部也进行了重返地球评估。NASA 维持着一个民用数据库也称为北美航空航天防御司令部（NORAD）两线系统。直到 2011 年 7 月④，世界数据中心每月出版《空间警告通报》。

在德国，空军在乌埃德姆（Weltraumlagezentrum）安装了一个空间态势感知基础设施，德国宇航中心实施了民用分支机构。如今，私营卫星运营商还开发了一套避免碰撞的监测系统。1999 年，国际通信卫星组织与航空航天公司签订了这种系统⑤。今天，空间数据协会，一个卫星运营商的非盈利组织，已经建立了一个监测和避免碰撞的网络⑥。

在苏联/俄罗斯，监测空间物体的设施是从太空时代开始发展起来的。从 1960 年代开始，政府决定建立适当的监测、控制和数据处理中心，以确保对近地空间的人造

① Jasentuliyana, Nandasiri/Lee, Roy S. K. (eds.), Manual on Space Law, Volume Ⅲ, Oceana Publications, New York 1981, p. 666.

② See US General Accounting Office (US GAO), Report to Congressional Requesters, Space Surveillance, 1 December 1997, GAO/NSIAD-98-42.

③ Klinkrad, Heiner, Space Debris: Models and Risk Analysis, Springer, Berlin 2006, p. 27.

④ Last Spacewarn Bulletin No. 692, July 2011. A monthly publication of the National Space Science Data Center/NASA. The past bulletins will remain accessible through NSSDC <http: //nssdc. gsfc. nasa. gov/spacewarn> accessed 26 April 2019.

⑤ Pelton, Joseph N. /Jakhu, Ram S., Space Safety Regulations and Standards, Elsevier Publisher, Amsterdam 2010, p. 133.

⑥ See Dal Bello, Richard/Mendelson, Michael, Private Risk Management in Orbital Operations, Inter-operator Liability and Space Data Association, Zeitschrift für Luft- und Weltraumrecht (60) 2011, pp. 218-230.

空间物体进行持续监测。与关于空间物体的其他数据来源一起，形成了一个外层空间控制系统（俄语首字母缩写为 SKKP）。1962 年 11 月 15 日，苏联共产党中央委员会和部委会议关于建立国家空间控制服务的法令，规定了 SKKP 的组织框架。

目前，俄罗斯的 SKKP 是永久战略信息系统。1970 年代初，外层空间控制中心（俄语首字母缩写为 TSKKP）利用 SKKP 提供的信息和从特殊来源获得的信息，追踪了登记在主要空间物体目录（俄语首字母缩写为 GKKO）中的 500 个物体；1976 年，TSKKP 已经追踪了超过 1500 个物体，到 2011 年，追踪了大约 12000 个物体①。自 2011 年 12 月以来，作为 TSKKP 继任者的主要空间情报中心（俄语首字母缩写为 GTSRKO）现今追踪到的空间物体总数的信息不再向公众提供。

1980 年 4 月 24 日关于改进和提高 SKKP② 工作的苏联法令为进一步发展 TSKKP 和 SKKP 提供了基础。TSKKP 开发了计算和预测空间物体可能影响的时间和区域，尤其是紧急情况下大型非受控的宇宙飞船和航天器③。这个系统既能通过确定目的、国籍和国际编号来检测宇宙飞船，又能监测宇宙飞船目前的退役状态，包括运行状态和紧急状态。在 1970 年代末，TSKKP 进行了调试，并且开始运行一个算法和软件子系统，用以确定宇宙飞船的运行寿命和可能重返大气层的时间和区域④。

苏联“宇宙-594”和“宇宙-1402”卫星上的核动力源（NPS）事故引起了国际社会的广泛关注。一旦完成飞行，这些 NPS 空间物体通常会被送入更高的所谓“坟场轨道”。然而，在上述情况下，这一尝试失败了，导致它重新进入地球大气层⑤。在这种情况下，TSKKP 在其进入密集大气层之前提供了支撑，高精度确定了事故发生的时间和区域（加拿大北部为宇宙-954 号，大西洋南部为宇宙-1402 号）。

SKKP 在控制外层空间的国际重要性以及它所提供的重大机会，可以从获取关于

---

① A. Shironin, “They Control Outer Space”, PolitRu, 21 September 2011, <http://m. polit. ru/article/2011/09/21/space_ control_ cenrer> accessed 26 April 2019.

② О работах по совершенствованию и развитию СККП, 24 апреля 1980 г.

③ See Воздушно-космического оборона, Система контраля космического пространства, <http://old. vko. ru/article. asp? pr_ sign=archive. 2004. 19. 29> accessed 26 April 2019. Reference publication of this article is Анисимов, В. Д. /Батырь, Г. С. /Меньшиков, А. В. /Шилин, В. Д., Корпоратсия “вымпел”: Системы пракетно-космическоы обороны, Оружие и токхнологии, Moscow 2004.

④ A brief general overview on the SKKP system is provided by Гаврилин, Евгений Васильевич, Эпоха《классической》ракетно-космической обороны, Техносфера, Moscow 2008, p. 13.

⑤ National Research Council, Limiting Future Collision Risk to Spacecraft, An Assessment of NASA’s Meteoroid and Orbital Debris Programme, The National Academies Press, Washington DC 2011, p. 61.

礼炮 7 号——宇宙-1686 号空间复合体[①]的时间和可能影响区域的信息中看出。复合碎片重返大气层的时间和地点（阿根廷南部）被提前以高精度确定。SKKP 的结果似乎比来自类似系统的数据更精确。

今天，确保执行上述功能的系统的一个关键要素被授予俄罗斯国家航天公司“俄罗斯国家航天集团”的“重大空间情报中心”（GTsRKO）和“任务控制中心”（俄语首字母缩写为 TSUP）[②]。俄罗斯联邦空间部队能够侦测到本国和外国发射的所有弹道导弹和运载火箭，以及外国和国内卫星的机动。他们监测轨道飞船，并对脱离轨道的空间物体进行控制。俄罗斯空间部队经常提醒主管实体注意空间物体和国际空间站（ISS）的危险结合。

在乌克兰，相应的设施是乌克兰国家航天局[③]国家空间设施控制和试验中心的特别控制中心。在哈萨克斯坦共和国，可用于追踪宇宙飞船和控制外层空间的天线综合体位于萨雷莎干试验场的设施内。

八、第七条（政府间国际组织）

1. 除本公约第八条至第十二条［含第八条和第十二条在内］外，凡提及国家时，应视为也适用于从事外空活动的任何政府间国际组织，但该组织须声明接受本公约规定的权利和义务，并且该组织的多数会员国须为本公约和《关于各国探索和利用包括月球和其他天体在内外层空间的活动的原则的条约》的缔约国。

2. 为本公约缔约国的任何这种国际组织的会员国，应采取一切适当行动，保证该组织依照本条第一款规定发表声明。

Bohlmann

① Cosmos 1686 docked to the Soviet space station Salyut 7 in order to test systems for the later MIR core module. The complex massed 43 tons and re-entered 7 February 1991 with debris over Argentina.

② See the website of the Mission Control Center <http：//www. mcc. rsa. ru> accessed 26 April 2019.

③ <http：//zakon. rada. gov. ua/cgi-bin/laws/main. cgi？ nreg = 698 %2F96>；<http：//www. nkau. gov. ua/nsau/catalogNEW. nsf/ByNamesU/232114C754525191C3256BF8004BF972？ OpenDocument&Lang = U> both accessed 26 April 2019.

目录

（一）谈判和起草历史

《登记公约》第七条的阐述方式等同于先前协商的《责任公约》第二十二条第 1 款和第 2 款。涉及特殊的程序和连带及个别责任问题的《责任公约》第二十二条第 3 款和第 4 款没有被《登记公约》采纳，两者在这方面不相关。关于国际组织的条款早在加拿大第一份草案中已有体现①。

1972 年 4 月 4 日加拿大草案②中首次出现了“如果该组织的大多数成员国是本公约和《关于各国探索和利用包括月球和其他天体在内外层空间活动的原则条约》的缔约国”的表述，但该表述显然是仿照《营救协定》第六条和《责任公约》第二十二条。由于《登记公约》的准备工作文件对提法及其可能引起的讨论保持沉默，因此，可以从导致早期条约中纳入类似条款的发展中获得一些见解。在《营救协定》的谈判过程中，提出了两种截然相反的政府间国际组织参与的解决方案：③ 一方面，有人建议该组织本身的一项声明就足以允许有限的参与④，另一方面，有人假设该组织的所有成员国都必须是《营救协定》和《外空条约》的缔约国，以便该组织能够正式宣布接受相应的权利和义务⑤。最终为《营救协定》所采用的解决方案分别出现在 1967

① UN Doc. A/AC. 105/C. 2/L. 82, 4 April 1972, Art. VI.

② Ibid.

③ See chapter on ARRA in this Volume, Historical Background and Context, mn. 16.

④ See UN Doc. WG. 1/30, Art. 7 Joint Australian and Canadian Draft in: UN Doc. A/AC. 105/21, Report of the Legal Sub-Committee on the Work of the Second Part of its Third Session (5-23 October 1964), Annex 1, Proposals and Amendments Relating to Assistance to and Return of Astronauts and Space Vehicles, Australia and Canada Proposal, 23 October 1964, p. 12.

⑤ Intermediate solutions according to which at least one Member State needed to be State Party were also put forward, see UN Doc. A/AC. 105/C. 2/L. 8, USA: Revised proposal-Convention concerning liability for damage caused by the launching of objects into outer space, in: UN Doc. A/AC. 105/19, Report of the Legal Sub-Committee on the Work of its Third Session (9-26 March 1964) Annex Ⅱ, Proposals and amendments relating to liability for damage caused by objects launched into outer space, 26 March 1964.

年12月12日和12月14日公布的两个草案文本[①]中，作为基于欧洲和澳大利亚代表团提出的想法而形成的务实的和创造性的折衷解决方案[②]，其考虑到基本的理论方法是不可调和的。

（二）评注

1. 接受声明

认识到空间活动国际合作的不断加强和融合，《登记公约》第七条规定，国际政府间组织有可能在某些条件下获得几乎等同于《登记公约》缔约国的地位，但有一个明确的区别，即《登记公约》第九条所预见的对公约提出修正案和发起并参与公约修订的权利仍然是缔约国的特权。与《营救协定》第六条、《责任公约》第二十二条和《月球协定》第十六条的平行条款一起，这一条款在承认政府间国际组织在国际公共空间法中的客观法律人格方面迈出了一步，因为他们脱离了《外空条约》第十三条中较狭隘的概念[③]。

为了获得“尽可能接近缔约国”[④]的地位，政府间国际组织需要满足两个条件，即该组织的大多数成员国是《登记公约》和《外空条约》的缔约国，同时该组织宣布接受《登记公约》规定的权利和义务。

鉴于《登记公约》的两个基本期望，正如在序言第九段所阐述的，即加强空间物体的识别并促进关于探索和利用外层空间的国际法的适用和发展，由此为什么《登记公约》应当设立附加条件的问题出现了，即该组织的大多数成员国是《登记公约》和《外空条约》的缔约国，以便政府间国际组织能够按照《登记公约》第七条的规定做

---

① UN Doc. A/AC. 105/C. 2/L. 28, Draft agreement on the rescue of astronauts, the return of astronauts and the return of objects launched into outer space, 12 December 1967 and UN Doc. A/AC. 105/C. 2/L. 28/Rev. 1, Draft agreement on the rescue of astronauts, the return of astronauts and the return of objects launched into outer space, 14 December 1967.

② The wording had been developed in the Working Group on the United Nations Committee on the Peaceful Uses of Outer Space that had been established by the European Space Conference, see Lafferranderie, Gabriel, The Outer Space Treaty and the International Organisations conducting Space Activities, in: IISL, Proceedings of the 40th Colloquium on the Law of Outer Space, 6-10 October 1997 Turin (Italy), AIAA, 1998, pp. 161ff.

③ For details see Bohlmann, Ulrike M./Suess, Gisela, Article XIII, in: Hobe, Stephan/Schmidt-Tedd, Bernhard/Schrogl, Kai-Uwe (eds.), Cologne Commentary on Space Law, Volume I, Carl Heymanns, Cologne 2009, pp. 215-222.

④ Lafferranderie, Gabriel, The European Space Agency (ESA) and international space law (1999), in: Proceedings of the 3rd ECSL Colloquium on International Organisations and Space Law, 6-7 May 1999 Perugia, pp. 19, 21.

出声明。这一附加条件暂时不包括国际移动卫星组织（IMSO）[①]、阿拉伯卫星通信组织（ARABSAT）[②] 和欧洲通信卫星组织（EUTELSAT）[③] 的声明。另一方面，国际空间通信组织（INTERSPUTNIK）将符合这一标准。[④]

这一条件可被视为对国际组织的声明及其内部决策机构的运作表示一定程度的不信任。在公认的理论案例中，它可被理解为一个组织宣布其接受《登记公约》越权的权利和义务的正式保护。不仅是该组织的成员国受益于这种保护，整个国际社会也受益于这种保护，因为虚假地认为一个政府间国际组织的登记得到大多数会员国支持的风险将会减少。然而，鉴于《登记公约》的意图，将保护作为开展空间活动的政府间国际组织成员但本身并不是《登记公约》和《外空条约》的缔约国的国家作为《登记公约》意图的核心，似乎不符合逻辑。

对《责任公约》中相应条款的讨论集中在允许政府间国际组织有限地参与《责任公约》的制度这一方面，确保“扩大该组织空间活动造成的任何损害的赔偿责任，并

① As of 30 November 2018, IMSO has got 104 Member States, of which 73 are States Parties to OST, but only 52 Parties to REG, see UN Doc. A/AC. 105/C. 2/2018/CRP. 3, Status of International Agreements relating to activities in outer space as at 1 January 2018, 9 April 2018 with regular updates published on http://www.unoosa.org/documents/pdf/spacelaw/treatystatus/AC105_ C2_ 2018_ CRP03E. pdf.

② ARABSAT has got 21 Member States, of which fourteen are States Parties to OST, but only eight States Parties to REG, see UN Doc. A/AC. 105/C. 2/2018/CRP. 3, Status of International Agreements relating to activities in outer space as at 1 January 2018, 9 April 2018 with regular updates published on http://www.unoosa.org/documents/pdf/spacelaw/treatystatus/AC105_ C2_ 2018_ CRP03E. pdf.

③ The case of EUTELSAT is a little peculiar: As of 1 December 2018, it had 49 Member States, of which 35 are States Parties to the OST and 27 are States Parties to the REG, but only 24 are States Parties to both, see UN Doc. A/AC. 105/C. 2/2018/CRP. 3, Status of International Agreements relating to activities in outer space as at 1 January 2018, 9 April 2018 with regular updates published on http://www.unoosa.org/documents/pdf/spacelaw/treatystatus/AC105_ C2_ 2018_ CRP03E. pdf. Even though the majority of Member States of EUTELSAT are Parties to the OST and another majority of its Member States are Parties to the REG, a grammatical interpretation of Art. Ⅶ REG excludes a valid declaration by EUTELSAT since there is not a majority of Member States that are parties to both. Nonetheless, EUTELSAT's Assembly of Parties has already adopted a resolution in favor of such a declaration at the occasion of its 6th session, should the conditions be met in the future, see Roisse, Christian, EUTELSAT et le droit de l'espace-considérations juridiques, in: Proceedings of the 3rd ECSL Colloquium on International Organisations and Space Law, 6-7 May 1999 Perugia, pp. 63, 65.

④ As of December 2018, INTERSPUTNIK had 26 Member States, of which 21 are States Parties both to OST and REG and another 14 are States Parties only to OST, see UN Doc. A/AC. 105/C. 2/2018/CRP. 3, Status of International Agreements relating to activities in outer space as at 1 January 2018, 9 April 2018 with regular updates published on http://www.unoosa.org/documents/pdf/spacelaw/treatystatus/AC105_ C2_ 2018_ CRP03E. pdf.

按照《外空条约》规定的原则执行这些活动。”① 由于在一个国家登记处登记空间物体不是直接导致有关发射国承担国际责任的决定性因素，也不会对作为发射国的另一个国家的质量产生任何影响，因此，所涉发射国之一，包括任何适当的政府间国际组织，登记空间物体的问题主要与管辖权和控制权有关。然而，通过登记，一个国家能确信其具有发射国的特征。因此，从实体责任法的角度来看，将政府间国际组织纳入《登记公约》制度不如《责任公约》制度重要，这也可能解释了《登记公约》谈判期间明显缺乏对该条款的讨论。此外，必须牢记国际组织不可能成为唯一的“发射国”，因为总有一个国家从其领土上发射空间物体，而国际组织由于显而易见的原因而永远无法成为该类发射国。根据一种解释，政府间国际组织发射空间物体的行为不应被视为有关组织的成员国为登记的目的而联合发射②。

承担条约缔约方权利和义务的政府间国际组织的成员国的立场所产生的后果这一一般性问题是一个复杂且备受争议的问题，迄今为止未能达成一致。这可通过参考1986年的《关于国家和国际组织间或国际组织相互间条约法的维也纳条约法》草案的第三十六条的讨论来说明。③ 如果以条约相对性的一般概念为出发点，则国际组织的成员国应被视为相对于条约的其他缔约国的第三方，如《登记公约》。反对的立场

① See UN Doc. A/AC. 105/C. 2/SR. 120, Draft Agreement on Liability for Damage Caused by Space Objects Launched into Outer Space, 19 June 1969, and in particular the statement by the UK delegate Mr. Freeland.

② See the letter by Erik Suy, Legal Counsel of the United Nations to ESA (Mr. Kaltenecker, International Affairs) dated 19 September 1975 making reference to the intention of the Registration Convention, letter reproduced in Proceedings of the 3rd ECSL Colloquium on International Organisations and Space Law, 6-7 May 1999 Perugia, p. 31, according to which the launching by an international intergovernmental organisation should not be regarded as a joint launching by its Member States, nevertheless "[…] the organization, when considering the registration of the space object, should consider also the question as to which of its member States could most appropriately exercise jurisdiction over the space object and its personnel"; see also Zhukov, Gennady P. /Kolosov, Yuri (Belitzky, Boris (tr.)), International Space Law, Praeger, New York 1984, p. 88. "[…] member-states have to reach agreement as to which of them shall exercise jurisdiction and control over the space objects by the organization, since the organization itself cannot have such powers.".

③ Vienna Convention on the Law of Treaties between States and International Organizations or between International Organizations (opened for signature on 21 March 1986, not yet in force) <http://untreaty.un.org/ilc/texts/instruments/english/conventions/1_2_1986.pdf> accessed 26 April 2019.

是在一个组织的成员国和条约缔约国之间建立一个“附带协议”①。在为达成该问题的一般性解决办法而提出的不同草案进行了长时间讨论之后，1986 年公约将确定该组织成员国权利和义务的国际组织缔结的条约问题留给了每个组织的国内法②。

这一问题不可能得出一个最后结论的事实表明，自《登记公约》生效以来，一般性讨论进展不大。国家一方面对国际组织的法律独立程度感到不安，另一方面对他们的问责制及其成员国的问责制仍然感到不安。就《登记公约》而言，这种矛盾心理导致了上文所述的混合解决办法，它向《登记公约》的其他缔约国提供了关于国际组织所作声明可靠性的保证，但不一定能回答所有相关问题。

《登记公约》没有特别指出国际政府间组织声明接受权利和义务所需采取的形式。迄今为止，这两项声明均已根据 ESRO③ 和 EUMETSAT 的内部法律秩序由各自组织在理事会决议中通过。这两个文本都在序言中回顾了接受声明的条件得到满足的事实，并在其业务部分宣布各组织接受《登记公约》的权利和义务。在向联合国秘书长提交这些声明时，两个组织都正式同意受《登记公约》适用条款的约束④。

2. 政府间国际组织成员国的行动

《登记公约》第七条第 2 款规定，《登记公约》的缔约国也是开展空间活动组织的成员国，有义务努力促使有关组织根据《登记公约》第七条第 1 款作出声明。《登记公约》的缔约国如何履行这项义务，将由相关国际组织的内部法律秩序决定，由有关缔约国斟酌决定。

---

① For more detailed information see Brölmann, Catherine, The Institutional Veil in Public International Law-International Organisations and the Law of Treaties, Hart Publishing, Oxford and Portland 2007, pp. 212ff.; Fitzmaurice, Malgosia, Third Parties and the Law of Treaties, in: Frowein, Jochen A./Wolfrum, Rüdiger, Max Planck Yearbook of United Nations Law, Volume 6, Kluwer Law International, The Hague 2002, pp. 37-137.

② Art. 74 para. 3 together with Preambular para. 13 Vienna Convention on the Law of Treaties.

③ With the succession of ESRO by ESA, this declaration is attributed to ESA, see in general on the evolution from ESRO/ELDO to ESA Lafferranderie, Gabriel, European Space Agency, in: Wouters, Jan (ed.), International Encyclopaedia of Laws: Intergovernmental Organizations, Kluwer Law International, The Hague 2005, pp. 23ff.

④ ESRO lodged its declaration on 2 December 1979 and EUMETSAT followed on 10 July 1997.

九、第八条（签署/批准/加入/生效）

1. 本公约应听由所有国家在纽约联合国总部签字。凡在本公约按照本条第 3 款生效以前尚未签字于本公约的任何国家得随时加入本公约。

2. 本公约应经各签字国批准。批准书或加入书应交存联合国秘书长。

3. 本公约应于向联合国秘书长交存第五件批准书时在已交存批准书的国家间发生效力。

4. 对于在本公约生效后交存批准书或加入书的国家，本公约应自其交存批准书或加入书之日起开始生效。

5. 秘书长应将每一签字日期、交存本公约的每一批准书和加入书日期、本公约生效日期和其他通知事项，迅速告知所有签字国和加入国。

Schmidt-Tedd

目录

（一）谈判和起草历史

结构和主要内容首次出现在美国草案的第七条中[①]。

（二）评注

该条款结构如下：

1. 公开签署
2. 批准书/加入书
3. 生效
4. 后期交存和生效
5. 秘书长提供的资料

---

① UN Doc. A/AC. 105/C. 2/L. 85，19 March 1973.

该公约于 1974 年 7 月 5 日得到 UNCOPUOS 的认可，并于 1974 年 11 月 12 日在第 3235（XXIX）号决议中获得联合国大会的通过。《登记公约》在 1975 年 1 月 14 日提交签署，并在第五份批准文件交存后于 1976 年 9 月 15 日生效。第一个批准的国家是 1975 年 12 月 17 日递交的法国，随后是 1976 年的保加利亚、瑞典、加拿大和美国。

十、第九条（拟议修正案）

本公约任何缔约国得对本公约提出修正案。修正案对于每一接受修正案的缔约国应在过半数缔约国接受该修正案时发生效力，嗣后对于其余每个缔约国应在该缔约国接受修正案之日起发生效力。

Schmidt-Tedd

目录

（一）谈判和起草历史

该条款与《责任公约》第二十五条相同，相当于《营救协定》的第八条。该条款在《登记公约》上下文中的完整措辞首次出现在美国草案的第八条中[①]。

（二）评注

在《登记公约》第一个十年之后，在学术讨论会上提出了修订提案，但是缔约国没有正式的修订提案[②]。

① UN Doc. A/AC. 105/C. 2/L. 85, 19 March 1973.

② Diederiks-Verschoor, I. H. Philepina/Kopal, Vladimir, An Introduction to Space Law, 3rd edn. , Kluwer Law International, The Hague 2008, p. 46.

十一、第十条（复核/修订）

本公约生效十年以后，应在联合国大会的临时议程内列入复核本公约的问题，以便按照公约过去施行情形，考虑其是否需要修订。但在本公约生效五年以后的任何时期，如经缔约国三分之一的请求并征得多数缔约国的同意，应即召开缔约国会议复核本公约。此种复核应特别计及任何相关的技术发展情形，包括有关识别空间物体的技术发展情形。

Schmidt-Tedd and Tennen

目录

（一）谈判和起草历史

复核条款的前两句在很大程度上与《责任公约》的复核条款第26条类似。第三句考虑到与空间物体识别相关的技术发展，是专门针对《登记公约》的。它反映了关于“空间物体自愿或强制标记”替代方案的争议性讨论，并为后来的强制性制度敞开了大门。

（二）评注

1986年，在《登记公约》生效的十年后，联合国大会确实考虑了对公约的审查。结果于1986年12月3日联合国大会第41/66号决议中阐述[①]，强调了所有航天国家和政府间国际组织批准或者加入公约的重要性。秘书长编写的关于公约适用情况的报告已经提交给法律小组委员会[②]。尽管有一些批评意见，但讨论并未导致对公约的任

① UNGA Res. 41/66, Question of the review of the Convention on Registration of Objects Launched into Outer Space, 3 December 1986.

② UN Doc. A/AC. 105/382, Application of the Convention on registration of objects launched into outer space, 2 March 1987.

何改编①。后来，20 个欧洲国家提出了一个新的议程项目“改进《登记公约》”，当时没有达成共识。继这一一般性审查方法之后，于 2000 年就“审查发射国概念”这一单方面的三年工作计划达成了协议②。

总之可以得出一个积极的结论，《登记公约》符合国家对非政府空间活动的责任，并阻碍了“方便旗”的做法。尽管对一般司法内容有一些批评，但“鉴于目前商业航天活动的发展，《登记公约》似乎没有很大的空白需要新条款或者对其现有措辞进行实质性修正来填补。”③ 真正的问题是在当事方之间缺乏协议的情况下的合理应用和备用解决方法。

一国的通知做法可能存在不一致，向联合国秘书长登记空间物体的国家做法也可能存在差异和不一致之处。各国习惯登记已经完成轨道运行或已到达或超过逃逸速度的物体④。然而，有些国家只登记已经到达轨道的物体。⑤ 除此之外，有关卫星在使用寿命结束时脱离轨道的信息披露是不一致的，而美国是报告碎片的为数不多的行动者之一⑥。基本信息报告存在不一致，如美国只提供国际名称，而俄罗斯联邦只提供物体的名称⑦。这些例子表明需要进一步统一登记做法。

在法律文献中，已经提出了许多不同的修正《登记公约》的提案。《登记公约》

---

① Kopal, Vladimir, The 1975 Convention on Registration of Objects Launched into Outer Space in View of the Growth of Commercial Space Activities, in: Benkö, Marietta/Kröll, Walter (eds.), Luft- und Weltraumrecht im 21. Jahrhundert (Air and Space Law in the 21st Century) -Liber Amicorum Karl-Heinz Böckstiegel, Carl Heymanns, Cologne 2001, p. 374.

② Ibid., pp. 372f.

③ Ibid., p. 380.

④ Zhukov, Gennady/Kolosov, Yuri (Belitzky, Boris (tr.)), International Space Law, Praeger, New York 1984, p. 87.

⑤ Ospina, Sylvia, Revisiting the Registration Convention: A Proposal to Meet the Need to Know "What Is Up There", in: IISL, Proceedings of the 43rd Colloquium on the Law of Outer Space, 2-6 October 2000 Rio de Janeiro (Brazil), AIAA, 2001, p. 204.

⑥ Cocca, Aldo A., Convention on Registration of Objects Launched into Outer Space, in: Jasentuliyana, Nandasiri/Lee, Roy S. K. (eds.), Manual on Space Law, Volume I, Oceana Publications, New York 1979, p. 180.

⑦ Hörl, Kay-Uwe/Hermida, Julian, Change of Ownership, Change of Registry? Which Objects to Register, What data to be Furnished, When, and Until When?, in: IISL, Proceedings of the 46th Colloquium on the Law of Outer Space, 29 September-3 October 2003 Bremen (Germany), AIAA, 2004, p. 456.

第四条的披露要求建立了通知联合国登记册的信息的最低基准格式[①]，然而各国报告格式的变化和不一致阻碍了条约的效力[②]。《登记实践决议》是解决问题的一个步骤。需要披露的信息的有限性进一步阻碍了该条约的效力。例如，要求披露的轨道参数不足以确定物体在空间中的实际位置和运动[③]，因此对于避免碰撞和碎片观测几乎没有用处[④]。

建议在规定的时限内向联合国秘书长发出通知[⑤]，该时限可按国家标准衡量，如发放非政府有效载荷许可证。有人提议可对不遵守行为实施制裁，例如将保险视发射前登记情况而定[⑥]。《登记公约》并未明确要求对空间物体进行标记，尽管迄今为止大多数发射物体都已被标记。有人指出，这种做法已经形成了一种国际惯例，因此未作标记可能被视为恶意并透露出不遵守《登记公约》的意图[⑦]。有学者质疑《登记公约》的范围，因为该公约中没有关于对天体上的站点和设施进行登记的规定，这些站点和设施由无法再与运送它们的空间物体识别为一体的材料制成，从而导致出现未登记的空间物体[⑧]。然而，这一解释可能超出了“发射进入或越出地球轨道”这一短语的限度，因为该站点或设施不是从地球发射，而是用来自地球（也许其他地方）的材料建造。在任何情况下，部件的组装地点不会影响作为空间物体的资格[⑨]。

① Qizhi, He, The Registration Convention and Maintenance of Peaceful Uses of Outer Space, in: Jasentuliyana, Nandasiri (ed.), Maintaining Outer Space for Peaceful Uses: Proceedings of a Symposium held in The Hague, March 1984, United Nations University, Tokyo 1984, pp. 117ff.

② Perek, Lubos, The 1976 Registration Convention, in: IISL, Proceedings of the 41st Colloquium on the Law of Outer Space, 28 September-2 October 1998 Melbourne (Australia), AIAA, 1999, p. 377.

③ Ibid., p. 376.

④ Hörl, Kay-Uwe/Hermida, Julian, Change of Ownership, Change of Registry? Which Objects to Register, What data to be Furnished, When, and Until When?, in: IISL, Proceedings of the 46th Colloquium on the Law of Outer Space, 29 September-3 October 2003 Bremen (Germany), AIAA, 2004, p. 456.

⑤ Ospina, Sylvia, Revisiting the Registration: Convention A Proposal to Meet the Need to Know "What Is Up There", in: IISL, Proceedings of the 43rd Colloquium on the Law of Outer Space, 2-6 October 2000 Rio de Janeiro (Brazil), AIAA, 2001, p. 205.

⑥ Ibid., p. 206.

⑦ Williams, Maureen, The "Surprise" Convention on the Registration of Space Objects, Zeitschrift für Luft- und Weltraumrecht (28) 1979, p. 127.

⑧ Cheng, Bin, Space Objects and their Various Connecting Factors, in: Lafferanderie, Gabriel/Crowther, Daphné (eds.), Outlook on Space Law over the Next 30 Years: Essays published for the 30th Anniversary of the Outer Space Treaty, Kluwer Law International, The Hague 1997, p. 205.

⑨ See chapter on MOON in this volume, Commentary MOON, Article 12, mn. 220.

有人提议扩大《登记公约》要求的披露范围以涵盖不同的主题事项。一项建议涉及在国际统一私法协会（UNIDROIT）《移动设备国际利益公约》，包括《空间资产特定问题议定书》[①]（现为《柏林议定书》[②]）的范围内列入关于空间物体经济利益的数据。但是，如果能修改《登记公约》以包括披露财务数据，则也可以修改该公约以包括其他数据，包括许可、轨道、频率和其他权利[③]。然而，《登记公约》旨在发射后提供所需信息的通知，而《柏林议定书》所考虑的财务数据一般涉及发射前的情况，旨在用于与《登记公约》不同的目的。

将联合国登记册转变为一般信息数据库将对其主要功能产生负面影响，即告知公众对空间物体的管辖权和控制权。此外，还会有许多实际限制。扩大联合国登记册以构成一个包括许可证、轨道、频率、资助者利益和其他权利的全面记录，需要就哪些信息可以记录、哪些信息必须记录、记录所需信息的时限以及确定对不遵守行为的制裁制定适当的规则和程序。这些职能一般不是由秘书长履行的，因此，其他实体履行这些职责似乎更切实可行，国际电信联盟空间总登记册协调轨道和无线电频率的情况就是如此。[④] 出于标识目的，这可能不排除交叉引用。

十二、第十一~十二条（最后条款）

第十一条

本公约任何缔约国应在本公约生效一年以后以书面通知联合国秘书长退出本公约。退出公约应自接获该通知之日起一年后发生效力。

① Ospina, Sylvia, Revisiting the Registration Convention: A Proposal to Meet the Need to Know "What Is Up There", in: IISL, Proceedings of the 43rd Colloquium on the Law of Outer Space, 2-6 October 2000 Rio de Janeiro (Brazil), AIAA, 2001, p. 206.

② Schmidt-Tedd, Bernhard/Pellander, Erik, From Cape Town to Berlin-a new instrument for financing space assets, The Aviation and Space Journal (11) 2012, pp. 32ff.

③ Ospina, Sylvia, Revisiting the Registration Convention: A Proposal to Meet the Need to Know "What Is Up There", in: IISL, Proceedings of the 43rd Colloquium on the Law of Outer Space, 2-6 October 2000 Rio de Janeiro (Brazil), AIAA, 2001, pp. 205f.

④ Schmidt-Tedd, Bernhard/Gerhard, Michael, Registration of Space Objects: Which Are the Advantages for States Resulting from Registration?, in: Benkö, Marietta/Schrogl, Kai-Uwe (eds.), Space Law: Current Problems and Perspectives for Future Regulation, Eleven International Publishing, Utrecht 2005, p. 135.

第十二条

本公约原本应交存联合国秘书长，其阿拉伯文、中文、英文、法文、俄文及西班牙文本同样作准。秘书长应将本公约经证明的副本分送所有签字国和加入国。

为此，下列签字人，经各别政府正式授权，签字于本公约，以昭信守。

本公约于 1975 年 1 月 14 日在纽约由各国签署。

Schmidt-Tedd

目录

（一）谈判和起草历史

在谈判的最后阶段，阿根廷提出了对美国草案第七条第 2 款的修正案，根据该决议，联合国秘书长应为公约保存人[①]，而不是如《外空条约》第十七条，《责任公约》第二十八条所述的一些主要国家（保存政府）。联合国大会于 1973 年开创了《关于防止和惩治侵害受国际保护人员包括外交代表的罪行的公约》的先例[②]。最终版本据此制定，因此确定联合国秘书长为保存人。

（二）评注

1. 第十一条（退出）

《登记公约》第十一条几乎完全符合《营救协定》第九条，《责任公约》第二十七条和《月球协定》第二十条的相关规定。尚未有国家退出公约的报告。

---

① UN Doc. A/AC. 105/115, Report of the Legal Sub-Committee on the Work of its Twelfth Session (26 March-20 April 1973), Annex Ⅱ, Documents Relating to the Draft Convention on Registration of Objects Launched into Space for the Exploration or Use of Outer Space, Argentina: Working Paper, 20 April 1973.

② See Report of the Chairman of the Working Group on the Draft Convention on Registration in: Jasentuliyana, Nandasiri/Lee, Roy S. K. (eds.), Manual on Space Law, Volume Ⅲ, Oceana Publications, New York 1981, p. 689.

2. 第十二条（公约的作准语言/交存）

《登记公约》第十二条中首次将联合国条约中的阿拉伯文作为正式语言,[①] 自1973年12月18日起成为联合国的官方和工作语言。

与《外空条约》《营救协定》和《责任公约》中关于保存国政府的表达不同,《登记公约》第十二条确定联合国秘书长为保存人。

① Jasentuliyana, Nandasiri/Lee, Roy S. K. (eds.), Manual on Space Law, Volume I, Oceana Publications, New York 1979, p. 187.

第三章　前景展望

Schmidt-Tedd

目录

一、有待解决的实践问题

为进一步发展登记实践，仍有三个主要问题需要解决：

1. 鉴于《登记公约》第二条第2款的规定，如果两个或两个以上发射国未就登记国达成一致，需要一个备用解决方案。按照向第三国客户提供发射服务的既定做法，一项原则是，发射服务提供商登记进入轨道或者越出轨道的较高阶段，有效载荷客户登记其有效载荷。

2. 在国际政府组织的情况下，如果不登记，还需要一个后备的解决方案。最自然的做法是要求该组织的主要所在地国进行登记。此外，这个国家可以是填补管辖权和控制范围内的完全国家主权和国际政府组织有限主权之间差距的国家。

3. 一个普遍的问题是根据《登记公约》第二条第2款签订的协议的可执行性。即使发射服务提供商和客户之间（分别在这些非政府实体背后的国家之间）就客户登记有效载荷的义务达成了一项发射前协议，但在实践中，如果不遵守就没有措施来履行这项义务[1]。打破这种不遵守僵局的办法可以是发射成功的情况下发出发射前通知/登记授权，然后交由发射服务提供商转交给有关登记处和联合国，发射后不能无故撤回。

二、展望/联合国模板

《登记实践决议》[2] 以及《关于加强国家和国际政府间组织登记空间物体的做法的建议》是在解决和实际问题不一致方面向前迈出的重要一步。根据该决议，联合国外空事务办公室和成员国协商制定了一个模板，以实施这些建议并支持更加统一的登记做法[3]。这项决议和模板将成为《科隆空间法评注（第三卷）》的主题之一[4]。

① Hucteau, Mario, Registration Issues-French National Registry (1965-2012), Presentation UNCOPUOS Legal Subcommittee 2012, Vienna, 21 March 2012, online accessible at <http: //www. oosa. unvienna. org/pdf/pres/lsc2012/tech-03F. pdf> accessed 26 April 2019; Hucteau, Mario, Space Debris Activities and Registration Issues, Presentation UNCOPUOS Legal Subcommittee 2011, Vienna, April 2011, online accessible at <http: //www. oosa. unvienna. org/pdf/pres/lsc2011/tech-01. pdf> accessed1 October 2012.

② UNGA Res. 62/101, Recommendations on Enhancing the Practice of States and International Intergovernmental Organizations in Registering Space Objects, 17 December 2007.

③ The template is attached to this commentary-part below.

④ See Hobe, Stephan/Schmidt-Tedd, Bernhard/Schrogl, Kai-Uwe (eds.), Cologne Commentary on Space Law, Volume Ⅲ, Carl Heymanns, Cologne (forthcoming).

1979 年《关于各国在月球和其他天体上活动的协定》

Stephan Hobe, Ram Jakhu, Steven Freeland, Fabio Tronchetti and Peter Stubbe *

联合国大会通过：1979 年 12 月 5 日

开放签署：1979 年 12 月 18 日

生效：1984 年 7 月 11 日

来源：联合国条约集第 1363 卷第 3 页

《月球协定》文本

经大会在其 1979 年 12 月 5 日第 34/68 号决议中通过

本协定各缔约国，

注意到各国在月球和其他天体的探索和利用方面所获得的成就，

认识到构成地球的天然卫星的月球在探索外层空间方面起着重大的作用，

决心在平等基础上促成各国在探索和利用月球和其他天体方面合作的进一步发展，

切望不使月球成为国际冲突的场所，

---

* All commentaries to all articles of the MOON have been extensively discussed among all five participating authors. The indication of authorship attributed to each article refers, however, to the kind of special scientific responsibility the commentators take for a particular commentary to a specific article. The authors would like to thank George Robinson and Oliver Funke for their comments on the chapter.

铭记着开发月球和其他天体的自然资源所可能带来的利益，

回顾《关于各国探索和利用包括月球与其他天体在内外层空间活动的原则条约》《关于营救宇航员、送回宇航员和归还射入外层空间的物体的协定》《空间物体所造成损害的国际责任公约》和《关于登记射入外层空间物体的公约》，

考虑到对于此类有关月球和其他天体的国际文书的各项条款必须参照外层空间的探索和利用的继续进展，加以阐释和发展，

达成协议如下：

第一条

1. 本协定内关于月球的条款也适用于太阳系内地球以外的其他天体，但如任何此类天体已有现已生效的特别法律规则，则不在此限。

2. 为了本协定的目的，“月球”一词包括环绕月球的轨道或其他飞向或飞绕月球的轨道。

3. 本协定不适用于循自然方式到达地球表面的地球外物质。

第二条

月球上的一切活动，包括其探索和利用在内，应按照国际法，尤其是联合国宪章的规定，考虑到一九七〇年十月二十四日大会通过的关于各国依联合国宪章建立友好关系和合作的国际法原则宣言，顾及维持国际和平与安全及促进国际合作与相互谅解的利益并适当顾及所有其他缔约国的相应利益予以进行。

第三条

1. 月球应供全体缔约国专为和平目的而加以利用。

2. 在月球上使用武力或以武力相威胁，或从事任何其他敌对行为或以敌对行为相威胁概在禁止之列。利用月球对地球、月球、宇宙飞行器、宇宙飞行器或人造外空物体的人员实施任何此类行为或从事任何此类威胁，也应同样禁止。

3. 缔约国不得在环绕月球的轨道上或飞向或飞绕月球的轨道上，放置载有核武器或任何其他种类的大规模毁灭性武器的物体，或在月球上或月球内放置或使用此类武器。

4. 禁止在月球上建立军事基地、军事装置及防御工事，试验任何类型的武器及举行军事演习。但不禁止为科学研究或为任何其他和平目的而使用军事人员。也不禁止使用为和平探索和利用月球所必要的任何装备或设备。

第四条

1. 月球的探索和利用应是全体人类的事情并应为一切国家谋福利，不问它们的经济或科学发展程度如何。应依照联合国宪章规定，充分注意今世与后代人类的利益、以及提高生活水平与促进经济和社会进步和发展的需要。

2. 缔约国应遵循合作和互助原则从事一切有关探索和利用月球的活动。按照本协定进行的国际合作，应尽量扩大范围，并可在多边基础上、双边基础上或通过政府间国际组织进行。

第五条

1. 缔约国应在实际可行的范围内尽量将它们在探索和利用月球方面的活动告知联合国秘书长以及公众和国际科学界。每次飞往月球的任务的时间、目的、位置、轨道参数和期间的情报应在发射后立即公布，而关于每次任务的结果，包括科学结果在内的情报则应在完成任务时公布。如果一次飞行任务的期间超过六十天，应将任务进行情况的情报，包括科学结果在内，每隔三十天公布一次。如飞行任务超过六个月，则在六个月以后，只须将这方面的重要补充情报予以公布。

2. 如一个缔约国获知另一缔约国计划同时在月球上的同一区域或环绕月球的同一轨道或飞向或飞绕月球的同一轨道进行活动时，应立即将其自己进行活动的时间和计划通知该缔约国。

3. 缔约各国在进行本协定所规定的活动时，应将其在外层空间，包括月球在内所发现的可能危及人类生命或健康的任何现象以及任何有机生命迹象，通知联合国秘书长、公众和国际科学界。

第六条

1. 所有缔约国都享有不受任何种类的歧视，在平等基础上，并按照国际法的规定在月球上从事科学研究的自由。

2. 缔约国为促进本协定各项规定的实施而进行科学研究时，应有权在月球上采集并移走矿物和其他物质的标本。发动采集此类标本的缔约国可保留其处置权，并可为科学目的而使用这些标本。缔约国应顾及宜否将此类标本的一部分供给感兴趣的其他缔约国和国际科学界作科学研究之用。缔约国在进行科学研究时，也可使用适当数量的月球矿物和其他物质以支援它们的任务。

3. 缔约国同意于派遣人员前往月球或在其上建立装置时，在实际可行的范围内宜尽量交换科学和其他人员。

第七条

1. 缔约国在探索和利用月球时，应采取措施，防止月球环境的现有平衡遭到破坏，不论这种破坏是由于在月球环境中导致不利变化，还是由于引入环境外物质使其环境受到有害污染，或由于其他方式而产生。缔约国也应采取措施防止地球环境由于引入地球外物质或由于其他方式而受到有害影响。

2. 缔约国应将它们按照本条第 1 款所采取的措施通知联合国秘书长，并应尽一切可能预先将它们在月球上放置的一切放射性物质以及放置的目的通知秘书长。

3. 缔约国应就月球上具有特殊科学重要性的地区向其他缔约国和秘书长提出报告，以便在不损害其他缔约国权利的前提下，考虑将这些地区指定为国际科学保护区，并经同联合国各主管机构协商后，对这些地区商定特别保护办法。

第八条

1. 缔约国可在月球的表面或表面之下的任何地点进行其探索和利用的活动，但须遵守本条约的其他规定。

2. 为此目的，缔约国特别可以：

（1）在月球上降落及从月球发射外空物体；

（2）将它们的人员、外空运载器、装备、设施、站所和装置放置在月球的表面或表面之下的任何地点。人员、外空运载器、装备、设施、站所和装置可在月球表面或表面之下自由移动或自由被移动。

3. 缔约国依据本条第 1 款和第 2 款进行的活动不应妨碍其他缔约国在月球上的活动。发生此种妨碍时有关缔约各国应依照第十五条第 2 款和第 3 款规定进行协商。

第九条

1. 缔约国可在月球上建立配置人员及不配置人员的站所。建立站所的缔约国应只使用为站所进行业务所需要的地区，并应立即将该站所的位置和目的通知联合国秘书长。以后每隔一年该缔约国应同样将站所是否继续使用，及其目的有无变更通知秘书长。

2. 设置站所应不妨碍依照本协定及关于各国探索和利用外层空间包括月球与其他天体活动所应遵守原则的条约第一条规定在月球上进行活动的其他缔约国的人员、运载器和设备自由进入月球所有地区。

第十条

1. 缔约国应采取一切实际可行的措施，以保护在月球上的人的生命和健康。为此目的，缔约各国应视在月球上的任何人为关于各国探索和利用外层空间包括月球和其他天体活动所应遵守原则的条约第五条所称的宇宙航行员，并视其为《营救宇航员、送回宇航员和归还射入外层空间的物体的协定》所称外空飞行器人员的一部分。

2. 缔约国应以其站所、装置、运载器、及其他设备供月球上遭难人员避难之用。

第十一条

1. 月球及其自然资源均为全体人类的共同财产，这将在本协定的有关条款，尤其是本条第 5 款中表现出来。

2. 月球不得由国家依据主权要求，通过利用或占领，或以任何其他方法据为已有。

3. 月球的表面或表面下层或其任何部分或其中的自然资源均不应成为任何国家、政府间或非政府国际组织、国家组织或非政府实体或任何自然人的财产。在月球表面或表面下层，包括与月球表面或表面下层相连接的构造物在内，安置人员、外空运载器、装备设施、站所和装置，不应视为对月球或其任何领域的表面或表面下层取得所有权。上述条款不影响本条第 5 款所述的国际制度。

4. 缔约各国有权在平等基础上和按照国际法和本协定的规定探索和利用月球，不得有任何性质的歧视。

5. 本协定缔约国承诺一俟月球自然资源的开发即将可行时，建立指导此种开发的国际制度，其中包括适当程序在内。本款该按照本协定第十八条的规定予以实施。

6. 为了便利建立本条第 5 款所述的国际制度，缔约各国应在实际可行的范围内尽量将它们在月球上发现的任何自然资源告知联合国秘书长以及公众和国际科学界。

7. 即将建立的国际制度的主要宗旨应为：

（1）有秩序地和安全地开发月球的自然资源；

（2）对这些资源作合理的管理；

（3）扩大使用这些资源的机会；

（4）所有缔约国应公平分享这些资源所带来的惠益，而且应当对发展中国家的利益和需要，以及各个直接或间接对探索月球作出贡献的国家所作的努力，给予特别的照顾。

8. 有关月球自然资源的一切活动均应适当进行，以便符合本条第 7 款所订各项宗旨以及本协定第六条第 2 款的规定。

第十二条

1. 缔约国对其在月球上的人员、运载器、装备、设施、站所和装置应保有管辖权和控制权，外空运载器、装备、设备、站所和装置的所有权不因其在月球上而受影响。

2. 凡在预定位置以外的场地发现的运载器，装置及装备或其组成部分应依照《关于营救宇航员、送回宇航员和归还射入外层空间物体的协定》第五条处理。

3. 缔约国如遇足以威胁生命的紧急情况时，可使用其他缔约国在月球上的装备、运载器、装置、设施或供应品。此种使用应迅速通知联合国秘书长或有关缔约国。

第十三条

一个缔约国获悉并非其本国所发射的外空物体在月球上坠毁、强迫着陆或其他非出自本意的着陆时，应迅速通知发射该物体的缔约国和联合国秘书长。

第十四条

1. 本协定缔约国对于本国在月球上的各种活动应负国际责任，不论这类活动是由政府机构或非政府团体所进行的，并应负国际责任保证本国活动的进行符合本协定所载的各项规定。缔约国应保证它们所管辖的非政府团体只有在该缔约国的管辖和不断监督下方可在月球上从事各种活动。

2. 缔约国承认，由于在月球上的活动的增加，除关于各国探索和利用外层空间包括月球与其他天体活动所应遵守原则的条约和空间物体所造成损害的国际责任公约内的条款以外或许需要有关在月球上引起的损害赔偿责任的细节办法。对任何此类办法的拟订均应依照本协定第十八条所规定的程序。

第十五条

1. 每一缔约国应查明其他缔约国从事探索及利用月球的活动确是符合本协定的规定。为此目的，在月球上的一切外空运载器、装备、设施、站所和装置应对其他缔约国开放。这些缔约国应于合理期间事先发出所计划的参观通知，以便举行适当协商和采取最大限度的预防措施，以保证安全和避免干扰被参观设备的正常操作。为实行本条，任何一个缔约国可使用其自己的手段，亦可在任何其他缔约国的全面或局部协助下，或经由联合国体制内的适当国际程序，遵照宪章的规定采取行动。

2. 一个缔约国如有理由相信另一缔约国未能履行依照本协定所负的义务或相信另一缔约国妨害其在本协定规定下所享有的权利时，可要求与该国举行协商。接获此种要求的缔约国应立即开始协商，不得迟延。任何其他缔约国如提出要求，应有权参加协商。每一参加此等磋商的缔约国，应对任何争议寻求可以互相接受的解决办法，并应体念所有缔约国的权利和利益。磋商结果应通知联合国秘书长，并由秘书长将所获情报转送一切有关缔约国。

3. 如果磋商结果未能导致一项可以互相接受而又适当顾及所有缔约国权利和利益的解决办法，有关各国应采取一切措施，以他们所选择的并且适合争端的情况和性质的其他和平方法解决这项争端。如果在开展协商方面发生困难或协商结果未能导致一项可以互相接受的解决办法，任何缔约国可无须征求任何其他有关缔约国的同意要求联合国秘书长协助解决争端。一个缔约国如果没有同另一有关缔约国保持外交关系，则应自行选择由其自己出面参加协商或经由另外的缔约国或秘书长作为中间人参加协商。

第十六条

除第十七条至第二十一条外，凡在本协定内提及国家时，应视为适用于进行外空活动的任何政府间国际组织，但该组织须声明接受本协定内所规定的权利和义务，并且该组织的多数会员国须为本条约及《关于各国探索和利用包括月球与其他天体在内外层空间活动原则的条约》的缔约国。为本协定缔约国的任何此等组织的会员国，应采取一切适当行为，以保证该组织依照上述规定发表声明。

第十七条

本协定任何缔约国均可对本协定提出修正案。修正案对于每一接受修正案的本协定缔约国在本协定多数缔约国接受修正案时发生效力，其后对于本协定其余每个缔约国，在该缔约国接受修正案之日发生效力。

第十八条

本协定生效后十年，联合国大会应在临时议程内列入审查本协定的问题，以便参照本协定过去的实施情况，审议是否需加修正。但在本协定生效五年后的任何时候，作为协定保存人的联合国秘书长，经本协定三分之一的缔约国提出要求，并经多数缔约国同意，即应召开缔约国会议，以审查本协定。审查会议还应按照第十一条第 1 款所述原则，并且在特别考虑到任何有关的技术发展的情况下，审议执行第十一条第 5 款的各项规定的问题。

第十九条

1. 本协定应开放给所有国家在纽约联合国总部签署。

2. 本协定应经各签字国批准。在本协定按照本条第 3 款生效前未在本协定签字的任何国家可随时加入本协定。批准书和加入书应交存联合国秘书长。

3. 本协定应在五国政府交存批准书后第三十天生效。

4. 对于本协定生效后交存批准书或加入书的国家，本协定应自其交存批准书或加入书之日后第三十天开始生效。

5. 秘书长应将每次签字的日期，交存每项批准或加入本协定文书的日期，本协定生效日期，和接到其他通知的情况立即通知所有签字国和加入国。

第二十条

任何缔约国可在本协定生效后一年书面通知联合国秘书长退出本协定。这种退出应在接得通知后一年生效。

第二十一条

本协定的阿拉伯文、中文、英文、法文、俄文及西班牙文六种文本具有同等效力，并应交存联合国秘书长，由秘书长将本协定正式核证的副本分送各签署国和加入国。

为此，下列签字人，经本国政府正式授权，在本协定上签字，以昭信守。

本公约于一九七九年十二月十八日在纽约开放供各国签署。

目录

四、第三条（和平目的/去军事化）
五、第四条（人类的共同事情）
六、第五条（任务信息/科学界）
七、第六条（科学考察/标本/矿产）
八、第七条（环境/放射性物质）
九、第八条（探索利用/磋商）
十、第九条（站所/自由进入）
十一、第十条（生命安全保障）
十二、第十一条（人类共同遗产/国际制度）
十三、第十二条（管辖权和控制权/所有权/紧急情况）
十四、第十三条（坠毁、强迫着陆或非出自本意的着陆）
十五、第十四条（国际责任/赔偿责任）
十六、第十五条（核查/进入/磋商/争议解决）
十七、第十六条（政府间国际组织）
十八、第十七条（提出修正案）
十九、第十八条（审查/修正）
二十、第十九条（签署/批准/加入/生效）
二十一、第二十至二十一条（最后条款）
第三章　前景展望

文献精选

Agreement Governing the Activities of States on the Moon and Other Celestial Bodies（adopted 05 December 1979, entered into force 11 July 1984）1363 UNTS 3（MOON）

UN Doc. A/AC. 105/32, Draft Treaty Governing the Exploration of the Moon and Other CelestialBodies: Letter dated 16 June 1966 from the Permanent Representative of the United States of America addressed to the Chairman of the Committee on the Peaceful Uses of Outer Space, Annex, 17 June 1966

UN Doc. A/AC. 105/C. 2/L. 71 and Corr. 1, Argentina: Draft Agreement on the Principles Governing Activities in the Use of the Natural Resources of the Moon and other

Celestial Bodies, 23 June 1970

UN Doc. A/8391, Treaty Concerning the Moon: Letter dated 27 May 1971 from the Minister for Foreign Affairs of the Union of Soviet Socialist Republics addressed to the Secretary-General, Annex, 4 June 1971

UN Doc. PUOS/C. 2/WG (XI) /15/Rev. 1, Draft Treaty Concerning the Moon: Text formulated by the Working Group, 4 May 1972, in: UN Doc. A/AC. 105/101, Report of the Legal Sub-Committee on the Work of its Eleventh Session (10 April-5 May 1972), 11 May 1972

Working Paper submitted by Bulgaria-Draft Treaty Relating to the Moon, 27 March 1973, in: UN Doc. A/AC. 105/115, Report of the Legal Sub-Committee on the Work of its Twelfth Session (26 March-20 April 1973), Annex I, Documents Relating to Agenda Item 2 (Draft Treaty Relating to the Moon), 27 April 1973

Union of Soviet Socialist Republics: Working Paper-Draft Treaty Relating to the Moon (Question of the "common heritage of all mankind"), 28 March 1973, in: UN Doc. A/AC. 105/115, Report of the Legal Sub-Committee on the Work of its Twelfth Session (26 March-20 April 1973), Annex I, Documents Relating to Agenda Item 2 (Draft Treaty Relating to the Moon), 27 April 1973

Argentina: Working Paper-Draft Treaty Relating to the Moon (Question of the "common heritage of all mankind"), 17 April 1973, in: UN Doc. A/AC. 105/115, Report of the Legal Sub-Committee on the Work of its Twelfth Session (26 March-20 April 1973), Annex I, Documents Relating to Agenda Item 2 (Draft Treaty Relating to the Moon), 27 April 1973

UN Doc. A/AC. 150/C. 2/L. 93, Bulgaria: Working Paper-Draft Treaty Relating to the Moon, 8 May 1974

UN Doc. WG. I (1978) /WP. 2, Austria: Working Paper-Agreement Governing the Activities of States on the Moon and other Celestial Bodies, 3 April 1978, in: UN Doc. A/AC. 105/218, Report of the LegalSub-Committee on the Work of its Seventeenth Session (13 March-7 April 1978), Annex I, Report of the Chairman of Working Group I, Appendix, 13 April 1978

Working Paper Reflecting the Outcome of the Review at the Present Session of Working

Paper WG. I (1978) /WP. 2 of 3 April 1978, in: UN Doc. A/AC. 105/240 Report of the Legal Sub-Committee on the Work of its Eighteenth Session (12 March-6 April 1979), Annex Ⅲ, Report of the Chairman of Working Group I, Appendix A, 10 April 1979

参考文献精选

Bashor, Harold W., Interpretation of the Moon Treaty-Recourse to Working Papers and Related International Documents, Annals of Air and Space Law (XXXII) 2007, pp. 149-200

Baslar, Kemal, The Concept of Common Heritage of Mankind in International Law, Martinus Nijhoff Publishers 1998

Bini, Antonella, The Moon Agreement: Its effectiveness in the 21st century, ESPI Perspectives (14) 2008, pp. 1-7

Crawford, Ian A., The scientific case for renewed human activities on the Moon, Space Policy (20) 2004, pp. 91-97

Christol, Carl Q., The modern international law of outer space, Pergamon Press, New York 1982, pp. 253-311

Christol, Carl Q., The 1979 Moon Agreement: Where is it Today?, Journal of Space Law (27) 1999, pp. 1-33

Christol, Carl Q., The Moon Treaty and the Allocation of Resources, Annals of Air and Space Law (XXII/ II) 1997, pp. 31-47

Christol, Carl Q., The Moon Treaty enters into force, American Journal of International Law (79) 1985, pp. 163-168

Diederiks-Verschoor, I. H. Philepina/ Kopal, Vladimir, An Introduction to Space Law, 3rd edn., Kluwer Law International, The Netherlands 2008, pp. 50-54

Doyle, Stephen E., Using Extraterrestrial Resources Under the Moon Agreement of 1979, Journal of Space Law (26) 1998, pp. 111-128

von der Dunk, Frans G., The Moon Agreement and the Prospect of Commercial Exploitation of Lunar Resources, Annals of Air and Space Law (XXXII) 2007, pp. 91-113

von der Dunk, Frans G., The dark side of the Moon-The status of the Moon: public concepts and private enterprises, in: IISL, Proceedings of the 40th Colloquium on the Law of

Outer Space, 6-10 October 1997 Turin (Italy), AIAA, 1998, pp. 119-124

Hobe, Stephan, ILA Resolution 1/2002 with Regard to the Common Heritage of Mankind Principle in the Moon Agreement, in: IISL, Proceedings of the 47th Colloquium on the Law of Outer Space, 4-8 October 2004 Vancouver (Canada), AIAA, 2005, pp. 536-544

Hobe, Stephan, The Moon Agreement-Let's Use the Chance!, Zeitschrift für Luft- und Weltraumrecht (59) 2010, pp. 372-381

Hobe, Stephan, Adequacy of the Current Legal and Regulatory Framework Relating to the Extraction and Appropriation of Natural Resources, Annals of Air and Space Law (32) 2007, pp. 115-130

Hofmann, Mahulena, Recent Plans to Exploit the Moon Resources Under International Law, in: IISL, Proceedings of the 47th Colloquium on the Law of Outer Space, 4-8 October 2004 Vancouver (Canada), AIAA, 2005, pp. 425-434

Jakhu, Ram, Twenty Years of the Moon Agreement: Space Law Challenges for Returning to the Moon, Zeitschrift für Luft- und Weltraumrecht (54) 2005, pp. 243-260

Jakhu, Ram/ Buzdugan, Maria, The Role of Private Actors: Commercial Development of the Outer Space Resources, Including Those of the Moon and other Celestial Bodies: Economic and Legal Implications, Astropolitics (6) 2008, pp. 201-250

Jasentuliyana, Nandasiri, The Moon Treaty, in: Jasentuliyana, Nandasiri (ed.), Maintaining Outer Space for Peaceful Uses: Proceedings of a Symposium held in The Hague, March 1984, United Nations University, Tokyo 1984, pp. 121-139

Kopal, Vladimir, Exploration of the Moon and Exploitation of Its Resources: Present State of Legal Regulation and Coming Issues, in: Proceedings of the 8th European Summer Course on Space Law and Policy, 29 August-12 September 1999 Geneva (Switzerland), pp. 20-47

Lochan, Rajeev/ Gopalakrishnan, V., Lunar Exploration-The Road Ahead, in: IISL, Proceedings of the 50th Colloquium on the Law of Outer Space, 24-28 September 2007 Hyderabad (India), AIAA, 2008, pp. 56-67

Lyall, Francis, On the Moon, Journal of Space Law (26) 1998, pp. 129-138

Matte, Nicolas M., Treaty Relating to the Moon, in: Jasentuliyana, Nandasiri/ Lee,

Roy S. K. （eds.）, Manual on Space Law, Volume I, Oceana Publications, New York 1979, pp. 253-282

Rogers, Thomas F., Magnifying our world: Why we must extend civilization to the Moon, Space Policy (22) 2006, pp. 128-132

Tronchetti, Fabio, The exploitation of natural resources of the Moon and other celestial bodies: a proposal for a legal regime, Martinus Nijhoff/Brill Publishers, Leiden 2009

Tucker, Cody, How Current International Law addresses Rights to Use and Exploit Lunar Resources, Annals of Air and Space Law (XXXIV) 2009, pp. 591-620

第一章　历史背景和上下文

Hobe，Stubbe and Tronchetti

目录

一、引言

《关于各国在月球和其他天体上活动的协定》（以下简称《月球协定》）[①] 是联合国谈判达成的关于外层空间活动的第五个国际协定。该协定于 1979 年 12 月 5 日由联合国大会第 34/68 号决议通过[②]，1979 年 12 月 18 日开放签署，于 1984 年 7 月 11 日

① Agreement Governing the Activities of States on the Moon and Other Celestial Bodies (done 18 December 1979, entered into force 11 July 1984) 1363 UNTS 3 (MOON).

② UNGA Res. 34/68, Agreement Governing the Activities of states on the Moon and Other Celestial Bodies, 5 December 1979.

生效[①]。尽管 1979 年联合国外空委经协商一致通过了该协定，并随后在联合国大会上作为一项决议通过，但它并未得到主要航天大国和国际社会的广泛支持。然而即便多数国家参与探月任务的财政和现实可行性有限，还是可以从该条约的整体优势中获得惠益。至今，只有 18 个国家[②]批准了该条约，远远低于其他联合国外空公约的批准国数目（一般为 50~100）[③]。

“人类共同遗产”（以下简称“CHM”）[④] 概念仍然被一些国家认为是《月球协定》不被广泛接受的主要阻碍[⑤]，主要原因是缺乏这一概念的明确定义。然而，自《月球协定》谈判以来，世界无论从政治还是技术层面都发生了变化，毫无疑问，《月球协定》将重回视野。由于《月球协定》是唯一一部专门关于月球及其资源探索利用的法律文本，因此分析和理解其条文是非常重要的。

在分析其条文时，应牢记《月球协定》是唯一在 1969 年《维也纳条约法公约》（以下简称《条约法公约》）[⑥] 生效后才生效的国际空间条约。因此，《条约法公约》关于条约解释的规则适用于对《月球协定》条款的解释。此外需要注意的是，近年来又有五个国家批准了《月球协定》，联合国和平利用外层空间委员会（以下简称联合

① See United Nations Treaty Collection, Status of Treaties: Agreement Governing the Activities of States on the Moon and Other Celestial Bodies, <http://treaties.un.org/pages/ViewDetails.aspx?src=TREATY&mtdsg_no=XXIV-2&chapter=24&lang=en> accessed 26 April 2019.

② See United Nations Treaty Collection, Status of Treaties: Agreement Governing the Activities of States on the Moon and Other Celestial Bodies, <http://treaties.un.org/pages/ViewDetails.aspx?src=TREATY&mtdsg_no=XXIV-2&chapter=24&lang=en> accessed 26 April 2019; and UN Doc. A/AC.105/C.2/2018/CRP.3, Status of International Agreements relating to activities in outer space as at 1 January 2018, 9 April 2019 with regular updates published on http://www.unoosa.org/documents/pdf/spacelaw/treatystatus/AC105_C2_2018_CRP03E.pdf.

③ The exact number of States Parties to the UN space treaties is published annually by the UN Office for Outer Space Affairs. The information as of January 2019 is available in: UN Doc. A/AC.105/C.2/2018/CRP.3, Status of International Agreements relating to activities in outer space as at 1 January 2018, 9 April 2019 with regular updates published on http://www.unoosa.org/documents/pdf/spacelaw/treatystatus/AC105_C2_2018_CRP03E.pdf.

④ The present commentary uses the word 'mankind', rather than 'humankind', to ensure consistency with the original terminology of the text of the MOON. This choice is not intended to make any specific statement.

⑤ See UN Doc. A/AC.105/917, Report of the Legal Subcommittee on its Forty-Seventh Session, (31 March-11 April 2008), 18 April 2008; UN Doc. A/AC.105/935, Report of the Legal Subcommittee on its Forty-Eighth Session (23 March-3 April 2009), 20 April 2009; and UN Doc. A/AC.105/942, Report of the Legal Subcommittee on its Forty-Ninth Session (22 March-1 April 2010), 16 April 2010.

⑥ Vienna Convention on the Law of Treaties (done 23 May 1969, entered into force 27 January 1980) 1155 UNTS 331 (VCLT).

国外空委）的法律小组委员会也讨论了迄今为止参与国数目不多的原因①。

二、谈判的历史背景

首先，毫无疑问应将《月球协定》置于特定的历史背景进行考量。《月球协定》的谈判和起草与联合国第三次海洋法会议相伴而生，一些非常类似的问题也在第三次会议上进行了讨论。1982 年《海洋法公约》（以下简称 UNCLOS）② 第 136 条规定深海海底及其资源为人类共同遗产，可视为佐证之一。虽然关于深海海底制度的讨论影响了关于月球资源利用部分的谈判，但《月球协定》的其他方面沿循了 1959 年《南极条约》③ 的模式，该条约已经影响了 1967 年“关于各国探索和利用包括月球和其他天体在内的外层空间活动所应遵守的原则的条约”④（“外层空间条约”，以下称《外空条约》）。其中诸如自由进入、去军事化和相互检查等要素已在《南极条约》中有所体现⑤。

《月球协定》谈判也必须置于当时美苏关系的背景下来审视。1962 年爆发严重的古巴导弹危机，此后，两个超级大国开始趋于不断加强军备控制，这一趋势也延伸到了外层空间。1963 年缔结的《部分核禁试条约》⑥ 禁止在外层空间进行核试验，也是意识到这种试验对载人航天非常不利。此外，两国越来越认识到外层空间对于被动式

---

① See UN Doc. A/AC. 105/891, Report of the Legal Subcommittee on its Forty-Sixth Session (26 March-5 April 2007), Annex I, Report of the Chairman of the Working Group on the Status and Application of the Five United Nations Treaties on Outer Space, 2 May 2007. Already ten years after the entry into force of the MOON, in 1994, UNCOPUOS-in view of Art. 18 MOON-considered the question of the review of the Agreement and recommended to the UN General Assembly not to take action. See UN Doc. A/49/20, Report of the Committee on the Peaceful Uses of Outer Space, General Assembly Official Records, Forty-Ninth Session, Supplement No. 20, 12 August 1994, paras. 150-153.

② See United Nations Convention on the Law of the Sea (done 10 December 1982, entered into force 16 November 1994) 1833 UNTS 396 (UNCLOS).

③ Antarctic Treaty (done 1 December 1959, entered into force 23 June 1961) 402 UNTS 71.

④ Treaty on Principles Governing the Activities of States in the Exploration and Use of Outer Space, including the Moon and Other Celestial Bodies (done 27 January 1967, entered into force 10 October 1967) 610 UNTS 205 (OST).

⑤ See Art. I, II and Ⅶ Antarctic Treaty; and-also on the influence of the Antarctic Treaty as well as the parallel development of the UNCLOS on the MOON negotiations-Peterson, Mildred J., International Regimes for the Final Frontier, State University of New York Press, Albany 2005, pp. 154-156.

⑥ Treaty Banning Nuclear Weapon Tests in the Atmosphere, in Outer Space and under Water (done 5 August 1963, entered into force 10 October 1963) 480 UNTS 43.

军事应用，特别是卫星通信和卫星侦察的价值①。两国在外层空间中关于部分去军事化的共同利益促成了1967年《外空条约》采纳了去军事化的条款，即禁止在外层空间放置大规模毁灭性武器，并达成“专为和平目的使用月球和其他天体”的共识②。七十年代两个超级大国之间的军控合作进一步扩大，由此签订了1972年《反弹道导弹条约》和《削减和限制进攻性战略武器条约》。侦察卫星作为核查的技术手段，在执行军备控制条约方面发挥了至关重要的作用。美国和苏联在民用航天方面的合作也有所加强，并在1975年达到顶峰，完成了阿波罗号和联盟号宇宙飞船之间的在轨载人交会对接任务③。在《月球协定》谈判期间，两个超级大国之间关系的特点是在军控领域加强合作。

与此同时，《月球协定》谈判的开端是以两个太空超级大国之间的太空竞赛为特征的。苏联（月球1号）和美国（先驱者4号）都已经成功地进行了一次月球飞越。1969年7月20日，美国实现了前总统约翰·肯尼迪在1961年宣称的目标，即在六十年代结束之前将人类送上月球并安全返回地球。

三、近年来的科技发展/经济意义

在编写本评注时，有几个进一步探索外层空间和天体的项目正在进行④。虽然有时月球和火星对一些国家来说似乎是非常重要的优先事项，但在其他时候，这些国家对它们的兴趣却显得似乎微乎其微。中国和印度都制定了探月战略。中国分别于2007

① See Moltz, James C., The Politics of Space Security, 2nd edn., Stanford University Press, Stanford 2008, pp. 135-142.

② See Peterson, Mildred J., International Regimes for the Final Frontier, State University of New York Press, Albany 2005, pp. 146-149. On the demilitarization provision of the OST see Schrogl, Kai-Uwe/Neumann, Julia, Article IV, in: Hobe, Stephan/Schmidt-Tedd, Bernhard/Schrogl, Kai-Uwe (eds.), Cologne Commentary on Space Law, Volume I, Heymanns, Cologne 2009, pp. 75-78, mn. 18-28.

③ See Moltz, James C., The Politics of Space Security, 2nd edn., Stanford University Press, Stanford 2008, pp. 164-173.

④ However, there are private initiatives for the promising development of asteroid resources, see Leone, Dan, Asteroid Mining Venture to Start with Small, Cheap Space Telescopes, SpaceNews, 24 April 2012 <http://www.spacenews.com/venture_space/120424-asteroid-mining-venture.html> accessed 26 April 2019.

年 10 月 24 日、2010 年 10 月 1 日和 2013 年 12 月 14 日成功发射嫦娥一号、嫦娥二号①和嫦娥三号月球探测器。2019 年初，嫦娥四号探测器在南极艾特肯盆地的“月球背面”着陆。印度于 2008 年 10 月 22 日发射了首个月球探测器“月船一号”②，原本计划在 2013 年发射第二次登月任务“月船 2 号”，截至 2019 年 1 月，这项发射计划拟定于 2019 年 4 月进行。美国在奥巴马总统第一届任期（2009—2012）期间，似乎对重返月球失去了兴趣，取而代之的是开始着手在 2030 年前完成首次载人登陆火星的任务③。但是最近，美国航空航天局又试图与全球伙伴合作重返月球④。在国际层面，一些领先的航天机构在未来的空间探索上存在着一定程度的合作。国际空间探索协调小组于 2011 年发布了全球探索路线图，其最终目标是探索火星。为了实现这一共同目标，需要根据各国探索政策，通过对月球或近地天体开展过渡式的探索活动以开发和演示关键技术。因此，该战略代表了各航天机构参与方来决策、协调以探索火星为最终目标的人类探索活动的共同努力⑤。

月球和其他天体存在着对潜在的“殖民者”和去往其他目的地的宇航人员有着重要意义的自然资源，这些国家对太阳系进行探索的兴趣盎然与此不无关系⑥。

科学研究表明，月球表面覆盖着一层疏松的颗粒物质（月球风化层），这些颗粒主要是由陨石的侵蚀力造成的⑦。月球表面的岩石暴露在宇宙射线和太阳辐射以及太

① See www. space. com, Chinese Moon Probe Begins Deep Space Exploration, Space. com, 15 June 2011. <http://www. space. com/11971-china-moon-probe-begins-deep-space-exploration. html >; Xin, Dingding, China's moon goal right on schedule, China Daily, 2 October 2010 <http://www. chinadaily. com. cn/china/2010-10/02/content_ 11373487. htm> (accessed 26 April 2019).

② ISRO, Chandrayaan-1: India's First Scientific Mission to the Moon <http://www. isro. org/chandrayaan/htmls/home. htm>; ISRO, What is Chandrayaan-2 <http://www. chandrayaan-i. com/index. php/chandrayaan-2. html> accessed 26 April 2019.

③ On the relevant statement by US President Barack Obama on 15 April 2010 seeAmos, Jonathan, Obama sets Mars Goal for America, BBC News, 15 April 2010 <http://news. bbc. co. uk/2/hi/8623691. stm> accessed 26 April 2019.

④ NASA's Campaign to Return to the Moon with Global Partners, 19 January 2019. <https://www. nasa. gov/feature/nasa-s-campaign-to-return-to-the-moon-with-global-partners> accessed 26 April 2019.

⑤ See International Space Exploration Coordination Group, The Global Exploration Roadmap, Washington, September 2011, pp. 8, 36 <http://www. nasa. gov/pdf/591067main_ GER_ 2011_ small_ single. pdf> accessed 26 April 2019.

⑥ See Faure, Gunter/Mensing, Teresa M., Introduction to Planetary Science: The Geological Perspective, Springer Verlag, Dordrecht 2007, p. 159.

⑦ See King, Elbert A., Space Geology: An Introduction, Wiley & Sons, New York 1976, p. 165.

阳风之下①。

太阳风主要由电子和质子（电离氢）以及 α 粒子（电离氦-3 和氦-4）组成。当这些粒子撞击月球表面时，它们被困在月球土壤中自然形成的风化层矿物的晶体中。这一过程已经持续进行了大约 45 亿年，并积累了大量的太阳能气体②。

据估计，月球上的静海地区的风化层含有至少 10000 公吨的氦-3③。为了理解这一点的重要性，目前估计，一旦可行的核聚变技术可用，大约 370 公吨氦-3 足以为人类提供一整年的能量④。

氦-3 是一种不具有放射性的中子氦同位素，当用中子轰击时，它可以与在聚变过程中施加的电磁力相互作用。该过程可以直接发电，而不会产生放射性中子作为副产品。实际上，据说氦-3 由于其非放射性性质，而几乎不产生放射性废物或副产品⑤。

然而，氦-3 需要大约 1000 万摄氏度的温度才能自然发生碰撞。这样的温度在地球上只能存在很短的时间（例如，在热核氢弹中）⑥。为了便于直接从月球表层中提取可商用的数量，需由精密的机器人进行采矿和精炼，并且需要高水平的专家来监督采矿和返回地球运输的过程。为了实现这一目标，地月运输必须变得更加普及和便宜⑦。具有讽刺意味的是，这可以通过氦-3 聚变火箭来实现⑧。然而尽管在回收和使

① See Crawford, Ian A., The scientific case for renewed human activities on the Moon, Space Policy (20) 2004, p. 91; and King, Elbert A., Space Geology: An Introduction, Wiley & Sons, New York 1976, p. 188.

② See Faure, Gunter/Mensing, Teresa M., Introduction to Planetary Science: The Geological Perspective, Springer Verlag, Dordrecht 2007, p. 164.

③ See Neal, Clive R., The Moon 35 years after Apollo: What's left to learn?, Chemie der Erde (69) 2009, p. 21.

④ See Reinke, Niklas, No Helium-3 from Moon-Commentary on the Current Moon Debate, DLR Countdown 03/07, p. 24.

⑤ Ibid.

⑥ See Faure, Gunter/Mensing, Teresa M., Introduction to Planetary Science: The Geological Perspective, Springer Verlag, Dordrecht 2007, p. 165.

⑦ See Reinke, Niklas, No Helium-3 from Moon-Commentary on the Current Moon Debate, DLR Countdown 03/07, p. 24.

⑧ See Faure, Gunter/Mensing, Teresa M., Introduction to Planetary Science: The Geological Perspective, Springer Verlag, Dordrecht 2007, p. 159.

用氦-3方面存在困难，中国和印度都宣布了提取这种物质并将其带回地球的目标。①

除了这两个国家的兴趣点以外，值得注意的是，为了促进开发月球表层的新技术的发展，月球发掘挑战于2009年启动，由美国航空航天局百年挑战计划项目资助。这一挑战要求竞争对手使用移动式机器人挖掘机，能够挖掘至少330磅的风化层，并在30分钟或更短的时间内将其放回容器中。这次挑战的获胜者是伍斯特的保罗机器人公司，它在规定的时间内挖掘了965磅的风化层材料，获得了50万美元的奖金②。

另一项竞赛是谷歌的X奖，但它比的不是挖掘，而是挑战私人资助的团队谁能够安全地将机器人降落在月球表面，使机器人在月球表面上行进500米，并将视频、图像和数据传回地球③。

除了氦-3，月球地壳还有其他多种基本元素，包括铀、钍、钾、氧、硅、镁、铁、钛、钙、铝和氢④。此外，风化层含有玄武岩和辉长岩的角砾，这些岩石是通过自然发生的撞击从下基岩中挖掘出来的⑤。

月球上另一种有价值的资源是阳光，它可以通过融化月球土壤来制造玻璃，还可以从硅酸盐或氧化物矿物中提取氧气。它也可以直接转换成电或热⑥。

在宣布在月球上发现水分子一年后，美国宇航局又于2010年10月21日宣布，科学家们从美国宇航局月球陨坑观测与传感卫星研究机构（LCROSS）发现的数据中显示，月球上存在的不仅仅是水。在这些任务中发现的证据表明，月球阴暗环形山内的

---

① See statement by senior officials of the Indian Government, in: Nelson, Dean, India to spend £ 1. 7bn sending man to the moon, The Telegraph, 23 February 2009 <http: //www. telegraph. co. uk/news/worldnews/asia/india/4788143/India-to-spend-1. 7bn-sending-man-to-the-moon. html> accessed 26 April 2019; and on the Chinese plans to send a manned lunar mission, see David, Leonard, China Mulls Plans for New Moon Rock Lab, Space. com, 16 March 2010 <http: //www. space. com/8050-china-mulls-plans-moon-rock-lab. html> accessed 26 April 2019.

② See NASA, Regolith Excavation Challenge <http: //www. nasa. gov/offices/oct/early_ stage_ innovation/centennial_ challenges/regolith/index. html> accessed 26 April 2019; and NASA, College Team Wins NASA Lunar Robot Prize <http: //www. nasa. gov/offices/oct/early_ stage_ innovation/centennial_ challenges/cc_ regolith_ feature_ first_ prize. html> accessed 26 April 2019.

③ Google Lunar X-Price, Price details <http: //www. googlelunarxprize. org/prize-details> accessed 26 April 2019; for information on the XPrize Foundation and the Google Lunar XPrize see <http: //www. xprize. org> accessed 26 April 2019; and <http: //www. googlelunarxprize. org/prize-details> accessed 26 April 2019.

④ See Robens, Erich/Bischoff, Addi/Schreiber, Andreas/Unger Klaus K., Investigation of surface properties of lunar regolith Part II, Journal of Thermal Analysis and Calorimetry (94) 2008, p. 627.

⑤ See Faure, Gunter/Mensing, Teresa M., Introduction to Planetary Science: The Geological Perspective, Springer Verlag, Dordrecht 2007, p. 143.

⑥ See ibid., p. 159.

土壤富含有用物质，而且月球似乎具有化学活性，例如，它有一个完整的水循环。根据这些信息，科学家们可证实，月球上的水在一些地方以纯冰晶的形式存在①。显然，发现月球土壤中水的存在对未来月球及其资源的探索和利用具有特别的意义。

在美国于 1969 年、1971 年和 1972 年返回月球之后，上述愿景可能促使人类再次重返月球。一旦永久性载人月球站成为现实，并且可以证明其有助于在月球上进行采矿，这就可以成为在太阳系其他陆地行星上，特别是在火星上，执行类似任务的第一步。此外，在火星和木星之间的小行星带内进行完全自动化的小行星采矿，在技术上看来已经是可行的。用于这一目的的采矿机器人也可以自行生产它们自己的燃料，这些燃料是将勘探到的矿物和矿石送回地球所必需的。至少科学家已经证实存在赤铁矿和水冰②。可能取得的进一步发展是难以预料的，这可能也会对月球法律制度的前景产生影响。

四、起草历史

（一）概述：在联合国外空委的谈判

早在 1966 年 6 月，在《外空条约》通过之前，美国在给联合国外空委主席的信中便要求在法律小组委员会制定一个条约草案，该草案应在同年提交大会③。然而，联合国外空委直到 1969 年才提出这个问题，当时一些提案首次提出细化关于月球

① For an overview of the Lunar Crater Observation and Sensing Satellite mission see NASA, Lunar Crater Observation and Sensing Satellite <http://www.nasa.gov/mission_ pages/LCROSS/main/index.html> accessed 26 April 2019; and for a description of the results of this mission see Phillips, Tony (ed.), Lunar impact Uncovered More Than Just Moon Water, NASA Science News, 1 October 2010 <http://science.nasa.gov/science-news/science-at-nasa/2010/21oct_ lcross2/> accessed 26 April 2019.

② See NASA, Near Earth Object Program <neo.jpl.nasa.gov/neo/resource.html> accessed 26 April 2019; and SolStation.com, Main Asteroid Belt <http://www.solstation.com/stars/asteroid.htm> accessed 26 April 2019.

③ UN Doc. A/AC. 105/32, Draft Treaty Governing the Exploration of the Moon and Other Celestial Bodies: Letter dated 16 June 1966 from the Permanent Representative of the United States of America addressed to the Chairman of the Committee on the Peaceful Uses of Outer Space, Annex, 17 June 1966; the document is reproduced in: UN Doc. A/AC. 105/35, Report of the Legal Sub-Committee on the Work of its Fifth Session (12 July-4 August and 12-16 September 1966), Annex I, 16 September 1966.

（及其他天体）上人类活动以及有关利用在月球上发现的资源的规则[①]。阿根廷是倡导制定月球条约的国家之一[②]。有时，阿根廷被认为是发起讨论与月球和其他天体有关的条约或协议的国家[③]，尽管美国已于1966年提出对该主题进行讨论，并在1966年的第五届联合国外空委大会上提出了条约草案[④]。这可能是由于阿根廷后来在1970年提交的条约草案[⑤]中提出了一个成为谈判焦点之一的问题：即人类共同遗产原则适用于月球资源。

1971年，苏联向联合国秘书长提交了条约草案，并要求将制定月球条约列入联合国大会的议程项目[⑥]。作为回应，联合国大会于1971年要求联合国外空委及其法律小组委员会考虑将拟订月球条约草案作为优先事项[⑦]。因此，法律小组委员会列入了一个新的议程项目"与月球有关的问题"[⑧]，并在第十一届大会开始时成立了一个工作

① UN Doc. A/AC. 105/C. 2/L. 53, Poland: Working Paper, 13 June 1969; UN Doc. A/AC. 105/C. 2/L. 54, Argentina: Proposal, 13 June 1969; UN Doc. A/AC. 105/C. 2/L. 66, Argentina and Poland: Proposal, 27 June 1969; UN Doc. A/AC. 105/C. 2/L. 69, Argentina, France and Poland: Proposal, 1 July 1969, those documents are reproduced in: UN Doc. A/AC. 105/58, Report of the Legal Sub-Committee on the Work of its Eighth Session (9 June-4 July 1969), 4 July 1969, Annex I, Proposals Concerning Questions Relative To The Definition Of Outer Space And The Utilization Of Outer Space And Celestial Bodies, Including The Various Implications Of Space Communications, pp. 4, 6-7; and ibid., para. 10.

② UN Doc. A/AC. 105/C. 2/L. 54, Argentina: Proposal, 13 June 1969; UN Doc. A/AC. 105/C. 2/L. 66, Argentina and Poland: Proposal, 27 June 1969; UN Doc. A/AC. 105/C. 2/L. 69, Argentina, France and Poland: Proposal, 1 July 1969.

③ See e. g. Kopal, Vladimir, Exploration of the Moon and Exploitation of Its Resources: Present State of Legal Regulation and Coming Issues, in: ECSL, Proceedings of the 8th European Summer Course on Space Law and Policy, 2008, p. 24.

④ See UN Doc. A/AC. 105/35, Report of the Legal Sub-Committee on the Work of its Fifth Session (12 July-4 August and 12-16 September 1969), 16 September 1966, para. 2.

⑤ UN Doc. A/AC. 105/C. 2/L. 71 and Corr. 1, Argentina: Draft Agreement on the Principles Governing Activities in the Use of the Natural Resources of the Moon and other Celestial Bodies, 23 June 1970; The document is reproduced in: UN Doc. A/AC. 105/85, Report of the Legal Sub-Committee on the Work of its Ninth Session (8 June-3 July 1970), Annex II, Proposals Concerning Questions Relative to the Definition of Outer Space and the Utilization of Outer Space and Celestial Bodies, Including the Various Implications of Space Communications, 3 July 1970, p. 1.

⑥ UN Doc. A/8391, Treaty Concerning the Moon: Letter dated 27 May 1971 from the Minister for Foreign Affairs of the Union of Soviet Socialist Republics addressed to the Secretary-General, 4 June 1971; the document is reproduced in: International Legal Materials (10) 1971, pp. 839-846.

⑦ See UNGA Res. 2779 (XXVI), Preparation of an international treaty concerning the Moon, 29 November 1971.

⑧ See UN Doc. A/AC. 105/101, Report of the Legal Sub-Committee on the Work of its Eleventh Session (10 April-5 May 1972), 11 May 1972, para. 5.

组来详细讨论[1]。该工作组在 1972 年形成了一版草案[2]，这个草案是在工作组的讨论和各种工作文件基础上形成的[3]。随后的谈判主要集中在两个具体问题上——资源的利用和适用范围[4]——而对工作组在 1972 年制订的许多条款的实质内容没有争议。最终在 1978 年，奥地利提交了一份协定草案[5]，该草案是非正式谈判的结果[6]，并为 1979 年最终草案的通过铺平了道路[7]。

（二）早期提案草案

1966 年，受约翰逊总统指示，美国大使亚瑟·戈德堡在联合国框架内寻求能达成有关月球和其他天体的国际协议的讨论[8]。他这样描述美国的利益："正如美国致力于帮助实现地球和平一样，我们尽其所能的确保对月球和其他天体的探索将仅用于和平目的。我们希望确保我们的宇航员和其他国家的宇航员能够自由地对月球进行科学考察。"[9] 亚瑟·戈德堡在给联合国外空委主席的信中提出了这些观念[10]，其中包含了要

---

① See ibid. , para. 9.

② UN Doc. PUOS/C. 2/WG （XI） /15/Rev. 1, Draft Treaty Concerning the Moon：Text formulated by the Working Group, 4 May 1972, in：UN Doc. A/AC. 105/101, Report of the Legal Sub-Committee on the Work of its Eleventh Session（10 April-5 May 1972）, 11 May 1972, para. 21.

③ See UN Doc. A/AC. 105/101, Report of the Legal Sub-Committee on the Work of its Eleventh Session （10 April-5 May 1972）, 11 May 1972, Annex I, Proposals and other Documents relating to Agenda Item 3 （Questions relating to the Moon）.

④ See below Historical Context and Background, mn. 26ff.

⑤ UN Doc. WG. I （1978） /WP. 2, Austria：Working Paper, AgreementGoverning the Activities of States on the Moon and other Celestial Bodies, 3 April 1978, in：UN Doc. A/AC. 105/218, Report of the Legal Sub-Committee on the Work of its Seventeenth Session （13 March-7 April 1978）, Annex I, Report of the Chairman of Working Group I, Appendix, 13 April 1978, p. 2.

⑥ See UN Doc. A/AC. 105/240 Report of the Legal Sub-Committee on the Work of its Eighteenth Session （12 March-6 April 1979）, 10 April 1979, para. 34.

⑦ See UN Doc. A/34/20, Report of the Committee on the Peaceful Uses of Outer Space, General Assembly Official Records, Thirty-Fourth Session, Supplement No. 20, 14 August 1979, para. 66.

⑧ See Senate Committee on Aeronautical and Space Sciences, Space Treaty Proposals by the United States and U. S. S. R. -Staff Report Prepared for the Use of the Committee on Aeronautical and Space Sciences, 89th Congress, 2nd Session, U. S. Government Printing Office, Washington 1966, p. 1.

⑨ Ibid.

⑩ UN Doc. A/AC. 105/32, Draft Treaty Governing the Exploration of the Moon and Other Celestial Bodies：Letter dated 16 June 1966 from the Permanent Representative of the United States of America addressed to the Chairman of the Committee on the Peaceful Uses of Outer Space, Annex, 17 June 1966.

列入天体条约的、需要进一步细化的十二个基本要素[1]。信中附有《探索月球和其他天体的条约》草案[2]。在重复《外空条约》草案许多条款的同时，它强调了探索和利用天体的自由以及科学考察天体的重要性[3]，并特别强调禁止在月球和其他天体上部署大规模毁灭性武器以及其他军事设施[4]。

在美国提案所强调的主题背景下，阿根廷的提案显得别具一番意义。1970 年 7 月 3 日，阿根廷代表奥尔多・科卡提出了“关于利用月球和其他天体自然资源活动原则的协定草案”[5]，该草案当时也得到了美国的支持[6]。如果将该草案与美国早期提案进行比较，可以看出各自着眼不同的优先事项。除了重复一些基本自由之外，美国提案似乎集中在探索利用月球和其他天体的自由、环境关切，以及其在《外空条约》中就关注的主权和所有权主张问题[7]。而阿根廷提案首要的也是唯一的聚焦点是开发月球资源的问题。以“月球和其他天体的自然资源应是人类共同遗产”为前提[8]，阿根廷提案集中于这些资源的法律性质和从这些资源获得的利益如何分配的问题[9]。基于阿

① The essential elements contained in the letter must not be mistaken for the actual fully formulated draft treaty annexed to the letter. This is sometimes not correctly perceived in literature as, apparently, in Bashor, Harold W., Interpretation of the Moon Treaty-Recourse to Working Papers and Related International Documents, Annals of Air and Space Law (XXXII) 2007, pp. 154-155.

② The treaty proposal was reproduced in a separate document: UN Doc. A/AC. 105/C. 2/L. 12, Draft Treaty Governing the Exploration of the Moon and Other Celestial Bodies, Proposal United States of America, 11 July 1966.

③ See UN Doc. A/AC. 105/32, Draft Treaty Governing the Exploration of the Moon and Other Celestial Bodies: Letter dated 16 June 1966 from the Permanent Representative of the United States of America addressed to the Chairman of the Committee on the Peaceful Uses of Outer Space, Annex, 17 June 1966, Art. 1 and 2.

④ See ibid., Art. 8 and 9.

⑤ UN Doc. A/AC. 105/C. 2/L. 71 and Corr. 1, Argentina: Draft Agreement on the Principles Governing Activities in the Use of the Natural Resources of the Moon and other Celestial Bodies, 23 June 1970.

⑥ See Bashor, Harold W., Interpretation of the Moon Treaty-Recourse to Working Papers and Related International Documents, Annals of Air and Space Law (XXXII) 2007, p. 153.

⑦ See UN Doc. A/AC. 105/32, Draft Treaty Governing the Exploration of the Moon and Other Celestial Bodies: Letter dated 16 June 1966 from the Permanent Representative of the United States of America addressed to the Chairman of the Committee on the Peaceful Uses of Outer Space, Annex, 17 June 1966, Art. 1, 10 and 7, respectively.

⑧ UN Doc. A/AC. 105/C. 2/L. 71 and Corr. 1, Argentina: Draft Agreement on the Principles Governing Activities in the Use of the Natural Resources of the Moon and other Celestial Bodies, 23 June 1970, Art. 1.

⑨ Ibid., Art. 4 reads as follows: “The benefits obtained from the use of the natural resources of the Moon and other celestial bodies shall be made available to all peoples without discrimination of any kind.” As to the distribution of the benefits, Art. 5 further makes reference to aims enshrined in Art. 55 lit. (a) UN Charter as well as the interests and requirements of developing countries. See Charter of the United Nations (done 26 June 1945, entered into force 24 October 1945) 1 UNTS 16 (UN Charter).

根廷提案，人类共同遗产的概念在关于月球和其他天体人类活动法律框架的谈判中成为了关键。

1971 年，苏联提交的要求筹备制定月球条约的信函中载有六项基本原则，主张具体内容的起草应当以此为基础。它还在信函的附件中列入了题为“关于月球条约”的完整草案①。苏联的条约草案没有提及有关“协定应包括除月球的其他天体”的建议②。与阿根廷在其草案中提出人类共同遗产概念相比③，苏联在原则上反对这个概念④。苏联提案明确指出，无论是月球的表面还是底土都不能成为任何国家或个人的财产⑤。

美国和苏联的提案强调了和平利用，均包括了禁止在月球上部署或安装核武器和任何其他大规模杀伤性武器。⑥ 因此有关条约的适用范围，特别是地外资源经济开发问题，在谈判伊始即存争议，并在后续谈判中占主导地位。

（三）讨论的主要问题

联合国外空委讨论的两个主要问题：一是月球和其他天体的自然资源的地位，尤其是人类共同遗产概念的适用和解释；二是“月球”一词的范围。关于第一个问题，苏联坚决反对人类共同遗产概念，而美国则对其持积极态度。美国于 1972 年提交了

---

① UN Doc. A/8391, Treaty Concerning the Moon: Letter dated 27 May 1971 from the Minister for Foreign Affairs of the Union of Soviet Socialist Republics addressed to the Secretary-General, Annex, 4 June 1971.

② The draft treaty only refers to “the Moon”, the “circumlunar space” and “orbit around the Moon”; see e. g. UN Doc. A/8391, Treaty Concerning the Moon: Letter dated 27 May 1971 from the Minister for Foreign Affairs of the Union of Soviet Socialist Republics addressed to the Secretary-General, Annex, 4 June 1971, Art. I and Art. II.

③ See UN Doc. A/AC. 105/C. 2/L. 71 and Corr. 1, Argentina: Draft Agreement on the Principles Governing Activities in the Use of the Natural Resources of the Moon and other Celestial Bodies, 23 June 1970, Art. 1.

④ See Union of Soviet Socialist Republics: Working Paper-Draft Treaty Relating to the Moon (Question of the “common heritage of all mankind”), 28 March 1973, in: UN Doc. A/AC. 105/115, Report of the Legal Sub-Committee on the Work of its Twelfth Session (26 March-20 April 1973), Annex I, Documents Relating to Agenda Item 2 (Draft Treaty Relating to the Moon), 27 April 1973, p. 24.

⑤ See UN Doc. A/8391, Treaty Concerning the Moon: Letter dated 27 May 1971 from the Minister for Foreign Affairs of the Union of Soviet Socialist Republics addressed to the Secretary-General, Annex, 4 June 1971, Art. VIII.

⑥ See UN Doc. A/AC. 105/32, Draft Treaty Governing the Exploration of the Moon and Other Celestial Bodies: Letter dated 16 June 1966 from the Permanent Representative of the United States of America addressed to the Chairman of the Committee on the Peaceful Uses of Outer Space, Annex, 17 June 1966, Art. 8 and 9; and UN Doc. A/8391, Treaty Concerning the Moon: Letter dated 27 May 1971 from the Minister for Foreign Affairs of the Union of Soviet Socialist Republics addressed to the Secretary-General, Annex, 4 June 1971, Art. II.

几份工作文件[①]，其中第八条规定：“月球和其他天体的自然资源应是人类共同遗产。”[②]

关于第二个问题，苏联主张将协定的适用范围限制在月球[③]，而美国则赞成更广泛的适用范围，既包括月球，也包括其他天体。在美国递交的材料中，每每提及此类协议，它总是称之为有关“月球和其他天体”加以讨论[④]。

至于发展中国家而言，埃及和印度联合提交了一份工作文件，详细阐述了共同遗产原则，认为该原则意味着所有签署国应共同分享利益[⑤]。

1972年，法律小组委员会批准了第一个条约草案[⑥]。关于人类共同遗产概念的范围和后果，尚未达成一致。

值得注意的是，此后1973年美国代表团提案[⑦]中的第十条成为了《月球协定》第十一条的大部分实质性内容的出处。尤其是第十条第五段勾勒出了未来月球国际制度的主要目的。

---

① The submitted Working Papers each contain one article, which altogether constitute a complete draft treaty. See A/AC. 105/101, Report of the Legal Sub-Committee on the Work of its Eleventh Session (10 April-5 May 1972), Annex I, Proposals and other Documents relating to Agenda Item 3 (Questions relating to the Moon), 11 May 1972.

② There is an original and a revised version of the Working Paper: UN Doc. A/AC. 105/C. 2 (XI) /WP. 12, United States of America: Working Paper, 13 April 1972; and UN Doc. A/AC. 105/C. 2 (XI) /WP. 12/Rev. 1, United States of America: Working Paper, 17 April 1972. Both documents are reproduced in: A/AC. 105/101, Report of the Legal Sub-Committee on the Work of its Eleventh Session (10 April-5 May 1972), Annex I, Proposals and other Documents relating to Agenda Item 3 (Questions relating to the Moon), 11 May 1972, p. 13.

③ The Soviet position was also supported by other States such as Japan, UN Doc. A/AC. 105/C. 2/SR. 187, 2 May 1972, pp. 3-4; Hungary, UN Doc. A/AC. 105/C. 2/SR. 187, 2 May 1972, p. 14; Poland, UN Doc. A/AC. 105/C. 2/SR. 187, 2 May 1972, p. 15; Egypt, UN Doc. A/AC. 105/C. 2/SR. 188, 3 May 1972, p. 19; Bulgaria, UN Doc. A/AC. 105/C. 2/SR. 188, 3 May 1972, p. 29; and Czechoslovakia, UN Doc. A/AC. 105/C. 2/SR. 188, 3 May 1972, p. 30.

④ See e. g. UN Doc. A/AC. 105/32, Draft Treaty Governing the Exploration of the Moon and Other Celestial Bodies: Letter dated 16 June 1966 from the Permanent Representative of the United States of America addressed to the Chairman of the Committee on the Peaceful Uses of Outer Space, Annex, 17 June 1966.

⑤ See UN Doc. A/AC. 105/C. 2/ (XI) /WP, Egypt and India: Working Paper, 14 April 1972, , in: A/AC. 105/101, Report of the Legal Sub-Committee on the Work of its Eleventh Session (10 April-5 May 1972), Annex I, Proposals and other Documents relating to Agenda Item 3 (Questions relating to the Moon), 11 May 1972, p. 17.

⑥ See UN Doc. PUOS/C. 2/WG (XI) /15/Rev. 1, Draft Treaty Concerning the Moon: Text formulated by the Working Group, 4 May 1972, in: UN Doc. A/AC. 105/101, Report of the Legal Sub-Committee on the Work of its Eleventh Session (10 April-5 May 1972), 11 May 1972, para. 21.

⑦ See United States of America: Working Paper, 17 April 1973, in: UN Doc. A/AC. 105/115, Report of the Legal Sub-Committee on the Work of its Twelfth Session (26 March-20 April 1973), Annex I, Documents Relating to Agenda Item 2 (Draft Treaty Relating to the Moon), 27 April 1973, pp. 33-34.

1973年，外空委以协商一致的方式通过了一些条款，然而这些条款都与关键问题无关[①]。

苏联在1973年3月28日提交的一份工作文件中，更为坚决地反对人类共同遗产概念。苏联认为，“遗产”和“继承”是民法术语，不应在空间法中使用，空间法是国际公法的一部分。苏联更倾向于阐释《外空条约》中“共同事情”的概念[②]。

阿根廷迅速做出回应，称人类共同遗产概念有坚实的法律先例支撑，其载于联合国大会关于深海海底的第2749（XXV）号决议。阿根廷认为，这一概念可用于详细阐述诸如有关利益获取、公平分享的权利资格，以及国际制度的机构建设等重要问题[③]。

历经了几轮大会辩论，尤其是在苏联进一步坚持其反对人类共同遗产概念的立场之后[④]，美国、保加利亚、印度、埃及、尼日利亚和蒙古[⑤]向联合国外空委递交了工作文件。1974年，法律小组委员会第十三届会议的审议工作集中于“条约的范围、探月任务的透明度和月球自然资源的使用”[⑥]。保加利亚的一项协议草案提出召开一次大

① See UN Doc. A/AC. 105/115, Report of the Legal Sub-Committee on the Work of its Twelfth Session (26 March-20 April 1973), p. 5.

② See Union of Soviet Socialist Republics: Working Paper-Draft Treaty Relating to the Moon (Question of the "common heritage of all mankind"), 28 March 1973, in: UN Doc. A/AC. 105/115, Report of the Legal Sub-Committee on the Work of its Twelfth Session (26 March-20 April 1973), Annex I, Documents Relating to Agenda Item 2 (Draft Treaty Relating to the Moon), 27 April 1973, p. 24.

③ See Argentina: Working Paper-Draft Treaty Relating to the Moon (Question of the "common heritage of all mankind"), 17 April 1973, in: UN Doc. A/AC. 105/115, Report of the Legal Sub-Committee on the Work of its Twelfth Session (26 March-20 April 1973), Annex I, Documents Relating to Agenda Item 2 (Draft Treaty Relating to the Moon), 27 April 1973, p. 29.

④ See UN Doc. A/AC. 105/C. 2/SR. 187, 12 July 1972, reproduced in: UN Doc. A/AC. 105/C. 2/SR. 187-191, Legal Sub-Committee, Eleventh Session, Summary Record of the One Hundred and Eighty-Seventh to the One Hundred and Ninety-First and Meetings (2-5 May 1972), 12 July 1972, p. 8; and UN Doc. A/AC. 105/PV. 175, Verbatim Record of the One Hundred and Seventy-First Meeting (28 June 1977), 25 July 1977, pp. 47-50.

⑤ See UN Doc. A/AC. 105/C. 2/L. 91 and Corr. 1, United States of America: Working Paper, 6 May 1974; UN Doc. A/AC. 105/C. 2/L. 93, Bulgaria: Working Paper, 8 May 1974; UN Doc. A/AC. 105/C. 2/L. 95, Egypt and India: Working Paper, 13 May 1974; UN Doc. A/AC. 105/C. 2/L. 96, India: Working Paper, 13 May 1974; UN Doc. A/AC. 105/C. 2/L. 97, Egypt, India and Nigeria: Working Paper, 13 May 1974; and UN Doc. A/AC. 105/C. 2/L. 98/Rev. 1, Mongolia: Working Paper, 20 May 1974. All these documents are reproduced in: UN Doc. A/AC. 105/133, Report of the Legal Sub-Committee on the Work of its Thirteenth Session (6-31 May 1974), Annex I, Documents Relating to Agenda Item 2, 6 June 1974.

⑥ Bashor, Harold W., Interpretation of the Moon Treaty, Recourse to Working Papers and Related International Documents, Annals of Air and Space Law (XXXII) 2007, p. 149.

会，以落实治理月球自然资源开发的国际制度[1]。阿根廷则强调有必要取得可与海洋法会议相媲美的进一步发展[2]，而苏联则不断重申其对于人类共同遗产确切含义的严重质疑[3]。

直到 1978 年，在奥地利代表团主导的非正式谈判中，以上观点之间的差距才有所缩小。随即形成的奥地利条约草案[4]体现了各方努力的结果，并作为妥协案文成为就《月球协定》最终达成一致的基础[5]。

即便联合国外空委已经耗费了一定时间才取得了基于奥地利提案的共识，但巴西还是就协定第十一条提出了修正案[6]："月球及其自然资源均为人类的共同遗产，这将在本协定的有关条款，尤其是本条第五款中表现出来。"。由此，苏联便撤回其反对将人类共同遗产纳入协定的立场，并接受了协议的文本，自此再未提出反对意见。

由此，联合国大会于 1979 年 12 月 5 日经表决一致通过了《月球协定》草案。该协定于 1979 年 12 月 18 日在联合国总部纽约开放供签署[7]。

---

① See Art. X-bis para. 2 and 4 of the Bulgarian draft agreement, UN Doc. A/AC. 105/C. 2/L. 93, Bulgaria: Working Paper, 8 May 1974, in: UN Doc. A/AC. 105/133, Report of the Legal Sub-Committee on the work of its Thirteenth Session (6-31 May 1974), Annex I, Documents Relating to Agenda Item 2, 6 June 1974.

② See UN Doc. A/AC. 105/PV. 164, Verbatim Record of the Hundred and Sixty-Fourth Meeting (25 June 1976), 25 June 1976, pp. 30-35.

③ See ibid., pp. 8-11.

④ See UN Doc. WG. I (1978) /WP. 2, Austria: Working Paper, Agreement Governing the Activities of States on the Moon and other Celestial Bodies, 3 April 1978, in: UN Doc. A/AC. 105/218, Report of the Legal Sub-Committee on the Work of its Seventeenth Session (13 March-7 April 1978), Annex I, Report of the Chairman of Working Group I, Appendix, 13 April 1978, p. 2.

⑤ UN Doc. A/33/20, Report of the Committee on the Peaceful Uses of Outer Space, General Assembly Official Records, Thirty-Third Session, Supplement No. 20, 7 August 1978, p. 11 (Statement by the Chairman Dr. Peter Jankowitsch).

⑥ See Bashor, Harold W., Interpretation of the Moon Treaty-Recourse to Working Papers and Related International Documents, Annals of Air and Space Law (XXXII) 2007, p. 199.

⑦ See UNGA Res. 34/68, Agreement Governing the Activities of States on the Moon and Other Celestial Bodies, 5 December 1979.

第二章 《月球协定》的评注

目录

一、前言

本协定各缔约国，

注意到各国在月球和其他天体的探索和利用方面所获得的成就，

认识到构成地球的天然卫星的月球在探索外层空间方面起着重大的作用，

决心在平等基础上促成各国在探索和利用月球和其他天体方面合作的进一步发展，

切望不使月球成为国际冲突的场所，

铭记着开发月球和其他天体的自然资源所可能带来的利益，

回顾《关于各国探索和利用包括月球与其他天体在内外层空间活动的原则条约》《关于援救宇航员、送回宇航员和归还射入外层空间的物体的协定》《空间物体所造成损害的国际责任公约》和《关于登记射入外层空间物体的公约》，

考虑到对于此类有关月球和其他天体的国际文书的各项条款必须参照外层空间的探索和利用的继续进展，加以阐释和发展，

达成协议如下：

（一）谈判与起草历史

阿根廷1970年提案的序言部分强调指出，《外空条约》没有关于月球和其他天体自然资源利用的具体规定。确定此类规定是必要的，但必须同时牢记利用外层空间及其资源应为所有国家谋福利和利益，并应是全人类的共同事情①。阿根廷采用了早先在讨论海洋法条约时的概念，将月球的自然资源也界定为全人类共同遗产，并纳入协定②。

苏联在其1971年提案中强调防止月球成为战场的重要性，并强调了在探索和利用月球及其底土和绕月空间方面进一步合作的需求。③ 该提案没有提及有关月球和其他天体资源法律地位的问题。

美国1972年提案的序言与苏联提案类似，但没有提及月球底土或绕月空间。但提出该协议应该适用于“月球和其他天体”④。

1972年联合国有关月球的首个条约草案结合了美国和苏联的草案，将整个条约草案中的“和其他天体”字样置于方括号内⑤。

1978年，奥地利提出的妥协方案同样结合了美国和苏联的草案，但也提及了《关

① See UN Doc. A/AC. 105/C. 2/L. 71 and Corr. 1, Argentina: Draft Agreement on the Principles Governing Activities in the Use of the Natural Resources of the Moon and other Celestial Bodies, 23 June 1970, Preamble para. 3 and 5.

② There, it was the Maltese representative to the UN, Arvid Pardo, who proposed to qualify the bottom of the oceans as a common heritage of mankind. See Sohn, Louis B., *Managing the Law of the Sea: Ambassador Pardo's Forgotton Second Idea*, Columbia Journal of Transnational Law (36) 1998, p. 285-287; UN Doc. A/C. 1/PV. 1515, UNGA Official Records, Twenty-Second Session, Agenda Item 92, 1 November 1967; and UN Doc. A/C. 1/PV. 1516, UNGA Official Records, Twenty-Second Session, Agenda Item 92, para. 13; see also Christol, Carl Q., *The Moon Treaty and the Allocation of Resources*, Annals of Air and Space Law (XXII/II) 1997, p. 33.

③ See UN Doc. A/8391, Treaty Concerning the Moon: Letter dated 27 May 1971 from the Minister for Foreign Affairs of the Union of Soviet Socialist Republics addressed to the Secretary-General, Annex, 4 June 1971.

④ See UN Doc. A/AC. 105/C. 2 (XI) /WP. 9, United States of America: Working Paper, 12 April 1972. The document is reproduced in: UN Doc. A/AC. 105/101, Report of the Legal Sub-Committee on the Work of its Eleventh Session (10 April-5 May 1972), Annex I, Proposals and other Documents relating to Agenda Item 3 (Questions relating to the Moon), 11 May 1972, p. 12.

⑤ UN Doc. PUOS/C. 2/WG (XI) /15/Rev. 1, Draft Treaty Concerning the Moon: Text formulated by the Working Group, 4 May 1972, in: UN Doc. A/AC. 105/101, Report of the Legal Sub-Committee on the Work of its Eleventh Session (10 April-5 May 1972), 11 May 1972, para. 21.

于援救宇航员、送回宇航员和归还射入外层空间的物体的协定》（以下简称《营救协定》）[①]，《空间物体所造成的损害的国际责任公约》（以下简称《责任公约》）[②] 和《关于登记射入外层空间物体的公约》（以下简称《登记公约》）[③]。但这并没有使序言发生实质改变。

（二）评注

与大多数国际协定一样，《月球协定》也有序言，用以阐明缔约各方的目标和愿景[④]。

细读序言会发现，《月球协定》意欲调整两个主要方面。一是特别关注月球对于未来探索（乃至）利用外空的重要性，尤其是开发所得利益的分配问题，这是《月球协定》需要规制的第一个重要问题。二是军事利用被明确提及，有必要避免使月球成为国际冲突的另一场所。

整个序言起草非常简洁明了，省略了其他条约间或出现的一些为显示庄严性的冗余措辞。该序言就是为了明确制定《月球协定》的两个动机，即一方面是形成关于探索和开发月球的法律框架，另一方面是防止这颗地球的天然卫星成为冲突之地[⑤]。早在 1979 年，人们便察觉到及时确定月球活动的必要性，特别是开发活动[⑥]。

二、第一条（适用范围）

1. 本协定内关于月球的条款也适用于太阳系内地球以外的其他天体，但如任何此类天体已有现已生效的特别法律规则，则不在此限。

---

① Agreement on the Rescue of Astronauts, the Return of Astronauts and the Return of Objects Launched into Outer Space (done 22 April 1968, entered into force 3 December 1968) 672 UNTS 119 (ARRA).

② Convention on International Liability for Damage Caused by Space Objects (done 29 March 1972, entered into force 1 September 1972) 961 UNTS 187 (LIAB).

③ Convention on Registration of Objects Launched into Outer Space (done 14 January 1975, entered into force 15 September 1976) 1023 UNTS 15 (REG).

④ See generally on preambles: Treviranus, Hans-Dietrich, *Preamble*, in: Bernhardt, Rudolf (ed.), *Encyclopedia of Public International Law*, Volume Ⅲ, Elsevier, Amsterdam 1997, pp. 1097ff.

⑤ See also Diederiks-Verschoor, I. H. Philepina/Kopal, Vladimir, *An Introduction to Space Law*, 3rd rev. edn., Kluwer Law International, The Netherlands 2008, p. 48.

⑥ See also von der Dunk, Frans G., *The Moon Agreement and the Prospect of Commercial Exploitation of Lunar Resources*, Annals of Air and Space Law (XXXII) 2007, pp. 100-104.

2. 为了本协定的目的，“月球”一词包括环绕月球的轨道或其他飞向或飞绕月球的轨道。

3. 本协定不适用于循自然方式到达地球表面的地球外物质。

（一）谈判与起草历史

从一开始，美国就主张《月球协定》的适用范围不限于月球，应扩至其他天体①，而苏联草案则将适用范围限定于月球②。其他一些国家如保加利亚、波兰、埃及、法国和日本也反对将条约适用于除月球以外的其他天体③。而另外一些国家或明确或含蓄地赞成将《月球协定》适用范围延伸至太阳系其他行星。这些国家除了美国外，还有英国、加拿大、澳大利亚、比利时、罗马尼亚和伊朗④。1972 年联合国关于

① See the various Working Papers submitted by the USA：UN Doc. A/AC. 105/C. 2（XI）/WP. 1, United States of America：Working Paper（Article I）, 11 April 1972；UN Doc. A/AC. 105/C. 2（XI）/WP. 4, United States of America：Working Paper（Article IV）, 11 April 1972；UN Doc. A/AC. 105/C. 2（XI）/WP. 9, United States：Working Paper（Preamble）12 April 1972. The documents are reproduced in UN Doc. A/AC. 105/101, Report of the Legal Sub-Committee on the Work of its Eleventh Session（10 April-5 May 1972）, 11 May 1972, Annex I, Proposals and other Documents relating to Agenda Item 3（Questions relating to the Moon）.

② See UN Doc. A/8391, Treaty Concerning the Moon：Letter dated 27 May 1971 from the Minister for Foreign Affairs of the Union of Soviet Socialist Republics addressed to the Secretary-General, Annex, 4 June 1971.

③ See UN Doc. A/AC. 105/C. 2/SR. 187, 2 May 1972 reproduced in：UN Doc. A/AC. 105/C. 2/SR. 187-191, Legal Sub-Committee, Eleventh Session, Summary Record of the One Hundred and Eighty-Seventh to the One Hundred and Ninety-First and Meetings（2-5 May 1972）, 12 July 1972, pp. 4, 8, 14, 15；and UN Doc. A/AC. 105/C. 2/SR. 188, 3 May 1972, reproduced in：UN Doc. A/AC. 105/C. 2/SR. 187-191, Legal Sub-Committee, Eleventh Session, Summary Record of the One Hundred and Eighty-Seventh to the One Hundred and Ninety-First and Meeting（2-5 May 1972）, 12 July 1972 pp. 19, 26, 29.

④ See UN Doc. A/AC. 105/C. 2/SR. 187, Canada（2 May 1972）, reproduced in：UN Doc. A/AC. 105/C. 2/SR. 187-191, Legal Sub-Committee, Eleventh Session, Summary Record of the One Hundred and Eighty-Seventh to the One Hundred and Ninety-First Meetings（2-5 May 1972）, 12 July 1972, p. 10；UN Doc. A/AC. 105/C. 2/SR. 188, 3 May 1972, reproduced in：UN Doc. A/AC. 105/C. 2/SR. 187-191, Legal Sub-Committee, Eleventh Session, Summary Record of the One Hundred and Eighty-Seventh to the One Hundred and Ninety-First Meetings（2-5 May 1972）, 12 July 1972, pp. 22, 24, 28, 32；and UN Doc. A/AC. 105/C. 2/SR. 189, 4 May 1972, reproduced in：UN Doc. A/AC. 105/C. 2/SR. 187-191, Legal Sub-Committee, Eleventh Session, Summary Record of the One Hundred and Eighty-Seventh to the One Hundred and Ninety-First Meetings（2-5 May 1972）, 12 July 1972, pp. 38, 39, 44.

月球的首个草案[1]将适用范围留作一个待讨论的议题[2]，目的是想让《月球协定》“适用于除了地球以外的所有其他天体”。1978 年奥地利提交的妥协案文[3]同样将适用范围扩至太阳系的其他行星。在此版本提出之后，再无关于适用范围的异议。

另一个与协定适用范围有关的问题就是“绕月空间”。它源自苏联草案第一条第一款[4]，苏联认为包括《联合国宪章》在内的国际法适用于月球和绕月空间的活动，由于未给出相关定义，继而法律小组委员会将其置于括号中。虽然未能就此达成最终协议，但是 1972 年草案第一条[5]仍初步界定“月球和其他天体”包括了“围绕（月球）的轨道或围绕其他天体的轨道”[6]。

此外，这份《月球协定》草案首次提及该协定“不适用于循自然方式到达地球表面的地球外物质”的条款[7]。以上两条——适用于绕月空间以及不适用于以自然方式到达地球表面的地球外物质——未遇异议，继而体现在 1978 年的奥地利妥协案文中[8]。

（二）评注

与其他四个有关人类外空活动的国际条约不同，《月球协定》首先从界定适用范围着手。这具有积极的意义，因为一直以来人们都期许《外空条约》也能界定“外层

---

① See UN Doc. PUOS/C. 2/WG（XI）/15/Rev. 1, Draft Treaty Concerning the Moon: Text formulated by the Working Group, 4 May 1972, in: UN Doc. A/AC. 105/101, Report of the Legal Sub-Committee on the Work of its Eleventh Session (10 April-5 May 1972), 11 May 1972, para. 21.

② Throughout the text of the UN Draft Treaty, the formulation "and other celestial bodies" was put in square brackets, thus indicating that no agreement could be reached on the issue. See UN Doc. A/AC. 105/101, Report of the Legal Sub-committee on the Work of its Eleventh Session (10 April-5 May 1972), 11 May 1972, para. 19.

③ See UN Doc. A/33/20, Report of the Committee on the Peaceful Uses of Outer Space, General Assembly Official Records, Thirty-Third Session, Supplement No. 20, 7 August 1978, p. 11 (Statement by the Chairman Dr. Peter Jankowitsch).

④ UN Doc. A/8391, Treaty Concerning the Moon: Letter dated 27 May 1971 from the Minister for Foreign Affairs of the Union of Soviet Socialist Republics addressed to the Secretary-General, Annex, 4 June 1971.

⑤ See UN Doc. PUOS/C. 2/WG（XI）/15/Rev. 1, Draft Treaty Concerning the Moon: Text formulated by the Working Group, 4 May 1972, in: UN Doc. A/AC. 105/101, Report of the Legal Sub-Committee on the Work of its Eleventh Session (10 April-5 May 1972), 11 May 1972, para. 21.

⑥ Ibid., Art. I, para. 1 (ii).

⑦ Ibid., Art. I para. 2.

⑧ See UN Doc. WG. I（1978）/WP. 2, Austria: Working Paper, Agreement Governing the Activities of States on the Moon and other Celestial Bodies, 3 April 1978, in: UN Doc. A/AC. 105/218, Report of the Legal Sub-Committee on the Work of its Seventeenth Session (13 March-7 April 1978), Annex I, Report of the Chairman of Working Group I, Appendix, 13 April 1978, Art. 1, para. 2 and 3.

空间”的含义。只有《月球协定》通过限定太阳系内以及地外空间，为界定外层空间提供了重要参考。这是人类活动极可能触及的区域。毋庸置疑，人类法律只能适用于人类行为。在探知宇宙的其他地方是否有以其他形式存在的生命方面，人类技术，无论积极地或消极地，都是极其有限的。因此，将国际空间法的适用范围限定在地月环境和太阳系中是谨小慎微和深谋远虑的。

1. 月球以及太阳系内其他天体

第一条第一款明确指出了本协定除了着重讨论月球本身外，还包括了太阳系内其他天体（比如围绕太阳运行的行星，即水星、金星、火星、木星、土星、天王星、海王星和以前的冥王星）。此外还适用行星以外的天体，如小行星、流星和彗星，只要它们位于太阳系内[①]。至此，太阳系内所有的固体天体均被协定适用范围所覆盖。特别是在谈及不得据为己有原则时，没有一个联合国外空条约对大天体和小天体进行区分。关于太阳系的限定值得注意，因为人类制定的国际条约应明智地限于适用人类已发现的领域。将人类规范适用于纵深约有 700 亿光年的整个宇宙中的人类活动，是不可能的[②]。因此，将适用范围限定在太阳系内以及包含地外月球空间是有道理的。其他四个国际条约虽未规定此类适用范围的限定，但可从《月球协定》借鉴此种限定。将这样的限定适用于其他几个主要的外空条约也是说得通的，毕竟这些条约也用于调整人类在外空的活动。

2. 绕月轨道

第一条第二款明确指出本协定所称“月球”应包括环绕月球的轨道或其他飞向或飞绕月球的轨道。[③] 这对于去军事化目标具有特别重要的意义，根据该定义，不仅禁

---

① The term ‘celestial body’ is understood as “［a］ny aggregation of matter in space constituting a unit for astronomical study, such as the sun, moon, a planet, comet, star, or nebula.” Parker, Sybil P., *McGraw-Hill Dictionary of Scientific and Technical Terms*, McGraw-Hill Book Company, New York 1989, p. 313.

② A light-year, (also light year or lightyear), is a unit of length, equal to just under 10 trillion kilometers (10^{16} meters, 10 petameters or 6 trillion (6, 000, 000, 000, 000) miles). The International Astronomical Union (IAU) defines a light-year as the distance that light travels in a vacuum in one Julian year. See International Astronomical Union, *Measuring the Universe-The IAU and astronomical units*<http://www.iau.org/public/measuring/> accessed 26 April 2019.

③ For a description on this point see Cheng, Bin, *Studies in International Space Law*, Clarendon Press, Oxford 1997, pp. 363f.

止在月球上部署武器，在飞向或飞绕月球的轨道上也不能部署[①]。

3. 外星物质

第一条第三款规定了《月球协定》的适用范围不包含以自然方式落到地球表面的外来物质[②]。值得注意的是，《月球协定》的第十一条规定了月球的采矿权利。因此，只有月球上的资源由此协定规制，不包含地球上自然资源的分解与沉降。

三、第二条（国际法和国际合作）

月球上的一切活动，包括其探索和利用在内，应按照国际法，尤其是联合国宪章的规定，考虑到一九七〇年十月二十四日大会通过的关于各国依联合国宪章建立友好关系和合作的国际法原则宣言，顾及维持国际和平与安全及促进国际合作与相互谅解的利益并适当顾及所有其他缔约国的相应利益予以进行。

（一）谈判和起草过程

《月球协定》第二条的用词源自埃及和印度在 1973 年 3 月 27 日联合提交的一个工作文件[③]。该文件是对由工作组制定、法律小组委员会 1972 年第 190 次工作会议上通过的草案条约的述评[④]。

① See Jasentuliyana, Nandasiri, *The Moon Treaty*, in: Jasentuliyana, Nandasiri (ed.), Maintaining Outer Space for Peaceful Purposes, The United Nations University, Tokyo 1984, p. 130.

② The text of Art. I para. 3 was drafted following a proposal made by the United Kingdom in 1972, see UN Doc. A/AC. 105/C. 2 (XI) /WP. 24, United Kingdom: Working Paper, 20 April 1972, in: UN Doc. A/AC. 105/101, Report of the Legal Sub-Committee on the Work of its Eleventh Session (10 April-5 May 1972), Annex I, Proposals and other Documents relating to Agenda Item 3 (Questions relating to the Moon), 11 May 1972, p. 18.

③ Egypt and India: Working Paper-Draft Treaty Relating to the Moon, 27 March 1973, in: UN Doc. A/AC. 105/115, Report of the Legal Sub-Committee on the Work of its Twelfth Session (26 March-20 April 1973), Annex I, Documents Relating to Agenda Item 2 (Draft Treaty Relating to the Moon), 27 April 1973, p. 21.

④ UN Doc. PUOS/C. 2/WG (XI) /15/Rev. 1, Draft Treaty Concerning the Moon: Text formulated by the Working Group, 4 May 1972, in: UN Doc. A/AC. 105/101, Report of the Legal Sub-Committee on the Work of its Eleventh Session (10 April-5 May 1972), 11 May 1972, para. 21.

1966 年美国起草了首个治理月球和其他天体探索活动的条约草案①，此后“根据国际法”或类似提及国际法适用性的表述，被纳入了《月球协定》草案中，“根据国际法”一词同样规定在《外空条约》第三条中②。合作原则和适当顾及义务源自 1971 年苏联草案③。这些原则和义务全部为最终的《月球协定》第二条所采纳。之后的讨论只是措辞不同，实质内容无变化，一直到 1978 年奥地利草案，确定了现有措辞④。

（二）评注

第二条除了援引 1970 年《国际友好合作宣言》（以下简称《友好合作宣言》）⑤，

---

① UN Doc. A/AC. 105/32, Draft Treaty Governing the Exploration of the Moon and Other Celestial Bodies: Letter dated 16 June 1966 from the Permanent Representative of the United States of America addressed to the Chairman of the Committee on the Peaceful Uses of Outer Space, Annex, 17 June 1966.

② Ibid., Art. 1; UN Doc. A/8391, Treaty Concerning the Moon: Letter dated 27 May 1971 from the Minister for Foreign Affairs of the Union of Soviet Socialist Republics addressed to the Secretary-General, Annex, 4 June 1971, Art. I para. 1; UN Doc. PUOS/C. 2/WG (XI) /15/Rev. 1, Draft Treaty Concerning the Moon: Text formulated by the Working Group, 4 May 1972, in: UN Doc. A/AC. 105/101, Report of the Legal Sub-Committee on the Work of its Eleventh Session (10 April-5 May 1972), 11 May 1972, para. 21, Art. II para. 1; Working Paper submitted by Bulgaria-Draft Treaty Relating to the Moon, 27 March 1973, in: UN Doc. A/AC. 105/115, Report of the Legal Sub-Committee on the Work of its Twelfth Session (26 March-20 April 1973), Annex I, Documents Relating to Agenda Item 2 (Draft Treaty Relating to the Moon), 27 April 1973, p. 11, Art. II para. 1; UN Doc. A/AC. 150/C. 2/L. 93, Bulgaria: Working Paper-Draft Treaty Relating to the Moon, 8 May 1974, Art. II para. 1; UN Doc. WG. I (1978) /WP. 2, Austria: Working Paper, Agreement Governing the Activities of States on the Moon and other Celestial Bodies, 3 April 1978, in: UN Doc. A/AC. 105/218, Report of the Legal Sub-Committee on the Work of its Seventeenth Session (13 March-7 April 1978), Annex I, Report of the Chairman of Working Group I, Appendix, 13 April 1978, p. 2, Art. II; only the Argentinean draft of 25 June 1970 did not address the issue. As this rather short proposal (5 articles) only dealt with questions of the exploitation of resources on celestial bodies, it just refers to Art. 55 lit. (a) UN Charter in the distribution of the benefits gained from the activities, UN Doc. A/AC. 105/C. 2/L. 71 and Corr. 1, Argentina: Draft Agreement on the Principles Governing Activities in the Use of the Natural Resources of the Moon and other Celestial Bodies, 23 June 1970.

③ UN Doc. A/8391, Treaty Concerning the Moon: Letter dated 27 May 1971 from the Minister for Foreign Affairs of the Union of Soviet Socialist Republics addressed to the Secretary-General, Annex, 4 June 1971, Art. Ⅲ para. 1 and 2.

④ UN Doc. WG. I (1978) /WP. 2, Austria: Working Paper, Agreement Governing the Activities of States on the Moon and other Celestial Bodies, 3 April 1978, in: UN Doc. A/AC. 105/218, Report of the Legal Sub-Committee on the Work of its Seventeenth Session (13 March-7 April 1978), Annex I, Report of the Chairman of Working Group I, Appendix, 13 April 1978, p. 2, Art. II.

⑤ UNGA Res. 2625 (XXV), Declaration on Principles of International Law Concerning Friendly Relations and Co-operation among States in Accordance with the Charter of the United Nations, 24 October 1970 (Friendly Relations Declaration).

没有创设任何关于人类外空活动的新规则。它将有关人类天体活动的法律置于一般国际法的视野当中。它继而说明空间法并非无本之木，而是作为国际法的一部分，必须在国际法语境中予以考量。

1. 根据国际法开展的外空活动

这一规定背后的理念与1967年《外空条约》第三条是一致的①。人类在月球和其他天体上活动必须有法可依，而不能处于法律真空，并且所适用的空间法作为国际法的一部分，必须在国际法的语境下讨论。《月球协定》同《外空条约》一样②，并非自洽的法律制度③。不过，与一般国际法规则相比，《月球协定》的规则应被视为特别法④。这意味着，《月球协定》适用于其规定的具体情形，与此同时，一般国际法仍然保持适用性。此外，具体的空间法必须在一般国际的框架下来解释。因此，国际公法应该适当地适用于国家在月球和其他天体上的具体活动，包括国际习惯法规则，但效力低于《月球协定》中的明文规定。这也意味着，对于解释《月球协定》的具体条款而言，《条约法公约》不仅适用而且十分重要。

2. 《联合国宪章》和《友好合作宣言》

《联合国宪章》和《友好合作宣言》是证明存在被广泛接受的国际法原则的有力证据⑤。以上两者都列举了重要且普遍的国际公法原则，如互不干涉、互不侵犯，不得使用武力原则等，每一原则都必须为了确保外空和平与安全而予以诠释。《月球协定》第二条具体规定的这些相互谅解的原则在《友好合作宣言》中被特别提及。

3. 执行前景

第二条在未来的角色尚有待观察。至于究竟会有多少国际环境法的学说⑥、规则、原则将在此领域适用于或解释人类在天体上可能开展的活动，则是引人关注的。外空

---

① See Ribbelink, Olivier, Article Ⅲ, in: Hobe, Stephan/Schmidt-Tedd, Bernhard/Schrogl, Kai-Uwe (eds.), Cologne Commentary on Space Law, Volume I, Heymanns, Cologne 2009, pp. 64-69.

② See ibid., p. 64, mn. 1.

③ Simma, Bruno/Pulkowski, Dirk, *Of planets and the universe: self-contained regimes in international law*, European Journal of International Law (17) 2006, pp. 483-529.

④ For a similar conclusion see Ribbelink, Olivier, Article Ⅲ, in: Hobe, Stephan/Schmidt-Tedd, Bernhard/Schrogl, Kai-Uwe (eds.), Cologne Commentary on Space Law, Volume I, Heymanns, Cologne 2009, p. 65, mn. 1.

⑤ See Rosenstock, Robert, *The Declaration of Principles of international law Concerning Friendly Relations: A Survey*, American Journal of International Law (65) 1971, pp. 714f.

⑥ See e. g. Viikari, Lotta, *The environmental element in space law*, Martinus Nijhoff Publishers, Leiden 2008, pp. 125-140.

条约的一般适用和《月球协定》的特殊适用在这种情况下都是不准确和不详细的。毕竟整体上的《外空条约》和特别领域的《月球协定》都不够明确和细化。

四、第三条（和平目的/去军事化）

1. 月球应供全体缔约国专为和平目的而加以利用。

2. 在月球上使用武力或以武力相威胁，或从事任何其他敌对行为或以敌对行为相威胁概在禁止之列。利用月球对地球、月球、宇宙飞行器、宇宙飞行器或人造外空物体的人员实施任何此类行为或从事任何此类威胁，也应同样禁止。

3. 缔约各国不得在环绕月球的轨道上或飞向或飞绕月球的轨道上，放置载有核武器或任何其他种类的大规模毁灭性武器的物体，或在月球上或月球内放置或使用此类武器。

4. 禁止在月球上建立军事基地、军事装置及防御工事，试验任何类型的武器及举行军事演习。但不禁止为科学研究或为任何其他和平目的而使用军事人员。也不禁止使用为和平探索和利用月球所必要的任何装备或设备。

（一）谈判和起草过程

《月球协定》第三条奠定了该协定去军事化的基调。在 1966 年 2 月 3 号苏联月球 9 号航天器在月球上软着陆之后，美国的担忧和关切是：一是月球和其他天体可能出现的军事化；二是月球和其他天体自然资源的获取和控制。于是，美国总统林登·约翰逊在联合国倡议起草有关月球和其他天体的条约时，便表明了美国的利益诉求，即月球以及其他天体上的探索只能用于和平目的①。

相应地，美国在联合国提交的关于制定月球国际条约的倡议中强调了对军事活动的限制。在美国提交给联合国外空委主席的信中，其中一条原则被美国认为是制定未来相关条约的基础，该原则表述如下：“天体应仅用于和平目的。不允许任何国家在

---

① See Senate Committee on Aeronautical and Space Sciences, Space Treaty Proposals by the United States and U. S. S. R. -Staff Report Prepared for the Use of the Committee on Aeronautical and Space Sciences, 89th Congress, 2nd Session, U. S. Government Printing Office, Washington 1966, p. 1.

天体上放置大规模杀伤性武器。军事防御工事、武器试验和军事演习应在禁止之列。”① 值得注意的是，美国总统表达了起草条约的紧迫性和应有的信念，“不仅是为了我们这一代人，也是为了子孙后代——确保太空活动不会引发严重的政治冲突”②。

因此，对军事活动的限制性规定成为美国提交的早期条约草案的一部分。美国提案的序言部分提到 1963 年大会第 1884 号决议，该决议呼吁各国避免在月球和其他天体上安装大规模杀伤性武器③。草案第 9 条具化了限制的内容：“天体应只用于和平目的。所有国家承诺避免在天体进行诸如建造军事防御工事、进行军事演习或试验任何类型的武器等活动。不禁止军事人员、设施或设备用于科学研究或任何其他和平目的”④。

1970 年，阿根廷提交的条约草案主要关切的是月球自然资源的利用，除了在草案序言中提及和平利用月球外，没有类似的规定⑤。相比之下，苏联外交部长 1971 年 5 月 27 日致联合国秘书长的信中最早提出了苏联关于月球的条约草案⑥，其序言中有关乎于此的明确表述，用以表达“防止月球成为国际冲突的领域”的诉求⑦。为了实现这一目标，苏联的条约草案包含以下两条：

“第一条”：

1. 各缔约国应根据包括《联合国宪章》在内的国际法，在月球和绕月空间开展活动。

---

① UN Doc. A/AC. 105/32, Draft Treaty Governing the Exploration of the Moon and Other Celestial Bodies: Letter dated 16 June 1966 from the Permanent Representative of the United States of America addressed to the Chairman of the Committee on the Peaceful Uses of Outer Space, 17 June 1966, p. 2.

② Senate Committee on Aeronautical and Space Sciences, *Space Treaty Proposals by the United States and U. S. S. R. -Staff Report Prepared for the Use of the Committee on Aeronautical and Space Sciences*, 89th Congress, 2nd Session, U. S. Government Printing Office, Washington 1966, p. 1.

③ See UNGA Res. 1884 (XVIII), Question of general and complete disarmament, 17 October 1963, para. 2 lit. (a).

④ UN Doc. A/AC. 105/32, Draft Treaty Governing the Exploration of the Moon and Other Celestial Bodies: Letter dated 16 June 1966 from the Permanent Representative of the United States of America addressed to the Chairman of the Committee on the Peaceful Uses of Outer Space, Annex, 17 June 1966.

⑤ See UN Doc. A/AC. 105/C. 2/L. 71 and Corr. 1, Argentina: Draft Agreement on the Principles Governing Activities in the Use of the Natural Resources of the Moon and other Celestial Bodies, 23 June 1970, Preamble, para. 2.

⑥ See UN Doc. A/8391, Treaty Concerning the Moon: Letter dated 27 May 1971 from the Minister for Foreign Affairs of the Union of Soviet Socialist Republics addressed to the Secretary-General, Annex, 4 June 1971.

⑦ Ibid., Preamble.

2. 根据《联合国宪章》的原则，在月球上应禁止以任何形式使用武力或以武力相威胁，以及任何其他敌对行动或威胁采取此类行动。还应禁止使用月球进行与地球或空间物体有关的任何上述行动。

“第二条”：

1. 所有缔约国专为和平目的利用月球。

2. 各缔约国承诺不在月球轨道上携带核武器或任何其他种类的大规模毁灭性武器的物体，或在月球表面或其底土上安装此类武器。

3. 应禁止建立军事基地、设施和防御工事、试验任何类型的武器以及在月球上进行军事演习”①。

在法律小组委员会工作组范围内的进一步谈判中，讨论的提案包括美国在 1972 年提交的 18 份关于月球军事活动的工作文件：

“第一条”：（国际法，使用或威胁使用武力，自卫）

1. 条约缔约国应按照国际法，包括《联合国宪章》和其他现行条约，在月球和其他天体上开展活动。

2. 除根据《宪章》第五十一条行使单独或集体自卫的固有权利外，各缔约方应避免对月球和其他天体使用或威胁使用武力，或任何其他敌对行为或以敌对行为相威胁。缔约国不得利用月球或其他天体对地球、月球、宇宙飞行器、宇宙飞行器或人造外空物体的人员实施任何此类行为或从事任何此类威胁②。

“第二条”：（和平目的，核武器，军事禁例）

1. 所有缔约国均应专为和平目利用月球和其他天体。

2. 各缔约方不得在月球或其他天体周围或其周围的轨道上或其他轨道上或在此类天体上携带核武器或任何其他种类武器或安装大规模毁灭性物体或将前述武器放置在月球或其他天体上。

3. 应禁止在月球上建立军事基地、设施和防御工事、测试任何类型的武器以及在月球和其他天体上进行军事演习。不禁止军事人员用于科学研究或任何其他和平目

---

① Ibid.

② UN Doc. A/AC. 105/C. 2（XI）/WP. 1, Unites States: Working Paper, 11 April 1972, in: UN Doc. A/AC. 105/101, Report of the Legal Sub-committee on the Work of its Eleventh Session (10 April-5 May 1972), Annex I, Proposals and Other Documents Relating to Agenda Item 3 (Questions Relating to the Moon), 11 May 1972, p. 7.

的。也不得禁止以和平探索方式使用月球和其他天体所需的任何设备或设施”①。

从《月球协定》第三条的起草历史可以看出，其最终条款基于上述苏美的条约草案。可见两个航天强国非常关切月球和其他天体的军事化问题。在评价《月球协定》的谈判历史时，郑斌准确无误地总结到：“当多数其他代表团盛赞人类共同遗产概念的采纳时，苏联阵营更热衷于强调第三条月球和天体的去军事化的立场重申。事实上，对于超级大国来说，规制外层空间的政治和军事方面的重要性远远超过其经济方面。”②《月球协定》第三条的谈判历史表明了该条约旨在确保两个超级大国之间的军事竞赛不在月球和其他天体上重演③。

（二）评注

《月球协定》第三条规制在月球和其他天体上的军事活动。其规定明确指出，月球应专为和平目的而加以利用，月球上的军事人员只能为进行科学研究而存在。

1. “专为和平目的”一词

《月球协定》第三条所设定的义务比其他空间法的规定更加细致④。第三条第 1 款规定缔约国有义务遵守专为和平目的利用月球。这一义务也适用于太阳系内除地球以外的天体⑤，并适用于一个国家不论是由政府或非政府实体实施的任何本国活动，以及适用于《月球协定》缔约国加入的国际组织⑥。但是，“和平”一词可有不同解释，可被解释为“非侵略性的”，这意味着未必否定“军事的”，或是更近一步，解释为“非军事的”⑦。对“和平”一词的理解分歧同样可能会引起有关月球活动的争议。“专

① Ibid.

② Cheng, Bin, Studies in International Space Law, Clarendon Press, Oxford 1997, p. 362.

③ See Peterson, Mildred J., International Regimes for the Final Frontier, State University of New York Press, Albany 2005, p. 156.

④ See Hobe, Stephan, The Moon Agreement-Let’s Use the Chance!, Zeitschrift für Luft- und Weltraumrecht (59) 2010, p. 380.

⑤ Art. 1 para. 1 MOON specifies that the “provisions of this Agreement relating to the moon shall also apply to other celestial bodies within the solar system, other than the earth”.

⑥ Art. VI OST obliges States Parties to the Treaty to assure that the activities of their non-governmental entities or those of the international organizations to which they are Parties are “carried out in conformity with the provisions set forth in the present Treaty.” With regard to the activities of non-governmental entities, this obligation is contained again in Art. 14 para. 1 MOON.

⑦ On the interpretation of the term ‘peaceful’ see Schrogl, Kai-Uwe/Neumann, Julia, Article IV, in: Hobe, Stephan/Schmidt-Tedd, Bernhard/Schrogl, Kai-Uwe (eds.), Cologne Commentary on Space Law, Volume I, Heymanns, Cologne 2009, p. 82, mn. 44.

为和平目的”的表述一般被理解为提出了“完全非军事化”的要求[①]（即不得在月球和其他天体上进行军事活动）。实际上，这些措辞可以理解为禁止军事活动，否则如此严厉的措辞就成了空话。此外，《月球协定》第三条第 4 款关于军事人员的例外规定，也可理解为原则上应是全面去军事化的立场。

第三条是两条公认的国际法原则的结合，一个规定于《外空条约》第四条，另一个则源于《联合国宪章》第二条第 4 款。后者在《友好关系宣言》中得到了全面细化。根据《月球协定》第二条，该宣言适用于月球和其他天体。它是对《联合国宪章》现有原则的重大澄清，因此有着重要的分量。尽管其作为联合国大会决议而言，表面看并不意味着具有法律约束力[②]。因此，《月球协定》第三条在谈判中几乎没有经历什么讨论和争议[③]。

2. 使用武力或以武力相威胁、从事其他敌对行为或以敌对行为相威胁

根据《月球协定》第三条第 2 款，在月球上使用武力或以武力相威胁，或从事任何其他敌对行为或以敌对行为相威胁概在禁止之列。利用月球对地球、月球、宇宙飞行器、宇宙飞行器或人造外空物体的人员实施任何此类行为或从事任何此类威胁，也应同样禁止。《外空条约》虽然没有明确禁止在月球上使用武力或以武力相威胁。但第三条第 2 款根植于《联合国宪章》第二条第 4 款，即不得使用武力原则。它的解释有时会引起争论，尤其是将其与《联合国宪章》第五十一条中赋予的各国单独和集体的自卫权一并考虑时[④]。然而，禁止威胁或使用武力是国际法最基本的规则之一，从

① See Cheng, Bin, Studies in International Space Law, Clarendon Press, Oxford 1997, p. 366.

② See Rosenstock, Robert, The Declaration of Principles of international law Concerning Friendly Relations：A Survey, American Journal of International Law (65) 1971, pp. 714f.

③ The demilitarization was in the interest of both, the USA and the USSR. See Cheng, Bin, Studies in International Space Law, Clarendon Press, Oxford 1997, p. 362.

④ See Thomas, Frank, Who Killed Article 2 (4)? Or Changing Norms Governing of the Use of Force by States, The American Journal of International Law (64) 1970, pp. 809f.; and Thomas, Frank, What Happens Now? The United Nations After Iraq, The American Journal of International Law (97) 2003, pp. 607f.

其强制法的地位可见一斑①。所以它也适用于外层空间和天体②。因此，法国签署《月球协定》时宣称："法国认为，从协定致力实现的目标来看，与其说第三条第 2 款有关不得使用武力的规定是创设性的，不如说是一种重申，是对不得使用武力原则的重申，这是各国在国际关系中必须遵守的义务，一如《联合国宪章》规定的那样。"③

3. 携带核武器或其他大规模毁灭性武器的物体

第三条第 3 款提出了月球非武器化的要求④。它禁止在环绕月球的轨道上或飞向或飞绕月球的轨道上，放置核武器或任何其他种类的大规模毁灭性武器⑤。此外，不得在月球上使用此类武器。这项规定包含的内容比《外空条约》所禁止的范围更广，后者未在其第四条中提及在月球和其他天体上使用核武器或大规模毁灭性武器⑥。但是，与《外空条约》第四条类似，《月球协定》第三条第 3 款也没有明确禁止在月球的轨道和其他轨道上放置核武器和大规模毁灭性武器之外的武器，尽管如同《外空条约》第四条第 2 款，《月球协定》第三条第 4 款也禁止在月球上进行任何类型的武器试验。

4. 军事设施、武器试验、军事演习和军事人员

除了禁止武器试验，第三条第 4 款还禁止在月球和其他天体上建立军事基地、军

---

① See Evans, Malcolm D. , International Law, Oxford University Press, Oxford 2006, p. 591; Shaw, Malcolm N. , International Law, Cambridge University Press, Cambridge 2008, p. 1123; and Kadelbach, Stefan, Jus Cogens, Obligations Erga Omnes and Other Rules-The Identification of Fundamental Rules, in: Tomuschat, Christian/Thouvenin, Jean-Marc (eds.), The fundamental rules of the international legal order, Martinus Nijhoff Publishers, Leiden 2006, p. 32.

② Ribbelink, Olivier, Article Ⅲ, in: Hobe, Stephan/Schmidt-Tedd, Bernhard/Schrogl, Kai-Uwe (eds.), Cologne Commentary on Space Law, Volume I, Heymanns, Cologne 2009, p. 67, mn. 13.

③ United Nations Treaty Collection, Status of Treaties: Agreement Governing the Activities of States on the Moon and Other Celestial Bodies, Declarations and Reservations: Interpretative statement of France (upon signature), 29 January 1980 <http://treaties.un.org/pages/ViewDetails.aspx? src = TREATY&mtdsg _ no = XXIV-2&chapter = 24&lang=en> accessed 26 April 2019.

④ Pursuant to Art. 1 para. 1 MOON, reference to the Moon includes other celestial bodies.

⑤ On the notion of a nuclear weapon and other weapons of mass destruction see the comprehensive analysis in Schrogl, Kai-Uwe/Neumann, Julia, Article IV, in: Hobe, Stephan/Schmidt-Tedd, Bernhard/Schrogl, Kai-Uwe (eds.), Cologne Commentary on Space Law, Volume I, Heymanns, Cologne 2009, pp. 75-78, mn. 18-28.

⑥ In its advisory opinion on the legality of the threat or use of nuclear weapons, the ICJ generally found that in view of international humanitarian law a lawful use of nuclear weapons was hardly imaginable, while recognizing that it has not sufficient evidence of establishing with certainty whether such use would in any event be inadmissible. See Legality of the Threat of Use of Nuclear Weapons (Advisory Opinion) [1996] ICJ Rep. 226, para. 95.

事装置、防御工事以及进行军事演习，但它允许军事人员开展科学研究和和平的活动。然而，这并不意味着未被明文禁止的就在允许之列，因为《月球协定》第三条第1款的“专为和平目的”设定的是广泛而严格的去军事化标准。在此标准下，何为可为，何为不可为，要根据活动的目的和本质来判断，而非活动实施的形式。如前所述，“专为和平目的”的“公式”表征了月球和其他天体广泛而深远的去军事化，因此在月球上使用军事人员的活动必须既不是“侵略的”，也不是“军事的”。

总体来讲，第三条确立了有关月球探索利用的“专为和平”和免受威胁环境的法律规则，这是吸引月球活动所需财政投资的一个非常重要的因素。

五、第四条（人类的共同事情）

1. 月球的探索和利用应是全体人类的事情并应为一切国家谋福利，不问它们的经济或科学发展程度如何。应依照联合国宪章规定，充分注意今世与后代人类的利益、以及提高生活水平与促进经济和社会进步和发展的需要。

2. 缔约各国应遵循合作和互助原则从事一切有关探索和利用月球的活动。按照本协定进行的国际合作，应尽量扩大范围，并可在多边基础上、双边基础上或通过政府间国际组织进行。

（一）谈判和起草过程

《月球协定》第四条产生的基本义务在起草过程中的大多数草案中都有提出①，

① UN Doc. A/AC. 105/32, Draft Treaty Governing the Exploration of the Moon and Other Celestial Bodies: Letter dated 16 June 1966 from the Permanent Representative of the United States of America addressed to the Chairman of the Committee on the Peaceful Uses of Outer Space, Annex, 17 June 1966, Art. 3; UN Doc. A/8391, Treaty Concerning the Moon: Letter dated 27 May 1971 from the Minister for Foreign Affairs of the Union of Soviet Socialist Republics addressed to the Secretary-General, Annex, 4 June 1971, Art. Ⅲ; UN Doc. PUOS/C. 2/WG（XI）/15/Rev. 1, Draft Treaty Concerning the Moon: Text formulated by the Working Group, 4 May 1972, in: UN Doc. A/AC. 105/101, Report of the Legal Sub-Committee on the Work of its Eleventh Session (10 April-5 May 1972), 11 May 1972, para. 21, Art. Ⅳ para. 1 and 2; Working Paper Reflecting the Outcome of the Review at the Present Session of Working Paper WG. I（1978）/WP. 2 of 3 April 1978, in: UN Doc. A/AC. 105/240 Report of the Legal Sub-Committee on the Work of its Eighteenth Session (12 March-6 April 1979), Annex Ⅲ, Report of the Chairman of Working Group I, Appendix A, 10 April 1979, p. 4, Art. Ⅳ.

仅是措辞有所不同，而且并不总是作为单一的条款提出，而是分散在不同的条款中。

虽然自 1966 年以来就有三份草案和若干提案①，但联合国外空委法律小组委员会直到 1972 年才开始关于月球条约/协议的第一次讨论。随后成立的工作组提交了一份条约草案，该草案基本上使用了当前的措辞②。表述几乎是无争议的，除了“人类共同事情”一词，尤其是发展中国家更倾向于使用“人类共同遗产”这一措辞。该条的讨论与第十一条紧密相关，第十一条最终包含了人类共同遗产原则。《月球协定》第四条重复了《外空条约》第一条第 1 款的表述，“全人类共同事情”，来强调《外空条约》第一条第 1 款的权利和义务同样的适用于月球。

（二）评注

第四条首先提到了探索和利用月球和其他天体的自由，这些自由与外空条约第一条第 2 款类似，不论各国经济或科学发展的程度如何，都应为所有国家谋福利和利益。这一原则被《月球协定》第四条的合作原则所扩大。如此，国际社会愿意将这些自由权利也建立在《外空条约》所包含的相同原则之上。由此不会产生新的原则。

1. 探索自由

虽然第四条第 1 款没有具体提到，但人类共同事情条款的基本前提当然是探索和利用自由是有效存在的。这种自由意味着任何开展各自活动的国家都无须寻求其他国家的许可。它既可以探索——如发现是否可利用——也可以利用月球和其他天体。在外空和利用外空的活动都包含在《外空条约》第一条第 2 款所描述的自由之内③。

《月球协定》第四条通过共同利益条款所施加的限制也同样真实不虚。与《外空条约》一样，全人类共同事情条款旨在阻止任何国家垄断外空活动，并确保外层空间的探索和利用仍然是一个“全社会的努力”，以便全人类都能从这些活动中获益④。

引人注意的是，《月球协定》第四条第 1 款包含了另一项限制。根据该条，应适

① Jasentuliyana, Nandasiri/Lee Roy S. K. （eds.）, Manual of Space Law, Volume IV, Oceana Publications, New York 1981, p. 6.

② UN Doc. PUOS/C. 2/WG（XI）/15/Rev. 1, Draft Treaty Concerning the Moon：Text formulated by the Working Group, 4 May 1972, in：UN Doc. A/AC. 105/101, Report of the Legal Sub-Committee on the Work of its Eleventh Session（10 April-5 May 1972）, 11 May 1972, para. 21, Art. IV para. 1 and 2.

③ On this provision see Hobe, Stephan, Article I, in：Hobe, Stephan/Schmidt-Tedd, Bernhard/Schrogl, Kai-Uwe（eds.）, Cologne Commentary on Space Law, Volume I, Heymanns, Cologne 2009, pp. 34-43, mn. 34-70.

④ See ibid., pp. 36-41.

当顾及今世后代的利益以及顾及《联合国宪章》提及的提高生活水平的需要[①]。这些措辞源于苏联提交的草案，为空间立法引入了一个新的概念。[②] 代际公平的概念更具有呼吁的性质，可以说要求所有探索和利用都应与保护环境的需要相权衡，使下一代所继承的环境不会呈现比上一代面临的环境更糟糕的状态[③]。

这一重要的环保关注点，以及特别提到提高生活水平和经济及社会进步条件的必要性，表明《月球协定》承认需要探索和使用自由。这项规定要求探索和使用月球和其他天体的人应保护其环境以供子孙后代使用，扩大了《外空条约》第一条人类共同事情概念的范围[④]。除了禁止为了一个国家的利益而垄断这种勘探和使用，并注意保护环境外，这项规定还要求国际层面具有一定的社会意识，虽然没有明确用言语具体描述[⑤]。

2. 合作互助原则

第二款呼吁缔约国在加强基于双边或多边、特别是通过国际政府间组织的国际合作。本条款不涵盖跨国公司，即私人实体。这种呼吁国际合作的实际相关性必须在整体成本和全人类可得利益的语境下予以考量[⑥]。

---

① Art. 55 lit. (a) UN Charter sets forth that the United Nations shall promote "higher standards of living, full employment, and conditions of economic and social progress and development". The Members of the United Nations committed themselves to work to achieve these goals according to Art. 56 UN Charter.

② See UN Doc. A/8391, Treaty Concerning the Moon: Letter dated 27 May 1971 from the Minister for Foreign Affairs of the Union of Soviet Socialist Republics addressed to the Secretary-General, Annex, 4 June 1971.

③ On the concept of intergenerational equity see Brown-Weiss, Edith, Our rights and obligations to future generations for the environment, American Journal of International Law (84) 1990, pp. 198f.; and on principles of environmental law see Birnie, Patricia/Boyle, Alan/Redgwell, Catherine, International Law and The Environment, 3rd edn., Oxford University Press, New York 2009.

④ See Hobe, Stephan, The Moon Agreement-Let's Use the Chance!, Zeitschrift für Luft - und Weltraumrecht (59) 2010, pp. 377-378. On the province of all mankind concept see Hobe, Stephan, Article I, in: Hobe, Stephan/Schmidt-Tedd, Bernhard/Schrogl, Kai-Uwe (eds.), Cologne Commentary on Space Law, Volume I, Heymanns, Cologne 2009, pp. 34-43, mn. 34-70.

⑤ See von der Dunk, Frans G, The dark side of the Moon-The status of the Moon: public concepts and private enterprises, in: IISL, Proceedings of the 40th Colloquium on the Law of Outer Space, 6-10 October 1997 Turin (Italy), AIAA, 1998, p. 121.

⑥ Doyle, Stephen E., Using Extraterrestrial Resources under the Moon Agreement of 1979, Journal of Space Law (26) 1998, pp. 118ff.

六、第五条（任务信息/科学界）

1. 缔约国应在实际可行的范围内尽量将它们在探索和利用月球方面的活动告知联合国秘书长以及公众和国际科学界。每次飞往月球的任务的时间、目的、位置、轨道参数和期间的情报应在发射后立即公布，而关于每次任务的结果，包括科学结果在内的情报则应在完成任务时公布。如果一次飞行任务的期间超过六十天，应将任务进行情况的情报，包括科学结果在内，每隔三十天公布一次。如飞行任务超过六个月，则在六个月以后，只须将这方面的重要补充情报予以公布。

2. 如一个缔约国获知另一缔约国计划同时在月球上的同一区域或环绕月球的同一轨道或飞向或飞绕月球的同一轨道进行活动时，应立即将其自己进行活动的时间和计划通知该缔约国。

3. 缔约各国在进行本协定所规定的活动时，应将其在外层空间，包括月球在内所发现的可能危及人类生命或健康的任何现象以及任何有机生命迹象，通知联合国秘书长、公众和国际科学界。

（一）谈判和起草过程

阿根廷草案[①]和苏联 1972 年提案都没有提到向国际社会、联合国秘书长以及其他缔约国提供信息的一般性义务[②]。只有在美国 1972 年的提案中第三条第 5 到 7 款[③]，包含了相应的义务。工作组在 1973 年达成共识的其中一个条款非常接近最终《月球协定》第五条的表述[④]。

① See UN Doc. A/AC. 105/C. 2/L. 71 and Corr. 1, Argentina: Draft Agreement on the Principles Governing Activities in the Use of the Natural Resources of the Moon and other Celestial Bodies, 23 June 1970.

② See UN Doc. A/AC. 105/101, Report of the Legal Sub-Committee on the Work of its Eleventh Session (10 April-5 May 1972), Annex I, Proposals and Other Documents Relating to Agenda Item 3, 11 May 1972, p. 2.

③ See UN Doc. A/AC. 105/C. 2 (XI) /WP. 3, United States of America: Working Paper, 11 April 1972, in: UN Doc. A/AC. 105/101, Report of the Legal Sub-Committee on the Work of its Eleventh Session (10 April-5 May 1972), Annex I, Proposals and Other Documents Relating to Agenda Item 3 (Questions relating to the Moon), 11 May 1972, pp. 8f.

④ It is the text of Art. IV para. 3 which is reproduced in UN Doc. A/AC. 105/115, Report of the Legal Sub-Committee on the Work of its Twelfth Session (26 March-20 April 1973), 27 April 1973, para. 17.

美国和苏联之间的另一个分歧点是有关月球任务信息的提供时间问题。前者希望在每次发射之前提供相关信息，后者则不同意在任务开始前承担任何披露信息的义务[①]。最终，苏联意见占了上风，按照《月球协定》第五条第1款的规定，应当在发射后尽快给出关于时间、目的、位置、轨道参数和期间的信息。

（二）评注

第五条规定了缔约国对其他缔约国和国际空间社会所承担的相关责任。该条款包含提供信息的各种职责。缔约国有责任向联合国秘书长以及公众和科学界提供信息。“探索和利用月球的相关活动的信息必须在实际可行的范围内尽量”予以通知。这类信息应包含目的、位置、轨道参数和期间。

此外，如一个缔约国获知另一缔约国计划同时在月球上的同一区域或环绕月球的同一轨道或飞向或飞绕月球的同一轨道进行活动时，则该缔约国有义务将其活动情况通知该缔约国。该条明确提到“同时活动”，目的是避免在月球上的活动的多个国家相互干扰。该条款需要与《月球协定》第十五条和《外空条约》第九条一并考量。

此外，还有一项特别职责，即将任何可能危及正在执行具体任务的人类生命的现象，通知联合国秘书长以及一般公众。

第5条规定的内容是对各国已承担的《外空条约》第十一条所规定义务的细化。本条规定中各种告知义务更加明确，但并未创设新的义务。[②] 唯一超出了现有义务范围的规定是第五条第3款，即缔约国有义务将任何危害人类生命或健康的现象以及外层空间有机生命的任何迹象通知秘书长。《外空条约》第五条第3款侧重于保护宇航员，因为它要求各国告知宇航员生命和健康危险，而不包括告知有机生命迹象的义务。

七、第六条（科学考察/标本/矿产）

1. 所有缔约国都享有不受任何种类的歧视，在平等基础上，并按照国际法的规定在月球上从事科学研究的自由。

---

① See Cheng, Bin, Studies in International Space Law, Clarendon Press, Oxford 1997, p. 360.

② See for a similar opinion, Doyle, Stephen E., Using Extraterrestrial Resources under the Moon Agreement of 1979, Journal of Space Law (26) 1998, p. 119.

2. 缔约国为促进本协定各项规定的实施而进行科学研究时，应有权在月球上采集并移走矿物和其他物质的标本。发动采集此类标本的缔约国可保留其处置权，并可为科学目的而使用这些标本。缔约国应顾及是否将此类标本的一部分供给感兴趣的其他缔约国和国际科学界作科学研究之用。缔约国在进行科学研究时，也可使用适当数量的月球矿物和其他物质以支援它们的任务。

3. 缔约国同意于派遣人员前往月球或在其上建立装置时，在实际可行的范围内宜尽量交换科学和其他人员。

（一）谈判和起草过程

该条阐述了科学调查的自由，使其成为除一般的探索和利用自由之外一种特殊的自由。第 2 款对有关收集标本的科学调查的范围作了详细界定，这是一项特别具有创新性的规定。它曾包含在美国早期的工作文件中，其原有表述为："缔约国在开展科学调查时，可以使用适当数量的月球和其他天体资源，以便利协定其他条文的实施，无论是支持在月球或其他天体进行科学调查，或取走此类资源移至地球进行分析，或在外空中或月球和其他天体上进行分析①。

保加利亚、瑞典、英国和澳大利亚也提出了关于使用样品的建议②。英国和瑞典共同提议"月球和其他天体的科学调查结果应向国际社会免费提供"③。然而这个建议未被采纳。

---

① UN Doc. A/AC. 105/C. 2（XI）/WP. 12, United States of America：Working Paper, 13 April 1972, in：UN Doc. A/AC. 105/101, Report of the Legal Sub-Committee on the Work of its Eleventh Session（10 April-5 May 1972）, Annex I, Proposals and Other Documents Relating to Agenda Item 3（Questions Relating to the Moon）, 11 May 1972.

② See UN Doc. A/AC. 105/C. 2（XI）/WP. 10, Sweden and United Kingdom：Working Paper, 12 April 1972；UN Doc. A/AC. 105/C. 2（XI）/WP. 10/Rev. 1, Sweden and United Kingdom：revised Working Paper, 13 April 1972；UN Doc. A/AC. 105/C. 2（XI）/WP. 11, Australia：Working Paper, 13 April 1972；UN Doc. A/AC. 105/C. 2（XI）/WP. 13, Australia：Working Paper, 13 April 1972；and UN Doc. A/AC. 105/C. 2（XI）Working Paper 25, Bulgaria：Working Paper, 27 April 1972. All these Working Papers are reproduced in：UN Doc. A/AC. 105/101, Report of the Legal Sub-Committee on the Work of its Eleventh Session（10 April-5 May 1972）, Annex I, Proposals and Other Documents Relating to Agenda Item 3（Questions Relating to the Moon）, 11 May 1972.

③ UN Doc. A/AC. 105/C. 2（XI）/WP. 10, Sweden and United Kingdom：Working Paper, 12 April 1972, in：UN Doc. A/AC. 105/101 Report of the Legal Sub-Committee on the Work of its Eleventh Session（10 April-5 May 1972）, Annex I, Proposals and Other Documents Relating to Agenda Item 3（Questions Relating to the Moon）, 11 May 1972.

第3款关于交换科研人员和其他人员的意愿的提议源自美国[①]。

（二）评注

第六条概述了缔约国基于科学原因探索和利用月球及其他天体时的权利义务范围和程度。

1. 科学调查的自由

《月球协定》第六条第1款是对《外空条约》第一条第2款的复述，它重申根据国际法，各缔约国享有在平等和不受任何歧视的基础上进行科学调查的自由[②]。

2. 采集并移走矿物和其他物质的标本

第六条第2款与《外空条约》相比，有重大区别，它允许移走和采集月球标本。根据该款规定，各国、各国政府机构和在国家监管下的私人实体可以为科学目的采集和移走月球材料和其他物质，并将其用于支援它们的空间任务[③]。此时应考虑该权利是否也存在于《外空条约》之中，这很重要。而相关的《外空条约》第二条的规定却相当模糊，其虽明确禁止在外层空间或天体上征用任何领土，但对标本采集只字未提。由于《月球协定》的明确许可，并根据后法优于前法原则，鼓励投资，以便发展用于确定月球资源开发可行性的各项能力[④]。

第六条第2款允许对资源（标本）的采集和处置，并不意味允许据为己有和赋予

① See UN Doc. A/AC. 105/C. 2（XI）/WP. 3, United States of America: Working Paper, 11 April 1972, in: UN Doc. A/AC. 105/101, Report of the Legal Sub-Committee on the Work of its Eleventh Session (10 April-5 May 1972), Annex I, Proposals and Other Documents Relating to Agenda Item 3 (Questions Relating to the Moon), 11 May 1972.

② See Tucker, Cody, How Current International Law addresses Rights to Use and Exploit Lunar Resources, Annals of Air and Space Law (XXXIV) 2009, p. 604.

③ Doyle, Stephen E., Using Extraterrestrial Resources under the Moon Agreement of 1979, Journal of Space Law (26) 1998, p. 120; Cheng, Bin, Studies in International Space Law, Clarendon Press, Oxford 1997, p. 375; and Diederiks-Verschoor, I. H. Philepina/Kopal, Vladimir, An Introduction to Space Law, 3rd rev. edn., Kluwer Law International, The Netherlands 2008, p. 49.

④ Jakhu, Ram, Twenty Years of the Moon Agreement: Space Law Challenges for Returning to the Moon, Zeitschrift für Luft - und Weltraumrecht (54) 2005, p. 257.

转让出售的权利。不应忽略缔约国[1]使用月球材料和其他物质时所应受的限制。本条所赋予的采集使用月球资源的权利仅限于科学和探索目的。至于移走、使用和开发月球物质的权利——可能出于商业原因，例如一个私人实体在缔约国授权下开展相关活动——则可由另一法律框架调整，即《月球协定》第十一条，以及根据第十一条“一俟月球自然资源的开发即将可行时”建立的国际制度。

而且，各国可使用适当数量的月球材料和其他物质以支援它们的任务。虽然“适当数量”具有主观性，但可以在科学语境下加以界定[2]。此外，该款明确了关于使用的授权。材料使用的程度范围由任务定义或情况以及目的和目标来确定[3]。

3. 交换科学和其他人员的意愿

第 3 款为科学和其他人员的交换铺平了道路。但是该款并未设定法律义务，仅是指向这种交换的意愿和需求[4]。

八、第七条（环境/放射性物质）

1. 缔约国在探索和利用月球时，应采取措施，防止月球环境的现有平衡遭到破坏，不论这种破坏是由于在月球环境中导致不利变化，还是由于引入环境外物质使其环境受到有害污染，或由于其他方式而产生。缔约国也应采取措施防止地球环境由于引入地球外物质或由于其他方式而受到有害影响。

2. 缔约国应将它们按照本条第一款所采取的措施通知联合国秘书长，并应尽一切可能预先将它们在月球上放置的一切放射性物质以及放置的目的通知秘书长。

---

① Hofmann, Mahulena, Recent Plans to Exploit the Moon Resources Under International Law, in: IISL Proceedings of the 47th Colloquium on the Law of Outer Space, 4-8 October 2004 Vancouver (Canada), AIAA, 2005, p. 427; Tronchetti, Fabio, The exploitation of natural resources of the Moon and other celestial bodies: a proposal for a legal regime, Martinus Nijhoff/Brill Publishers, Leiden 2009, pp. 43, 225-226; and Gal, Gyula, Acquisition of Property in the Legal Regime of Celestial Bodies, in: IISL Proceedings of the 39th Colloquium on the Law of Outer Space, 7-11 October 1996 Beijing (China), AIAA, 1997, p. 47.

② See Lochan, Rajeev/Gopalakrishan, V. , Lunar Exploration-The Road Ahead, in: IISL Proceedings of the 50th Colloquium on the Law of Outer Space, 24-28 September 2007 Hyderabad (India), AIAA, 2008, pp. 62f.

③ See Doyle, Stephen E. , Using Extraterrestrial Resources under the Moon Agreement of 1979, Journal of Space Law (26) 1998, pp. 119f.

④ See Matte, Nicolas M. , Treaty Relating to the Moon, in: Jasentuliyana, Nandasiri/Lee, Roy S. K. (eds.), Manual on Space Law Volume I, Oceana, New York 1979, p. 261.

3. 缔约国应就月球上具有特殊科学重要性的地区向其他缔约国和秘书长提出报告，以便在不损害其他缔约国权利的前提下，考虑将这些地区指定为国际科学保护区，并经与联合国各主管机构协商后，对这些地区商定特别保护办法。

（一）谈判和起草过程

《月球协定》的国际谈判，包括第七条，恰逢被称之为“国际环境法运动”的开端。自 1972 年 6 月 16 日《联合国人类环境会议宣言》（以下简称 1972 年《斯德哥尔摩宣言》）[①] 之后的几十年里，发展了大量的国际环境法，该宣言是有关保护（地球）环境基本国际原则的第一份重要声明。

与此同时，阿波罗载人任务的成功，以及对带回地球的月球岩石样本的科学研究，为人们带来了一种期待，即开发（例如采矿）月球和其他（近地）天体的自然资源并非天方夜谭。联合国大会鼓励缔结一项协议，以规定“治理使用月球和其他天体的所有自然资源和物质的活动的特别规则”[②]。

《月球协定》的讨论考虑了如何纳入与开采活动环境影响有关的问题。保护月球和其他天体环境已被列为“人类共同遗产”概念[③]的一个重要基本要素，这一概念明确适用于月球和其他天体的自然资源[④]。

从意欲建立的国际制度的目的上，也可见一斑。《月球协定》规定“要建立的国际制度”的一个具体目标便是“合理管理”月球和其他天体的自然资源。[⑤]

1971 年 6 月，苏联条约草案首次提交给联合国大会[⑥]，然后提交法律小组委员会

---

① UN Doc. A/CONF. 48/14/Rev. 1, Report of the United Nations Conference on the Human Environment, Stockholm 5-16 June 1972, Declaration of the United Nations Conference on the Human Environment, 16 June 1972, pp. 3-5; Stockholm Declaration of the United Nations Conference on the Human Environment of 16 June 1972, 11 ILM 1416.

② UNGA Res. 2779（XXVI）Preparation of an international treaty concerning the Moon, 29 November 1971, Preamble para. 7.

③ See Tuerk, Helmut, The Negotiation of the “Moon Agreement”, in: IISL-ECSL, Proceedings of the Space Law Symposium, ‘30th Anniversary of the “Moon Agreement”: Retrospect and Prospects’, 48th Session of the UNCOPUOS Legal Subcommittee, 23 March 2009 Vienna（Austria）, 2010, pp. 491, 499.

④ See Art. 11 para. 1 MOON.

⑤ See Art. 11, para. 7 lit.（b）MOON.

⑥ UN Doc. A/8391, Treaty Concerning the Moon: Letter dated 27 May 1971 from the Minister for Foreign Affairs of the Union of Soviet Socialist Republics addressed to the Secretary-General, Annex, 4 June 1971.

审议，其规定保护月球环境的第四条内容是：

1. 各缔约国应以合理方式探索和利用月球，避免破坏月球环境的现有平衡。

2. 各缔约国在探索和利用月球时，应防止由于引入星外物质而使月球环境发生不利变化和受到污染。必要时，有关缔约国应进行协商①。

联合国外空委法律小组委员会讨论提出了后续版本，包括披露和报告的要求，最后在 1973 年达成一致意见②。经过一些微小修改之后，最终成为《月球协定》的第七条。

（二）评注

《月球协定》的定位之一便是“明确和发展”之前四项联合国外空条约的条款③。第 7 条即具备该特点，尤其是针对《外空条约》中与外空环境相关的条款。

《外空条约》第九条特别提到了探索月球和其他天体的相关义务，即“避免使其遭受有害污染，以及避免由于引入地球以外物质而使地球环境发生不利变化”④，但国际空间法整体上并没有提供关于保护包括月球和其他天体在内的外空环境的一个全面的法律框架⑤。但是仍需谨记除了联合国外空系列条约之外，还有一些与外空环境有关的其他（非约束性的）国际文件，包括那些关于所谓“行星保护”的文件，特别是空间研究委员会发布的文件⑥。

《外空条约》第九条还要求缔约国“在必要时”为了以上目的而“采取适当措施”。

---

① Ibid.

② For details of the different drafts considered at various stages during the negotiation process by the Legal Sub-Committee of UNCOPUOS see Tennen, Leslie, Evolution of the Planetary Protection Policy: Conflict of Science and Jurisprudence?, in: IISL Proceedings of the 45th Colloquium on the Law of Outer Space, 10-19 October 2002 Houston (Texas), AIAA, 2003, pp. 466, 470f.

③ See Preamble para. 7 MOON.

④ For a general discussion of the legal regulation relating to the environment of outer space, see Viikari, Lotta, The Environmental Element in Space Law: Assessing the Present and Charting the Future, Martinus Nijohff Publishers, Leiden 2008.

⑤ Art. IX OST.

⑥ See Committee on Space Research (COSPAR) Planetary Protection Policy (adopted 20 October 2002, amended 24 March 2005) <http://cosparhq. cnes. fr/Scistr/Pppolicy. htm> accessed 26 April 2019. The International Academy of Astronautics (IAA) in 2010 published a study on the protection of the environment of celestial bodies which among others includes a legal appraisal of planetary protection. See Hofmann, Mahulena/Williamson, Mark/Rettberg, Petra (eds.), Protecting the Environment of Celestial Bodies, International Academy of Astronautics (IAA), Paris 2010, pp. 55-67.

《月球协定》调整“开发月球以及其他天体自然资源”的活动[1]，第七条旨在强调这些活动的后果。开发行为一旦最终付诸实施，几乎必定会对它们的自然环境造成影响。

《月球协定》第七条一方面确认了与《外空条约》第九条关于正反向【译者注：去时污染外空、回来污染地球】污染的原则[2]，另一方面又对外空活动环境影响行为规定了更多和更具体的义务，《月球协定》对《外空条约》的很多条款都是如此处理的。

1. 正反向污染原则

《月球协定》第七条第1款首先规定缔约国有义务在探索利用月球和其他天体时“采取措施防止破坏其现有平衡”。必须执行这些措施以避免正反向污染，和避免由于其他任何活动（或其他任何形式）造成月球和其他天体环境的“不利变化”。

因此，第七条第1款规定的义务非常广泛。乍看起来，这些规定似乎很全面。

缔约国负有积极义务，对可能造成环境损害的多个方面“采取措施”，其范围超过了《外空条约》第九条，然而，对于这些措施应采取的形式，并未说明。

此外，条文中没有直接明确这些措施是否应以“主观”方式（即有关缔约国认为适当）或“客观”方式（即为避免这种环境损害而实际必要的方式）确定，尽管鉴于该条文的广度，后者更有可能发生。与《外空条约》第九条（要求缔约国“采取适当措施”）不同，形容词“适当”没有包含在内。

实际上，任何对月球和其他天体自然资源的开发都将包括一个勘察和提取过程，并最终将这些自然资源永久地从其原位移走。一旦这些自然资源被提取和移走，它们很可能会被加工或以某种方式使用，从而不可逆转地改变它们的自然形态。

因此，对其自然资源的开发将不可避免地改变月球或相关天体环境的现有平衡。基于此种认识，联合国外空委在其提交联合国大会的报告中明确表达，《月球协定》第七条并非禁止月球和其他天体的开发活动，而是旨在保护其现有的环境平衡[3]。

---

① See Preamble para. 5 MOON.

② See, e. g. , Art. 4 MOON containing the province of all mankind clause.

③ See, Tennen, Leslie, Evolution of the Planetary Protection Policy: Conflict of Science and Jurisprudence?, in: IISL Proceedings of the 45th Colloquium on the Law of Outer Space, 10-19 October 2002 Houston (Texas), AIAA, 2003, pp. 466, 471 and the corresponding footnotes.

如何才算是“破坏”现有平衡，条文未提及。然而，需谨记《月球协定》的目标和宗旨[①]，即规制月球和其他天体自然资源的开发，由此，“破坏”并不是指环境平衡的任何变化，即便是永久性变化，而仅指对该环境具有负面影响和可能导致环境的不稳定性。这可从“不利的”（环境变化）、“有害的”（污染）等限定词的使用上得到印证，这些限定词都指向不能被接受的破坏平衡的方式。

虽然何为“不利的”并未被界定（《外空条约》第九条也没界定），但它意味着一种消极的和破坏性的环境变化。它使如下成为可能，即一些环境变化也许不会被认为是不利的，因为它们不会危及现有环境平衡。

但是，这给评估某种行动是否符合第 7 条所要求的标准带来了困难。如前所述，任何与开发月球和其他天体自然资源有关的活动都会“改变”（更改）它们的自然环境，且很可能是不可逆转的。

例如，2009 年 10 月 9 日，为了确定月球是否以及在多大程度上可能含有水的沉积物，以便将来进行勘探，由美国宇航局发射的作为“月球环形山观测和遥感卫星（LCROSS）”计划一部分的阿特拉斯 V 型火箭，其载有的探测器的上面级故意猛烈撞击月球南极的坎布斯撞击坑，产生大约 350 公吨碎片，并升至空中两公里处[②]。

目前尚不清楚上述蓄意行为会对环境造成什么样的长期影响，以及这些行为是否可被认为是第七条第 1 款所说的“不利”变化[③]。虽然 LCROSS 项目的结果可能具有科学价值，并可能有助于规划和实施未来对月球的探索和利用，但它对月球自然环境的影响显然是永久性和不可逆转的。第七条的焦点是关于开发活动对环境的不良影响，因此这些活动可能产生的积极利益与决定其是否违反禁止性规定并无关系。

要求采取措施避免月球和其他天体遭受“有害污染”的义务类似于《外空条约》第九条的规定。与上述不利变化的概念一样，对于什么构成“有害污染”也没有定

---

① SeeArt. 31 para. 1 VCLT, which also reflects customary international law, see e. g. Territorial Dispute（Libyan Arab Jamahiriya v. Chad）（Judgment）[1994] ICJ Rep. 6, para. 41; Maritime Delimitation and Territorial Questions（Qatar v. Bahrain）（Judgment）[1995] ICJ Rep. 6, para. 33; and Legal Consequences of the Construction of a Wall in the Occupied Palestinian Territory（Advisory Opinion）[2004] ICJ Rep. 136, para. 94.

② See Freeland, Steven, Fly Me to the Moon: How Will International Law Cope with Commercial Space Tourism?, Melbourne Journal of International Law（11）2010, p. 90.

③ Of course, the United States is not a State Party to the MOON. However, the LCROSS example is illustrative of the difficulties that may emerge in attempting to apply the obligations under Art. 7.

义。有时这被称为“广义概念”①，但任何不确定性都会使其在特定情况的应用变得更加困难。

然而，该条款指出，这种污染可能“通过引入外界环境物质”而产生，乍一看，感觉是任何此类物质引入月球和其他天体的环境都将被视为“有害”。这可能与《月球协定》更为高远的目标不一致，因为一些外界环境物质在开发过程中是必需的（比如引爆性物质）。

第七条第1款重申了《外空条约》第九条对避免通过“引入地球以外物质”造成对地球环境有害或不利影响的规定。然而，这并不是试图禁止将天体标本②，或是最终具有商业性质的月球和其他天体的自然资源带回地球。

如上所述，不仅具体提到的各种活动需要进一步讨论，而且这种“无所不包”的措辞方式实则意味着任何形式导致的破坏都是不被允许的。然而，这也必须按照上述讨论的对“破坏”的不同解释来理解。

2. 通知义务：根据第1款采取的措施以及放射性材料的放置

外空国际规则设定的一般性义务之一即缔约国向联合国（秘书长）通知其外空活动。联合国外空系列条约中的确贯穿着有关信息的强制性条款【译者注：不同意该观点】③。

《月球协定》第七条第2款重申了这一义务，即缔约国按照第七条第1款的要求采取措施，并“尽一切可能”预先通知在月球和其他天体上放置的“放射性物质”以及放置的目的。

因此这一条款已经考虑到，在某些情况下，缔约国可以合法地放置这些材料。目

---

① See Marchisio, Sergio, Article IX, in: Hobe, Stephan/Schmidt-Tedd, Bernhard/Schrogl, Kai-Uwe (eds.), Cologne Commentary on Space Law, Volume I, Heymanns, Cologne 2009, p. 176, mn. 29.

② See also Art. 6 para. 2 MOON. State practice appears to support this general view-e. g. in June 2010, the Japanese Hayabusa probe returned to earth, landing in Australia, with samples recovered from the Itokawa asteroid after a 600 million kilometer round journey. Australia (although not Japan) is a State Party to the MOON and did not object to this, in fact playing an active role in the Hayabusa mission and authorizing the return of the probe: for further details, see Freeland, Steven, Sensing a Change? The re-launch of Australia's Space Policy and Some Possible Legal Implications, Journal of Space Law (36) 2010, p. 381.

③ See e. g. Art. V and XI OST; Art. 1 lit. (b), Art. 2, 3 and 5 para. 1 ARRA; Art. II para. 1, IV para. 1 and 3, and Art. V REG; Art. 5 para. 1 and 3, Art. 7 para. 2 and 3, Art. 9 para. 1, Art. 11 para. 6, Art. 12 para. 3, Art. 13, 15 para. 2 MOON.

前尚不清楚这些情况可能是什么，可无论如何，放置此类材料仍可能构成对月球或天体环境的有害污染，从而违反第七条第 1 款，因此需要进行个案分析。

虽然根据第七条第 1 款向联合国秘书长通知其采取措施的义务是绝对的义务（shall），但谈及有关放射性物质放置的预先通知义务却仅要求“尽一切可能”。这并不奇怪，因为这些信息可能涉及缔约国核能力的各个方面，通常被视为国家安全问题。

虽然此类措辞【译者注：指代不明，是指“尽一切可能”还是“通知义务”？结合 126，似乎是前者】未出现在其他国际空间法中，但一般来说，关于缔约国公开披露其探索利用外空信息的义务，会以类似的形式被提及①。

这种限定词赋予缔约国重要的自由裁量权，来决定何时以及在何种程度上提供信息。虽然不确定是在客观还是主观的基础上确定这种“可行性”，但联合国外空系列条约的缔约国有义务根据国际法的基本原则，诚信地履行其条约所规定的义务（条约必须遵守原则）。②。

所以，缔约国对此类信息的提供有积极履行的义务，而不能无视这项义务。

3. 具有特殊科学利益的领域：国际科学保护区

第七条第 3 款格外顾及了月球和其他天体的特定区域，最终可能被指定为国际科学保护区，并在未来得到更全面的保护。这一过程的进展速度取决于各缔约国之间（也包括联合国）信息交流的程度，而且这种指定要有“不损害其他缔约国权利”的考量③。

因此，此类指定更可能仅通过合作实现，这样每一个缔约国都有机会评估自己的权利可能受到的影响，并提出相应主张。

虽然向其他缔约国和联合国秘书长报告这些区域的义务是强制性的（shall），但没有强制性义务（may）予以考虑和最终决定这样的指定。这再次强调了这种考虑应具有合作性质。

---

① See e. g. Art. XI OST（‘to the greatest extent feasible and practicable’）; Art. IV para. 3 REG（‘to the greatest extent feasible and as soon as practicable’）and Art. VI REG（‘to the greatest extent feasible’）; Art. 5 para. 1 MOON（‘to the greatest extent feasible and practicable’）and Art. 11 para. 6 MOON（‘to the greatest extent feasible and practicable’）.

② See e. g. Case concerning rights of nationals of the United States in Morocco,（France v. United States of America）(Judgment) [1952] ICJ Rep. 176, 212; and Art. 26 VCLT.

③ Art. 7 para. 3 MOON.

目前尚无建立上述区域的具体程序。任何有关安排“应与联合国主管机构协商达成协议”①。尽管联合国外空委在这方面起着很大作用，但并未确切说明到底哪个机构具备“资格”。

第七条的前两款规定是对月球和其他天体开发活动环境问题的原则性规定。至于指定“国际科学保护区”并非受环境保护因素的驱使，而是基于特殊区域是否有“特殊的科学利益”。

因此可推测，这类区域的指定不是由环境关切或月球和其他天体环境的“固有价值”② 来决定的。

此外，尚不清楚科学利益是否必然延伸到所谓的“历史意义”。在这个方面，第七条第 3 款并非是指向最终“外空遗产”条约的前置程序，“外空遗产”条约则不仅着眼于保护具有科学用途的重要区域，还保护可能具有重要历史意义的区域③。

九、第八条（探索利用/磋商）

1. 缔约国可在月球的表面或表面之下的任何地点进行其探索和利用的活动，但须遵守本条约的其他规定。

2. 为此目的，缔约国特别可以：

（1）在月球上降落及从月球发射外空物体；

（2）将它们的人员、外空运载器、装备、设施、站所和装置放置在月球的表面或表面之下的任何地点。人员、外空运载器、装备、设施、站所和装置可在月球表面或表面之下自由移动或自由被移动。

3. 缔约国依据本条第 1 款和第 2 款进行的活动不应妨碍其他缔约国在月球上的活动。发生此种妨碍时有关缔约各国应依照第十五条第 2 款和第 3 款规定进行协商。

---

① Ibid.

② Bohlmann, Ulrike M., *Planetary Protection in Public International Law*, in: IISL Proceedings of the 46th Colloquium on the Law of Outer Space, 29 September-3 October 2003 Bremen (Germany), AIAA, 2004, pp. 18, 21.

③ For further reading on this issue, see Rogers, Thomas F., *Safeguarding Tranquility Base: Why the Earth's Moon Base Should Become a World Heritage Site*, Space Policy (20) 2004, pp. 5f.

（一）谈判和起草过程

第八条的内容是在1971年苏联草案中首次提出的①，在此后工作组的各个草案中都被采纳，没有作出任何显著更改②。当时的草案有些仅指月球，而有些除了月球还包含了其他天体，反映了当时关于《月球协定》整体适用范围的普遍讨论。

（二）评注

开发月球和其他天体自然资源必然要求从事此类活动的缔约国应被允许进入和离开（使用的术语是“发射”）月球或相关天体，并被允许使用适当人员和设备从事此类活动。

第八条规定，缔约国被允许实施促进开发活动的必要职能，尽管这总体上应受“自由”原则的调整，自由原则亦包含不得妨碍其他缔约国活动之意。

1. 在月球表面或表面之下进行的活动

该条承认，各缔约国为科学研究进行的探索利用月球包括在月球表面和表面以下的“提取”。

这些活动都受到《月球协定》相关限制的规制，例如，有关环境关切③和实施人类共同遗产原则的规定④。

在《月球协定》的其他部分，“表面之下（below the surface）”被表述为月球“表面下层（subsurface）”⑤，但结合其上下文语境可知，这些表述没有明显差别。

---

① UN Doc. A/8391, Treaty Concerning the Moon: Letter dated 27 May 1971 from the Minister for Foreign Affairs of the Union of Soviet Socialist Republics addressed to the Secretary-General, Annex, 4 June 1971, Art. V.

② UN Doc. PUOS/C.2/WG (XI) /15/Rev. 1, Draft Treaty Concerning the Moon: Text formulated by the Working Group, 4 May 1972, in: UN Doc. A/AC. 105/101, Report of the Legal Sub-Committee on the Work of its Eleventh Session (10 April-5 May 1972), 11 May 1972, para. 21, Art Ⅶ; Working Paper submitted by Bulgaria-Draft Treaty Relating to the Moon, 27 March 1973, in: UN Doc. A/AC. 105/115, Report of the Legal Sub-Committee on the Work of its Twelfth Session (26 March-20 April 1973), Annex I, Documents Relating to Agenda Item 2 (Draft Treaty Relating to the Moon), 27 April 1973, p. 11, Art. Ⅶ; UN Doc. WG. I (1978) /WP. 2 Austria: Working Paper, Agreement Governing the Activities of States on the Moon and other Celestial Bodies, 3 April 1978, in: UN Doc. A/AC. 105/218 Report of the Legal Sub-Committee on the Work of its Seventeenth Session (13 March-7 April 1978) 13 April 1978, Annex I, Report of the Chairman of Working Group I, Appendix, p. 2, Art. Ⅷ.

③ See e. g. Art. 4 and 7 MOON.

④ Art. 11 MOON.

⑤ Art. 11 para. 3 MOON.

2. 特许之行为

（1）空间物体降落在月球上和从月球发射

第八条第2款第（1）项强调了《外空条约》第一条所规定的“自由”原则，确认各缔约国为了探索利用的目的，可将其空间物体降落在月球和其他天体上，也可从月球和其他天体上发射空间物体。该条明确授权可从月球和其他天体上发射，这是《外空条约》起草时无从考虑的①。

第八条没有定义“空间物体”，其在本条中的含义一般来讲可在其他联合国外空条约空间物体的定义中找到②，但众所周知，这不当然意味着空间物体的应有或可有的范围是十分清楚的。不管怎样，“空间物体”一词应该被广义理解为一切由人类发射入外空的物体，包括从月球和其他天体上发射的物体③。

空间物体只能是指携带有效载荷的飞行器（包括运载工具），在缔约国操作控制下，降落在月球和其他天体上或从月球和其他天体上发射。因此，它不包括那些只是设计为最终仅在月球或相关天体表面上或下方使用，但自身却不能作为单独空间物体“发射”的有效载荷。但该条款引言部分明确指出，这条不仅仅限于携带其他空间物体的空间物体（其用词是“尤其是”）。因此，本条没有明确禁止被另一个空间物体携带的有效载荷的登陆或发射。这样的结论与《登记条约》的登记义务也是一致的。

（2）人员、外空运载器、装备、设施、站所和装置在月球表面或表面之下的部署和放置

《外空条约》禁止在月球和其他天体上建立“军事基地、军事设施和军事工事”④。但是，它确实考虑到了人员的部署问题（为了科学或其他和平目的），不论是明示的军事人员，或暗示的非军事人员。此外，装备、设施可为和平探索月球及和其他天体而做必要的使用⑤。《月球协定》第三条第4款重申了这些原则。

---

① See Griffin, Nancy L., *Americans and the Moon Treaty*, Journal of Air Law and Commerce (46) 1981, pp. 729, 741.

② See Art. 1 lit. (d) LIAB.

③ See Kerrest, Armel/Smith, Jane, *Article* Ⅷ, in: Hobe, Stephan/Schmidt-Tedd, Bernhard/Schrogl, Kai-Uwe (eds.), Cologne Commentary on Space Law, Volume I, Heymanns, Cologne 2009, p. 140, mn. 51.

④ Art. IV OST.

⑤ Art. IV OST.

此外，《外空条约》也假定了“驻地、设施、设备和宇宙飞行器”可以放置在月球和其他天体上，所以才能“以互惠基础”对其他缔约国开放①。

《外空条约》没有定义这些不同类别的物体②。鉴于《外空条约》是在月球和其他天体的语境下提到它们的，并且《月球协定》第三条第 4 款也很大程度上在映射《外空条约》，所以对这些相应条款应做出一致解释。

第八条第 2 款第（1）项重申了上述提及的《外空条约》第四条和第十二条中的原则，特别规定人员、外空运载器、设备、设施、驻地和装置【译者注：与《外空条约》译文不同，后者采用的是站所、设施】可以放置在月球和其他天体上，并可以“在月球表面或表面以下”自由移动或被自由移动。

它还进一步扩展了这一原则，规定它们可为利用月球和其他天体而使用。这沿循了《月球协定》的宗旨，即用于明确开发月球和其他天体自然资源的法律制度。第八条第 2 款、第（2）项中提到“在月球和其他天体表面上或之下的任何地方”的放置，则进一步强调了这一点。

第八条第 2 款所列第（2）项没有提及任何关于此类人/物的放置的“合理性”要求，唯一的义务性要求是要以探索和利用月球和其他天体为目的。这似乎比《外空条约》第四条所规定的设备或设施应为和平探索之“必须”的要求更为宽泛，从而赋予有关缔约国决定何为“为此目的”之适当的一定程度的自由裁量权。但此类决策仍受《月球协定》其余部分，包括第八条第 3 款（见下文）所约束。

起初，第八条第 2 款第（2）项所使用的“外空运载器”【译者注：与 OST 不同，宇宙飞行器】一词的含义，还存在一定程度的不确定性。“外空运载器”和“空间物体”有时被互换使用。实际上，“外空运载器【译者注：OST 中文版本为宇宙飞行器】”是在《外空条约》中有关登记国的语境下第一次被使用③，也可被认为是指空间物体。

---

① Art. XII OST.

② For a discussion of these terms, see Schrogl, Kai-Uwe/Neumann, Julia, Article IV, in: Hobe, Stephan/Schmidt-Tedd, Bernhard/Schrogl, Kai-Uwe (eds.), Cologne Commentary on Space Law, Volume I, Heymanns, Cologne 2009, pp. 84f., mn. 53-57, 62ff.; and Smith, Lesley Jane, Article XII, in: Hobe, Stephan/Schmidt-Tedd, Bernhard/Schrogl, Kai-Uwe (eds.), Cologne Commentary on Space Law, Volume I, Heymanns, Cologne 2009, pp. 209f., mn. 9f.

③ See Art. V OST.

《责任公约》[1] 和《登记公约》[2] 都定义了空间物体。自“空间物体”在联合国外空系列条约中被正式定义之后，就成为了空间法专门的法律概念。《月球协定》第八条使用的各种术语，如外空运载器、装备、设施、站所和装置等都被认为是可能在月球上使用的空间物体。由于空间物体这一法律术语太过宽泛，因此以上只是列举而非穷举。

3. 禁止妨碍其他缔约国的活动

第八条第 3 款规定缔约国在根据前两款进行探索利用月球和其他天体的活动时，“不应妨碍其他缔约国的活动”。这既符合《外空条约》的自由原则，也深化了《月球协定》第六条第 1 款有关科学调查自由和第四条第 2 款的合作互助原则。

该项禁止与其他国家的“活动”相关。尽管未明文说明这些活动仅限于第八条第 1、2 款规定范围内的活动。但如果是指任何活动，也不尽合理。由此似乎可得出，妨碍其他缔约国的不法活动应该是不被禁止的。

一般而言，妨碍的概念比必然造成伤害/损害的概念范围更宽，这从《外空条约》[3] 的用词可见一斑。“对其他缔约国的有害妨碍”，它更指向对其他缔约国活动[4]的“物理性侵犯”。缔约国依据本条第 1 款和第 2 款进行的活动不应妨碍其他缔约国在月球上的活动。发生此种妨碍时有关缔约各国应依照第十五条第 2 款和第 3 款规定进行协商。

该款要求，当“可能发生”此类妨碍时，应按照《月球协定》第十五条第 2 款和第 3 款进行协商。这表示，在任何潜在的妨碍可能发生之前应进行协商。这就给缔约国设定了一个更广的义务，若意欲开展第八条 1、2 款中特定的活动，则应首先考虑是否会妨碍其他缔约国的活动，如果会造成妨碍，应先与其进行协商。

该款规定提及的第十五条第 2 款，其处理的（可能出现的）妨碍的情况有稍许不同。其情况是，对另一缔约国权利的妨碍已经被确信发生。两个条款并用，可确保若某一缔约国错误的或故意的不提前寻求协商，另一缔约国同样可以要求对方进行协

① See Art. I lit. (d) LIAB.

② See Art. I lit. (b) REG.

③ Art. IX OST (emphasis added).

④ Cocca, Aldo A./Esquivel de Cocca, Maria M./Sterns, Patricia M./Tennen, Leslie I., Autonomous Settlements and Environmental Protection in the Law of Outer Space, in: IISL Proceedings of the 44th Colloquium on the Law of Outer Space, 1 October-5 October 2001 Toulouse (France), AIAA, 2002, pp. 337, 342.

商，只要确信其“权利”受到了妨碍。

十、第九条（站所/自由进入）

1. 缔约国可在月球上建立配置人员及不配置人员的站所。建立站所的缔约国应只使用为站所进行业务所需要的地区，并应立即将该站所的位置和目的通知联合国秘书长。以后每隔一年该缔约国应同样将站所是否继续使用，及其目的有无变更通知秘书长。

2. 设置站所应不妨碍依照本协定及《关于各国探索和利用外层空间包括月球与其他天体活动所应遵守原则的条约》第一条规定在月球上进行活动的其他缔约国的人员、运载器和设备自由进入月球所有地区。

（一）谈判和起草背景

在月球上建立配置人员及不配置人员的站所的权利是在苏联 1971 年草案[①]中首次提及的。除了通知义务以外，这项权利没有受到质疑，也几乎没有更改。通知义务是在法律小组委员会 1972 年通过的草案中[②]提出的，就此形成了最终《月球协定》第九条的系列权利和义务。

建立“站所”，几乎为探索利用月球和其他天体之必然需要，不仅为人类栖息与协作提供驻地，也可成为当航天人员遇到危难时的庇护所[③]。

（二）评注

在相关天体表面被认为适于特定活动的地点，可以建立永久或半永久性的建筑，作为站所。正如这个单词显示的，站所一般是“固定物体”[④]，尽管《月球协定》第

① UN Doc. A/8391, Treaty Concerning the Moon: Letter dated 27 May 1971 from the Minister for Foreign Affairs of the Union of Soviet Socialist Republics addressed to the Secretary-General, Annex, 4 June 1971, Art. VI.

② UN Doc. PUOS/C. 2/WG (XI) /15/Rev. 1, Draft Treaty Concerning the Moon: Text formulated by the Working Group, 4 May 1972, in: UN Doc. A/AC. 105/101, Report of the Legal Sub-Committee on the Work of its Eleventh Session (10 April-5 May 1972), 11 May 1972, para. 21, Art. Ⅷ.

③ Art. 10 para. 2 MOON.

④ See Smith, Lesley J., Article XII, in: Hobe, Stephan/Schmidt-Tedd, Bernhard/Schrogl, Kai-Uwe (eds.), Cologne Commentary on Space Law, Volume I, Heymanns, Cologne 2009, pp. 208f., mn. 9f.

八条第 2 款假设它们是可移动的。

为了和“浓缩（encapsulated）”于《外空条约》而又确认于《月球协定》中的自由原则保持一致，有必要分析建立此类站所具体情形。《外空条约》第十二条假定可以在月球和其他天体上建立驻地【译者注：即“站所”，OST 原文如此】。实际上，站所与“装置、设备以及宇宙飞行器”有所区别，后者一般被认为在大多数情况下会更易移动。

《月球协定》设定了一些与此类站所相关的其他义务。

1. 站所的建立以及将有关信息通知联合国秘书长

第九条第 1 款规定站所可以配置人员也可不配置人员，这主要取决于站所的位置和装置的条件，以及规定应通报给联合国秘书长相关具体信息①。

这一条限制了站所覆盖的区域只能是“为站所进行业务所必须”。这可能就要求缔约国随着站所功能的变化，不时调整站所所在的区域。

该款也规定了缔约国有“立即”将站所设立位置和设立宗旨通知联合国秘书长的强制性义务。可以预见，这些信息随后应该可以公开获得，尽管《月球协定》没有提及联合国秘书长应通过怎样的机制来实现②。

缔约国有义务每隔一年通知联合国秘书长其站所是否仍继续使用，以及目的有无变更。这代表一种严格而持续性的执行程序，旨在确保缔约国在月球和其他天体上建立的任何站所都要符合《月球协定》的宗旨。这不仅包括了环境关切和符合自由探索原则，还涉及到《月球协定》第三条第 1 款设立的“专为和平目的”的要求③。

2. 站所设置不得妨碍月球所有区域之进入

该项条文对站所的设置提出了限制条件。目的是为了不妨碍其他缔约国自由进入月球和其他天体。它以成文的形式强调了《外空条约》第一条的自由原则和《月球协

---

① In a 2008 Joint Statement, several of the States Parties to the MOON (Australia, Belgium, Chile, Mexico, the Netherlands, Pakistan and Philippines) described these conditions as “reasonable substantive and procedural conditions”, UN Doc. A/AC. 105/C. 2/L. 272, Joint statement on the benefits of adherence to the Agreement Governing the Activities of States on the Moon and Other Celestial Bodies by States parties to the Agreement, Annex, 3 April 2008, para. 7 lit. (c), lit. (i).

② This can be contrasted with the express requirement under REG for the United Nations Secretary-General to maintain a Register, to which there will be ‘full and open access’, in which the information it receives pursuant to that instrument is recorded; see Art. Ⅲ para. 1 and para. 2 REG.

③ See also Art. IV OST.

定》的站所设置以及其他条款。

此项义务是绝对的，因为它专门指出不得妨碍进入月球和其他天体的“所有区域”，但是也存在潜在可操作性问题。站所一旦设置完成，可以预见，它将坐落于和覆盖区域表面的某个区域（如果需要地基，可能也包括会在地表之下）。在这种情况下，完全不妨碍其他缔约国进入这些区域是现实的。

为了走出这种困境，需要将第九条第 2 款置于第 1 款的从属地位理解。第 1 款允许缔约国在“为站所进行业务所必需的地区”设置和使用站所。

根据自由探索原则，站所的安置（以及人员、外空运载器、设备、设施和装置）并不能创设对月球和其他天体表面以及表面之下的所有权①。

十一、第十条（生命安全保障）

1. 缔约国应采取一切实际可行的措施，以保护在月球上的人的生命和健康。为此目的，缔约国应视在月球上的任何人为关于各国探索和利用外层空间包括月球和其他天体活动所应遵守原则的条约第五条所称的宇宙航行员，并视其为《营救宇航员、送回宇航员和归还射入外层空间的物体的协定》所称外空飞行器人员的一部分。

2. 缔约国应以其站所、装置、运载器、及其他设备供月球上遭难人员避难之用。

① See Art. 11 para. 3 MOON.

（一）谈判和起草过程

除了1970年的阿根廷草案之外①，其他草案②都提到了为在月球上从事活动的人提供协助。考虑到阿根廷草案仅涉及月球和其他天体资源的地位、开发和分配，而并未涉及相关的人类活动，所以该草案中缺少此项规定不足为奇。1966年的美国草案相当笼统，规定“在提出请求或情况需要”③时，各国应提供援助，而1971年苏联草案第七条与协定最终文本④的行文方式类似，一直到1978年才有实质性的修改。1978年的奥地利草案⑤建议删除苏联草案第七条第3款，并加入一般性的通知义务，包括通知可能危害人类的现象的义务，以及报告有机生命现象。该建议最终被采纳。

（二）评注

《月球协定》第十条没有提出任何新的、重要的空间法原则或规则，因为它只是重申了《外空条约》和《营救协定》相关条文的适用。因此，毫无意外的，此项规定是在联合国外空委中引发讨论最少的条款之一，空间法专家对此条款也鲜有评论。

---

① UN Doc. A/AC. 105/C. 2/L. 71 and Corr. 1, Argentina: Draft Agreement on the Principles Governing Activities in the Use of the Natural Resources of the Moon and other Celestial Bodies, 23 June 1970.

② UN Doc. A/AC. 105/32, Draft Treaty Governing the Exploration of the Moon and Other Celestial Bodies: Letter dated 16 June 1966 from the Permanent Representative of the United States of America addressed to the Chairman of the Committee on the Peaceful Uses of Outer Space, Annex, 17 June 1966, Art. 5; UN Doc. A/8391, Treaty Concerning the Moon: Letter dated 27 May 1971 from the Minister for Foreign Affairs of the Union of Soviet Socialist Republics addressed to the Secretary-General, Annex, 4 June 1971, Art. Ⅶ; UN Doc. PUOS/C. 2/WG (XI) /15/Rev. 1, Draft Treaty Concerning the Moon: Text formulated by the Working Group, 4 May 1972, in: UN Doc. A/AC. 105/101, Report of the Legal Sub-Committee on the Work of its Eleventh Session (10 April-5 May 1972), 11 May 1972, para. 21, Art. IX; Working Paper submitted by Bulgaria-Draft Treaty Relating to the Moon, 27 March 1973, in: UN Doc. A/AC. 105/115, Report of the Legal Sub-Committee on the Work of its Twelfth Session (26 March-20 April 1973), Annex I, Documents Relating to Agenda Item 2 (Draft Treaty Relating to the Moon), 27 April 1973, p. 11, Art. IX; UN Doc. WG. I (1978) /WP. 2, Austria: Working Paper, Agreement Governing the Activities of States on the Moon and other Celestial Bodies, 3 April 1978, in: UN Doc. A/AC. 105/218, Report of the Legal Sub-Committee on the Work of its Seventeenth Session (13 March-7 April 1978) 13 April 1978, Annex I, Report of the Chairman of Working Group I, Appendix, p. 2, Art. V.

③ UN Doc. A/AC. 105/32, Draft Treaty Governing the Exploration of the Moon and Other Celestial Bodies: Letter dated 16 June 1966 from the Permanent Representative of the United States of America addressed to the Chairman of the Committee on the Peaceful Uses of Outer Space, Annex, 17 June 1966, Art. 5.

④ UN Doc. A/8391, Treaty Concerning the Moon: Letter dated 27 May 1971 from the Minister for Foreign Affairs of the Union of Soviet Socialist Republics addressed to the Secretary-General, Annex, 4 June 1971, Art. Ⅶ.

⑤ UN Doc. WG. I (1978) /WP. 2, Austria: Working Paper, Agreement Governing the Activities of States on the Moon and other Celestial Bodies, 3 April 1978, in: UN Doc. A/AC. 105/218 Report of the Legal Sub-Committee on the Work of its Seventeenth Session (13 March-7 April 1978) 13 April 1978, Annex I, Report of the Chairman of Working Group I, Appendix, p. 2, Art. V.

即便如此，第十条所提出的安全保障义务的光芒不容掩盖，重要性不宜贬损，因为它是致力于保护和捍卫那些勇敢承担或即将承担在月球和其他天体极为艰苦环境下工作或即将开展工作的人类的生命和健康。

保障所有在月球和其他天体上的人员的生命和健康安全，对于鼓励国家资本和社会力量开展与月球探索乃至其自然资源开发相关的活动至关重要。其含义包括了工作环境和对月球环境的保护①。采取"一切切实可行的措施"的义务，包含了国家和国际层面起草和现实执行合理的技术安全标准和程序，以此保障不仅是本国人，还有外国人的生命健康。

1. 保障生命健康的可行措施

根据第十条第1款，"月球上的任何人"（包括本国人和外国人）均被视为《外空条约》第五条的"宇宙航行员"和《营救协定》中的"航天器人员"。任何外空法条约中都没有定义"宇宙航行员"以及"航天器人员"。外空法条约中的这些术语似乎存在重叠。虽然"宇宙航行员"似乎假定为那些经过专门训练、有熟练太空飞行技能的人②，但实际上，"宇航员"同"航天器人员"本质上含义相同，都是指在外空中或在月球和其他天体上的任何人③。《月球协定》第十条第1款，要求缔约国应将专业和非专业的宇宙航行人员均视为享有《外空条约》和《营救协定》项下权利和特权的宇宙航行员和外空飞行器人员。引人注意的是，凡批准《月球协定》的缔约国都有义务分别遵守《外空条约》和《营救协定》中的有关"宇宙航行员"和"航天器人员"的规定，而无论这些缔约国是否也为这两个条约的缔约国。

2. 站所、装置、运载器及其他设备作为庇护所

《月球协定》第十条第2款规定为所有在月球上遇险的人提供庇护所，因此扩大了《外空条约》第五条的适用范围，其仅规定适用于"宇宙航行员"。《月球协定》没有定义"危难"一词，但是可以理解为，是一种保护（庇护）因不利天气或其他

---

① For a corresponding discussion on planetary protection in the context of Mars exploration, see Conley, Catharine, A. /Rummel, John D., Planetary protection for human exploration of Mars, Acta Astronautica (66) 2010, pp. 793f.

② Senate Committee on Commerce, Science, and Transportation, The Moon Treaty-Hearings before the Subcommittee on Science, Technology, and Space, 96th Congress, 2nd Session, U. S. Government Printing Office, Washington 1980, p. 25.

③ See chapter on ARRA in this Volume, Commentary ARRA, Article I, mn. 100f.

灾难导致紧张局势、重大危急情况、恶劣天气或紧急情况时，生命健康安全受到危及的、在月球和其他天体上的人员的需要。《月球协定》的第十二条也规定了出现“威胁人命的紧急情况”时的援助义务。

十二、第十一条（人类共同遗产/国际制度）

1. 月球及其自然资源均为全体人类的共同遗产【译者注：官方文本翻译不准确，建议直接改动，否则会引起重大误解。】，这将在本协定的有关条款，尤其是本条第 5 款中表现出来。

2. 月球不得由国家依据主权要求，通过利用或占领，或以任何其他方法据为已有。

3. 月球的表面或表面下层或其任何部分或其中的自然资源均不应成为任何国家、政府间或非政府国际组织、国家组织或非政府实体或任何自然人的财产。在月球表面或表面下层，包括与月球表面或表面下层相连接的构造物在内，安置人员、外空运载器、装备设施、站所和装置，不应视为对月球或其任何领域的表面或表面下层取得所有权。上述条款不影响本条第 5 款所述的国际制度。

4. 缔约各国有权在平等基础上和按照国际法和本协定的规定探索和利用月球，不得有任何性质的歧视。

5. 本协定缔约国承诺一俟月球自然资源的开发即将可行时，建立指导此种开发的国际制度，其中包括适当程序在内。本款该按照本协定第十八条的规定予以实施。

6. 为了便利建立本条第 5 款所述的国际制度，缔约各国应在实际可行的范围内尽量将它们在月球上发现的任何自然资源告知联合国秘书长以及公众和国际科学界。

7. 即将建立的国际制度的主要宗旨应为：（1）有秩序地和安全地开发月球的自然资源；（2）对这些资源作合理的管理；（3）扩大使用这些资源的机会；（4）所有缔约国应公平分享这些资源所带来的惠益，而且应当对发展中国家的利益和需要，以及各个直接或间接对探索月球作出贡献的国家所作的努力，给予特别的照顾。

8. 有关月球自然资源的一切活动均应适当进行，以便符合本条第 7 款所订各项宗旨以及本协定第六条第 2 款的规定。

（一）谈判和起草过程

《月球协定》第十一条第 1 款规定“月球及其自然资源均为全体人类的共同遗产，这将在本协定的有关条款，尤其是本条第 5 款中表现出来”。1970 年 7 月 3 日，奥尔多·科卡大使在阿根廷同年关于“利用月球和其他天体自然资源活动的原则草案”的提案中首次提出了本协定中的人类共同遗产原则①。该提案全文如下：

“本协定各缔约国，

铭记使用月球自然资源的活动已经开始，

重申人类在促进和平利用月球和其他天体在内的外层空间方面具有共同利益，

顾及到 1967 年 1 月 27 日的《外空条约》没有制定为使用月球和其他天体自然资源活动的专门规则，

坚信有必要完善该条约关于使用此类资源活动的法律制度，

铭记在 1967 年条约框架下就使用月球和其他天体自然资源达成的一般性共识中迅即建立起的各项原则带来的惠宜，

回顾利用外层空间必须为所有国家谋福利和利益，并应为人类共同的事情，

达成以下协议：

第一条

月球和其他天体的自然资源应是全人类的共同遗产。

第二条

所有来自月球或其他天体的物质均应视为自然资源。

① UN Doc. A/AC. 105/C. 2/L. 71 and Corr. 1, Argentina: Draft Agreement on the Principles Governing Activities in the Use of the Natural Resources of the Moon and other Celestial Bodies, 23 June 1970.

第三条

利用原有自然资源的法律体系应有别于利用已带回地球的资源的法律体系。

第四条

利用月球和其他天体自然资源所获得的利益应不受任何歧视的惠及所有人。

第五条

利益的分配，应考虑《联合国宪章》第五十五条提到的“促进较高之生活程度，及经济与社会进展条件”的需要，并考虑发展中国家的利益与要求，以及从事这些活动的国家的权利。

虽然一般认为首个提出人类共同遗产原则的是阿根廷，但美国的官方立场是“人类共同遗产的概念，最初由阿根廷提出，但正式建议是由美国在 1972 年提出的”①。

在进一步探讨第十一条的起草历史并分析人类共同遗产原则以充分理解其在《月球协定》中的确切含义、实质和范围之前，有必要研究其在一般国际法中所处的语境，尤其是在海洋法方面，即在《联合国海洋法公约》谈判中得到的更详细的讨论和阐述。

二十世纪六七十年代的特点之一就是，新独立的发展中国家致力于构建一个新的国际经济秩序。由于这些国家的前身一般都是未获独立的殖民地，而国际经济秩序依然建立，因此它们急于寻求平等参与国际经济关系的机会②。几个世纪以来，经济发达军事强大的国家都被认为在经济上使较弱的发展中国家处于不利地位。因此，在讨论国际区域，例如公海或深海海床的开发时，诸如强制性的从发达国家向发展中国家的技术转让，以及（来自全球公域的）国际货物的许可制度等义务性要求，被发展中

① Statement by Ambassador Richard W. Petree, in: Senate Committee on Commerce, Science, and Transportation, Agreement Governing the Activities of States on the Moon and Other Celestial Bodies-Prepared at the Request of Hon. Howard W. Cannon (Chairman), Part 4, 96th Congress, 2nd Session, U. S. Government Printing Office, Washington 1980, Appendix K, p. 514 (emphasis added).

② A typical statement of this time was the one by Castaneda, Jorge, The Underdeveloped Nations and the Development of International Law, International Organization (15) 1961, pp. 41ff.

国家视为各种必要机制的重心所在①。

海洋法第三次会议（1973 年至 1982 年）为倡导此类理念提供了机会和平台。1982 年《联合国海洋法公约》的通过使之到达一个巅峰，国际管理制度得以建立，使得相关区域不再是行动国的随心所欲之地。根据《海洋法公约》第 136 条（以及《联合国海洋法公约》的第 11 部分和附件 3），深海海床被宣布为“人类的共同遗产”，并建立了以重新定位资源开发的国际关系为目的的法律制度，此类资源例如位于深海海床底部的锰结核②。

由此建立的组织机构，即有自己的企业部门的国际海底管理局，旨在限制经济技术强大的国家专为一己之利而使用深海海床资源。国际海底管理局被授权将从这些资源中的获利分配给所有国家，使其都能从中获益③。

但是人类共同遗产原则的引入，导致一些工业化发达的国家对《联合国海洋法公约》的反对，危及了条约的有效性。如果被寄予厚望来帮助发展中国家的工业化国家及其工业不受《联合国海洋法公约》的调整或约束，那么该公约的整个机制将难以发挥作用。因此，经由联合国秘书长哈维尔主持下的大量谈判，在 1994 年 7 月 28 日，达成了关于 1982 年 12 月 10 日《联合国海洋法公约》第 11 部分的执行协议（以下简称《联合国海洋法公约》1994 年修正案）④，它对“人类共同遗产原则”进行了重要修改，赋予其更加宽松的含义和范围。⑤ 于是，强制性技术转让将不复存在，发展中国家也不再强烈坚持在国际海底区域管理局理事会中占据多数席位，并减少对发达国

---

① Antarctica, although also a global common, has a different international legal development. See the Antarctic Treaty, which had established a treaty system with some privileged States of the so-called Antarctic Club, consisting of those States that have made claims to Antarctica and those that have proven their interest in Antarctica through financial and scientific contributions. In fact, the States in the Club control the international regulation of the Antarctic region. See i. a: Wolfrum, Rüdiger, Die Internationalisierung staatsfreier Räume: die Entwicklung einer internationalen Verwaltung für Antarktis, Weltraum, Hohe See und Meeresboden, Springer, Heidelberg 1984, pp. 30-100, with further references.

② On the role of the CHM principle in the UNCLOS see Baslar, Kemal, The Concept of Common Heritage of Mankind in International Law, Martinus Nijhoff Publishers 1998, pp. 206-220.

③ See Wolfrum, Rüdiger, Die Internationalisierung staatsfreier Räume: die Entwicklung einer internationalen Verwaltung für Antarktis, Weltraum, Hohe See und Meeresboden, Springer, Heidelberg 1984, pp. 591-607.

④ Agreement relating to the Implementation of Part XI of the United Nations Convention on the Law of the Sea of 10 December 1982 (done 28 July 1994, entered into force provisionally 16 November 1994, entered into force definitively 28 July 1996) 1836 UNTS 3; see Charney, Jonathan I., Entry into Force of the 1982 Convention on the Law of the Sea, Virginia Journal of International Law (35) 1995, p. 381.

⑤ See also Lyall, Francis, On the MOON, Journal of Space Law (26) 1988, p. 133.

家的强制性义务要求。

从《联合国海洋法公约》谈判历史的简述中，可以得出两个重要结论：第一，至上世纪 90 年代初，发展中国家同意放弃建立在工业化国家承担不对等义务基础上的国际经济秩序，相反，商品服务贸易市场的开放模式将决定国际经济关系 。第二，《联合国海洋法公约》1994 年修正案中人类共同遗产原则的新含义和新范围在比之 1982 年的公约版本①，其实现路径有了相当不同的改变（更加宽松和自由）。因此《联合国海洋法公约》中的人类共同遗产原则对于理解《月球协定》中的该原则的含义和范围来说，并无多少特别之处，但它表明该原则并非是一成不变的，而是与时俱进，随着国际政治与具体所处环境的独特要求而不断演进。

在 1982《联合国海洋法公约》谈判逐步推进之时，七十年代初，关于人类在月球和其他天体上的活动法律框架的谈判也揭开序幕。联合国外空委的谈判已促成了 1967 年《外空条约》的通过，但其中并没有特别提及人类共同遗产原则。而是提到探索和利用外空应是为所有国家谋福利，是“全人类共同的事情”。毫无疑问，《外空条约》第一条第 1 款的“全人类共同的事情”原则，比《月球协定》的“人类共同遗产原则”更加笼统，但仍对缔约国专为本国利益的行动自由设置了一般性的限制②。

值得注意的是，苏联在 1971 年 11 月 5 日提交的提案③中没有包含任何关于人类共同遗产原则的条文，1972 年 5 月 3 日美国参加联合国外空委法律小组委员会的代表，在提及月球自然资源时说道：“主张这些资源是‘人类共同遗产’的一部分似乎也是正确的”。这与当时尼克松总统提出的相关政策并行不悖，他提出所有国家应将公海 200 米深处以下的海床资源视为人类共同遗产④。为反映这一政策，美国的 12 号

① See Evans, Malcolm D. (ed.), International Law, Oxford University Press, Oxford 2006, pp. 645f.

② See, for a thorough interpretation of this provision, Hobe, Stephan, Article I, in: Hobe, Stephan/Schmidt-Tedd, Bernhard/Schrogl, Kai U., (eds.), Cologne Commentary on Space Law, Volume I, Heymanns, Cologne 2009, pp. 36f., mn. 45ff.

③ UN Doc. A/8391, Treaty Concerning the Moon: Letter dated 27 May 1971 from the Minister for Foreign Affairs of the Union of Soviet Socialist Republics addressed to the Secretary-General, Annex, 4 June 1971.

④ See Senate Committee on Commerce, Science, and Transportation, Agreement Governing the Activities of States on the Moon and Other Celestial Bodies-Prepared at the Request of Hon. Howard W. Cannon (Chairman), Parts 1 and 2, 96th Congress, 2nd Session, U. S. Government Printing Office, Washington 1980, p. 14.

工作文件中①，列了一项有关自然资源法律地位的草案条文，其大意是“月球和其他天体上的自然资源是人类共同遗产”。美国一贯积极地维护这一政策，并且最终促成其纳入第十一条。美国的立场得到了发展中国家的支持，1972年4月14日埃及和印度共提的工作文件中明确指出“月球和其他天体及其自然资源应是全人类的共同遗产”②。

另一方面，苏联始终到最后一刻还在坚决反对将人类共同遗产原则纳入《月球协定》，直至代表发展中国家立场的巴西修改了提案中关于第十一条第1款的措辞，即“月球及其自然资源是人类共同遗产，这将在本协定的有关条款，尤其是本条第5款中表现出来”③，苏联这才放弃了反对立场。《月球协定》被通过时，联合国外空委美国代表团的团长尼尔·霍森鲍尔指出，之所以能对最终版本达成一致，“一方面由于苏联接受了巴西关于‘共同遗产’原则的表述，另一方面，发展中国家放弃了‘在建立国际制度治理自然资源开发之前，应冻结此类开发’的立场”④。联合国大会特别政治委员会美国大使理查德重申了霍森鲍尔先生的观点，他表述了美国对于《月球协定》草案的理解，“不冻结国家及其国民对天体自然资源的开发，是众多代表团妥协的结果之一”⑤。冻结事宜对美国至关重要，美国设法保全联合国外空委向联合国大会提交的委员会报告中达成的三个谅解。其中之一是关于《月球协定》的进一步澄清，“该协定并非旨在禁止开发除了地球以外的其他天体上的自然资源”⑥。

---

① UN Doc. A/AC. 105/C. 2（XI）/WP. 12/Rev. 1, United States of America：Working Paper, 17 April 1972, in：UN Doc. A/AC. 105/101, Report of the Legal Sub-Committee on the Work of its Eleventh Session（10 April-5 May 1972）, Annex I, Proposals and other Documents relating to Agenda Item 3（Questions relating to the Moon）, 11 May 1972, p. 13.

② UN Doc. A/AC. 105/C. 2（XI）/WP, Egypt and India：Working Paper, 14 April 1972, in：UN Doc. A/AC. 105/101, Report of the Legal Sub-Committee on the Work of its Eleventh Session（10 April-5 May 1972）, Annex I, Proposals and Other Documents Relating to Agenda Item 3（Questions Relating to the Moon）, 11 May 1972.

③ See Hosenball, Neil, The United Nations Committee on the Peaceful Uses of Outer Space：Past Accomplishments and Future Challenges, Journal of Space Law（7）1979, p. 100.

④ Ibid.

⑤ Statement by Ambassador Richard W. Petree, in：Senate Committee on Commerce, Science, and Transportation, Agreement Governing the Activities of States on the Moon and Other Celestial Bodies-Prepared at the Request of Hon. Howard W. Cannon（Chairman）, Part 4, 96th Congress, 2nd Session, U. S. Government Printing Office, Washington 1980, Appendix K, p. 514.

⑥ UN Doc. A/34/20, Report of the Committee on the Peaceful Uses of Outer Space, General Assembly Official Records, Thirty-Fourth Session, Supplement No. 20, 14 August 1979, para. 65.

在第十一条起草期间，几个具有争议性和重要性的问题引发了广泛的讨论。

重要问题之一是关于从月球和其他天体上自然资源中获益的共享问题。该问题引起了极大关注，因为发展中国家认为其获益应用于促进其经济和社会发展。然而最终的妥协案文确立的是在直接或间接贡献基础上的公平分享，以及顾及发展中国家需求。美国认为“这种草案也反映了电信等其他空间应用领域国际合作的实践，例如在国际通信卫星组织、苏联全球卫星通信组织、国际海事卫星组织中，成员国耗费大量公共和私人资源发展空间系统来开发其应用，并与国际社会公平的分享其惠益”①。该原则在将来建立月球自然资源开发国际制度时应予以考虑。

某个《月球协定》的缔约国可能会加入，也可能不会加入未来开发月球自然资源的国际制度，尽管“加入”更为人所期待。美国大使理查德·佩特里表示美国“政府将……，竭诚努力促成此类谈判。当然，参加‘国际制度’讨论大会的各方必然着眼本国利益来评估会议上可能达成的任何条约。与美国而言，希望达成的条约是均衡合理的。”②

最后，为了充分理解《月球协定》的起草历史，不受错误言论左右也是很重要的。可惜对“共同遗产”的含义仍存在重大误解。例如《美军空间政策法律指南文本》就错误的断言，根据《月球协定》，“月球是全人类共同遗产，这意味着所有国家都应平等的分享从月球开发中所获得的利益。一旦美国签署了该条约，它将很难得到私人公司在未来月球项目上的投资，如果这些公司被要求分摊其利润”③。有一些言论宣称，苏联是在发展中国家支持下在《月球协定》中引入了人类共同遗产原则，目的是阻止秉承市场开放经济理念的自由企业从事月球探索、利用乃至开发月球资源。然而，如前文所述，协定的谈判历史清楚表明，实际反而是美国强烈支持发展中国家

① Statement by Ambassador Richard W. Petree, in: Senate Committee on Commerce, Science, and Transportation, Agreement Governing the Activities of States on the Moon and Other Celestial Bodies-Prepared at the Request of Hon. Howard W. Cannon (Chairman), Part 4, 96th Congress, 2nd Session, U. S. Government Printing Office, Washington 1980, Appendix K, p. 514.

② Ibid.

③ Space Policy and Law, (US) Army Space Reference Text, Chapter 3, <http://www.fas.org/spp/military/docops/army/ref_text/chap3im.htm> accessed 26 April 2019, (emphasis added). This document was prepared by Space Division, HQ TRADOC. The purpose of this Reference Text is to provide information on space systems and their use as they relate to US Army operations. The intended users are US Army commanders, staff officers and Non-commissioned Officers, students attending Army courses of instruction and their instructors.

保留人类共同遗产原则，苏联则是坚决反对。还有类似的，诸如“苏联和欠发达国家准备了一个仅为其利益服务的条约”，为驳斥该子虚乌有之说，卡尔·克里斯托强调，《月球协定》“在联合国大会通过之前已然获得联合国外空委全部 47 个成员国的认同。外空委包含了所有主要的具有航天资源的国家，以及遍布各大洲的多个发展中国家，囊括了具有各种不同的社会经济观点和意识形态的国家。”①

《月球协定》的起草历史同时表明起草者并不认为自然资源开发是一个紧迫事项。而是具有远见的预判，未来只有当自然资源开发现实可行时，才可能达成任何关于新经济秩序的协定。因此，《月球协定》虽然建立了月球和其他天体自然资源探索的法律制度，但关于这些资源未来的开发，仅提供给了一些有限的指引。

第十一条的案文应根据其简短的起草历史来解释和理解。

（二）评论

《月球协定》最为重要的理念根植于其第十一条，其最为创新性的条款也规定在第十一条，因为是该条首次将人类共同遗产原则引入空间法领域，并创设了探索月球和其他天体自然资源的法律条件，明确了开发这些自然资源的法律地位。本条是《月球协定》的核心条款，也是最具争议的条款，起草过程中对该条的讨论是十分深入的，各国和法律学者也对此进行了广泛的研究。但第十一条仍具争议，并且是整个《月球协定》是被全盘接受还是全盘推翻的决定性因素。

1. 人类共同遗产

分析《月球协定》第十一条，应从第四条第 1 款开始，它主要重申了《外空条约》第一条第 1 款的“全人类共同事情”条款。但是它比《外空条约》更加强调代际平等的观念，因为它将环境因素与“全人类共同事情”的观点相结合，即保护环境为后人所用。

《月球协定》第十一条第 1 款宣布月球自然资源是“人类共同遗产”。尤为重要的是，人类共同遗产原则不能依其在《月球协定》之外使用的情形来确定其含义。而只

① Christol, Carl Q., The Moon Treaty: fact and fiction, The Christian Science Monitor, 2 April 1980, reprinted at <http://www.csmonitor.com/1980/0402/040234.html> accessed 26 April 2019.

能在协定之内，尤其是依照第十一条第5款①来理解其内涵。这表明，该原则的含义和范畴不是由《联合国海洋法公约》、联合国教科文组织的《世界文化多样性宣言》(2001年11月2日)② 或任何其他国际文件来决定的。第十一条第5款呼吁缔约国建立月球资源开发的国际制度，但应仅是在开发切实可行的时候。后文将提及，《月球协定》第十一条第7款制定了用于调整未来可能适用于月球自然资源开发的国际制度的主要特征和指导方针。因此，为了充分理解人类共同遗产原则的含义、范畴、适用以及效用，绝不能极端和孤立地解读第十一条1款，而是要和第十一条的其他款项以及本协议的其他条文相结合予以一致解释。如上所述，在《联合国海洋法公约》的语境下，人类共同遗产原则的本质是动态的、多样化的，某种意义上，从其所有的外在表现来看，它不存在独一无二的特征或特定的含义。各种不同的解释正在被提出或可能被提出，然而人类共同遗产原则的适当含义只能由将该原则置于其中并创设相关国家具体权利义务可适用的管理性制度的语境和宗旨来决定。换言之，任何赋予人类共同遗产原则的某个方面的含义，是无法适用于国际法的整个体系的。

2. 禁止国家据为己有

《月球协定》第十一条第2款只是对《外空条约》第二条的复述，并未增加其范畴。同《外空条约》第二条一样，此款规定也应理解为禁止国家（单独地或者通过其参加的国际组织集体地）或其私人企业（包括法人和自然人）通过主张主权【译者注：当然此点仅适用于国家】、利用或占领以及其他方式将其据为己有。更为重要的是，该款未提及月球的自然资源，似乎表明禁止据为己有不代表限制自然资源的开

---

① See for an analysis of the Common Heritage of Mankind concept, i. e. Wolfrum, Rüdiger, The Principle of the Common Heritage of Mankind, Zeitschrift für ausländisches Öffentliches Recht und Völkerrecht (43) 1983, pp. 312ff.; Pinto, Moragodage C. W., "Common Heritage of Mankind": From Metaphor to Myth and the Consequences of Constructive Ambiguity, in: Makarczyk, Jerzy (ed.), Theory of International Law at the Threshold of the 21st Century: Essays in honour of Krzysztof Skubiszewski, Kluwer Law International, The Hague 1996, pp. 249ff.; Joyner, Christopher C., Legal Implications of the Concept of Common Heritage of Mankind, The International and Comparative Law Quarterly (35) 1986, pp. 190ff.; Hobe, Stephan, Was bleibt vom gemeinsamen Erbe der Menschheit?, in: Dicke, Klaus and others (eds.), Weltinnenrecht: Liber amicorum Jost Delbrück, Duncker und Humblot, Berlin 2005, pp. 329ff.; and Hobe, Stephan, ILA Resolution 1/2002 with Regard to the Common Heritage of Mankind Principle in the Moon Agreement, in: IISL, Proceedings of the 47th Colloquium on the Law of Outer Space, 4-8 October 2004 Vancouver (Canada), AIAA, 2005, pp. 541f.

② UNESCO Universal Declaration on Cultural Diversity (adopted at the 31st Session of the General Conference of UNESCO in Paris 2 November 2001) proclaims in its Art. 1, that cultural diversity "is the common heritage of humanity and should be recognized and affirmed for the benefit of present and future generations.".

发。这种开发将受制于《月球协定》第十一条第 5 款和第 7 款[①]中待建的国际制度的宗旨。此外，第十一条第 2 款是一般性的原则，其效力可能被特别规则所覆盖，例如，第十一条第 5 款中潜在的国际制度，因为特别法优于一般法。

3. 不得主张财产权或所有权

《月球协定》第十一条第 3 款进而将所禁止的主权主张扩展至财产权主张，即禁止对月球的表面或表面下层或其任何部分或其在位自然资源主张财产权。本款明确规定与月球相关的活动不能成为任何国家、政府间或非政府国际组织、国家组织或非政府实体或任何自然人主张财产权和所有权的法律基础。通过明确主体范围，强调任何实体，无论公私，都无资格取得这些权利。这与《外空条约》第二条和《月球协定》第十一条第 2 款的解释是一致的[②]。

但是，这些禁止不影响预想中将在未来创设的国际制度，这点下文将提及。更为重要的是，这些禁止不适用于根据《月球协定》其他具体条款已经合法移走的自然资源，如第六条第 2 款。换言之，通过使用已移走的矿物质和其他自然资源将其据为己有是不被禁止的，只要其符合第六条第 2 款的限定条件，即应将这些资源用于科学调查（探索），以及可使用适当数量支援其任务。对据为己有和所有权的一般禁止做出例外规定，是为了允许、鼓励和便利月球和其他天体自然资源的开发，这是合乎情理的，但前提是，相关国家（包括其各自的实体）应是《月球协定》的缔约国。因此如果仅是《外空条约》而非《月球协定》的缔约国，就不能享受该协定下的关于月球和其他天体自然资源所有权的益处。

4. 关于探索利用的权利

第十一条第 4 款反映了《外空条约》第一条第 2 款的措辞，同时是对《月球协定》第六条第 1 款的补充，明确规定了探索利用的权利。这些条款规定了在平等基础上、不受任何歧视依照国际法自由探索利用月球和在月球上进行科学调查的权利，前提是必须遵守《月球协定》的相关规定。所有《月球协定》缔约国都享有该项权利，

---

① See Freeland, Steven/Jakhu, Ram, Article II, in: Hobe, Stephan/Schmidt-Tedd, Bernhard/Schrogl, Kai-Uwe (eds.), Cologne Commentary on Space Law, Volume I, Heymanns, Cologne 2009, p. 59, mn. 64f.

② See ibid., p. 53, mn. 32; see for further details Hobe, Stephan, Adequacy of the Current Legal and Regulatory Framework Relating to the Extraction and Appropriation of Natural Resources, Annals of Air and Space Law (32) 2007, pp. 115-130.

并且根据《外空条约》第六条以及《月球协定》第十四条，其公私实体也可各自开展在月球上的活动。如郑斌指出的第十一条第 4 款项下的探索利用的权利，“并未给予有关自然资源的附加权利，但与探索利用的形式有关，例如着陆起飞、安置人员、建立配置人员和不配置人员的站所等”①。

5. 建立指导开发自然资源的国际制度

如上所述，人类共同遗产原则的含义和范畴将由《月球协定》缔约国在第十一条第 5 款规定之下建立的国际制度来决定。这个预想中的国际制度应包括关于规制月球自然资源开发的适当程序及规定，但前提是这种开发变得切实可行。建立此种制度的时机只能由缔约国根据其关于自然资源的现实探索以及预备开发活动的基础来予以确定，并按照《月球协定》第十八条建立的程序，通过召集缔约国间的国际审议大会来实现。

谈及该设想中的国际制度，有必要回顾一下美国律师协会国际法部门主席罗纳德·斯托在美国参议会对《月球协定》的听证会上的证词，他提出了各种美国应批准该协定的理由，特别提及这对美国公私实体致力于从月球自然资源开发中获益是一种支持。他提醒到，“拒绝批准这个条约对于提供此类支持毫无益处。我认为批准该条约不会对未来投资产生威胁，因为该条约自身就没有此类威胁。实际上，存在何种投资不安全因素与美国批准或不批准该条约关系不大，问题在于早晚会到来的关于资源制度的谈判。不批准本条约并不会消除这种不安全因素，而只会使美国在保护自身利益方面更加困难”②。

需要理解的很重要的一点是，在未来的开发制度建立之前，人类共同遗产原则对当下的月球资源探索利用活动并不产生影响，虽然它在之后可能会变得重要，但也只有在这种开发变得切实可行时（实则与未来技术和商业发展有关）以及在尚待谈判的、设想中的国际制度之下，才能发挥作用。自然资源开发之现实可行也许还需要 30 到 40 年，再需 10 到 20 年谈判建立设想中的国际制度。缔约国应竭诚努力召集国际大会来为达成一致协议而进行谈判，但不应局限于为达成有关国际制度的协议。关于国

---

① Cheng, Bin, Studies in International Space Law, Clarendon Press, Oxford 1997, p. 377.

② Senate Committee on Commerce, Science, and Transportation, The Moon Treaty-Hearings before the Subcommittee on Science, Technology, and Space, 96th Congress, 2nd Session, U. S. Government Printing Office, Washington 1980, p. 75.

际大会的提议应是缔约国自决自定的，因此也可能不是为了建立该设想的国际制度。即便是为了建立该制度，也完全可以不采用人类共同遗产原则，或者给予该原则一个新的、不受拘泥的范畴，就像《联合国海洋法公约》1994 年修正案一样。

《月球协定》第 11 条对已有的探索利用月球和其他天体并没有什么影响，但它为未来的开发制度铺设了道路。这个未来制度需要澄清根据《月球协定》第六条第 2 款认可范围内的对标本、矿产及其他物质的使用与在非主权领域的（商业的）开发之间的界限。因此，《月球协定》尤其是第十一条，是面向未来的开发活动的。

6. 告知发现的自然资源

第十一条第 6 款旨在规定有关自然资源发现的透明度问题。从事月球活动的缔约国有义务将其未来在月球上发现的自然资源告知于联合国秘书长以及公众和国际科学界。该项义务的设定是为了促进设想中的国际制度的建立。尽管缔约国应根据第十一条第 6 款诚信履行其义务，但对信息性质、范围的要求，仍被表述为在“实际可行的范围内尽量提供。这将由各国在提交此类信息时决定。

7. 即将建立的国际制度的主要宗旨

第十一条第 7 款似乎与美国原住民一句谚语背后的哲理是一脉相承的，即“我们的世界并非承继于祖先，而是借用于子孙”。它规定了设想的国际制度中将创设的未来经济秩序的四项基本特征：

（1）有序和安全发展

任何月球和其他天体自然资源的开发活动都应有秩序地和安全地进行。

（2）资源作合理管理

这些自然资源应该合理管理。实践中，这意味着应避免所有浪费资源的行为。这是对于任何不合理的利用的明文限制，特别关于自然资源的使用。

（3）扩大使用自然资源的机会

扩大使用自然资源的机会是第三个要素，应被理解为是原则上鼓励各国优化利用资源的技术。这是一个颇具远见的限制性条件，因为能够防止缔约国在尚未真正了解可能造成的环境影响前，过早的利用资源。

（4）从自然资源所获利益的公平分享

第十一条第 7 款第（4）项是最具争议的，其中规定“所有缔约国应公平分享这些资源所带来的惠益……”。本条款关键是“公平”分享的概念。该句的后半段解释了“公平”的具体体现，即“对发展中国家的利益和需要，以及各个直接或间接对探索月球作出贡献的国家所作的努力，给予特别的照顾”。显然，所有缔约国的利益都应顾及。同样不言自明的是，特别是对月球探索作出了重要贡献的国家应会受该规定的保护。因此，“公平”并不意味着“平等”，因此不能仅因为发展中国家利益而采取片面的做法。它要寻求投资国（贡献方）和非投资国之间的平衡。在这后一类国家中，尤其应该考虑到发展中国家的利益。

这可能是第十一条第7款的公平概念唯一偏离所谓“对等回报”观念的地方。该条的理念是即便发展中国家毫无投资或者投资很少的情况下仍可在开发中获益。因此，不发达缔约国从中获得的此种非对称利益，可能会引发争议。投资缔约国的利益也应该被顾及。

因此，认为勾勒了未来月球资源开发国际法律制度广泛和普遍特征的《月球协定》第十一条，仅是片面的有利于发展中国家的观点，显然是不正确的。这些国家的确有一定的特权地位，然而只是获得为改善其不发达状态的一些“好处”（尽管这在本质上也未必是财政层面的好处）。这种“补偿性受益”也体现在“共同但有区别责任”的理念中①。为了所有人的福祉（包括自然和环境本身），总有一些人要做出更多贡献来帮助他人。总而言之，“未做出贡献的发展中国家却应受益”的观念，是唯一可能影响未来自然资源开发法律制度构建的不平等因素。

因此，人类共同遗产原则的存在没有限制月球自然资源的探索和利用，并且有可能不被最终接受或适用于开发这些资源的活动。牢记“探索”和“开发”之间的区别尤为重要。就自然资源而言，“探索”一般是指通过各种手段搜寻、勘探矿产资源，以确定其存在、程度、数量和质量，并评估开发的可行性或可能性，而“开发”通常是指在探索后进行的，与生产前的开发和提取（采掘）矿产以进行加工、使用或出售牟利有关的任何活动。

如果从事月球活动的国家未加入《月球协定》，那么包括探索利用自然资源在内的与月球有关的活动，将受《外空条约》的规制。与此直接相关的是，《外空条约》

① See Stone, Christopher D., Common but Differentiated Responsibilities in International Law, American Journal of International Law (98) 2004, p. 276; and for a comprehensive appraisal of this concept Kellersmann, Bettina, Die gemeinsame, aber differenzierte Verantwortlichkeit von Industriestaaten und Entwicklungsländern für den Schutz der globalen Umwelt, Springer, Berlin 2000.

第二条，它严格而又泛泛地禁止了国家据为己有①。另一方面，《月球协定》第六条第 2 款明确赋予缔约国从月球上采集和移走矿产和其他物质并将其用于支持其探索任务的权利。这是对《外空条约》第二条以及《月球协定》第十一条第 2 款一般性规定的改进，且作为特别规定优于这些一般性条款【译者注：不同意该观点。】换言之，比之《外空条约》，《月球协定》是后法（lex posterior），因此它的规定优先前法。当前一个条约的所有缔约国同为后一个条约的缔约国时，“先订条约仅于其规定与后订条约规定相合之范围内适用。”② 因此，有观点认为，《月球协定》相比于《外空条约》，似乎更有利于有意探索开发月球和其他天体自然资源的公私实体。

8. 符合第十一条第 7 款的宗旨和第六条第 2 款的规定

《月球协定》第十一条的最后一款将协定中所有与月球自然资源有关的重要的条款相关联。这意味着，任何一条都不能单独的、排他的用于决定协定中建立的关于月球自然资源活动的法律制度。此类活动应尤其符合《月球协定》第十一条第 7 款各项的宗旨和第六条第 2 款的规定③。该款与《月球协定》的整体是息息相关的，该款试图建立一个适于有序安全开采宗旨以及激励月球和其他天体自然资源开发的法律制度，为一旦开发现实可行时构建更为细致明确的未来国际制度铺平道路。

第十一条第 8 款作为总括性和非常笼统的规定，并非高于或取代第十一条第 7 款和第六条第 2 款的规定，只是通过规定这些条款适用于“与月球自然资源有关的所有活动”而起到加强其适用程度的作用。因此，资源开发开采受第十一条的规制，而其探索和科学研究，以及可行的样本采集和移走受第六条规制。

总体而言，关于如何在可能尚且遥远的将来构建月球和其他天体的资源开发国际

---

① See Freeland, Steven/Jakhu, Ram, Article II, in: Hobe, Stephan/Schmidt-Tedd, Bernhard/Schrogl, Kai-Uwe (eds.), Cologne Commentary on Space Law, Volume I, Heymanns, Cologne 2009, pp. 44-63.

② Art. 30 VCLT.

③ According to the US Ambassador Richard W. Petree, the provisions of Art. 11 para. 7 and para. 8 and Art. 6 para. 2 collectively set “the standards for the general right to exploit natural resources” and are “intended to ensure that the unrestricted right to collect samples of natural resources is not infringed upon and that there is no limit upon the rights of States Parties to utilize in the course of scientific investigations, such quantities of those natural resources found on celestial bodies as are appropriate for the support of their missions.” See Senate Committee on Commerce, Science, and Transportation, Agreement Governing the Activities of States on the Moon and Other Celestial Bodies-Prepared at the Request of Hon. Howard W. Cannon (Chairman), Part 4, 96th Congress, 2nd Session, U. S. Government Printing Office, Washington 1980, Appendix K, p. 515.

制度的问题，《月球协定》第十一条对此持完全开发的立场，即便它确实提供了一些指导意见。因此，人类共同遗产原则的准确含义和有效适用是无法预先确定的，因为第十一条第7款建立的只是相关制度的一般宗旨。

在第十一条第1、5、7款涉及的国际制度尚未建立之时，以及对于非《月球协定》缔约国的国家而言，《外空条约》第一条和第二条有关自然资源利用的最低标准是适用的。如资源的利用应为所有国家谋福利和利益，月球和其他天体及其自然资源不能为国家据为己有【译者注：不同意该观点】。

十三、第十二条（管辖权和控制权/所有权/紧急情况）

1. 缔约国对其在月球上的人员、运载器、装备、设施、站所和装置应保有管辖权和控制权，外空运载器、装备、设备、站所和装置的所有权不因其在月球上而受影响。

2. 凡在预定位置以外的场地发现的运载器，装置及装备或其组成部分应依照《关于营救宇航员、送回宇航员和归还射入外层空间物体的协定》第五条处理。

3. 缔约国如遇足以威胁生命的紧急情况时，可使用其他缔约国在月球上的装备、运载器、装置、设施或供应品。此种使用应迅速通知联合国秘书长或有关缔约国。

（一）谈判和起草过程

美国1966年草案将给予月球上人员和运载器的权威指派给了将其“运至”月球的国家，并未提及“登记国”的概念，并确立这些物体的所有权不因其在月球上而受影响[①]。苏联1971年草案提及了《外空条约》第八条，只明确提及了财产权问题[②]。

① UN Doc. A/AC. 105/32, Draft Treaty Governing the Exploration of the Moon and Other Celestial Bodies: Letter dated 16 June 1966 from the Permanent Representative of the United States of America addressed to the Chairman of the Committee on the Peaceful Uses of Outer Space, Annex, 17 June 1966, Art. 7.

② UN Doc. A/8391, Treaty Concerning the Moon: Letter dated 27 May 1971 from the Minister for Foreign Affairs of the Union of Soviet Socialist Republics addressed to the Secretary-General, Annex, 4 June 1971, Art. IX.

1972 年，工作组起草了该条款，该草案最终获得通过①。条款措辞的讨论虽然简短②，但还是被美国接受③，并随后得到小组委员会的批准④。

（二）评注

第十二条前两款主要重申了空间法已有的原则【译者注：这个观点不准确】，但着重强调了它们对在月球和其他天体上的活动的具体适用。第三款是个创新。除了之前第十条，它再次强调了以人道主义为宗旨开展国际合作的必要性，以救助处在不利环境以及从事新的、不熟悉的因此充满危险的工作的人员。

1. 管辖权和控制权/所有权

《月球协定》第十二条第 1 款规定了各缔约国对其在月球上的人员、运载器、装备、设施、站所和装置应保有管辖权和控制权，此条重申了《外空条约》第八条的内容【译者注：实则与第八条完全不同】。类似的，外空运载器、设施的所有权不因其在月球上而受影响，与其在地球上一样。《外空条约》第八条赋予登记国管辖权和控制权。因此，《月球协定》第 12 条第 1 段含蓄的假定相关物体已经有序登记。根据《登记公约》第二条，当发射国对某特定空间物体进行国内登记后，即成为登记国，这当然只能是在发射完成后。如果在《外空条约》第八条规定之外分配管辖权和控制权，那么也会削弱《外空条约》关于责任分配的规定。但是，尚没有证据表明该款有意偏离这一既定的法律制度。

---

① UN Doc. PUOS/C. 2/WG（XI）/15/Rev. 1, Draft Treaty Concerning the Moon：Text formulated by the Working Group, 4 May 1972, in：A/AC. 105/101, Report of the Legal Sub-Committee on the Work of its Eleventh Session（10 April-5 May 1972）, 11 May 1972, para. 21, Art. IX.

② UN Doc. A/AC. 105/C. 2（XI）/WP. 14, United States of America：Working Paper, 13 April 1972, in：UN Doc. A/AC. 105/101, Report of the Legal Sub-Committee on the Work of its Eleventh Session（10 April-5 May 1972）, 11 May 1972, Annex I, Proposals and other Documents relating to Agenda Item 3（Questions relating to the Moon）, p. 14, Doc. no. 18; UN Doc. PUOS/C. 2/WG（XI）/9, Text formulated by the Working Group, 18 April 1972, in：UN Doc. A/AC. 105/101, Report of the Legal Sub-Committee on the Work of its Eleventh Session（10 April-5 May 1972）, 11 May 1972, Annex I, Proposals and other Documents relating to Agenda Item 3（Questions relating to the Moon）, p. 24, Doc. no. 39.

③ UN Doc. A/AC. 105/C. 2（XI）/WP. 26, United States of America：Working Paper, 28 April 1972, in：UN Doc. A/AC. 105/101, Report of the Legal Sub-Committee on the Work of its Eleventh Session（10 April-5 May 1972）, 11 May 1972, Annex I, Proposals and other Documents relating to Agenda Item 3（Questions relating to the Moon）, p. 20, Doc. no. 30.

④ UN Doc. PUOS/C. 2/WG（XI）/15/Rev. 1, Draft Treaty Concerning the Moon：Text formulated by the Working Group, 4 May 1972, in：UN Doc. A/AC. 105/101, Report of the Legal Sub-Committee on the Work of its Eleventh Session（10 April-5 May 1972）, 11 May 1972, para. 21, Art. XI.

2. 在预定位置以外的场地发现的运载器，装置及装备或其组成部分

根据《月球协定》第十二条第2款，按照《营救协定》处理，《外空条约》第八条要求这些物体或组成部分必须返还给登记国。本条仅适用于已经被“射入外空”的物体以及其组成部分①。但根据《月球协定》，返还的义务似乎扩大到那些不是从地球发射到外层空间而是在月球和其他天体上制造或建造的“运载器、装置及装备或其组成部分”②。不过这种区别的意义可能不大，特别是对可移动物体而言，因为这些在月球上更为复杂的环境中建成的“物”，其各部分很可能也需从地球带到月球。这些物被制造加工时所处的月球上的位置，并不会改变它们作为空间物体的法律地位，不论是单个物件还是作为复杂建筑的不可分割的一部分。

3. 足以威胁人命的紧急情况

根据第十二条第3款，出于人道主义原因，月球上的生命安全被定位为很高的优先级。在出现足以威胁人命的紧急情况时，属于其他正从事月球活动缔约国的装备、运载器、装置、设施或供应品，可以在不提前征求同意下，根据紧急程度而被使用。这种使用权反映了该规定的理念，即人道主义考虑，这也是整个《营救协定》③ 的基础。要求事先通知装备、运载器、装置、设施或供应品所属缔约国或获得其许可可能是不现实的，也不符合本规定的宗旨④。这种使用权必须合法、合理地行使，而且只能在紧急情况下行使，不得滥用。行使此项权利的国家有义务迅速将此事实通知联合国秘书长或其他有关缔约国。虽然需要“迅速通知”，但由于事出紧急，所以这种通知可以在事后发出。更重要的是，《月球协定》第十二条第3款所规定的使用权仅授予该协定的缔约国，并适用于其国民或是由其私人实体雇佣的人。非缔约国无资格享有这项权利，但是任何相关人员都可以成为这项规定的受益者。

---

① See chapter on ARRA in this Volume, Commentary ARRA, Article 6, mn. 199.

② Under Art. 6 ARRA, the term ‘launching authority’ refers “to the State responsible for launching, or, where an international intergovernmental organization is responsible for launching, that organization, provided that this organization declares its acceptance of the rights and obligations provided for in this Agreement and a majority of the States members of that organization are Contracting Parties to this Agreement and to the [OST] ”.

③ The Preamble of the ARRA mentions “sentiments of humanity” as a motivation for the agreement.

④ See Senate Committee on Commerce, Science, and Transportation, The Moon Treaty-Hearings before the Subcommittee on Science, Technology, and Space, 96th Congress, 2nd Session, U. S. Government Printing Office, Washington 1980, p. 64.

十四、第十三条（坠毁、强迫着陆或非出自本意的着陆）

一个缔约国获悉并非其本国所发射的外空物体在月球上坠毁、强迫着陆或其他非出自本意的着陆时，应迅速通知发射该物体的缔约国和联合国秘书长。

（一）谈判和起草过程

《月球协定》第十三条的义务是在苏联 1971 年草案第十条[①]中首次出现。1972 年工作组[②]对该条文本的表述稍作修改，未改动实质内容。自此之后，本条文没有再改动。

（二）评注

《月球协定》旨在通过使相关信息广为人知，来促进发生意外事故时的国际合作与互助。该条对《月球协定》其他条文起到了补充作用，特别是第十条和第十二条。

第十三条适用于空间物体或其组成部分在月球上坠毁、强迫着陆或其他非出自本意的着陆时的情形。该条款与《外空条约》的不同之处是，它设立了一种关于缔约国获悉的空间物体意外着陆的通知义务。《外空条约》第五条是与宇航员有关的义务，而非空间物体，第八条第 3 句则是关于空间物体返还的义务，而非通知义务。但是，《营救协定》第五条第 1 款与《月球协定》第十三条是可比较的，前者要求在空间物体返回地球时通知发射当局和联合国秘书长[③]。《月球协定》第十三条是关于月球活动的相应义务；而《营救协定》第五条第 1 款不直接适用于这些活动，因为它明确指出是返回地球的空间物体。

《月球协定》缔约国的义务是，将坠毁、强迫着陆或其他非出自本意的着陆的情况迅速通知发射国（如果可知）和联合国秘书长。该义务在有关缔约国“获悉”这

① UN Doc. A/8391, Treaty Concerning the Moon: Letter dated 27 May 1971 from the Minister for Foreign Affairs of the Union of Soviet Socialist Republics addressed to the Secretary-General, Annex, 4 June 1971.

② UN Doc. PUOS/C. 2/WG（XI）/15, Text formulated by the Working Group, 27 April 1972, in: UN Doc. A/AC. 105/101, Report of the Legal Sub-Committee on the Work of its Eleventh Session (10 April-5 May 1972), Annex I, Proposals and other Documents relating to Agenda Item 3 (Questions relating to the Moon), 11 May 1972, p. 27, Art. IX.

③ See chapter on ARRA in this Volume, Commentary ARRA, Article 5, mn. 174ff.

种着陆，即一国获悉事件相关信息后旋即产生①。可以推测，如果一个从事探月活动的国家知悉和传播有关另一个从事探月活动的国家或其他国家的宇宙飞行器着陆事故的信息，那么在这种紧急情况下，该国应该会提供可能的援助。但第十三条的通知义务不包括对空间物体进行保护和返还的要求，也未包括对可能发生的事故的宇宙飞行器人员的救援、协助以及返还。这些义务已经包含在《月球协定》第十二条第2款有关空间物体和第十条有关人员的规定中。前者确认了《营救协定》第五条对于月球活动的适用性，后者陈述了《外空条约》第五条有关宇航员的条文，以及明确《营救协定》中关于宇宙飞行器人员的规定适用于在月球上的活动。

十五、第十四条（国际责任/赔偿责任）

1. 本协定缔约国对于本国在月球上的各种活动应负国际责任，不论这类活动是由政府机构或非政府团体所进行的，并应负国际责任保证本国活动的进行符合本协定所载的各项规定。缔约国应保证它们所管辖的非政府团体只有在该缔约国的管辖和不断监督下方可在月球上从事各种活动。

2. 缔约国承认，由于在月球上的活动的增加，除关于各国探索和利用外层空间包括月球与其他天体活动所应遵守原则的条约和《空间物体所造成损害的国际责任公约》内的条款以外或许需要有关在月球上引起的损害赔偿责任的细节办法。对任何此类办法的拟订均应依照本协定第十八条所规定的程序。

（一）谈判和起草过程

美国1966年草案对一般责任和损害赔偿责任只字未提，但苏联1971年草案提到了《外空条约》第七条，进而建立了发射国及其人员的任何作为或不作为导致的基于

① ‘Learn’ might be regarded as equivalent to the formulation ‘receives information or discovers’ as used i. a. in Art. 1 and 5 para. 1 ARRA, thus covering situations in which the State passively as well as actively gains knowledge of an incident. See chapter on ARRA in this Volume, Commentary ARRA, Article 1, mn. 121.

过错的赔偿责任[①]。1972 年工作组[②]起草文本的第十一条第 1 款中首次提及一般责任，同时采纳了苏联 1971 年草案，作为第十一条第 2 款[③]。这一文本措辞没有改变，除了关于“月球条约”还是“月球协定”的措辞选择，因为在当时还未最终确定该条约的名称。

（二）评注

本条款阐述了政府和非政府团体的一般责任和赔偿责任的问题，从而参考了有关“国家责任”的一般原则，以及《外空条约》和《责任公约》中的特定条款。

1. 国际责任/非政府团体活动

这项规定包括两个不同的概念：一方面，是本国活动的责任概念，不论这些活动是由非政府团体或政府机构进行。这项规定与《外空条约》第六条第 1 句相对应。此外，第十四条第 1 款第 2 句还规定，对非政府团体具有管辖权的国家应确保其在月球上的活动仅在该缔约国的授权和持续监督下方可进行。非政府团体的活动必须在有关国家的监督下进行的规定也对应了《外空条约》第六条第 2 句[④]。根据一般国际法，政府实体的活动显然归于国家自身[⑤]。另外，如果一个非政府团体的活动由有关国家批准，或与有关国家存在真实联系，则可归于该国[⑥]。该条没有任何新规定【译者注：事实并非如此】。实际上，可根据《外空条约》和一般国际法的各种原则来推定各国自身的义务。

---

① UN Doc. A/8391, Treaty Concerning the Moon: Letter dated 27 May 1971 from the Minister for Foreign Affairs of the Union of Soviet Socialist Republics addressed to the Secretary-General, Annex, 4 June 1971, Art. XI.

② UN Doc. PUOS/C. 2/WG（XI）/15, Text formulated by the Working Group, 27 April 1972, in: UN Doc. A/AC. 105/101, Report of the Legal Sub-Committee on the Work of its Eleventh Session（10 April-5 May 1972）, Annex I, Proposals and other Documents relating to Agenda Item 3（Questions relating to the Moon）, 11 May 1972, p. 27, Art. XI.

③ UN Doc. A/8391, Treaty Concerning the Moon: Letter dated 27 May 1971 from the Minister for Foreign Affairs of the Union of Soviet Socialist Republics addressed to the Secretary-General, Annex, 4 June 1971, Art. XI.

④ See Doyle, Stephen E., Using Extraterrestrial Resources under the Moon Agreement of 1979, Journal of Space Law（26）1998, p. 119; and von der Dunk, Frans G., The Moon Agreement and the Prospect of Commercial Exploitation of Lunar Resources, Annals of Air and Space Law（XXXII）2007, p. 104.

⑤ See Articles on Responsibility of States for internationally wrongful acts of the International Law Commission, as endorsed by the UN General Assembly in: UNGA Res. 56/83, Responsibility of States for internationally wrongful acts, Annex, 12 December 2001, Art. 4-8.

⑥ The ICJ accepts the concept of effective control, according to which actions of a non-governmental entity can be attributed to a State. This concept has been developed in the Military and Paramilitary Activities in and against Nicaragua（Nicaragua v. United States of America）［1986］ICJ Rep. 14.

2. 关于责任的安排

第十四条第 2 款基于以下的认识，即考虑到月球活动可能或越来越频繁，除了基于《外空条约》第七条和第六条以及《责任公约》国家应为其机构、非政府团体行为（导致的损害［译者按］）承担一般性的赔偿责任之外，或许需要有关在月球上引起的损害赔偿责任的细节办法。一旦制定更为细致的法律为形势所必须，此项规定就成为其授权依据，可见其立足长远。例如，如果法律允许对月球资源进行商业开发，则可能有必要规定更详细的赔偿责任条款。一个类似的例子①是 1988 年 6 月 2 日在惠灵顿通过的《南极矿产资源活动管理公约》②。该公约十分详细，但最后没有被“南极俱乐部”的所有国家通过，其第六十七条的规定相当详尽，关于实体在南极采矿活动中如果发生损害赔偿时应承担的赔偿责任，其设置了非常严苛的条件。由于对月球资源的开发制度仍在探索阶段，《月球协定》第十一条也没有对该制度的具体形态作出任何详细说明，因此，第十四条第 2 款至少为引入这种明确的赔偿责任制度提供能够了可能性和可行性。

十六、第十五条（核查/进入/磋商/争议解决）

1. 每一缔约国应查明其他缔约国从事探索及利用月球的活动确是符合本协定的规定。为此目的，在月球上的一切外空运载器、装备、设施、站所和装置应对其他缔约国开放。这些缔约国应于合理期间事先发出所计划的参观通知，以便举行适当协商和采取最大限度的预防措施，以保证安全和避免干扰被参观设备的正常操作。为实行本条，任何一个缔约国可使用其自己的手段，亦可在任何其他缔约国的全面或局部协助下，或经由联合国体制内的适当国际程序，遵照宪章的规定采取行动。

2. 一个缔约国如有理由相信另一缔约国未能履行依照本协定所负的义务或相信另一缔约国妨害其在本协定规定下所享有的权利时，可要求与该国举行协商。接获此种要求的缔约国应立即开始协商，不得迟延。任何其他缔约国如提出要求，应有

---

① See Tronchetti, Fabio, The exploitation of natural resources of the Moon and other celestial bodies: a proposal for a legal regime, Martinus Nijhoff/Brill Publishers, Leiden 2009, pp. 162 and 264.

② Convention on the Regulation of Antarctic Mineral Resource Activities (done 2 June 1988, not in force) 27 ILM 868 (CRAMRA).

权参加协商。每一参加此等磋商的缔约国，应对任何争议寻求可以互相接受的解决办法，并应体念所有缔约国的权利和利益。磋商结果应通知联合国秘书长，并由秘书长将所获情报转送一切有关缔约国。

3. 如果磋商结果未能导致一项可以互相接受而又适当顾及所有缔约国权利和利益的解决办法，有关各国应采取一切措施，以他们所选择的并且适合争端的情况和性质的其他和平方法解决这项争端。如果在开展协商方面发生困难或协商结果未能导致一项可以互相接受的解决办法，任何缔约国可无须征求任何其他有关缔约国的同意要求联合国秘书长协助解决争端。一个缔约国如果没有同另一有关缔约国保持外交关系，则应自行选择由其自己出面参加协商或经由另外的缔约国或秘书长作为中间人参加协商。

（一）谈判和起草过程

第十五条第 1 款源自 1966 年美国草案，其第六条规定了自由进入月球上所有区域和装置的权利①。草案第十一条也规定了争端解决条款，该条款明确将争端提交国际法院，而不是由有关国家自行选择争端解决程序。苏联 1971 年草案仅规定在缔约国有理由相信条约被违反的情况下可以提出磋商②。自 1972 年工作组文本③形成之后，本条规定基本内容保持不变，只是提案的结构和措词一直在调整。

（二）评注

《外空条约》第十二条规定，月球和其他天体上的驻地、设施、设备和宇宙飞行器“在互惠的基础上”开放。

《月球协定》第十五条规定了缔约国的检查权，既确认了规定在包括《月球协

---

① UN Doc. A/AC. 105/32, Draft Treaty Governing the Exploration of the Moon and Other Celestial Bodies: Letter dated 16 June 1966 from the Permanent Representative of the United States of America addressed to the Chairman of the Committee on the Peaceful Uses of Outer Space, Annex, 17 June 1966, Art. 6.

② UN Doc. A/8391, Treaty Concerning the Moon: Letter dated 27 May 1971 from the Minister for Foreign Affairs of the Union of Soviet Socialist Republics addressed to the Secretary-General, Annex, 4 June 1971, Art. Ⅲ para. 3.

③ UN Doc. PUOS/C. 2/WG（XI）/15, Text formulated by the Working Group, 27 April 1972, in: UN Doc. A/AC. 105/101, Report of the Legal Sub-Committee on the Work of its Eleventh Session (10 April-5 May 1972), Annex I, Proposals and other Documents relating to Agenda Item 3 (Questions relating to the Moon), 11 May 1972, p. 27, Art. XIV.

定》第四条第2款①在内的空间法一般原则之中的互助合作义务，又总结和拓展了《外空条约》中的原则。

第十五条可视为《月球协定》的执行机制，不仅规定了检查权，并且建立了当一缔约国相信另一缔约国违反条约或妨碍其条约之下的权利时的争端解决程序。

1. 开放进入/计划参观的通知

本条为缔约国设立了关于在月球和其他天体上的“所有外空运载器、装备、设施、站所和装置”的检查权。因此，严格意义上讲，它可能比《外空条约》相应条款规定的范围更广，因为它还包含了“设施”。美国1966年《月球协定》草案中第六条②没有提及该术语，它是之后新增的，也是唯一增加的术语。

顺便提及，《外空条约》第十二条第2句【译者注：应当是第1句】与《月球协定》第15条第3句都暗含了“设施”是一个通用术语，涵盖站所、装置、装备和外空运载器（指将被参观的“设施”）。

1966年《月球协定》草案最初将可检查权利的范围扩大到“天体所有区域”，但未被纳入《月球协定》第十五条的最终版本。然而，《月球协定》第九条第2款中对月球和其他天体“自由进入所有区域”的规定，实则增强了检查权。

在《月球协定》第十五条中没有“互惠”要求（《外空条约》第十二条有此要求）。虽未明确提及，但鉴于以上所有的“物”都可以成为检察权行使的对象，那么只要缔约国依据条款设定的前提条件行使其检察权，被检查的缔约国则无理由拒绝。

该权利的目的（“to this end”）是为了使得缔约国能“自我确信”其他缔约国对月球的开发利用符合《月球协定》的规定。根据条约法的一般原则，缔约国在行使其条约项下权利时必须善意履行之③，因此，不能基于不符合此要求的目的而提出检查要求。

---

① See also UN Doc. A/AC. 105/C. 2/L. 272, Joint statement on the benefits of adherence to the Agreement Governing the Activities of States on the Moon and Other Celestial Bodies by States Parties to the Agreement, Annex, 3 April 2008, para. 7 lit. (c), lit. (v).

② UN Doc. A/AC. 105/32, Draft Treaty Governing the Exploration of the Moon and Other Celestial Bodies: Letter dated 16 June 1966 from the Permanent Representative of the United States of America addressed to the Chairman of the Committee on the Peaceful Uses of Outer Space, Annex, 17 June 1966.

③ Art. 26 VCLT reads as follows: “Every treaty in force is binding upon the parties to it and must be performed by them in good faith”. On the meaning of this provision see Villiger, Mark E., Commentary on the 1969 Vienna Convention on the Law of Treaties, Martinus Nijhoff Publishers, 2009, p. 367, mn. 8.

《月球协定》第十五条第 1 款第 3 句反映了《外空条约》第十二条有关通知的要求①。

该条还规定，意欲进行检查的缔约国可寻求另一缔约国的协助，或者根据《联合国宪章》经由联合国框架内的适当程序进行。《外空条约》和习惯规则确认了探索利用月球和其他天体应“根据包括《联合国宪章》在内的国际法”②，鉴于此，本条对《联合国宪章》程序的援引是对《联合国宪章》之于外空活动适用性的再次确认。

2. 缔约国之间的磋商

“联合国系列外空条约缔约国间磋商”的概念贯穿国际空间法始终，它是便利国家间合作和保障条约具体条款执行的一个基本机制。

如上文《月球协定》第八条所述，协定中规制缔约国各项权利义务执行的机制便与磋商有关。第十五条第 2 款假定的情形是，当某一缔约国相信另一缔约国违反了《月球协定》的义务，抑或是妨碍了自己权利。该条没有局限在仅提及缔约国的“活动”（“积极”视角），而是暗示任何缔约国的不作为也可能导致其义务之违反或妨碍了另一缔约国的权利。由此，这项规定代表了一种“无所不包（catch all）”的机制，以期通过磋商谋求解决问题的“方案”。

在这种情况下，“如此认为（so believing）”的缔约国可以要求进行磋商，而进入磋商对被请求缔约国来说是强制性的。此类磋商也向其他缔约国开放，因此也包括其他未必认为被磋商国已违反条约或请求磋商国权利一定已被妨碍的国家。

关于请求磋商的缔约国对另一缔约国的作为或不作为进行判断的“合理性”是否为必备前提，协定并没有给出具体指示，也没有提及其他缔约国要求加入磋商是否也需要有合理理由。但是协定提及了所有参加协商的缔约国有“寻求相互接受的解决办法”的义务，并应体念所有缔约各国（包括没有参加磋商的国家）的权利和利益。这样的规定再次重申缔约国应通过合作共同保证协定的各相关要求得到遵守。

协商结果应通知给联合国秘书长，秘书长将所获情报转送一切有关缔约国。因此，联合国秘书长根据《月球协定》的规定履行管理职能。这些工作的执行也是《月

① See for the discussion of these notice requirements: Smith, Lesley J., Article XII, in Hobe, Stephan/Schmidt-Tedd, Bernhard/Schrogl, Kai-Uwe (eds.), Cologne Commentary on Space Law, Volume I, Heymanns, Cologne 2009, pp. 211-213, mn. 18-25.

② Art. Ⅲ OST.

球协定》（联合国外空系列条约之一）缔约国的基本期待。

3. 和平解决争端和联合国秘书长的协助

联合国关于外空的条约规定了一些争端解决机制。在大多数情况下，它们与国际公法和《联合国宪章》中的一般原则保持一致，并通过这些原则适用于探索利用外空，包括月球和其他天体的活动①。这些原则也指示各缔约国应以和平方式解决争端②。

这些和平解决争端的方法都可能涉及磋商，例如谈判、调查、调解、和解、仲裁、司法解决或其他（缔约国）自行选择的和平手段"③。此外，一些条约制度特别将国际法院作为解决争端的途径④，虽然联合国关于外空的条约没有这样规定。

这个联合国关于外空的条约的一般特点也存在例外，《责任公约》设置的赔偿委员会，就是一个特殊的争端解决机制⑤。

《月球协定》第十五条第3款与《南极条约》体现了一样的思路，即规定如果磋商不能解决问题，则有关各国应"采取一切措施，以他们所选择的其他和平方法解决这项争端"。

该条款在解决争端方面比其他联合国外空条约（除《责任公约》外）更具规范性，因为该条款明确规定，如果磋商已无可能或者磋商不会促成"相互接受的解决方案"，则可以寻求联合国秘书长的协助。这样的措辞可能会比第十五条第二款使用的"争议解决"有更加正式要求。

该条款没有规定联合国秘书长介入的方法和确切范围。

该条款还建立了一种机制，使不保持外交关系的《月球协定》的缔约国仍可根据第十五条第二款【译者注：应是第3款】进行磋商。

---

① Ibid.

② See Art. 2 no. 3 UN Charter. The concrete means of dispute settlement are set out in Art. 33 para. 1 UN Charter. See also Tomuschat, Christian, Article 33, in: Simma, Bruno (ed.), The Charter of the United Nations-A Commentary, C. H. Beck, München 2002, pp. 584 and 588-592, mn. 3 and 26-36.

③ Art. 11 para. 1 Antarctic Treaty. This means of dispute settlement is almost congruent with the means enunciated in Art. 33 UN Charter.

④ See e. g. Art. 11 para. 2 Antarctic Treaty.

⑤ See, Art. XIV-XX LIAB.

十七、第十六条（政府间国际组织）

除第十七条至第二十一条外，凡在本协定内提及国家时，应视为适用于进行外空活动的任何政府间国际组织，但该组织须声明接受本协定内所规定的权利和义务，并且该组织的多数会员国须为本条约及《关于各国探索和利用包括月球与其他天体在内外层空间活动原则的条约》的缔约国。为本协定缔约国的任何此等组织的会员国，应采取一切适当步骤，以保证该组织依照上述规定发表声明。

（一）谈判和起草过程

工作组在 1972 年形成的草案①中，首次提出了这条规定，允许政府间组织作为《月球协定》权利和义务的主体，之后就成了每一版本草案的一部分，直到为最终版本所采纳②。

（二）评注

《月球协定》第十六条用来解决政府间国际组织问题。《外空条约》第十三条确认了可在“政府间国际组织的框架内”进行外空探索利用活动（第 1 款）。第 2 款还考虑到这样的活动可能由“政府间国际组织”开展。鉴于外空活动的合作性质以及政府间国际组织开展外空活动的可能性（无论法律还是实践视角），具体说明在何种情

① UN Doc. PUOS/C. 2/WG（XI）/15, Text formulated by the Working Group, 27 April 1972, in: UN Doc. A/AC. 105/101, Report of the Legal Sub-Committee on the Work of its Eleventh Session (10 April-5 May 1972), Annex I, Proposals and other Documents relating to Agenda Item 3 (Questions relating to the Moon), 11 May 1972, p. 27, Art. XII.

② Working Paper submitted by Bulgaria-Draft Treaty Relating to the Moon, 27 March 1973, in: UN Doc. A/AC. 105/115, Report of the Legal Sub-Committee on the Work of its Twelfth Session (26 March-20 April 1973), Annex I, Documents Relating to Agenda Item 2 (Draft Treaty Relating to the Moon), 27 April 1973, p. 11, Art. XIV; UN Doc. A/AC. 150/C. 2/L. 93, Bulgaria: Working Paper-Draft Treaty Relating to the Moon, 8 May 1974, Art. XIV; UN Doc. WG. I（1978）/WP. 2, Austria: Working Paper, Agreement Governing the Activities of States on the Moon and other Celestial Bodies, 3 April 1978, in: UN Doc. A/AC. 105/218, Report of the Legal Sub-Committee on the Work of its Seventeenth Session (13 March-7 April 1978), Annex I, Report of the Chairman of Working Group I, Appendix, 13 April 1978, p. 2, Art. XVI; Working Paper Reflecting the Outcome of the Review at the Present Session of Working Paper WG. I（1978）/WP. 2 of 3 April 1978, in: UN Doc. A/AC. 105/240 Report of the Legal Sub-Committee on the Work of its Eighteenth Session (12 March-6 April 1979), Annex III, Report of the Chairman of Working Group I, Appendix A, 10 April 1979, p. 4, Art. XVI.

况下联合国关于外空的条约适用于该组织就显得十分必要①。

如在《科隆空间法评注》（第一卷）② 中所讨论的那样，尽管联合国关于外空的条约中未界定国际组织的构成要素，但还是存在基本共识的。修饰词“政府间”即强调该组织是国家共同创建的，并且成员是国家，虽然这种强调也许没有必要③，但表明这些实体与私人实体是截然不同的④。

《月球协定》第十六条与《责任公约》⑤ 和《登记公约》⑥ 的规定是一致的，即在特定条件下，国际组织遵守联合国有关外空的条约的执行协议是可行的。《营救协定》第六条也有类似规定，它规定了“发射当局”这个术语。同《责任公约》《登记公约》《月球协定》相比，作为基础的《外空条约》没有谈及政府间国际组织声明接受条约项下权利义务的可能性，尽管这些组织外空活动已被考虑在内。

就其真正性质而言，政府间国际组织是法人实体，而且不同于创立该组织的国家⑦。政府间国际组织的权利义务与组成该组织的、具有完全主权的各个国家的权利义务是不同的⑧。国际组织不具有与国家一样的完全主权。《外空条约》意欲防止国家将其外空活动或国际组织的活动引发的国家责任不当稀释和淡化。因此，《外空条约》第六条第 3 句规定，责任由政府间国际组织及其会员国共同承担⑨。

沿循这种总体进路，国际组织一方面可以声明接受《月球协定》项下的权利义务，以及执行上述联合国有关外空的条约。另一方面，条约（修正、审查）的处置权仍保留给缔约国。《月球协定》中适用于政府间国际组织的例外条款，从第十七条到

---

① See Bohlmann, Ulrike/Suess, Gisela, Article XIII, in: Hobe, Stephan/Schmidt-Tedd, Bernhard/Schrogl, Kai-Uwe (eds.), Cologne Commentary on Space Law, Volume I, Heymanns, Cologne 2009, p. 220, mn. 11-12.

② See ibid., pp. 217f., mn. 3f.

③ E. g. for the purposes of the VCLT, an intergovernmental organization is equated with an ‘international organization’, Art. 2 para. 1 lit. (i) VCLT.

④ See Bohlmann, Ulrike/Suess, Gisela, Article XIII, in: Hobe, Stephan/Schmidt-Tedd, Bernhard/Schrogl, Kai-Uwe (eds.), Cologne Commentary on Space Law, Volume I, Heymanns, Cologne 2009, pp. 217f., mn. 4, 5.

⑤ See Art. XXII para. 1 and 2 LIAB.

⑥ See Art. VII para. 1 and Art. VII para. 2 REG.

⑦ See e. g. Reparation for Injuries Suffered in the Service of the United Nations (Advisory Opinion) [1949] ICJ Rep. 174.

⑧ See e. g. Maclaine Watson and Co Ltd v. Department of Trade and Industry (High Court of England, Chancery Division) (1987) 80 ILR 39 (‘Tin Council Case’).

⑨ Bohlmann, Ulrike/Suess, Gisela, Article XIII, in: Hobe, Stephan/Schmidt-Tedd, Bernhard/Schrogl, Kai-Uwe (eds.), Cologne Commentary on Space Law, Volume I, Heymanns, Cologne 2009, pp. 219f., mn. 10.

第二十一条（含本条），基本呼应了《责任公约》和《登记公约》中的类似条款。

《月球协定》第十九条第 1 款和第 2 款表明，只有国家可以成为该文件的正式缔约国。《月球协定》第十六条规定的条件，以及《责任公约》和《登记公约》中的相应规定，提供了一种实用方法，旨在解决任何条约规定适用于非缔约方（某一政府间国际组织）的法律不确定性。

《月球协定》第十六条第 2 款明确规定了缔约国的强制性义务（shall）“采取一切步骤以保证”与其相关的政府间国际组织在此种情况下声明接受《月球协定》项下的权利义务。迄今还未出现根据第十六条做出的此类声明[1]。

十八、第十七条（提出修正案）

> 本协定任何缔约国均可对本协定提出修正案。修正案对于每一接受修正案的本协定缔约国在本协定多数缔约国接受修正案时发生效力，其后对于本协定其余每个缔约国，在该缔约国接受修正案之日发生效力。

（一）谈判和起草过程

除了工作组 1972 年制定的草案[2]外，所有草案均包含一条规定，允许缔约国提出修正案。联合国五个空间法条约均设置了程序条款。

（二）评注

第十七条允许缔约国对《月球协定》提出修正案。任何此类修改将仅按照特定的程序生效。

联合国各项空间法条约均载有对条约提出修正案的权利，而且这项权利也符合条约法的一般原则和国际法实践[3]。

---

① See United Nations Treaty Collection, Status of Treaties: Agreement Governing the Activities of States on the Moon and Other Celestial Bodies, <http://treaties.un.org/Pages/ViewDetails.aspx? src = TREATY&mtdsg_ no = XXIV-2&chapter = 24&lang = en> accessed 26 April 2019.

② UN Doc. PUOS/C.2/WG (XI) /15, Text formulated by the Working Group, 27 April 1972, in: UN Doc. A/AC.105/101, Report of the Legal Sub-Committee on the Work of its Eleventh Session (10 April-5 May 1972), Annex I, Proposals and other Documents relating to Agenda Item 3 (Questions relating to the Moon), 11 May 1972, p. 27.

③ For the general rules of treaty law concerning the amendment and modification of treaties see Art. 39-41 VCLT.

《月球协定》第十七条与其他联合国空间法条约中关于“修正案”的规定是一致的，包括《外空条约》第十五条（除了用词是“条约”而不是“协定”）[①]。

第十七条应与第十八条一并解读，后者涉及《月球协定》的“修正”以及召开审议此类修正会议的机制。

迄今，还没有缔约国根据第十七条的规定和程序，提出有关《月球协定》的实质修正案。

十九、第十八条（审查/修正）

本协定生效后十年，联合国大会应在临时议程内列入审查本协定的问题，以便参照本协定过去的实施情况，审议是否需加修正。但在本协定生效五年后的任何时候，作为协定保存人的联合国秘书长，经本协定三分之一的缔约国提出要求，并经多数缔约国同意，即应召开缔约国会议，以审查本协定。审查会议还应按照第十一条第 1 款所述原则，并且在特别考虑到任何有关的技术发展的情况下，审议执行第十一条第 5 款的各项规定的问题。

（一）谈判和起草过程

《月球协定》第十八条的第二句是工作组在 1972 年草案[②]中提出的，随后每个草案版本都有该表述。1978 年奥地利草案建议在第一句[③]中增加审查要求，之后再无异议。《责任公约》（第二十六条）和《登记公约》（第二十六条）都有类似的条款。

---

① The relevant provisions in the other space treaties are：Art. XV OST，Art. 8 ARRA，Art. XXV LIAB and Art. IX REG.

② UN Doc. PUOS/C. 2/WG（XI）/15，Text formulated by the Working Group，27 April 1972，in：UN Doc. A/AC. 105/101，Report of the Legal Sub-Committee on the Work of its Eleventh Session（10 April-5 May 1972），Annex I，Proposals and other Documents relating to Agenda Item 3（Questions relating to the Moon），11 May 1972，p. 27，Art. XV.

③ UN Doc. WG. I（1978）/WP. 2，Austria：Working Paper，Agreement Governing the Activities of States on the Moon and other Celestial Bodies，3 April 1978，in：UN Doc. A/AC. 105/218，Report of the Legal Sub-Committee on the Work of its Seventeenth Session（13 March-7 April 1978），Annex I，Report of the Chairman of Working Group I，Appendix，13 April 1978，p. 2，Art. XVIII.

（二）评注

《月球协定》第十一条第 5 款设想建立一个管理月球和其他天体开发活动的国际制度，“一俟此种开发即将可行”。这个设想将按照第十八条规定的程序执行，即在审查会议上审议这一问题。

第十八条具体规定了缔约国召集审查会议的具体情形，并规定协定生效十年后（即 1994 年）将协定的审查列入联合国大会临时议程。

《月球协定》于 1984 年 7 月 11 日，即第五份批准书交存后 30 天生效①。考虑到第十八条第一句规定的要求，联合国外空委在 1994 年第 37 次会议上审议了《月球协定》的审查问题。经审议后，外空委建议联合国大会“它决定暂不针对”《月球协定》修正“采取任何措施”②。联合国大会于 1994 年 12 月将这一建议记录在案③。

直到近年来，联合国外空委开始重拾审查《月球协定》的可能性，并进行了一系列针对性的讨论和研究④，但还未向联合国大会提出任何有关修正《月球协定》的建议。

第十八条第二句规定了审查会议召开的前提是“经本协定三分之一的缔约国提出要求，并经多数缔约国同意”。

这样的会议将是“［仅］缔约国”的审查会议。鉴于《月球协定》的缔约国数量不多，目前并不包括任何一个“主要的”航天发达国家，仅在缔约国《月球协定》审查会议上提出的修正案不会得到广泛的支持，更无现实意义。因此，迄今为止，缔约国尚未根据这些条款召集审查会议。

但鉴于近年来探索利用月球的热情重新高涨，《月球协定》的若干缔约国基于其经验发布了一项联合声明，目的是总结“反映外空委旨在发展和扩大外空法适用的相

① See, Art. 19 para. 3 MOON.

② UN Doc. A/49/20, Report of the Committee on the Peaceful Uses of Outer Space, General Assembly Official Records, Forty-Ninth Session, Supplement No. 20, 12 August 1994, para. 153.

③ UNGA Res. 49/34, International cooperation in the peaceful uses of outer space, including the question of the review of the Agreement governing the Activities of States on the Moon and Other Celestial Bodies, 9 December 1994, para. 42.

④ For further details, see Bini, Antonella, The Moon Agreement in the 21st Century, Acta Astronautica (67) 2010, pp. 499-501.

关工作中的要素”，以供外空委参考①。

第十八条的最后一句是呼应《月球协定》第十一条第 1 款和第 5 款。它规定审查会议应考虑执行用于建立管理月球和其他天体自然资源的国际制度的各项程序，并以第十一条第 1 款规定的“人类共同遗产”原则为基础，同时应特别考虑到“任何有关技术的发展”。

当召开审查会议时，参会缔约国也可能最终决定该项国际制度未必需要面面俱到地反映《月球协定》规定的人类共同遗产原则。因此，第十一条所勾勒的人类共同遗产原则未必一定会体现在根据第十八条召开的审查会议所达成的实施标准和原则中。

第十八条中提到了任何有关技术发展，尽管现实中此类发展不会被忽略，但关于如何衡量这些发展【译者增：与审查惠益的关系】，尚不清楚。

无论如何，鉴于从未召开过此类审查会议，并且对月球和其他天体自然资源进行商业或其他开发似乎尚不可行，因此迄今为止第十八条最后一句规定的义务还未派上用场。

二十、第十九条（签署/批准/加入/生效）

1. 本协定应开放给所有国家在纽约联合国总部签署。

2. 本协定应经各签字国批准。在本协定按照本条第 3 款生效前未在本协定签字的任何国家可随时加入本协定。批准书和加入书应交存联合国秘书长。

3. 本协定应在五国政府交存批准书后第三十天生效。

4. 对于本协定生效后交存批准书或加入书的国家，本协定应自其交存批准书或加入书之日后第三十天开始生效。

5. 秘书长应将每次签字的日期，交存每项批准或加入本协定文书的日期，本协定生效日期，和接到其他通知的情况立即通知所有签字国和加入国。

① UN Doc. A/AC. 105/C. 2/L. 272, Joint statement on the benefits of adherence to the Agreement Governing the Activities of States on the Moon and Other Celestial Bodies by States parties to the Agreement, Annex, 3 April 2008, para. 5.

（一）谈判和起草过程

《月球协定》第十九条的程序事项早已包含在 1966 年的美国提案中，虽然结构和措辞不一样。美国提案不是以单一条款的形式提出的，而是散见在其提案的第 12、13、14、还有 17 条中[①]。1966 年美国草案与当前的第十九条有所不同，它只允许某些国家签署该协议，并且只需要两个批准书即可使协议生效。随后 1971 年苏联草案已具备当前结构，并需要五国批准才能使协定生效。其第六段明确要求，根据《联合国宪章》第一百零二条对条约进行登记[②]。此外，苏联希望指定保存国，这在草案中并没有规定。该草案版本一直沿用到 1978 年奥地利提出新草案，提议秘书长担任保存人，并删除了苏联草案的第 6 款[③]。1978 年法律小组委员会的工作文件同时包含了这两种方案[④]。最终，奥地利提案胜出，被最终采纳。

（二）评注

第十九条涉及了《月球协定》一些程序问题[⑤]，比如签署、批准、生效、加入条约以及保存主体。第十九条包括的条款有签署（第 1 款）、批准（第 2 款和第 4 款）、生效（第 3 款）还有保存职责（第 5 款）。

1. 签署

第十九条第 1 款规定，所有国家在位于组约的联合国总部签署《月球协定》。1978 年奥地利草案规定了《月球协定》确切签署地点，之前的草案都没有提及。

---

① UN Doc. A/AC. 105/32, Draft Treaty Governing the Exploration of the Moon and Other Celestial Bodies: Letter dated 16 June 1966 from the Permanent Representative of the United States of America addressed to the Chairman of the Committee on the Peaceful Uses of Outer Space, Annex, 17 June 1966.

② UN Doc. A/8391, Treaty Concerning the Moon: Letter dated 27 May 1971 from the Minister for Foreign Affairs of the Union of Soviet Socialist Republics addressed to the Secretary-General, Annex, 4 June 1971, Art. XII.

③ UN Doc. WG. I（1978）/WP. 2, Austria: Working Paper, Agreement Governing the Activities of States on the Moon and other Celestial Bodies, 3 April 1978, in: UN Doc. A/AC. 105/218, Report of the Legal Sub-Committee on the Work of its Seventeenth Session（13 March-7 April 1978）, Annex I, Report of the Chairman of Working Group I, Appendix, 13 April 1978, p. 2, Art. XIX.

④ Working Paper Reflecting the Outcome of the Review at the Present Session of Working Paper WG. I（1978）/ WP. 2 of 3 April 1978, in: UN Doc. A/AC. 105/240 Report of the Legal Sub-Committee on the Work of its Eighteenth Session（12 March-6 April 1979）, Annex Ⅲ, Report of the Chairman of Working Group I, Appendix A, 10 April 1979, p. 4, Art. XIX.

⑤ Doyle, Stephen E., Using Extraterrestrial Resources under the Moon Agreement of 1979, Journal of Space Law（26）1998, p. 124; and Christol, Carl Q., The Modern International Law of Outer Space, Pergamon Press, New York 1982, p. 49.

2. 批准和加入

第十九条第 2 款规定所有国家可以签署《月球协定》，如果一国在条约生效前没有签署，可根据本条第 3 款随时签署。另外，第 2 款指定《月球协定》的保存人为联合国秘书长。这一选择不同于《外空条约》等其他外空公约，如《外空条约》指定美国、苏联和英国作为条约文本的交存国①，这很难解释，因为谈判记录中未见任何此类迹象。如上所述，唯一可能有关联的是，1971 年苏联草案和 1972 年联合国草案建议指定某些政府作为交存政府②，但 1978 年奥地利草案提议由联合国秘书长担任此角色，这个方案最终为所有谈判方所接受③。

3. 生效

第十九条第 3 款规定《月球协定》在向五国政府交存批准书后第三十天生效。不同于《外空条约》和《营救协定》，《月球协定》不需要美国、苏联和英国的接受即可生效④。《月球协定》的谈判记录未能提供各国做此选择的原因。也许这是为了使《月球协定》能更快、更容易的生效。

1979 年 7 月 3 日，《月球协定》最终文本在联合国外空委获得一致核可，并于 1979 年 12 月 5 日在联合国大会获得一致通过。在联合国秘书长交存第五份批准书之后，协定于 1984 年 7 月 11 日生效⑤。截至 2018 年 1 月，只有 18 个国家批准了该协

---

① See Goh, Gerardine, Articles XIV-XⅦ, in: Hobe, Stephan/Schmidt-Tedd, Bernhard/Schrogl, Kai-Uwe (eds.), Cologne Commentary on Space Law, Volume I, Heymanns, Cologne 2009, p. 226, mn. 7.

② See UN Doc. A/8391, Treaty Concerning the Moon: Letter dated 27 May 1971 from the Minister for Foreign Affairs of the Union of Soviet Socialist Republics addressed to the Secretary-General, Annex, 4 June 1971; and UN Doc. PUOS/C. 2/WG (XI) /15/Rev. 1, Draft Treaty Concerning the Moon: Text formulated by the Working Group, 4 May 1972, in: UN Doc. A/AC. 105/101, Report of the Legal Sub-Committee on the Work of its Eleventh Session (10 April-5 May 1972), 11 May 1972, para. 21, Art. XVIII para. 2.

③ UN Doc. WG. I (1978) /WP. 2, Austria: Working Paper, Agreement Governing the Activities of States on the Moon and other Celestial Bodies, 3 April 1978, in: UN Doc. A/AC. 105/218, Report of the Legal Sub-Committee on the Work of its Seventeenth Session (13 March-7 April 1978), Annex I, Report of the Chairman of Working Group I, Appendix, 13 April 1978, p. 2; and UN Doc. A/33/20, Report of the Committee on the Peaceful Uses of Outer Space, General Assembly Official Records, Thirty-Third Session, Supplement No. 20, 7 August 1978, p. 11 (Statement by the Chairman Dr. Peter Jankowitsch).

④ See Christol, Carl Q., The Moon Treaty Enters into Force, American Journal of International Law (79) 1985, p. 163.

⑤ See the fifth State to deposit its ratification was Austria, which followed Chile, the Philippines, Uruguay and the Netherlands. United Nations Treaty Collection, Status of Treaties: Agreement Governing the Activities of States on the Moon and Other Celestial Bodies, <http://treaties.un.org/Pages/ViewDetails.aspx?src=TREATY&mtdsg_no=XXIV-2&chapter=24&lang=en> accessed 26 April 2019.

定，另有 4 个国家仅签署了该协定[①]。

4. 生效后的批准或者加入

第十九条第 4 款规定了《月球协定》对于在其生效后批准或加入的国家的生效日期。各缔约国自其交存批准书或加入书之日后第三十天开始，将受本协定的约束。

5. 关于签字、保存、生效的信息和其他通知

第十九条第 5 款规定了联合国秘书长作为交存人的义务，即将每次签字的日期、交存的每项批准或加入本协定文书的日期、本协定生效日期和接得其他通知的情况立即通知所有签字国和加入国。美国 1966 年提出的关于月球的草案，苏联 1971 年草案以及 1972 年法律小组委员会通过的草案，都包含了一项条款，要求交存政府根据《联合国宪章》第一百零二条登记《月球协定》[②]，它规定条约或国际协定的交存政府尽快在联合国秘书长处登记的义务。1978 年决定由联合国秘书处作为《月球协定》的交存机构，因此于《月球协定》而言，是否登记也就不是必要的了。

---

① See the thirteen States which have ratified the Moon Agreement are: Australia, Austria, Chile, Mexico, Morocco, the Netherlands, Pakistan, the Philippines, Uruguay, Kazakhstan, Belgium, Peru and Lebanon. The four States which have signed it are: France, Guatemala, India and Romania. See UN Doc. A/AC. 105/C. 2/2018/CRP. 3, Status of International Agreements relating to activities in outer space as at 1 January 2018, 9 April 2019 with regular updates published on http://www. unoosa. org/documents/pdf/spacelaw/treatystatus/AC105 _ C2 _ 2018 _ CRP03E. pdf.

② See UN Doc. A/8391, Treaty Concerning the Moon: Letter dated 27 May 1971 from the Minister for Foreign Affairs of the Union of Soviet Socialist Republics addressed to the Secretary-General, Annex, 4 June 1971, Art. XII para. 6; UN Doc. A/AC. 105/32, Draft Treaty Governing the Exploration of the Moon and Other Celestial Bodies: Letter dated 16 June 1966 from the Permanent Representative of the United States of America addressed to the Chairman of the Committee on the Peaceful Uses of Outer Space, Annex, 17 June 1966, Art 18; and UN Doc. PUOS/C. 2/WG (XI) / 15/Rev. 1, Draft Treaty Concerning the Moon: Text formulated by the Working Group, 4 May 1972, in: UN Doc. A/AC. 105/101, Report of the Legal Sub-Committee on the Work of its Eleventh Session (10 April-5 May 1972), 11 May 1972, para. 21, Art. XVIII, para. 6. Art. 102 United Nations Charter reads: "1. Every treaty and every international agreement entered into by any Member of the United Nations after the present Charter comes into force shall as soon as possible be registered with the Secretariat and published by it. 2. No party to any such treaty or international agreement which has not been registered in accordance with the provisions of paragraph 1 of this Article may invoke that treaty or agreement before any organ of the United Nations".

二十一、第二十~二十一条（最后条款）

第二十条

任何缔约国可在本协定生效后一年书面通知联合国秘书长退出本协定。这种退出应在接得通知后一年生效。

第二十一条

本协定的阿拉伯文、中文、英文、法文、俄文及西班牙文六种文本具有同等效力，并应交存联合国秘书长，由秘书长将本协定正式核证的副本分送各签署国和加入国。

为此，下列签字人，经本国政府正式授权，在本协定上签字，以昭信守。

本公约于一九七九年十二月十八日在纽约开放供各国签署。

（一）谈判和起草过程

最后条款的起草方式与其他联合国外空条约相同。值得注意的是，只有《登记条约》和《月球协定》包含了阿拉伯语作为正式语言，于《月球协定》而言，该提议是奥地利在 1978 年提出的①。

这必须放在当时联合国将阿拉伯语作为官方语言这一背景下来看。联合国大会是在 1973 年 12 月 18 日的第 3190 号决议（XXⅧ）② 将阿拉伯语作为联合国大会及联合国主要委员会的官方语言，随后在 1980 年又将其作为联合国大会和安理会下属机

① UN Doc. WG. I (1978) /WP. 2, Austria: Working Paper, AgreementGoverning the Activities of States on the Moon and other Celestial Bodies, 3 April 1978, in: UN Doc. A/AC. 105/218, Report of the Legal Sub-Committee on the Work of its Seventeenth Session (13 March-7 April 1978), Annex I, Report of the Chairman of Working Group I, Appendix, 13 April 1978, p. 2, Art. XXI.

② UNGA Res. 3190 (XXⅧ), Inclusion of Arabic among the official and working languages of the General Assembly and its Main Committees, 18 December 1973.

构的官方语言①。

（二）评注

第二十条和第二十一条规定了《月球协定》其他非实质性的未决程序问题。具体而言，这两条包括了退出和不同语言文本效力的问题。

在《月球协定》谈判期间，第二十条和第二十一条并不是任何重要讨论的对象。

第二十一条末尾，也是整个协定的结尾，是留作“经正式授权”的各国政府代表签字的格式和留白。

1. 第二十条（退出）

第二十条为意欲退出《月球协定》的缔约国设立了相关程序。必须书面通知联合国秘书长，这种退出应在接得通知后一年生效。

迄今，尚无国家退出任何联合国外空法条约，包括《月球协定》。

2. 第二十一条（正式语言/协定保存）

第二十一条规定阿拉伯文、中文、英文、法文、俄文及西班牙文六种文本具有同等效力②。该条款除上述提及的阿拉伯文之外，与《外空条约》《营救协定》《责任公约》《登记公约》中所含内容相呼应，与《联合国宪章》第一百一十一条类似③。

这六种语言的真实性和权威性与《维也纳条约法公约》的第三十三条第 1 款④和第 3 款⑤规定相一致。

虽然以上五种【译者注：应是六种】语言同一作准，但是也可能出现一些解释上

① UNGA Res. 35/219, Use of Arabic in the subsidiary organs of the General Assembly in the Security Council and in the Economic and Social Council: amendments to rules 51, 52, 54 and 56 of the rules of procedure of the Assembly, 17 December 1980.

② On the interpretation of multilingual treaties see Shelton, David, Reconcilable Differences? The Interpretation of Multilingual Treaties, Hastings International and Comparative Law Review (20) 1997, pp. 611-638; and Tabory, Mala, Multilingualism in International Law and Institutions, Sijthoff and Noordhoff International, Alphen aan den Rijn 1980.

③ Art. 111 UN Charter reads: “The present Charter, of which the Chinese, French, Russian, English, and Spanish texts are equally authentic, shall remain deposited in the archives of the Government of the United States of America. Duly certified copies thereof shall be transmitted by that Government to the Governments of the other signatory states”.

④ Art. 33 para. 1 VCLT reads: “When a treaty has been authenticated in two or more languages, the text is equally authoritative in each language, unless the treaty provides or the parties agree that, in case of divergence, a particular text shall prevail”.

⑤ Art. 33 para. 3 VCLT reads: “The terms of the treaty are presumed to have the same meaning in each authentic text”.

的问题。实际上，由于法律传统不同，同一词或概念在各个语言中的含义可能有所不同。例如，一旦关于《月球协定》中、英文文本的解释有争议，则可能得由法院来决定以哪一个文本作准。此时应与《维也纳条约法公约》第三十三条第 4 款保持一致，即“倘比较作准约文后发现意义有差别而非适用第三十一条及第三十二条所能消除时，应采用顾及条约目的及宗旨之最能调和各约文之意义”。

第三章　前景展望

Hobe

目录

一、整体评论

迄今已实施了 6 次载人登月任务，即 1969 年 7 月 16 日的阿波罗 11 号、1969 年 11 月的阿波罗 12 号、1971 年 1 月的阿波罗 14 号、1971 年 7 月的阿波罗 15 号、1972 年 4 月的阿波罗 16 号和 1972 年的阿波罗 17 号。

一些其他国家和组织，例如中国、欧空局、印度、日本和苏联，已经发射或正在计划进行无人月球任务，并且近来一些全球合作计划已被宣布，如月球上建立“月球村”①、在地月空间建立“月球门户”②，目前尚不清楚这些计划的细节。此外，关于人类将何时重返月球、是否以及在何种条件下，诸如氦-3 之类的自然资源可被提取，尚有待观察。

根据《月球协定》第十八条，协定生效之后 10 年，联合国外空委考虑在 1994 年

① See <https：//m. esa. int/About_ Us/Ministerial_ Council_ 2016/Moon_ Village> accessed 26 April 2019.

② See < https：//www. nasa. gov/feature/nasa-s-lunar-outpost-will-extend-human-presence-in-deep-space > accessed 26 April 2019.

第37次会议上第一次审议了该协议以及国际制度的前景问题。结果可能是因为委员会届时对《月球协定》没有特殊关切①，它建议联合国大会在第49次会议上暂时不采取进一步措施②。

如今，随着跨国的、国家的外空活动以及外空商业化带来的前所未有的影响，《月球协定》以及“人类共同遗产”概念再次被讨论③。

法律小组委员会第46届会议讨论了《月球协定》缔约国数量不多的原因，提出了有关促使更多国家加入该条约的各种建议④。

“联合国五项外层空间条约的现状和适用情况”工作组商定：（1）讨论在月球和其他天体上正在或将要开展的活动；（2）识别有关在月球和其他天体上活动的国际规则；（3）评估现有的国际规则是否足以调整月球和其他天体上的活动；（4）收集缔约国提供的有关加入该协定的益处的资料⑤。

2008年3月，法律小组委员会第47届会议上，所有缔约国发表了“缔约国有关加入《关于各国在月球和其他天体上活动的协定》益处的联合声明”⑥。联合声明认定《月球协定》是国际法的一部分，因为其根据《联合国宪章》第102条⑦进行了登记。它还提供了专门的国际法律框架，供联合国大会讨论并期待能为国际社会所接受⑧。

---

① See Christol, Carl Q., The 1979 Moon Agreement: Where Is It Today?, Journal of Space Law (27) 1999, pp. 22-24.

② See UNGA Res. 49/34, International cooperation in the peaceful uses of outer space, including the question of the review of the Agreement governing the Activities of States on the Moon and Other Celestial Bodies, 9 December 1994.

③ See also Hobe, Stephan, The Moon Agreement-Let's Use the Chance!, Zeitschrift für Luft- und Weltraumrecht (59) 2010, pp. 372-381. As indication of the growing interest towards the Moon Agreement it should also be mentioned that in 2004 at its 43rd Session of the Legal Subcommittee a symposium on space law was held, with the title "New developments and the legal framework covering the exploitation of the resources on the Moon". Then in 2007, the High-Level Panel on Space Exploration discussed the multitude of motivations behind the ongoing and planned exploration efforts, including the projects aimed at returning to the Moon (The documents relating to the Panel are available at <http://www.oosa.unvienna.org/oosa/COPUOS/2007/panel.html> accessed 26 April 2019).

④ See UN Doc. A/AC. 105/891, Report of the Legal Subcommittee on its Forty-Sixth Session (26 March-5 April), Annex I, Report of the Chairman of the Working Group on the Status and Application of the Five United Nations Treaties on Outer Space, 2 May 2007.

⑤ See ibid.

⑥ UN Doc. A/AC. 105/C. 2/L. 272, Joint statement on the benefits of adherence to the Agreement Governing the Activities of States on the Moon and Other Celestial Bodies by States parties to the Agreement, 3 April 2008, Annex.

⑦ See ibid., para. 6 lit. (c).

⑧ See ibid., para. 6 lit. (e).

关于《月球协定》中争议更大的第十一条，缔约国指出，这是联合国有关外空的条约中唯一从根本上预见开发外空资源可能性的条款。因此，该条款可能提供了一个触手可及的法律解决方案。此外，它强调《月球协定》赋予缔约国建立国际制度和定义、执行人类共同遗产概念的职责，以及一俟开发即将可行时，建立其他与开发月球和其他天体自然资源相关的原则①。

最重要的是，该声明指出“该协定没有预先排除任何形式的公私实体开发，也没有禁止商业用途，只要这种开发与人类共同遗产制度相符”②。此外，该声明鼓励各国批准《月球协定》，因为该协定是“寻求多边解决方案的相互承诺”，特别是“考虑到可能即将开展或参与天体探索任务或项目”的国家③。

在法律小组委员会 2009 年和 2010 年会议期间，这个联合声明及《月球协定》成为进一步讨论的主题④。一些代表团认为“有关加入《月球协定》益处的联合声明”为讨论提供给了有益基础，另一些代表团则认为，声明的某些方面需要进一步澄清。其他国家声称应深入分析批准《月球协定》的缔约国数目较少的原因，于此，人类共同遗产的概念也应予以进一步考量。

二、未来月球资源经济开发的国际经济秩序蓝图

有三种模式可用于根据《月球协定》第十一条第 5 款建立的未来国际制度的讨论：（1）规定一种或多或少具有国际化性质的制度；（2）规定在强有力的环境保护条件下，为国家和私人主体提供一定的行动自由；（3）规定附有一些限制条件的自由行动制度。

（一）国际制度

基于授予许可证而建立一个独立的、将月球和其他天体的任何利用都国际化的法

---

① See ibid. , para. 7 lit. （d）, lit. （e）.

② Ibid. , para. 7 lit. （e）.

③ Ibid. , para. 8.

④ See UN Doc. A/AC. 105/935, Report of the Legal Subcommittee on its Forty-Eighth Session (23 March-3 April 2009), 20 April 2009; and UN Doc. A/AC. 105/942, Report of the Legal Subcommittee on its Forty-Ninth Session (22 March-1 April 2010), 16 April 2010.

律秩序，似乎并不现实[1]。1982年《海洋法公约》就首次试图建立这样的框架。但事实证明，正是这种思路严重限制了国家和私人主体的自由，从而出现了从根本上修正这一版本海洋法公约的需求[2]。有理由认为，当谈及月球资源利用时，此种解决方案很难得到支持。

（二）生态保护框架

1988年《南极矿产活动管理公约》（以下简称CRAMRA）[3] 可为建立天体上与资源相关活动的强有力的生态框架，做出了好的示范。根据这一法律制度，所有此类活动都受到本公约的严格管理。基本上，本公约所设立的有关机构必须在非常严格的生态条件下颁发开发许可（第39条f款）[4]。考虑到对外空和天体生态整体性的高度关注，CRAMRA的模式可能是一种选择，尽管该条约尚未生效。众所周知，法国未加入该条约，但非常支持将南极宣布为自然保护区的解决方案，在之后的30年都可能不得经济利用。

（三）最低限度监管的制度

第三种选择是允许各国政府和私人主体开展经济活动，但对这些活动施加一些限制[5]。分析《月球协定》，其特点是赋予开发开采和利用自由，同时规定禁止一些军事活动的限制，以及包含在第四条和第七条中的一些环境保护限制，它们宣称探索利用月球和其他天体是全人类的共同事情，并且应为所有国家谋福利和利益。此外，这些自由应以宣称月球和其他天体为人类共同遗产为前提。就如分析《外空条约》所体现的，"人类共同事情"的概念是有一定限制作用的，尽管对于在何种程度上去限制

---

① This idea is supported, e. g., by Mani, V. S., The common heritage of mankind: implications for the legal status of property rights on the Moon and other celestial bodies?, in: IISL Proceedings of the 39th Colloquium on the Law of Outer Space, 7-11 October 1996 Beijing (China), AIAA, 1997, pp. 31-38; van Traa-Engelman, Hanneke L., Clearness Regarding Property Rights on the Moon and Other Celestial Bodies, in: IISL Proceedings of the 39th Colloquium on the Law of Outer Space, 7-11 October 1996 Beijing (China), AIAA, 1997, pp. 38-44; and Cocca, Aldo A., Property Rights on the Moon and Other Celestial Bodies, in: IISL Proceedings of the 39th Colloquium on the Law of Outer Space, 7-11 October 1996 Beijing (China), AIAA, 1997, pp. 9-15.

② See Evans, Malcolm D. (ed.), International Law, Oxford University Press, Oxford 2006, pp. 645f.

③ CRAMRA.

④ A similar line of arguments is proposed in Tronchetti, Fabio, The exploitation of natural resources of the Moon and other celestial bodies: a proposal for a legal regime, Martinus Nijhoff/Brill Publishers, Leiden 2009, pp. 159ff.

⑤ Doyle, Stephen E., Using Extraterrestrial Resources under the Moon Agreement of 1979, Journal of Space Law (26) 1998, p. 124; and von der Dunk, Frans G., The Moon Agreement and the Prospect of Commercial Exploitation of Lunar Resources, Annals of Air and Space Law (XXXII) 2007, pp. 111ff.

自由还没有清楚精准的答案。但很明确的是，不允许任何国家仅出于自己的利益而排它式的利用外空，相反，这些活动应是能够惠益国际社会的。

现在来看《月球协定》规定的人类共同遗产问题，对它的唯一描述是《月球协定》第十一条的第 7 款①。根据人类共同遗产概念而建立的制度应带来自然资源有序和安全的开发、合理的管理、使用资源机会的扩大，以及所有缔约国公平分享获益，同时应特别照顾发展中国家利益和需求以及做出贡献国家所做的努力。基于这一原则的法律制度要求合理利用资源，并且至关重要的是，要确保维护投资国和私人企业的利益，以及与一些所谓的发展中国家，即非参与国分享红利。但是，《月球协定》第十一条第 7 款没有规定发展中国家的利益在多大程度上能得到保障，从《联合国海洋法公约》的经验中可以清楚看出，对可能的未来投资者，不论是私人企业或政府实体，必须有重要的激励。因此，可以思考某种制度禁止军事活动，且对外空经济活动施加一定的生态限制。后者要求各国确保其经济活动不会破坏天体环境。这样的制度允许有关各方开发资源，但要求其一旦提取某些重要矿产时应将相关信息公之于众。可以考虑建立一个基金，将一定比例的收益注入其中。这清楚表明人类共同遗产概念已被予以顾及，所有国家都会在一定程度上从这一共同财产中获益。

上述勾勒的制度也许可作为今后讨论月球和其他天体资源经济开发法律制度的基础。未决问题是，谁来进行这种法律制度的谈判？仅是《月球协定》缔约国或是联合国外空委的所有成员国，尽管其大多数尚未批准该协定，又或者仅是主要参与月球活动的国家？

基于对法律形势预估，似乎不应采用仅“月球活动国家”参与的路径。这一曾用于修正南极制度的路径，是基于存在个别国家对南极各部分的领土诉求。然而根据《月球协定》建立的法律制度，不得对天体任何区域提出此类诉求。

如果谈判只限于《月球协定》成员国，那么能否增加批准国家的数目，是令人怀疑的，并且国际社会应该被更为广泛的代表。因此，任何有关月球和其他天体商业活动的法律制度都应在联合国框架内进行谈判，并由联合国和平利用外层空间委员会予以筹备。

① See Hobe, Stephan, The Moon Agreement-Let's Use the Chance!, Zeitschrift für Luft - und Weltraumrecht (59) 2010, pp. 377-380.